B.A. Carmichael

W9-AXZ-220

# TOURISM
## PRINCIPLES, PRACTICES, PHILOSOPHIES

# TOURISM
## PRINCIPLES, PRACTICES, PHILOSOPHIES

SIXTH EDITION

**ROBERT W. McINTOSH**
*Professor Emeritus*
*Michigan State University*

**CHARLES R. GOELDNER**
*University of Colorado*

**WILEY**

**JOHN WILEY & SONS, INC.**
New York • Chichester • Brisbane • Toronto • Singapore

Publisher: Therese A. Zak
Editor: Claire Thompson
Managing Editor: Frank Grazioli
Copyediting, design, and production: Progressive Typographers
Cover Design: David Levy

Cover Photos
**Top Left** French Government Tourist Office **Top Right** Mark Nohl/New Mexico Economic & Tourism Dept **Bottom Right** Singapore Tourist Promotion Board **Bottom Left** Singapore Tourist Promotion Board **Center** Swiss National Tourist Office

Part-Opening Photo Credits
**Part One** Courtesy British Tourist Authority **Part Two** Courtesy Italian Government Travel Office **Part Three** Courtesy Greater New Orleans Tourist and Convention Commission **Part Four** Courtesy Vermont Travel Division- **Part Five** Courtesy Kodak

Copyright © 1972, 1977, 1980, 1984, 1986, 1990 by John Wiley & Sons, Inc.

All rights reserved. Published simultaneously in Canada.

Reproduction or translation of any part of this work beyond that permitted by Sections 107 and 108 of the 1976 United States Copyright Act without the permission of the copyright owners is unlawful. Requests for permission or further information should be addressed to the Permissions Department, John Wiley & Sons.

**Library of Congress Cataloging-In-Publication Data**

McIntosh, Robert W.
        Tourism principles, practices, philosophies  sixth edition / Robert W. McIntosh, Charles R. Goeldner

        ISBN 0-471-62255-9

Printed in the United States of America

90 91 10 9 8 7 6 5 4 3

# The Tourist Business

**ARTHUR HAULOT, PAST PRESIDENT, WTO**
*From* World Travel *published by World Tourism Organization*

We in the tourist business have to be more and more aware of our responsibilities toward our fellow citizens. We are the people who over the years have put tourism in the world spotlight. In this advanced technological era, with leisure time growing, wages increasing, with more time and opportunity for education, we are encouraging our citizens to discover the world, its fascinating riches, its variety, and its basic and profound unity. We are presenting tourism to the world with all its wonderful possibilities.

But it is not enough to proclaim tourism as an international force promoting the happiness and enrichment of our peoples. We must make this a reality for all our fellow citizens of the world. We must endeavor to maintain tourism at the highest cultural and spiritual levels. We must organize tourism so that it is not only a good business, but an opportunity to create a more cultivated and peaceful world.

In our business we have the chance of acting as if we were in a play whose stars are ancient and modern art, old and modern culture, beautiful landscapes, archaeological and historical souvenirs. In other words, we use as our capital not only money but also the greatest traditions and most remarkable achievements of mankind throughout history.

Thus, millions of people rely on us to supply not only the perfect technical conditions for tourism—that is, transportation, accommodations, and arrangements—but also to arrange what they do and where they will go on what they must regard as the most important days of their year.

These are the special days they have saved for and dreamed about—the days of their holidays, removed from routine and full of the adventure of new discovery.

We must, then, deserve this confidence they place in us by allowing us to arrange these special days for them, with the greatest repect for the tourist values of our world, and that much respect for the traveler himself.

# Preface

"The world should no longer regard tourism merely as a business, but as a means by which men may know and understand one another; human understanding being so essential in the world, at this time."

> Gustavo Diaz Ordaz
> Constitutional President of the
> United States of Mexico

Tourism can be defined as the science, art, and business of attracting and transporting visitors, accommodating them, and graciously catering to their needs and wants. (See additional definitions in Chapter 1.)

All progressive states in the world are interested in tourism. Political and industrial leaders have almost universally recognized the economic (if not the social) advantages of tourism—particularly in-tourism. What these countries have done about making tourism a viable, growing segment of their economies presents the widest possible divergence—from virtually nothing to superbly organized, highly productive tourism plants.

This book explores major concepts in tourism, what makes tourism possible, and how tourism can become an important factor in the wealth of any nation. It is written in broad global terms, setting forth principles, practices, and philosophies of tourism that have been found advantageous. Some of the topics included are introductory principles, study approaches, the importance of tourism, some tourism history and careers, the organization of tourism, travel motivations, elements of tourism demand and supply, economics, planning and development principles, marketing, research, consumerism, and some hypotheses for the future.

It is our intention that this book be used as a textbook for college and university courses in tourism. However, the material should also provide useful information and guidance for chambers of commerce, tourism promotion and development organizations, tourist accommodations and other businesses, transport and carrier firms, oil companies, automobile manufactures and dealers, and any other organization interested or involved in the movement of persons from their homes to vacation or business destination areas.

As the Sixth Edition goes to press, we celebrate the thousands of students who have already begun their education in travel and tourism with previous editions of this book. We also acknowledge their participation by writing to us or our publisher. Our goal has been to maintain the book's comprehensiveness and to keep it up to date with an ever more rapidly changing industry. Many readers have responded positively to the readings at the ends of chapters. Therefore we have retained those that were still pertinent and added some new ones.

We are grateful for the help of the following educators who contributed to this edition through their constructive comments on the previous one: Linda L. Lowry, University of Massachusetts at Amherst; Jeannie Fagan, Community College of the Finger Lakes; Mark Bonn, University of South Carolina; Marianne Ansbro, Tompkins Cortland Community College; Courtland Carrier, Mt. Hood Community College; John Baker, Indiana University, PA; Frederick Piellusch, Mansfield University; Richard Howell, Clemson University; Barbara McGill-Rudolph, State University College of Technology, Delhi, NY.

*Robert W. McIntosh*
*Charles R. Goeldner*

# Contents

## CHAPTER 3
### *How Tourism Is Organized: Industry Segments and Trade Associations*

# TOURISM
## PRINCIPLES, PRACTICES, PHILOSOPHIES

# Understanding Tourism: Its Nature, History, and Organization

# CHAPTER 1

# Introductory Principles, Study Approaches, Importance, History, and Careers

## LEARNING OBJECTIVES

- Understand what tourism is and its many definitions.
- Examine the various approaches to studying tourism and determine which one is of greatest interest to you.
- Appreciate how important this industry is to the economy of many countries.
- Know and appreciate some history of travel.
- Learn about careers in the travel industry.

## WHAT IS TOURISM?

When we think of tourism, we think mainly of people who are visiting a particular place for sightseeing, visiting friends and relatives, taking a vacation, and having a good time. They may spend their leisure time engaging in various sports, sunbathing, talking, singing, taking rides, touring, reading, or simply enjoying the environment. If we consider the subject further, we may include in our definition of tourism people who are participating in a convention, a business conference, or some other kind of business or professional activity, as well as those who are taking a study tour under an expert guide or doing some kind of scientific research or study.

These visitors use all forms of transportation, from hiking in a wilderness park to flying in a jet to an exciting city. Transportation can also include taking a chairlift up a Colorado mountainside or standing at the rail of a cruise ship looking across the blue Caribbean. Whether people travel by one of these means or by car, motorcoach, camper, train, taxi, motorbike, or bicycle, they are taking a trip and thus are engaging in tourism. That is what this book is all about—why people travel (and why some don't) and the socioeconomic effects that their presence and expenditures have on a society.

Any attempt to define tourism and to describe fully its scope must consider the various groups that participate in and are affected by this industry. Their perspectives are vital to the development of a comprehensive definition.

Four different perspectives of tourism can be identified:

1. *The tourist.* The tourist seeks various psychic and physical experiences and satisfactions. The nature of these will largely determine the destinations chosen and the activities enjoyed.
2. *The businesses providing tourist goods and services.* Businesspeople see tourism as an opportunity to make a profit by supplying the goods and services that the tourist market demands.
3. *The government of the host community or area.* Politicians view tourism as a wealth factor in the economy of their jurisdictions. Their perspective is related to the incomes their citizens can earn from this business. Politicians also consider the foreign exchange receipts from international tourism as well as the tax receipts collected from tourist expenditures, either directly or indirectly.
4. *The host community.* Local people usually see tourism as a cultural and employment factor. Of importance to this group, for example, is the effect of the interaction between large numbers of international visitors and residents. This effect may be beneficial or harmful, or both.

Thus, *tourism* may be defined as *the sum of the phenomena and relationships arising from the interaction of tourists, business suppliers, host governments, and host communities in the process of attracting and hosting these tourists and other visitors.* (See the Glossary for definitions of *tourist* and *excursionist*.)

Tourism is a composite of activities, services, and industries that delivers a travel experience, namely, transportation, accommodations, eating and drinking establishments, shops, entertainment, activity facilities, and other hospitality services available for individuals or groups that are traveling away from home. It encompasses all providers of visitor and visitor-related services. Tourism is the entire world industry of travel, hotels, transportation, and all other components, including promotion, that serves the needs and wants of travelers. Finally, tourism is the sum total of tourist expenditures within the borders of a nation or a political subdivision or a transportation-centered economic area of contiguous states or nations. This economic concept also considers the income multiplier of these tourist expenditures (discussed in Chapter 9).

One only has to consider the multidimensional aspects of tourism and its interactions with other activities to understand why it is difficult to come up with a meaningful definition that will be universally accepted. Each of the many different definitions that have arisen is aimed at fitting a special situation and solving an immediate problem, and the lack of uniform definitions has hampered study of tourism as a discipline. Development of a field depends on (1) uniform definitions, (2) description, (3) analysis, (4) prediction, and (5) control.

Modern tourism is a discipline that has only recently attracted the attention of scholars from many fields. The majority of studies have been conducted for special purposes and have used narrow operational definitions to suit particular needs of researchers or government officials; these studies have not encompassed a systems approach. Consequently, many definitions of "tourism" and "the tourist" are based on distance traveled, the length of time spent, and the purpose of the trip. This makes it difficult to gather statistical information that scholars can use to develop a database, describe the tourism phenomenon, and do analyses.

The problem is not a trivial one. It has been tackled by a number of august bodies over the years, including the League of Nations, the United Nations, the

Airport ticket counter personnel provide pleasant and competent service for departing air travelers. (Photo courtesy of American Airlines)

World Tourism Organization (formerly IUOTO), the Organization for Economic Cooperation and Development (OECD), the National Tourism Resources Review Commission, and the U.S. Senate's National Tourism Policy Study.

The following review of related definitions illustrates the problems of arriving at an operational definition.

### Foreign Tourist

Starting with the definition of the Committee of Statistical Experts of the League of Nations in 1937, we find a "foreign tourist"[1] described as

---

[1] Organization for Economic Cooperation and Development, *Tourism Policy and International Tourism in OECD Member Countries* (Paris: OECD, 1980), pp. 5–7.

Any person visiting a country, other than that in which he usually resides, for a period of at least 24 hours.

The following are considered tourists:

1. Persons traveling for pleasure, for family reasons, for health, and the like
2. Persons traveling to meetings, or in a representative capacity of any kind (scientific, administrative, diplomatic, religious, athletic, etc.)
3. Persons traveling for business reasons
4. Persons arriving in the course of a sea cruise, even when they stay less than 24 hours (the latter should be reckoned as a separate group, disregarding if necessary their usual place of residence)

The following are not considered tourists:

1. Persons arriving, with or without a contract of work, to take up an occupation or engage in any business activity in the country
2. Other persons coming to establish a residence in the country
3. Students and young persons in boarding establishments or schools
4. Residents in a frontier zone and persons domiciled in one country and working in an adjoining country

Serving guests on shipboard is a pleasant assignment. (Photo courtesy of Royal Cruise Line)

5. Travelers passing through a country without stopping, even if the journey takes more than 24 hours

## Excursionist

Persons traveling for pleasure for a period of less than 24 hours are treated as "excursionists."[2]

## Visitor

In 1963, the United Nations Conference on International Travel and Tourism (held in Rome) considered a definition and recommended that it be studied by the United Nations Statistical Commission. The conference considered an overall definition of the term "visitor"[3] that, for statistical purposes,

> describes any person visiting a country other than that in which he has his usual place of residence, for any reasons other than following an occupation remunerated from within the country visited.

This definition covered

1. "Tourists," that is, temporary visitors staying at least 24 hours in the country visited and the purpose of whose journey can be classified under one of the following headings:
   a. Leisure (recreation, holiday, health, study, religion, and sport)
   b. Business, family, mission, meeting
2. "Excursionists," that is temporary visitors staying less than 24 hours in the country visited (including travelers on cruises)

The "excursionists" definition excludes travelers who, in the legal sense, do not enter the country (e.g., air travelers who do not leave an airport's transit area).

An expert statistical group on international travel statistics convened by the United Nations Statistical Commission recommended in 1967 that countries use the definition of visitor proposed by the United Nations' 1963 conference in Rome. The group considered that it would be preferable to distinguish within the definition of visitor a separate class of visitors who might be described as "day visitors" or "excursionists;" these are defined as those on day excursions and other people crossing a national border for purposes other than employment, cruise passengers, and visitors in transit who do not stay overnight in accommodations provided within the country. The special characteristic of this category of visitor, distinguishing it from the main class of visitor, is that there is no overnight stay.

## Domestic Tourist

The National Tourism Resources Review Commission, which published its work in 1973, developed the following working definition of a domestic tourist:[4]

[2] Ibid.
[3] Ibid.
[4] National Tourism Resources Review Commission, *Destination U.S.A.*, Volume 2, *Domestic Tourism* (Washington, D.C.: Government Printing Office, 1973), p. 5.

A tourist is one who travels away from his home for a distance of at least 50 miles (one way) for business, pleasure, personal affairs, or any other purpose except to commute to work, whether he stays overnight or returns the same day.

The government of Canada classifies a tourist as one who travels at least 25 miles beyond the boundary of his or her community. The Canadian definition is consistent with the concept employed by the U.S. Bureau of Labor Statistics in its *Consumer Expenditure Survey,* in which expenditures for food and lodging "out of the home city" are tabulated. The BLS does not specify a distance that will take a traveler out of his or her home city, but the effect is to distinguish "travel" expenditures from local expenditures in a meaningful way.[5]

## A Trip

The U.S. Census Bureau is responsible for conducting a national travel survey and defines a trip as "each time a person goes to a place at least 100 miles away from home and returns." This definition was used in both the 1972 and 1977 *National Travel Surveys;* however, the 1963 and 1967 surveys used a slightly different definition, adding "or is out-of-town one or more nights." The 1972 and 1977 surveys omit all travel under 100 miles regardless of whether one night or more was spent away from home. This creates problems for a major market such as Denver, where a Denver tourist can go to nearby resorts such as Estes Park, Keystone, Copper Mountain, Breckenridge, and Grand Lake; stay a weekend or month; and not be recorded as having taken a trip. Consequently, the *National Travel Survey* understates national tourist travel.

The U.S. Travel Data Center, located in Washington, D.C., uses a definition similar to the U.S. Census Bureau in its travel work—100 miles away from home. However, in 1986 it also started collecting data on trips of less than 100 miles which included one or more nights spent in paid accommodations. The U.S. Travel Data Center now uses the following definition of a domestic traveler:[6]

> any resident of the United States regardless of nationality who travels to a place 100 miles or more away from home within the United States or who stays away from home one or more nights in paid accommodations.

This includes trips that can be classified under one or more of the following purpose categories: pleasure, recreation, holiday, sport, religion, shopping, vacation, visiting friends or relatives, business, commerce, meeting, conference, convention, trade show, health, or study. Like the Census Bureau, the Travel Data Center excludes the following kinds of trips: (1) travel as part of an operating crew on a train, airplane, bus, or ship; (2) commuting to a place of work; and (3) student trips to or from school.

---

[5] Ibid., p. 4.
[6] U.S. Travel Data Center, *The 1988–89 Economic Review of Travel in America* (Washington, D.C.: USTDC, 1989), p. B-2.

## *Travel, Tourism, and Recreation*

For the purposes of this text, the terms travel and tourism will be synonymous. Tourism may also be defined as people taking trips away from home, and it embraces the whole range of transportation, lodging, food service, and other activities relating to and serving the traveler. Consequently, a tourist is someone who travels away from home. The term "tourist industry" is used to describe the economic sectors (transportation, lodging, etc.) supplying the tourist, who is the consumer of the industry's products. The term "visitor," which is common in international travel, will be synonymous with tourist. These definitions of tourism, travel, and tourist admittedly are very broad, but they permit the development of additional subcategories to define market segments, such as out-of-state visitors, recreationists, con-

The definition of a trip typically requires travel 100 miles away from home. Many trips are taken on the Blue Ridge Parkway, America's most popular scenic parkway. It is a unique mountain-top drive designed solely for vacation travel. Approximately 250 miles of the Parkway are in North Carolina. (Photo by William Russ, courtesy of North Carolina Travel and Tourism Division)

ventioneers, the sports minded, and others. The definitions are also in keeping with those used by the *National Tourism Policy Study*, which construed the three terms, travel, tourism, and recreation, as follows:

1. *Travel* — the action and activities of people taking trips to a place or places outside of their home communities for any purpose except daily commuting to and from work.
2. *Tourism* — a term that is synonymous with "travel."
3. *Recreation* — the action and activities of people engaging in constructive and personally pleasurable use of leisure time. Recreation may include passive or active participation in individual or group sports, cultural functions, natural and human history appreciation, nonformal education, pleasure travel, sightseeing, and entertainment.[7]

## BASIC APPROACHES TO THE STUDY OF TOURISM

Tourism commonly is approached through a variety of methods. However, there is little or no agreement on how the study of tourism should be undertaken. The following are several methods that have been used.

### Institutional Approach

This major approach to the study of tourism considers the various intermediaries and institutions that perform the tourism activities. It emphasizes institutions such as the travel agency. This approach requires an investigation of the organization, operating methods, problems, costs, and economic place of travel agents who act on behalf of the customer, purchasing services from airlines, rental car companies, hotels, and so on. An advantage of this approach is that the U.S. Census Bureau conducts a survey every five years on selected services that includes travel agents and lodging places, thus providing a database for further study.

### Product Approach

The product approach involves the study of various tourism products and how they are produced, marketed, and consumed. For example, one might study an airline seat — how it is created, who are the people engaged in buying and selling it, how it is financed, how it is advertised, and so on. Repeating this procedure for rental cars, hotel rooms, meals, and other tourist services gives a full picture of the field. Unfortunately, the product approach tends to be too time consuming; it does not allow the student to grasp the fundamentals of tourism quickly.

### Historical Approach

This approach is not widely used. It involves an analysis of tourism activities and institutions from an evolutionary angle. It searches for the cause of innovations,

[7] *National Tourism Policy Study Final Report* (Washington, D.C.: Government Printing Office, 1978), p. 5.

A dude ranch pack trip leader explains ranch life to a guest. (Photo courtesy of Snowmass Resort Association, Colorado)

their growth or decline, and shifts in interest. Because mass tourism is a fairly recent phenomenon, this approach has limited usefulness.

## Managerial Approach

The managerial approach is firm oriented (microeconomic), focusing on the management activities necessary to operate a tourist enterprise, such as planning, research, pricing, advertising, control, and the like. It is a popular approach, using insights gleaned from other approaches and disciplines. Although a major focus of this text is managerial, readers will recognize that other perspectives are also being used. Regardless of which approach is used to study tourism, it is important to know the managerial approach. Products change, institutions change, society changes; this means that managerial objectives and procedures must be geared to change to meet shifts in the tourism environment. The *Journal of Travel Research* and *Tourism Management* both feature this approach.

Employment in a travel agency is a demanding yet stimulating, educational, and enjoyable occupation. (Photo courtesy of American Airlines)

## Economic Approach

Because of its importance to both domestic and world economies, tourism has been closely examined by economists who focus on supply, demand, balance of payments, foreign exchange, employment, expenditures, development, multipliers, and other economic factors. This approach is useful in providing a framework for analyzing tourism and its contributions to a country's economy and economic development. The disadvantage of the economic approach is that, while tourism is an important economic phenomenon, it has noneconomic impacts as well. The economic approach does not usually pay adequate attention to environmental, cultural, psychological, sociological, and anthropological approaches.

## Sociological Approach

Tourism tends to be a social activity. Consequently, it has attracted the attention of sociologists who have studied the tourism behavior of individuals, groups of people, and the impact of tourism on society. This approach examines social classes, habits, and customs of both hosts and guests. The sociology of leisure is a relatively undeveloped field, but it shows promise of progressing rapidly and becoming more widely used. As tourism continues to make its massive impact on society, it will be studied more and more from a social point of view.

A prime reference in this area is *The Tourist, A New Theory of the Leisure Class,* by Dean MacCannell (Schocken Books, New York, 1976). Erik Cohen, of the Hebrew University of Jerusalem, has made many contributions in this area (see Chapter 6). Roy Buck of Pennsylvania State University has also been a leader in this area, producing a number of studies of the Amish sect and tourism.

## Geographical Approach

Geography is a wide-ranging discipline, so it is natural that geographers should become interested in tourism and its spatial aspects. The geographer specializes in the study of location, environment, climate, landscape, and economic aspects. The geographer's approach to tourism sheds light on the location of tourist areas, the movements of people created by tourism places, the changes that tourism brings to the landscape in the form of tourism facilities, dispersion of tourism development, physical planning, and economic, social, and cultural problems. Since tourism touches geography at so many points, geographers have investigated the area more thoroughly than have scholars in many other disciplines. Because the geographers' approach is so encompassing—dealing with land use, economic aspects, demographic impacts, and cultural problems—a study of their contributions is highly recommended. Recreational geography is a common course title used by geographers studying this specialty. Because tourism, leisure, and recreation are so closely

The flight deck crew has a myriad of controls and indicators necessary for their passengers' comfort and safety. Pilots are among the highest paid transportation employees. (Photo courtesy of the Boeing Company)

related, it is necessary to search for literature under all these titles to discover the contributions of various fields. Geographers were instrumental in starting both the *Journal of Leisure Research* and *Leisure Sciences,* which should be read regularly by all serious students of tourism.

## Interdisciplinary Approaches

Tourism embraces virtually all aspects of our society. We even have cultural tourism, which calls for an anthropological approach. Because individuals behave in different ways and travel for different reasons, it is necessary to use a psychological approach to determine the best way to promote and market tourism products. Since tourists cross borders and require passports and visas from government offices, and since most countries have government-operated tourism development departments, we find that political institutions are involved and are calling for a political science approach. Any industry that becomes an economic giant affecting the lives of many people attracts the attention of legislative bodies (along with the sociologists, geographers, economists, and anthropologists), which create the laws, regulations, and legal environment in which the tourist industry must operate; so we also have a legal approach. The great importance of transportation suggests passenger transportation as another approach. The fact simply is that tourism is so vast, so complex, and so multifaceted that it is necessary to have a number of approaches to studying the field, each geared to a somewhat different task or objective. Figure 1.1 illustrates the interdisciplinary nature of tourism studies and their reciprocity and mutuality. *The Annals of Tourism Research,* an interdisciplinary social sciences journal, is another publication that should be on the serious tourism student's reading list.

*The Systems Approach*    What is really needed to study tourism is a systems approach. A system is a set of interrelated groups coordinated to form a unified whole and organized to accomplish a set of goals. It integrates the other approaches into a comprehensive method dealing with both micro and macro issues. It can examine the tourist firm's competitive environment, its market, its results, its linkages with other institutions, the consumer, and the interaction of the firm with the consumer. In addition, a system can take a macro viewpoint and examine the entire tourism system of a country, state, or area and how it operates within and relates to other systems, such as legal, political, economic, and social systems.

## TOURIST SUPPLIERS AND ACTIVITIES

The tourist industry can be described as shown in Figure 1.2. Accommodations include all forms of lodging, even camping and caravanning, and all types of food and beverage services. Shopping encompasses any form of retail purchase such as souvenirs, arts and crafts, clothing, groceries, and others. Activities comprise services such as entertainment, sports, sightseeing, local tours, cultural events, festivals, and gambling. Transportation includes all forms by land, air, or water.

The entire tourism industry rests on a base of natural resources. Such a base must be wholesome and attractive, preferably possessing unusual natural beauty

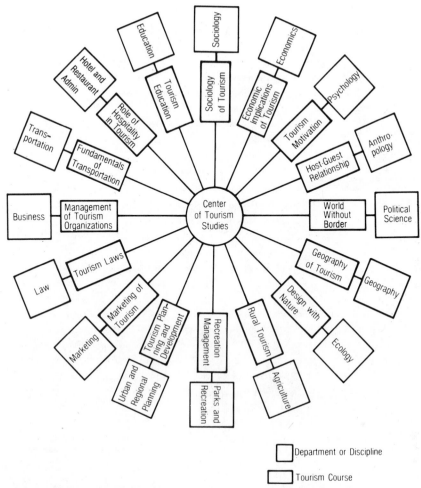

**Figure 1.1** Study of Tourism Choice of Discipline and Approach. *Source:* Jafar Jafari, University of Wisconsin-Stout

and appeal to vacationers. These natural resources must be adequate in dimension to avoid crowding, and they should be free from hazards such as pollution, dangerous or poisonous plants, animals, or insects. Likewise, development of tourism should be on sites free from natural disasters such as floods, droughts, landslides, or earthquakes. (See Chapter 7 for additional considerations of natural resources.)

Strictly speaking, tourism, like recreation and leisure, is typically not defined as an industry. There is no Standard Industrial Classification (SIC) code for tourism. Yet tourism is a major economic activity. There is a market for, a demand for, travel, lodging, food, shops, entertainment, and other tourism services. This demand has created the need for tour operators, travel agents, airlines, cruise ships, buses, accommodations, food and beverage facilities, and other goods and services that supply tourist needs. This economic activity *is* the tourist industry or, properly designated, simply tourism.

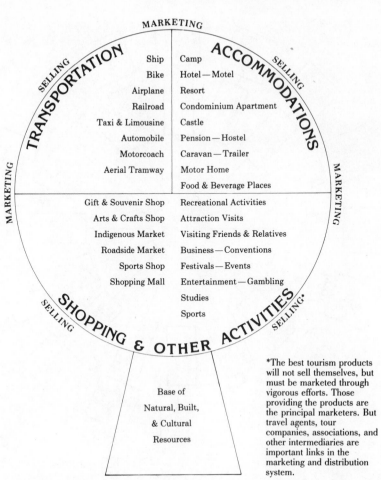

**Figure 1.2** Tourist suppliers and activities.

Tourism is a fragmented industry with many parts and varied activities. As a young industry, it has not yet achieved the cohesiveness necessary for all components to work together for the common good. Each segment makes its own separate contributions to the total tourism picture, yet the segments are interrelated and depend on each other. For example, the success of a Colorado ski resort depends on transportation to bring skiers to the slopes, housing to accommodate them, restaurants to feed them, and other services (medical facilities, après ski lounges, and retail shops) to take care of their needs. Most of the enterprises affiliated with skiing are small. They have a variety of operating policies and, while they are operated as independent businesses, they do in fact depend on each other and serve as small parts of the total picture. This dependence calls for cooperative effort and similar policies; however, the fact that the businesses often compete with each other for the consumer's dollar makes cooperation difficult. Many of them are fiercely independent, dominated by their own self-interest. As tourism grows and matures, the industry will become more united and speak with a single voice on major issues.

Professional chefs find much satisfaction in creating tasty, nutritious, and almost irresistable buffet food items. (Photo courtesy of Royal Cruise Line)

Firms will become larger, and the weak links in tourism's chain of services will be eliminated. Thus, the future of tourism promises to be bright, dynamic, and exciting.

---

### STATISTICAL DATA AVAILABILITY

One of the problems in collecting and reporting statistical data for a book is the data lag. As this text was being revised, 1987 data and some 1988 data were just becoming available. Unfortunately data lags are increasing rather than decreasing. This disturbing reality is especially upsetting when one considers that travel is a dynamic and changing industry. The data in this book provide a perspective on the size and importance of the industry and its sectors. Users are encouraged to access the sources provided to update the information and determine if trends are continuing or changing.

---

## Expenditure Patterns

The expenditure breakdown of the vacation travel dollar is shown in Figure 1.3. Transportation is the largest item in the typical household travel budget, accounting

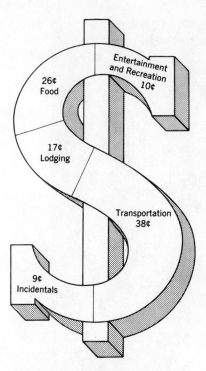

**Figure 1.3** Travel Expenditure
Patterns. *Source:* U.S. Travel Data
Center.

for about 38 cents out of every dollar spent. Food requires the second highest outlay
at 26 cents, followed by 17 cents for lodging. Entertainment and recreation account
for 10 cents, and incidentals require 9 cents.

## ECONOMIC IMPORTANCE

Tourism has grown to be an activity of worldwide importance and significance. For a
number of countries, tourism is the largest commodity in international trade. In
many others it ranks among the top three industries. Tourism has grown rapidly to
become a major social and economic force in the world.

As tourism has grown, it has moved from being the province of the rich to
accessibility to the masses, involving millions of people. The World Tourism Organization attempts to document tourism's growth in an annual publication entitled
*Tourism Compendium.* The 1989 edition estimates that some 390.0 million international tourist arrivals were recorded in 1988, up from the 358.7 peak recorded in
1987. The series shows strong growth from 1950. See Table 1.1.

The Organization for Economic Cooperation and Development (OECD) reports
that the top nine countries ranked by international tourism receipts are (1) United
States, $12.9 billion; (2) Spain, $11.9 billion; (3) Italy, $9.8 billion; (4) France, $9.5

**Table 1.1** International Tourist Arrivals
1950, 1960, and 1970–1986

| Years | Arrivals (in millions) | Percent of Growth |
|-------|------------------------|-------------------|
| 1950 | 25.3 | — |
| 1960 | 69.3 | 173.9 |
| 1970 | 159.7 | 130.4 |
| 1971 | 172.2 | 7.8 |
| 1972 | 181.9 | 5.6 |
| 1973 | 190.6 | 4.8 |
| 1974 | 197.1 | 3.4 |
| 1975 | 214.4 | 8.8 |
| 1976 | 220.7 | 2.9 |
| 1977 | 239.1 | 8.3 |
| 1978 | 257.4 | 7.7 |
| 1979 | 274.0 | 6.4 |
| 1980 | 284.8 | 3.9 |
| 1981 | 288.8 (r) | 1.4 |
| 1982 | 286.7 (r) | −.7 |
| 1983 | 284.4 (r) | −.8 |
| 1984 | 311.2 (r) | 9.4 |
| 1985 | 325.7 (r) | 4.7 |
| 1986 | 332.9 (r) | 2.2 |
| 1987 | 358.7 (r) | 7.8 |
| 1988 | 390.0 (p) | 8.7 |

(r) = revised figures
(p) = preliminary
*Source:* World Tourism Organization and Somerset R. Waters, *Travel Industry World Yearbook,* (New York: Child & Waters, 1989).

billion; (5) United Kingdom, $7.9 billion; (6) West Germany, $7.8 billion; (7) Austria, $6.9 billion; (8) Switzerland, $4.2 billion; and (9) Canada, $3.8 billion.

Americans are prolific travelers. On the average, each day of the year, the number of Americans traveling exceeds the number of residents in New York City. According to the U.S. Travel Data Center, 14.8 million people per day are traveling on a trip that takes them 100 or more miles from home and requires an overnight stay. Over 147 million Americans travel each year out of a nationwide population of 245 million — over 60 percent. Obviously, many more take shorter trips not involving overnight stays.

These travelers create a tremendous economic impact, making the U.S. travel business the third largest retail and service industry in the country, exceeded only by the auto and food industry in size. According to the U.S. Travel Data Center's *1989 Travel Tab,* in 1988 international and domestic travelers in this country spent $313 billion, directly supported 5.5 million jobs, and generated $38.8 billion in tax revenue. To appreciate these figures, consider that each minute you spend reading this chapter, travelers are spending $595,510, the federal government is collecting $40,335 in travel-generated taxes, and state and local governments collect $33,295.

---

**ECONOMIC IMPORTANCE OF TOURISM**

International travel to the United States:

- in 1988, accounted for 34 million arrivals and receipts of $37.1 billion, including international transportation payments to U.S. carriers;
- in 1988, resulted in Federal, state and local tax revenues of more than $3.4 billion, of which $1.5 billion was in Federal tax revenues;
- annually supports over 500,000 U.S. jobs; and
- accounts for one-third of business services exports.

Combining the impact of *international and domestic* travel, tourism in the United States:

- is the third largest retail industry, following food stores and automotive dealers;
- is the second largest private employer in the Nation;
- is one of the top three employers in 39 states;
- accounts for $323 billion in domestic and foreign visitor spending, exceeding 6.4 percent of the gross national product;
- directly employs 5.5 million Americans at every level of skill;
- generates more than $70 billion a year in wages and salaries, and more than $36 billion a year in Federal, state, and local tax revenues; and
- is a highly diversified industry with more than one million component companies ranging from small travel agencies, restaurants and souvenir shops to large airlines and hotel chains, with 99 percent of these companies classified as small businesses.

---

*Source:* U.S. Travel and Tourism Administration

The top 10 states by travel expenditures as reported by the U.S. Travel Data Center are California, which leads with $33.7 billion, followed by Florida with $20.4 billion, New York with $16.8 billion, Texas with $15.2 billion, New Jersey with $13.0 billion, Pennsylvania with $10.1 billion, Illinois with $9.6 billion, Michigan with $7.6 billion, Nevada with $7.3 billion, and Ohio with $6.9 billion.

As already indicated, the travel industry is also a major employer, directly supporting 5.5 million jobs. Travel jobs make up 5.1 percent of the total nonagricultural payroll in the United States. Also, travel-generated employment has been growing at the rate of 2.4 percent, which is somewhat faster than the 1.9 percent growth rate in total U.S. nonagricultural employment.

While these figures are impressive, Somerset Waters, a noted travel consultant and author of the *Travel Industry Yearbook—The Big Picture*, argues that we have been underestimating the size of the travel industry in the United States because we base our estimates of domestic tourism spending on people who travel 100 miles or more from home. He states that if travel between 25 miles to 99 miles were counted,

U.S. travel spending would have totaled $537 billion in 1987, about 86 percent higher than the estimate of the U.S. Travel Data Center.

## Technological Marvels

Four key technologies have made possible the present $2.5 trillion dollar global mass tourism industry. These are: (1) an enormously expanded air transport system serving most of the world's population in an amazingly efficient manner; (2) remarkable technological improvements in cruise ships, motorcoaches, trains, and automobiles, making these types of equipment more comfortable, safer, and beautiful — even resplendent, especially the newer cruise ships; (3) telecommunications spanning the globe with voice as well as written messages; and (4) information processing which links reservations for hotels, transportation systems, travel agencies, tour companies, and other services, all of which can be thousands of miles apart or continents away. Through these technologies, a prospective traveler can make arrangements for a trip to almost anywhere. The trip can be by motorcoach, airplane, passenger ship, or any combination, supplemented by taxi or limousine service, hotel, tour bus, rental car, and even providing entertainment. If the trip is by auto, arrangements for accommodations can easily be made by calling a toll-free telephone number and arranging payment by credit card. If by public carrier, similar telephone or telex reservations can be made. Should the trip be somewhat complicated and require a

Airlines reservation staff members must be accurate, efficient, and courteous. (Photo courtesy of Pan American World Airways)

combination of public transportation, accommodations, transfers, tours or other services, a convenient procedure is to contact a travel agent. The agent integrates the travel services of all suppliers so that the trip will be smooth and trouble free. Virtually all travel agencies are computerized. In the United States, examples of "automated" reservations systems are Sabre (American Airlines), Apollo (United Airlines), and DeltaStar (Delta Airlines). To illustrate, Sabre's worldwide travel information and services network includes 17,500 hotel properties, over 650 airlines, more than 35 tour companies, and 39 major automobile rental agencies. The system can access more than 43 million air fares and discounts.

## Future Projections

In his books *World Economic Development: 1979 and Beyond* (Westview Press, Boulder, Colorado, 1979) and *The Next 200 Years—A Scenario for America and the World* (Morrow, New York, 1976), the late Herman Kahn stated that by the year 2000 tourism will be one of the largest industries in the world. The January 1979 issue of *Travel Trade* magazine, its fiftieth anniversary issue, examined travel from 1929 to the year 2029 and presented additional predictions from Herman Kahn. The May 19, 1989, issue of *Travel Trade,* 60th anniversary issue, contained update information. Figure 1.4, reprinted from the *Travel Trade 60th Anniversary Edition,* presents an excellent review of tourism and provides a framework for future analysis of the industry. It emphasizes the point made earlier that mass tourism is a recent phenomenon: From the time *Travel Trade* was founded in 1929, the birth of modern tourism has taken place. The dramatic breakthroughs in transportation and the growth of a tourist infrastructure have been recorded recently. In the span of the lifetime of one person, all of this has taken place. With growth and technology accelerating, it is difficult to comprehend the dynamic future ahead for tourism.

## A BRIEF HISTORY—TOURISM THROUGH THE AGES

A brief review of the history of travel and tourism is essential to provide background on tourism's roots and to indicate lessons and relationships that still exist today. Even though mass tourism is a recent phenomenon, which has evolved since World War II to become an industry of worldwide importance, there are numerous references to travel and tourism throughout history.

From earliest times, people traveled, mainly driven by hunger or to escape danger; their remains are widely distributed. For example, fossil remains of the first true people *(Homo erectus)* have been found in Western Europe, Africa, China, and Java. This fact indicates the remarkable ability of such early people to travel great distances under primeval conditions.

The invention of money by the Sumerians (Babylonia) and the development of trade, beginning about 4000 B.C., probably mark the beginning of the modern era of travel. The Sumerians not only first grasped the idea of money and used it in their business transactions, but they also invented cuneiform writing and the wheel, and so should be credited as the founders of the travel business; people could now pay for transportation and accommodations either with money or by barter.

Five thousand years ago, cruises were organized and conducted from Egypt. Probably the first journey ever made for purposes of peace and tourism was made by Queen Hatshepsut to the lands of Punt (believed to be what is now Somalia) in 1490 B.C. Descriptions of this tour have been recorded on the walls of the Temple of Deit El Bahari at Luxor. These texts and bas reliefs are some of the rarest artworks and are universally admired for their wonderous beauty and artistic qualities. The Colossi of Memnon at Thebes have on their pedestals the names of Greek tourists of the fifth century B.C.

The Phoenicians were probably the first real business travelers in the modern sense that they went from place to place as traders. Early travel in the Orient, particularly in China and India, was also largely based on trade.

## Early Travelers

*Oceanians*  Among early voyages, those in Oceania are amazing. Small dugout canoes, not over 40 feet in length, were used for voyages from Southeast Asia southward and eastward through what is now called Micronesia across the Pacific to the Marquesas Islands and the Tuamotu Archipelago and the Society Islands. At about 500 A.D., Polynesians from the Society Islands traveled to Hawaii, a distance of over 2000 miles. Navigation was accomplished by observing the position of the sun and stars, ocean swells, clouds, and bird flights. Considering the problems of fresh water and food supplies, such sea travel was astonishing.

*Mediterranean Peoples*  In the ancient cradle of Western civilization, travel for trade, commerce, religious purposes, medical treatment, or education developed at an early date. There are numerous references to caravans and traders in the Old Testament.

In ancient Greece, people traveled to the Olympic Games, begun in 776 B.C., giving rise to the peripheral business of providing accommodations; they were needed by both the participants and the spectators, as well as other travelers. Today the Olympics and other sporting events continue to be major tourist attractions; the National Football League's annual Super Bowl is a prime example.

Ancient Rome provided another important early chapter in tourism history. The Romans' affluence and vast empire were the primary ingredients needed for tourism. To manage their empire, the Romans built a magnificent network of roads, on which they could travel as much as 100 miles a day using relays of horses furnished from rest posts five or six miles apart. Romans also journeyed to see famous temples in the Mediterranean area, particularly the pyramids and monuments of Egypt. Greece and Asia Minor were popular destinations, offering the Olympic Games, medicinal baths and seaside resorts, theatrical productions, festivals, athletic competitions, and other forms of amusement and entertainment. The Roman combination of empire, roads, the need for overseeing the empire, wealth, leisure, tourist attractions, and the desire for travel created a demand for accommodations and other tourist services that came into being as an early form of tourism.

This pattern, clearly evident in the Roman days, can be observed over and over again in the cycle of tourism development. Building roads and applying military

# SOME PAST, PRESENT AND FUTURE

| Chart prepared by Dr. Herman Kahn for Travel Trade 50th Anniversary Issue, 1979. Present Decade facts compiled and updated by Doris and Phil Davidoff. | **1929** | **1949** | **1969** |
|---|---|---|---|

## Travel Modes, Speeds, Times & Costs

| | 1929 | 1949 | 1969 |
|---|---|---|---|
| **TRAVEL MODES** | Air: Ford, Fokker Trimoters. Rail: first streamliners; 60–70 mph cruise. Auto: Model T/A; ~35 mph; roads poor. Ship: All overseas travel 25 mph | DC-4; DC-6, Constellation; many DC-3s. Railroads near peak. Bus travel growing. Cars ~60 mph; roads good. | 707, DC-8, Electra, DC-9; 727 Air travel booming (Jets introduced end of 1950's) Rail, bus declining relatively. Cars ~70 mph; Interstate hiway system 80% completed. |
| **APPROX. MAX. TRAVEL SPEEDS** | 100–125 MPH | 250–300 MPH | 500–600 MPH |

### TIME NEEDED FROM N.Y. TO:

| | 1929 | 1949 | 1969 |
|---|---|---|---|
| Sydney (10,000mi) | 2 weeks | 2 days | 1 day |
| Moscow (4,700mi) | 1 week | 1 day | 9 hours |
| London (3,500mi) | 5 days | 18 hours | 7 hours |

| | Hrs. | Car | Rail | Air | Hrs. | Car | Rail | Air | Hrs. | Car | Rail | Air |
|---|---|---|---|---|---|---|---|---|---|---|---|---|
| LA (2,500mi) | | 120 | 70 | 25 | | 80 | 5 | 12 | | 60 | 55 | 5 |
| Chicago (700mi) | | 25 | 16 | 9 | | 15 | 14 | 5 | | 13 | 13 | 3 |
| Wash., DC (200mi) | | 9 | 5 | 3 | | 6 | 4 | 3 | | 4 | 4 | 1½ |

| **ILLUSTRATIVE MINIMUM TRAVEL FARES (1979 DOLLARS)** | NY—San Francisco: ~$725 one way (plane or train) ~28¢/mi | *1947* NY—San Francisco: ~$470 or 19¢/mi NY—London: ~$1070 or 31¢/mi NY—Sydney: ~$2500 or 25¢/mi | NY—San Francisco: ~$210 or 8¢/mi NY—London: ~$280 or 8¢/mi NY—Sydney: ~$882 or 8¢/mi |

## Progress in Technology

| | 1929 | 1949 | 1969 |
|---|---|---|---|
| **DESTINATIONS/ ACCESSIBILITY** | Only nearby destinations practical for *most* tourists & many businesspersons. | Continental travel possible for many tourists. Overseas travel still limited. | Continental travel for most; overseas travel for many; growing rapidly. |
| **CONVENIENCES** | Very limited, but luxury and personal services available at high price | Improving rapidly, e.g., car rentals, credit cards, handy motels. | "Convenience technology" e.g., moving sidewalks, improved baggage handling |
| **INFORMATION AND RESERVATIONS: TIME NEEDED** | By mail or office visits to carrier or travel agent; weeks to hours | Much by phone; hours to minutes | Phone/computer; minutes to seconds |
| **STAYING IN TOUCH WITH HOME** | Mail; days Telegraph; hours | Mail/phone; days/minutes | Phone: direct dialing credit cards; minutes/seconds. |
| **WEATHER PREDICTION** | Barely useful next day predictions in a few localities | Useful nationwide predictions | Some tourist planning on basis of weather |

## Economic & Social

| | 1929 | 1949 | 1969 |
|---|---|---|---|
| **"TOURIST POLLUTION" ISSUES** | Practically none | Negligible | Emerging |
| **ROLE OF TRAVEL/ TOURIST AGENT** | Clerk—"Mom & Pop" store | Clerk, sometimes counselor; still "Mom & Pop" | More specialization; clerking aspects easier |
| **TRAVEL/ TOURISM/ LEISURE** | Some leisure; travel expensive; tourism for relative few | More leisure; travel cheaper; tourism available to many | $\dfrac{(\text{Tourism} = T)}{(\text{Leisure} = L)}$ growing Booming business travel; Specialized tourism activity orientation and conventions |
| | U.S. average work week ~48 hours | Av. work week ~41 hrs. | Av. work week ~40 hrs. |
| **TRAVEL/TOURISM AND ECONOMIC GROWTH** | Economy good (just before depression) Travel & tourism growing | End of two decades of depression and war Beginning of new economic growth & new era of travel and tourism. War-increased awareness of other places | Travel & tourism growth about double overall economic growth rate since 1949. |

**Explanations: ALL prices have been computed in terms of 1979 U.S. dollars. Symbol: ~ = approximate.**    *Copyright © 1989*

**Figure 1.4** Tourism trends. *Source:* Prepared by Dr. Herman Kahn of the Hudson Institute for the Travel Trade 50th Anniversary Issue in 1979 and updated by Doris and Phillip Davidoff. Reproduced from the 60th Anniversary Edition of *Travel Trade* 1989.

# TRENDS IN THE TRAVEL INDUSTRY

| 1979 | PRESENT | 2009 | 2029 |
|---|---|---|---|
| 747; various wide bodied craft, Limited Concorde service. Rail, bus declining relatively; some technological & comfort improvements. Cars (temporarily?) held to nominal 55 mph | No real change in either subsonic or supersonic aircraft. Concorde routes unchanged: no second generation supersonic aircraft. 747-400 carries more people over longer range. ATC improvement just beginning. General aviation declined during decade. Fast rail expanded in Europe and Japan, but not U.S. No increase in car speed. | HST ($H_2$ fuel?) 3rd generation SST. Many various, big jets Guided surface (various "rail" ~ 200–400 mph); Cars ~ 100–200 mph (with auto. control) Personal planes (V/STOL). Limited commercial & government space travel & accommodations. | Revolutionary new modes; e.g. "transplanetary tunnel." Many HSTs; still much subsonic air travel. Suborbital travel. Private space travel and tourism accommodations. Various fast automated private vehicles. |
| 500–1300 MPH | 500–1300 MPH | 500–3000 MPH | 500–6000 MPH |
| 1 day | 1 day | 8 hours | 3 hours |
| 9 hours | 9 hours | 4 hours | 2 hours |
| 4 hours | 4 hours | 3 hours | 2 hours |
| Hrs.  Car 70 / 15 / 4½   Rail — / 13 / 3.5   Air 5 / 2 / 1 | Hrs.  Car 70 / 15 / 4½   Rail — / 13 / 3.5   Air 5 / 2 / 1 | 2 hours / 1 hour / 1 hour | 1 hour / 1 hour / .5 |
| NY—San Francisco: ~$125 or 5¢/mi  NY—London: ~$150 or 4.5¢/mi  NY—Sydney: ~$800 or 8¢/mi | Increased competition lowered fares, especially as shown in terms of 1979 dollars (approximately 60% of 1989 dollars). London $118, 3.3 cents San Francisco $101, 4.0 cents Sydney $450, 4.5 cents | 0–5¢ per mile  →  Some transportation "free" as a public service | 0–5¢ per mile  Much transportation "free" as public service. |
| Overseas travel possible for most people. New range of destinations opening up. | More frequent, shorter vacations, weekend commuting in some professional families. | Very extensive, frequent worldwide travel All destinations (e.g., subsea, some space) accessible. | Cheap, fast, convenient travel to everywhere (but space travel may be expensive). |
| More frequent, shorter vacations, weekend commuting in some professional families. | Room-to-room baggage and simple, universal credit cards not attained. Bank credit cards more universal than 1979. | "Red-tape" problems largely eliminated. Fast and comfortable room-to-room service. | What is incremental convenience? |
| Phone/computer; Improved, multi-enquiry computer; seconds | PC's have become base for agencies; databases increased and more information easily available. | All data of interest & all reservations by instantaneous home video, "everything in living room" | Various formats e.g., holography in living room, for display, consideration of unlimited information |
| Phone at widely acceptable cost; seconds | Long distance rates lower, but not cheap. | Phone/video slight cost domestic & worldwide | Whole world videophone at negligible cost |
| Good short-term predictions; days | No real change. | Consistent travel planning by weather; weeks ahead. Resorts with controlled environments | Planning months ahead; cost discounts for bad weather periods |
| Frequent discussion; sometimes limiting | Little change from 1979. | Receding as a controversial issue; largely controlled by local option and improved management | Not conceived as problem; fully managed; but various local limits are understood |
| Specialized "leisure counselor" Large agency chains grow | Increased market share of domestic tickets. Travel supermarkets did not develop. | Real-time pictures available from point-of-destination agencies; home video connections | Distinction between local and distant may have largely eroded—Every place is "next door" |
| T/L still growing; new leisure options proliferate; Pleasure travel increasing relative to business travel | Vast growth even though great increase in competition. Average workweek unchanged. | T/L stabilized, but all options growing absolutely; Diverse specialized tourism | Vast range of pleasant aesthetically satisfying, fulfilling activities (incl. travel); discretionary choices among them |
| ------------------------------- Av. work week ~ 38 hrs. | ------------------------------- Av. work week ~ 35 hrs. | ------------------------------- Individual work week reflects choices; could be about 20 hours | ------------------------------- Work time largely a matter of individual choice; could be slight; very many choices |
| Rapid expansion of tourism as a way of life  → | Both business and pleasure travel grew at rates well beyond the economic growth rate. | Business travel partly or greatly superseded by new telecommunications Tourism & leisure fraction of economy still increasing slowly | "Steady state" for travel & leisure, but in overall slowly growing economy Many present categories (e.g., discretionary spending & leisure time) no longer meaningful |

*Travel Trade Publications*

technology (e.g., aircraft) to civilian use are examples. The national system of inter-state highways in the United States and the jet airplane have both been tremendous boons to tourism, yet neither was developed expressly for that purpose.

In Asia Minor, beginning with the installation of a democratic government in Ephesus by Alexander the Great in 334 B.C., some 700,000 tourists would crowd into Ephesus (in what is now Turkey) in a single season to be entertained by the acrobats, animal acts, jugglers, magicians, and prostitutes who filled the streets. Ephesus also became an important trading center and, under Alexander, was one of the most important cities in the ancient world.

History can teach us many lessons. The Roman Empire and that of Alexander the Great provide another history lesson for tourism—tourists wish to go where they will be safe and comfortable. When these empires were at their height, tourism flourished and travel was safe. Water-based recreation and summer holidays were as popular then as they continue to be today. But the decline of the empire was accompanied by the decline of tourism. The wealthy class was greatly reduced, roads deteriorated, and the countryside became overrun with bandits, thieves, and scoundrels, making travel unsafe. Today's traveler, just like the ancient Greeks and Romans, does not want to travel in places that have a reputation for being unsafe.

*Europeans*  The collapse of the Roman Empire in the fourth and fifth centuries spelled disaster for pleasure travel and tourism in Europe. During the Dark Ages (from the fall of the Western Roman Empire, 476 A.D., to the beginning of the modern era, 1450 A.D.), only the most adventurous persons would travel. A trip during this period in history was dangerous; no one associated travel with pleasure. The most notable exception to this in Europe during the period was the Crusades and, by the end of the Dark Ages, the pilgrimages of Europeans who were traveling to the religious shrines on that continent.

Epic sea travels by the Scandinavians to Greenland and North America about 982 A.D. were great feats of navigation and courage.

*The Grand Tour*  The "Grand Tour" of the seventeenth and eighteenth centuries was made by diplomats, businesspeople, and scholars who traveled to Europe, mainly to the cities of France and Italy. It became fashionable for scholars to study in Paris, Rome, Florence, and other cultural centers. While making the Grand Tour began as an educational experience, it has been criticized as eventually degenerating into the simple pursuit of pleasure. The following paragraph from *A Geography of Tourism* describes the Grand Tour.

> One of the interesting aspects of the Grand Tour was its conventional and regular form. As early as 1678 John Gailhard, in his *Compleat Gentlemen*, had prescribed a three-year tour as customary. A generally accepted itinerary was also laid down which involved a long stay in France, especially in Paris, almost a year in Italy visiting Genoa, Milan, Florence, Rome and Venice, and then a return by way of Germany and the Low Countries via Switzerland. Of course, there were variations to this itinerary but this was the most popular route: it was generally believed that "there was little more to be seen in the rest of the civil world after Italy, France and the Low Countries, but plain and prodigious barbarism."[8]

[8] H. Robinson, *A Geography of Tourism* (London: Macdonald and Evans, 1976), p. 13.

The term *Grand Tour* persists today, and the trip to Europe — the Continent — can be traced back to the early Grand Tour. Today's concept is far different, however; the tour is more likely to be three weeks, not three years.

*Americans*   The vast continent of North America, principally in what is now Florida and in the Southwest, was originally explored by the Spanish in the sixteenth century. Remarkably long journeys were made, often under severe conditions. The Spanish used horses, which were unknown to the American Indians until that time. In the East, Cape Cod was discovered by Gosnold in 1602 and the Plymouth Colony was established in 1620.

Early travel was on foot or on horseback, but travel by small boat or canoe provided access to the interior of the country. Generally, travel was from east to west. As roads were built, stagecoach travel became widespread, and "ordinaries" (small hotels) came into common use. Among the most remarkable journeys were those by covered wagon to the West across the Great Plains. This movement followed the Civil War (1861 – 1865). Construction of railroads across the country (the first transcontinental link was at Promontory, Utah, in 1869) popularized rail travel. The Wells-Fargo Company organized the American Express Company in 1850. This pioneer company issued the first travelers checks in 1891 and began other travel services, later becoming travel agents and arranging tours. Today, American Express is known throughout the world for its travelers checks, credit cards, and various travel and financial services.

One of the most significant events in America's travel history is the amount of travel done by servicemen and women during World War II. Over 12 million Americans served in the armed forces from 1941 to 1945. Most of these were assigned to duty at places far removed from their homes, such as the European and Pacific war theaters. Extensive domestic travel was commonplace, introducing the military traveler to different and often exotic places and bringing a broader perspective of what the North American continent and foreign countries had to offer visitors. Travel thus became a part of their life experience. Following the war, a large increase in travel occurred when gasoline rationing was removed and automobiles were again being manufactured. Air, rail, and bus travel also expanded.

## Early (and Later) Tourist Attractions

Sightseeing has always been a major activity of tourists; this has been true since ancient times. Most of us have heard of the seven wonders of the ancient world, but few could win a trivia contest by naming them:

1. The Great Pyramids of Egypt, including the Sphinx
2. The Hanging Gardens of Babylon, sometimes including the Walls of Babylon and the Palace, in what is now Iraq
3. The Tomb of Mausolus at Halicarnassus, in what is now Turkey
4. The Statue of Zeus at Olympia in Greece
5. The Collosus of Rhodes in the Harbor at Rhodes, an island belonging to Greece
6. The Great Lighthouse (Pharos) in Alexandria, Egypt
7. The Temple Artemis (also called the Temple of Diana) at Ephesus — at the time part of Greece, now in Turkey

The Great Pyramids of Egypt are the sole remaining wonder.

Just as tourists in ancient times traveled to see these wonders, modern tourists travel to see such natural wonders as the Grand Canyon, Yosemite National Park, Yellowstone, Niagara Falls, the oceans, the Great Lakes, and human-built wonders such as great cities, museums, dams, and monuments.

## Spas, Baths, Seaside Resorts

Another interesting aspect in the history of tourism was the development of spas, after their original use by the Romans, which took place in Britain and on the continent. In the eighteenth century, spas became very fashionable among members of high society, not only for their curative aspects but also for the social events, games, dancing, and gambling that they offered. The spa at Bath, England, was one such successful health and social resort.

Sea bathing also became popular, and some believed that salt water treatment was more beneficial than was that at the inland spas. Well known in Britain were Brighton, Margate, Ramsgate, Worthing, Hastings, Weymouth, Blackpool, and Scarborough. By 1861 these successful seaside resorts indicated that there was a pent-up demand for vacation travel. Most visitors did not stay overnight but rather made one-day excursions to the seaside. Patronage of the hotels at these resorts was still limited to those with considerable means.

Tourism thus owes a debt to medical practitioners who advocated the medicinal value of mineral waters and sent their patients to places where mineral springs were known to exist. Later on, physicians also recommended sea bathing for its therapeutic value. While spas and seaside resorts were first visited for reasons of health, they soon became centers of entertainment, recreation, and gambling, attracting the rich and fashionable with or without ailments. This era of tourism illustrates that it is usually a combination of factors rather than one element that spells the success or failure of an enterprise. Today one finds that hot springs, although they are not high on travelers' priority lists, are still tourist attractions. Examples in the United States are Hot Springs, Arkansas; French Lick, Indiana; and Glenwood Springs, Colorado. The sea, particularly in the Sunbelt, continues to have a powerful attraction and is one of the leading forces in tourism development, which is evident by the number of travelers to Hawaii, Florida, the Caribbean, and Mexico.

## Early Economic References

As tourists traveled to see pyramids, visit seaside resorts, and attend festivals and athletic events, they needed food and lodging, and they spent money for these services. Traders did the same. Then as now, the economic impact of these expenditures was difficult to measure, as evidenced by the following quotation from Thomas Mun, who in 1620 wrote in *England's Treasure by Foreign Trade*, ''There are yet some other petty things which seem to have a reference to this balance of which the said officers of His Majesty's Customs can take no notice to bring them into the account; as mainly, the expenses of the travelers.''[9] In contrast, a present-day statement

---

[9] George Young, *Tourism, Blessing or Blight?* (Middlesex, England: Pelican Books, 1973), p. 1.

Scuba diver in Sea Base Alpha demonstrates deep sea exploration systems for Walt Disney World guests at "The Living Seas," Epcot Center adventure in Future World. Crystal-clear windows in the futuristic sea base enable visitors to look directly into a six-million gallon "ocean" with a Caribbean coral reef teeming with tropical fish and other sea creatures. The clear acrylic "scuba tube" enables researchers to show how they would enter the ocean from an underwater research center of the future. Attractions provide many such unique jobs, plus those of tour guides who give explanations. (Photo courtesy of Walt Disney Productions, 1986)

reads, "Today we have moved from tourism being an accounting nuisance to the largest item in the world trade and for many countries the principal source at foreign exchange earnings." [10]

[10] John Hamilton, Robert Clerindon, and Quentin Claugh, *International Tourism* (London: The Economist Intelligence Unit, 1970), p. 1.

### The First Travel Agents

In 1822, Robert Smart of Bristol, England, announced himself as the first steamship agent. He began booking passengers for steamers to various Bristol Channel ports and to Dublin, Ireland.

In 1841 Thomas Cook began running a special excursion train from Leicester to Loughborough (in England), a trip of 12 miles. On July 5 of that year, Cook's train carried 570 passengers at a round-trip price of 1 shilling per passenger. This is believed to be the first publicly advertised excursion train. Thus, Cook can rightfully be recognized as the first rail excursion agent; his pioneering efforts were eventually copied widely in all parts of the world. Cook's company grew rapidly, providing escorted tours to the Continent and later to the United States and around the world. The company continues to be one of the world's largest travel organizations.

The first specialist in individual inclusive travel (the basic function of travel agents) was probably Thomas Bennett (1814–1898), an Englishman who served as secretary to the British consul-general in Oslo, Norway. In this position, Bennett frequently arranged individual scenic tours in Norway for visiting British notables. Finally, in 1850 he set up a business as a "trip organizer" and provided individual tourists with itineraries, carriages, provisions, and a "traveling kit." He routinely made advance arrangements for horses and hotel rooms for his clients.

### Historic Transportation

Another element in the tourism equation is transportation. The early tourists traveled on foot, on beasts of burden, by boat, and on wheeled vehicles.

*Stagecoach Travel*   Coaches were invented in Hungary in the fifteenth century and provided regular service there on prescribed routes. By the 1800s, stagecoach travel had become quite popular, especially in Great Britain. The development of the famous English tavern was brought about by the need for overnight lodging by stagecoach passengers.

*Water Travel*   Market boats picked up passengers as well as goods on ship canals in England as early as 1772. The Duke of Bridgewater began such service between Manchester and London Bridge (near Warrington). Each boat had a coffee room from which refreshments were sold by the captain's wife. By 1815 steamboats were plying the Clyde, the Avon, and the Thames. A poster in 1833 announced steamboat excursion trips from London. By 1841 steamship excursions on the Thames were so well established that a publisher was bringing out a weekly *Steamboat Excursion Guide.*

*Rail Travel*   Railways were first built in England in 1825 and carried passengers beginning in 1830. The newly completed railway between Liverpool and Manchester featured special provisions for passengers. The railroad's directors did not expect much passenger business, but time proved them wrong. The typical charge of only 1 penny per mile created a sizable demand for rail travel—much to the delight of the rail companies. As these fares were much lower than stagecoach fares, rail travel became widely accepted even for those with low incomes.

Early rail travel in Britain was not without its detractors, however. Writers in the most powerful organs of public opinion of that day seemed to consider the new form of rail locomotion a device of Satan. When a rail line was proposed from London to Woolrich to carry passengers at a speed of 18 miles per hour, one aghast contributor to the *Quarterly Review* wrote, "We should as soon expect the people of Woolrich to be fired off upon one of Congreve's ricochet rockets as trust themselves to the mercy of such a machine going at such a rate." Another writer deemed the railroads for passenger transportation as "visionary schemes unworthy of notice."

*Automobile and Motorcoach Travel*  Automobiles entered the travel scene in the United States when Henry Ford introduced his famous Model T in 1908. The relatively cheap "tin lizzie" revolutionized travel in the country, creating a demand for better roads. By 1920 a road network became available, leading to the automobile's current dominance of the travel industry. Today the automobile accounts for about 84 percent of intercity miles traveled and is the mode of travel for approximately 80 percent of all trips. The auto traveler brought about the early tourist courts in the 1920s and 1930s, which have evolved into the motels and motor hotels of today. Motorcoaches also came into use soon after the popularization of the automobile and remain a major mode of transportation.

*Air Travel*  Nearly 16 years after the airplane's first flight at Kitty Hawk, North Carolina, in 1903, regularly scheduled air service began in Germany. This was a Berlin-Leipzig-Weimar route, and the carrier later became known as Deutsche Lufthansa. Today, Lufthansa is a major international airline. The first transatlantic passenger was Charles A. Levine, who flew with Clarence Chamberlin nonstop

Pleasant, prompt service by flight attendants adds much to a relaxing and happy trip. (Photo courtesy of Delta Airlines)

from New York to Germany. The plane made a forced landing 118 miles from Berlin, their destination, which they reached on June 7, 1927. This was shortly after Charles Lindbergh's historic solo flight from New York to Paris.

The first U.S. airline, Varney Airlines, was launched in 1926 and provided scheduled airmail service. However, this airline was formed only 11 days before Western Airlines, which began service on April 17, 1926. Varney Airlines later merged with three other lines to form United Airlines. On April 1, 1987, Western merged with Delta Airlines. At first, only one passenger was carried in addition to the mail, if the weight limitations permitted. The first international route appears to have been Pan American Airways' flight from Key West, Florida, to Havana, Cuba, on October 28, 1927.

The various U.S. airlines gradually expanded their services to more cities and international destinations. During World War II, their equipment and most staff were devoted to war service. Development of the DC-3 and the Boeing 314A trans-oceanic Clipper in the early 1940s established paying passenger traffic and brought about much wider acceptance of air travel. The jet engine, invented in England by Frank Whittle, was used on such military planes as the B-52. The first American commercial jet was the Boeing 707. The first United States transcontinental jet flight was operated by American Airlines on January 25, 1959, from Los Angeles to New York City, and the jumbo jet era began in January 1970 when Pan American World Airways flew 352 passengers from New York to London using the new Boeing 747 equipment.

Because of its speed, comfort, and safety, air travel is the leading mode of public transportation today, as measured in revenue passenger miles (one fare-paying passenger transported one mile).

### Accommodations

The earliest guest rooms were parts of private dwellings, and travelers were hosted almost like members of the family. In the Middle East and in the Orient, caravan-saries and inns go back into antiquity. In more modern times, first the stagecoach, and then railroads, steamships, the automobile, motorcoach, and airplane, expanded the need for adequate accommodations. The railroad brought the downtown city hotel, the automobile and motorcoach the motel, and the airplane the boom in accommodations within or near airports. Housing, feeding, and entertaining travelers is one of the world's most important industries, and because of this importance, further detail is provided in Chapters 3 and 7.

## CAREERS IN TOURISM

Every student eventually must leave the college or university campus and seek a career-oriented job. This is a difficult decision-making time, often filled with doubt as to what goals or ambitions should be pursued. Coming face to face with the problem of getting a first major career-oriented job is a challenging task. You are marketing a product — yourself — and you will have to do a good job of communicating to convince a prospective employer that you have the abilities needed and that you will be an asset to the firm.

## Employment Forecasts

Generally, occupations in which current participants have the most education are projected to have the most rapid growth rates. Service-producing industries will account for much of the projected growth. These industries will expand (1986 to 2000) by more than 10 million jobs. In 1986, service industries accounted for about 23 percent of all nonfarm wage-paying and salaried jobs. In 2000, they will account for somewhat over 27 percent. More than 32 million payroll jobs will be in the services division in the year 2000 — an awesome growth. Business services will be important contributors as they continue to produce new services that greatly add to their overall demand and employment growth.[11]

Table 1.2 provides employment projections for various tourism-related industries.

## Career Possibilities

Tourism today is one of the world's largest industries. It is made up of many segments, the principal ones being transportation, accommodations, food service, shopping, travel arrangement, and activities for tourists, such as history, culture, adventure, sports, recreation, entertainment, and other similar activities. The businesses that provide these services require knowledgeable business managers.

Familiarity with tourism, recreation, business, and leisure equips one to pursue a career in a number of tourism-related fields. Even during times of severe economic downturn, tourism has performed well. Tourism skills are critically needed, and there are many opportunities available in a multitude of fields.

Because tourism is very fragmented and each sector has many job opportunities and career paths, it is virtually impossible to list and describe all the jobs one might consider in this large field. However, as a student interested in tourism, you could examine the following areas, many of which are discussed in more detail in Chapter 3.

*Airlines*  The airlines are a major travel industry employer, offering a host of jobs at many levels ranging from entry level to top management. Illustrative jobs are reservation agents, flight attendants, pilots, flight engineers, aircraft mechanics, maintenance staff, baggage handlers, airline food service jobs, sales representatives, sales jobs, computer specialists, training staff, office jobs, clerical positions, ticket agents, and research jobs. Since airlines have to meet safety and other requirements, opportunities also exist with the Federal Aviation Administration. The FAA hires air traffic controllers and various other specialists. Airports also use a wide range of personnel from parking attendants to managers. Other air-related jobs are available with associations such as the Air Transport Association.

*Bus Companies*  Bus companies require management personnel, ticket agents, sales representatives, tour representatives, hostesses, information clerks, clerical positions, bus drivers, personnel people, and training employees.

[11] U.S. Department of Labor, *Projections 2000* (Washington, D.C.: Government Printing Office, 1988).

**Table 1.2** Tourism Employment Forecasts to Year 2000

| Industry | Employment (thousands) | | | | | Annual Rate of Change (percent) | |
|---|---|---|---|---|---|---|---|
| | 1979 | 1986 | Projected, 2000 | | | Employment | Output |
| | | | Low | Moderate | High | | |
| Transportation | 3021 | 3041 | 3315 | 3500 | 3568 | 1.0 | 2.4 |
| Local passenger | 263 | 282 | 300 | 308 | 315 | .6 | 1.3 |
| Air transportation | 438 | 570 | 690 | 721 | 725 | 1.7 | 3.7 |
| Arrangement of passenger trans. | — | 158 | 217 | 227 | 230 | 2.6 | 5.9 |
| Miscellaneous trans. services | — | 126 | 153 | 164 | 172 | 1.9 | 3.0 |
| Eating & drinking places | 4513 | 5879 | 8084 | 8365 | 8501 | 2.6 | 1.9 |
| Miscellaneous shopping stores | 569 | 746 | 1038 | 1085 | 1103 | 2.7 | — |
| Hotels & other lodging places | 1060 | 1401 | 1848 | 1971 | 2061 | 2.5 | 1.9 |
| Advertising | 146 | 202 | 284 | 302 | 310 | 2.9 | 3.5 |
| Research, management & consulting services | — | 788 | 1186 | 1301 | 1394 | 3.6 | 4.3 |
| Automotive rentals without drivers | 120 | 161 | 210 | 233 | 241 | 2.7 | 2.6 |
| Amusement & recreation services | 712 | 915 | 1143 | 1204 | 1235 | 2.0 | 4.6 |
| Business & professional assn's. | 118 | 135 | 144 | 159 | 165 | 1.2 | 2.2 |

*Source:* U.S. Department of Labor, *Projections 2000* (Washington, D.C.: Government Printing Office, 1988).

*Cruise Companies* The cruise industry is the fastest growing segment of the tourism industry today. Job opportunities include those for sales representatives, clerical workers, market researchers, and recreation directors. Because of its similarity in operations, the cruise industry has many of the same jobs as the lodging industry.

*Railroads* Passenger rail service is currently dominated by Amtrak, which hires passenger service representatives, sales representatives, reservation clerks and other types of clerks, conductors, engineers, firemen, and station agents.

*Rental Car Companies* With increased air travel and the growth of fly/drive programs, rental car companies are becoming an even more important segment of

Vital engineering and maintenance of jet engines must be performed by expert personnel. (Photo courtesy of Pan American World Airways)

the travel industry. This sector of tourism employs reservation agents, rental sales agents, clerks of various kinds, service agents, mechanics, and district and regional managers.

*Hotels, Motels, and Resorts*   The range of jobs in hotels and motels is extremely broad. The following list is representative: general manager, resident manager, comptroller, accountants, management trainees, director of sales, director of convention sales, director of personnel, director of research, mail clerks, room clerks, reservation clerks, front office manager, housekeepers, superintendent of service, bellhops, lobby porters, doormen, maids, chefs, cooks, kitchen helpers, storeroom employees, dishwashers, waiters, bartenders, apprentice waiters, heating and air conditioning personnel, maintenance workers, engineers, electricians, plumbers, carpenters, painters, and laundry workers.

Resorts tend to have the same jobs as those mentioned for hotels and motels; however, larger resorts will have greater job opportunities and require more assistants in all areas. Resorts also have a number of additional job opportunities in the areas of social events, entertainment, and recreation, such as for tennis and golf pros. At ski resorts there will be ski instructors, members of a safety patrol, and so on. The American Hotel and Motel Association estimates the lodging industry employs approximately 1.4 million people and creates 100,000 new jobs a year.

*Travel Agencies*   Travel agencies range from very small to very large businesses. The smaller businesses are very much like any other small business. Very few people carry out all the business operations, and jobs include secretarial, travel counseling, and managerial activities. In large offices job opportunities are more varied and include commercial account specialists, domestic travel counselors, international travel counselors, research directors, and advertising managers. Trainee group sales consultants, accountants, file clerks, sales personnel, tour planners, tour guides, reservationists, group coordinators, trainees, operations employees, administrative assistants, advertising specialists, and computer specialists are other possibilities.

*Tour Companies*  Tour companies offer employment opportunities in such positions as tour manager or escort, tour coordinator, tour planner, publicist, reservations specialist, accountant, sales representative, group tour specialist, incentive tour coordinator, costing specialist, hotel coordinator, office supervisor, and managerial positions. Often a graduate will begin employment as a management trainee, working in all the departments of the company before a permanent assignment is made.

*Food Service*  Many job opportunities are available in the rapidly growing food service industry such as head waiters, captains, waiters, waitresses, bus persons, chefs, cooks, bartenders, restaurant managers, assistant managers, personnel directors, dieticians, menu planners, cashiers, food service supervisors, purchasing agents, butchers, beverage workers, hostesses, kitchen helpers, and dishwashers.

*Tourism Education*  As tourism continues to grow, the need for training and education grows. In recent years many colleges and universities have added travel and tourism programs, existing programs have expanded, vocational schools have launched programs, trade associations have introduced education and certification programs, and private firms have opened travel schools. There are job opportunities for administrators, teachers, professors, researchers, and support staff.

*Tourism Research*  Tourism research consists of the collection and analysis of data from both primary and secondary sources. The tourism researcher plans market studies, consumer surveys, and the implementation of research projects. Research jobs are available in tourism with airlines, cruise lines, management consulting firms, state travel offices, and so on.

*Travel Journalism*  There are a number of opportunities available in travel writing as editors, staff writers, and freelance writers. Most major travel firms have a need for public relations people who write and edit, disseminate information, develop communication vehicles, obtain publicity, arrange special events, do public speaking, plan public relations campaigns, and so on. A travel photographer could find employment either in public relations or travel writing.

*Recreation*  Jobs in recreation include life guards, tennis and golf instructors, coaches for various athletic teams, drama directors, and so on. Many recreation workers teach handicrafts. Resorts, parks, and recreation departments often employ recreation directors who hire specialists to work with senior citizens or youth groups, to serve as camp counselors, or to teach such skills as boating and sailing. Management, supervisory, and administrative positions are also available.

*Attractions*  Attractions such as amusement parks and theme parks are a major source of tourism employment. Such large organizations as Disney World, Disneyland, Six Flags, Worlds of Fun, and Sea World provide job opportunities ranging from top management jobs to clerical and maintenance jobs.

*Tourist Offices and Information Centers*  Numerous jobs are available in tourist offices and information centers. Many chambers of commerce function as informa-

Employment as an animal trainer is a highly specialized position. (Photo courtesy of Circus World Museum, operated by the State Historical Society in Baraboo, Wisconsin)

tion centers and hire employees to provide this information. Many states operate welcome centers. Job titles found in state tourism offices are: director, assistant director, deputy director, travel representative, economic development specialist, assistant director for travel promotion, statistical analyst, public information officer, assistant director for public relations, marketing coordinator, communications specialist, travel editor, media liaison, media specialist, photographer, administrative assistant, information specialist, media coordinator, manager of travel literature, writer, chief of news and information, marketing coordinator, market analyst, research analyst, economist, reference coordinator, secretary, package tour coordinator, and information clerk.

*Convention and Visitors Bureaus*   As more and more cities enter the convention and visitor industry, employment opportunities in this segment grow. Many cities are devoting public funds to build convention centers to compete in this growing market. Convention and visitors bureaus require managers, assistant managers, research directors, information specialists, marketing managers, public relations staff, sales personnel, secretaries, and clerks.

*Meeting Planners*   A growing profession is meeting planning. Many associations and corporations are hiring people whose job responsibilities are to arrange, plan, and conduct meetings.

Children are special at resorts, and special activities keep them entertained and smiling. Clowns and face painters are frequent visitors to Snowmass festivals. (Photo courtesy of Snowmass Resort Association)

*Other Opportunities* A fairly comprehensive list of career opportunities has been presented. Others that do not fit the general categories listed are club management, corporate travel departments, hotel representative companies, in-flight and trade magazines and trade and professional associations.

## Other Sources of Career Information

Most of the career opportunities available in the travel field have been listed. It is hoped that this overview will provide you with a guide and point out that industries are so large that they are worthy of much further study by themselves. In considering career opportunities, it is important to gather information before you invest a great deal of time looking for a job. The following are good references:

Milne, Robert Scott. *Opportunities in Travel Careers.* Lincolnwood, Ill: National Textbook Company, 1985.

Stevens, Laurence. *Your Career in Travel and Tourism.* Albany, N.Y.: Delmar Publishers, 1988.

Whitzky, Herbert K. *Your Career in Hotels and Motels.* New York: Dodd Mead, 1971.

Rubin, Karen. *Flying High in Travel, A Complete Guide to Careers in the Travel Industry.* New York: John Wiley and Sons, 1986.

These books discuss tourism jobs. One book on how to get a job is particularly recommended:

Bolles, Richard. *What Color Is Your Parachute?* Berkeley, Calif.: Ten Speed Press, 1989.

The information provided in this section should be an important starting point for you. However, it is really just the tip of the iceberg. It is up to you to explore the subject further and to gain additional information. You not only need to learn about careers in tourism and travel-related fields, but also about the task of marketing yourself — how to work up resumes and how to conduct yourself during interviews. General books on getting a job will help you in this task.

# SUMMARY

This chapter examines the subject of tourism. The rapid growth in the movement of people, both domestically and internationally, has brought about an industry of vast proportions and diversity. Also, it is universal — found in all countries of the world, but in greatly varied qualities and proportions. It is this growth and diversity that accounts for the variety of employment opportunities. Most of the businesses that serve the needs and wants of travelers are labor intensive. They require planners, builders, managers, staff, and support businesses. All of these have career possibilities. Thus, one of the results of your study of this chapter could be an awareness of a field of work that might interest you.

Anyone who has a serious interest in the study of tourism needs to know something of the history of travel, famous early travelers, and equally famous pioneers in the business of travel. The economic importance and future prospects are also worthy of careful study. These considerations lead to the ways in which the study of tourism can be undertaken. There are a number of basic approaches to your study of tourism, and this text includes all of them in the various chapters. By the time you complete the book, you will know a great deal about the social and economic implications of tourism, and you will likely have developed a keen interest in our world and the fascinating panorama of places, peoples, cultures, beauty, and learning that travel so richly provides.

## Key Concepts

accommodations
basic parts of tourism
business or convention travel
careers
domestic tourist
economic contributions
excursionist
expenditure patterns
foreign tourist
future projections
history of travel
host community
host community government
importance of tourism
marketing and selling

natural resources
numbers or groups of visitors
recreation
shopping
study approaches to tourism
the tourist
tourism definitions
tourist activities
tourist attractions
tourist businesses
transportation
travel agents
travel modes
trip
visitor

## For Review and Discussion

1. Identify and describe the four perspectives contained in the definition of tourism, in terms of your home community.
2. Why do bodies such as the United States need specific tourism definitions? Why does a state or country need them? A county? A city?
3. What approach to tourism study does this course take? Which approach interests you most?
4. Is there a relationship between early democratic forms of government in the Mediterranean basin and tourism? Explain.
5. Does the concept of the Roman combination of roads, empire, leisure, and wealth apply to today's tourism? Can you give examples?
6. Discuss the relationship between health and travel.
7. Have travel patterns changed a great deal in the past 20 years? What elements have not changed?
8. Why has air travel become dominant in long-distance public transportation? Is this true in countries other than the United States?
9. How important are tourist attractions?
10. Does tourism stimulate the economy of your college's community?
11. For a career in tourism, what type of position appeals to you? What preparation will be needed? What are the likely rewards?
12. Why are geographers, sociologists, anthropologists, and economists interested in tourism?
13. Who was the first travel agent, and what basic concepts of travel services did he formulate?
14. What will the tourism industry be like in the year 2000?

## Selected References

Antil, Frederick H. "Career Planning in the Hospitality Industry." *The Cornell Hotel and Restaurant Administration Quarterly*, Vol. 25, no. 1 (May 1984), pp. 46–52.

Antil, Frederick H. "Learning Hospitality Management Through a Rigorous Work-Study Experience." *Hospitality and Tourism Educator*, Vol. 1, no. 2 (Summer/Fall 1988), pp. 24–29.

Belasco, Warren James. *Americans on the Road: From Autocamp to Motel, 1920-1945*. Cambridge, Mass.: The M.I.T. Press. 1979.

Boniface, Brian G., and Christopher Cooper. *The Geography of Travel and Tourism*. London: Heinemann, 1987.

Burkart, A. J., and S. William Medlik. *Tourism, Past, Present, and Future*. London: Heinemann, 1981.

Casson, Lionel. *Travel in the Ancient World*. London: George Allen & Unwin, 1974.

Crafts, Peter C. "Career Development Programs: How to Recruit and Retain Growing People in a Shrinking Market." *Hospitality and Tourism Educator*, Vol. 1, no. 2 (Summer/Fall 1988), pp. 30–33.

Crossley, John C., and Lynn M. Jamieson. *Introduction to Commercial and Entrepreneurial Recreation*. Champaign, Ill.: Sagamore Publishing, 1988.

Doswell, Roger. *Case Studies in Tourism*. London: Barrie and Jenkins, 1978.

Fedler, Anthony J. "Are Leisure, Recreation, and Tourism Interrelated?" *Annals of Tourism Research*, Vol. 14, no. 3, 1987, pp. 311–313.

Gay, Jeanne. *Travel and Tourism Bibliography and Resources Handbook*. 3 vols. Santa Rosa, Calif.: Travel and Tourism Press, 1981.

Gee, Chuck, James Makens, and Dexter Choy. *The Travel Industry*. New York: Van Nostrand Reinhold, 1989.

Goeldner, C. R., and Karen Dicke. *Bibliography of Tourism and Travel Research Studies, Reports and Articles*. 9 vols. Boulder: Business Research Division, University of Colorado, 1980.

Goeldner, Charles R., and Karen Duea. *Travel Trends in the United States and Canada*. Boulder: Business Research Division, University of Colorado, 1984. Published in cooperation with the Travel and Tourism Research Association.

Gunn, Clare A. *Tourism Planning*. New York: Taylor & Francis, 1988.

Hawkins, Donald E., Elwood L. Shafer, and James M. Rovelstad. *Summary and Recommendations International Symposium on Tourism and the Next Decade*. Washington, D.C.: George Washington University Press, 1980.

Holloway, J. Christopher. *The Business of Tourism*. London: Macdonald and Evans, 1983.

Hudman, Lloyd E. *Tourism: A Shrinking World*. New York: John Wiley, 1980.

Howell, David W. *Passport, An Introduction to the Travel and Tourism Industry*. Cincinnati: South-Western Publishing Company, 1989.

Jafari, Jafar. "Anatomy of the Travel Industry." *The Cornell Hotel and Restaurant Administration Quarterly*, Vol. 24, no. 1 (May 1983), pp. 71–77.

Jansen-Verbeke, Myriam, and Adri Dietvorst. "Leisure, Recreation, Tourism: A Geographic View on Integration." *Annals of Tourism Research*, Vol. 14, no. 3 (1987), pp. 361–375.

Kaiser, Charles, Jr., and Larry E. Helber. *Tourism Planning and Development*. Boston: CBI, 1978.

Krippendorf, Jost. *The Holiday Makers*. London: Heinemann, 1987.

Leighfield, M. A., ed. *Leisure, Recreation, and Tourism Abstracts*. Quarterly. Wallingford, Oxon, United Kingdom: CAB International.

Leiper, Neil. "The Framework of Tourism: Towards a Definition of Tourism, Tourist and the Tourism Industry." *Annals of Tourism Research*, Vol. 6, no. 4 (October-December 1979), pp. 390–407.

Lundberg, Donald E. *The Tourist Business*. Boston: CBI, 1980.

Metekla, Charles J. *The Dictionary of Tourism*. Wheaton, Ill.: Merton House Travel and Tourism, 1986.

Mill, Robert Christie, and Alastair M. Morrison. *The Tourism System*. Englewood Cliffs, N.J.: Prentice-Hall, 1985.

National Tourism Resources Review Commission. *Destination USA*. Volume 1, *Summary Report*. Washington, D.C.: NTRRC, June 1973.

*The President's Commission on Americans Outdoors: A Literature Review*. Washington, D.C.: U.S. Government Printing Office, 1986.

Robinson, H. *A Geography of Tourism*. London: Macdonald and Evans, 1976.

Rosenow, John E., and Gerreld L. Pulsipher. *Tourism: The Good, the Bad, and the Ugly*. Westport, Conn.: AVI, 1979.

Rubin, Karen. *Flying High in Travel*. New York: John Wiley & Sons, Inc., 1986.

Rugoff, Milton. *The Great Travelers*. New York: Simon & Schuster, 1960.

Smith, Stephen L. J. "Defining Tourism: A Supply-Side View." *Annals of Tourism Research*, Vol. 15, no. 2 (1988), pp. 179–190.

Starr, Nona. *Travel Career Development*. Wellesley, Mass.: Institute of Certified Travel Agents, 1987.

Towner, John. "Approaches to Tourism History." *Annals of Tourism Research*, Vol. 15, no. 1 (1988), pp. 47–62.

Towner, John. "The Grand Tour: A Key Phase in the History of Tourism." *Annals of Tourism Research*, Vol. 12, no. 3 (1985), pp. 297–333.

Towner, John. "The Grand Tour—Sources and a Methodology for an Historical Study of Tourism." *Tourism Management*, Vol. 5, no. 3 (September 1984), pp. 215–222.

Travel and Leisure. *World Travel Overview 1988/1989*. Annual. New York: American Express Publishing Corporation, 1988.

Travel Industry Association of America. *The U.S. Travel and Tourism Industry, 1984*. Washington D.C.: TIAA, 1984.

*Travel Market Yearbook, 1982*. New York: Ziff-Davis, 1982.

Travel Trade Publications. *Travel Trade 50, 1929-1979 Golden Anniversary Edition*. New York: Travel Trade, 1979.

Travel Trade Publications. *Travel Trade: Our 60th Anniversary Edition*. New York: Travel Trade, 1989.

Turner, Louis, and John Ash. *The Golden Hordes*. London: Constable, 1975.

U.S. Travel Data Center. *The 1988-89 Economic Review of Travel in America*. Washington, D.C.: U.S. Travel Data Center, 1989.

U.S. Travel Data Center. *1989 Travel Tab: A Quick Reference Guide to Current Travel Trends*. Washington, D.C.: U.S. Travel Data Center, 1989.

University of Colorado, Business Research Division. *Tourism's Top Twenty*. Boulder: University of Colorado, 1988. Published in cooperation with the U.S. Travel Data Center.

Van Doren, Carlton S., and Sam A. Lollar. "The Consequences of Forty Years of Tourism Growth." *Annals of Tourism Research*, Vol. 12, no. 3 (1985), pp. 467–489.

Wahab, Salah. *Managerial Aspects of Tourism*. Turin, Italy: Center International de Perfectionnement Professionel et Technique, 1976.

Waters, Somerset R. *Travel Industry World Yearbook. The Big Picture—1989*. Annual. New York: Child & Waters, 1989.

Witt, Stephen F., and Luiz Moutinho. *Tourism Marketing and Management Handbook*. London: Prentice-Hall, 1989.

World Tourism Organization. *Definitions Concerning Tourism Statistics*. Madrid: WTO, 1983.

Young, George. *Tourism, Blessing or Blight?* Baltimore, Md.: Penguin Books, 1973.

# How Tourism Is Organized: World, National, and Regional Organizations

## LEARNING OBJECTIVES

- Understand the magnitude of world tourism in terms of the vast numbers of organizations that serve the needs of their diverse memberships.
- Recognize the variety of types and functions of tourism organizations.
- Know why states support official offices of tourism.
- Learn how national, regional, and trade organizations are structured and operated.

The complex organization of tourism involves literally hundreds of thousands of units. Tourism organizations can be reviewed (1) geographically with the following breakdowns—international, regional within world, national, regional within nation, state or provincial, regional within state or province, and local categories; (2) by ownership, such as government, quasi-government, or private; (3) by function or type of activity, such as regulators, suppliers, marketers, developers, consultants, researchers, educators, publishers, professional associations, trade organizations, and consumer organizations; (4) by industry, such as transportation (air, bus, rail, auto, cruise), travel agents, tour wholesalers, lodging, attractions, and recreation; and (5) by motive, profit or nonprofit.

The purpose of Chapters 2 and 3 is to discuss the major types of tourist organizations and how they interrelate and operate, focusing on *illustrative examples*. The discussion begins with official international tourism groups in this chapter and ends with the private organizations and firms that make up the tourism industry covered in Chapter 3. Additional important supplemental areas that facilitate the tourism process, such as education, publishing, and marketing and publicity, are also included in Chapter 3.

## INTERNATIONAL ORGANIZATIONS

### World Tourism Organization

The World Tourism Organization (WTO) is the most widely recognized organization in tourism today. Located in Madrid, Spain, it is the only organization that represents all national and official tourist interests. Private commercial interests are allied members. The WTO is an official consultative organization to the United Nations, particularly to ECOSOC (the Economic and Social Council of the UN), and has the following objectives:

1. To accelerate and enlarge the contribution of tourism (international and domestic) to peace, understanding, health, and prosperity throughout the world
2. To facilitate, in travel, people's access to education and culture
3. To raise standards of living in the less developed areas of the world by helping to provide facilities for foreign tourism and the promotion of tourist traffic to these areas
4. To improve the conditions of country dwellers and so to contribute to an expanding world economy
5. To act as an international agency of coordination and cooperation to spread tourism
6. To provide a service to members valuable to them in their national operations in the field of tourism
7. To provide a point for meeting and coordination of all tourist interests of member countries concerning both the national tourist organizations and professional sectors and organizations representing the interests of the travelers
8. To establish permanent liaison and consultation with the various sectors of tourist operators
9. To do all this in the most efficient way

Generally, WTO concentrates on the informed promotion of tourism, spreading an appreciation of tourism and its advantages and dangers and recommending positive measures like the creation of new facilities. The organization attempts to harmonize tourist policies among nations through formulating and applying principles of international tourism. As mentioned, WTO is instrumental in the representation of tourism in the United Nations and acts as the central authoritative voice for world tourism and the tourist, complementing the central authority and position of the national tourist organizations. Additionally, WTO concludes multilateral international instruments and supports their implementation, as well as the implementation of the appropriate existing instruments, and fosters settlement of international technical tourism disagreements.

Other activities of WTO include helping developing countries and organizing and stimulating cooperation among all countries in technical matters affecting tourism. This is done through standardization of equipment, terms, phraseology, and signs as an aid to easier travel and comprehension for foreign visitors. WTO also acts as an international clearinghouse for information and encourages the application of new knowledge to tourism development and marketing. One important contribution of WTO is research, which includes studying the features of international tourism and devising methods of measurement, forecasting, development, and marketing that would be of use to national tourist organizations in their own activities. Research activities lead to improvement in the comparability of statistics. WTO carries out a regular survey of world tourism, appraising and measuring both progress and obstacles to further progress. WTO attempts to facilitate world travel through elimination or reduction of governmental measures for international travel as well as standardization of requirements for passports, visas, police registration, frontier formalities, and so forth. WTO also provides technical help to developing countries, primarily through the United Nations.

## International Air Transport Association

The International Air Transport Association (IATA) is the global organization for virtually all the international air carriers. The principal function of IATA is to facilitate the movement of persons and goods from any point on the world air network to any other by any combination of routes. This can be accomplished by a single ticket bought at a single price in one currency and valid everywhere for the same amount and quality of service. The same principles apply to the movement of freight and mail.

Resolutions of the traffic conferences of IATA standardize not only tickets but waybills, baggage checks, and other similar documents. These resolutions coordinate and unify handling and accounting procedures to permit rapid interline bookings and connections. They also create and maintain a stable pattern of international fares and rates. In effect, they permit the linking of many individual international airline routes into a single public service system.

Setting rates is the most significant part of IATA work. The need for agreement on rates among the IATA airlines is both practical and political — the fares and rates of international airlines are controlled by the governments of the individual countries that are served. Each country is absolute in its own airspace, and each country can bar or admit whom it pleases and set what conditions it likes.

IATA traffic conferences are held after governments have decided bilaterally on the exchange of rights and after each government decides individually what air carriers are going to serve its area. The IATA traffic conferences are, in effect, an important adjunct to government. Also, the rules that IATA formulate must be approved by the governments involved.

To be a member of IATA and the conferences, an airline must hold a certificate for scheduled air carriage from a government eligible for membership in the International Civil Aviation Organization (ICAO), a specialized agency of the United Nations.

IATA's travel agency accreditation services are conducted by its Passenger Network Services (PNS) Corporation.

There are three IATA traffic conferences — Western Hemisphere; Europe, Africa, and the Middle East; Asia and Australia.

## International Civil Aviation Organization

ICAO is an organization of some 80 governments joined to promote civil aviation on a worldwide scale. This organization, established in 1944, has the following specific objectives:

1. To ensure the safe and orderly growth of international civil aviation throughout the world
2. To encourage the arts of aircraft design and operation for peaceful purposes
3. To encourage the development of airways, airports, and air navigation facilities for international civil aviation

4. To meet the needs of the people of the world for safe, regular, efficient, economical air transport
5. To encourage economic means to prevent unreasonable competition
6. To ensure that the rights of contracting countries are fully respected and that every contracting country has a fair opportunity to operate international airlines
7. To avoid discrimination between contracting countries
8. To promote safety of flight in international air navigation
9. To promote generally the development of all aspects of international civil aeronautics

## DEVELOPMENTAL ORGANIZATIONS (INTERNATIONAL AND NATIONAL)

Financing is always a major problem in tourism development. Large financial organizations are willing to make developmental loans. Examples include the World Bank (U.S.), International Bank for Reconstruction and Development (U.S.), United Nations Development Program (U.S.), Asian Development Bank (Philippines), Overseas Private Investment Corporation (U.S.), Inter-American Development Bank (U.S.), Colonial Development Corporation (U.K.), Kreditanstalt fuer Wiederaufbau (W. Germany), Export-Import Bank (U.S.), and Agency for International Development (U.S.). Examples of national organizations are FONATUR (Mexico) and EMBRATUR (Brazil). Further sources include governments of countries that want additional hotel development or other supply components and are willing to make low-interest loans or grants or offer other financial inducements for such types of development.

## REGIONAL INTERNATIONAL ORGANIZATIONS

### Organization for Economic Cooperation and Development

The Organization for Economic Cooperation and Development (OECD) was set up under a convention, signed in Paris on December 14, 1960, that provides that the OECD shall promote policies designed to (1) achieve the highest sustainable economic growth and employment and a rising standard of living in member countries while maintaining financial stability, and thus to contribute to the development of the world economy; (2) contribute to sound economic expansion in member as well as nonmember countries in the process of economic development; and (3) contribute to the expansion of world trade on a multilateral, nondiscriminatory basis in accordance with international obligations.

Members of OECD are Australia, Austria, Belgium, Canada, Denmark, Finland, France, the Federal Republic of Germany, Greece, Iceland, Ireland, Italy, Japan, Luxembourg, The Netherlands, New Zealand, Norway, Portugal, Spain, Sweden, Switzerland, Turkey, the United Kingdom, and the United States. OECD's Tourism Committee fosters development of tourism in member countries and in Yugoslavia (an associated member) by studying the tourism problems confronting the governments and sectors of the economy in view of the large development of transit traffic in recent years, and by making recommendations based on its findings. The Tourism Committee actively seeks standard definitions and methods for compiling tourism statistics and issues an annual report entitled *Tourism Policy and International Tourism in OECD Member Countries.*

### Pacific Asia Travel Association

The Pacific Asia Travel Association (PATA) represents 34 countries in the Pacific and Asia that have united to achieve a common goal — excellence in travel and tourism growth in this vast region. Its work has been to promote tourism through programs of research, development, education, and marketing. PATA has gained a reputation for outstanding accomplishment among similar world organizations. For this reason a more detailed look at this association's organization and activities is presented as a reading at the end of this chapter.

## NATIONAL ORGANIZATIONS

### United States Travel and Tourism Administration

The United States Travel and Tourism Administration (USTTA) is the prime government agency in the United States responsible for the promotion of tourism. USTTA was established by the National Tourism Policy Act of 1981. Its mission is to develop travel to the United States from abroad as a stimulus to economic stability, growth of the U.S. travel industry, and expanded foreign exchange earnings.

Because the act mandates tourism's importance to the nation's economic and social well-being, it is a significant step forward for the travel industry and the traveling public. The act increases federal involvement in promoting the United States as a destination for international tourists and attempts to increase cooperation between the federal government and private industry through the creation of a Travel and Tourism Advisory Board comprised of representatives of the travel industry, organized labor, the academic community, and the public interest sector.

The law sets forth 12 broad national tourism policy goals. By creating USTTA, the act upgraded the functions and status of the United States Travel Service, which was established 20 years earlier under the International Travel Act. USTTA is headed by an Under Secretary of Commerce, who reports directly to the Secretary of Commerce.

The legislation also established a Tourism Policy Council, headed by the Secretary of Commerce, that coordinates governmental policies, issues, and programs that affect tourism. It includes high-level representatives of the Office of Management and Budget and the U.S. Departments of Transportation, Interior, Labor, State, and Energy.

The organization structure of USTTA is shown in Figure 2.1. A reading at the end of the chapter provides more information on USTTA.

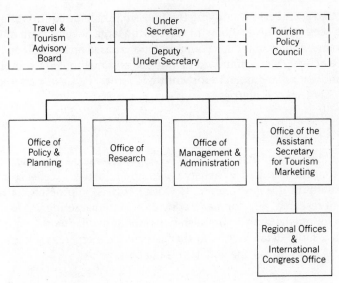

**Figure 2.1** Organization Chart of the United States Travel and Tourism Administration.

## Tourism Canada

Tourism Canada, the Canadian agency responsible for maintaining the orderly growth of tourism in Canada, has one of the most comprehensive tourism programs in the world and serves as a model that many other nations strive to equal. For this reason a detailed look at the scope, structure, and operations of Tourism Canada is presented as a reading at the end of this chapter.

## Federal Aviation Administration

Numerous responsibilities for efficient and safe air travel are assigned to the Federal Aviation Administration (FAA). This U.S. government organization in the Department of Transportation formulates regulations and supervises or controls various aspects of airline and airport operations. Examples of these functions are air traffic control, air safety, flight standards, aviation engineering, airport administration districts, airways facilities, and certification of new aircraft. The FAA also examines and licenses pilots and flight engineers. The FAA is illustrative of governmental regulating bodies.

## Department of Transportation

The Department of Transportation has the federal authority to protect air travelers and to police industry practices. It has responsibility for in-flight smoking rules, charters, denied boarding compensation, baggage liability, handicapped traveler rules, passenger notices, computer reservations bias, and antitrust authority.

Newer types of aircraft undergoing testing and inspection
required by the Federal Aviation Administration. (Photo courtesy
of the Boeing Company)

## Other Government Agencies

Numerous other government agencies play an active role in tourism. The Department of State issues passports, the Customs Bureau monitors international travel, Statistics Canada and the U.S. Bureau of Census compile travel statistics and data, the Interstate Commerce Commission regulates bus transportation, the National Maritime Commission deals with ships, and the National Park Service and the Forest Service provide and administer many scenic attractions and facilities.

## Travel Industry Association of America

The Travel Industry Association of America (TIA) is the leading private organization that promotes tourism in the United States, and it serves as the voice for the diverse segments of the industry. Originally incorporated in 1941, TIA has grown from a small association of travel officials into a national nonprofit organization with a membership that now represents all components of the travel industry: airlines, attractions, hotels and motels, travel agents, tour operators and brokers, convention and visitors bureaus, state government travel offices, area and regional tourism organizations, food service establishments, intercity bus and rail lines, cruise lines, and other components of what is known today as the travel industry.

TIA has always worked to benefit the travel industry as a whole by coordinating private industry efforts toward common goals and encouraging and promoting travel within and to the United States. In recent years, the association has increasingly supported research and has become more involved with government policies that affect tourism. TIA's objectives are to (1) promote and facilitate travel to and within the United States, (2) unify the travel industry by seeking and presenting consensual positions on matters of common concern, (3) promote a wider understanding of travel as a major U.S. industry that contributes substantially to the economic and social well-being of the nation, (4) develop and implement programs beneficial to the travel supplier and traveler, (5) encourage reciprocal travel between nations and oppose any restrictions on such travel, and (6) initiate and cooperate with positive tourism programs, policies, and legislation in the federal government and protect the interests of the industry in government decisions that affect tourism.

TIA has also taken a leadership role in organizing industry councils to provide a unified voice for segments of the industry that enables them to address legislative issues of mutual concern, carry out educational programs unique to their industry components, and offer guidance in the development of TIA policies and programs. Each of the councils is described briefly.

The National Council of State Travel Directors (NCSTD) is the nationally recognized coordinating body of state and territorial government travel directors. The council provides a forum for its members to exchange ideas and information on issues common to state/territorial offices. It is through the NCSTD that newly appointed travel directors gain a thorough orientation of the industry and its importance to the U.S. economy. The council also affords state travel directors the opportunity to participate in educational programs offering, among others, information on destination travel promotion, marketing, communications, and press and public relations.

The National Council of Area and Regional Travel Organizations (CARTO) was formed in 1976 in response to those destination promotion organizations representing a specific area or region of the United States. This grass-roots group stands ready to respond to legislative calls to action and is involved in providing its members with educational, communications, and marketing vehicles by which they may better themselves and therefore strengthen their voice in the industry. CARTO members are (1) area or regional travel promotion organizations at the county or district level, (2) organizations that service areas larger than a city, (3) multicounty agencies or associations within a state, and (4) statewide or multistate organizations whose concern is the promotion of travel. CARTOGRAM, a quarterly communiqué, supplies CARTO members with current information relating specifically to area and regional travel promotion organizations and provides a vehicle for sharing the planning, development, and production of projects undertaken by individual CARTO members, marketing tips, and other items of interest to all CARTO members.

The National Council of Travel Attractions (NCTA) was organized in 1976 to unify the travel attractions, arts, and cultural institutions component within the association. This unification gives the NCTA the strength and resources necessary to assist its members by improving communications, providing marketing tools specifically geared to this segment, and assuring adequate representation to all levels of government. A quarterly newsletter keeps NCTA members abreast of council activities, relays TIA information pertinent to attractions, arts, and cultural institutions members, and provides research and marketing information specifically produced for them. Membership is representative of historic, cultural, scientific, entertainment, natural, and human-made attractions, as well as attraction-related service organizations.

The National Council of Urban Tourism Organizations (NCUTO) was formed in 1976 by TIA in conjunction with the International Association of Convention and Visitors Bureaus (IACVB) to ensure representation of cities in domestic tourism development. The council fulfills two very important functions for its urban destination promotion organization members. The council works to ensure that national policies and legislation reflect the significance of cities as integral components of the national tourism product, and it monitors trends and developments in the travel industry that affect U.S. urban destinations. Working closely with the Travel and Tourism Government Affairs Council, NCUTO members remain actively prepared to testify before House and Senate groups on legislative issues affecting the travel industry. Membership includes convention and visitors bureaus and chambers of commerce.

To further reflect its leadership role in the U.S. travel industry, TIA created and provides major support for the following organizations:

The Travel and Tourism Government Affairs Council was established on March 17, 1982, as an affiliate of the Travel Industry Association of America, to represent a unified industry viewpoint on legislative and regulatory issues of common concern in Washington, D.C.

Other responsibilities of the council include representing the industry on government issues that have potentially broad impacts on the industry and maintaining contact with Congress and other federal entities to develop programs and policies that respond to government initiatives affecting the industry. The council also provides a range of professional services, such as research and statistical resources.

The council's membership is made up of a coalition of major national tourism and recreation organizations, including representatives from the sectors of transportation, accommodations, food services, travel agents, tour sales, and attractions. Literally thousands of travel industry companies are represented on the council through their membership in national travel industry organizations.

The U.S. Travel Data Center, the research affiliate of TIA, is the national nonprofit center for travel and tourism research.

TIA established the Center in 1972 for the purpose of "advancing the common interests of the travel industry and the public it serves by encouraging, sponsoring, and conducting statistical, economic, and scientific research concerning travel, the travel industry, and travel-related industries; by gathering, analyzing, publishing and disseminating the results of such research, and by cooperating with all federal, state, and other government agencies, and all organizations with similar purposes in pursuit of its objectives."

Today, the U.S. Travel Data Center devotes its resources to measuring the economic impact of travel and monitoring changes in travel markets. The Data Center has become the recognized source of current data used by business and government to develop tourism policies and marketing strategies.

## REGIONAL ORGANIZATIONS

Regional tourism organizations have the goal of attracting tourists to their specific geographic region. There are several types of regional associations such as multicountry, multistate, and multicounty. Examples range from PATA, which covers the Pacific region of the world, to groups such as Travel South, USA, which promotes travel in the southern states, to the East Michigan Tourist Association, which promotes only a region in Michigan—the northeastern section. Another multistate organization is Foremost West, which promotes tourism in Colorado, Utah, Arizona, New Mexico, Nevada, and Wyoming. Pennsylvania probably has more regional tourism organizations within its boundaries than any other state—59 tourist promotion agencies represent Pennsylvania's 67 counties.

To understand how regional tourism organizations function, turn to Reading 2-4, which describes promotion by area and regional organizations.

## STATE AND CITY ORGANIZATIONS

### State

Traditionally, states have promoted tourism as a tool for economic development. In most states, a tourism office has been established by statute and charged with the orderly growth and development of the travel and tourism industry in the state. These offices conduct programs of information, advertising, publicity, and research relating to the recreational, scenic, historic, highway, and tourist attractions in the state at large.

Each of the 50 states has an official government agency responsible for travel development and promotion. Hawaii and Texas each have two entities devoting funds and resources to tourism development. In Hawaii, responsibility for travel development rests primarily with a privately operated nonprofit organization, the Hawaii Visitors Bureau, that receives money from the state. The services performed and programs administered by the Hawaii Visitors Bureau are similar to those of the official state travel offices; thus all states are supporting tourism activity. The majority of states house their tourism offices in Departments of Economic Development (or Commerce).

Any review of state travel offices must start with the U.S. Travel Data Center's annual *Survey of State Travel Offices.* The report covering the fiscal year 1988-89 published in January 1989 shows that the average U.S. state travel office had a budget of $6.3 million, an advertising budget of $2.4 million, and a staff of 36 people. The average term of the director was 4.4 years. There are 504 highway welcome centers in 46 states, 44 states have one or more toll-free telephone numbers for travel information inquiries, 48 states sponsor a travel conference, 36 states offer matching funds programs for groups participating in promotion programs, 41 states conduct press or travel writer tours, and 44 states publish a travel newsletter. A list of official state travel offices can be found in Appendix A.

### City

Most major cities have also recognized the importance of tourism and have established convention and visitors bureaus. In many smaller communities, the chambers of commerce perform this function. Larger cities now own the central convention

State travel organizations furnish publicity pictures for newspapers, magazines, and other media. This changing autumn landscape is an example of the type of photos made available by the Vermont Travel Division. (Photo courtesy of Vermont Travel Division)

facilities. A great deal of promotion and sales effort is then devoted to backing these facilities.

*Convention and Visitors Bureaus*   A convention and visitors bureau is a not-for-profit umbrella organization that represents a city or urban area in the solicitation and servicing of all types of travelers to that city or area, whether they visit for business, pleasure, or both.

It is the single entity that brings together the interests of city government, trade and civic associations, and individual "travel suppliers" — hotels, motels, restaurants, attractions, local transportation — in building outside visitor traffic to the area.

Urban tourism is an increasingly important source of income and employment in most metropolitan areas — and therefore warrants a coordinated and concerted effort to make it grow. This growth is best nurtured by the role a convention and visitors bureau can play in continually improving the scope and caliber of services the city provides to corporate and association meeting planners, to individual business travelers, and to leisure travelers.

The Jacob K. Javits Convention Center is a splendid new facility in New York City. (Photo courtesy of New York Division of Tourism)

The bureau is the city's liaison between potential visitors to the area and the businesses that will host them when they come. It acts as an information clearinghouse, convention management consultant, and promotional agency for the city and often as a catalyst for urban development and renewal.

Typical services offered to meeting planners include orientation to the city, liaison between suppliers and meeting planners, and meeting management.

The meetings and conventions market is huge. *Meetings and Conventions* magazine conducts a biannual survey of this market and reports that their readers planned 1,001,600 meetings in 1987, spent $31.9 billion, and generated more than 74 million attendees.[1]

*International Association of Convention and Visitors Bureaus* Most of the city convention and visitors bureaus belong to the International Association of Convention and Visitors Bureaus (IACVB), P.O. Box 758, Champaign, Illinois 61820. This group was founded in 1914 as the International Association of Convention Bureaus to promote sound professional practices in the solicitation and servicing of meetings and conventions. In 1974, the words "and Visitors" were added to IACB's name to reflect most bureaus' increasing involvement in the promotion of tourism. Since its inception, the association has taken a strong position of leadership in the travel industry. The organization has over 320 members in 25 countries. IACVB provides its members with numerous opportunities for professional dialogue and exchange of industry data on convention-holding organizations.

[1] Helen Zia, "The Meetings Market Report '87," *Meetings and Conventions,* April 1988, pp. 83–85.

IACVB's convention data exchange is the most complete available on the association meetings market. It is an invaluable aid to the member bureau in maximizing its ability to effectively and efficiently serve convention holding organizations.

Members receive regular reports from IACVB on future convention bookings in all member cities. Professional members also receive detailed postconvention reports on all meetings within the sphere of their marketing influence.

To encourage exchange between its members, IACVB holds an annual convention, organizes annual educational seminars leading to certificates in sales or bureau operations, organizes topical workshops and seminars, makes regular studies of convention industry trends, maintains a consulting service, and provides its members with government and industry liaison.

## SUMMARY

The World Tourism Organization represents governmental tourist interests and aids in the world tourism development. Individual countries, states, and provinces have their own tourist promotion and development organizations that work to promote tourism in their area and coordinate tourism promotion with other groups. Most governments play a regulatory as well as developmental role in tourism through such agencies as civil aeronautics boards, federal aviation administrations, customs offices, passport bureaus, and so on. Government agencies typically compile research statistics and gather data. Governments also operate tourist enterprises such as airlines, national parks, and sometimes hotels and campgrounds.

### *About the Readings*

There are five readings in this chapter. The first two deal with national tourism organizations — USTTA and Tourism Canada. The third covers PATA, the fourth promotion by regional organizations, and the fifth the New York Convention and Visitors Bureau.

USTTA was established following the passage of the National Tourism Policy Act and replaced the United States Travel Service. This reading examines the role and position of USTTA in promoting tourism.

One of the world's best national tourism organizations is Tourism Canada. Although it operates on a large scale, its basic functions and structure become a model for any country aspiring to improve tourism. Note the breadth of concern of this organization and how its functions aid all facets of Canada's tourism.

Similarly recognized is the Pacific Asia Travel Association. This is a regional association within the world group. It is unique in having a worldwide network of PATA chapters. It is also respected for its outstanding conferences and travel marts that are highly successful and valuable for the attendees.

Within a state, region, or area, tourist associations play a vital part in the promotion of tourism. The East Michigan Tourist Association is a notable example of such an organization. Although of much smaller dimensions than those previously described, the association performs most of the basic functions of larger ones.

City convention and visitors bureaus are growing in importance. The reading on this topic describes the efforts of the New York Convention and Visitors Bureau to build cooperation with other industry sectors to develop both convention and leisure travel business.

## READING 2-1

### *Current Role of the U.S. Government in Tourism*

#### *Role and Position of USTTA*

The United States Travel and Tourism Administration (USTTA) promotes U.S. export earnings through trade in tourism. To increase U.S. exports of goods and services in tourism, USTTA stimulates foreign demand, works to remove barriers to international tourism, facilitates the entry of additional small and medium size U.S. exporters into the international marketplace, provides accurate and timely data to the travel industry, and promotes cooperation between local, state, and national tourism interests, both public and private, to achieve collective goals.

USTTA has endeavored to maintain field offices in those foreign markets which have traditionally accounted for the bulk of the United States' international tourism business and which represent the highest potential for growth. Offices are now located in Canada (Toronto, Montreal, and Vancouver); Mexico (Mexico City); Japan (Tokyo); the United Kingdom (London); France (Paris); the Netherlands (Amsterdam); Italy (Milan); the Federal Republic of Germany (Frankfurt); and Australia (Sydney). A twelfth office, which covers Brazil, Argentina, Colombia, and Venezuela, is located in Miami. An International Congress Office, which promotes the United States as a site for international meetings and conventions, is headquartered in Paris. USTTA's liaison with the domestic U.S. travel industry and potential cooperative partners are orchestrated out of Washington.

#### *Role of the Field Offices*

The USTTA field offices focus on three basic strategies:

- To educate and motivate tour wholesalers/operators and travel agents to sell the United States as a destination
- To persuade the traveling public in the market that the United States is a price-affordable destination which offers value for money, is to be preferred over competing destinations, and should be experienced now
- To assist U.S. and foreign tourism interests in the market to promote and sell the VISIT USA travel product

#### *Role of USTTA Headquarters/Activities Within the United States*

*Recruiting New Tourism "Exporters"*  USTTA participates in and conducts Export Now Regional Conferences throughout the country to convey the message that goods and services sold to a foreign tourist visiting the United States contribute to U.S. export earnings. In 1988, 10 conferences were held and attended by regional, state, city, or local tourism officials, appropriate private sector representatives from the travel industry, and USTTA staff from Washington and the regional offices abroad. USTTA has participated in many other state and organizational conferences in the promotion of international tourism. The seminar programs generate export awareness and also serve to recruit new U.S. exporters from the seminar participants.

At the same time, USTTA aggressively solicited participation by public and private sector tourism organizations in cooperative marketing programs abroad. Emphasis began in late FY 1984 and has grown consistently since then. In FY 1986, USTTA funded $1.8 million to seven categories of cooperative projects, to which industry partners contributed $9.7 million. In FY 1987, USTTA contributed $900,000, with 3579 partners adding $10.4 million. Through the first two quarters of FY 1988, USTTA contributed more than $500,000, with partner contributions of nearly $9.9 million. There were 3066 partner participations.

### Research

The Office of Research responds to the information needs of the travel industry. Information provided includes international arrivals and departures to and from the United States, characteristics of the travelers, consumer behavior data for inbound travelers from the United States's major markets, and visitor forecasts. These data are available at the national level and, in some cases, at the state and city level. Because accurate state- and city-level data are so critical, the Office of Research is seeking private sponsors of its In-Flight Survey. Incremental funds will allow USTTA to increase the accuracy of the information on states and cities with smaller visitation levels.

The Office of Research responded to about 6000 telephone inquiries and 3000 written requests during FY 1988. Publications prepared by this office provide the travel industry with information about foreign travelers to the United States. Some of these publications are for sale and are a rare source of revenue for the agency.

USTTA's research staff also makes customized presentations to suppliers and regional, state, and city organizations. These groups are provided the latest information on international tourism to their respective areas and its impact on their economies.

*World Fairs and International Expositions*  World fairs and international expositions have a significant impact on a country's economic growth and are important instruments of national policy, particularly in the exchange of ideas and the demonstration of cultural achievements between peoples.

The Office of World Fairs and International Expositions (WOFIE) coordinates all Department of Commerce activities involving the Bureau of International Expositions (BIE) in Paris. WOFIE counsels potential fair organizers on the application requirements of the BIE, reviews private sector applications for compliance with BIE requirements, and makes recommendations to the Secretary concerning the viability and feasibility of individual projects.

*Special Events*  One-time commemorations, international sporting events, and major conferences add incrementally to America's ability to generate export income through trade in tourism.

The Office of Special Events coordinates the U.S. government's role in activities such as the Christopher Columbus Quincentennial Jubilee and the 1994 World Cup soccer tournament. In addition, the Office, in cooperation with WOFIE, coordinates the Department of Commerce's role in world fairs and international expositions held outside the United States.

The Office manages USTTA's annual international marketing conference, represents USTTA on the National Tourism Week Coalition, and serves as the secretariat for the Travel and Tourism Advisory Board.

### Role of the Foreign Commercial Service

Travel development activities in countries without direct USTTA representation are carried out under the direction of USTTA regional directors in cooperation with VISIT USA committees comprised of representatives of the U.S. and foreign travel industry in those countries, and the U.S. and Foreign Commercial Service of the International Trade Administration.

## READING 2-2

### Tourism Canada

Tourism Canada, a branch of Industry, Science and Technology Canada (ISTC), is the federal agency responsible for encouraging and supporting the economic growth, excellence, and international competitiveness of the tourism industry in all parts of Canada.

Tourism Canada has five main objectives:

- To define and communicate a medium-term (four-year) direction for tourism market and product development activities of Canada's tourism partners — federal, provincial, and private sector — that also spells out the strategy of the federal government itself
- To define new federal government programming to come into effect once the current generation of subagreements expires, that places more emphasis on the provision of intelligence, facilitation and advocacy services, and on the development of internationally competitive destinations and products
- To provide information on the Canadian tourism product and its relationship to the emerging needs of Canada's markets, that facilitates the decision making of investors both public and private
- To influence federal government decision making in programs and policies that reflect the interests of the tourism industry, and
- To facilitate the efforts of the Canadian tourism industry in selling in the international marketplace, in obtaining financing, in negotiating joint ventures of all types, and in marketing product development, including human resource development and research.

### A Brief History

The Canadian federal government's involvement in tourism can be traced back to 1887, when Parliament established the Rocky Mountains Park Branch to protect what is now known as Banff National Park. It took a distinctly passive approach in those days.

An earnest beginning in federal tourism promotion began in 1934, when the Canadian Travel Bureau was created, largely as an anti-Depression measure. It later became the Canadian Government Travel Bureau, then in 1973 the Canadian Government Office of Tourism, and in 1983 Tourism Canada. The original bureau was created to promote travel to Canada from the United States, but its mandate was later extended to cover a number of overseas countries.

The first field office was opened in New York City in 1951, followed shortly by offices in Chicago and San Francisco. The first overseas location, London, opened in 1963. Then, in the mid-1960s, inspired in part by the approach of Canada's centennial in 1967, 14 more offices sprang up in the United States and overseas. In 1975, the first regional offices were opened in Canada to help develop the major market at home (almost four-fifths of the annual tourism income was from Canadians traveling in Canada).

Expo '67, in Montreal, and other celebrations helped to draw a record 40.5 million visitors from the United States and abroad in that year. Uncertainty about the ability of Canadian facilities and services to meet the demand led to the conclusion that the supply side of Canadian tourism needed more attention. This led to the creation, in 1968, of what was then called the Travel Industry Branch, now called Product Development.

In 1982, the overseas tourism field force was transferred to an enlarged Department of External Affairs (DEA), the field force members becoming DEA officers (titled "Trade Commissioners—Tourism"). Notwithstanding, ISTC remains responsible for the federal tourism program overall; DEA is responsible only for its delivery outside Canada.

Within Canada, ISTC has an extensive field force across the country. ISTC regional executive directors, one per province, have staffs deployed in principal and satellite offices in each province. They are responsible for delivering the department's services within the office's territory. This responsibility extends to delivering all the tourism operations.

Tourism Canada gives functional guidance to the tourism delivery officers across Canada and joins with them in determining work plans for tourism, using computer-based systems for mutual planning and operational monitoring.

A national consultative process on future directions and strategies for the Canadian tourism industry arose from one of the federal-provincial/territorial conferences of tourism ministers and culminated in the National Tourism Tomorrow Conference in October 1985. The result has been an ongoing dialogue between government and industry as well as a consensus on tourism issues.

Another result of the conference was the setting up of a national task force on tourism data. This body in turn recommended the establishment of an institute which would pool public and private tourism research and expertise. The Canadian Tourism Research Institute opened in 1987 and has increased the visibility of tourism as an industrial sector.

*An Inside Look*

Tourism Canada has four branches: Market Development, Product Development, Research, and Management Services and Liaison.

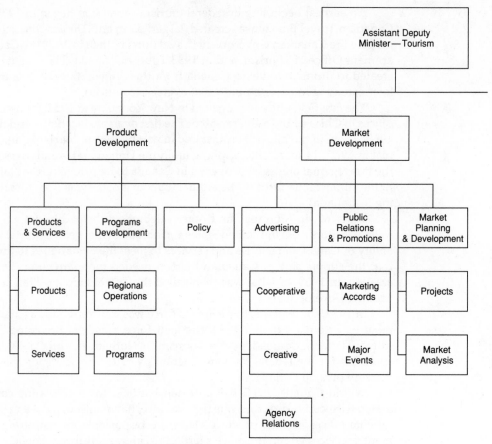

Organization Chart of Tourism Canada.

*Market Development*  The people in Tourism Canada's marketing area have the enviable task of selling the world on Canada as a travel destination. This branch is divided into three divisions—advertising, public relations and promotions, and planning and program development.

While Tourism Canada traditionally markets Canada as a travel destination to two broad groups—consumers and the travel trade—special attention is paid to selected high potential markets such as meetings and conventions, incentive travel and the mature market (aged 40 to 65).

Some of the initiatives of Market Development are summarized here.

Advertising.  Tourism Canada's advertising campaigns are focused on upscale travelers in Canada's top five international markets to be most effective in augmenting Canada's share of international travel receipts. Market research is more and more important as a guide to advertising priorities and cost-effectiveness. Consultations, coordination, and cooperative ventures with public and private sector partners are increasingly used to integrate marketing efforts and maximize resources and opportunities.

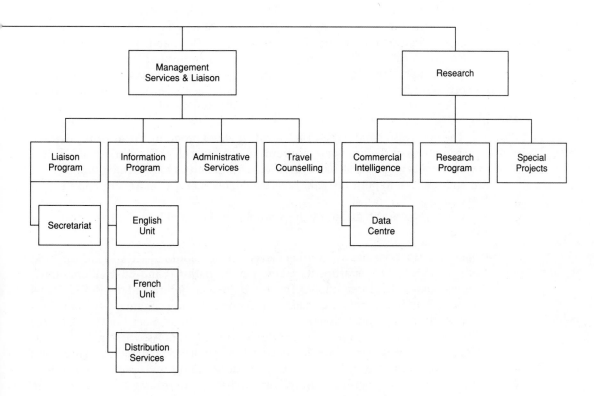

American travelers still represent the majority (84.7 percent in 1987) of foreign visitors. The primary regions targeted in the United States are the East North Central, Mid-Atlantic, Pacific, and New England states, and the vertical or specialty markets include meetings and conventions, ski, outdoor/fishing, and the travel trade.

The core campaign, which is consumer-oriented, runs from March through May each year and consists of television commercials supported by magazine ads. With the addition of campaigns for fall and winter, Canada has had a year-round presence in the United States since 1987.

While the overall picture of foreign travel to Canada shows an upward trend, there is a steeper increase in overseas travel to Canada. Compared with 1985, for example, the number of U.S. overnight visits to Canada in 1987 was 5.3 percent higher; the number of visits from overseas countries, however, was 39.6 percent higher.

Canada's primary overseas markets are the United Kingdom, Japan, West Germany, and France. They each surpassed 100,000 overnight visits in 1987, and their combined total accounted for nearly half (49.0 percent) of the overseas market.

Planning and Promotion.   Market Development provides strategic direction to the 20 field offices that deliver the tourism program in the United States and overseas for ISTC. It evaluates the programs and then plans and budgets for the next cycle.

The overseas field offices, under the jurisdiction of the Department of External Affairs, include London (for the United Kingdom and Ireland), Frankfurt, Paris, The Hague, Tokyo (for Japan and Korea), Hong Kong, and Sydney. The U.S. field offices are located in Atlanta, Boston, Buffalo, Chicago, Cleveland, Dallas, Detroit, Los Angeles, Minneapolis, New York, San Francisco, Seattle, and Washington, D.C.

These offices provide leadership, coordination, and support for government and private sector marketing activities. Their major activities include market intelligence reporting, cooperative promotions, and trade development familiarization programs.

The posts also handle the Visit Canada (media) program. Within this program, representatives of the print and electronic media from all major markets are invited to visit Canada to gain first-hand knowledge of Canada's tourism attractions, facilities, and services. Reports on their travel experiences serve to motivate people to visit Canada.

Other programs handled by the Market Development branch of Tourism Canada are

- Major promotional events.  Market Development coordinates travel industry and provincial tourism departments taking part in national and international trade shows, such as the International Tourism Bourse, in Berlin, and the World Travel Mart, in London. Tourism Canada also participates in convention-type marketplaces put on by organizations such as the American Bus Association, the National Tour Association, and the United States Tour Operators Association.
- Joint marketing agreements.  Market Development has negotiated numerous joint marketing accords and memoranda of understanding with public and private sector partners, recognizing the private sector as the driving force for tourism development and growth.
- Distribution.  Federal, provincial, and private sector promotional material (publications, maps, display material, and merchandising aids) is sent out from a distribution center in Yarmouth, Nova Scotia, in response to requests from the field offices, associations, and the travel trade.
- Canadian marketplaces.  Rendez-vous Canada is an annual travel industry marketplace which brings international travel trade buyers to do business with providers of the Canadian tourism product in order to increase the number of package tours featuring Canadian destinations. TourCanada is a marketplace designed to sell Canadian tourism products to buyers from Canada, the United States, and Mexico.

*Product Development*   Product Development is concerned with the Canadian tourism product and overall federal tourism policy. Objectives in this area are to ensure that the Canadian tourism product is internationally competitive and that the economic climate is favorable to its optimal development.

Product Development staff gather, analyze and disseminate information on product and policy; advocate on behalf of the industry both within the government and outside; develop and implement programs; and assist industry in regard to issues such as human resource development, financing/investment, transportation, taxes, and environment. The aim is to develop an internationally competitive product in a number of key areas indicated by research: cities, touring, specialty outdoor/wilderness products, and resort destinations.

Other activities include liaising with provincial tourism authorities and international tourism organizations (e.g., the Organization for Economic Cooperation and Development and the World Tourism Organization); developing a tourism sector strategy, tripartite policy consultation, and collaboration with the industry and provincial and territorial governments; developing, drafting, and presenting policy proposals to Cabinet; negotiating ISTC-Tourism policy positions; and influencing the formulation of federal policies affecting tourism.

While perfecting a five-year federal tourism development plan, the branch is elaborating regional and provincial tourism development strategies. These would be specific to geographic areas, but would also integrate the findings of product assessments presently being carried out on international destinations, touring corridors, resort areas, and specialty products such as outdoor sport, cruises, and adventure, culture, and native-related products.

Tourism facilities, events, and attractions in many parts of the country are now being improved as a result of the tourism subsidiary agreements between the federal government, provinces, and territories. ISTC-Tourism works with the provinces and territories to stimulate investment by the private sector in tourism that contributes to improve the competitiveness of the tourism sector. These agreements have a cost-share ratio ranging from 50 : 50 to 70 : 30, normally effective for a period of up to five years.

The subagreements are delivered through the ISTC provincial offices, in St. John's, Charlottetown, Halifax, Moncton, Montreal, Toronto, Winnipeg, Regina, Edmonton, Vancouver, Whitehorse, and Yellowknife.

In order to keep Canada's tourism industry competitive, there is now greater emphasis on collecting data on the markets, the competition, and Canada's own tourism products, and making the resulting intelligence available to the industry.

*Research*   Research activities include market and product research studies, travel surveys, economic analyses, and the collection and dissemination of commercial intelligence information on tourism to the other branches, the industry, industry associations, federal agencies, and other countries.

In initiating market research material, Research contributes to the longer-term marketing strategy. In 1985, an in-depth pleasure travel market study of the United States — Canada's largest market — was conducted. In 1986, a five-year agreement was signed between Tourism Canada and the United States Travel and Tourism Administration to undertake jointly funded long-haul pleasure travel market studies in key overseas countries. Tracking studies are also carried out in countries in which Tourism Canada advertises, to evaluate the effectiveness of its campaigns.

In addition to analyzing data from market studies, Research staff collect economic data to assess the impact of tourism in Canada. In 1988, a study was made of the economic impact of tourism in the Niagara Falls (Ontario) area, and a model developed that could be adapted for use in other communities.

The commercial intelligence program sends out a monthly bulletin to keep the

Canadian tourism industry informed about the activities of governments and the private sector that might have an impact on tourism in Canada.

The Tourism Reference and Documentation Centre has the most comprehensive collection of tourism-related information in Canada, with more than 7000 documents—research papers, statistical reports and studies, analyses, journals, conference proceedings, speeches, feasibility studies, legislation, guide books and bibliographies. Information about this material is stored in a data bank.

*Management Services and Liaison*  Management Services and Liaison is responsible for relations with the provinces and territories, which includes coordination of federal-provincial/territorial tourism conferences. It is also responsible for liaison with the major national tourism associations.

The branch puts out a newsletter, packages and distributes information to client groups including the media and the associations, and provides Tourism Canada with administrative services.

## READING 2-3

### *Pacific Asia Travel Association*

 Founded in Hawaii in 1951 to develop, promote, and facilitate travel to and among the destination areas in and bordering the Pacific Ocean, the Pacific Asia Travel Association brings together governments, airline and steamship companies, hoteliers, tour operators, travel agents, and a wide range of other tourism-related organizations.

Members exchange ideas, seek solutions to problems, and participate in shaping the future of travel in Asia and the Pacific Area. Membership totals about 2000. Since its founding, the Association has become an important source of accurate, up-to-date information for its members in the fields of marketing, development, research, education, and other travel-related activities. PATA's activities and long-range plans are examined and adjusted each year at the Association's annual conference.

### *Committees*

Standing committees on management, marketing, development, and research carry out the Association's ongoing program. A publications division publishes a variety of textbooks, reports, studies, publicity materials, directories, and periodicals. The principal periodical is *Pacific Travel News,* a monthly journal with three regional editions and a combined circulation of about 58,000 copies. The main objective of the *News* is to promote travel to and within the Asia Pacific region. Eighty percent of the editorial content is feature material based on research and photographs obtained by the editors in the field.

PATA's marketing efforts are directed to influencing more individuals to travel to and within the Pacific area. The committee also strives to improve marketing skills at the point of sale and in destination areas.

Development activities are geared to improving and advancing facilities and services in new destinations, increasing the handling capacity of existing destinations, and preserving their heritage and quality.

In research, PATA concentrates on the operation of an annual travel research conference, the publication of an annual Pacific area statistical report, and the conduct of cooperative research studies.

### PATA Conferences and Marts

Two of the more visible activities are the annual Conference and the Pacific Travel Marts. The Conference, held in a member country each year, brings together up to 2,000 people who join in discussions of the current needs and problems of Pacific tourism and participate in the Association's annual business meeting. Sessions of the Conference offer selected themes to assist members in gaining a better working knowledge of tourism. The Pacific Travel Marts bring to a single location the buyers and sellers of travel who meet to negotiate contracts for future business. An example would be a tour operator who meets with travel agents in countries which might supply travelers to participate in that company's tour offerings. Specifically, a tour operator in Australia would meet with travel agents from the United States who might be sending clients to Australia or a tour operator in the United States who is operating tours to Australia would be meeting with a ground operator (such as a local tour company) from Australia, who would supply a local tour for this tour group when it arrived in Sydney.

The work of the official PATA organization is greatly augmented by an international network of PATA chapters. They comprise over 10,000 members worldwide. Chapter members meet regularly to learn about the various PATA designations through educational presentations and out-of-country familiarization trips.

The PATA secretariat is located in San Francisco, California. Divisional offices are located in Singapore to serve the Asia Region, in Sydney to serve the Pacific, and in San Francisco for the Americas/Europe Division.

## READING 2-4

### Travel Promotion by Area and Regional Tourism Organizations

By James H. Hall, Sr., Former President/CEO
East Michigan Tourist Association
Bay City, Michigan

### History and Purpose of Area Tourist Promotion Organizations

The automobile and mass public transportation, at the beginning of the twentieth century, provided traveler access to nearly every location on the globe. As travel costs tumbled, increased millions of travelers vented their desires to follow the pathways of Marco Polo and Charles A. Lindberg. With the growing demand for travel, far-sighted travel industry business and government leaders responded by organizing "area" groups for the purpose of attracting travelers to their respective geographical locations.

Groups like the All-Year-Club of Southern California and the Michigan Tourist Association pioneered this action after World War I. Thus were created nonprofit area tourism marketing organizations. In the 1940s they established the first national group, "National Association of Travel Officials" (later "Organizations") now known as the Travel Industry Association of America, headquartered in Washington, D.C. Their simple goal was to create traveler spending as a form of economic development in their areas.

From these pioneer bands grew a collection of business and local government associations, bureaus, councils, trade boards, chambers of commerce, and so on, that impacted the world travel market by enlarging newspaper travel sections, creating travelogues, printing maps, directories, guides, and magazines, and creating broadcast communications. This massive communications network was directed at the exploding numbers of travelers. State government programming was created after World War II, bolstering area and local organization efforts.

That these groups were successful, and remain so today, is proven by the involvement in tourism marketing by nearly all countries of the world—in the United States by all fifty states and territories and thousands of areas, regions, and communities within their boundaries. The principles of their purpose have not changed over the years.

Successful marketing programs of business enterprises today include a program of product or service promotion. It is a recognized marketing function and is the action that creates consumer demand. Promotion is an integral function of marketing tourism products and services. In fact, it carries *more* importance because of the unique characteristics of tourism marketing.

In the selling of most manufactured products, the consumer can inspect the product prior to purchase. Even in the area of services, this feature is available to the consumer. Not so for the tourism product. It is simply impossible to place the total aspect of a vacation trip on a store shelf or showroom or in a home.

The purpose, then, of tourist promotion is to perform the vital marketing function of "making the sale" without the consumer's being able to touch, inspect, smell, or even see with his or her own eyes. And while the key "sale" factor is the sale of the lodging accommodation or the attraction ticket away from home, the total sale involves a great deal more.

Tourist promotion programs are generated to motivate people to travel away from their home communities. Area and/or community programs are geared, in most instances, to complement and supplement the programs generated by the state travel promotion agency.

Individual business enterprises pool their promotion dollars into a cooperative organizational fund to perform promotion functions they cannot afford by themselves. All forms of promotion are used in varying degrees in the individual action programs. The challenge constitutes a communications problem in relating the values of a total experience to the consumer for a decision. Competition between areas provides additional challenge to the promotion organization.

Impulse buying of vacation trips (last-minute decisions), especially of the packaged variety, is the fastest growing element of the travel industry today. Price is a factor for midweek and off-season trips, thus filling the sales valleys of tourism businesses.

The fact that vacations are usually decided long before the start of the actual trip creates additional problems. However, new promotions are successful in creating impulse buying of vacation trips, especially of the short, weekend variety.

The final sale for tourism is the deposited reservation, the package prepayment, and/or the scheduled trip decision by the travel party. The party can work directly with the hotel, motel, resort, or transportation company, or can work via a travel agent in the home city. This is the final objective of the promotion program as generated by all segments of the tourism industry. Area programs are geared, in varying degrees, to fulfilling this purpose.

### Types of Promotion Organizations

While organizing for area tourism promotion can take several directions, the basic purpose is the same. Nearly all involve the private sector, and there are variations of local and state government (public sector) involvement. Private businesses can pay dues, purchase print and broadcast advertising sponsored by the organization, and/or collect local tourist taxes earmarked for promotion. The latter is usually done through a local area, city, or county room tax or assessment.

Support can come from all types of businesses, those receiving direct or indirect benefits from traveler spending in the area. Some states in the United States and other countries offer support grants as an additional source of funding. The Michigan system of regional/local area groups has gained state support since 1929. Amounts vary from a few thousand to more than $100,000 per year. Most organizations are state-registered nonprofit corporations with local business/government leadership.

### Operation Policies and Procedures

The action program is the heart of tourist promotion organization and is designed to carry out the organizational policies in fulfillment of the association's purpose. The policies can be clearly stated. The program elements can vary from one organization to another. The purpose is to advertise and publicize in an unbiased manner the individual areas and their businesses and to attract *tourist and convention* business for the area or region. The action activities are designed to "make the sale" for the tourist operator, luring the traveler away from home and headed in his or her direction. This is where the product is taken to market.

### Advertising

Display advertising space in print media and time on broadcast media are purchased to expose the name of an area to the general public and/or to special segments of the general public. Most major newspapers contain regular Sunday or weekday "travel sections," where people look for vacation ideas. Many consumer magazines have a similar section. Magazines like *Sunset, Southern Living, The New Yorker, Better Homes and Gardens,* auto club magazines, and travel industry journals are classified as travel publications. They provide a medium to reach travel-minded people. Print media offer the best source of write-in coupon inquiries to obtain detailed information.

Radio and television also offer opportunity to reach the public. However, it is more difficult to obtain a written inquiry for additional information using broadcast media, though it is done. Television, regular and cable, though expensive, offers a unique marketing tool for tourist promotion. Motion picture photography of various lures can be used in a commercial of one minute or less to actually expose a product to the general consuming public. No other advertising medium can offer this advantage. Use of WATS line service has expanded response to broadcast media advertising. Both print and broadcast media offer unique opportunities to elicit inquiries for detailed information and to generate impulse travel.

An unusual advertising feature offered by the media is the "banner" method, whereby an area organization or state travel office purchases a "banner" space or time, with cooperating businesses and groups placing their advertisements in the same page space(s) or time slot(s). This cooperation gains increased response. Another unusual media offering is the actual reproduction of a brochure — in color or black and white — with standard copy space for all advertisers, printed in a special newspaper or magazine section. This method has produced high volumes of inquiries.

Additional advertising media include outdoor billboards, house organs, and direct mail. These are not utilized as much as the more formal media, but direct mail to "occupants" or to names on purchased lists holds promise of producing meaningful results.

While many areas of the United States have extended their traditional vacation seasons, few can boast a truly year-round vacation offering with the same advantages. Thus seasonality does affect most promotion programs. Promotion programs are geared to those seasonal changes. Advertising schedules follow suit and are slated to run from two to six months ahead of the actual season to allow time for response to the advertising and response from the area purchasing the advertising. This is very important. Advertising is mainly geared to inquiries for additional information. Time is a key factor in answering the inquiries; sometimes several inquiries must be answered before the sale is made to a single inquiring party. Impulse buying of travel products is on the increase in recent years and is geared to price, including packaging.

Seasonal schedules call attention, in copy and illustration (or music), to the special advantages of a given season. The seasons are becoming better understood by the consuming public. Of course, most programs are geared to the traditional school vacation period, but this is changing as time becomes available to more and more people and tourism marketing programs of areas and states are adapted.

Miami Beach, for example, advertises in each of the twelve months. But its advertising messages are geared to seasonal activities, attractions, and availability of vacation time by the customer. The seasonal barrier, a virtual stone wall to tourist promoters for a hundred years, will be broken before the end of the century.

The objective of most advertising campaigns is twofold. The first is to obtain inquiries — names of people interested in a vacation in a destination area or resort. The second is to establish a positive image of an area as a vacation area. The former can be measured very effectively as to cost and is easily researched. The latter is much more difficult to measure in terms of direct results for an area. Inquiries coming from coupons, spoken requests to "write in," or telephone calls are answered with detailed printed information about an area.

*Sales Promotion*

Sales promotion techniques have produced proven results for many tourism organizations. Among them are travel shows, staged in major city markets in the United States and Canada and worldwide. As a promotion technique, travel shows offer the unique opportunity to attract tourists by direct contact with the prospective travelers. In addition, sales literature, shipped in bulk to travel show sites, is distributed to people interested in vacations, at a cost well below that incurred through advertising. Research has proved that travel shows produce inquiries of equal quality to advertising inquiries. Community shopping malls stage boat and recreation shows offering good promotion opportunities.

Travel shows require investment in booth exhibit displays; they offer space units of ten feet wide, minimum. Area organizations can purchase any number of units, depending upon budget and available manpower to work the exhibit. The average travel show attracts more than 100,000 people during a ten-day show period. To exhibit at a travel show costs from $40 to $80 per foot of display space, and staff to work the booth from $200 to $450 per day for two people.

Other types of shows allied to tourism include boat, outdoor, camping, and home shows. Seasonal shows for skiing, boating, and camping, home and garden shows, and weekend shopping mall shows also offer good opportunities to promote an area.

Sales promotion specialty items are good travel motivators. Bumper stickers, buttons, lapel pins and stick-ons, car banners, highway information centers on state entry points and major freeways, and the like can bring the name of an area to the attention of many prospective tourists.

Some promotion organizations also utilize their staff to make direct sales calls to sell their areas. This is expensive, but it pays off in terms of quality response. Distribution of sales literature—reference and consumer—in person at travel agencies, auto club offices, and other locations is a plus factor for any promotion program. This activity can use counter cards with inquiry reply cards, as well as sales literature and posters.

The promotion of group motorcoach business is an important segment of the sales promotion programs of area organizations. Methods involve working with individual bus companies and bus-tour operators and with groups of these people. The proven technique is the use of a familiarization trip designed to orient bus-tour decision makers to potential destination areas. The trip is usually one of two to four days, with stops at natural and human-made attractions and facilities in the area. This kind of trip allows a liaison of decision makers with host operators. The "fam trip" may have up to 20 to 30 participants. Other techniques involve contact at national meetings of the American Bus Association (ABA) and the National Tour Association (NTA), both requiring membership affiliation on the part of the area organization. Personal sales calls also contribute to the success of this promotional method. Several states have specialized organizations with promotion programs aimed exclusively at the motorcoach market, gaining excellent results.

New broadcast media promotion is another promotional method that area organizations can take advantage of, involving public broadcasting (PBS) stations and cable television companies. The technique involves actual filming of attractions, facilities, and activities in an area by a videotape film crew and subsequent production of shows to be offered to PBS stations or cable TV companies. The area organization is the underwriter of the show. This technique is a supplement to the traditional travelogue, not a replacement.

*Publicity and Public Relations*

As a partner to advertising and sales promotion, the functions of publicity and public relations can produce positive results for an area tourist promotion organization. The basic elements of these activities are the preparation and release of news stories, photographs, film, and videotape to the general press and broadcast media: they can also be used as an assist to free-lance journalists. A key factor in these activities is that they must consist of newsworthy subjects for stories, photographs, film, and tape. They cannot resemble advertising or they will not be used.

Topics for coverage include the specific and unique attractions and people of an area. Festivals and special events also are good subjects. Stories must be well written. Photos, film, or tape sent on an exclusive basis receive the most use. Black-and-white, 8- by 10-inch photograph prints of high quality and 35mm color slides may be used. Only outstanding photographs can be reproduced for quantity distribution with any meaningful results. Direct work with cable companies can also produce excellent results, if this capability is offered by the organization.

Distribution of publicity is most effective if sent to special travel editors, to travel newspapers and magazines, or to specialty personnel in radio and television (i.e., sports directors, feature directors, weather announcers, etc.), by name.

Publicity and public relations talents, such as creative feature writing and photographic, and video services for special promotions may be purchased from agencies if the organization budget does not allow for full-time staff.

A successful method of public relations is to stage a special promotion by inviting a group of writers and photographers to an event involving direct participation. Again, the program must be newsworthy. To promote a certain area, it would be appropriate to host outdoor writers in small groups, or a statewide or regional organization of writers, for a hunting and fishing trip of a few days or a week. This kind of action always gains outstanding results in the media, including national publications. Local and area press clubs, and state and regional travel-writing and sports-writing groups are organizations that respond to invitations for such visits to tourist areas and events. Keep in mind that regular contact with media people and free-lancers is also vital to the success of public relations programs.

*Sales Literature*

Perhaps the most important promotional tool for selling tourism is sales literature. Literature can carry the tourism sales message to the consumer in his or her home better than any other promotion method. It is, in fact, the "hard sell" of the tourist industry. It can make the sale.

A great variety of literature is created and produced by area organizations, ranging from business cards and one-color brochures to full-color guide books of 100 or more pages. Included as major items are maps, post cards, directories of travel service businesses and public facilities, posters, calendars of festivals and events, and many special-subject brochures, flyers, and direct-mail pieces.

Variety of literature, its quality, and its quantity are greatly dependent upon available budget. A promotion program budget must allocate adequate funding of promotional methods to allow for the production of meaningful literature in sufficient quantities to meet the demand produced by advertising, sales promotion, publicity, public relations, and word-of-mouth communications.

The most important elements in literature preparation include a fair description of the general appeals of an area, specific information on the available activities and basic lodging and dining facilities, map directions and information on festivals and events. As recreation becomes more specialized, detailed information on activities and facilities are necessary to make the sale (i.e., a golfer wants to know details about the facilities for his sport; likewise for the fisherman, hunter, skin diver, spelunker, culture-seeker, etc.).

Literature should also give ample space to the uniqueness of the area. This is the appeal that differs from those of other areas.

Because so many area tourist organizations are promoting today, literature must be of high quality. It is almost useless to use one-color literature, except for specialty folders. It cannot effectively compete with the full-color material which is the "average" today. Quality of literature is growing in importance as competition increases.

Next to quality, the most important consideration for literature is efficiency of handling the inquiry. The time factor for the inquirer is vital to the decision-making process. For a tourist promotion organization, the day's inquiries delivered by mail or received by phone are the most important messages received. All inquiries should be processed as quickly as possible, using the most effective class of mail possible within the budget allocation. An increasing number of organizations are now using UPS or first-class mail. The information contained in the literature should be as current as possible. While an image-type folder can be used for more than one year, detailed literature on activities and facilities should be printed new on at least an annual basis. This is especially important for literature containing lodging rate information.

Literature should be designed and organized to make it readily understandable by the inquirer. Inclusion of information on costs is always a plus factor.

Proof of the value of literature as a promotion tool is reflected in reservations generated for lodging operators listed or advertised in the literature, and in the use of literature by tourists while on their vacation trips.

The sharing of inquiries with travel business supporters of the area organization can help produce direct sales for lodging, dining, attractions, and other features in the local area. The methods of making this information available include the use of computer print-outs for the various segments of the industry (i.e., camping, lodging, special activity inquiries). Names can be printed in list form or on mailing labels.

*Information Services*

Tourist promotion organizations located in close proximity to tourist traffic can prove an added bonus to promotion programs. The information office should be well stocked with area literature, as well as literature of members. Most important are maps and directories of lodging, dining facilities, and area attractions. Personnel answering walk-in inquiries should be adequately informed about the area. Hours of operation would necessarily be seasonal, based on demand. Adequate signage from major traffic routes is also essential.

Information personnel are usually those who answer mail and phone inquiries. Theirs is a key service to tourists and a vital element of the tourist promotion program.

An information office with high traffic can also utilize "home grown" products of the area as give-away items to visitors. This action can produce extra days of visitation for an area; it is also of great public relations value.

*Coordination with Other Organizations*

With the advent of new organizations and the expansion of existing organizations working full time in tourism marketing, the need for coordination of promotional programming is greater than ever. This is true for an in-state region and for a state or group of states. The objective of such coordination is to avoid duplication of promotional activities. A second objective is to bolster specific activities such as publicity and public relations. A communications system is vital to the success of reaching these objectives. Petty "area" competition must be shunted aside in sustaining a good system.

Many times, cooperative promotion projects can be an effective method of improving the efficiency of promotional funds. The sharing of promotional costs may dilute the inquiry result, but it lowers the cost by expanding the effectiveness of the promotional message.

Several states have systems that coordinate programs from the state level down to individual operators. Many states and area organizations are utilizing the best elements of these two systems.

Programs directed from the state level down to area and local groups and businesses are successful only when leadership is industry represented. Coordination is a two-way street that requires statesmanship on the part of state travel office personnel and industry representatives. The many benefits accruing from successful coordination programs are well worth the time and money invested.

*Organization Structure*

Tourist promotion organizations, like other nonprofit corporations, are required to file articles of incorporation with their respective state governments and with the federal government to obtain an employment number for the handling of taxes (payroll). These are normal organizational procedures, listing name, purpose, and names and signatures of incorporating citizens. The bylaws of the organization establish the organizational structure.

The bylaws set up the membership structure, including dues and classes of membership, the governing body which is usually a board of directors, officers and staff, annual meeting, committees, and amendment procedures. To a varying degree the duties of members, officers, and staff are detailed in the bylaws. Basically, the bylaws set the ground rules under which the organization can legally function. Each year a form is required by the state asking for the names of current officers and a review of the program, income, expenditure data, and some may require an audited report filed in addition to the form.

*Membership*   Nearly all area tourist promotion organizations have business firm (private enterprise) members who pay dues to the association. If the tourist promotion program is a part of a larger business organization or chamber of commerce program, the tourist promotion program is a budgeted item in the total program, or a percentage is taken from annual dues. Few organizations in this field have restrictive clauses, so the field is open to any and all kinds of business enterprise. In the main, it is tourist-service type businesses that make up the major portion of the members. This is not always true in terms of dues paid (i.e., wholesale and utility firms and others may pay a multiple-unit membership which may total more than a larger number of smaller unit memberships).

Dues are paid on an annual basis and are often by contract. This enforces a continuing program with annual billing. Some organizations may have a staggered schedule for the payment of dues for differing sizes of businesses, or one based on sales volume. An example is a 10-unit motel paying one unit of dues and a 200-room hotel paying a multiple-unit dues amount.

Membership, many times, is also open to governmental units below the state level. This allows cities, villages, townships, and counties to support tourist promotion. Performance contracts are sometimes used for governmental unit support of the nonprofit promotional organization. In Michigan and some other states, state law must permit the expenditure of local funds for this purpose. Laws in Michigan in this regard date back to 1910. Under some statutes, a special promotional tax may be levied to be earmarked for tourist promotion by local units of government.

The most widely used form of tax is the room tax levied on transient room rentals to support local or area convention, visitor, and tourist promotion groups. Tax funds may also be used for capital improvements of travel service facilities (public sector), such as convention centers or welcome centers.

Thus, tourist promotion organizations can be supported by both private enterprise and government. Many call this a "quasi-governmental organization." Members usually hold at least one annual meeting at which appropriate policies and programs are approved.

*Board of Directors*  The administrative board oversees the operation of the program and meets during the interim between official annual meetings. It is usually the board's function to hire and direct the executive officer and the other office staff. It functions as the go-between for members of staff and organizations with working relationships, including governmental units. Officers are nominated from the list of directors. Directors can serve specific terms of office or can serve indefinitely, as set up in the bylaws. The board runs its affairs in a manner similar to any corporate board or governmental commission. All officers and the chief executive officer (staff) are responsible to both the board of directors and the membership.

*Executive Committee*  Although the board of directors has responsibility to the members between annual meetings, it may be necessary to have an executive committee which functions on behalf of the board between board meetings. In addition, the executive committee, usually made up of at least one past president plus the current officers and executive officer, can be assigned specific responsibility in the area of legal and financial affairs.

*Committees*  While not absolutely necessary in fulfilling the purpose of a tourist promotion organization, the committee system can be of great benefit. Committees can help officers and staff in carrying out the total program responsibilities of the organization. Examples of types of committees include nominating, resolutions, promotion or advertising, publications, publicity, annual meeting, product improvement, education and training, hospitality, special promotion, natural resource management, and transportation.

A committee can assist in any area of internal or external operation of the organization. Committees should involve members and directors, as well as resource people such as educators and promotion purveyors. Size of budget, promotion, and staff may also affect the number of committees needed for directing the affairs of the organization. Committee action can provide excellent opportunities to develop the talents of the involved people to gain needed and experienced industry leadership.

*Staff*   As tourism in the United States has grown to be recognized for its total economic impact, the need for better qualified management has expanded. Increased programs of promotion and development require full-time management in many tourism organizations in the country today. New programs have developed as well, adding to the demand for management.

As programs and management have expanded, so, too, has the need for skilled personnel in tourist promotion offices. Demand for special services also has expanded in the contractual service field.

Tourist promotion organizations — separate corporations — always have at least one employee, a director. Traditionally, staff managers have come from closely related fields of organization management, such as the chamber of commerce field. Communications and advertising have also proved to be a source. Few, if any, managers come from college campuses because of lack of knowledge of opportunity or lack of curriculum for training. This situation is changing as university curricula now provide degree-earning opportunities in the tourism field.

The program and the budget are usually the factors that spell out the size of staff. For an average organization, the following chart can be used as a guideline.

| Number of Members | Budget for Promotion | Staff Needs* |
|---|---|---|
| 100 – 200 | $40,000 – $85,000 | 1 – 2 |
| 150 – 1000 | $100,000 – $250,000 | 3 – 5 |
| 1500 plus | $250,000 plus | 6 – 8 |

For larger programs, the personnel needs expand into field sales and membership services, inquiry-handling specialist, bookkeeper and records specialist, publicity and publications director/editor, and stenographer/word processor. Computer operation is increasingly being used by tourism offices, especially for information storage and inquiry processing. Many of these responsibilities in larger programs can be contracted for on a special basis if available in the community. Inquiry handling and publicity are two that are commonly handled in this manner, thus keeping overhead low. If the program warrants, an advertising agency can also perform some staff functions.

* Total is dependent also upon degree of contractual services purchased. Following the manager, a secretary/bookkeeper is most necessary. Between them, the basic jobs of administration, promotion, and inquiry handling can be taken care of for the small program.

Tourism office equipment involves normal business office machines — typewriters, file cabinets, dictating and copying machines. In addition, special attention must be given to handle literature and direct mail processing, including storage, folding, weighing, inserting, postage application, sorting, packaging, and delivery for postal service or UPS handling. Computerized inquiry processing and information storage (such as membership directories of area facilities), even in a small office, can be of enormous value to the tourism organization administrative office.

*Model Structure for an Area Tourist Promotional Organization*

The majority of the United States and Canadian provinces promote tourism using a regional or area breakdown within the state. The reason for doing this is consumer demand for "area" information versus statewide information. It is more easily understood and responded to by consumers of the tourism product. This holds true for all attractions, activities, and facilities being promoted.

Factors for a promotional regional breakdown are mainly geographic, but political, transportation, and personal factors are also involved. The geographic factor involves basic natural resources. Lakes or groups of lakes, river systems, mountain groups, forest areas, and tourism development within them separate a state into from three to a dozen "natural" areas. Such regional breakdowns are natural for area tourist promotion organizations.

Individual resort areas, such as Lake of the Ozarks in Missouri, can and do operate successfully without full statewide regional breakdown.

Regional systems today are usually established in cooperation with the state travel office. The regions in California and Michigan, however, were established at local levels prior to state promotion programs. Nearly all regional systems use county or city lines for boundary limits.

Regardless of whether a state has one operating region or a dozen, the regional or area tourist promotion programs can operate successfully.

The name of the organization is important. The name is used on all signatures in promotion and in fund-raising. Geographic description is paramount here; use of directions and/or major natural resources and city names are commonly used.

Steps to organize a tourist promotional organization are the same for any group that wishes to establish formally a program of activity on a cooperative basis. Registration is required at state and sometimes local levels. The initial step, following organizational meeting(s), is to file articles of incorporation. The next step is a general meeting to adopt the bylaws which establish basic organization and program functions. From this point, annual meetings are usually the most basic function for organizational reporting to members.

Organizations involving local tax funding usually require organization representation by elected officials and/or government professional staff personnel for liaison purposes (or full participation of the governing body). Government involvement can also establish guidelines to the organization for use of government funds involved in the overall program. Such programs are also subject to auditing by the government unit involved. In these instances there is a great need for mutual understanding by people involved to ensure efficiency and effectiveness.

Charts depicting model organizations for an "area or regional" tourist promo-

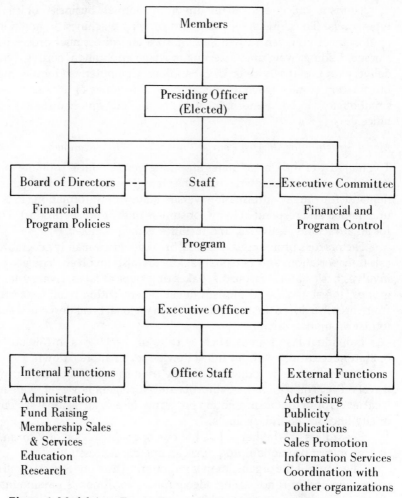

**Figure 1** Model Area Tourist Promotion Organization Chart.

tion organization and a state system for tourist promotion are shown in Figures 1 and 2.

## READING 2-5

### *Report on a 50-Year Love Affair*

By Charles Gillett, Immediate Past President
New York Convention and Visitors Bureau, Inc.

(Excerpts from a speech to the Big Apple Chapter of the Hotel Sales and Marketing Association International in 1987)

Our success in New York in marketing the visitor product is based on the continuing ability of the various components of the hotel industry to work in har-

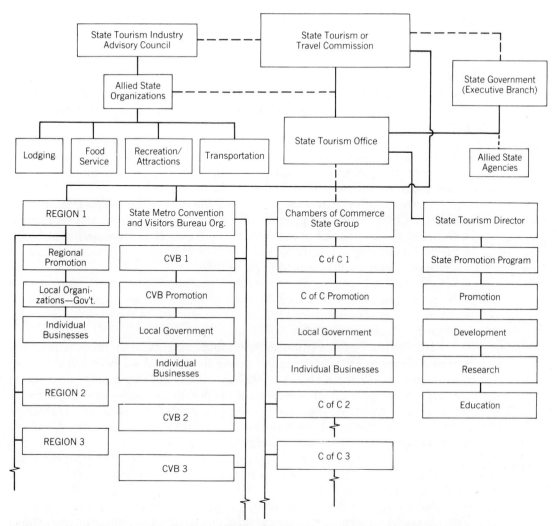

**Figure 2**  Model for State System for Tourist Marketing (patterned after the Michigan system)

mony with the Bureau staff. Wherever I go and whenever I speak, I recommend harmony and cooperation between the bureau or tourist promotion agency and the hotels in an area as the proven prescription for success in selling any destination, regardless of size.

Together we've come a long way since 1937. Today tourism is the city's leading economic resource and New York City is the world's top visitor destination.

Our major resource is the strong bonds of common purpose and professional respect that exist between hotel salespeople and the professionals of the Bureau. Because we work together on a day-to-day basis we have created a cooperative atmosphere. This is our "secret weapon."

We at the New York Convention and Visitors Bureau recognize the tremendous importance of this harmony and so do the leaders of the hotel industry. The Bureau is always available to work with the individual hotel salespeople in building convention sales, exposition sales, group sales, vacation visitor sales, package sales, and foreign visitor sales.

### Support Is Vital

What we ask from the hotels, of course, is support — in terms of being boosters of the Bureau and in terms of tuning in to the Bureau's marketing and promotional programs.

Hotel occupancy for 1986 was 75 percent, compared to 72 percent in 1985. This compares to the national average of 63 percent projected for 1986. We enjoyed the highest occupancy of any major city in the country despite the large number of hotel rooms which have come on line in the last 10 years.

The very positive performance in 1986 is the result of long-term promotion of New York City tourism, an upturn in visitor traffic from overseas, and very strong convention business, some booked as much as a decade ago. Of course, there was the tremendous impetus of Liberty Weekend, the World Series and the Jacob K. Javits Convention Center which opened in April 1986.

Let's look back for a moment at Liberty Weekend. What an extravaganza! What great publicity for New York City! How about the 98 percent hotel occupancy we enjoyed over the Fourth of July Weekend, usually one of the lowest periods for occupancy of the year? It didn't just happen.

At the Bureau we set out to avoid the disappointments of other cities which have hosted big events. From early on in beating the drums for Liberty Weekend we emphasized that New York has 100,000 hotel rooms and would not be sold out. In the last weeks before Liberty Weekend we kept tabs on exactly how many rooms were available and where they were. We kept the public informed of this availability until the final hurrah of Liberty Weekend. Thus, the 98 percent occupancy. That's a great example of how the Bureau and hotels work together.

How about next month, next year, ten years from now? How about the economy, the new tax laws, the possibility of another fuel crisis, and growing competition?

That we worry — and do something about it — is essential. It keeps us alive. Euphoria is the father of complacency and complacency is a privilege no one in hotel sales can afford. When we start taking business for granted, then we're in bad trouble.

The facts of life in our business are that no matter how good our product may be it has to be sold and resold. The really successful marketeers in our industry understand that the better business is the more money must be plowed back into advertising, direct mail, promotion, and, most important, salesmanship. That's how success breeds success.

It takes a lot of work to build five or ten points increase in occupancy and it doesn't take much to lose it. So, the future is now. We have to look at our best markets for developing opportunities; we have to identify new markets and exploit the opportunities they represent.

Convention and business travel is the backbone of the visitor industry for New York. This will continue to be true in the years ahead. But, in my opinion, what we do in selling the leisure market may be the difference between red and black ink, and between seasonal and weekend lows and year-round consistency.

Fortunately, one of the best ways to generate leisure travel is to do a good job in selling conventions and business travel. Today's business traveler is tomorrow's pleasure traveler, often multiplied by the family accompanying him. We have found that businesspeople who have "discovered" New York City — the convention delegates or business travelers who have found that they won't be mugged in the streets, won't be shoved off the sidewalks, won't be ripped off at the restaurants — want to come back and share their enjoyment with families and friends.

*Where to Find Business*

So the business or convention traveler is a hot prospect in developing vacation travel. His or her name and address can be found right on your registration forms.

In today's world where time, not miles, is the true measure of distance, we can realistically expect to sell the leisure market as near as Scarsdale and as far as Tokyo, London, Frankfurt, or Caracas.

At the New York Convention and Visitors Bureau we have been using hotel packages for many years to attract the leisure market, especially from the massive population zone within 250 miles of New York. We were first with the idea of a tour packages directory, and it has been copied by cities throughout the country. We have been highly encouraged to see so many of the city's hotels advertising these same packages in suburban dailies and other nearby markets. It's one reason that we're enjoying such good weekend and holiday traffic in the Big Apple.

Today, too, the overseas traffic is a prime target for our sales campaigns. We have had a generous taste of foreign business and it has whetted our appetite for more. In 1986, we had 2,684,000 overseas visitors — an all-time high.

The overseas market is just one of several prime markets we focus on at the Bureau. Some of the others we spend time and resources on are the incentive market and the motorcoach market. And like you, we have to recognize and adapt to the changing mores as well as changing markets.

## Key Concepts

| | |
|---|---|
| chambers of commerce | Organization for Economic Cooperation and Development |
| convention and visitors bureaus | |
| Department of Transportation | Pacific Asia Travel Association |
| Federal Aviation Administration | regulators |
| International Air Transport Association | state tourism offices |
| | Tourism Canada |
| International Association of Convention and Visitors Bureaus | Travel Industry Association of America |
| | World Bank |
| multicountry | World Tourism Organization |
| multistate | |
| multicounty | |

## For Review and Discussion

1. For a manager in any kind of tourist business, why is it necessary to know about world, national, and regional tourism organizations?
2. How does the work of the FAA affect your career in tourism?

3. Describe how the Federal State Department and the Customs Bureau affect international tourism.
4. Is there a relationship between the work of the U.S. Travel and Tourism Administration and our trade deficit?
5. What official tourism organizations should be responsible for helping to prevent terroristic attacks upon transportation carriers?
6. Is it proper for a state promotion organization to spend taxpayers' money to promote tourism to that state?
7. What specifically does a city convention and visitors bureau do? How is it usually financed?
8. What are the best ways for a regional tourism association to raise necessary funds?
9. If you were the manager of a lodge, what arguments would you present to your board of directors in favor of financial support for your local and regional tourism promotion organizations?
10. Why is the name of a promotional organization so important?
11. As a motel manager, how would you find out whether your membership plus an advertisement in an area or regional tourism promotion publication was paying off?
12. Is a local chamber of commerce likely to be just as effective in promoting tourism as a convention and visitors bureau?
13. What attributes of Tourism Canada make it an outstanding organization?
14. Suppose that you were director of tourism of a small developing country. What assistance could you obtain for your country from WTO?

## Case Problems

1. You have been asked to serve on a committee to reorganize your local chamber of commerce. Up to now, there has been no formal recognition of tourism, even though tourism has become a growing factor in the community's economy. Make recommendations as to how tourism interests could become represented in the new chamber organization.
2. Mr. J. C. has been newly appointed Minister of Tourism in a small emerging nation. He soon realizes that his department must compete vigorously (and at some disadvantage) with other departments of the government for money. He must formulate specific steps to enhance his government's support for his organization and its vital work. What might these be?

## Selected References

Council of State Governments. *Tourism: State Structure, Organization, and Support.* Lexington, Ky.: The Council, 1979.
Gartrell, Richard B. *Destination Marketing for Convention and Visitor Bureaus.* Dubuque, Iowa: Kendall/Hunt, 1988.
*National Tourism Policy Study—Ascertainment Phase.* Washington, D.C.: Superintendent of Documents, Government Printing Office, 1977.
*National Tourism Policy Study—Final Report.* Washington, D.C.: Superintendent of Documents, Government Printing Office, 1978.

Organization for Economic Cooperation and Development. *Tourism Policy and International Tourism in OECD Member Countries.* Paris: OECD, 1989.

Pritchard, Garth. "Tourism Promotion Pays Off for the States." *The Cornell Hotel and Restaurant Administration Quarterly,* Vol. 23, no. 1 (August 1982), pp. 48–57.

Ronkainen, Ilkka A., and Richard J. Farano. "United States Travel and Tourism Policy." *Journal of Travel Research,* Vol. 25, no. 4 (Spring 1987), pp. 2–8.

Travel Industry Association of America. *Competitiveness in the International Tourism Market —A Proposed Marketing Plan for the United States.* Washington, D.C.: TIAA, 1984.

U.S. Travel Data Center. *Survey of State Travel Offices, 1988-89.* Washington, D.C.: The Center, 1989.

World Tourism Organization. *Budgets of National Tourism Administrations, 1981-1982-1983.* Madrid: WTO, 1984. Accompanied by appendices.

# CHAPTER 3

# How Tourism Is Organized: Industry Segments and Trade Associations

## LEARNING OBJECTIVES

- Comprehend the magnitude and importance of transportation organizations and the volume of passengers carried each year.
- Understand the role of travel agents.
- Learn the composition of the lodging sector and how it operates.
- Examine the food service industry and its contribution to tourism.
- Study the attractions industry.

## PRIVATE BUSINESS FIRMS AND ORGANIZATIONS

When we discuss the private sector we typically think of the firms that furnish the travel product to the consumer. These are commonly referred to as suppliers. Suppliers are those organizations that actually supply the transportation, offer the accommodations, make the arrangements, and provide entertainment for travelers. Examples are airlines, cruise lines, rail lines, motorcoach lines, ground operators who provide local transportation and local tours, taxi companies, auto rental firms, charter boat services, and aerial tramways.

Accommodations suppliers include hotels, motels, resorts, clubs, condominiums, timesharing (sometimes called interval ownership) resorts, youth hostels, bed and breakfast homes, tourist homes, camps, and others. Along shores are marinas, boat rental operators, and other water-oriented sports equipment suppliers, for example, suppliers of wind surfing gear. In resort areas are suppliers of tennis, golf, and other activities.

Suppliers of arrangements are dominated by retail travel agencies. However, there are also tour operators and wholesalers, consolidators, tour organizers and managers, tour guides, couriers, escorts, tour directors, and others who may assume a leadership position with a traveling group. Restaurants, cafes, caterers, food stores, bars/taverns, and similar eating and drinking places make up the components of the food and food service group. Finally, there are places of amusement and entertainment, such as theme parks; national, state, and local parks; public forests; wilderness

82

areas; lakes, streams, seashores, and beaches; night clubs; sports facilities and events; and theaters.

Supplementing all these are stores and shops of various kinds that provide opportunities for travelers to obtain whatever type of goods and services they need or want in any particular place. Each of the major components of the private sector will be examined separately in the following sections.

## THE AIRLINE INDUSTRY

In the span of 50 years the airline industry has grown from infant to giant; by 1988 the air share of the common carrier passenger mile market was 92.1 percent (Table 3.1). Airlines now account for 335.8 billion passenger miles a year.

The airlines have revolutionized travel, and the range and speed of jet travel has greatly expanded what tourists or business travelers could once accomplish with the equivalent time and funds at their disposal. Today, for example, it is possible to fly around the globe in less time than it takes to drive across the United States. The system is also incredibly efficient: you need only make one call to an airline or a travel agent and purchase a ticket to your desired destination; then all you have to do is go to the airport and check your bags through to the final destination. The logistics that make it happen are complex, but the system works well. For example, American Airlines serves over 1100 domestic pairs of points on its system, not including its connections with domestic airlines and worldwide airlines. Other airlines have similar structures and combine to make a total system that blankets the country.

Although the major advantage of air travel is speed, which results in more time for other activities, there are negative aspects for those who wish to travel by air. These include some people's fear of flying and lack of geographic accessibility — many communities in the country are not served by air transportation. An additional problem is the length of time spent getting to and from the airport. Frequently, this time exceeds that spent en route.

The $50 billion air transportation industry in the United States is dominated by a small number of large firms; the major carriers — American, Continental, Delta, Eastern, Northwest, Pan American, Piedmont, TWA, United, and U.S. Air — all

**Table 3.1** Intercity Passenger Travel in the United States 1978 vs 1987 and 1988 (passenger miles in millions)

|  | 1978 | 1987 | 1988 |
| --- | --- | --- | --- |
| Common carriers |  |  |  |
| Airlines | 182,677 | 329,100 | 335,800 |
| Amtrak | 10,222 | 5,200 | 5,800 |
| Motor buses | 25,100 | 22,800 | 23,000 |
| Total | 217,999 | 357,100 | 364,600 |
| Air share estimate, % | 83.8% | 92.2% | 92.1% |

*Source:* Air Transport Association, *Air Transport 1989* (Washington, D.C.: ATA, 1989), p. 7.

Efficient aircraft such as this one can transport passengers swiftly and comfortably. In the United States commercial airlines carry 92.1 percent of intercity passenger miles. (Photo courtesy of the Boeing Company)

record over $1 billion in revenue annually. In spite of the domination by the large carriers, there are a number of small firms in the market. In 1988 there were over 77 domestic operators flying some 5022 aircraft, enplaning 455 million passengers, and employing over 480,553 workers.

A number of publications report on the rapidly occurring changes in this industry, including *Air Transport World, Aviation Week and Space Technology,* and the *Journal of Air Law and Commerce.* One of the best sources of data on the airline industry is an annual report entitled *Air Transport,* published by the Air Transport Association of America, 1709 New York Avenue N.W., Washington, D.C. 20006. Another useful source of information on the airline industry is the Federal Aviation Administration. Consumer protection is the responsibility of the Department of Transportation.

With the advent of deregulation, the airline industry has undergone a dramatic change. However, because transportation by definition is an essential ingredient in travel and tourism, the future of the airline industry continues to remain linked to the performance of the entire tourism industry.

Although some additional changes will occur in the airline industry, there will be a slowing and finally an end to airline consolidation. Air traffic is expected to increase at about 5 percent annually. The popular frequent-flyer programs are expected to become more restrictive.

A 1987 survey of air travelers by the Gallup organization revealed that a record number, 126 million people, or 72 percent of the entire adult population in the United States, has flown. Nearly one out of every three U.S. citizens flew during the past year. The survey found that 52 percent of airline trips during the past year were for pleasure or other personal reasons, and 48 percent were for business. The average air traveler made 3.4 round-trips over the past year.

The airline industry is supported by three major organizations. IATA and ICAO have already been discussed under international organizations; they are two key associations controlling air travel. The major U.S. organization is the Air Transport Association of America, or the ATA.

## Air Transport Association of America

In 1936, fourteen fledgling airlines met in Chicago to form the Air Transport Association (ATA) "to do all things tending to promote the betterment of airline business, and in general, to do everything in its power to best serve the interest and welfare of the members of this association and the public at large."

Today, from its headquarters in Washington, D.C., and six regional offices, the ATA represents virtually all of the scheduled airlines in the United States, plus two associate member carriers in Canada, with responsibilities ranging from the continual improvement of safety to planning for the industry's role in national defense.

ATA is the meeting place where the airlines cooperate in noncompetitive areas to improve airline service, safety, and efficiency. The mission of the ATA is to support and assist its member carriers by promoting aviation safety, advocating industry positions, conducting designated industry-wide programs, and assuring public understanding.

Thus, while the carriers are intensely competitive among themselves and with other forms of transportation in their individual promotion of airline service for the traveling and shipping public, they are equally intense in their mutual cooperation on matters of industrywide importance, such as safety, technological progress, and passenger service improvement.

The focus of ATA activities is to

- Work effectively with the Federal Aviation Administration and other federal agencies on a broad range of matters affecting safety and operations
- Represent the industry before Congress and before agencies and regulatory bodies of federal, state, and local governments
- Conduct selected industrywide programs that can be carried out more efficiently on a common-industry basis

Following are examples of industrywide programs that meet important common needs of the ATA membership: Airline Scheduling Committees at high-density airports; Airline Clearing House; Airline Inventory Redistribution System (AIRS); Universal Air Travel Plan; and Scheduled Airline Traffic Offices, Overseas (SATO-OS). Many of these programs serve both ATA member and nonmember airlines.

The ATA headquarters is located at 1709 New York Avenue N.W., Washington, D.C. 20006-5206.

## THE RAIL INDUSTRY

Rail passenger transportation, once the major mode of travel in the United States, reached its peak volume in 1920. Major railroads have wished to rid themselves of the passenger business, and today the survival of service (other than commuter service) depends largely on Amtrak.

## Amtrak

Amtrak is the marketing name for the National Railroad Passenger Corporation, an operating railroad corporation, the controlling stock of which is owned by the United States government through the U.S. Department of Transportation. Amtrak's business is providing rail passenger transportation in the major intercity markets of the United States. The National Railroad Passenger Corporation was established by the Rail Passenger Service Act of 1970.

Although it receives financial support from the federal government, Amtrak is not a government agency. It is a corporation structured and managed like other large businesses in the United States and competes with all other modes in the transportation marketplace.

Amtrak's business is providing rail passenger transportation in the major intercity markets of the United States. (Photo courtesy of Amtrak)

Serving 43 states and 500 destinations, Amtrak carried more than 20.4 million intercity passengers 5.2 billion miles in 1987. In addition, Amtrak carried 10.2 million commuters on trains operated under contract for the Massachusetts Bay Transportation Authority and the Maryland Department of Transportation.

Amtrak's fortunes appear to be on the upswing. The Amtrak railway system surpassed previous records in revenues, the number of passengers carried, and the distance they traveled during the fiscal year (FY) that ended September 30, 1988.

Passenger miles for FY 1988 rose to 5.7 billion from FY 1987's previous record of 5.2 billion passenger miles systemwide (a passenger mile is one passenger carried one mile). This 9 percent rise reflects the longer average distance traveled by each Amtrak passenger during the fiscal year, up from 255 miles in FY 1987 to 264 in FY 1988.

Setting another all-time record was Amtrak's revenue-to-cost ratio, up from 65 percent in 1987 to 69 percent in FY 1988. Revenue earned during FY 1988 covered a larger percentage of Amtrak's costs than at any other time in the company's history. As recently as 1981, Amtrak's revenue-to-cost ratio was only 48 percent.

The record-setting trend at Amtrak can be attributed to several factors. Aggressive marketing, including service enhancements on several routes, has played a major role. Also contributing to the marketing success has been Amtrak's membership in the Airline Reporting Corporation, a national clearinghouse for travel agencies' billing systems, as well as reservations and ticketing accessibility on most major airline computer systems. These factors enable travel agents to look up Amtrak information, reserve space, and generate tickets, using the same computers they use for airline transactions. As a result, sales by travel agents increased by 21 percent in FY 1988 over FY 1987, rising by $49 million to $280 million.

One of Amtrak's major problems is raising capital to expand its passenger car fleet, because Amtrak has only limited capacity and pales in comparison to rail systems in other countries. Amtrak's approximately 2000 cars operate over a 24,000-mile network, whereas countries like France and Germany each have some 17,000 cars serving approximately the same route structures. Japan has 26,000 cars for approximately 13,000 route miles. Amtrak has been testing its new viewliner car series, the prototypes of their future long-distance passenger car fleet.

Because Amtrak is subsidized, suppliers of the other modes of transportation (especially bus) feel that Amtrak is attracting its customers with taxpayer assistance. However, even with the controversy, Congress is likely to see that Amtrak remains in business for the foreseeable future.

## THE MOTORCOACH INDUSTRY

The motorcoach companies are the second most important common carrier in intercity passenger travel in the United States, having a 6.3 percent share of the market in 1988. The industry accounts for 23.0 billion passenger miles (see Table 3.1). Over the past decade bus passenger volume appeared to be setting a long-term downward trend. The fares and routes of the intercity bus industry were closely regulated by the Interstate Commerce Commission (ICC) until 1982, when deregulation eliminated many of the most restrictive regulations while maintaining a regulatory framework for the industry.

In 1987 two very significant events took place in the intercity bus industry. First, Greyhound Lines, Inc., was sold by the Greyhound Corporation in Phoenix, Arizona, to a Dallas firm whose primary business was leasing intercity buses to other bus carriers. Second, this "new" Greyhound Lines bought Trailways Lines, Inc.

The sale of Greyhound Lines was consummated on March 18, 1987. The Greyhound Corporation had diversified and become a company involved in packaged goods, food service, and cruise ships, rather than emphasizing the intercity bus business. The result was a decline in ridership. The sale and the move to Dallas brought new management dedication to providing good quality, low-cost bus transportation to the people of the United States.

In July 1987 the "new" Greyhound Lines purchased Trailways Lines, creating an intercity bus network of about 2600 sales facilities serving more than 15,000 points in the continental United States. Thus, the Greyhound/Trailways Lines consolidation produced a route and schedule network that provides a traveler with more choices and travel options than ever before. In addition, the employees of these two companies were merged to form the best and most experienced personnel in the bus industry. The result has been a dramatic rebound in passenger traffic.

Although Greyhound attracts the attention, the intercity bus industry is not a one-company industry but a small-business industry with a great deal of flexibility. There are over 1000 companies ranging from the giant Greyhound to small family operations. The companies operate more than 20,000 buses over 250,000 miles of scheduled routes, providing not only regular route services but charter and tour services as well.

The industry is the largest, most pervasive form of intercity transportation, providing service to more than 15,000 communities. Of the communities served by motorcoaches, approximately 14,000 have no other form of transportation. In contrast, Amtrak provides service to about 500 locations, and the airlines to about 700. This means that accessibility is the bus industry's greatest advantage over train and airline service.

The intercity bus passenger is different from other travelers, according to the U.S. Travel Data Center. Its data show that 43 percent of total person-trips are taken for pleasure, but only 15 percent of bus trips are taken for this purpose. The intercity bus passenger is less affluent than travelers by other modes. Fifty-seven percent of bus passengers have family incomes of less than $20,000 a year, compared with 24 percent of all travelers.

College students, active-duty military, foreign visitors, and the rapidly expanding Hispanic market are important passenger segments that are expected to grow. The senior citizen passenger is also an extremely important part of the industry's customer mix. Greyhound Lines is trying to make travel more attractive to the senior citizen market segment through an expansion of its "Golden Savers Club" and other seniors programs.

Bus industry advocates believe that this form of transportation is particularly well suited to certain needs of tourism, especially one-way trips of 150 miles or less. The increase in foreign visitors who frequently are bus travelers has benefited the industry. However, one of the problems that bus companies have faced over the

The motorcoach industry is the most pervasive form of intercity
public transportation in the United States. Motorcoaches serve
more than 15,000 communities and provide both scheduled and
charter service. (Photo courtesy of National Tour Association)

years is the public's perception and attitude toward bus travel; that is, bus travel has
had a largely negative image. Moreover, buses are perceived as being slow and
uncomfortable, even though their fares are inexpensive and they allow the passenger to see the countryside. In response, the bus industry has done a great deal to
upgrade its product, putting in restrooms, heating and air-conditioning controls,
reclining seats, and tinted glass windows and building modern terminals.

## Bus Organizations

The American Bus Association (ABA) is the national organization of the intercity bus
industry and serves as the prime source of industry statistics. ABA members are bus
operating companies, other travel industry participants, and others associated with
providing bus transportation. Bus operating companies include some 450 carriers
throughout the United States and Canada. Collectively, these carriers provide more
than 90 percent of all intercity bus travel in the United States and Canada. The travel
industry category includes hotel/motel chains and properties, food service organizations, attractions and theme parks, and local, state, regional, and federal promotion organizations interested in working with bus companies to expand tourism in
North America.

The United Bus Owners of America (UBOA) is the largest trade association
serving intercity bus owners. With a membership of almost 2000, UBOA members
own all types of bus companies, ranging from the smallest to the largest. Bus manufacturers and other industry suppliers are also members. Major programs of the
association are safety, insurance, credit, computer services, resident agent services,
meetings, lobbying, and communications.

In 1984 the National Tour Association (NTA) and UBOA announced a joint agreement between the two trade associations for the exchange of certain membership benefits because the relationship between bus companies and tour operators are many with the most fundamental being the use of the motorcoach by both parties for tour and charter business. Many tour operators have become bus owners, and bus owners have opened tour and charter departments. UBOA members will benefit from the tour expertise of NTA members, and NTA tour operator members will gain valuable insights into the bus industry.

## THE AUTOMOBILE

According to the U.S. Travel Data Center, in its *National Travel Survey*, automobile travel accounts for about 76 percent of all travel away from home and 83 percent of the intercity miles. Two-thirds of households use automobiles as their means of taking a family vacation. Additionally, the recreational vehicle is an important part of the automobile travel component. While the RV market has had its ups and downs because of the energy crisis, the market for recreation vehicles is very much alive, and its long-term prospects are positive.

When we look at the intercity passenger travel in the United States, we find that approximately 81.3 percent of all travel is by automobile. Table 3.2 extends Table 3.1 to include all common carriers and the automobile. It shows that the common carrier share is 18.7 percent and that the air share of the total is 17.2 percent, reflecting the importance of air and auto for passenger travel in the United States. The table shows the clear dominance of the automobile over other means of transportation.

All studies show the automobile's dominance, whether the study is from the Air Transport Association, the Highway Administration, the Census Bureau, or the *National Travel Survey* of the U.S. Travel Data Center. There is no doubt that the great bulk of intercity transportation of passengers is by automobile. Data also

**Table 3.2** Intercity Passenger Travel in the United States, 1978 vs. 1987 and 1988

|  | (Passenger Miles in millions) | | |
|---|---|---|---|
|  | *1978* | *1987* | *1988* |
| Common Carriers |  |  |  |
| Airlines | 182,677 | 329,100 | 335,800 |
| Amtrak | 10,222 | 5,300 | 5,800 |
| Motor Buses | 25,100 | 23,000 | 23,000e |
| Total | 217,999 | 357,400 | 364,600 |
| Air Share (%) | 83.8 | 92.1 | 92.1 |
| Private Automobiles | 1,162,000 e | 1,520,000 | 1,588,000 |
| Total Common Carrier and Auto | 1,379,999 | 1,877,400 | 1,952,600 |
| Common Carrier Share (%) | 15.8 | 19.0 | 18.7 |
| Air Share (%) | 13.2 | 17.5 | 17.2 |

e = Estimate

*Source:* Air Transport Association, *Air Transport 1989* (Washington, D.C.: ATA, 1989).

indicate that this has been constant for several decades. The energy crisis made some inroads into auto travel, causing some shifts to common carriers, but these inroads have been small. However, because of the great dominance of the automobile in travel, only a small shift in automobile travel to the common carriers can result in enormous increases in the carriers' business.

The interstate highway system significantly encouraged vacation travel and especially encouraged long-distance travel. It made automobile travel much faster and more comfortable. A major concern of tourism groups today is the maintenance of the highway network. There is growing evidence that the highway system is in need of substantial repair to prevent it from suffering further deterioration. A poor road system costs the individual driver, the bus operator, and other users additional funds in terms of increased fuel use and vehicle maintenance, and the knowledge that a highway is in poor condition may cause the traveler to select another destination to avoid the problem.

On the whole, people's attitudes are very favorable toward travel by automobile. The key feature of the automobile is immediate accessibility and convenience. The automobile owner can leave from his or her own doorstep at any hour of the day or night and travel by a chosen route to a chosen destination. When two or more persons travel by automobile, the per person cost of travel is more favorable than it is with the other transportation modes. Air is the primary competitor to the automobile when it comes to travel, especially for long trips.

The advantages of air travel—the quality of service, speed, and comfort— must be weighed by travelers against the automobile's advantages of price and accessibility.

## Rental Cars

An important aspect of automobile travel is the rental car industry, whose growth has been paralleling or exceeding the growth in air travel. While there is no question about the rental car business having heavy use by businesses, it also has substantial vacation use and frequent combination trip use.

According to data compiled annually by the Hertz Corporation, the rental car industry grossed $7.2 billion in 1987. In the United States the companies operated a fleet of more than 766,000 cars in 1986. In addition, there are about 5000 small operators such as car dealers and service stations that rent cars at about 20,000 locations.

Major companies in the rental car business are Hertz, Avis, National, and Budget, which dominate the airport locations and claim the majority of the market. The big four are being challenged by a host of small companies, including Alamo, Dollar, Thrifty, American International, and others.

Many of the auto rental systems are international and have services in virtually every tourist destination area in the world. These companies arrange for the purchase, lease, or rental of automobiles domestically and abroad. Companies representative of this type of organization are Americar Rental Systems; Auto-Europe, Inc.; Europe-by-Car; Hertz International, Ltd.; The Kemwel Group, Inc.; National Car Rental Systems, Inc.; and Open Road International, Inc.

Airports are key locations for car rental companies. Vans
commonly carry rental car customers from airport doors to the
rental car site. (Photo courtesy of National Car Rental)

## Taxi and Limousine Service

Taxi and limousine companies play an exceedingly important part in tourism. Local
transportation companies perform vital services for airlines in servicing departing
and arriving passengers as well as providing similar services for bus, rail, and
shipping lines. Businesspersons and tourists alike would have a difficult time getting
from place to place if these services were not available.

Inclines and aerial trams serve as a form of taxi service and are of a special
interest to visitors in scenic tourist destination areas as a form of recreation and
sightseeing.

The International Taxicab Association (ITA) in Kensington, Maryland, is the
major taxicab association. It was formed in 1966 by a merger of the National Association of Taxicab Owners, the Cab Research Bureau, and the American Taxicab
Association. ITA has 600 members who are fleet taxicab owners operating 30,000
vehicles. The association sponsors an annual convention and trade show, is involved
with political action, and publishes *Taxicab Management*.

## Oil Companies

Oil companies the world over have a very important stake in automobile tourism
and thus are organized in many ways to serve the wants and needs of travelers. In
the United States, many of the major oil companies publish road maps as a touring
service. Some companies have organized motor clubs, such as the American Oil

Motor Club, which provides travel information and routing services for its members, among other services. An example of special travel services is the *Mobil Travel Guide,* which has seven regional editions and lists over 20,000 hotels, motels, and restaurants. These accommodations are rated from one to five stars in quality and indicate the prices of typical meals and accommodations to suit every budget. Each *Guide* also contains a variety of special sightseeing tours with easy-to-follow maps.

## Automobile Clubs and Organizations

The American Automobile Association (AAA) is the world's largest single membership travel group. With a membership of over 29 million, this organization promotes travel in several different forms among its members, including auto travel as a primary form of transportation. It also operates worldwide travel services similar to those provided by a travel agency or tour company. The AAA Travel Department also provides travel services for nonmembers and is thus competitive with other tour companies and retail travel agencies. This additional service gives the club a certain glamour and status in the community, and nonmembers who are brought into the club office through the travel service become prospects for new members in the automobile club.

The AAA provides insurance protection to motorists through its various state and city affiliate organizations (such as the Automobile Club of Michigan), publishes travel maps and *Tour Books,* and has a national touring board as well as a national touring bureau staff. The principal function of the *Tour Books* is to describe the history, attractions, points of interest, and accommodations in hotels, resorts, motels, and restaurants that have been inspected and approved by AAA field representatives. All accommodations listed have been selected on the basis of a satisfactory report submitted by the AAA field representative.

An organization of wider geographic membership is the World Touring and Automobile Organization, with headquarters in London, England. Other organizations of a similar nature are the International Road Federation of Washington, D.C.; the Pan American Highway Congress, Washington, D.C.; Inter-American Federation of Automobile Clubs, Buenos Aires; and the International Automobile Federation, with headquarters at Paris.

# THE CRUISE INDUSTRY

Cruising is currently the fastest-growing segment of the travel industry. It is experiencing a surge of growth in both passengers and ship and passenger capacity. Cruise lines are expanding their fleets, adding new amenities and new ports of call.

Within the last 10 years, the demand for cruising has doubled. In 1970, an estimated 500,000 people took cruises; in 1987 over 3 million people cruised. From 1980 to 1987 the cruise industry has grown at a compounded 9 percent rate. The market demands for cruising are currently 10 times the size of the existing business.

Growth has affected not only passenger and ship capacity, but also the ports of embarkation as well. In the last 20 years, cruise traffic in Miami has more than doubled, with 24 ships sailing regularly from the city's modern port facilities. Other ports experiencing substantial growth include Ft. Lauderdale, Port Canaveral, Tampa, New Orleans, San Diego, Los Angeles, and San Juan.

The cruise industry contributes over $1.2 billion annually to the U.S. economy in direct purchase of goods and services. Over 10,000 U.S. citizens derive their entire income from the cruise industry.

Cruise revenues have grown to an estimated $5 billion annually in 1987 (a 10 percent increase over 1986 figures), representing commissions of some $50 million for travel agents, who sell 95 percent of all sea vacations.

Trends in the cruise industry include the building of new ships of all sizes, from yacht-like vessels to superliners, new programs and itineraries, and new on-board facilities. Vessels are of all sizes, carrying from 75 to 2600 passengers. There are new adventure and theme cruises, health and fitness cruises, and food and wine cruises.

In this decade, more than 40 new ships have been built or announced, and another 55 have been refurbished. By 1990, 16 new ships will join the cruise fleet, and more than $3 billion will be spent on construction. Architectural breakthroughs and innovations have resulted in larger "hotel-like" vessels with expansive interiors, as well as smaller vessels and unique adventure-type crafts. There are new and unusual amenities on board and new programs available to today's cruise passengers. New and exotic itineraries include cruises to ports in South America, the Far East, Europe, and a renewed interest in the Mediterranean.

Cruise passengers come from all walks of life—there is a cruise for every interest and pocketbook. A study conducted by the Cruise Lines International Association (CLIA) shows that cruisers come from a wide range of income levels; nearly half are under 45 years of age, and one-third are under 35. California is the home state of more cruise passengers than any other state, accounting for almost 20 percent of the total. Florida is a close second, followed by New York, Illinois, Pennsylvania, and Texas.

Sailing on weekly round trips from Miami to the Western Caribbean, Royal Caribbean Cruise Line's *Song of America* leads a new generation of luxury resorts-at-sea with a complete range of recreational and entertainment features, as well as Royal Caribbean's award-winning passenger service. (Photo courtesy of Royal Caribbean Cruise Lines)

### Cruise Lines International Association

Cruise Lines International Association (CLIA) is a marketing and promotional trade organization comprised of 35 of the major cruise lines serving North America, representing over 100 ships. CLIA was formed in 1975 out of a need for the cruise industry to develop a vehicle to promote the general concept of cruising. CLIA exists to educate, train, promote, and explain the value, desirability, and profitability of the cruise product.

When, in mid-1984, the Federal Maritime Commission consolidated other industry organizations into CLIA, it became the sole marketing organization of the cruise industry. CLIA represents almost 97 percent of the cruise industry, and more than 18,500 travel agents are affiliated with CLIA and display the CLIA seal, which identifies them as authorities on cruise vacations.

The Cruise Lines International Association headquarters is located at 500 Fifth Avenue, Suite 1407, New York 10110.

## TRAVEL AGENTS

Travel, whether for business or pleasure, requires arrangements. The traveler usually faces a variety of choices regarding transportation, accommodations, and, if the trip is for pleasure, destinations, attractions, and activities. The traveler may gather information on prices, value, schedules, characteristics of the destination, and available activities directly, investing a considerable amount of time and possibly money on long-distance telephone calls to complete the trip arrangements. Alternatively the traveler may use the services of a travel agency, obtaining all these arrangements at no cost.

### What Is a Travel Agent?

A travel agency is a middleman — a business or person selling the travel industry's individual parts or a combination of the parts to the consumer. In marketing terms a travel agent is an agent middleman, acting on behalf of the client, making arrangements with suppliers of travel — airlines, hotels, tour operators — and receiving a commission from the suppliers.

In legal terms, a travel agency is an agent of the principal, specifically transportation companies. The agency operates as a legally appointed agent, representing the principal in a certain geographic area. The agency functions as a broker, bringing buyer and seller together, for the other suppliers like hotels, car rentals, ground operators, and tour companies.

A travel agent is thus an expert, knowledgeable in schedules, routing, lodging, currency, prices, regulations, destinations, and all other aspects of travel and travel opportunities. In short, the travel agent is a specialist and counselor.

The *Travel Weekly* studies conducted by Louis Harris and Associates define the travel agent as follows:

A travel agent, besides selling prepared package tours, also prepares individual itineraries. He arranges for hotels, motels, accommodation at resorts, meals, sightseeing,

Automation is now a necessary ingredient in travel agency operations. Agency staff receives instruction from an airline representative. (Photo courtesy of United Airlines)

transfers of passengers and luggage between terminals and hotels; furthermore, he can provide the traveler with a host of other information (for example, on rates, quality and so on) which would normally be hard to get. The travel agent is paid for his services through commissions. For example, if a travel agent writes up an air ticket or makes a reservation in a hotel for a client, he gets paid by the carrier or the hotel in the form of a commission. In short, the travel agent saves the customer both time and money.

Thanks to the reports sponsored by *Travel Weekly* magazine and conducted by Louis Harris and Associates, excellent data are available on the travel agency business. Started in 1970, these studies conducted every two years are regarded as the benchmark research in the retail travel industry. The latest *Travel Weekly—Louis Harris Study* was published in June 1988 and represents the ninth in a series of studies on the character and volume of the U.S. travel agency market. The 1985 and 1987 studies provide a comprehensive examination of the industry since deregulation and computerization. Even though it has slowed, the growth of the travel agency business has been remarkable.

## The Dimension of the Travel Agency Business

The *Travel Weekly* survey reported that at the end of 1987 there were 29,584 agency locations in the United States, 9 percent over 1985 (27,193), and 442 percent above the 6700 agencies first reported in 1970 (see Figure 3.1).[1] Since airline deregulation took effect in 1978, the number of agency locations in the United States has more than doubled, from 14,804 to 29,584. The average agency has 5.9 full-time employees, up from 5.4 in 1985.

The *Travel Weekly* study found that the median salary for travel agents with three to five years of experience, working full time on straight salary, was $16,510 in 1987.

Median salaries for agency employees with other levels of experience were: less than one year, $11,781; one to three years, $14,260; five to ten years, $18,600, and more than ten years, $21,636.

Just as the number of travel agencies has increased, so has the dollar volume. The annual estimated dollar volume for agencies reached $64.2 billion in 1987, an increase of 18 percent over the $54.3 billion reported in 1985 and an increase of 1284 percent over the $5.0 billion reported in 1970 (see Figure 3.2). Today 9 percent of the agencies reach $5 million or more, 26 percent reach $2.5 million, 34 percent reach $1 to 2 million, and 41 percent under $1 million. The average annual gross volume per agency is $2.1 million.

In spite of many predictions that the independent travel agent would disappear, the species is alive and well as today's industry is dominated by single-office enterprises. Among the locations in the *Travel Weekly* study, 68 percent are single-office firms, 19 percent branch offices, and 12 percent head offices.

Computerized reservations systems have become the rule, as 95 percent of all travel agency locations are now automated. This compares with 90 percent in 1985, 85 percent in 1983, and 69 percent in 1981.

Forty percent of the agencies were found to be located in the central cities, 48 percent in suburban areas, and 12 percent in towns and rural areas.

Another source of information on travel agencies is the American Society of Travel Agents (ASTA). ASTA reports that more than 77 percent of ASTA member travel agencies are incorporated, 9 percent are partnerships, and 14 percent are sole proprietorships. Most travel agencies are small businesses, over two-thirds having an annual volume of gross sales of less than $2 million. Women comprise 76 percent of ASTA agency employees, and 55 percent of ASTA agency owners.

More than half of ASTA agency owners have been in the business for more than ten years; 70 percent of agency managers have been in the travel business for more than five years. Over half of all travel agency employees have been in the travel business for more than three years. Approximately 80 percent of ASTA agency owners, 66 percent of managers, and 53 percent of agency employees have attended or have been graduated from college.

Leisure travel is the primary business for 56 percent of the member agencies of ASTA, 37 percent specialize in commercial travel, and 8 percent specialize in group or incentive travel.

[1] *Travel Weekly*, Louis Harris Study Issue, Vol. 47, no. 57 (June 1988), pp. 4–142.

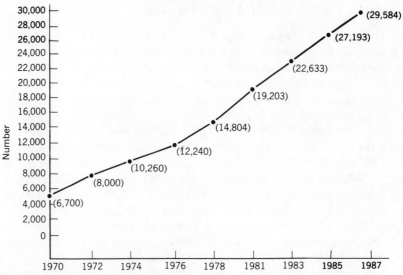

**Figure 3.1** Total U.S. Travel Agencies. *Source: Travel Weekly,* copyright ©
1988, Murdoch Magazines.

## Types of Travel Arrangements Made

As would be expected, the most common type of travel arrangement made is for air
transportation. In 1987, 59 percent of total dollar volume was for air travel, the first
time the proportion fell below 60 percent. Cruise sales accounted for 16 percent —
an all time high — up from 14 percent in 1985 and 11 percent in 1978. Much smaller
proportions of the total dollar volume are attributable to lodging, car rentals, rail,
and miscellaneous arrangements; these activities accounted for 25 percent of total
agency dollar volume. See Figure 3.3.

## Travel Agency Organizations

The American Society of Travel Agents (ASTA) is the largest (over 21,000 members)
and most influential trade association of travel and tourism professionals worldwide. Established in 1931, ASTA continues to serve the best interests of the travel
industry and the traveling public. ASTA's purpose is

- To promote and encourage travel among people of all nations
- To promote the image and encourage the use of professional travel agents world-
  wide
- To promote and represent the views and interests of travel agents to all levels of
  government and industry
- To promote professional and ethical conduct in the travel agency industry world-
  wide
- To serve as an information resource for the travel industry worldwide
- To promote consumer protection and safety for the traveler

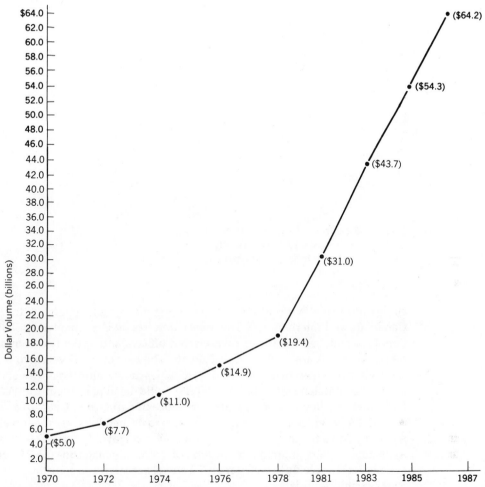

**Figure 3.2** Agency Annual Dollar Volume. *Source: Travel Weekly,* copyright © 1988, Murdoch Magazines.

- To sponsor and conduct educational programs for travel agents on subjects related to the travel industry, and
- To engage in any lawful activity the members of the association shall deem fit and appropriate for the promotion of their common welfare

    To be an active ASTA member, a travel agency must be currently accredited with the Airlines Reporting Corporation (ARC), the International Airlines Travel Agent Network (IATAN), National Tour Association (NTA), Cruise Lines International Association (CLIA), or Amtrak. All ASTA members agree to comply with the Society's Principles of Professional Conduct and Ethics.

    ASTA is managed by a Board of Directors elected by travel agency members. Although travel agencies, through an official firm representative, are the voting members, other categories of membership include individual associate, allied (in-

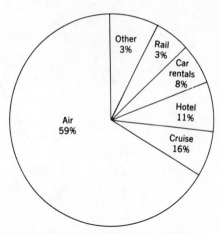

**Figure 3.3** Sources of Agency Revenues
by Travel Sector. *Source: Travel Weekly,*
copyright © 1988, Murdoch Magazines.

cludes most of the world's major travel suppliers), tour operator, travel school, Canadian, and international. The association has 30 U.S. chapters and 35 international chapters, each with its own elected officers and appointed committees. All officers of ASTA are working travel agents. They are elected every two years by the society's active members. Day-to-day activities are administered by a staff of more than 90 professionals located at ASTA's world headquarters in the Washington, D.C., metropolitan area, and a regional office in San Diego, California.

ASTA provides a wide range of services to its members and the travel industry, including educational seminars, the annual World Travel Congress and Trade Show, a consumer affairs program, publication of a monthly magazine *(ASTA Agency Management)* and a weekly newsletter *(ASTA Notes)*, research and statistics programs, and a scholarship foundation.

A smaller organization of travel agents is the Association of Retail Travel Agents (ARTA). The purpose of this organization is similar to ASTA's, but ARTA does not supply the range of services provided to the members of ASTA.

For travel agencies that have specialized and sell only cruises, there is the National Association of Cruise Only Agencies (NACOA). This group provides promotional and management assistance to its members.

On a global scale, travel agent organizations include the International Federation of Travel Agencies, the Universal Federation of Travel Agents Association, and the World Association of Travel Agents.

Particularly in the British Commonwealth and in the United States, there are travel agents' organizations whose purpose is to raise business and professional competency and to award certification. In the United States, the Institute of Certified Travel Agents provides an educational and certification program leading to the designation CTC (Certified Travel Counselor). Candidates for the certification must successfully pass four-hour examinations in travel agency business management, marketing, sales management, and international travel and tourism. An original research paper or a seminar evaluation report must be submitted. The candidate needs five years of experience in the industry, two of which can be with a carrier or other tourism organization and three years with a travel agency. Similar programs are operated in the British Commonwealth by the Institute of Travel Agents in cooperation with the Association of British Travel Agents. The institute awards the designation M.T.A.I. indicating that the recipient has fulfilled the academic requirements by passing examinations leading to the certification.

## THE TOUR WHOLESALER

The tour wholesaler[2] (also called tour operator) puts together a tour and all its components and sells the tour through his or her own company, through retail outlets, and/or through approved retail travel agencies. Wholesalers can offer vacation packages to the traveling public at prices lower than an individual traveler can arrange because wholesalers can buy services such as transportation, hotel rooms, sightseeing services, airport transfers, and meals in large quantities at discounted prices.

Tour wholesaling became an important segment of the U.S. travel industry after World War II. It has expanded substantially since the 1960s, largely because air carriers wanted to fill the increasing numbers of aircraft seats. The tour wholesale business consists primarily of planning, preparing, and marketing a vacation tour, including making reservations and consolidating transportation and ground services into a tour assembled for a departure date to a specific destination. Tours are then sold to the public through retail outlets such as travel agents and airline ticket offices.

Approximately 300 independent tour wholesalers operate in the United States today, with 10 major independent tour wholesalers accounting for about 30 percent of the industry's business. Consequently, unlike the retail travel agent industry, the tour wholesaler industry is concentrated among a small number of large operators.

Independent tour wholesalers provide significant revenue to transportation and ground service suppliers. They also provide the retailer and the public with a wide selection of tours to a large number of destinations at varying costs, for varying durations, and in various seasons. Furthermore, they supply advance notice and increased assurance of future passenger volumes to suppliers.

The independent tour wholesaler's business is characterized by relative ease of entry, high velocity of cash flow, low return on sales, and the potential for high return on equity because the investment necessary to start such a business is small.

Tour wholesaling businesses are usually one of three kinds: (1) the independent tour wholesaler, (2) the airline working in close cooperation with a tour wholesaling business, and (3) the retail travel agent who packages tours for its clients. These three entities, along with incentive travel companies and travel clubs, comprise the industry.

Figure 3.4 illustrates the position of the tour wholesaler in the basic structure of the travel industry. The public or the consumer is the driving force and can purchase travel services from a retail travel agent or directly from the suppliers of travel

---

[2] Touche Ross, *Tour Wholesaler Industry Study* (New York: Touche Ross, 1975), pp. 1–24.

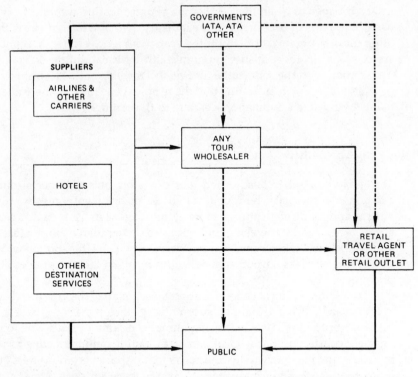

**Figure 3.4** Basic Structure of the U.S. Travel Industry. *Source: Tour Wholesaler Industry Study,* Touche, Ross & Co.

services — the airlines, hotels, and other providers of destination services. The tour wholesaler's role is that of consolidating the services of airlines and other carriers with the ground services needed into one package, which can be sold through travel agents to the consuming public.

The package tour industry generates more than $10.5 billion annually in North America. The typical group tour produces more than $3500 in sales for each overnight stay in an average-sized North American city. Tour and charter business accounted for nearly half of total bus company revenues in 1987, and 60 percent of total bus passenger volume.

## Tour Wholesaler Organizations

The National Tour Association (NTA) founded in 1951 is the primary group tour industry association in North America. Its membership includes group tour operators, who package and sell group tours in the United States, Canada, and Mexico, and suppliers, whose businesses include hotels, attractions, restaurants, bus companies, airlines, passenger vessels, sightseeing companies, destination marketing organizations, and other travel and tourism entities.

The Association provides marketing assistance, educational programs, governmental representation and communications for its membership, and annually produces the NTA Convention and Tour and Travel Exchange. This event is one of the largest travel industry gatherings held in North America, offering members the opportunity to conduct intensive business sessions and attend education seminars that increase professionalism in the industry. The Association also produces the Spring Tour and Travel Exchange, which provides members with a second opportunity each year to conduct business and participate in educational programs.

The National Tour Association requires its members to adhere to a strict code of ethics that assures proper business activity between individual members for the ultimate good of the traveling public. The Association acts as the primary advocate for consumers of the group tour product in North America and works to promote consumer awareness of that vacation alternative.

The U.S. Tour Operators Association (USTOA) also represents tour operators. The goals of USTOA are to ensure consumer protection and education; to inform the travel industry, government agencies, and the public about tour operators' activities and objectives; to maintain a high level of professionalism within the industry; and to facilitate travel on a worldwide basis.

USTOA's members must subscribe to the organization's strict code of ethics. Members are required to represent all information pertaining to tours, to maintain a high level of professionalism, and to state clearly all costs and facilities in advertising and promotional materials.

Most tour operators and wholesalers belong to the American Society of Travel Agents. Many also belong to the various promotional groups such as PATA (Pacific Asia Travel Association), ACTO (Association of Caribbean Tour Operators), and TIA (Travel Industry Association of America).

Local or short tours are conducted by sightseeing companies, and many of them are organized into American Sightseeing International and Grayline. These organizations aid sightseeing companies by providing local sightseeing services and competent personnel. Many sightseeing tour companies are also affiliated with the organizations already mentioned.

## THE LODGING INDUSTRY

The most important concept of accommodations in relation to tourism is that these businesses are an essential part — but only a part — of the wide array of tourism suppliers. A traveler is in a particular destination area because he or she had a certain motivation, either for business or pleasure. In order to prosper, the accommodations manager must recognize the integral relationship that exists between accommodations and the volume of tourists attracted to an area. Success of the accommodations will thus be dependent upon the effectiveness of the tourism marketing program conducted in behalf of that destination. The extent of the lodging industry's financial support for its local convention and visitors bureau, chamber of commerce, area and/or regional tourism promotion organization will determine such marketing success.

The lodging industry is made up of hotels, motor hotels, motels, condos, tourist

The Hong Kong Hilton serves as an example of international hotel development. (Photo courtesy of Hilton International)

courts, sporting and recreational camps, and trailer parks and campsites for transients, that is, establishments engaged primarily in providing lodging or lodging and meals to the general public. While the Bureau of the Census includes these categories in the *Census of Service Industries,* sporting and recreational camps and trailer parks and campsites for transients have a quite different operating structure from hotels and motels, and most industry analysts do not include these categories.

Since the mid-1970s the U.S. lodging industry has been experiencing the greatest building boom in its history. Consequently, the number of hotel rooms offered by the hotel and motel industry in the United States reached a record 2.79 million in 1987, a net increase of 120,000 rooms over the previous year, which was also a record total. Industry revenues grew to $51 billion in 1987, an 11 percent increase over $45.9 billion in sales in 1986. Room occupancy reached 62.9 percent in 1987, a slight increase over the 62.4 percent occupancy in 1986.

It is projected that the additions to the supply of overall rooms available will level off in the 1990s and that occupancy rates will increase. Room rates are expected to continue to rise about 3 to 4 percent a year.

A dramatic marketing innovation is the introduction of "yield management" to the lodging industry. By using computerized systems similar to programs employed by airlines, hotels and motels will be able to monitor guest-room inventories and measure them against demand on a day-by-day, or even hour-by-hour, basis.

The lodging industry has practiced market segmentation in recent years. Many of the big chains offer products at almost every price level—full-service luxury hotels, luxury all-suite hotels, moderately priced full-service hotels, moderately priced all-suites, moderately priced limited service, and economy or budget motels. The two fastest growing segments of the industry are the all-suites and economy segments.

Excellent sources of information on the lodging industry are Laventhol and Horwath, 1845 Walnut Street, Philadelphia, Pennsylvania 19103, and Pannell, Kerr, Forster, 262 North Belt East, Houston, Texas 77060. Both of these CPA firms publish reports on the U.S. and worldwide lodging industries. Both firms define the lodging industry as hotel and motor hotel operations. Examples of the types of information available from these firms are shown in Figures 3.5 and 3.6.

Hotels and motels are classified in a variety of ways. One of the most common is by location, such as resort, city center, airport, suburban, or highway. There are a number of very large companies in the lodging industry, and many of the major chains are growing rapidly. *Hotels and Restaurants International,* published by Cahners Publishing Company, 1350 East Touhy Avenue, Des Plaines, Illinois 60018-3358, compiles an annual listing of the world's 200 largest corporate hotel chains. Holiday Inns, headquartered in Memphis, Tennessee, is the world's largest lodging chain, with 1868 hotels and 360,958 rooms in 1988.

Between 1960 and 1990, the trend in the lodging industry has been away from independently owned and operated properties toward chain and franchise affiliations. There are also referral groups or voluntary membership associations. Both independents and chains have found it profitable to join together to market their properties. In 1988 Best Western International, headquartered in Phoenix, Arizona, was the largest referral group, with 3306 properties and 255,217 rooms. Although the third-ranking Federation de Logis et Auberges in Paris, France, numbers 4658 properties, they are smaller inns, totalling only 77,985 rooms.

The trend toward consolidation and acquisition will continue in the 1990s because chains have the potential for improvement in productivity and the advan-

1,000 Hotels and Motels
**Source and Disposition of the Industry Dollar**

Revenues

Costs and Expenses

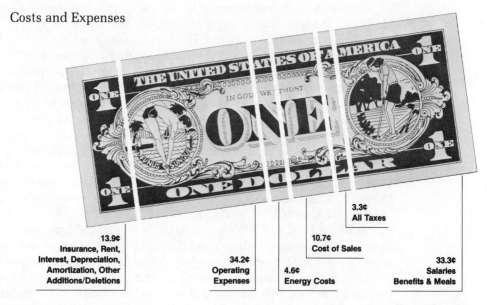

*Prepared by Pannell Kerr Forster*

**Figure 3.5** Source and Disposition of the U.S. Lodging Industry Dollar. Source: Reprinted with permission from *Trends in the Hotel Industry,* USA Edition 1988, a publication of Pannell Kerr Forster.

International Hotels—Regional Analyses—1987
**Source and Disposition of the Industry Dollar**

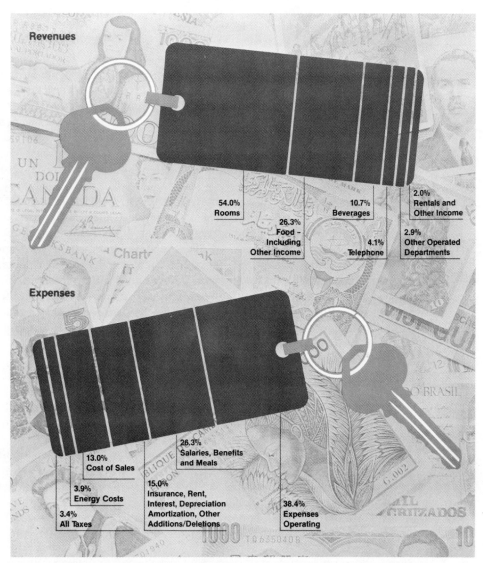

**Figure 3.6** Source and disposition of the International Hotel Industry Dollar. *Source:* Reprinted with permission from *Trends in the Hotel Industry*, International Edition 1988, a publication of Pannell Kerr Forster.

tages that accrue to large size. Chains can most effectively use training programs, employee selection programs, major equipment such as computers, and research. They can experiment with different layouts, prices, advertising, equipment, and so on, and what works well in one property can be employed chainwide.

One reason for the popularity of the referral groups is that members who are independent operators achieve the marketing benefits of chains without chain membership.

Franchising is also well known in the lodging industry and has made a rapid penetration into the marketplace. However, franchising generates mixed reports. Many managements believe that it is difficult to control the franchisees and maintain the quality that the chain advertises and the standards that are supposed to be met. Thus, many chains are buying back franchises to ensure that management maintains the quality level desired. In other cases, firms are moving ahead rapidly with franchising because they can conserve cash and expand more rapidly by franchising. In addition, the franchisee, having invested his or her own capital, has great motivation to succeed.

Franchisees have the advantage that they receive the knowledge, advice, and assistance of a proven operator. Franchising also spreads the costs of promotion, advertising, and reservation systems over all outlets, making the unit cost much lower. If the franchisor has an excellent reputation and image, the franchisee benefits greatly. Most of the companies with franchise operations also operate company-owned units. Industry predictions are that as the industry grows and matures, there will be less franchising, which will give the chains more control over their properties and operations so that they can maintain the desired quality control. Increased competitiveness and improved properties will necessitate having the ability to make these improvements.

A trend in the lodging industry appears to be that more large properties will be operated under management contracts. Investors, such as insurance companies, frequently purchase hotel properties and turn them over to chains or independents to manage, a process that has advantages to both parties. The owner has the financial resources and the manager has the reputation and experience to manage the property profitably.

A discussion of the lodging industry would not be complete without mentioning the burgeoning bed and breakfast (B and B) segment. It is made up of over 10,000 privately owned homes, inns, and reservation services. It is the fastest-growing segment of the accommodations industry in the nation. B and Bs provide both luxury and economy accommodations in many areas where major hotel and motel chains do not build. This brings tourism dollars into communities often neglected by most tourists.

B and Bs provide the best possible avenue for travelers of all ages and from all locations to experience first-hand the life-styles in areas of the country previously unknown to guests. The B and B host can become an area's best ambassador.

For many single and retired people, B and Bs provide additional income. In many cases around the nation, the institution of a B and B has saved a historic property that might have otherwise been destroyed.

B and B reservation services inspect and approve B and B homes and inns, maintain ongoing quality control, and provide one-stop shopping for the traveler.

A beautiful and spacious lobby provides a relaxing setting for hotel guests. (Photo courtesy of the Sheraton Corporation)

They can provide the traveler with a chain of recourse in case of a problem. Reservation services are privately owned corporations, partnerships, or single proprietorships, each representing from 35 to 100 host homes and inns.

## Lodging Organizations

There are a large number of accommodations organizations—international, regional, state, and local. Of these, the American Hotel and Motel Association (AH&MA) is the largest and most prominent in the United States.

AH&MA is a federation of hotel and motel associations located in the 50 states, the District of Columbia, Puerto Rico, and the U.S. Virgin Islands and speaks as the trade association for the U.S. lodging industry. Founded in Chicago in 1910, AH&MA now represents 1.3 million transient rooms comprising more than 8900 individual hotels, motels, and resorts. This is essentially 53.4 percent of the total rooms inventory in the United States, accounting for 82.6 percent of total revenues generated by the industry. AH&MA works for favorable amendments to existing laws and coordinates with almost 100 related groups for maximum industry support and impact. In the past year, for example, AH&MA has spoken out on fire safety regulations, lodging industry labor shortages, liquor liability, and state taxation on advertising.

Internationally, organizations representing accommodations include the European Motel Federation in the Netherlands; the International Hotel Association, in Paris, France; the International Organization of Hotel and Restaurant Associations, in Zurich, Switzerland; and the Caribbean Hotel Association, in Santurce, Puerto Rico. For hostels, there is the International Youth Hostel Federation in Welwyn Garden City, England; and for camping, the International Federation of Camping and Caravanning of Brussels, Belgium.

These organizations provide information and educational services to members, help to avoid unfair legislation and encourage favorable legislation among governmental bodies, and promote the use and development of their facilities and services by the traveling public.

Bed & Breakfast Reservation Services World-Wide (B&BRSWW) was formed in 1985 to promote the use of B and Bs and reservation services (RSOs), educate the traveling public about B and Bs and RSOs, and set standards of excellence in accommodations and services provided by member RSOs and their hosts. Its members include B and Bs from around the world. The association is currently developing a code of ethics for member services and host homes and inns. They have also recently developed an innovative program whereby host homes will be inspected and certified annually through the association.

## THE FOOD SERVICE INDUSTRY

Eating and drinking places are big business. While much of this activity is local, eating and drinking are favorite pastimes of travelers, and the food service industry would face difficult times without the tourist market.

In 1989, the National Restaurant Association projected that food industry sales for that year would total $227.3 billion, 6.7 percent above the $213.0 billion recorded in 1988. The industry currently employs more than 8 million people. By the year 2000, eating and drinking places are expected to employ 2.5 million more people, generating the largest number of new jobs in any industry. Nearly two-thirds of all those in food-service occupations are women, and one-fourth are teenagers. The food-service industry employs more minority managers than any other retail industry.

Travelers contribute about $73 billion to food service sales each year, whether for a coffee shop breakfast, a dinner on an airline, a sandwich from a bus station vending machine, or a ten-course dinner on a cruise ship. Travelers, including foreign visitors, spend more money on food than anything else except transportation, and travelers account for about one-third of the total sales in the food service industry.

The food service industry consists of restaurants, travel food service, and vend-

Trying different foods while traveling is an important part of the trip. (Photo courtesy of the Florida Division of Tourism)

ing and contract institutional food service. Local restaurants are made up of establishments that include fast-food units, coffee shops, specialty restaurants, family restaurants, cafeterias, and full-service restaurants with carefully orchestrated "atmosphere." Travel food service consists of food operations in hotels and motels, roadside service to automobile travelers, and all food service on airplanes, trains, and ships. Institutional food service in companies, hospitals, nursing homes, and so on, is not considered part of the tourism industry.

Over the past two decades, the food and beverage business has grown at a phenomenal rate. This has been especially true for the fast-food segment, with the franchising portion in the fast-food segment becoming the dominant growth sector. This remarkable increase has been gained at the expense of other food service operators and supermarkets. Franchisees control approximately three-fourths of the fast-food outlets, whose hamburgers, chickens, steaks, and pizzas dominate the fast-food business. The *Statistical Abstract of the United States, 1989,* shows that in 1970, 32,600 restaurants were franchises; in 1988, the total was 90,800.

Fast-food chains have enjoyed great success in part because they limit their menus, which gives them greater purchasing power, less waste, and more portion control, and, of importance to the consumer, lower operating costs. They are leaders in labor productivity in the restaurant industry. Most fast-food operations use disposable paper and plastic; the expense for these materials is more than offset by the savings resulting from not providing regular service and from not employing the personnel required to wash the dinner service. Fast-food operations also enjoy the advantages of specialization; they have become specialists in menu items, job simplification, and operating systems. Franchising has been used extensively in both the restaurant field and the lodging field as a means of achieving rapid growth. Using the franchisee's capital, the entrepreneur can get much more rapid penetration of the marketplace.

As noted earlier, franchise units account for approximately three-fourths of the growing fast-food portion of the industry. Advantages of franchising accrue to both sides. The franchisee gets the start-up help, advice from experienced management, buying power, advertising, and low unit costs from spreading fixed costs over large numbers of units. The franchisor has the advantage of a lower capital investment, rapid growth, and royalty income. The fast-food franchise operators have a great deal of concentration in their segment of the industry. The seven largest account for almost half of the fast-food units and almost half of the sales. Franchise firms are household words: McDonald's, Kentucky Fried Chicken, A&W Root Beer, Wendy's, Dairy Queen, Tastee Freeze, Burger King, Pizza Hut, Arby's, and Shakey's.

Although the fast-food segment is the most rapidly growing segment, the high-quality segment of the restaurant industry must not be overlooked. Much of this business is based on customers seeking a special or different experience in dining out. This demand has been most effectively satisfied by local entrepreneurs who emphasize special menus, varying atmospheres, and high-quality food and service. New concepts or trends include ethnic restaurants, especially those with an oriental or Mexican flavor; increased demand for health foods, fish, local produce, and regional dishes; and variety in portion sizes.

### Restaurant Organizations

The National Restaurant Association (NRA), a full-service trade association with about 12,000 members, is the most important trade association in the food service field. Membership is diverse, running the gamut from the New Jersey prison system to Club 21 and including white table cloth and fast-food members, institutional feeders, and vending machine operators.

The goals and objectives of NRA are channeled in three directions: (1) political action, (2) information, and (3) promotion. Through their Political Action and Political Education Committees, NRA promotes the political and legislative concerns of the industry and combats any potentially harmful attempts by government to regulate the operational aspects of the industry.

The recently formed Educational Foundation satisfies the current and future training and educational/informational needs of the food service industry.

NRA works to position the industry and its services before the public in a favorable light. NRA, working in unison with 14 other associations, introduced "Ours Is a Special World," an ongoing program designed to promote the hospitality industry as a source of rewarding careers.

NRA regularly publishes surveys and reports on a variety of topics, ranging from employee management to consumer attitudes toward smoking in restaurants. Through its library's information service, NRA responds to thousands of requests for information. NRA is located at 1200 17th Street N.W., Washington, D.C. 20036.

## ATTRACTIONS

Natural and developed attractions are the "mainspring" that drives much of humanity to travel. The great national parks of the United States and other countries such as those in Canada, India, Australia, and Japan are examples. National forests in the United States attract millions of recreationists. State parks exist in many areas that have tourist appeal. The same is so for botanical, zoological, mountain, and seaside parks. Thus, these natural wonders lure travelers to enjoy the natural beauty, recreation, and inspiration that they provide.

Human-built attractions such as historical sites and prehistory and archeological sites such as the ancient monuments of Egypt, Greece, Israel, Turkey, Indonesia, India, Mexico, and Peru also have appeal for those inspired to learn more about contemporary and long-vanished civilizations.

Great modern cities with their cultural treasures of many sorts provide powerful attractions to millions of visitors each year. Sightseeing tours are provided in most cities, giving easy access to the city's attractions. Theaters, museums, special buildings, cultural events, festivals, shopping, and dining are some of the appeals.

## The Attractions Industry

The attractions industry consists of fixed-location amusement parks and attractions in the United States and 40 other countries. They are primarily private businesses, although there are a number of publicly operated facilities. Amusement parks and attractions in the United States generate approximately $4 billion in annual revenues. Over 275,000 people are employed seasonally by the industry in the United States, and an estimated 235 million visits to U.S. parks and attractions are recorded annually.

The attractions industry is dominated by Disneyland and Disney World, which have been two of the most successful attractions ever developed. However, while theme parks are a major tourist attraction, there are more than 10,000 natural scenic, historical, cultural, and entertainment attractions that appeal to travelers. Attractions include not only theme parks, but the entertainment park, amusement park, animal park, museum, scenic railway, historic village, preserved mansion, scenic cruise, natural wonder, restaurant, music festival, industry exhibit, cave, theater, historic farm, scenic overlook, resort complex, historic site, botanical garden, arboretum, plantation, hall of fame, water show, zoo, sports complex, cultural center, state park, national park, county park, outdoor theater, native American reservation, and transportation exhibit.

The U.S. Census Bureau measures amusement and recreation services in its *1982 Census of Selected Services.* This group includes establishments primarily engaged in providing amusement, recreation, or entertainment on payment of a fee or admission charge, including motion pictures. Symphony orchestras, ballet and opera companies, and similar entertainment groups as well as membership sports and recreation clubs, commercial museums, and botanical and zoological gardens are included in this group. In its "other amusement and recreation services" category, 33,515 establishments (with payroll) recorded over $10 billion in receipts. Under amusement parks (establishments with payroll), 466 are recorded. The 1987 Census of Selected Services data is expected to be available in early 1990.

## Theme Parks

The theme park business has enjoyed spectacular expansion since the opening of Disneyland in 1955 in Anaheim, California. The opening of Disneyland changed the local amusement park business considerably because it expanded the concept of amusement parks from simply rides and carnival barkers to include shows, shops,

Exciting rides and live shows with a history theme are the
attraction of Libertyland, the Memphis theme park at the huge
Mid-South Fairgrounds where hundreds of thousands of visitors
gather each September for one of the largest fairs in the South.
(Photo courtesy of Tennessee Tourist Development)

and restaurants in theme settings with immaculate cleanliness, promising adventure, history, science fiction, or fantasy.

The success of Disneyland brought Disney World, the largest and grandest theme park in the world with its Magic Kingdom as the focal point of the resort complex. Disney World lures over 23.8 million visitors annually (see Table 3.3) and is far more than a theme park. It has a 7500-acre conservation project for the preservation of fauna and wildlife of the everglades, an experimental prototype community of tomorrow (EPCOT), and the Disney World Showcase where several nations feature exhibits of their country's attractions and culture.

As would be expected, the success of the Disney theme parks brought imitators

**Table 3.3** Top 20 Theme Parks in North America by Attendance

| Park | 1988 (millions) |
|------|:---------------:|
| 1. Disney World/EPCOT Orlando, Florida | 23.8* |
| 2. Disneyland, Anaheim, California | 12.7* |
| 3. Sea World, Orlando, Florida | 4.3 |
| 4. Universal Studios, Universal City, Calif. | 3.8 |
| 5. Knott's Berry Farm, Buena Park, California | 3.5 |
| 6. Sea World, San Diego, California | 3.5 |
| 7. Busch Gardens, Tampa, Florida | 3.3 |
| 8. Cedar Point, Sandusky, Ohio | 3.1* |
| 9. Kings Island, Kings Island, Ohio | 3.0 |
| 10. Six Flags, Magic Mountain, Valencia, Calif. | 2.9 |
| 11. Sea World, San Antonio, Texas | 2.7 |
| 12. Six Flags, Great America, Gurnee, Illinois | 2.5 |
| 13. Six Flags Over Texas, Arlington, Texas | 2.3 |
| 14. Great America, Santa Clara, California | 2.3 |
| 15. Opryland, Nashville, Tennessee | 2.2 |
| 16. Six Flags Over Georgia, Atlanta, Georgia | 2.3 |
| 17. Kings Dominion, Doswell, Virginia | 2.2 |
| 18. Canada's Wonderland, Toronto, Ontario | 2.2 |
| 19. Busch Gardens, Williamsburg, Virginia | 2.1 |
| 20. Six Flags Great Adventure, Jackson, New Jersey | 1.9 |

* 1987 Attendance

and large corporations to the business. Some of the prominent ones are (1) Six Flags, Inc., which operates Six Flags over Texas at Arlington, Six Flags over Georgia at Atlanta, Six Flags over Mid-America at Eureka, Missouri, Astroworld at Houston, and Great Adventure at Jackson, New Jersey; (2) Kings Entertainment, which operates Kings Island in Kings Island, Ohio, Kings Dominion in Doswell, Virginia, Carowinds in Charlotte, North Carolina, and Canada's Wonderland in Vaughan, Ontario; and (3) Anheuser-Busch, which operates the Dark Continent in Tampa, Florida, and the Old Country in Williamsburg, Virginia. Other well-known parks are Knott's Berry Farm in California, Cedar Point in Ohio, Magic Mountain in California, and Opryland in Tennessee.

The nation's major theme parks appear to be concentrated in Florida and California. Disney has projects in both states, and the Orlando, Florida, area probably has the single largest number of theme parks and attractions in any one location.

This concentration is likely to continue, as new attractions or expansions are still taking place in the area. There are two new Disney projects. Pleasure Island, a six-acre nighttime entertainment center, includes six innovative themed night clubs and a number of shops and specialty food outlets. Disney-MGM Studio and Studio Tour facilities include an animation building, four soundstages, a back lot of streets and sets, crafts, and specialty shops. These Florida studios will provide facilities for live-action filming and animation and television production work. Visitors can view all aspects of production, including live demonstrations and filmed stunts; participate in TV-show segments; and experience ride-through adventures such as "Great Moments at the Movies." The Disney-MGM Studio is located one mile southwest of EPCOT Center, and the 100-acre studio site will be linked by monorail to the rest of the Disney World complex.

The various Sea World parks have attracted international attention for pioneering marine mammal research and working with injured or endangered species. The new Sea World Airship is now at its winter home in the Florida park. The Airship is a new operation of Sea World's parent company, publisher Harcourt Brace Jovanovich, Inc. (HBJ). It is being used in various educational, broadcast, and promotional efforts on behalf of the company's family entertainment parks, which include the Florida, California, Ohio, and Texas (opened 1988 in San Antonio) Sea World parks, Florida's Cypress Gardens, and Boardwalk and Baseball.

An imaginative "first" in the theme park world, Boardwalk and Baseball occupies the 135-acre cite near Orlando at the intersection of I-4 and U.S. 27, formerly known as Circus World. The park reflects the heydays of Coney Island and Atlantic City, with an actual boardwalk connecting 32 rides, live magic and Western shows, a family-themed midway, and other new attractions. The park has more than doubled in size as compared with the previous attraction.

Industry representatives predict that an area to watch for the future is the development of theme parks in conjunction with shopping malls. The activity at the West Edmonton, Canada mall complex has encouraged this prediction.

### International Association of Amusement Parks and Attractions

The goals and objectives of the International Association of Amusement Parks and Attractions (IAAPA) include increasing education and instituting training seminars, both regionally and overseas.

The association plans to establish an International Institute for amusement industry management. It has also targeted its efforts towards coordinating safety regulations and standards among various countries. IAAPA has scheduled an increase in activities beneficial to members outside the United States.

The long-term goal of the association is to continue as the sole international parks association by increasing the participation of international members, conducting a major trade show and seminar for the industry each year, and raising the standards of management and service in the industry.

## GAMING

Gambling, or the gaming industry, has become a major force in the tourism industry. The gaming industry has grown from a narrow Nevada base with limited acceptance in the financial and public sector to a recognized growth industry. While gaming has always been a popular form of recreation, it has also been controversial. At present casino gambling is allowed only in Nevada and New Jersey, although elections have been held in other cities and states. Gaming is being promoted in some states as a means of attracting tourists and creating economic development.

There is no question that gaming generates travel. Nevada has been the leader in gambling, which has made tourism the number one industry in the state. Las Vegas is considered the casino capital of the world. It is interesting to note the differences in the types of tourists and their modes of transportation when comparing Las Vegas and Atlantic City. Las Vegas attracts destination visitors from long distances who fly or drive, while Atlantic City is located in a densely populated area and attracts nearby (within 150 miles) residents. Atlantic City has successfully promoted short-duration motorcoach tours to increase its numbers.

Gaming is available in many parts of the world, as well as on cruise ships. Well-known areas for casino gambling include Monaco, the Caribbean, London, Nice, Macau, and Rio de Janeiro.

As new casinos go up in Atlantic City and in the Bahamas, one sees the impact of gaming on tourism and the local economy. Given the current growth in gaming, it is

Gaming is an important part of hotel operations in Nevada, in Atlantic City, New Jersey, and in San Juan, Puerto Rico. Gambling is likewise popular with cruise ship passengers. (Photo courtesy of Costa Lines)

safe to predict that it will continue to play a role in tourism and economic development.

# RECREATION

Recreation is a diverse industry, representing over $350 billion in expenditures each year. The industry generates millions of jobs in the manufacturing, sales, and service sectors.

Nearly 50 percent of Americans describe themselves as "outdoor people." They enjoy a wide variety of activities to keep fit, to add excitement to their lives, to have fun with family and friends, to pursue solitary activities, and to experience nature first-hand.

The draw of recreation opportunities throughout the United States is one factor in the rise of domestic travel, as well as in the increase in international visits to the United States. Outdoor adventure travel is gaining in popularity, and travel professionals have better access to information on recreational travel options. People are seeking higher quality services and amenities.

Illustrative of the range of businesses within the recreation industry are recreation vehicle (RV) manufacturers and dealers, boat manufacturers and dealers, full-line recreation product manufacturers, park concessioners, campground owners, resorts, enthusiast groups, snowmobile manufacturers, recreation publications, motorcoach operators, bicycling interests, and others.

Companies manufacturing recreation products tend to be large. For example, the manufacturing of new RVs is an $8 billion per year industry. According to the Recreation Vehicle Dealers Association, another $6.5 billion is generated through the used and rental RV markets and the sales of after-market parts, accessories, and services. On the road, the nation's 25 million RV users travel an average of 23 days per year, stay at the nation's 16,000 public and private campgrounds, and spend an estimated $58 daily, thus pumping even more dollars into tourism and, ultimately, the overall U.S. economy.

The Recreation Vehicle Industry Association (RVIA) is located in Reston, Virginia, and is a primary source of shipment statistics, market research, and technical data. The association also supplies campground directories, publications covering RV maintenance, trip preparation, and safety issues.

In contrast to the large companies involved in manufacturing RVs, boats, pools, mountain bikes, skis, and so on, the private service sector is made up primarily of small businesses, ranging from campgrounds to marinas to wilderness guides. There is also the public sector providing services through the National Park Service, Forest Service, and state and local agencies.

## *Parks, Forests, Campgrounds, and Trailer Parks*

Both private and government enterprises operate various kinds of parks, including amusement parks. National parks are often very important parts of a nation's or state's tourism. In some countries (Africa for example), national parks are their primary attractions. Typical are Kenya, Nwanda, Uganda, Tanzania, Botswana, and

South Africa. Figure 3.7 documents the importance of national parks in tourism in the United States. There were over 287 million visits in 1987. Table 3.4 shows the number of visits from 1980 to 1987 and forecasts to the year 2020.

In the United States many individual states operate park systems, some of the most outstanding being New York, California, Tennessee, Oregon, Indiana, Kentucky, Florida, and Michigan. Parks are also operated by other units of government such as county or park districts like the Huron-Clinton Metropolitan Authority of the greater Detroit area in southeastern Michigan. This system has six parks within easy access of residents of the Detroit metropolitan area. Counties, townships, and cities also operate parks and often campgrounds as parts of parks.

Campgrounds are often maintained by forest services such as United States Forest Service, or they may be part of a system operated by the Bureau of Reclamation, the Corps of Engineers, the National Park Service, or the Tennessee Valley Authority. State campgrounds may be included as part of the state park system, and campgrounds may be provided by state forest installations.

Trailer parks are organized into two major divisions: mobile home parks, which are permanent year-round types of establishments, and recreational vehicle parks, which cater to tourists.

National forests are also major tourist attractions. In 1988 242.3 million visitor days spent in U.S. national forests were reported, as shown in Table 3.5. Especially enjoyed are hiking, hunting, camping, canoeing, fishing, and other water sports. In

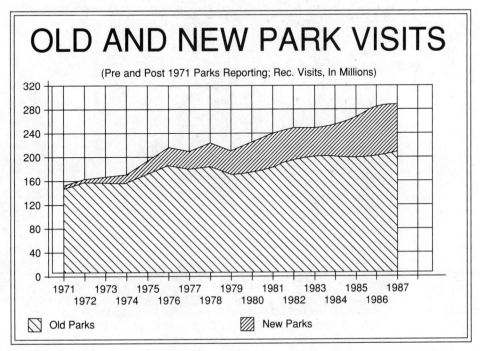

**Figure 3.7** National Park Visits, 1971 to 1987. *Source:* National Park Service, *Statistical Abstract,* U.S. Department of Interior, National Park Services, 1987.

**Table 3.4** Recreation Visits and Forecasts of Visits to the
National Park System

| Year | Visits | Percent Change |
|------|--------|----------------|
| 1980 | 220,463,211 | +7.4% |
| 1981 | 238,592,669 | +8.2% |
| 1982 | 244,924,579 | +2.8% |
| 1983 | 243,616,747 | −0.5% |
| 1984 | 248,785,509 | +2.1% |
| 1985 | 263,441,808 | +5.9% |
| 1986 | 281,094,850 | +6.7% |
| 1987 | 287,244,998 | +2.2% |
| 1988 | 287,593,000 | +0.1% (Forecast) |
| FORECAST | | |
| 1995 | 320–335 million | |
| 2000 | 350–375 million | |
| 2010 | 450–500 million | |
| 2020 | 575–675 million | |

*Source:* National Park Service, *National Park Statistical Abstract* (Denver: NPS
Statistical Office, 1987).

Sleeping Bear Dunes National Lakeshore, Michigan, is representative of the spectacular
natural wonders that the National Park Service administers and preserves for the
enjoyment of visitors. (Photo courtesy of the Michigan Travel Commission)

**Table 3.5** Recreational Use of U.S. National Forests 1988

| Top 15 States | Visitor Days (thousands) |
|---|---|
| California | 59,516.9 |
| Colorado | 21,484.0 |
| Oregon | 19,598.1 |
| Arizona | 18,831.2 |
| Washington | 15,477.6 |
| Texas | 14,454.8 |
| Idaho | 10,736.3 |
| Montana | 8,843.7 |
| New Mexico | 7,227.5 |
| Wyoming | 6,514.5 |
| North Carolina | 4,973.2 |
| Minnesota | 4,449.6 |
| Alaska | 4,354.5 |
| Michigan | 4,319.6 |
| Virginia | 3,804.0 |
| Total for all 50 states | 242,315.7 |

*Source:* U.S. Forest Service, U.S. Department of Agriculture.

some states, winter sports such as cross-country and downhill skiing, snowmobiling, and ice fishing are also popular.

## SHOPS

Shopping is an important part of any tourist's activities. To make shopping as convenient as possible, many hotels provide shops featuring gift items, particularly local handicrafts and artwork. In the shopping areas of each community that caters successfully to tourists are found quality gift and souvenir shops featuring items of particular interest to visitors. The chain hotel and motel companies have also organized gift shops as part of their operations. Holiday Inns of America, for example, has gift shops that also sell candy and cosmetics and similar products in virtually all of its motels and hotels. Host International maintains a system of gift and merchandise shops in most of the areas in which it has established airport dining rooms, cocktail lounges, snack bars, coffee shops, and in-flight food services. These gift and merchandise shops are an important part of the business operations. In addition, gift shops are provided along the toll roads, where Host International provides dining rooms, coffee shops, and snack bars.

Gift and souvenir shops and the companies operating them are commonly members of the local chambers of commerce, convention and visitors bureaus, and regional or local tourism promotional organizations.

## EDUCATION

Suppliers of the tourism product look to educational organizations as sources of talent for their industries. These include secondary schools, vocational schools, junior or community colleges, four-year colleges and universities, and trade association schools and institutes.

Most high schools, which are known by various terms in different countries, offer curricula and subjects of value to travel firms. Examples are native and foreign languages, geography, history, writing, use of computers, secretarial skills, bookkeeping, and food preparation. Many vocational schools produce entry-level employees for travel agencies, tour companies, airlines, accommodations, food service, and others, and junior and community colleges likewise offer education and training in various skills applicable to the travel industry.

Trade associations and professional societies also are active in education. Exam-

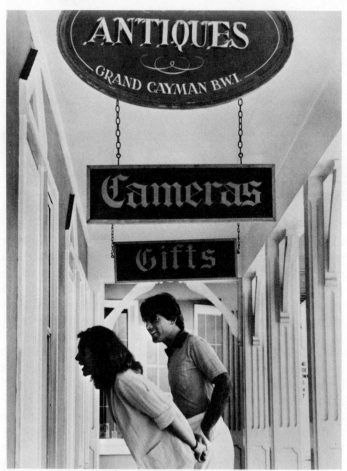

Shopping delights visitors and is an important tourism activity.
(Photo courtesy of Cayman Islands News Bureau)

ples of these are the educational programs and home study courses of the American Society of Travel Agents, the Institute of Certified Travel Agents, the Educational Institute of the American Hotel and Motel Association, the National Institute for the Foodservice Industry, and, in Britain, the Institute of Travel and Tourism. Most public carriers and especially the airlines provide rigorous training and educational programs for their own employees, as well as for those working for travel agencies and tour companies. The International Labour Organization (a U.N. affiliate in Geneva, Switzerland) has conducted numerous types of training programs in tourism-related vocations. Similarly, the World Tourism Organization conducts a correspondence course for those in official tourism departments.

Four-year colleges and universities provide instruction in similar skills and management education. In keeping with the diversity of the industry, courses are offered in schools of business and hotel and restaurant administration, colleges of natural resources, commercial recreation departments, sociology departments, and anthropology departments. A number of schools are offering graduate programs in travel and tourism. In addition to courses and educational programs, universities and colleges also conduct a great deal of research, which is available to the industry.

Finally, land grant schools provide services through the Cooperative Extension Service, which operates in all 50 states. Educational services are available to managers of hotels, motels, restaurants, resorts, clubs, marinas, small service businesses, and similar enterprises from some state organizations. Short courses and conferences are sometimes held for managers of these businesses in order to make them more efficient and productive. These educational services are provided by the land grant colleges and universities and the Cooperative Extension Service, which is supported in part by the U.S. Department of Agriculture.

### Educational Organizations

The Travel and Tourism Research Association has over 150 educational members and publishes an educators' page in its quarterly newsletter. In addition, educators' sessions are held at the annual conference. The National Park and Recreation Association has a section called the Society of Park and Recreation Educators (SPRE). This group works on appropriate curriculum and features programs on education and research. Hotel and restaurant educators formed the Council on Hotel, Restaurant, and Institutional Education (CHRIE), which fosters improved teaching methods and aids in curriculum development for all educational levels, from high school through four-year colleges and universities. Finally, there is the Society of Travel and Tourism Educators, which holds an annual workshop and publishes a newsletter.

## PUBLISHING

Producers of printed news, feature articles, advertising, and publicity constitute a very important type of business within tourism. Because the field is so fast changing, such news and feature articles must be read in order to keep up to date but also for current information needed for intelligent counseling and management.

Another vital group of publishers includes those who produce reference manuals, tariffs, guides, atlases, timetables, and operational handbooks. Without these, no travel organization could function. Counselors and others who contact travelers must be informed as to the nomenclature of their particular part of the business. They must also know rules and regulations, methods of operation, schedules, transit times, accommodations, equipment and service, tariffs, rates, commissions, and other, such as details of any travel destination. The list of these is long and they vary for each country. No single publication could possibly cover the needed information for any particular branch of the industry. References can be grouped as follows:

1. Independently published references for the travel industry, such as the *Official Airline Guide, Hotel and Travel Index, AH & MA Red Book,* the *ABC World Airways Guide,* and the *Official Steamship Guide*
2. Publications of the national tourism organizations
3. Hotel chain or hotel representatives references
4. Guides published mainly for the public but used in the travel industry such as Michelin, Fodor, Rand McNally, and Birnbaum
5. Specialized guides such as *Castle Hotels of Europe*

Trade papers and magazines are published in most countries and carry current information (some are published twice weekly) to the travel industry. Some examples are *Travel Weekly, Travel Agent, Travel Trade, Canadian Travel News,* and *British Travel News.* A more complete list and a better grasp of all the periodicals, studies, and research bulletins can be obtained by examining Appendix B.

## MARKETING AND PUBLICITY ORGANIZATIONS

Travel marketing consultants provide valuable assistance to any organization needing specialized sales services. A travel marketing consultant organization will provide assistance in planning a publicity and sales campaign, selecting markets, selecting media, providing market research, discovering new markets, and overall conducting of a sales and marketing program.

Most state-level tourism promotion programs are conducted through established advertising agencies. To conduct this program successfully, these agencies must do market analysis of the travel industry, and many of these agencies have developed an expertise in this field. The names of the advertising agencies serving the various state tourism organizations can be obtained by writing to the state organization. A list of the state tourism organizations can be found in Appendix A or obtained from the Travel Industry Association of America, 1133 21st Street N.W., Washington, D.C. 20036.

## MEETING PLANNERS

A growing area of interest to students of tourism is meetings and conventions. With the growth of more corporate and association meetings, there is a need for more meeting planners, meeting consultants, and suppliers of goods and services to meeting planners. Professional meeting planners are involved with such tasks as negotiating hotel contracts, negotiating with airlines, writing contracts, planning educational meetings and seminars, developing incentive meetings, negotiating with foreign countries and hotels for incentive travel, budgeting, promotion, public relations, and planning special events and postmeeting tours. Meeting planners are found in corporations, special interest associations, educational institutions, trade shows, and government.

The most prominent organization serving this group is Meeting Planners International (MPI). This organization, founded in 1972, numbers 5900 members and has the goal of improving meeting methods. The Society of Company Meeting Planners (SCMP) also serves this area. Company and corporate meeting planners and hotel convention service managers have united to promote continuing education and high standards among members. Another organization is the Society of Government Meeting Planners (SGMP), which is made up of individuals involved in planning government meetings on a full- or part-time basis. The association provides education in basic and advanced areas of meeting planning and facilitates professional contact with other government meeting planners.

## MISCELLANEOUS SERVICES

Many other organizations provide essential services to tourism. Examples are hospitals and medical services, police services, sanitary trash pickup and disposal services, laundry services, construction services, retail stores such as department stores, drugstores, clothing stores, newspapers (including tourist newspapers and special travel editions), travel writers, and magazines.

## SUMMARY

The complex organization of tourism involves hundreds of thousands of units. Although many large firms compete in the industry, tourism is basically an industry dominated by small business firms.

Private organizations exist in almost every sector of the tourism industry to influence public policy, gather statistics, develop industry programs, and further the cause of tourism and their sector's role in the industry.

Business firms complete the structure of the industry, providing the products and services that consumers enjoy. The thousands of firms that provide transportation, lodging, entertainment, and food and beverages and make travel arrangements form the backbone of the industry.

It is important to understand the role and significance of tourism organizations, regardless of your ultimate role in this industry. Your success will, in part, be determined by the effectiveness of those tourism organizations that influence your work and your community.

### Key Concepts

air transport industry    auto, rental car group
Amtrak    automobile clubs
attractions group    bus industry

| consultants | publishers |
| --- | --- |
| consumer groups | quasi-government |
| cruise industry | restaurant organizations |
| developers | shops |
| educators | suppliers |
| industry groups | theme parks |
| lodging industry | tour wholesalers |
| marketers | trade organizations |
| oil companies | travel agents |
| profit and nonprofit | |

## For Review and Discussion

1. How important is the airline industry in the total travel picture?
2. What might be the advantage of establishing a cruise-only agency?
3. Explain franchising. For what groups of tourism suppliers do franchising arrangements provide benefits? What are these benefits? From the franchisee's viewpoint, are there any disadvantages?
4. Evaluate the advantages and disadvantages of an agency's joining a cooperative; joining a consortium; buying air tickets from a consolidator.
5. What are "preferred suppliers"? Why would an agency employ such a list?
6. In your home community, what possibilities exist for an agency to create incentive travel awards programs?
7. Travel agencies are said to be selling dreams. Is this true?
8. Explain the relationship between tour wholesalers and retail travel agencies. How do they differ?
9. Assuming you become employed in the travel industry, why would you wish to become a Certified Travel Counselor (CTC)?
10. How does a travel agency relate to the ARC, IATAN, CLIA, and Amtrak?
11. Does ASTA have an educational function? If so, how is this responsibility fulfilled?
12. What might be some likely future trends in the food service industry?
13. Evaluate the importance of attractions as travel motivators.
14. Why has the automobile retained such a predominate position (80 percent plus) in vacation and business travel?

## Case Problems

1. Tanya B. will be graduated in June with a B.A. degree in travel and tourism management. She has two job offers: (1) as a lodging coordinator in a fairly large tour company, and (2) as a beginning travel counselor in a large city travel agency. The tour company's pay offer is slightly higher than the travel agency's. As she intends to make the travel industry her career, which job should she accept? Why?
2. A capable young assistant manager of a large retail travel agency has recently been promoted to manager. Soon after the promotion, this manager received a letter containing several reasons that the agency should become a member of ASTA. Should the agency join?

3. Each year several travel agency-related organizations, such as trade journals and associations, offer educational seminars and workshops. Speakers often describe techniques that have been successful in their own agencies. Additionally, specialists present various sales methods. What might be some reasons for attending? For not attending?
4. A city of 6000 people has two travel agencies and one bank. One of the agencies has received a direct-mail group tour promotion sponsored by the local bank. The manager has evaluated this tour offering as a "rip off." Her agency markets a far superior similar tour for less cost. As her policy has always been to provide the best values for the traveling public, what should she do about this situation, in light of public relations? In light of promotional considerations?
5. As an expert in tourism for an international management consulting firm, Mr. B. W. has been asked for recommendations about organizations by Ms. R. S., a resort hotel manager. Ms. R. S.'s hotel has 370 rooms and is well located in a newly developed, attractive tourist destination area. What advice should R. S. be given concerning any and all tourism organizations that would benefit her hotel? Prepare sound arguments in defense of each of B. W.'s recommendations. (Assume any actual or hypothetical geographic location.)

## Selected References

Air Transportation Association of America. *Air Transport 1989: The Annual Report of the U.S. Scheduled Airline Industry.* Washington, D.C.: ATA, 1989.

Association of American Railroads. *Yearbook of Railroad Facts.* Washington, D.C.: Economics and Finance Department, the Association, Annual.

Berkman, Frank W., David C. Dorf, and Leonard R. Oakes. *Convention Management & Service.* East Lansing, Mich.: The Educational Institute of the American Hotel and Motel Association, 1978.

Cammerman, James M., and Ronald Bordessa. *Wonderland Through the Looking Glass.* Ontario: Belsten, 1981.

Cunningham, Lawrence F., and Kenneth Thompson. "The Intercity Bus Tour Market: A Comparison Between Inquirers and Purchasers." *Journal of Travel Research,* Vol. 25, no. 2 (Fall 1986), pp. 8–12.

Curran, Patrick J. T. *Principles and Procedures of Tour Management.* Boston: CBI, 1978.

De Looff, James. *Commuter Airlines.* Hicksville, N.Y.: Exposition Press, 1979.

Elton, M. A. "U.K. Tour Operators and Retail Travel Agents — ABTA and the Public Interest." *Tourism Management,* Vol. 5, no. 3 (September 1984), pp. 223–228.

Hanlon, J. P. "Hub Operations and Airline Competition." *Tourism Management,* Vol. 10, no. 2 (June 1989), pp. 111–124.

Hoyle, Leonard H., David C. Dorf, and Thomas J. A. Jones. *Managing Conventions and Group Business.* East Lansing, Mich.: Education Institute of the American Hotel and Motel Association, 1989.

Laventhol & Horwath. *U.S. Lodging Industry, 1988.* Philadelphia: L&H, 1988.

Miller, Willis H. "The U.S. Cruise Ship Industry." *Journal of Geography,* Vol. 84, no. 5 (September–October 1985), pp. 199–204.

National Park Service. *National Park Service Statistical Abstract, 1988.* Denver: National Park Service Statistical Office, 1989.

National Restaurant Association. "1989 Foodservice Industry Forecast." *Restaurants USA,* Vol. 8, no. 11 (December 1988) pp. 21–44.

National Technical Information Service. *Airline Industry: Automated Reservations Systems.* Springfield, Va.: NTIS, 1989.

Nixon, Judith M. *The Hotel and Restaurant Industries: An Information Sourcebook.* Phoenix: Oryx Press, 1988.

Pannell, Kerr, Forster. *Trends in the Hotel Industry, USA Edition 1988.* Houston: PKF, 1988.

Powers, Thomas F. *Introduction to the Hospitality Industry.* New York: John Wiley, 1988.

Powers, Thomas F. *Introduction to Management in the Hospitality Industry.* New York: John Wiley, 1988.

Reilly, Robert T. *Handbook of Professional Tour Management.* Wheaton, Ill.: Merton House Travel and Tourism Publishers, Inc., 1982.

*Restaurants USA,* Vol. 8, no. 11 (December 1988), pp. 21–44.

Steadman, Charles E., and Michael L. Kasavana. *Managing Front Office Operations.* East Lansing, Mich.: The Educational Institute of the American Hotel and Motel Association, 1988.

Taneja, Nawal K. *Airlines in Transition.* Lexington, Mass.: D.C. Heath, 1981.

Taneja, Nawal K. *The Commercial Airline Industry.* Lexington, Mass.: D.C. Heath, 1976.

Thompson, Douglas, and Jon Schulberg. *The Complete Guide To Travel Agency Video.* San Francisco: Dendrobium Books, 1988.

Thompson-Smith, Jeanie M. *Travel Agency Guide to Business Travel.* Albany, N.Y.: Delmar Publishers, 1988.

*Travel Weekly's Louis Harris Study Issue: The U.S. Travel Agency Market.* New York: Murdoch Magazines, 1988.

Waters, Somerset R. *Travel Industry World Yearbook: The Big Picture, 1989.* New York: Child & Waters, 1989.

Winterbottom, Jeff, and William C. Gartner. "A Comparison of Tourism Transportation Modes from 1976–1984." *Proceedings of the National Outdoor Recreation Trends Symposium II,* Vol. 1, 1985, pp. 155–163. Atlanta, Ga.: National Park Service Science Publications Office.

Wyckoff, D. Daryl, and David H. Maister. *The Domestic Airline Industry.* Lexington, Mass.: Lexington Books-D.C. Heath, 1977.

Wyckoff, D. Daryl, and W. Earl Sasser. *The Chain-Restaurant Industry.* Lexington, Mass.: Lexington Books-D.C. Heath, 1978.

Wyckoff, D. Daryl, and W. Earl Sasser. *The U.S. Lodging Industry.* Lexington, Mass.: Lexington Books-D.C. Heath, 1981.

Zehnder, Leonard E. *Florida's Disney World: Promises and Problems.* Tallahassee, Fla.: Peninsular Publishing, 1975.

# PART TWO

# Motivation for Travel and Choosing Travel Products

# C H A P T E R   4

# Pleasure Travel Motivation

## L E A R N I N G   O B J E C T I V E S

- Determine the four basic travel motivators, realizing that engaging in pleasure travel is, in itself, learned behavior.
- Know the factors that make these motivations quite different in individual people.
- Examine the main reasons that some people do not travel and then look at what travel marketers can do to offset some of these barriers.
- Discover that people engage in various types of tourism based upon the category of destination area attraction or experience chosen for their trip.
- Learn that the traveler is mainly purchasing experiences.
- Recognize that the travel market can be divided psychologically into motivational groups.

Engaging in pleasure travel is, in itself, learned behavior. Thus, as tourism promoters, we have to induce people to travel for pleasure. Once they have tried it, they are likely to want to travel more. Travel brings about satisfactions obtained only by such experiences. Viewing pictures of a particular place is only a fraction as satisfying as an actual visit. Satisfactions often include a relaxation of tension as well. The pleasure trip thus becomes a highly complex and basically learned form of reducing tension.

An important part of the consideration of tourism psychology and motivation is the fact that a person usually travels for more than one reason. For example, if a person goes to an area for health reasons, the fact that a series of symphony concerts is being held at the same place during the time of the visit acts as an attraction and a reinforcement to the decision to go.

Basic travel motivators can be divided into four categories:

1. *Physical motivators* are those related to physical rest, sports participation, beach recreation, relaxing entertainment, and other motivations directly connected with health. Additional motivators might be a doctor's orders or recommendations and the use of health spas, curative baths, medical examinations, and similar health treatment activities. These motivations all have one feature in common, namely, the reduction of tension through physical activities.
2. *Cultural motivators* are identified by the desire to know about other areas — their food, music, art, folklore, dances, paintings, and religion.

The world-famous Banff Springs Hotel, set in the spectacular Canadian Rockies with wildlife populating its championship golf course, illustrates a variety of factors motivating tourists to visit a beautiful natural setting. (Photo courtesy of Banff Springs Hotel, Alberta)

3. *Interpersonal motivators* include a desire to meet new people, visit friends or relatives, escape from routine or from family and neighbors, or make new friendships.
4. *Status and prestige motivators* concern ego needs and personal development. Within this category are trips related to business, conventions, study, and the pursuit of hobbies and education. The desire for recognition, attention, appreciation, knowledge, and good reputation can be fulfilled through travel.

## TRAVEL MOTIVATION AS RELATED TO SEX, AGE, AND EDUCATION

Three areas in which individual differences are important when considering travel motivation are sex, age, and education. Sex differences appear to be due to two distinct factors: role conflict and training differences. Men may have a conflict between their family and business roles so the demands for allocation of time and energy may be in conflict. They may try to keep the two areas of their lives separate. In the United States, the rule is sometimes clearer for the woman; in case of conflict, home and family usually come first. However, roles are changing, so the differences between men and women in training, motivations, and interests are not as distinct as they once were. If children are involved, however, their needs may influence both parents' motivations and choices.

Age can also play a significant part in the types of experiences that appeal to an

Tourist attractions like the Magic Kingdom at Walt Disney World in Florida have great appeal for adults and children alike. (Photo copyright Walt Disney Productions, 1985)

individual. Youth may have a high tolerance for all types of new experiences. In animals, the immature animal seems to be less inclined toward the defense of a particular area of land and more toward vigorous exploration. Much the same can be said for young humans who are receptive to new ideas and may be less prone to embarrassment in social situations. The young person can always use his age as an excuse for social blunders; less may be expected from the young person. The younger age group is usually interested in new places and experiences.

During the middle years, a person's comfort may be more important. He or she has achieved a certain status and desires the comforts associated with this status. Another consideration for some members of an older age group is the desire to travel in groups. Two factors may be responsible for this: increased need for social comparison and companionship and reduced need for exploration. The middle-aged person will tolerate groups because he or she feels more secure when behavior can be adjusted to that of companions. This person may also prefer to travel in the family car. It is more comfortable in the sense that it is an extension of one's own home—secure and familiar.

In the later years of life, a person usually develops an increasing tolerance for immobility and a turning inward; however, there is no particular age at which this occurs and it may never take place.

Differences in educational level affect the types of new experiences a person is willing to accept. In discussing these differences, however, it must be remembered that these differences are intermixed with socioeconomic status and level of income. People with a high level of education generally earn more money and are of higher status than are those whose educational level is lower. College graduates usually appreciate change in their environment. They are more willing to take a chance and go somewhere unfamiliar. This group is increasingly mobile and is the initiator of a high percentage of social change. They make up a large percentage of the management personnel who are the most mobile individuals in our society. They are interested in travel and do not have to be sold on any particular travel concept. It may, in fact, be difficult to provide a truly novel experience for these people, and this offers a challenge to people who specialize in tourist services.

A new segment of Western society entering the area of travel is the high school graduate. This group was once thought to have little time for or interest in travel. But as income rises, high school graduates are accumulating the money and have the leisure time to enter the travel market. Conversely, while income has raised status, the interests of this population segment may continue to parallel those of parents who had limited travel opportunity and even less experience. This tourist, therefore, has to be sold on the *idea* of travel in spite of his or her needs for security and concern with proper travel behavior.

The graduate of grade school is the most static of all three education levels and is extremely concerned with familiarity and social appearance. This person may not travel at all because he or she may feel less cultured than the average traveler, even if this is not the case. The same pattern of travel may appear repeatedly, not because

Hundreds of green sea turtles like this one thrive at the Cayman Turtle Farm, a popular environmental attraction on Grand Cayman in the Cayman Islands. (Photo courtesy of Cayman Islands News Bureau)

the person desires to maintain the pattern, but because of fear of trying anything new. As with the high school graduate, it is necessary to reassure this person that a novel situation does not necessarily promote insecurity.

The factors of age, sex, and education are reviewed again in Chapter 12, "The Consumer Market," with numbers given showing the size and trends concerning these factors.

## BARRIERS TO TRAVEL

There are a number of reasons why people do not travel extensively, or do not travel at all. The reasons, products of psychological analysis, are not meant to be ultimate answers as to why people travel where they do. We can, however, look at the more concrete reasons why those studied did not go on a trip during a certain period of time. For most of these studies, barriers to travel fall into six broad categories:

1. *Cost.* Consumers operate within monetary constraints, and travel must compete with other allocations of funds. Saying that travel is too expensive is an indirect way of saying that travel is not important, but, even allowing this interpretation, costs are a principal reason for staying home.
2. *Lack of time.* Many people cannot leave their businesses, jobs, or professions for vacation purposes.
3. *Health limitations.* Poor health and physical limitations keep many persons at home.
4. *Family stage.* Parents of young children often do not travel because of family obligations and inconveniences in traveling with children. Widows and singles sometimes do not travel because of the lack of a traveling companion.
5. *Lack of interest.* Unawareness of travel destinations that would bring pleasurable satisfaction is a major barrier.
6. *Fear and safety.* Things unknown are often feared, and in travel, much is often not familiar to the would-be traveler. Wars, unrest, and negative publicity about an area will create doubt and fear in the mind of the prospective traveler. Terrorism has reared its ugly head in the last decade and is a deterrent to travel. Since the hijacking of TWA Flight 847 in Athens, the Achille Lauro cruise ship incident, violence at airports in Rome and Vienna, and the explosion of Pan Am flight 103 over Scotland, safety has been on the minds of tourists.

When motivation to travel is sufficiently powerful, the barriers may be overcome, but these forces may still influence means of travel and destinations selected.

Although travelers may be able to overcome the first four variables listed, tourism marketers need to modify the fifth barrier—lack of interest. To illustrate just how widespread this barrier is, the following approach was taken where the cost barrier was eliminated. The respondents were asked this incomplete sentence: "Mr. and Mrs. Brown were offered an expense-free tour of the United States, but they didn't want to go because . . ." Forty-two percent of the respondents said that the Browns wanted to go on the trip but couldn't due to job reasons, poor health, age, or responsibilities for children. However, 26 percent indicated that the Browns did not want to go on the trip at all; they would rather stay home, or they did not like to travel, or they were afraid to travel. It is evident that in spite of widespread desires to travel, some people would rather stay home. For others, a weak desire to travel is compounded by nervousness or fear of what the experience may bring. Such a reluctance to travel runs counter to the tide, but this segment is too large a group to be overlooked. With the proper motivational tools, a significant percentage of this untapped group of potential travelers might be convinced that there are places or things of interest outside the world in which they are now existing.

When analyzing some of the psychological reasons contributing to the lack of interest in travel, at least some are related to conflicts between exploration and safety needs. A person's home is safe, a place thoroughly known, and he or she is not required to maintain a facade there. On the other hand, the familiarity of home can also produce boredom and the need to explore. A person is thus possessed of two very strong drives—*safety* and *exploration*—and he or she needs to reduce this conflict.

One way to do this is by traveling in areas that the person knows well. He or she may go to the same cottage at the same lake with the same people he or she has known for years. Thus, a new experience that may threaten the need for safety is avoided, but this approach reduces the exploration need by the person's leaving home and traveling to a different place even though it is familiar.

## AIR TRAVEL OR AUTOMOBILE TRAVEL

Although a principal concern of tourism is motivating people with no desire to travel, the mode of transportation chosen by people when they do travel has significant effects on travel facilities. Certain variables are factors in motivating a person to choose air travel over auto travel for a nonbusiness trip. There are five independent variables:

1. Cost
2. Distance
3. Travel tastes and experience
4. Income
5. Time considerations

Cost is a major factor in deciding to travel by air or by auto. There are two measures of cost: the price of each trip and the number of people traveling. Only a small minority of trips are taken by adults who believe that air is less expensive. Air travel is not likely to be cheaper if more than one person goes on the trip.

Distance variables (time away and length of trip) may also be interpreted as cost variables because the cost of a trip is partly a function of trip distance and partly of time away. Costs of meals, hotel rooms, and so forth add up with each day away from home. There may be substantial pressure to minimize travel costs for trips involving lengthy stays. Air is likely to be cheaper than auto if the distance is over 1000 miles and time away is over 11 days. Auto travel has a clear edge over air travel for trips up to 300 miles.

High income consumers will have some preference for air travel over auto travel. Travel tastes and experience indicate that if the traveler perceived air as the

Fascinating creatures that lived millions of years ago populate the Museum of Geology in Rapid City. Being able to see these creates a powerful travel incentive. (Photo courtesy of the South Dakota Department of Tourism)

best way to travel and if he or she had experience as an air traveler, air travel would again have a slight edge as that person's choice of mode. Time consideration is a major factor in choosing air.

## THE ROMANCE OF PLEASURE TRAVEL

Perhaps the strongest of all individual travel motivations is simply that of satisfying a need for pleasure. Travel has the unique quality of being able to satisfy this desire to an extremely high degree. Not all trips are pleasurable, but some are more pleasurable than anticipated. The planning and anticipation period prior to the trip can be as enjoyable as the trip itself. Discussing prospects of the trip with friends and pursuing research, educational, and shopping activities relating to the trip and the area to be visited is a most important part of the total pleasure travel experience. In the formulation of marketing programs and advertising, in particular, the pleasurable aspects of the trip need to be emphasized. The prospective traveler should be told how much fun it is to go to the popular, as well as some of the most uncommon, destinations.

The romance of the trip is also a strong motivation, particularly in relation to honeymoon travel and for those who are thrilled with the romantic aspects of seeing, experiencing, and enjoying strange and attractive places. Thus, the romance and

The heritage and culture of American Indians is demonstrated at
the Red Earth celebration in Oklahoma. Tribes are represented by
their costumes, and traditional dances are performed. (Photo by
Fred W. Marvel, courtesy of Oklahoma Tourism Department)

pleasure of the trip are primary attributes of the travel experience and need to be
emphasized far more than they have been in the past. Sharing experiences with
members of the family or friends is another integral part of the enjoyment of the trip.
A trip can become a fine medium through which additional pleasure and romance is
experienced.

# TYPES OF DESTINATIONS—TRAVEL EXPERIENCES

The spatial and characteristic diversity among destinations has become so great that it is important to classify destinations so that a systematic discussion of tourism psychology and motivation can be undertaken. One way to do this is to build on Valene L. Smith's identification of several types of tourism.[1] That is, a classification of destinations can be developed on the basis of the types of travel experience provided at the various destinations.

Smith identified six categories of tourism:

*Ethnic Tourism* is traveling for the purpose of observing the cultural expressions and life-styles of truly exotic peoples. Such tourism is exemplified by travel to

Of great interest to Americans and foreign visitors alike is the restored Statue of Liberty, located in New York harbor. This dramatic statue and grounds are maintained by the National Park Service. (Photo courtesy of the New York Division of Tourism)

[1] Valene Smith, *Hosts and Guests* (Philadelphia: University of Pennsylvania Press, 1977), pp. 2–3.

Panama to study the San Blas Indians or to India to observe the isolated hill tribes of Assam. Typical destination activities would include visits to native homes, attending dances and ceremonies, and possibly participating in religious rituals.

*Cultural Tourism* is travel to experience and, in some cases, participate in a vanishing life-style that lies within human memory. The picturesque setting or "local color" in the destination area are the main attractions. Destination activities, typically, include meals in rustic inns, costume festivals, folk dance performances, and arts and crafts demonstrations in "old-style" fashion. Visits to Williamsburg, Virginia, and Greenfield Village in Dearborn, Michigan, or to Mystic Seaport, Connecticut, are examples of cultural tourism.

*Historical Tourism* is the museum-cathedral tour that stresses the glories of the past — Rome, Egypt, and Greece. Civil war sites in the United States such as Gettysburg, Pennsylvania, and Chancellorsville, Virginia, are other examples. Guided tours of monuments, visits to churches and cathedrals, sound and light performances that encapsulate the life-style of important events of a bygone era are favored destination activities. Such tourism is facilitated because the attractions are either in or are readily accessible from large cities. Typically, such attractions seem particularly adaptable to organized mass tourism.

*Environmental Tourism* is similar to ethnic tourism, drawing tourists to remote areas. But the emphasis here is on natural and environmental attractions, rather than on ethnic ones. Travel for the purposes of "getting back to nature" and to appreciate

The opportunity to engage in unique, exciting activities such as scuba diving is a prime tourism motivator. Reef dives, wreck dives, night dives, share dives, wall dives, and cave and tunnel exploring provide exhilarating experiences. (Photo courtesy of Cayman Islands News Bureau)

(or become sensitive to) people-land relationships belong in this category. Environmental tourism is primarily geographic and includes such destinations as Niagara Falls, the Grand Canyon, Yellowstone National Park, and other natural wonders. Typical destination activities include photography, hiking, mountain climbing, canoeing, and camping.

*Recreational Tourism*   centers on participation in sports, curative spas, sun bathing, and social contacts in a relaxed environment. Such areas often promote sand, sea, and sex through beautiful color photographs that make you want to be there on the ski slopes, on palm-fringed beaches, on championship golf courses, or on tennis courts. Such promotion is designed to attract tourists whose essential purpose is to relax. Las Vegas epitomizes another type of recreational travel—gambling, spectacular floor shows, and away-from-home freedom.

*Business Tourism*   as characterized by conventions/meetings/seminars, is another important form of travel. (The United Nations includes the business traveler in its definition of a tourist.) Business travel is frequently combined with one or more of the types of tourism already identified.

   This classification system is by no means unassailable. Destination areas can, and in most cases do, provide more than one type of tourism experience. For example, Las Vegas, which essentially provides recreational tourism, is also a popular

Conventions and trade show exhibits attract many travelers. (Photo courtesy of Las Vegas Convention Center)

convention destination. Resorts in Hawaii provide recreational, environmental, and cultural tourism, depending on what types of activities the tourist desires. A tourist vacationing in India, in addition to recreational tourism on one of the spectacular beaches in that country has the opportunity for ethnic tourist experiences. Visits can be made to the villages to observe the life-styles of remote populations.

Conversely, a tourist can select from myriad destinations that provide the same basic type of tourism. For instance, a tourist with an interest in historical tourism may travel to any country that has historical appeal.

## TYPES OF TOURISTS

Tourists are no more homogeneous than destinations. Therefore, it is equally critical to identify types of tourists, so that their travel patterns can be better understood and systematically analyzed. Usually markets are segmented on the basis of demographics. Demographics are the social statistics of population, such as income, age, sex, occupation, and geographic location. Increasingly, marketers are realizing that demand patterns are not fully explained by demographics alone, even in the case of tangible goods. Tourism is an intangible product (we are in the business of selling dreams). Except for small sums of money spent for souvenirs, most of the tourist dollar goes toward purchasing experiences. Since experiences are of a psychic nature, demand patterns for tourism depend rather intensely on the psychographic characteristics of tourists. Therefore, when considering the demand for tourism, it is essential to segment the market both in terms of demographics and psychographics.

Several models have been developed to classify people according to psychographic types. One such model was developed by Dr. Stanley C. Plog, who classified

Sportfishing has always been a strong travel motivator. (Photo courtesy of Cayman Islands News Bureau)

the U.S. population along a psychographic continuum — ranging from the psychocentric at one extreme to the allocentric at the other.[2]

The term "psychocentric" is derived from *psyche* or *self*-centered, meaning the centering of one's thought or concerns on the small problem areas of one's life. Allocentric, on the other hand, derives from the root word *allo*, meaning "varied in form." An allocentric person, thus, is one whose interest patterns are focused on varied activities. Such a person is outgoing and self-confident and is characterized by a considerable degree of adventure and a willingness to reach out and experiment with life. Travel becomes a way for the allocentric to express inquisitiveness and satisfy curiosity.

Plog found that the U.S. population was normally distributed along a continuum between these two extreme types. This is illustrated in Figure 4.1. Other groups have been identified between the allocentrics and psychocentrics. Most people fall in the midcentric classification.

Through further research, Plog identified the travel preferences of psychocentrics and allocentrics. These are summarized in Figure 4.2. In studying the population on the basis of income level, Plog discovered another interesting relationship. At the lower end of the income spectrum, he discovered a heavy loading of psychocentrics. People at the upper end of the income levels were found to be predominantly allocentric. However, for the broad spectrum in between — for most of America — interrelations are only slightly positive. This finding has several implications.

It is evident that at extremely low levels of family income, travel patterns may be determined largely by the income constraints. Regardless of the psychographic type, a person at the low end of the income spectrum may be compelled to take what Plog considers to be psychocentric-type vacations. College students are a good example of this. They may be allocentric by nature but cannot afford an allocentric-type vacation since such vacations are generally very expensive (a safari in Africa or a mountain climbing expedition in Nepal). They travel instead to nearby destinations, spend less money, and participate in familiar activities. Therefore, it may be erroneous to conclude that a person with a low income is likely to be psychocentric. The severe income constraint may distort the individual's classification in terms of psychographics.

Plog admits that middle-income groups exhibited only a small positive correla-

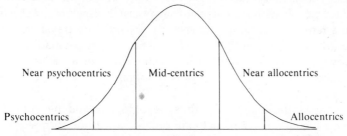

**Figure 4.1** U.S. Population Distribution by Psychographic Type.

[2] Stanley C. Plog, "Why Destination Areas Rise and Fall in Popularity," *The Cornell Hotel and Restaurant Administration Quarterly*, Vol. 14, no. 4 (February 1974), pp. 55–58.

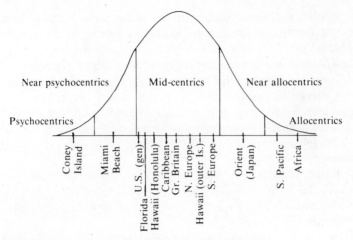

**Figure 4.2** Psychographic Positions of Destinations.

tion with psychographic types. Possessing greater flexibility in the choice of vacations (due to higher incomes), people in this category can choose the type of vacation they prefer — and, interestingly in this group, incomes and psychographics are not closely related.

Having defined types of destinations and types of tourists, one is tempted to link these two classifications directly, as Plog has done. Plog superimposed a list of destinations on the population distribution curve, suggesting that allocentrics would travel to such destinations as Africa or the Orient. Psychocentrics, on the other hand, would vacation in nearby destinations (such as Cedar Point, Ohio, theme park for a psychocentric from Toledo). The intervening psychocentric types are similarly identified with particular destinations (refer to Figure 4.2).

Such a direct linkage between the classification of tourists and of destinations does not consider the important fact that people travel with different motivations on different occasions. A wealthy allocentric may indeed travel to Africa on an annual vacation, but may also take weekend trips to a typically psychocentric destination during other times of the year. Similarly, though probably not as likely, psychocentrics could conceivably vacation in essentially allocentric destinations (with the exception of people with extremely low incomes). For instance, a psychocentric may travel to a remote area under the security provided by traveling with a group of similar tourists, which, being escorted at all times, may persuade a psychocentric to travel, say, to Asia. Is Asia, then, a psychocentric or an allocentric destination? Clearly, a direct relationship between psychographic types and destinations is tenuous at best.

What then is the link between the types of tourists and the types of destinations? To develop such a linkage, which will provide a method for predicting travel patterns, two things must be realized. First, as already pointed out, a tourist may travel for different reasons from one trip to the next. Second, a given destination can provide a variety of travel experiences, suitable to a wide range of tourists, depending on the manner in which the trip is planned. The only way in which a systematic linkage can be developed between the types of destinations and the types of tourists is to consider each trip in isolation and examine the motivations that have prompted the trip.

Figure 4.3 illustrates the relationship between types of tourists, travel motivations, and types of destinations.

As indicated in this figure, travel motivations link types of tourists and types of destinations in two ways:

1. The primary link is the tourist flow and client satisfaction that will result when a customer is directed to the appropriate type of destination. Such a choice is most likely to maximize satisfactions and produce the kind of travel experience that he or she seeks. A clear understanding is needed of the client's psychological and demographic profile and, hence, his or her travel motivations for that particular trip. Knowing this enables the purveyor of tourism services (such as a travel counselor) to recommend the types of tour packages (escorted or unescorted, fully planned or flexible), the types of destinations, and the types of travel experiences that will best suit the client or customer's needs. Travel experiences planned in this manner will yield the highest level of client satisfaction.
2. The secondary link relates to the promotion, development, and marketing of

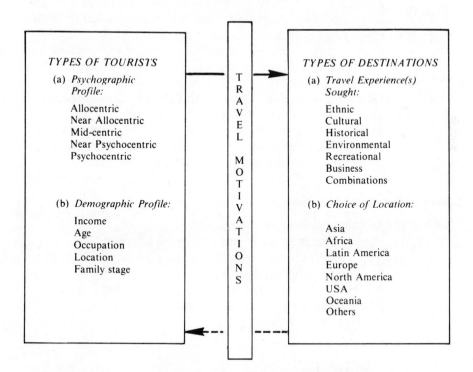

━━ PRIMARY LINK: TOURIST FLOW, CUSTOMER SATISFACTION
----------- SECONDARY LINK: DEVELOPMENT, PROMOTION, MARKETING

**Figure 4.3** Relationships Among Types of Tourists, Travel Motivations, and Types of Destinations.

destinations to appropriate target markets. Understanding the types of tourists in the target market and the travel motivations of this market will provide a sound basis for deciding the types of environments and services that should be provided at the destination. These understandings will also govern the message content of a promotion campaign.

The following list shows many travel motivations. It should be clear from this list that some motivations are shared by a wide variety of tourists (from allocentric to psychocentric), while other motivations relate to a more narrow spectrum of psychographic types.

On the basis of the foregoing discussion, it is clear that to maximize client satisfaction, it is imperative that travel motivations for a particular trip be clearly identified and understood. So doing will help the client select the type of travel experience that most closely matches his or her needs and wants.

## TRAVEL MOTIVATIONS LISTED

### Allocentric Motivations

1. Education and cultural motives — learning and increased ability for appreciation, scientific or purposeful; trips with expert leaders or lecturers
2. Study of genealogy
3. Search for the exotic — Hawaii, Polynesia, Japan, Thailand, East Africa, India
4. Satisfactions and sense of power and freedom — anonymity, flying, control, sea travel, fast trains
5. Gambling — Las Vegas, Atlantic City, Monte Carlo, Bahamas, Puerto Rico
6. Development of new friendships in foreign places
7. Sharpening perspectives — awaken senses, heighten awareness
8. Political campaigns, supporting candidates, government hearings
9. Vacation or second homes and condominiums

### Near-Allocentric Motivations

10. Religious pilgrimages or inspiration
11. Participation in sports events and sports activities
12. Travel as a challenge, sometimes a test of endurance such as exploring, mountain climbing, hiking, diving
13. Business travel, conferences, meetings, conventions
14. Theater tours, special entertainment
15. A chance to try a new life-style

### Midcentric Motivations

16. Relaxation and pleasure — just plain fun and enjoyment
17. Satisfying personal contacts with friends and relatives
18. Health — change in climate, sunshine, spas, medical treatment

The Ballet West Summer Dance School is a Snowmass tradition and an integral part of the Ballet-Aspen multicompany dance season. From the world-famous Aspen Music Festival to the Snowmass Repertory Theatre and Anderson Ranch Arts Center, culture and the arts create the special ambiance that is Snowmass/Aspen. Artistic appreciation is a growing travel incentive, motivating both parents and children attending schools and instructional centers for the arts. (Photo courtesy of Snowmass Resort Association)

19. The need for a change for a period of time
20. An opportunity to escape from life's problems
21. The real or imagined glamour of the destination
22. Appreciation of beauty—national and state parks, forests, lakes, wilderness areas, canoe trips, ocean shores
23. Sensual indulgence—food, comforts, luxuries for the body, romance, sexual enjoyment, rest, relaxation

24. Shopping—souvenirs, gifts, expensive possessions like cameras, jewels, furs, cars, antiques, art
25. Joys of transportation—cruise ships, gourmet meals, buffets, comfortable trains, buses, airplanes, autos
26. Pleasure of pre- and post travel—planning the trip, anticipation, learning, dreaming; then showing pictures and describing the trip after completion
27. Family or personal matters

### Near-Psychocentric and Psychocentric Motivations

28. Ego enhancement, quest for status
29. Travel for acceptance, to be comfortable socially
30. Travel as a cultural norm—paid vacations required by law
31. Visit to places seen or read about in the news
32. Visit to amusement parks

Dr. Plog first developed his model in 1972, some 18 years ago, and it has been widely cited in tourism literature since that time. It was one of the first attempts to provide a framework within which to analyze tourist behavior. The world has changed considerably since Dr. Plog introduced his model. For example, today there are fewer countries that are considered exotic. Also, there are now other ways to look at tourists, such as through life-style analysis or benefit segmentation. Dr. Plog's pioneering efforts, however, should not be overlooked. His model still provides a way to examine travel and think about developments using current market conditions.

## SUMMARY

Anyone marketing tourism should first identify the travel motivation(s) of prospective patrons or clients and then present the travel product that will best fulfill these desires and motivations. Knowledge of travel motivations is essential in planning advertising and other promotion programs.

A clear understanding of what motivates people to visit is essential to the successful promotion of any tourist destination area. Thus, it is the challenge of promoters to identify these motivations and reach the most likely prospects with convincing messages. This chapter identifies the principal travel motivators. Then it explains the specific relationship to demographic factors, modes of transportation, and types of destinations.

Understanding travel motivation importantly influences the nature of tourism developments. The location, design, characteristics, and features of the development must fulfill the travel motivations and expectations of those making up the principal target markets.

It is also useful to understand why some people do not travel and what the barriers to travel may be. Once defined, the barriers can often be overcome with skillful counseling and selling.

## Key Concepts

allocentrics
barriers to travel
business tourism
choice of location
choice of transportation mode
cultural tourism
demographic profile
distance variables
environmental tourism
ethnic tourism
historical tourism
income variables
midcentrics
near-allocentrics
near-psychocentrics

price variables
psychocentrics
psychographic profile
recreational tourism
romance of pleasure travel
sex, age, and education influences
travel, a learned behavior
travel experiences sought
travel motivators
travel tastes and experience
types of destinations
types of tourists
uses of motivations

## For Review and Discussion

1. Provide some examples of how a resort hotel's marketing director can use the four basic travel motivators in creating next year's marketing program.
2. Referring to the previous question, how might sex, age, and education of the hotel's present and prospective markets influence the hotel's upcoming annual marketing plan? Give examples.
3. If you were responsible for publicizing your attractive resort-type community, in what ways would you endeavor to overcome lack of interest in your potential major market cities?
4. From the standpoint of economic success in tourism, would it be better for a community to "specialize" in one or two of Valene Smith's six categories of tourism or to emphasize all six in marketing programs?
5. Might there be more than six categories (as proposed by Valene Smith)?
6. Evaluate the importance of pictures in sales literature as related to the main motivations identified for your particular business or destination.
7. As a tourism student, what are your most recognizable travel motivations? Do you think these will change over the years?
8. Airplane and airport bombings have created serious barriers to air travel in the minds of many people. What could airline marketing or public relations directors do to mitigate such feelings?
9. Cost is a major barrier to travel. Are there any psychological approaches to this problem that various suppliers could take?
10. Describe some communication devices that could be used by automobile clubs or retail travel agencies to overcome lack of interest in a particular travel experience.
11. Do you believe vacations are a necessity or a luxury in today's society?
12. In what ways do package tours overcome travel barriers?

## Case Problems

1. An astute architect who is familiar with Plog's psychographics and motivations is planning a new all-season resort. How might these motivations influence the design and make-up of the resort?

2. Samuel S. is a research-minded marketing director for a successful tour wholesaler. This firm specializes in general interest tours to Europe, Mexico, Hawaii, and the Caribbean. In a recent mail survey, he has discovered that about 20 percent of those who have the time and money for leisure travel do not travel and are not interested in his very attractive tours of excellent value. What sales recommendations might he make to his most productive retail travel agencies in order to reach this rather substantial market segment?

## Selected References

Brady, John, and Richard Widdows. "The Impact of World Events on Travel to Europe During the Summer of 1986." *Journal of Travel Research,* Vol. 26, no. 3 (Winter 1988), pp. 8–10.

Conant, Jeffrey S., Terry Clark, John J. Burnett, and Gail Zank. "Terrorism and Travel: Managing the Unmanageable." *Journal of Travel Research,* Vol. 26, no. 4, (Spring 1988), pp. 16–20.

Fridgen, Joseph D. "Environmental Psychology and Tourism." *Annals of Tourism Research,* Vol. 11, no. 1 (1984), pp. 19–39.

Hamilton-Smith, Elery. "Four Kinds of Tourism?" *Annals of Tourism Research,* Vol. 14, no. 3 (1987), pp. 332–334.

Krippendorf, Jost. *The Holiday Makers.* London: Heinemann, 1987.

Mayo, Edward J., and Lance P. Jarvis. *The Psychology of Leisure Travel.* Boston: CBI, 1981.

Morin, Michel. "A Socio-Psychological Approach to Vacation and Mobility in Touristic Sites." *Annals of Tourism Research,* Vol. 11, no. 1 (1984), pp. 113–127.

Neulinger, John. *The Psychology of Leisure.* Springfield, Ill.: Thomas, 1974.

Pasini, Walter. *Tourist Health: A New Branch of Public Health.* Madrid: World Tourism Organization, 1989.

Pearce, Philip L. *The Social Psychology of Tourist Behaviour.* Oxford: Pergamon, 1982.

Pizam, Abraham, and Roger Calantone. "Beyond Psychographics — Values as Determinants of Tourist Behavior." *International Journal of Hospitality Management,* Vol. 6, no. 3 (1988), pp. 177–181.

Reason, James. *Man in Motion: The Psychology of Travel.* New York: Walker, 1974.

Stringer, Peter. "Studies in the Socio-Environmental Psychology of Tourism." *Annals of Tourism Research,* Vol. 11, no. 1 (1984), pp. 147–166.

Stringer, Peter, and Philip L. Pearce. "Towards a Symbiosis of Social Psychology and Tourism Studies." *Annals of Tourism Research,* Vol. 11, no. 1 (1984), pp. 5–17.

Uzzell, David. "An Alternative Structuralist Approach to the Psychology of Tourism Marketing." *Annals of Tourism Research,* Vol. 11, no. 1 (1984), pp. 79–99.

Van Raaij, W. Fred, and Dick A. Francken. "Vacation Decisions, Activities, and Satisfactions." *Annals of Tourism Research,* Vol. 11, no. 1 (1984), pp. 101–112.

"Why Do People Travel?" *The Cornell Hotel and Restaurant Administration Quarterly,* Vol. 11, no. 4 (February 1971), pp. 2–12.

# Cultural and International Tourism for Life's Enrichment

## LEARNING OBJECTIVES

- Recognize that travel experiences are the best way to learn about other cultures.
- Identify the cultural factors in tourism.
- Appreciate the rewards of participation in life-seeing tourism.
- Become aware of the most effective promotional measures involving an area's cultural resources.
- Realize the importance of cultural attractions to any area promoting itself as a tourist destination.

The highest purpose of tourism is to become better acquainted with people in other places and countries, as this furthers the understanding and appreciation that builds a better world for all. International travel also involves the exchange of knowledge and ideas—another worthy objective. Travel raises levels of human experience, recognition, and achievements in many areas of learning, research, and artistic activity. In this chapter we discuss travel as it enriches our lives.

## IMPORTANCE

Cultural tourism covers all aspects of travel whereby people learn about each other's ways of life and thought. Tourism is thus an important means of promoting cultural relations and international cooperation. Conversely, development of cultural factors within a nation is a means of enhancing resources to attract visitors. In many countries, tourism can be linked with a "cultural relations" policy. It is used to promote not only knowledge and understanding but also a favorable image of the nation among foreigners in the travel market.

The channels through which a country presents itself to tourists can be considered its cultural factors. These are the entertainment, food, drink, hospitality, architecture, manufactured and hand-crafted products of a country, and all other characteristics of a nation's way of life.

Successful tourism is not simply a matter of having better transportation and hotels but of adding a particular national flavor in keeping with traditional ways of life and projecting a favorable image of the benefits to tourists of such goods and services.

A nation's cultural attractions must be presented intelligently and creatively. In this age of uniformity, the products of one nation are almost indistinguishable from those of another. There is a great need for encouraging cultural diversity. Improved techniques of architectural design and artistic presentation can be used to create an expression of originality in every part of the world.

Taken in their narrower sense, cultural factors in tourism play a dominant role chiefly in activities that are specifically intended to promote the transmission or sharing of knowledge and ideas. Consider the following factors:

1. Libraries, museums, exhibitions
2. Musical, dramatic, or film performances
3. Radio and television programs, recordings
4. Study tours or short courses
5. Schools and universities for longer-term study and research
6. Scientific and archaeological expeditions, schools at sea
7. Joint production of films
8. Conferences, congresses, meetings, seminars

In addition, many activities that are not educational or cultural in a narrow sense provide opportunities for peoples of different nations to get to know each other.

## LIFE-SEEING TOURISM

Traditionally, a person " sees the high points" of a given location and, thus, feels that he or she has "seen" this area. However, there is a growing belief among tourism specialists that such an approach, although traditionally valid, is by no means the best approach. Purposeful activities that match the travelers' interests are becoming more commonly accepted and recognized. (In popular tourist areas, such arrangements may have to be limited to the off-season periods of the year.) For example, a physician on a vacation might be interested in talking with local physicians and viewing interesting or progressive medical installations or facilities. He or she may wish to participate in a symposium or some type of educational endeavor there or have lunch with a group of physicians interested in the same particular specialty or in public health or medical practices in general. The visitor may also wish to visit the home of a well-known physician to exchange ideas.

Suggestions made by the travel agent and machinery provided to make such experiences come about are of growing importance to successful tourism. Any place that wishes to become a successful tourist destination must have more activities for visitors than the traditional recreational activities such as lying on the beach or patronizing a night club or visiting popular tourist attractions.

Axel Dessau, director of the Danish National Tourist Office, is credited with this concept of "life-seeing tourism." In Denmark, for example, the visitor is met by a graduate student or other person who is technically familiar with the field of interest that a visitor may have. This guide then arranges for purposeful visits in a schedule suited to the visitor.

Pago Pago Resort Hotel, American Samoa. Architectural design reflects the indigenous style of construction. When guests arrive at this hotel, they know they are in Polynesia!
*Source:* Wimberly, Allison, Tong and Goo, Architects, Honolulu, Hawaii.

For example, the visitor might be interested in reviewing social problems and city government. An expert in these matters would plan to visit city planning offices, schools, social welfare establishments, and rehabilitation centers; to attend meetings or seminars at which problems of this nature are discussed; and to provide other opportunities for the visitor to learn firsthand what is happening in his or her field in Denmark.

The plan is usually set up on a half-day basis, with the visitor spending afternoons to visit tourist highlights, go shopping, and pursue other traditional recreational activities. The mornings would be devoted to making visits to organizations and establishments with programs planned by a special expert guide. A travel agent can make these arrangements.

Another aspect of life-seeing tourism is the opportunity to have social intercourse with families. These families host the visitor or the visitor's family in the evening after dinner for conversation and sociability. Or the visitor can stay in a private home—an excellent way in which to become acquainted with the culture and life-style of persons in a different locality.

In the Bahamas, visitors can discover the island group's people and culture in a very personal way through their People-to-People Program. This stimulating and exciting program is organized by the Ministry of Tourism. It matches visitors with

Bahamian volunteers who host visitors having similar professions or interests. The Bahamian host or host family may choose to take guests to a local theater performance, a Sunday church service, or invite them to a home-cooked Bahamian dinner. A wide variety of other activities may be included, depending on the interests of the visitor(s). Such opportunities substantially increase visitor appreciation and understanding of the culture they are visiting, and often bring about lasting friendships.

## DEVELOPMENTAL AND PROMOTIONAL MEASURES

Measures taken to develop and promote the cultural elements in tourism through special activities can be considered from several different points of view.

### Development of Methods and Techniques

The examples just listed involve specialized methods, techniques, and skills, all of which can be developed in their own right, without any direct reference to the promotion of tourism. Theaters, libraries, museums, and other such national institutions are not usually created with tourism in mind, but they are a great asset in attracting the interest of visitors. Museums and monuments, especially, are among the expected features of a tourist itinerary. These and other activities that can assist in the development of tourism may also be desirable elements in the cultural development of the nation. The methods and techniques associated with each of the examples listed constitute a whole field of specialized knowledge. As in most other fields of expert knowledge, information and ideas can be acquired from abroad and adapted to national situations.

Even when the necessary facilities exist, it may be desirable to adapt them to the needs of tourism. Special courses will often have to be created for foreigners. Multilingual guides must be trained. Captions and instructions in museums and cinemas should be provided in at least two languages. Special arrangements may be made for tourists to be given free or inexpensive access to institutions of interest to them. Life-seeing arrangements can also be made.

### Improvement in Educational and Cultural Content of Tourism

There is always room for improvement in what a tourist may learn abroad. This applies chiefly to books, pamphlets, films, and all types of illustrated information material. There is a great need for the services of experts in such matters, not only in assembling material on the history or geography of a country, but also in the attractive and accurate presentation of the material in several languages.

Consideration might be given to the development, on a regional basis, of "cultural identity card" systems, such as that operated successfully by the Council of Europe, which would introduce the tourist to experts in the fields of education, science, and the arts.

Heritage interpretation as an academic discipline can be very useful in tourism. Courses can be developed to enable local citizens to become authentic interpreters of their area's cultural, historical, and natural heritage. Achievement of such knowledge builds a person's ability to become a fully qualified interpreter. One example might be a 40-hour course entitled "Tourism — Keeper of the Culture." Those who successfully complete the course would be fully aware of their area's resources and thus would be capable of providing guide services or other services in which their knowledge can be useful. All forms of tourism, from group to individual, can, in various ways, benefit from the assistance of such informed, enthusiastic individuals.

Such an educational effort, when publicized, also creates a new self-awareness and pride in the community and a resulting improvement in the quality of life. Local art events, for example, can be organized to be attractive to the community and tourists alike. "Heritage Trails" or "Cultural Highways" can be designated. "Art in the Park" and festivals with various cultural themes help show off the area's resources and help to lengthen the season or fill in low spots in visitor demand.

From the tourist's standpoint, engaging in such culturally oriented activities builds a heightened appreciation and respect for the qualities and abilities of their hosts.

## Concentration of Activities Around Important Themes

In recent years, much has been done to link up tourist-related activities with themes or events of widespread interest, as in the case of festivals that bring together a variety of dramatic, musical, or cinema performances. An example is the successful Seattle Ring Festival of Wagner's music and the Quebec, Canada, Winter Festival. Another way is to focus attention on large exhibitions or fairs. Events such as these give an opportunity for the combined sponsorship of many different types of activity. International congresses or meetings can be held at the same time as the exhibitions or festivals. Youth festivals or "jamborees" can take place to coincide with important sporting events or large conventions.

Another way of stimulating interest is through "twinning," whereby towns, communities, or regions in different countries establish relations with each other and send delegations to events arranged by their partners.

Special attractions like EPCOT near Disney World in Florida bring together in one location large-scale cultural exhibits and entertainment of several countries. Another example is the Polynesian Cultural Center in Hawaii. A map of the center is shown in Figure 5.1.

## Uses of Mass Media

Mass media are always important in the development of tourism. Whether for use outside a country as a means of attracting tourists or to inform and entertain them after their arrival, there is a great need for high-quality products by journalists, film producers, and artists. In many countries there are some who already specialize in the field of tourism whose services can be used to advantage. The Society of American Travel Writers is one professional group dedicated to good travel journalism.

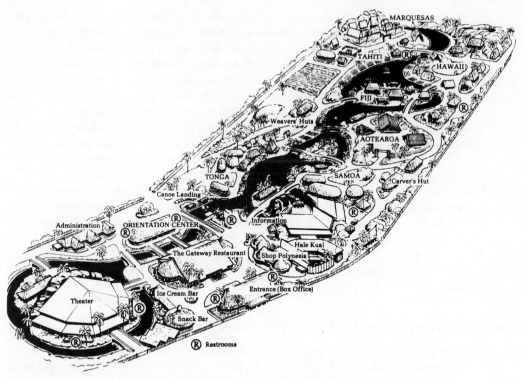

**Figure 5.1** *Polynesian Cultural Center, Hawaii.* There are many different villages at the Polynesian Cultural Center. Each is a combination of buildings, gardens, activities, and people as you would find them if you were to travel to the various island groups represented.

### *Development of Out-of-Season Tourism*

Educational and cultural activities are particularly well adapted to the "out-of-season" tourism development. International meetings and study courses do not depend on good weather and entertainment. Often their sponsors are glad to take advantage of off-season rates in hotels. Efforts should therefore be made to develop facilities and publicity to attract suitable activities and events. Theater tours are a good example.

## ANTHROPOGRAPHY (GEOGRAPHY OF HUMANKIND)

Anthropography is defined as the branch of anthropology that describes the varieties of humankind and its geographical distribution.

One of the most important motivations for travel is interest in the culture of other peoples. The Mexicans are not like the Swiss, and the Balinese are not like the Eskimos. Our natural curiosity about our world and its peoples constitutes one of the most powerful travel motivating influences. A travel agent or other travel counselor must be familiar with the basic differences in culture among the peoples of the world, where accessible examples of such cultures are located, and which of these cultures (or groups of culture) would be most interesting to a particular would-be traveler.

Most of the earth's 5 billion people are concentrated in a limited number of geographical areas. These population concentrations provide attractions in themselves. On the other hand, areas of the earth that are largely empty—such as Canada, parts of western United States, Siberia, Western China, Australia, most of Africa, and much of South America—have appeal because of the absence of humans. The landscape, with its towns and villages and rural, and perhaps nomadic, cultures, provides interesting contrasts to urban centers. Visits to primitive cultures are enriching and exciting travel experiences.

In the United States, such cultural groups as the Amish in Pennsylvania or the American Indian have tourist appeal.

## OTHER TOURIST APPEALS

Other representative expressions of a people provide powerful attractions for travel. Art, music, architecture, engineering achievements, and many other areas of activity have tourist appeal. See Figure 5.2.

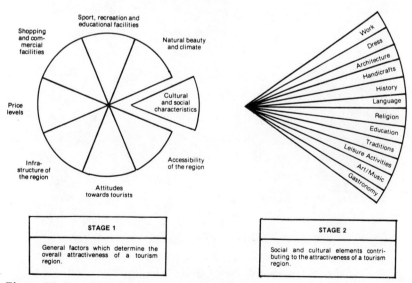

**Figure 5.2** Variables Influencing the Attractiveness of a Tourism Region. *Source:* J. R. Brent Ritchie and Michel Sins, "Culture as Determinant of the Attractiveness of a Tourism Region," *Annals of Tourism Research,* April–June 1978, p. 256.

*Fine Arts*

Such cultural media as painting, sculpture, graphic arts, architecture, and landscape architecture constitute an important motivation for travel. As a specific example, recall the beauty of art forms such as cloisonné or scroll paintings.

A recent trend in resort hotel operations has been the display of local art and craft objects within the hotel or in the immediate vicinity so that the guests may become acquainted with the art of the local people. These objects may be for sale and thus become valued souvenirs. Art festivals often include various types of fine arts together with other cultural expressions to make them more broadly appealing. There are many examples of these, such as the Edinburgh Festival in Scotland. This festival features not only displays of art, but also other forms of craft work, music, pageants, ceremonial military formations, and other cultural attractions.

Jazz, drifting down centuries-old streets, is everywhere in the Vieux Carre (old quarter) of New Orleans. The city where jazz was born has a long history of street entertainment, and these musicians carry on in that colorful tradition. (Photo courtesy of Louisiana Office of Tourism)

One of America's original contributions to the music of the world originated on Beale Street in Memphis. Blues Alley specializes in blues performances by a variety of entertainers. (Photo courtesy of Tennessee Tourist Development)

## Music and Dance

The musical expression and resources of a country are among its most appealing and enjoyable aspects. In fact, in some countries or states the music is a major source of enjoyment and satisfaction to visitors. Hawaii, Mexico, Haiti, Spain, various sections of the continental United States, and the Balkan states are examples.

Resort hotels, particularly, can bring to the guests opportunities for enjoyment of local music at its best. Evening entertainment programs, concerts, recordings, and sound reproduction systems all aid in presenting this aspect of the art of the country. Community concerts, parades, and welcoming ceremonies are appreciated by visitors. Phonograph or tape recordings that the visitor can purchase provide another effective means of keeping in touch with the culture of a particular area.

Ethnic dancing is another exciting and appealing aspect of a country's culture. The color, costumes, music, setting, and skill of forms and execution add to the appeal. Almost all countries have native or ethnic dancing. Local shows, nightclubs, and community programs present additional opportunities. Illustrations show a popular community festival scene and an example of ethnic dancers.

Notable examples of dance as a cultural expression are those of Polynesian dancers, the Ballet Folklorico of Mexico, the Russian ballet, folk dances of the

Eastern European countries, dances of many African nations, Thai dancing, the Kabuki dancers of Japan, and Philippine country dancing.

## *Handicraft*

To satisfy tourists, gifts and souvenirs offered for sale should be handcrafted or manufactured in the country or region where the purchase is made. There is much dissatisfaction in purchasing a craft article that you later discover was made in another country thousands of miles away. There is no substitute for genuineness. If the locally produced article is useful and appealing, it should be made available in conveniently located shops. A visit to shops where handicraft products for sale are actually being made is another effective form of guest entertainment.

The making of old-fashioned corn brooms absorbs the attention of these youngsters at the Henry Ford Museum, Dearborn, Michigan. (Photo courtesy of Michigan Travel Commission)

Visitors can observe the making of handcrafted quilts at the Ozark Folk Center. (Photo courtesy of the Arkansas Department of Parks and Tourism)

## *Industry and Business*

The industrial aspects of an area provide important motivation for travel. A large proportion of travelers, particularly international travelers, are intellectually curious about the economy of any state or country. They are interested in the country's industry, commerce, manufactured products, and economic base.

Industry tours are a good way to develop an interest in the culture of the area and provide a potential market for the product being made. Tourist organizations should encourage tours to factories or processing plants when such visits are appropriate and pleasant experiences. Lists of such industrial installations can be maintained by tourist promotional organizations, chambers of commerce, resort hotels, motels, restaurants, or other establishment or service organizations where tourist contacts are made.

Industrialists from one country are often interested in the industry of another. Group tours can be organized for manufacturers of a particular product who visit another country to see how the manufacture of that or a similar product is accomplished. Such visits are mutually beneficial as each country's representatives learn from the other.

Chambers of commerce or other business or industrial groups often conduct tours to become acquainted with markets and processors in other countries in an effort to develop more interest in their products and to increase sales in various market areas.

When visitors can watch this Miccosukee Indian woman making a
basket, they better appreciate its fine workmanship and
authenticity. (Photo courtesy of Florida Division of Tourism)

Business establishments, particularly retail stores, are of considerable interest to
visitors. Excellent examples are shopping centers near resort areas, where a wide
variety of stores is concentrated so that the visitor can readily find the products or
services desired.

Shopping is one of the most important elements in tourism. Attractiveness,
cleanliness, courtesy, and variety of products are among the most significant elements of the success of any shopping area. In fact, much goodwill can be created by
courteous and devoted store clerks who assist the visitor in finding just what is being
sought.

Probably the world's most notable example of businesses that cater to the
tourist is Hong Kong, where shopping and business activity are probably the most
important aspect of any visitor's experience.

### Agriculture

The agriculture of an area may be of interest to visitors. The type of farming
conducted — livestock, poultry, dairy, crops, vineyards and wine production, fresh
fruits and vegetables — is an interesting aspect of the culture.

Farmer's markets such as the well-known Los Angeles Farmer's Market or
roadside stands that offer local agriculture products are also an important part of

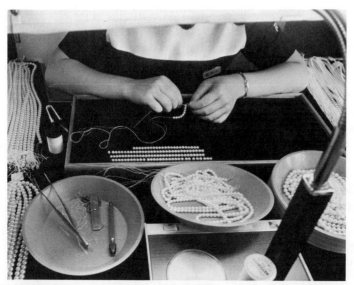

Skilled hands create genuine cultured pearl necklaces of great
beauty—a favorite souvenir or gift purchased by visitors to Japan.
(Photo courtesy of Japanese National Tourist Organization)

tourist services in many areas. This is particularly true of stands selling fresh fruits,
vegetables, honey, wine, cider and other drinks, and products from nearby farms
readily enjoyed by the traveler.

Exemplary agricultural systems provide a point of interest for farm groups who
may wish to visit a particular industry from another part of the country. Denmark,
with its outstanding pork industry, is of great interest to hog farmers in many parts of
the world.

Local tours should include agricultural developments and services so that visitors can see the agricultural products and operations within the country and perhaps
try some of the products. On the one-day tour of Oahu in Hawaii, visitors have a
chance to sample field-ripened pineapple at a stand adjacent to a great pineapple
plantation.

State and county fairs and livestock shows also have interesting tourist attractions.

## Education

Citizens of one country are concerned with education systems of another. The
college and university campuses of any country provide important attractions to
tourists. Many of these are beautifully landscaped and attractively situated for a
pleasant and enlightening visit. Well-known universities in England such as Oxford
or Cambridge are in themselves important tourist attractions.

The operation of high schools and grade schools as well as private schools and
other types of vocational training institutions are features of the culture of the area
that can be utilized to a considerable degree as attractions for visitors.

International education centers provide still another dimension of the relationship between tourism and education. Many universities conduct adult education programs within the university's continuing education service. Such educational opportunities attract learners from other states within their own country or from many countries around the world. This provides an incentive for travel. International conferences of business and industrial groups as well as scientific and educational organizations are often held on the campuses of colleges, universities, or other educational institutions.

Outstanding examples of this type of operation are the adult education centers similar to Kellogg Center at Michigan State University and the East-West Center at the University of Hawaii. These centers attract thousands of adults each year for continuing education courses, conferences, and meetings of an educational nature.

"Elderhostel" educational programs for senior citizens are held at many U.S. colleges and universities. These are short programs embracing a wide range of subject matter.

## Literature and Language

The literary achievements of a state or country, though having more limited appeal than some cultural aspects, still constitute a significant element of travel motivation. Books, magazines, newspapers, booklets, pamphlets, and other printed literary works are among the most important expressions of the culture of the country. Interestingly, the availability or absence of certain literature is indicative of the political system of the area. Consider the restriction on distribution of literature from various areas of the world practiced by the Soviet Union and in the Eastern European countries.

Libraries are favorite cultural institutions for the visitor. Many have well-appointed reading lounges and comfortable, attractive surroundings. Particularly on rainy days, the visitor can enjoy reading about the history, culture, arts, and folkways of the host area. Often guest entertainment programs will feature the reading of poetry or the discussion of various books or other literary works as a cultural enrichment opportunity for visitors.

A well-educated person is likely to speak or at least have studied more than one language. Interest in the language of another nation or state is a motivating force for travel. This is particularly true of students traveling to a particular area to practice the language and to become better acquainted with its colloquial usage.

Travel-study programs are particularly valuable learning experiences. Receiving instruction in a foreign language abroad might well be integrated into any comprehensive travel-study curriculum. Language study institutes flourish all over the world. They can be private or associated with universities. Some examples of the latter are the University of Geneva, Switzerland; University of Grenoble, France; and the University of California at Berkeley in the United States. Sophomore or Junior Year Abroad programs for college students provide excellent opportunities to learn a different language. Such programs are numerous in Europe and in other parts of the world. Elderhostel learning opportunities for senior citizens provide another example of travel-study in which a foreign language can be pursued.

Most travelers like to learn at least some of the language to use while they are in a foreign country. Usually, this is in the form of expressions related to ordering food in a restaurant or in talking with hotel or other tourism employees. Classes in language could be included in an entertainment or activities program within a tourist area.

## Science

The scientific activities of a country constitute an interest to visitors, particularly those in technical industries, education, or scientific research. Organizations responsible for tourist promotion can serve the scientific community by offering facilities for the exchange of scientific information, organization of scientific seminars, visits to scientific installations, and other activities that provide access to scientific information by visitors.

The most popular scientific appeals include museums of science and industry, planetariums, and visits to unusual scientific installations such as atomic power plants and space exploration centers. Zoos and aquariums are also popular.

An outstanding example is the John F. Kennedy Space Center in northeastern Florida. This installation attracts substantial numbers of visitors each year and provides educational and scientific knowledge for even the most unsophisticated visitor. Another is the Air and Space Museum in Washington, D.C.

Pathfinder, NASA's full-scale Space Shuttle orbiter mockup, bottom left, points the way to the new U.S. Space Camp Training Center. Built at a cost of $4.5 million, the 70,000-square-foot Training Center is part of The Space and Rocket Center complex—Earth's largest space museum. More than 23,000 young people have attended Space Camp programs, which have programs for youngsters 11 years old through adults. Space Camp and U.S. Space Academy programs for young people begin each spring and continue through the summer. The adult program is held each fall, and a special orientation program for teachers is conducted each summer. (Photo courtesy of the Space and Rocket Center, Huntsville, Alabama)

## Government

Systems of government vary throughout the world. Persons interested in political science and government find visits to centers of government, such as capitals, particularly valuable and highly motivating. Whenever a person visits another area, he or she is made aware of the type of government system in effect and notes the differences between this and the home country. Persons from Western countries are particularly aware of the differences between their form of government and that of Eastern Europe or the Soviet Union, for example. Probably the world's best example of this is the city of Berlin, which is divided between a Western democratic government and an Eastern totalitarian government.

Persons interested in politics and the ways in which other countries and areas solve their political problems represent another part of the market. Lawmakers often visit another state or country to observe the procedures developed to solve social or economic problems.

A visit to Washington, D.C., can show visitors the lawmaking process in the House of Representatives and in the Senate. Hearings on various proposed regulations or statutes are often open to visitors. As the center of the government of the United States, this city provides educational opportunities in many areas to both American and foreign travelers.

## Religion

Another motivation for travel through all of recorded history is the religious pilgrimage. Probably the best known are those to Mecca. Large numbers of people go to the headquarters of their church organizations and to areas well known in their religious literature. Often these are group trips, for example, a group of Protestants visiting magnificent churches and headquarters of various church denominations in different parts of the world. Similarly, missionaries travel with a religious mission. The large amount of travel to Israel is in part based on religious motivation, as are travels to the Catholic centers at Vatican City in Rome, Oberammergau, Lourdes, and Mexico City.

Visits to prominent houses of worship of all forms of religious doctrine are an important motivation for travel. Notre Dame cathedral in Paris, Saint Peter's basilica in Rome, and the sacred mosque at Mecca are examples.

## Food and Drink

Food and drink of a country are among its most important cultural expressions. The tourist enjoys native foods, particularly items of a local or ethnic nature. When traveling, trying out local dishes is part of the fun.

Restaurants and hotels can make a favorable impression on the tourist if they feature local dishes and also perhaps an explanation on the menu about what the dish consists of and how it is prepared. Of particular appeal is the type of restaurant in which the atmosphere is conducive to the type of food being served, such as seafood restaurants on the wharf.

The purchase of local food and drink is another source of tourist revenue. Advertising messages that include reference to local food are highly effective. The

San Jose Church in Old San Juan dates from 1532 and is the
second oldest church in the Western hemisphere. (Photo courtesy
of Puerto Rico Tourism News Bureau)

tourist considers eating and drinking important aspects of a vacation. How these
foods and drinks are prepared and presented are of great importance. Among the
happiest memories may be the experience of dining in a particularly attractive or
unusual eating place where local foods were prepared and served.

Encouragement from tourist organizations for restaurants and hotels to feature
local foods is highly recommended.

## History and Prehistory

The cultural heritage of an area is expressed in its historical resources. Some tourist
destination areas are devoted to history such as the Mackinaw City area of northern
Michigan, St. Augustine, Florida, the Alamo and San Juan Mission in San Antonio,
Texas, old gold mining tours in many Western states, Machu Picchu in Peru, and the
spectacular archeological find at Xian in east central China.

The preservation of history and the quality and management of museums is of
utmost importance for successful tourism. Becoming familiar with the history and
prehistory (archaeology) of an area can be one of the most compelling of all travel

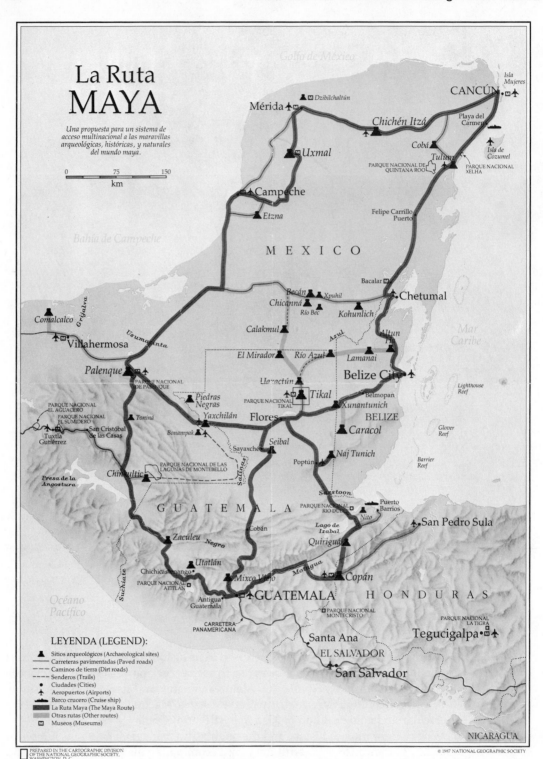

La Ruta
MAYA

Una propuesta para un sistema de
acceso multinacional a las maravillas
arqueológicas, históricas, y naturales
del mundo maya.

0        75        150
km

Golfo de México

Isla
Mujeres

CANCÚN

Dzibilchaltún

Mérida                    Chichén Itzá        Playa del
                                              Carmen

                                         Cobá        Isla de
                  Uxmal                              Cozumel
                                         Tulum
                              PARQUE NACIONAL DE    PARQUE NACIONAL
                              QUINTANA ROO          XELHA
        Campeche

        Etzna                      Felipe Carrillo
                                   Puerto

              M E X I C O

                                  Bacalar

                    Becán    Xpuhil          Chetumal
              Chicanná    Río Béc
                              Kohunlich
Comalcalco         Calakmul                  Altun
                                             Ha
                                                      Mar
              El Mirador    Río Azul    Lamanai        Caribe
Villahermosa
                                        Belize City
                       Uaxactún
Palenque                          Tikal        Lighthouse
PARQUE NACIONAL                                Reef
DE PALENQUE        Piedras    PARQUE NACIONAL
                  Negras      TIKAL        Belmopan
PARQUE NACIONAL        Yaxchilán              Xunantunich
EL AGUACERO        Toniná    Flores          BELIZE        Glover
PARQUE NACIONAL                                            Reef
EL SUMIDERO    San Cristóbal    Bonampak          Caracol
Tuxtla        de las Casas                              Barrier
Gutiérrez              Sayaxché                          Reef
                              Seibal
                  PARQUE NACIONAL DE LAS    Naj Tunich
Presa de la    Chinkultic  LAGUNAS DE MONTEBELLO
Angostura                              Poptún

              G U A T E M A L A
                              Sarstoon
                  PARQUE NACIONAL    Puerto
                  RÍO DULCE    Barrios
              Cobán        Nito
                        Lago de        San Pedro Sula
Océano    Zaculeu    Izabal    Quiriguá
Pacífico          Utatlán
       Chichicastenango              H O N D U R A S
       PARQUE NACIONAL    Mixco Viejo    Copán
       ATITLÁN
       Antigua    GUATEMALA        PARQUE NACIONAL    PARQUE NACIONAL
       Guatemala                   MONTECRISTO        LA TIGRA
              CARRETERA                              Tegucigalpa
              PANAMERICANA
                        Santa Ana
                        EL SALVADOR
                        San Salvador

LEYENDA (LEGEND):
▲  Sitios arqueológicos (Archaeological sites)
── Carreteras pavimentadas (Paved roads)
-- Caminos de tierra (Dirt roads)
- - Senderos (Trails)
●  Ciudades (Cities)
✈  Aeropuertos (Airports)
⛴  Barco crucero (Cruise ship)
▬  La Ruta Maya (The Maya Route)
▬  Otras rutas (Other routes)
Ⓜ  Museos (Museums)

                                                      NICARAGUA

PREPARED IN THE CARTOGRAPHIC DIVISION
OF THE NATIONAL GEOGRAPHIC SOCIETY,
WASHINGTON, D.C.                              © 1987 NATIONAL GEOGRAPHIC SOCIETY

motivations. One of the principal weaknesses observed in historical museums is that the explanations of the exhibits are provided in only one language. This is a serious limitation to many tourists' enjoyment of such historical exhibits.

The hours of operation of historical points of interest and museums are significant and should be arranged to provide access for visitors at convenient times. Admittance fees to museums and points of historical interest should be kept as low as possible to encourage maximum attendance. Promotion is necessary, and tourist contact organizations such as chambers of commerce, tourist information offices, hotels, resorts, restaurants, and other businesses should have available literature that describes the point of interest, hours, admittance fees, special events, and any other information needed by the tourist to visit this historical attraction.

Some notable examples of museums include the National Museum of Anthropology at Mexico City, the American Museum of Natural History of New York City, the various branches of the British Museum in London, the Hermitage in Leningrad, and the various museums of the Smithsonian in Washington, D.C.

Other types of historical preservation are national historic parks and monuments and national parks with a history or prehistory theme, such as Mesa Verde National Park, Colorado. Another are the "living history" farms in Iowa and Illinois.

Among the most outstanding innovations in the presentation of history are the "sound and light" programs found mainly in Europe, the Mediterranean countries, and Mexico. A series of loudspeakers, broadcasting recorded voices in several languages with sound effects, tell the history of an unusually significant structure or place. Varying lights intensify the effect and focus the attention of the audience on various parts of the location.

At the Forum in Rome, the history of Rome is presented at night in half a dozen languages. Visitors can hear the voices of the emperors and hear the crackling flames as Rome burns. At the pyramids of Teotihuacan, about 20 miles northeast of Mexico City, famous actors relate the history of the area in another sound and light presentation given in Spanish and English language versions. Egypt offers similar programs at its ancient monuments.

## SUMMARY

The cultural expressions of a people are of great interest to most travelers. These include fine arts, music and dance, handicrafts, food and drink, industry and busi-

**Figure 5.3** The Maya Route is a proposed system of paved roads, dirt roads, and trails connecting archeological sites of the magnificent culture shaped by people called the Maya. Between A.D. 250 and 900 "the Maya created one of the most distinguished civilizations of all antiquity" according to National Geographic author George Stuart. How the Maya raised their enormous pyramids and stone temples is one of the many mysteries confronting investigators. The Maya Route plan would also introduce visitors to Spanish Colonial architecture, marvelous tropical forests teeming with wildlife, miles of pristine beaches, excellent snorkeling, and villages of great charm. Preliminary work is now underway for creating and promoting this 4-nation eco-cultural tourism circuit. (Map courtesy of *National Geographic* magazine)

ness, agriculture, education, literature and language, science, government, religion, history, and prehistory. Tourists' experiences are enriched when they make a sincere effort to become better acquainted with local people.

Any country or area that seeks to attract tourists must plan and develop facilities and promote programs that invite access to such cultural expressions. A useful concept is "life-seeing tourism," a structured local program that arranges evening visits to local homes by tourists or, alternatively, a plan whereby interested tourists are accommodated for a few days in local homes.

Cultural interpretation in any area that hosts foreign tourists requires bilingual provisions. These include foreign language ability by guides, bilingual signs, labels, and literature.

Examination of the interrelationships of the cultural backgrounds of visitors and cultural expressions of the host society as provided by this chapter should provide useful guidance to hosts.

### About the Reading

In this section, the concept of "appropriate tourism" through heritage interpretation is outlined. Based on the application of heritage interpretation skills, appropriate tourism is proposed as an approach to aid in the perpetuation of an area's unique heritage. The writer gives examples of the empowerment of local hosts in facilitating heritage experiences for guests. Also discussed is the potential applicability of the appropriate tourism concept at all levels of tourism development.

An interesting focus on application possibilities in Hawaii, is given in an overview of the 1989 "think tank" on appropriate tourism in Honolulu. Preliminary principles of the appropriate tourism concept are listed, and future possibilities for concept development are discussed.

## READING 5-1

### Appropriate Tourism Through Heritage Interpretation

By Gabriel J. Cherem, Associate Professor, Heritage Interpretation
and Co-Director, Travel and Tourism
Department of Geography
Eastern Michigan University

### Introduction

There is growing interest throughout the world in the qualitative aspects of the tourism experience — expressed both on behalf of host populations, and on behalf of guest populations.

As significant symbolism in this regard, Frommer's (1988) *The New World of Travel* includes brilliant sections entitled "What's Wrong with Travel — and What We Can Do About It" and "Ethical Travel: Does Tourism Cause More Harm Than Good?" Frommer cites the seminal work of the Center for Responsible Tourism, and of the Ecumenical Coalition on Third World Tourism, in developing codes of ethics for tourists.

As a complement to the much-needed ethical preparation on the part of travelers, a philosophy of "appropriate tourism" planning and development is needed on the supply side of the tourism equation. The ethical and qualitative aspects of tourism development can help set the stage for both the behaviors and experiences of the guests.

### Appropriate Tourism

Eastern Michigan University's Travel and Tourism, and Historic Preservation, programs are developing the concept of "appropriate tourism." Appropriate tourism is tourism that actively aids in the perpetuation of an area's heritage — cultural, historical, and natural. It can be seen as tourism planning and development that springs from and emphasizes the heritage identity of an area (Cherem 1988a).

Indeed, in referring to the ideal, positive value of tourism (for small and medium-sized communities in Canada), Dalibard (1987) states: "The most significant reward is that the communities have retained and reinforced their identity, their sense of place."

A key feature of appropriate tourism is that it empowers local hosts to facilitate authentic heritage experiences for their guests. This empowerment is provided by a knowledge of the process and skills of heritage interpretation.

Appropriate tourism programs can be created at any level of tourism development — in areas where mass commercial tourism is well established, or in areas that are just beginning to develop their tourism potential. Hawaii is an example of the former; regional parks in France (Sax, 1986), the Navajo reservation in New Mexico (Robbins, 1988), and remote villages in Malaysia (Ashby, 1988) are examples of the latter.

Concerning the appropriate tourism concept, McLennan (1988) states:

> One principle that appeals to us is that it is desirable for representatives of the indigenous population to control, or at the very least, to have an equal voice in the planning of interpretive programs. The use of heritage should be as a conservation tool; it should not be exploitative or demeaning of the residents. Indigenous planners and participants can serve as the custodians of their culture, presenting authentic "heritage experiences" to guests, and training their youth to pridefully carry on these interpretive programs in the future.

Because every area on earth has its own unique heritage identity, appropriate tourism development for an area is based on the answers to the following questions:

1. What heritage experiences are available in this area that are not available anywhere else?
2. Specifically how should heritage interpretation of this area be implemented to empower local hosts to share these heritage experiences with visiting guests?

### Empowering Local Hosts

Appropriate tourism empowers local hosts to facilitate heritage experiences for their guests. The source of this empowerment lies in heritage interpretation training and planning.

The Interpret Hawaii program of Kapiolani Community College (1987) in Honolulu is a stellar example of the empowerment of local hosts in an area where mass commercial tourism is already well established:

> Interpret Hawaii serves Hawaii's people by making our community's heritage come to life. Visitor industry personnel, visitors and residents will find that our programs will be memorable experiences as they rediscover the beauty, history and mystery of our Island home.

> Hawaii No Ka Oi is a very special training program that provides hotel personnel, desk persons, activities coordinators, tour guides and museum personnel with an understanding of how to share the Hawaii experience. In addition to natural and cultural history, the trainees learn the skills of communication, self presentation, hospitality and coping with stress. Certified by the Hawaii Visitors Bureau, graduates of this 40-hour program receive the special "Warrior Pin," recognizing them as outstanding representatives of our island home. This is an important, exciting training program that will provide visitor industry personnel with concrete knowledge, skills and enthusiasm.

In a related development, the Waiaha Foundation in Hawaii is supporting a project called "Tourism, Keeper of the Culture" (State of Hawaii, 1987/88). Bobbee Mills and George Kanahele are instrumental in this program, which provides tourism industry employees with training in Hawaiian history, culture, and values. The employees learn how to use this information to build pride in Hawaiian heritage and to improve their guest relations and service skills.

Ashley (1988) writes of the efforts of Wilma Wood, the manager of an ecomuseum project in British Columbia, as she provides hospitality and interpretive techniques training to lumber workers, waitresses, and shopkeepers.

Gonsalves (1987), in a manual for Third World tourism, addresses the selection and training of local high school or university students as facilitators-interpreters for tours.

In speaking of the feelings of pride that tourism can bring to local hosts, Dalibard (1987) writes:

> The members of the community must want tourism not only because of the financial benefit it brings them but because they are proud of what they have and they want to share it. This approach to tourism might seem radical. It is, in fact, based on age-old human emotions and needs: pride and sharing. If tourism is approached from this point-of-view, the community will make the best use of its resources and offer visitors a meaningful and pleasant experience.

The traveler's perspective on the value of interacting with local hosts is well expressed by Frommer (1988) when he states, "Ultimately, the experienced traveler concludes that people are the highlight of any vacation trip and takes time to ensure that encounters with people will take place."

*Heritage Interpretation*

The role of heritage interpretation in empowering local hosts, and in facilitating heritage experiences, lies at the very core of appropriate tourism program development. We are increasingly aware that tourism is far more than an activity — it is an experience. More and more of today's tourists are demanding experiences that are *real*, authentic, and multidimensional.

Frommer (1988) writes:

After 30 years of writing standard guidebooks, I began to see that most of the vacation journeys undertaken by Americans were trivial and bland, devoid of important content, cheaply commercial, and unworthy of our better instincts and ideals. . . .

Those travels, for most Americans, consist almost entirely of "sight-seeing"—an activity as vapid as the words imply. We rove the world, in most cases, to look at lifeless physical structures of the sort already familiar from a thousand picture books and films. We gaze at the Eiffel Tower or the Golden Gate Bridge, enjoy a brief thrill of recognition, return home, and think we have travelled.

If sight-seeing can be viewed as a one-dimensional activity, then the heritage experiences provided by local hosts—empowered by interpretation skills—can be viewed as multidimensional and more meaningful.

Indeed, an excerpt from the classic definition of interpretation by Tilden (1977) from *Interpreting Our Heritage* reinforces this point. Interpretation is

. . . an activity which aims to reveal meanings and relationships through the use of original objects, by firsthand experiences, and by illustrative media. . . .

Ashley (1988) amplifies Tilden's definition by including "people" as well as "objects":

Interpreters have always realized that visitors to our sites are far more stimulated by their visit when they have been given the opportunity to interact with real objects or real people.

We have always understood that heritage experiences, whether they be natural or cultural, give tourists deep satisfaction when it helps them to understand their own world or the lives of other people.

It is significant to note that the process and scope of heritage interpretation have expanded dramatically in recent years.

Until the late 1970s, interpretation had traditionally occurred largely within the confines of historic sites, museums, and parks. The concept of interpretation as an "awakening giant" (Cherem, 1977)—applicable to a diverse array of settings and subject matters—is a relatively new development.

The elucidation of interpretation as a powerful process for leisure learning (Brown and Cherem, 1979) was followed by the development of the concept of community interpretation and tourism in 1980 (Brown, 1981; Cherem, 1988b). The latter conceptual development expanded the potential applications of interpretation to villages, towns, cities, and geographic regions throughout the world.

The evolving recognition that heritage interpretation has a major role to play in tourism (Cherem 1988a) was crucial to the creation of the appropriate tourism concept. In a statement of vision for the future, McLennan (1988) writes, "Perhaps it is not too optimistic to visualize the day when all major resort hotels employ a resident heritage interpretive planner."

Indeed, facilitated heritage experiences are becoming more common in hotels around the globe. The Regent Hotel in Auckland, New Zealand, has introduced a series of presentations for meetings and incentive tour groups on the history and culture of the country. Traditional music and dance of the native Maoris and a portrayal of New Zealand's gold rush are highlighted.

The Sheraton Hotels in Hawaii introduced a "Little Ones" weekly summer program in 1988. The program is open to guests' children, ages 5 to 12. A number of heritage experiences unique to Hawaii are featured, including hula lessons, lei making, shell crafts, Hawaiian folklore, and "the fine art of catching sand crabs."

*The Hawaiian Context*

A series of cooperative "interpretation institutes" have been initiated in Hawaii. The first institute, cosponsored by Kapiolani Community College and Eastern Michigan University, was held in the summer of 1987. It focused on the topic of "facilitating the visitor's experience in Hawaii," and stressed principles of interpretation, hospitality, experience planning (Kotler, 1984), and the experience industry (Ogilvy, 1986).

In early 1989, a second interpretation institute was held, to focus on the topic of "appropriate tourism through heritage interpretation." It took the form of a "think tank," with participants exploring the principles and potential applications of the appropriate tourism concept in Hawaii. The 1989 institute was jointly sponsored by Eastern Michigan University, Kapiolani Community College, and the University of Hawaii's Sea Grant Extension Service.

Hawaii presents an ideal setting to explore the applications of appropriate tourism. Its heritage identity includes a rich historical and contemporary mix of the Native Hawaiian, European, American, Japanese, Filipino, Chinese, Korean, and Samoan cultures. In addition Hawaii's being a very real meeting place of East and West, its volcanic origins, oceanographic setting, and flora and fauna are unique on earth. By some accounts, the natural ecosystem of Hawaii is more rare than even that of the famed Galapagos Islands.

From a tourism standpoint, Hawaii has been long established as a world-renowned tourist destination. Tabata (1988) states: "Visitor arrivals jumped from fewer than a million in the early 1960s to over 6 million last year — with projections of 10 million by the year 2000. Tourism is more important to the Hawaiian economy than the traditional mainstays of sugar, pineapple, and federal expenditures combined." In 1987, tourism contributed $5.6 billion to Hawaii's economy. Hawaii's guests come from virtually all over the world, including the rest of the United States, Canada, Europe, Latin America, and Japan.

At the same time, however, many aspects of Hawaii's unique cultural, historical, and natural heritage are not being addressed, nor interpreted, in the current scene of mass commercial "upscale" tourism. There is very real concern that important aspects of "Hawaiiana," the "Aloha Spirit," and other elements of Hawaii's heritage identity may soon be lost forever. Fueling this concern has been the high rate of investment in Hawaii by Japanese and other investors. For example, all but two hotels in Honolulu's Waikiki area are now owned by Japanese investors.

The 1989 "think tank" on appropriate tourism through heritage interpretation refined a preliminary list of principles of appropriate tourism. Participants then explored examples of potential application of each principle in Hawaii, and the group concurrently established a set of goals for the implementation of appropriate tourism programs in Hawaii. The potential application of the appropriate tourism concept on other Pacific islands was also addressed.

*Appropriate Tourism Principles*

The preliminary list of appropriate tourism principles generated to date is as follows:

1. Actively aids in the perpetuation of an area's heritage — cultural, historical, and natural
2. Emphasizes and showcases the heritage identity of an area as unique in the world
3. Is based on the application of heritage interpretation skills
4. Empowers local hosts to interpret their own heritage to guests
5. Builds the pride of local hosts in their heritage and improves their guest relations and service skills
6. Helps perpetuate local life-styles and values
7. Empowers local hosts to plan and facilitate authentic and meaningful multidimensional heritage experiences for their guests
8. Is "transcultural," in that both host and guest receive a mutually rewarding enrichment experience
9. Represents programming that can be implemented at any level of tourism development and in virtually any tourism setting
10. Represents a "value-added" approach to tourism, in that it increases the level and depth of genuine service provided to guests
11. Represents an approach to sustainable tourism development, because it respects and emphasizes an area's heritage and empowers its people as the true basis for tourism development

*Conclusion*

The concept of appropriate tourism development based on heritage interpretation skills is applicable in thousands of areas globally. The development of this concept provides a major opportunity for future tourism planning, development, and programming to become truly reflective of an area's heritage identity, its people, their values, and life-styles.

The potential for this concept to preserve and enhance the quality of tourism experiences is unlimited. To this end, the topic of appropriate tourism through heritage interpretation will become a major thematic emphasis of the Third World Congress on Heritage Presentation and Interpretation, slated for Honolulu in 1991. Sponsored jointly by units of Eastern Michigan University and units of the University of Hawaii, the Congress will provide a global forum for developments, directions, and opportunities for the growth of truly appropriate and sustainable tourism experiences.

*References*

Ashby, Phyllis. "42 Handshakes in Borneo." *The Christian Science Monitor*, January 11, 1988.

Ashley, Susan. "Tourism and the 'Heritage Experience'." *Interpscan: Interpretation Canada Journal*, Vol. 16, no. 2 (Summer 1988).

Brown, Barbara. "Community Interpretation in Chelsea." *The Historical Society of Michigan Newsletter*, Vol. 7, no. 2 (July–August 1981).

Brown, Barbara, and Gabriel J. Cherem. "Interpretation: A 'Brain-Compatible' Way to Learn." *Journal of Interpretation,* Vol. 4, no. 2 (November 1979).

Cherem, Gabriel J. "The Professional Interpretor: Agent for an Awakening Giant." *Journal of Interpretation,* Vol. 2, no. 1 (August 1977).

Cherem, Gabriel J. "Interpretation as the Vortex: Tourism Based on Heritage Experiences." *Proceedings of the Interpretation Canada National Conference.* Ottawa, Ontario (April 1988a).

Cherem, Gabriel J. "Community Interpretation and Tourism." Presented at the Second World Congress on Heritage Presentation and Interpretation. Warwick, England (August–September 1988b).

Dalibard, Jacques. "What do Tourists Want?" *Canadian Heritage,* Vol. 13, no. 2 (May–June 1987).

Frommer, Arthur. *The New World of Travel.* New York: Prentice-Hall, 1988.

Gonsalves, Paul S. *Alternative Tourism.* Equations, Equitable Tourism Options, Bangalore, India, 1987.

Kapiolani Community College. One-page promotional literature describing Interpret Hawaii program, 1987.

Kotler, Philip " 'Dream Vacations': The Booming Market for Designed Experiences." *The Futurist* (October 1984).

McLennan, Marshall S. "Heritage Interpretation Education at Eastern Michigan University: Evolving Conceptual Parameters." Presented at the Second World Congress on Heritage Presentation and Interpretation. Warwick, England (August–September 1988).

Ogilvy, James. "Experience Industry." *American Demographics* (December 1986).

Robbins, Catherine C. "In Navajo Country, Train Passengers Hear Insider's View of Indian Culture." *The New York Times* (April 1988).

Sax, Joseph L. "In Search of Past Harmony." *Natural History Magazine,* 1986.

State of Hawaii *i ka po'okela (toward excellence).* Tourism Training Council, Department of Labor and Industrial Relations, Vol. 1, no. 6. (December 1987–January 1988).

Tabata, Raymond S. "Implications of Special Interest Tourism for Interpretation and Resource Conservation." *Proceedings of the Interpretation Canada National Conference.* Ottawa, Ontario (April 1988).

Tilden, Freeman. *Interpreting Our Heritage.* Chapel Hill, N.C.: University of North Carolina Press, 1977.

## *Key Concepts*

achievements
agriculture
appreciation
appropriate tourism
artistic activity
attractiveness
communication
cultural attractions
cultural identity card
cultural tourism
education
festivals
fine arts

food and drink
government
handicraft
heritage interpretation
history and prehistory
industry and business
international travel
learning
life-seeing tourism
literature and language
multilingual guides and signs
music and dance
peace

recognition                    sound and light programs
religion                       twinning principle
research                       understanding
science                        ways of life and thought


## For Review and Discussion

1. Evaluate culture as a travel motivator.
2. Give an example of a cultural experience that would be most satisfying to a visitor in a country much different from his or her own.
3. Create a life-seeing tourism program in a familiar community.
4. What type of life-seeing experience would you particularly enjoy?
5. How much cultural difference can most tourists tolerate? Give examples.
6. Identify some of the rewards that international travel can bring to a perceptive, sensitive traveler.
7. For what reasons did the Minister of Tourism for the Bahamas promote their People-to-People Program?
8. Referring to the previous question, identify some other countries where a similar program would be equally successful.
9. A philosopher states that culture is what we know. Research changes our viewpoint. Thus, new discoveries make us change. Do you agree?
10. Does your community possess some distinctive cultural attraction?
11. Can you apply the concept of "appropriate tourism" to any tourist destination area? Give examples.
12. Explain the benefits tourists would enjoy if they participated in a heritage experience led by a graduate of a heritage interpretation training program of excellent quality.


## Case Problems

1. An attractive lakeside community of 5000 persons is presently a popular tourist center, primarily due to its appeal to sports enthusiasts and its proximity to a magnificent state park. However, tourist expenditures are low due principally to the lack of entertainment in the community. The movie theater closed three years ago, and there is virtually no entertainment except that to be found in a couple of beer taverns. The town and surrounding countryside are rich in history, but the only museum is a small one in the front part of a bar. How could a museum and other entertainment be provided?
2. As the director of an area tourism organization, you have been approached by a fine arts group to consider the feasibility of promoting a Shakespearian Festival in your community similar to the long-established festival at Stratford, Ontario, Canada. What factors would you consider in evaluating this request, and how would you work with your state and national tourism organizations to determine how this cultural event could be publicized?

## Selected References

Boniface, Brian G., and Christopher P. Cooper. *The Geography of Travel and Tourism.* London: Heinemann, 1987.

Buck, Roy C. "Making Good Business Better: A Second Look at Staged Tourist Attractions." *Journal of Travel Research,* Vol. 15, no. 3 (Winter 1977), pp. 30–32.

Cohen, Erik, and Robert L. Cooper. "Language and Tourism." *Annals of Tourism Research,* Vol. 13, no. 4 (1986), pp. 533–564.

Dernoi, Louis A. "Farm Tourism in Europe." *Tourism Management,* Vol. 4, no. 3 (September 1983), pp. 155–166.

Farrell, Bryan H. *Hawaii, the Legend That Sells.* Honolulu: University Press of Hawaii, 1982.

Frater, Julia M. "Farm Tourism in England." *Tourism Management,* Vol. 4, no. 3 (September 1983), pp. 167–179.

Graburn, Nelson H. H. "The Anthropology of Tourism." *Annals of Tourism Research,* Vol. 10, no. 1 (1983), pp. 9–33. Special Issue on the Anthropology of Tourism.

Graburn, Nelson H. H. *Ethnic and Tourist Arts.* Berkeley: University of California Press, 1976.

Haukeland, Jan Vidar. "Sociocultural Impacts of Tourism in Scandinavia." *Tourism Management,* Vol. 5, no. 3 (September 1984), pp. 207–214.

Hughes, Howard L. "Tourism and the Arts." *Tourism Management,* Vol. 10, no. 2 (June 1989), pp. 97–99.

International Association of Scientific Experts in Tourism. *Tourism and the Architectural Heritage—Cultural, Legal, Economic and Marketing Aspects.* St. Gallen, Switzerland: The Association, 1984.

Kemper, Robert V., John M. Roberts, and R. Swain Goodwin. "Tourism as a Cultural Domain: The Case of Taos, New Mexico." *Annals of Tourism Research,* Vol. 10, no. 1 (1983), pp. 149–171. Special Issue on the Anthropology of Tourism.

Lange, Frederick W. "The Impact of Tourism on Cultural Patrimony: A Costa Rican Example." *Annals of Tourism Research,* Vol. 7, no. 1 (1980), pp. 56–68. Special Anthropological Perspective Issue.

Lew, Alan A. "Authenticity and Sense of Place in the Tourism Development Experience of Older Retail Districts." *Journal of Travel Research,* Vol. 27, no. 4 (Summer 1989), pp. 15–22.

Lundberg, Donald E., and Carolyn B. Lundberg. *International Travel and Tourism.* New York: John Wiley, 1984.

Moscarfdo, Gianna M., and Phillip L. Pearce. "Historic Theme Parks: An Australian Experience in Authenticity." *Annals of Tourism Research,* Vol. 13, no. 3 (1986), pp. 467–479.

Ritchie, J. R., and Michel Sins. "Culture as Determinant of the Attractiveness of a Tourism Region." *Annals of Tourism Research,* Vol. 5, no. 2 (April–June 1978), pp. 252–267.

Smith, Valene L. "Anthropology and Tourism: A Science-Industry Evaluation." *Annals of Tourism Research,* Vol. 7, no. 1 (1980), pp. 13–33. Special Anthropological Perspectives Issue.

Smith, Valene L. *Hosts and Guests: The Anthropology of Tourism.* Philadelphia: University of Pennsylvania Press, 1989.

Stuart, George E. and Gene S. Stuart. *The Mysterious Maya.* Washington, D.C.: National Geographic Society, 1977.

Tighe, Anthony J. "The Arts/Tourism Partnership." *Journal of Travel Research,* Vol. 24, no. 3 (Winter 1986), pp. 2–5.

# CHAPTER 6

# Sociology of Tourism

## LEARNING OBJECTIVES

- Appreciate the inordinate social impact that travel experiences make on the individual, the family or group, and society as a whole—especially the host society.
- Recognize that a country's indigenous population may resent the presence of visitors, especially in large numbers. Also recognize that the influence of these visitors may be considered detrimental—both socially and economically.
- Discover that travel patterns change with changing life characteristics and social class.
- Become familiar with the concept of social tourism and its importance in various countries.
- Perceive that there are four extremes relating to the travel preferences of international tourists. Also, recognize that a sociologist has identified a typology of four tourist roles in international tourism.

Sociology is the science of society, social institutions, and social relationships. Visitors to a community or area create social relationships that typically differ greatly from the affiliations among the indigenous population.

In this chapter we shall identify and evaluate tourist-host relationships and then prescribe methods of managing these to create significant advantages for both groups. The ultimate effects of travel experiences on the population in areas of origin as well as in places of destination should determine to what extent societies encourage or discourage tourism.

## EFFECTS ON THE INDIVIDUAL

Someone who travels, particularly to a strange location, finds an unfamiliar environment not only geographically but personally, socially, and culturally. Thus, the traveler faces problems for which a solution must be found if the trip is to be fully enjoyable and rewarding. Travelers must manage their resources of money and time in situations much different from those at home. They also must manage their social interactions and social relations to obtain sustenance, shelter, and other needs and possibly to find companionship. Determining the extent of the "cultural distance" they may wish to maintain results in decisions as to just *how* unfamiliar the traveler wants his or her environment away from home base to be. People who travel do so with different degrees of contact with the new cultures in which they may find themselves. Life-seeing tourism, for example, is a structured method for those who wish deeper immersion in local ways of life to acquire such enrichment. Some travelers prefer a more selective contact experience as might be arranged by a tour company. Tours designed around cultural subjects and experiences such as an anthropological study tour or participation in an arts and crafts festival are examples. Regardless of the degree of local participation, the individual traveler must at least superficially study the country to be visited and reach some level of decision on how these problems in environmental differences are to be resolved. Advance preparation is an intelligent approach.

Travel experiences have a profound effect on the traveler as well as on society, as travel experiences often are among the most outstanding memories in the traveler's life.

## EFFECTS ON THE FAMILY

As a family is growing and the children are maturing, the trips taken as a family are highlights of any year. The excitement of preparation and anticipation and the actual travel experience are memorable occasions of family life. Travels with a measure of

Ten miles of beach and almost 12 miles of paved bicycle paths are ideal for family cycling on Kiawah Island, South Carolina. (Photo courtesy of Kiawah Island)

Snowmass is not only a place to ski, but a resort for family fun. In addition to downhill skiing there is cross-country skiing, dog sled rides, and swimming in heated pools. (Photo by Team Russell, courtesy of Snowmass Resort Association)

adventure are likely to be the most memorable. Family travel may also be educational. The more purposeful and educational a trip becomes, the more beneficial it is. Study before taking the trip and expert travel counseling greatly add to a maximization of the trip's benefits.

## EFFECTS ON SOCIETY

Travel has a significant influence on national understanding and appreciation of other people. Government policies in progressive and enlightened nations encourage travel, particularly domestic travel, as a means of acquainting citizens with other parts of their country and building appreciation for the homeland.

The presence of visitors in a country affects the living patterns of indigenous peoples. The way visitors conduct themselves and their personal relationships with citizens of the host country often have a profound effect on the mode of life and attitudes of local people. Probably the most pronounced effects of this phenomenon are noted when visitors from North America or Western Europe travel in an emerging country that has a primitive culture or a culture characterized by a low (economic) standard of living and an unsophisticated population.

Conversely the visitor, too, is influenced by the contrast in culture. Generally, however, this brings about an increased appreciation for qualities of life in the society visited that may not be present at home.

A favorable situation exists when visitors and those of the host country mingle socially and become better acquainted. This greatly increases the awareness of each other's character and qualities, building appreciation and respect in both groups.

## Tourism and Crime

Unfortunately, tourists can be easy prey for criminals. Tourists do not know about dangerous areas or local situations in which they might be very vulnerable to violent crimes. They become easy marks for robbers and other offenders as they are readily identified and are usually not very well equipped to ward off an attack.

Sometimes popular tourist attractions such as parks or beaches are within walking distance from hotel areas. However, a walking tour from the hotel may bring the tourist into a high-crime area lying directly in the path taken to reach this attraction. If such high-crime areas exist, active efforts to inform visitors and guests must be made. Hotels and others that publish maps of walking tours should route such tours into safe areas only. Also, they should warn guests of the danger that could arise if the visitor undertakes certain activities.

Crimes against tourists result in bad publicity and create a negative image in the minds of prospective visitors. So, tour companies tend to avoid destinations that have the reputation for crimes against tourists. Eventually, no matter how much effort is applied to publicize the area's benefits and visitor rewards, decreasing popularity will result in failure.

Pizam, Reichel, and Shieh found that tourism expenditures had a negligible effect on crime.[1] However, they suggested that tourism could be considered a potential determinant of crime, negatively affecting the quality of the environment. The tourist industry cannot be held responsible for the occurrence of crime. But one must be aware that tourists are a potential target of crime. Protecting them from offenders is essential to the survival and growth of the industry.

## Resentments

Resentment by local people toward the tourist can be generated by the apparent gap in economic circumstances, behavioral patterns, appearance, and economic effects. Resentment of visitors is not uncommon in areas where there is conflict of interests because of tourists. For example, in North America, local people may resent visiting sports enthusiasts because they are "shooting our deer" or "catching our fish." The demand for goods by tourists may tend to increase prices and cause bad feelings.

Another form of resentment may result in a feeling of inferiority among indigenous groups because of unfavorable contrasts with foreign visitors. Local persons employed in the service industries catering to visitors may be better paid and, thus, exhibit feelings of superiority toward their less fortunate fellow citizens. This creates a poor attitude toward the entire visitor industry.

[1] Abraham Pizam, Arie Reichel, and Chia Fian Shieh, "Tourism and Crime: Is There a Relationship?" *Journal of Travel Research,* Vol. 20, no. 3 (Winter 1982), pp. 7–10.

Financial dislocations can also occur. While a tourist may give a young bellhop a dollar tip for delivering bags, the bellhop's father may be working out in the fields as a farm laborer for a total daily wage of only a dollar or a dollar and a half.

Sensitive tourists become aware of another society's ways of life during a visit. For example, tourists might be interested in observing how different societies find solutions to common problems. An example of this is "welfare square" in Salt Lake City, Utah, where members of the Mormon Church work to recondition used clothes and other necessities of life for use by less fortunate members of the church. Publicly financed welfare is not welcome; they prefer to help each other.

As a rule, both hosts and guests in any society can learn from each other. Beneficial social contact and planned visits to observe local life and culture do much to build appreciation for the indigenous culture. At the same time, the visitors' interest in their ways of life increases the local people's respect for these visitors and gives them a feeling of pride in their own accomplishments.

Tourism, especially in-tourism, often facilitates a transition from rigid authoritarian social structure to one that is more sensitive to the individual's needs. When societies are "closed" from outside influences, they tend to become rigid. By encouraging visitors, this policy is changed to a more moderate one, for the benefit of hosts and guests.

The preservation of wildlife sanctuaries and parks as well as national monuments and other cultural resources is often encouraged when tourism begins to be a force in the society.

One-to-one interaction between hosts and guests can break down stereotypes, or the act of categorizing groups of people based upon a single dimension. By "labeling" people, often erroneously, individualism is lost. When a visitor gets to know people personally and is aware of their problems, hopes, and ways in which they are making life more pleasant, this visitor becomes much more sensitive to the universality of humankind. It is much easier to distrust and dislike indistinguishable groups of people than individuals one has come to know personally.

Some problems are often rooted in economic problems, such as unemployment or underemployment. The economic contributions of tourism can help to moderate such social difficulties.

Negative social effects on a host society have been identified as follows:

1. Introduction of undesirable activities such as gambling, prostitution, drunkenness, and other excesses
2. The so-called "demonstration effect" of local people wanting the same luxuries and imported goods as those indulged in by tourists
3. Racial tension, particularly where there are very obvious racial differences between tourists and their hosts
4. Development of a servile attitude on the part of tourist business employees
5. "Trinketization" of crafts and art to produce volumes of souvenirs for the tourist trade
6. Standardization of employee roles such as the international waiter—same type of individual in every country
7. Loss of cultural pride, if the culture is viewed by the visitor as a quaint custom or as entertainment

8. Too rapid change in local ways of life due to being overwhelmed by too many tourists
9. Disproportionate numbers of workers in low-paid, menial jobs characteristic of much hotel and restaurant employment

Many, if not all these negative effects can be moderated or eliminated by intelligent planning and progressive management methods. Tourism can be developed in ways that will not impose such a heavy social cost. Strict control of land use by zoning and building codes, enlightened policies on the part of the minister of tourism or similar official organization, proper phasing of supply components such as infrastructure and superstructure to match supply with demand for orderly development are some of the measures needed. Education and good public relations programs can accomplish much. Enforcing proper standards of quality in the marketing of local arts and crafts can actually enhance and "rescue" such skills from oblivion. As cited in the book *Hosts and Guests,*[2] the creative skills of America's Indians of the Southwest were kept alive, enhanced, encouraged, and ultimately expanded to provide tourists with authentic Indian rugs and turquoise jewelry particularly, but other crafts as well. The Fred Harvey Company, which still bears his name, is credited with encouraging Indians to continue these attractive crafts so that he could market them in his hotels, restaurants, and gift shops.

## Changing Population and Travel Interests

People change, group attitudes change, and populations change. All these factors affect travel interests. Travel interests also change. Some countries grow in travel popularity; others wane. World events tend to focus public attention on particular countries or regions of the world. The emergence of Japan and Korea as travel destinations following World War II and the Korean War and interest in visiting the Caribbean area, as well as Israel, Spain, Morocco, and East Africa are examples. Currently, travel to the People's Republic of China and Australia is of great interest. There is an old saying among travel promotors that "mass follows class." This has been proven beyond a doubt. Travel page publicity concerning prominent persons visiting a particular area inevitably produces a growth of interest in the area and subsequent increases in demand for travel to such well-publicized areas.

The growth of communication systems, particularly network and cable television, has broadened the scope of peoples' interests in other lands and other peoples. To be able to see, as well as hear, has a powerful impact on the viewer's mind and provides acquaintanceship with conditions in another country that may develop desire for a visit. As communications resources grow, awareness and interest also grow.

## LIFE CHARACTERISTICS AND TRAVEL

Rising standards of living, changes in the population age composition, the increasing levels of educational attainment, better communication, increased social conscious-

---

[2] Valene L. Smith (Ed.) *Hosts and Guests,* University of Pennsylvania Press, 1977, p. 176.

ness of people relating to the welfare and activities of other people throughout the world, and the psychological shrinking of the world by the jet plane have combined to produce an interest among nations in all other nations.

## Travel Patterns Related to Age and Residence

With age (late sixties and upward) the traveler may become more passive. Family recreation patterns are associated with life stages of the family. The presence of young children tends to reduce the number of trips taken, whereas married couples with no children are among the best travel prospects. As the children mature, however, families increase their travel activities, and families with children between the ages of 15 and 17 have a much higher family travel pattern than do those with

Motorcoach tours have the advantage allowing passengers to see the countryside without the responsibility of driving. Today's motorcoaches have restrooms, air conditioning, reclining seats, and large tinted windows to ensure comfortable traveling. (Photo courtesy of National Tour Association)

younger children. As the children grow up and leave home, the married couple (again without children) renews interest in travel. Also, couples in this life stage are more likely to have more discretionary income and are financially able to afford more travel. Persons living in urban centers are more travel inclined than are those in rural areas. Chapter 12, "The Consumer Market," examines these trends in some detail.

## Income and Social Class

Income and social class have an influence on travel. Wealthy persons and persons in higher social classes travel considerably. A glance at the society pages of any North American newspaper will substantiate that those in a high social status customarily travel south in the winter and north in the summer, as well as to overseas destinations.

The people at lower income and occupational levels tend to do the least traveling. But as their standards of living rise, democratization of travel should be much more widespread.

## Travel and the Handicapped

In the United States alone there are about 37 million physically handicapped people —more than the total population of Canada. This group constitutes an excellent potential market for travel if the facilities and arrangements are suitable for their use and enjoyment. Woodside and Etzel made a study of the degree to which physical and mental conditions restricted travel activities by households and how households with one or more handicapped persons were likely to adjust their vacation travel behavior.[3]

Findings in Table 6.1 indicate that many of the physical or mental conditions that limited travel were unobservable (such as heart condition or diabetes) by other travelers or by employees of tourist facilities. But this high percentage of disabled persons creates a substantial potential for emergency situations, and the planning and management of travel equipment and facilities must aim for a major reduction or elimination of such possibilities.

The effect of the presence of handicapped persons in a family on lengths of stays is summarized in Table 6.2. The number of nights away from home differed considerably between those traveling with handicapped persons and those without handicapped persons.

Many households reported little difficulty in using accommodations due to careful planning before making the trip. The majority of difficulties encountered seemed to be at recreational facilities. However, as shown in the Winter Park, Colorado, photo the handicapped can participate in difficult recreation activities. Winter Park is famous for its handicapped and blind skier programs. Over 250 handicapped competitors of all ages and disabilities participate in the annual Handicap National Championships.

---

[3] Arch G. Woodside and Michael J. Etzel, "Impact of Physical and Mental Handicaps on Vacation Travel Behavior," *Journal of Travel Research*, Vol. 18, no. 3 (Winter 1980), pp. 9–11.

A handicapped skier participating in the Handicap National Championships at Winter Park, Colorado. (Photo courtesy of Colorado Ski Country USA)

**Table 6.1** Physical or Mental Conditions Limiting Travel

| Condition | Number of Conditions | Percentage of Respondents |
|---|---|---|
| Heart condition | 20 | 33% |
| Crutches | 6 | 10 |
| Old age | 5 | 8 |
| Wheelchair | 3 | 5 |
| Stroke victim | 3 | 5 |
| Recent major surgery | 3 | 5 |
| Diabetes | 3 | 5 |
| Leg braces | 2 | 3 |
| Blindness | 2 | 3 |
| Other[a] | 15 | 23 |
| Total | 62 | 100% (n = 60) |

[a] For example, phobia of mountains, mental retardation, pregnancy, bad leg, dizziness, sprained back, flu, and stomach virus.

**Table 6.2** Number of Nights away from Home (as a percentage of total)

|  | Travel Parties | |
| Nights | With Handicapped Persons | Without Handicapped Persons |
| --- | --- | --- |
| 1–3 | 37% | 42% |
| 4–6 | 24 | 31 |
| 7–9 | 15 | 15 |
| 10–12 | 5 | 5 |
| 13–15 | 7 | 3 |
| 16 or more | 12 | 4 |
| Number of respondents | 60 | 530 |

Substantial improvements have been made by industry to serve this segment of the market. The airlines make special efforts to serve the handicapped, and there are now travel agents and tour companies specializing in the handicapped market. Architects are also designing hotel rooms with wide doors and other features to serve handicapped guests better.

# EMERGENCE OF GROUP TRAVEL PATTERNS

## Travel Clubs

These are groups, sometimes with a common interest (if only in travel), that have formed travel organizations for their mutual benefit. For example, some purchase an aircraft and then arrange trips for their members. Others join international membership clubs such as Club Méditerranée, which owns resort properties in many countries and provides package-type holidays at usually modest cost.

## Low-Priced Group Travel

Many tour companies cater to common interest groups such as the members of a religious group or professional or work group. A tour is arranged, often at reasonable cost, and is promoted to members of the group.

## Public Carrier Group Rates and Arrangements

Airlines and other public carriers make special rates available for groups — a common number is 15 at discounted rates. A free ticket is issued to the group's escort or leader. Chartering all or part of a public transportation vehicle, aircraft, or ship is also a special effort on the part of the carrier to accommodate travel groups.

## Incentive Tours

One of the fastest-growing group arrangements is that of incentive tours provided by a company to members and their spouses who are successful in achieving some objective, usually a sales goal. At the destination, the group is sometimes asked to review new products and receive some company indoctrination.

## Special Interest Tours

Special interest group travel is another segment growing in importance. Tours are arranged for those interested in agriculture, archaeology, architecture, art, bird watching, business, industry, castles and palaces, ethnic studies, fall foliage, festivals, fishing, hunting, flower arranging, gardening, gems and minerals, music, golf, history, literature, nature, opera, photography, professional interests, psychic research, safaris, skiing, skin diving, social studies, sports, study, theater, and wine, to name a few examples.

Social and fraternal organizations also are traveling more in groups. Some private clubs are taking group trips. Some are extensive trips around the world or trips lasting up to 60 days. Women's groups, social groups, youth groups, alumni, and professional societies commonly take extended trips together as a group. Preconvention and postconvention trips are also popular.

# SOCIAL (SUBSIDIZED) TOURISM

Although there is as yet no agreed definition of social tourism there has been considerable study of the question. Dr. W. Hunziker at the Second Congress of Social Tourism held at Vienna and Salzburg in 1959 proposed the following definition: "Social tourism is a type of tourism practiced by low income groups, and which is rendered possible and facilitated by entirely separate and therefore easily recognizable services." Another definition, that of M. Andre Poplimont, is as follows: "Social tourism is a type of tourism practiced by those who would not be able to meet the cost without social intervention, that is, without the assistance of an association to which the individual belongs."

From these definitions and from the reports of the three International Congresses on Social Tourism, it is clear that certain elements may be described. First is the idea of "limited means." Second, social tourism is subsidized by the states, local authorities, employers, trade unions, clubs, or other associations to which the worker belongs. Third, it involves travel outside the normal place of residence, preferably to a different environment that is usually within their own country or sometimes to a country nearby.

## Holidays with Pay

Paid holidays are now established all over the world, and in most countries a minimum duration (one, two, or three weeks) is specified either by law or by collective agreement. Some, however, consider this institution only a first stage, and believe that attention should now be turned to the way in which these holidays are used. One of the great subjects of discussion by twentieth-century sociologists is the use of the increased leisure time now available to workers and the cultural and educational development that such leisure time makes possible.

Large numbers of workers are obliged to spend their holidays at home, partly because of their lack of means or tourist experience and partly because of lack of information, transport difficulties, or shortage of suitable accommodation. Organized social tourism, if efficiently managed, can overcome most of these problems: finance through subsidies and savings schemes, experience and information through contacts elsewhere in the country concerned or abroad, transport problems through package deals with carriers, and accommodation through contracts with resorts. Thus organizations can bring tourism within the reach of many who would otherwise be unable to travel. There will be some, however, who for reasons of age, health, family responsibility, or disinclination are unwilling to join in such holidays even when all arrangements are made for them.

## Determination of Needs

Some countries carry out research in this field. In Belgium it was discovered that almost 60 percent of the respondents to an inquiry preferred a continuous stay to moving from place to place, but this preference was more marked among older than younger people. In the Netherlands, another inquiry revealed that about a million holiday makers preferred not to rely on the hospitality of relatives if other facilities within their means were provided. It was evident that existing facilities of this kind were inadequate.

It was also found that the tendency to take holidays away from home was increasing and that more attention should be given to the educational and cultural aspects of tourism. Studies in France and Italy have found orders of preference between the countryside, the seaside, the mountains, health resorts, and other places, and in Sweden and Italy, inquiries have been carried out into the types of accommodations favored.

## Examples of Social Tourism

Leysin, in Switzerland, is one of the best known examples of holiday centers for social tourism. Originally a famous health resort, advances in medicine meant that its clientele would gradually diminish, but with the cooperation of certain organizations, including the Caisse Suisse de Voyage, the resort was adapted to attract a new type of tourist. A small golf course, a swimming pool, tennis courts, and arrangements for skiing were established, and sanatoria and hotels were converted to meet the new demands. A publicity campaign was begun, and in its first year over 2000 tourists arrived and spent more than 50,000 bed-nights in the resort.

Camping and staying at hostels are popular with younger tourists and are also used by families. In recent years there has been a considerable development of caravan camps, particularly in Great Britain. Camping has the advantage of being one of the least expensive forms of holiday and makes possible more mobility. Financial aid is given to camps by the state in France and other countries. In Greece, camps are operated by some large industrial firms for the benefit of their employees, and in most countries, they are run by camping clubs and youth associations.

Table 6.3 illustrates ways in which social tourism is practiced.

## Provision of Information

In the development of social tourism, other problems arise, but these are largely common to tourism in general. The provision of information, however, deserves brief mention here, as many of the beneficiaries of social tourism will have little knowledge of the special attractions of different resorts. In some countries, government authorities, trade unions, national tourist organizations, and other bodies have given attention to this question. In the United States, for example, there are tourist information offices in the large cities, and publications are issued advising workers how they can spend their holidays. In Canada, bulletins are sent to the trade union offices and other organizations.

To date, most progress has been made in domestic tourism only, and although many workers are already traveling abroad, there is great opportunity for joint action between the official travel organizations of different states. Proposals have been made in some regions as how best to promote foreign travel by the lower-income groups, and the Argentine national tourist organization has invited the correspondent bodies in other South American states to arrange programs on a reciprocal basis.

**Table 6.3** Examples of Social Tourism

| Country | Type of Financial Aid |
| --- | --- |
| Argentina | Subsidized vacation accommodations for trade union workers |
| | Cheap excursion fares from large cities to holiday centers |
| Belgium | Trade union savings and subsidy |
| Czechoslovakia | Free rail tickets at holiday time |
| Denmark | Subsidized development of holiday centers |
| East Germany | Subsidy of holiday accommodations investments |
| | Reduced rail fares for groups |
| France | Trade union savings, subsidy |
| | Children's holiday homes |
| | Some types of accommodations tax exempt |
| Hungary | Rail travel discounts to workers taking holidays |
| Mexico | Subsidized vacation accommodations for low-income workers |
| Netherlands | Holiday bonuses paid to certain workers |
| New Zealand | Price reductions in hotels for certain classes of workers |
| Norway | Interest-free or reduced-rate state loans for development of holiday centers |
| Poland | Subsidy of workers' vacation costs |
| Soviet Union | Trade unions pay all or most of workers holiday costs |
| Switzerland | Discounted savings stamps for holiday use |
| | Trade union subsidies |
| United Kingdom | Holiday bonuses paid to certain workers |
| United States | Senior citizens discounts and free admissions |

# SUMMARY OF THE PRINCIPAL SOCIAL EFFECTS OF TOURISM

1. The vacation and special business trips a person takes are often among life's most vivid memories.
2. For families, vacation trips taken together are among the highlights of the year's activities.
3. The presence of visitors in a particular area can affect the living patterns of local people. The extent to which a local population is affected depends on the diversity of the mixing groups, including factors such as obvious differences in wealth, habits, appearance, and behavior.
4. On a national basis, people of a particular country can have their lives changed by tourism, particularly if there are large numbers of tourists in proportion to the indigenous population. Visitors may influence ways of dressing, consumption patterns, desire for products used by tourists, sexual freedoms, and a broadening outlook on the world.
5. For both hosts and guests, the most satisfying relationships are formed when they can meet and interact socially at a gathering such as a reception, a tea, or a cultural event; in "people to people" programs (home visitation); or in lifeseeing tourism (a structured learning-leisure program).
6. Tourism's effects on crime are negligible, but tourists can become easy victims of crime. Hosts must help them avoid dangerous places and areas.
7. Resentment of visitors by local (indigenous) people can occur. There may be conflicts over the use (or abuse) of local facilities and resources. Consumer prices may rise during the "tourist season."
8. Extensive tourism development can bring about undesirable social effects such as increased prostitution, gambling, drunkedness, rowdyism, unwanted noise, congestion, and other excesses.
9. Domestic and international tourism increases for people in a country that has a rising standard of living, a population age distribution favoring young adults or young marrieds with no children, and an increasing population of older, affluent adults.
10. People living in cities are more interested in travel than those living in small towns or rural areas.
11. Wealthy people and those in higher social classes are greatly inclined to travel.
12. Increase in the educational level in a population brings about an increase in travel.
13. Catering to handicapped persons substantially increases markets.
14. Group travel and tours are popular ways to travel.
15. Social tourism is a form of travel wherein the cost is subsidized by the traveler's trade union, government, public carrier, hotel, or association. Travelers thus assisted are in low-income groups, older age groups, or workers in organizations authorized to receive such subsidies or vacation bonuses.

# THE INTERNATIONAL TOURIST

International travel largely emanates from countries with a comparatively high standard of living, with high rates of economic growth, and with social systems characterized by declining inequality of incomes and a sizable urban population. In addition, these international travelers come from countries where large-scale industry and commerce comprise the foundations of the economy and where the communications and information environment is dominated by the mass media. The international market is largely made up of middle-income people, including the more prosperous minority of the working class, who normally live in large cities and earn their living in managerial, professional, white-collar, supervisory, and skilled occupations.

There are four extremes relating to the preferences of the international tourist: (1) complete relaxation to constant activity, (2) traveling close to one's home environment to a totally strange environment, (3) complete dependence on group travel to traveling alone, and (4) order to disorder. These extremes are not completely separate, and for most travelers there may be any number of combinations on any given trip. For example, a traveler may take a peaceful river cruise and then enjoy a strenuous swim in a quiet pool.

## Relaxation Versus Activity

Historically, the first wave of mass international travel (the interwar and postwar years) occurred at a time when there was a sharp differentiation between work and leisure and when the working week for most people, including the middle class, was long and exhausting. Under these circumstances it was not surprising the demand

A cruise vacation allows participants both relaxation and activity. Here Royal Caribbean Cruise Line passengers enjoy an early morning workout on the sports deck. (Photo courtesy of Royal Caribbean Cruise Lines)

concentrated on holidays that offered relaxation, recuperation, rest. Essentially they provided an opportunity for winding down and getting fit for the next 49 weeks of arduous activity. Since then the balance between work and leisure has shifted sharply in favor of the latter. Usually the weekend is free, and the annual holiday leave for some workers has been lengthened. In other words, over the past decade people have become used to greater slices of leisure time. Relaxation is possible throughout the year, and there is less need to use a holiday exclusively for this purpose.

With the arrival of year-round leisure, there seems to be a surfeit of opportunities for relaxation, so that increasingly the people have started to use their nonholiday leisure time to acquire and exercise new activity skills — sailing, climbing, sports, horseback riding. It is reasonable to forecast that the balance between leisure and work will continue to move in the direction of leisure and that the relative demand for activity-oriented travel will increase.

### Familiarity Versus Novelty

Most people, when they make their first venture abroad, tend to seek familiarity rather than novelty: people speaking the visitors' language, providing the meals and beverages they are accustomed to, using the same traffic conventions, and so on. Having found a destination where the traveler feels at home, this sort of tourist, at least for the first few ventures abroad, will be a "repeater," going back time and again to the same place. Not until more experience is gained will the traveler want to get away from a normal environment — to mix with people who speak differently, eat differently, dress differently.

In the Western world the general change in social conditions seems to be in the direction of speeding up the readiness for novelty. Where previously the social climate and rigid structure of society had reinforced a negative attitude to change, we now find increasingly a positive attitude to change. People accept and seek innovation in industry, education, family life, the arts, social relationships, and the like.

In particular, in countries with high living standards, manufacturers faced with quickly saturated markets concentrate on developing new products and encouraging the consumer to show greater psychological flexibility. More and more markets are dependent on the systematic organization of rapid change in fashion to sustain and expand. With the blurring of class differences and rising standards of living, travel demand will likely reflect this climate and express fragmentation of the total market as people move away from the traditional resorts to a succession of new places.

### Dependence Versus Autonomy

A widely accepted analysis of modern industrial society is based on the concept of alienation in work. Briefly, this view states that most people are inevitably employed in work that, though perhaps well paid, is not intrinsically rewarding and satisfying and that from this frustration results, among other things, a general sense of powerlessness, a withdrawal from political and social activities, and the pursuit of status symbols. In the field of leisure, this work alienation should lead to a demand for either passive, time-killing holidays or for holidays where the main gratification is the achievement of easily recognized status. Fundamental absence of significance in work, in other words, would lead to holidays during which the same sense of powerlessness and dependence would prevail—organized holiday camps, organized package trips, mass entertainment, and so forth.

In fact, there has been very little empirical research to substantiate this description of an industrialized society. Indeed, the data available suggest the very contrary—that many industrial workers, backed by strong trade unions and state-created full employment, feel that as workers they wield considerable power. Certainly, industry and social organization is moving in the direction of providing work that is intrinsically rewarding and satisfying, which should enhance life for today's workers, leading to a sense of personal autonomy in all aspects of their lives, including their leisure time. They are likely to seek holidays during which they feel independent and in control of what they do and how they do it. One would expect that for some time ahead, economic and social circumstances should generate a greater proportion of autonomous participants in the total demand for travel.

## Order Versus Disorder

Until recently in most Western societies, the training of children has been based on control and conformity, defined and enforced by an all-embracing circle of adult authority figures—parents, teachers, police officers, clergy, employers, civil authorities. With such a background, it is not surprising that most tourists sought holidays that reinforced this indoctrination—set meals at fixed times, guide books that told them the "right" places to visit, resorts where their fellow-tourists were tidy, well-behaved, "properly" dressed, and so on. They avoided situations where their sense of orderliness might be embarrassed or offended.

Tourists wishing a naval experience can explore jungle rivers.
(Photo courtesy of Wolfgang Kaehler/Society Expedition Cruises)

More recently child-rearing practices have changed in the direction of greater permissiveness, and the traditional incarnations of authority have lost much of their Victorian impressiveness. The newer generation of tourists no longer feels inhibited about what to wear and how to behave when on holiday; differences of others, opportunities for unplanned action, and freedom from institutionalized regulations are distinctive characteristics of the contemporary traveler.

Summing up, then, one would predict that because of deep and persisting social and economic changes in modern Western society, the demand for travel will be based less on the goals of relaxation, familiarity, dependence, and order and increasingly on activity, novelty, autonomy, and informality. One should not, of course, ignore the fact that, since international travel is a rapidly growing market, each year's total consumers will always include a minority who value familiarity, dependency, and order.

# SUMMARY

Sociologists are interested in tourism because travel profoundly affects individuals and families who travel, inducing behavioral changes. The new insights, understandings, and appreciations that travel brings are enlightening and educational.

An individual who travels to a strange environment encounters problems that must be resolved. How well the traveler solves these problems will largely determine the degree of the trip's success. In planning a trip the traveler must decide how much cultural distance (from the home environment) he or she desires. Tourists differ greatly in this regard.

This chapter has described various social phenomena related to mass tourism. Included are social tourism, international travel behavior extremes, and a typology of four tourist roles. Your understanding of these can help to provide a basis for determining tourist volume policy. Consideration must be given to the likely influence that masses of tourists will have on their hosts. Furthermore, applying the procedures explained in this chapter should minimize the negative sociological influences and enhance the positive effects of large numbers of tourists on their host society. Although tourism expenditures have a negligible effect on crime, tourists are potential targets for crime. It is essential that they be protected as much as possible.

## About the Readings

As you become educated in tourism, you will develop a growing awareness that international tourists differ greatly in their travel objectives, their manner of traveling, their spending habits, and their relationship to the tourist business establishment and to the citizens of the host country.

Each tourist must decide to what extent he or she wishes to become immersed into a different society when on a vacation trip. The degrees of involvement are divided or classified into a typology of four tourist roles by a sociologist, and these are described in detail in Reading 6-1 which has become a classic. Once understood, the classifications become very useful criteria for making decisions about who we wish to attract as tourists and what kinds of supply components are appropriate for each type of tourist.

Reading 6-2 reports the results of a study conducted in Central Florida to investigate residents' perceptions of the social consequences and impacts of tourism. Residents not only supported the current magnitude of the tourism industry, but also favored its expansion. Despite this overall favorable feeling, both positive and negative impacts were identified.

## READING 6-1

### *Toward A Sociology of International Tourism*

By Erik Cohen
Department of Sociology and Social Anthropology
The Hebrew University of Jerusalem

Reprinted from *Social Research*, Vol. 39, no. 1 (Spring 1972).

In recent years, there has been an enormous rise in both the number of people traveling for pleasure and the number of countries and places visited regularly by tourists.[1] Sociologists, however, seem to have neglected the study of tourism as a social phenomenon of international tourism, one which includes a typology of tourists on the basis of their relationship to both the tourist business establishment and the host country.[2]

*Varieties of Tourist Experience*
"After seeing the jewels of Topkapi, the fabled Blue Mosque
and bazaars, it's awfully nice to come home to
the Istanbul Hilton"

(Advertisement in *Time* magazine)

Tourism is so widespread and accepted today, particularly in the Western world,[3] that we tend to take it for granted. Traveling for pleasure in a foreign country by large numbers of people is a relatively modern occurrence, however, dating only from the early nineteenth century.[4]

It seems that mass tourism as a cultural phenomenon evolves as a result of a very basic change in man's attitude to the world beyond the boundaries of his native habitat. So long as man remains largely ignorant of the existence of other societies, other cultures, he regards his own small world as the cosmos. What lies outside is mysterious and unknown and therefore dangerous and threatening. It can only inspire fear or, at best, indifference, lacking as it does any reality for him.

A tremendous distance lies between such an orientation and that characteristic of modern man. Whereas primitive and traditional man will leave his native habitat only when forced to by extreme circumstances, modern man is more loosely attached to his environment, much more willing to change it, especially temporarily, and is remarkably able to adapt to new environments. He is interested in things, sights, customs, and cultures different from his own, precisely *because* they are different. Gradually, a new value has evolved: the appreciation of the experience of strangeness and novelty. This experience now excites, titillates, and gratifies, whereas before it only frightened. I believe that tourism as a cultural phenome-

non becomes possible only when man develops a *generalized* interest in things beyond his particular habitat, when contact with and appreciation and enjoyment of
strangeness and novelty are valued for their *own sake*. In this sense, tourism is a
thoroughly modern phenomenon.

An increased awareness of the outer world seems to lead to an increased readiness to leave one's habitat and to wander around temporarily, or even to emigrate to
another habitat. Although we have little real knowledge of the way in which this
awareness grows, it would seem that the technological achievements of the past two
centuries have been prime determinants. While the invention of increasingly effective means of communication and the increasingly widespread availability and use
of these means helped make man more aware of the outside world, at the same time
a parallel phenomenon occurred in transportation, making travel less arduous, less
dangerous, and less time-consuming. Also, the creation and growth of a monied
middle class in many societies made traveling for pleasure a possibility for large
numbers of people, whereas even as recently as the early nineteenth century only
the aristocracy could afford the necessary expenditure in money and time.

Though novelty and strangeness are essential elements in the tourist experience, not even modern man is completely ready to immerse himself wholly in an
alien environment. When the experience becomes too strange he may shrink back.
For man is still basically molded by his native culture and bound through habit to its
patterns of behavior. Hence, complete abandonment of these customs and complete
immersion in a new and alien environment may be experienced as unpleasant and
even threatening, especially if prolonged. Most tourists seem to need something
familiar around them, something to remind them of home, whether it be food,
newspapers, living quarters, or another person from their native country. Many of
today's tourists are able to enjoy the experience of change and novelty only from a
strong base of familiarity, which enables them to feel secure enough to enjoy the
strangeness of what they experience. They would like to experience the novelty of
the macroenvironment of a strange place from the security of a familiar microenvironment. And many will not venture abroad but on those well-trodden paths
equipped with familiar means of transportation, hotels, and food. Often the modern
tourist is not so much abandoning his accustomed environment for a new one as he
is being transposed to foreign soil in an "environmental bubble" of his native
culture. To a certain extent he views the people, places, and culture of that society
through the protective walls of his familiar "environmental bubble," within which
he functions and interacts in much the same way as he does in his own habitat.[5]

The experience of tourism combines, then, a degree of novelty with a degree of
familiarity, the security of old habits with the excitement of change.[6] However, the
exact extent to which familiarity and novelty are experienced on any particular tour
depends upon the individual tastes and preferences of the tourist as well as upon the
institutional setting of his trip. There is a continuum of possible combinations of
novelty and familiarity. This continuum is, to my mind, the basic underlying variable for the sociological analysis of the phenomenon of modern tourism. The division of the continuum into a number of typical combinations of novelty and familiarity leads to a typology of tourist experiences and roles. I will propose here a typology
of four tourist roles.[7]

*The Organized Mass Tourist*   The organized mass tourist is the least adventurous and remains largely confined to his "environmental bubble" throughout his trip. The guided tour, conducted in an air-conditioned bus, traveling at high speed through a steaming countryside, represents the prototype of the organized mass tourist. This tourist type buys a package tour as if it were just another commodity in the modern mass market. The itinerary of his trip is fixed in advance, and all his stops are well-prepared and guided; he makes almost no decisions for himself and stays almost exclusively in the microenvironment of his home country. Familiarity is at a maximum, novelty at a minimum.

*The Individual Mass Tourist*   This type of tourist role is similar to the previous one, except that the tour is not entirely preplanned, the tourist has a certain amount of control over his time and itinerary and is not bound to a group. However, all of his major arrangements are still made through a tourist agency. His excursions do not bring him much further afield than do those of the organized mass tourist. He, too, does his experiencing from within the "environmental bubble" of his home country and ventures out of it only occasionally—and even then only into well-charted territory. Familiarity is still dominant, but somewhat less so than in the preceding type; the experience of novelty is somewhat greater, though it is often of the routine kind.

*The Explorer*   This type of tourist arranges his trip alone; he tries to get off the beaten track as much as possible, but he nevertheless looks for comfortable accommodations and reliable means of transportation. He tries to associate with the people he visits and to speak their language. The explorer dares to leave his "environmental bubble" much more than the previous two types, but he is still careful to be able to step back into it when the going becomes too rough. Though novelty dominates, the tourist does not immerse himself completely in his host society, but retains some of the basic routines and comforts of his native way of life.

*The Drifter*   This type of tourist ventures furthest away from the beaten track and from the accustomed ways of life of his home country. He shuns any kind of connection with the tourist establishment, and considers the ordinary tourist experience phony. He tends to make it wholly on his own, living with the people and often taking odd-jobs to keep himself going. He tries to live the way the people he visits live, and to share their shelter, foods, and habits, keeping only the most basic and essential of his old customs. The drifter has no fixed itinerary or timetable and no well-defined goals of travel. He is almost wholly immersed in his host culture. Novelty is here at its highest, familiarity disappears almost completely.

The first two tourist types I will call *institutionalized* tourist roles; they are dealt with in a routine way by the tourist establishment—the complex of travel agencies, travel companies, hotel chains, etc., which cater to the tourist trade. The last two types I will call *noninstitutionalized* tourist roles, in that they are open roles, at best only very loosely attached to the tourist establishment.

*The Institutionalized Forms of Tourism:*
*The Organized and the Individual Mass Tourist*[8]
"Where were you last summer?"
"In Majorca."
"Where is that?"
"I don't know, I flew there."

(Conversation between two girls, reprinted in a German journal)

Contemporary institutionalized tourism is a mass industry. The tour is sold as a package, standardized and mass-produced.[9] All transportation, places to be visited, sleeping and eating accommodations are fixed in advance. The tourist establishment takes complete care of the tourist from beginning to end. Still, the package tour sold by the tourist establishment purportedly offers the buyer the experience of novelty and strangeness. The problem of the system, then, is to enable the mass tourist to "take in" the novelty of the host country without experiencing any physical discomfort or, more accurately, to observe without actually experiencing.

Since the tourist industry serves large numbers of people, these have to be processed as efficiently, smoothly, and quickly as possible through all the phases of the tour. Hence, it is imperative that the experience of the tourist, however novel it might seem to him, be as ordered, predictable, and controllable as possible. In short, he has to be given the illusion of adventure, while all the risks and uncertainties of adventure are taken out of his tour. In this respect, the quality of the mass tourist's experiences approaches that of vicarious participation in other people's lives, similar to the reading of fiction or the viewing of motion pictures. The tourist establishment achieves this effect through two interrelated mechanisms that I will call the *transformation of attractions* and the *standardization of facilities.*

Every country, region, or locality has something which sets it apart from all others, something for which it is known and worth visiting: scenic beauty, architecture, feasts or festivals, works of art, etc. In German there is a very appropriate term for these features, *Sehenswurdigkeiten,* or "things worth seeing," and I will call them "attractions." Some attractions are world renown, and become the trademark of a place; these attract tourists naturally. In other cases, they are created artificially — they are contrived "tourist attractions." [10]

The main purpose of mass tourism is the visiting of attractions, whether genuine or contrived. However, even if they are genuine, the tendency is to transform or manipulate them, to make them "suitable" for mass tourist consumption. They are supplied with facilities, reconstructed, landscaped, cleansed of unsuitable elements, staged, managed, and otherwise organized. As a result, they largely lose their original flavor and appearance and become isolated from the ordinary flow of life and natural texture of the host society.[11] Hawaiian dancing girls have to be dressed for public decency — but not much, so that they remain attractive; natural sights have to be groomed and guarded until they look like well-kept parks; traditional festivals have to be made more colorful and more respectable so tourists will be attracted but not offended. Festivals and ceremonies, in particular, cease being spontaneous expressions of popular feelings and become well-staged spectacles.[12] Even still-inhabited old quarters of otherwise modern cities are often turned into "living museums" to attract tourists, like the old town of Acre in Israel, Old San Juan, and Old Town in Chicago.

While the transformation of attractions provides controlled novelty for the mass tourist, the standardization of facilities serves to provide him with the necessary familiarity in his immediate surroundings. The majority of tourists originate today from the affluent Western countries, the U.S. and Western Europe, and increasingly from Japan. Hence, whatever country aspires to attract mass tourism is forced to provide facilities on a level commensurate with the expectations of the tourists from those countries. A tourist infrastructure of facilities based on Western standards has to be created even in the poorest host countries. This tourist infrastructure provides the mass tourist with the protective "ecological bubble" of his accustomed environment. However, since the tourist also expects some local flavor or signs of foreignness in his environment, there are local decorations in his hotel room, local foods in the restaurants, local products in the tourist shops. Still, even these are often standardized: the decorations are made to resemble the standard image of that culture's art, the local foods are made more palatable to unaccustomed tongues, the selection of native crafts is determined by the demands of the tourist.[13]

The transformation of attractions and the standardization of facilities, made necessary by the difficulties of managing and satisfying large numbers of tourists, have introduced a basic uniformity or similarity into the tourist experience. Whole countries lose their individuality to the mass tourist as the richness of their culture and geography is reduced by the tourist industry to a few standard elements, according to which they are classified and presented to the mass tourist. Before he even begins his tour, he is conditioned to pay attention primarily to the few basic attractions and facilities advertised in the travel literature or suggested by the travel agent, which are catalogued and sometimes even assigned a level of "importance."[14] This induces a peculiar kind of selective awareness: the tourist tends to become aware of his environment only when he reaches spots of "interest," while he is largely oblivious to it the rest of the time.[15] As a result, countries become interchangeable in the tourist's mind. Whether he is looking for good beaches, restful forests, or old cities, it becomes relatively unimportant to him where these happen to be found. Transportation by air, which brings him almost directly to his destination without his having to pass through other parts of the host country, contributes to the isolation of the attractions and facilities from the rest of the country—as well as the isolation of the tourist. And so mass tourism has created the following paradox: though the desire for variety, novelty, and strangeness are the primary motives of tourism, these qualities have decreased as tourism has become institutionalized.

In popular tourist countries, the tourist system or infrastructure has become separated from the rest of the culture and the natural flow of life. Attractions and facilities which were previously frequented by the local population are gradually abandoned. As Greenwich Village became a tourist attraction, many of the original bohemians moved to the East Village. Even sites of high symbolic value for the host society may suffer a similar fate: houses of government, churches, and national monuments become more and more the preserve of the mass tourist and are less and less frequented by the native citizen.

The ecological differentiation of the tourist sphere from the rest of the country makes for social separation; the mass tourist travels in a world of his own, surrounded by, but not integrated in, the host society. He meets the representatives of the tourist establishment—hotel managers, tourist agents, guides—but only seldom the natives.[16] The natives, in turn, see the mass tourist as unreal. Neither has much of an opportunity to become an individual to the other.

A development complementary to the ecological differentiation of the tourist sphere is the gradual emergence of an international tourist system, reaching across political and cultural boundaries. The system enjoys a certain independence and even isolation from its immediate surroundings, and an internal homogeneity in spite of the wide variations between the countries with which it intersects. The autonomy and isolation can be most clearly seen in those cases where tourists enjoy some special facilities that are out of bounds to the members of the host society, such as spas and nightclubs in Eastern European countries serving exclusively foreigners or the Berionka (dollar shop) in the Soviet Union, which caters only to tourists.

The isolation of the mass tourist from the host society is further intensified by a general communication gap. Tourist publications and travel literature are ordinarily written in the spirit of the tourist establishment—and often not by a native of the country—whose prime motive is selling, not merely informing. Such literature colors the tourist's attitudes and expectations beforehand. But probably more responsible than any other single factor mentioned thus far in creating and maintaining the isolation of the tourist is the fact that he seldom knows the language of the country he is traveling in. Not knowing the language makes forming acquaintances with the natives and traveling about on one's own so difficult that few tourists attempt it to any extent. Even worse, it leaves the tourist without any real feel for the culture of people in the country.

The sad irony of modern institutionalized tourism is that, instead of destroying myths between countries, it perpetuates them. The tourist comes home with the illusion that he has "been" there and can speak with some authority about the country he has visited. I would hypothesize that the larger the flow of mass tourists becomes, the more institutionalized and standardized tourism becomes and consequently the stronger the barriers between the tourist and the life of the host country become. What were previously formal barriers *between* different countries become informal barriers *within* countries.

### The Noninstitutionalized Forms of Tourism:
### The Explorer and the Drifter

Boorstin's vivid description of the evolution of the aristocratic traveler of yesterday into the tourist of modern times oversimplifies the issue to make a point. For Boorstin, there exists either the mass tourist or the adventurer, who contrives crazy feats and fabricates risks in order to experience excitement.[17] Even Knebel's less tendentious analysis postulates little variety in the role structure of the contemporary tourist. Both writers seem to have overlooked the noninstitutionalized tourist roles of explorer and drifter.

While the roles of both the explorer and the drifter are noninstitutionalized, they differ from each other chiefly in the extent to which they venture out of their microenvironment and away from the tourist system, and in their attitudes toward the people and countries they visit.

The explorer tries to avoid the mass tourist route and the traditional tourist attraction spots, but he nevertheless looks for comfortable accommodations and reliable means of transportation. He ventures into areas relatively unknown to the mass tourist and explores them for his own pleasure. The explorer's experience of the host country, its people, places and culture, is unquestionably much broader and deeper than that of the mass tourist. He tries to associate with the people he visits and to speak their language, but he still does not wholly immerse himself in the host society. He remains somewhat detached, either viewing his surroundings from an aesthetic perspective or seeking to understand the people on an intellectual level. Unlike the drifter, he does not identify with the natives emotionally or try to become one of them during his stay.

Through his mode of travel, the explorer escapes the isolation and artificiality the tourist system imposes on the mass tourist. Paradoxically, though, in his very attempts at escape he serves as a spearhead of mass tourism; as he discovers new places of interest, he opens the way for more commercialized forms of tourism, the managers of which are always on the lookout for new and unusual attractions. His experiences and opinions serve as indicators to other, less adventurous tourists to move into the area. As more and more of these move in, the tourist establishment gradually takes over. Thus, partly through the unwitting help of the explorer, the scope of the system expands.

As the tourist system expands, fewer and fewer areas are left that have mass tourist potential in terms of the traditional kinds of attractions. Recently, however, the ability of an area to offer a degree of privacy and solitude has, in itself, become a commodity of high value. Indeed, much of the mass tourist business today seems to be oriented to the provision of privacy *per se*. Obviously, mass tourism here reaches a point at which success is self-defeating.

While the explorer is the contemporary counterpart of the traveler of former years, the drifter is more like the wanderer of previous times. The correspondence is not complete, though. In his attitude toward and mode of traveling, the drifter is a genuine modern phenomenon. He is often a child of affluence, who reacts against it. He is young, often a student or a graduate, who has not yet started to work. He prolongs his moratorium by moving around the world in search of new experiences, radically different from those he has been accustomed to in his sheltered middle-class existence. After he has savored these experiences for a time, he usually settles down to an orderly middle-class career.

The drifter seeks the excitement of complete strangeness and direct contact with new and different people. He looks for experiences, happenings, and kicks. His mode of travel is adapted to this purpose. In order to preserve the freshness and spontaneity of his experience, the drifter purposely travels without either itinerary or timetable, without a destination or even well-defined purpose. He often possesses only limited means for traveling, but even when this is not true, he usually is concerned with making his money last as long as possible so as to prolong his travels. Since he is also typically unconcerned with bodily comfort and desires to live as simply as possible while traveling, he will travel, eat, and sleep in the most inexpensive way possible. He moves about on bicycle or motorcycle or hitchhikes rides in autos, private planes, freighters, and fishing boats. He shares rooms with fellow travelers he has met along the way or stays with a native of the area who has befriended him. When necessary, and often when not, he will sleep outdoors. And he will cook his own meals outdoors or buy food on the street more often than eat in a restaurant. If, in spite of such frugality, his money runs out before his desire to travel does, he will work at almost any odd-job he can get until he has enough to move on.

The particular way of life and travel of the drifter brings him into contact with a wide variety of people; these usually belong to the lower social groups in the host society. Often the drifter associates with kindred souls in the host society. In my study of a mixed Jewish-Arab town in Israel, I encountered a great deal of association between drifters and local Arab boys who also wanted to travel.[18]

An international subculture of drifters seems to be developing. In some places drifters congregate and create an ecological niche of their own. On the shore of the Red Sea in Eilat, Israel's southernmost port, there is a "permanently temporary" colony of squatters locally called "beatniks," who drifted there from many parts of the world. Similarly, the National Monument on the Dam, in the very center of Amsterdam, serves as a mass meeting place for young people who flock there from all over Europe and the U.S.

The drifter discards almost completely the familiar environment of his home country and immerses himself in the life of the host society. Moreover, as explained above, the drifter differs significantly from the explorer in the manner in which he relates to the host society. The drifter is, then, the true rebel of the tourist establishment and the complete opposite of the mass tourist.

*Discussion*

So far I have formulated a general approach to the sociology of tourism based on a typology of tourist roles. Here I will develop some implications of this approach and propose several problems for further research.

The fundamental variable that forms the basis for the fourfold typology of tourist roles proposed here is strangeness versus familiarity. Each of the four tourist roles discussed represents a characteristic form of tourist behavior and a typical position on the strangeness/familiarity continuum. The degree to which strangeness or familiarity prevail in the tourist role determines the nature of the tourist's experiences as well as the effect he has on the host society.

Initially, all tourists are strangers in the host society. The degree to which and the way they affect each other depends largely on the *extent* and *variety* of social contacts the tourist has during his trip. The social contacts of the mass tourist, particularly of the organized mass tourist, are extremely limited. The individual mass tourist, being somewhat more independent, makes occasional social contacts, but his conventional mode of travel tends to restrict them to the close periphery of the tourist establishment, thus limiting their number and their nature. The social contacts of the explorer are broader and more varied, while those of the drifter are the most intensive in quality and the most extensive in quantity.

The extent to which the tourist role is predefined and the social expectations of it spelled out determines to a large degree the *manner* in which tourists interact with members of the host society, as well as the images they develop of one another. The mass tourist generally does not interact at all, but merely observes, and even that from within his own microenvironment. The explorer mixes but does not become involved in the lives of members of the host society. Here the length of *time* spent in one place is as important a determinant of social involvement as attitude. The drifter, unlike the mass tourist, does not set a limit beforehand on the length of time he will spend in any one place; if he finds an area that particularly pleases him, he may stop there long enough for social involvement to occur.

Tourism has some important aggregate effects on the host society, in terms of its impact on the division of labor and on the ecology or the land-use patterns of that society. As the tourist role becomes institutionalized, a whole set of other roles and institutions develop in the host country to cater to his needs — what we have called the tourist establishment. This development gradually introduces a new dimension into the ecology of the host society, as attractions and facilities are created, improved, and set aside for tourist use. This primary impact of tourism has important secondary and tertiary consequences.[19] Predominantly agricultural regions may become primarily tourist areas, as agriculture is driven out by tourist facilities, and the local people turn to tourist services for their living. The "tourist villages" in the Austrian Alps are an example. Conversely, stagnant agricultural areas may receive a boost from increased demands for agricultural products in nearby tourist regions, such as the agricultural boom that has occurred in the hinterland of the Spanish Costa Brava. Without doubt, the impact of large-scale tourism on the culture, style of life, and world-view of inhabitants of tourist regions must be enormous. To my knowledge, however, the problem has not yet been systematically studied.[20]

The explorer and the drifter do not affect the general division of labor in the host society to the same degree as the mass tourist does, and consequently do not have the same aggregate impact on that society. Their effect on the host society is more subtle, but sometimes considerable, as I found in my own study of the impact of drifting tourist girls on Arab boys in a mixed Jewish-Arab city.

It is understood that foreign travel can have a considerable impact upon the traveler himself, and, through him, on his home country. In premodern times, travelers were one of the chief means through which knowledge and innovations were diffused and information about other countries obtained. How does the impact vary with the different kinds of experiences yielded by each type of tourist role, on the tourist himself, and, through him, on his own society? Is his image of his own society and his own style of life changed? In what ways? These are some of the questions that future studies of tourism might be organized around.

We also know very little about the way preferences for countries and localities are formulated in the mind of the tourist and later translated into the ways the tourist system expands or contracts geographically.[21] I have dealt with the role of the explorer in the dynamics of growth of the tourist system, but other mechanisms are undoubtedly at work, such as the planned creation of new attractions to foster mass tourism, like the building of Disneyland. It might be worthwhile to differentiate between the organic and the induced growth of the tourist system and look into the differential effect of the modes of expansion on the workings of the tourist system and the host society.

The problems raised in this paper have been dealt with in a most general form; any attempt to explore them in depth will have to make use of a comparative approach. Though tourism could be studied comparatively from several angles, the most important variables of comparison are probably the differences between the cultural characteristics of the tourist and the host[22] and the manner in which tourism is embedded in the institutional structure of the host country.[23]

## Conclusion

Growing interaction and interpenetration between hitherto relatively independent social systems is one of the most salient characteristics of the contemporary world. In

K. Deutsch's phrase, the world is rapidly becoming a "global village." No far-off island or obscure primitive tribe manages to preserve its isolation. Tourism is both a consequence of this process of interpenetration and one of several mechanisms through which this process is being realized. Its relative contribution to the process —in comparison to that of the major transforming forces of our time—is probably minor, though it seems to be increasing rapidly. Tourism already serves as the chief source of foreign currency in several countries, and its scope is growing at an accelerating rate.

It is interesting to speculate, then, about some of the broader sociological consequences of the increase in the scope of tourism for the society of the future. The picture which emerges is complex. On the one hand, as the numbers of mass tourists grow, the tourist industry will become more and more mechanized and standardized. This, in turn, will tend to make the interaction between tourist and host even more routinized. The effect of the host country on the mass tourist will therefore remain limited, whereas his effect on the ecology, division of labor, and wealth of the country will grow as his numbers do. On the other hand, as host societies become permeated by a wide variety of individually traveling tourists belonging to different classes and ways of life, increased and more varied social contacts will take place, with mixed results for international understanding.[24] Like-minded persons of different countries will find it easier to communicate with each other and some kind of new international social groupings might appear. Among the very rich such groups always existed; the fashionable contemporary prototype is the international "jet-set." And only recently drifter communities have emerged in many parts of the world, comprised of an entirely different kind of social category. The effect of such developments may well be to diminish the significance of national boundaries, though they also create new and sometimes serious divisions within the countries in which such international groups congregate. Some indication of the emergence of new foci of conflict can already be seen in the recent riots between drifters and seamen in Amsterdam, the hub of the European "drifter community."

Finally, the differential impact of tourism on various types of societies should be noted. As Forster pointed out,[25] the impact of tourism on a society with an unbalanced, developing economy might be much more serious than its impact on a mature, well-developed society. As tourism is eagerly sought for by the developing nations as an important source of revenue, it may provoke serious disruptions and cause ultimate long-range damage in these societies. The consequences can not yet be fully foreseen, but from what we already know of the impact of mass tourism it can safely be predicted that mass tourism in developing countries, if not controlled and regulated, might help to destroy whatever there is still left of unspoiled nature and of traditional ways of life. In this respect, the easy-going tourist of our era might well complete the work of his predecessors, also travelers from the West—the conqueror and the colonialist.

## Reading Endnotes

1. This paper was first written while I was a visiting scholar at the Institute of Urban Environment, Columbia University, New York. Thanks are due to the Institute as well as to Dr. R. Bar-Yoseph, Prof. Elihu Katz, and Dr. M. Skokeid, for their useful comments.

2. There exist very few full-length studies of tourism. One of the most comprehensive studies is that by H. J. Knebel, *Soziologische Struckturwandlungen in Modernem Touriusmus* (Stuttgard: F. Enke Verl, 1960). By far the most incisive analysis of American tourism has been performed by D. Boorstin, *The Image* (New York: Atheneum, 1961), pp. 71–117. There is a chapter on tourism in J. Dumazedier, *Towards a Society of Leisure* (New York: Free Press, 1967), pp. 123–128, and in M. Kaplan, *Leisure in America: A Social Inquiry* (New York: Wiley, 1960), Ch. 16.

3. For the contemporary tourist boom see S. K. Waters, "The American Tourist," The Annals of the American Academy of Social Science, 368 (November 1966), pp. 109–118.

4. Dumazedier, op. cit., p. 125n. For the scarcity of tourists even as late as 1860, see Boorstin, op. cit., p. 84.

5. Knebel speaks, following von Uexkull, of a *"touristische Eigenwelt,"* from which the modern tourist can no longer escape; op. cit., p. 147.

6. For a similar approach to modern tourism, see Boorstin, op. cit., pp. 79–80.

7. For a different typology of tourist roles ("travelers"), see Kaplan, op. cit., p. 216.

8. For a general description of the trends characteristic of modern mass tourism, see Knebel, op. cit., pp. 99ff.

9. See Boorstin, op. cit., p. 85.

10. Ibid., p. 103.

11. In Boorstin's language, they become "pseudo-events."

12. "Not only in Mexico City and Montreal, but also in the remote Guatemalan Tourist Mecca of Chichecastenango, out in far-off villages of Japan, earnest honest natives embellish their ancient rites, change, enlarge and spectacularize their festivals, so that tourists will not be disappointed." Ibid., p. 103.

13. Boorstin, talking of the Hilton chain of hotels, states: "Even the measured admixture of carefully filtered local atmosphere [in these hotels] proves that you are still in the U.S." Ibid., pp. 98–99.

14. For an analysis of the travel literature, see Knebel, op. cit., pp. 90–97. On the development of the guidebook, particularly the Baedeker, see Boorstin, op. cit., pp. 109ff, and Knebel, op. cit., pp. 24–26.

15. The tendency of the mass tourist to abide by the guidebook was noticed a hundred years ago by "A Cynic" who wrote in 1869: "The ordinary tourist has no judgment; he admires what the infallible Murray orders him to admire. . . . The tourist never diverges one hair's breadth from the beaten track of his predecessors, and within a few miles of the best known routes in Europe leaves nooks and corners as unsophisticated as they were fifty years ago; which proves that he has not sufficient interest in his route to exert his own freedom of will." "A Cynic: Vacations," *Cornhill Magazine, August 1869, reported in Mass Leisure,* E. Larrabee and K. Meyersohn (eds.), (Glencoe, Ill.: Free Press, 1952), p. 285.

16. Boorstin, op. cit., pp. 91ff.: Knebel, op. cit., pp. 102–104; see also Knebel's discussion of the primary tourist group, op. cit. pp. 104–106.

17. Boorstin, op. cit., pp. 116–117.

18. E. Cohen, "Arab Boys and Tourist Girls in a Mixed Jewish-Arab Community," *International Journal of Comparative Sociology,* Vol. 12, No. 4 (1971), pp. 217–233.

19. For some of these see J. Forster, "The Sociological Consequences of Tourism," *International Journal of Comparative Sociology,* Vol. 5, No. 2 (1964), pp. 217–227.

20. A study of this problem is in progress now in the region of Faro in southern Portugal; this is a backward region in which the sudden influx of mass tourism seems to have some serious disruptive effects.

21. This problem is discussed with reference to the rather special conditions of Hawaii and other Pacific Islands, by Forster, op. cit.

22. W. A. Sutton, "Travel and Understanding: Notes on the Social Structure of Touring,"

*International Journal of Comparative Sociology,* Vol. 8, No. 2 (1967), pp. 218–223, touches upon this point in a discussion of factors which make for harmony and tension in the tourist-host encounter.

23. Forster's argument about the differential impact of tourism on a society with an underdeveloped as against an advanced economy is one example of such an approach. Another would be to compare the effects of tourism on closed (totalitarian) as against open (democratic) societies.

24. See Sutton, op. cit.

25. See Forster, op. cit.

# READING 6-2

## Social Impacts of Tourism on Central Florida

By Ady Milman and Abraham Pizam

Dick Pope Institute of Tourism Studies
University of Central Florida

Reprinted from *Annals of Tourism Research,* Vol. 15, No. 2, 1988.

### Introduction

Apart from obvious manifestations of physical damage to the environment, tourism can contribute to social conditions that may lead to serious problems in the host society, including changes in value systems, individual behavior, family relationships, collective lifestyles, traditional ceremonies, or community organization.

Unfortunately, it is often difficult to measure the known social impacts of tourism. To a large extent, they are indirect. One may also suspect that there are other impacts yet to be discovered. In general, hosts' attitudes and perceptions toward tourism vary on a continuous scale between negative to positive (Belisle and Hoy 1980; Cant 1980; Pearce 1980; Pizam 1978; Sethna and Richmond 1978; Thomason, Crompton and Kamp 1979).

Tourism also impacts directly and indirectly on employment and entrepreneurship opportunities and, therefore, affects the attitudes of those dependent on it. Several studies indicate a correlation between economic dependency on tourism and residents support for it. Liu and Var's study (1986) of residents' attitudes toward tourism in Hawaii revealed that respondents strongly agreed that tourism provided many economic and cultural benefits, but were ambivalent about environmental benefits. They were reluctant to attribute social and environmental costs to tourism. Another example of the impacts of tourism was provided by Sternquist-Witter (1985) who compared attitudes about a resort area for a sample of tourists and a sample of local retailers. The findings revealed that retailers evaluated their resort area significantly more favorably than tourists did.

In a survey conducted on Cape Cod, Massachusetts, Pizam (1978) indicated that tourism-employed residents were more favorably disposed towards tourists than those who were not tourism-employed. Similarly, Rothman's (1978) assessment of the impact of seasonal tourism upon two beach resort communities in Delaware concluded that those residents that were economically dependent upon visitors were generally satisfied with tourism.

Employment generation by the tourism industry can have a positive impact on social preservation. A study undertaken by Boissevain (1979) found that development of tourism in Gozo, Malta's underdeveloped sister island, created permanent jobs for several hundred residents, and as a result avoided disintegration of the local community whose youth had traditionally migrated to look for new jobs. Finally, occupation transformation can result from the introduction of a new industry. Gamper's study (1981) of two communities in south Austria revealed that tourism caused local farmers to abandon their fields and rent rooms to tourists.

*Tourism Development in Central Florida*   Tourism is the largest industry in the state of Florida and especially large in Central Florida. In 1985, close to 30 million domestic and international tourists visited the state. These visitors purchased goods and services worth $19 billion. The Florida Division of Tourism estimated that in 1985, Central Florida was one of the most popular destinations in the State, hosting 23% of all auto visitors and 19% of all air visitors.

Central Florida attractions have always been very popular. In 1985, Walt Disney World's Magic Kingdom and EPCOT Center accounted for over 50% of Florida's air and auto attraction visitors. Other attractions like Sea World of Orlando, Church Street Station, and Cypress Gardens have also increased significantly the share of Central Florida for statewide attractions visits.

Tourism within Central Florida is expected to expand further and retain its position as the largest component of the region's economy. While currently it has not met with any vocal opposition from the resident population, the local community can be seriously affected by the various social consequences of this tourism-oriented economy. Therefore, the purpose of this study was to investigate the residents' perceptions of the social consequences and impacts of tourism, and later on compare them with residents in other regions of the world in which tourism plays a major economic role (Figure 1).

*Methodology*

*Instrument*   This study was part of an international comparative study on the social impacts of tourism sponsored by The International Social Science Council– European Coordination Centre for Research and Documentation in Social Sciences (also known as the Vienna Center). The study is conducted currently in Poland, Spain, Yugoslavia, Bulgaria, Hungary, United Kingdom, and the United States. The questionnaire developed for the Central Florida study (representing the USA) was not identical to the one developed for the Vienna Center because of differences in interviewing methods and budgetary constraints (the Vienna Center questionnaire was conducted through personal interviews while the Central Florida questionnaire was administered via telephone interviews). Nevertheless the questionnaire was based on several topics included in the Vienna Center survey, as well as additional items that were considered relevant to the unique environmental setting in which this study was undertaken. Since the study was exploratory in nature, no formal hypotheses were developed.

*Sampling*   A sample of Central Florida residents was drawn from both the local telephone directory (from where the first three digits of the local telephone ex-

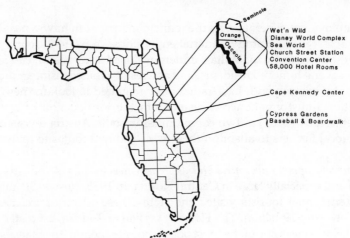

Wet'n Wild
Disney World Complex
Sea World
Church Street Station
Convention Center
58,000 Hotel Rooms

Cape Kennedy Center

Cypress Gardens
Baseball & Boardwalk

**Figure 1** Central Florida Attractions.

changes were drawn) and computer generated random tables (for the last four digits of the telephone number).

Strata sampling of residents of Orange, Seminole, and Osceola counties was drawn proportionally to the number of residents in each county (60.1%, 35.0%, and 4.9%, respectively). The response rate for each stratum was uniform.

Interviews were conducted by experienced telephone interviewers of a local marketing research company. The interviewers introduced themselves as working for the Tourism Institute at the University of Central Florida. Calls were made to households during weekdays between 5:00 pm–9:00 pm. Interviewers who encountered "no answer" or "busy" tones attempted to get the same number at three different times before the telephone number was omitted from the total valid sample. Interviewers asked to speak with adult male or female heads of households. Calls were made to 351 households, with respondents completing interviews in 203 households, for a response rate of 57.8%.

*Limitations*  Several limitations in the research methodology should be noted here. The practice of interviewing only willing respondents may create problems of representation. Since there was no control over who participated in the study, the results could be biased by either favorable or unfavorable responses.

In addition, respondents were generally aware that their opinions were sought by the Tourism Institute at their local state university, and consequently, they *might* have been less likely to express dissatisfaction with various aspects of the tourism industry. Finally, because the telephone numbers were drawn from published lists, the sample may be biased against those respondents who have unlisted numbers.

*Results*

*General Profile of the Respondents*  The majority of the respondents (about 60%) have lived in Central Florida over ten years, had a college degree (about 55%), and their median age was between 40 and 50 years. Most of them were married (about 72%) and had no children under 18 living in their household (about 65%). Those respondents who had children living with them reported an average of two children.

About 60% of the respondents were employed full time, 8% were employed part time, 22% were retired, and the rest were unemployed, homemakers, or students. Of those respondents who were employed, 11% were employed in the tourism industry. About 14% of the respondents also reported that at least one family member was employed in the tourism industry. The annual income of the respondents was in the range of $30,000–40,000.

The demographic profile of this sample represents the population of Central Florida as reported by continuous surveys conducted by Florida state authorities (Bureau of Economic and Business Research 1986).

*Overall Attitude Toward Tourism* In general, Central Florida residents had a positive attitude toward tourism. About 78% of the respondents favored somewhat or strongly favored the presence of tourism in Central Florida (Table 1). A majority (about 63%) also felt that the image of Central Florida improved somewhat or significantly improved as a result of tourism activities (Table 2).

Respondents were also asked to express their opinions on the impact that the tourism industry had on a variety of areas. Sixteen areas (variables) were evaluated with regard to the impact of tourism, where "1" indicated that the variable had been "significantly worsened" by the tourism industry and "5" "significantly improved."

As can be seen from Table 3, employment opportunities, income, and standard of living, town's overall tax revenue, and quality of life were perceived to improve as a result of tourism in Central Florida. On the other hand, traffic conditions, individual crimes, organized crime (crimes which are the product of groups or organizations), and alcoholism were perceived to worsen from tourism in Central Florida. Traffic conditions were perceived to worsen more significantly than any other variable.

It is important to note the moderate standard deviation among most variables indicates consensus among Central Florida residents as to the impact of tourism. The only notable exception was the impact of tourism on the town's overall tax revenue, where opinions varied among the respondents. Apparently some residents perceive the contribution of tourism to the "town's overall tax revenue" to be negative or to contribute very little; an opinion which still exists among some residents despite numerous state and local reports that prove otherwise.

**Table 1** Feelings About the Presence of Tourists in Central Florida

| Support for Tourist Presence | Percentage |
|---|---|
| Strongly oppose the presence of tourism (1) | 1.5 |
| Oppose somewhat the presence of tourists (2) | 4.5 |
| Neither oppose nor favor (3) | 15.8 |
| Favor somewhat (4) | 36.1 |
| Strongly favor (5) | 42.1 |
| | 100.0 |

Mean 4.2
Standard Deviation 0.9

**Table 2** The Impact of Increased Presence
of Tourism on the Image of Central
Florida

| Impact | Percentage |
|---|---|
| Significantly worsen (1) | 3.0 |
| Worsen somewhat (2) | 12.6 |
| Not make any difference (3) | 21.2 |
| Improve somewhat (4) | 46.0 |
| Significantly improve (5) | 17.2 |
| | 100.0 |

Mean 3.6
Standard Deviation 1.0

As to the rest of the variables, their mean (around 3.0) may indicate that the current level of tourism had no impact on them. Among these variables were morality, politeness and manners, sexual permissiveness, people's honesty, attitude toward work, and mutual confidence among people.

**Table 3** Impact of the Current Level of Tourism on Selected
Sociocultural Issues

| Issue | Mean[a] | Standard Deviation |
|---|---|---|
| Employment opportunities | 4.0 | 0.9 |
| Income and standard of living | 3.8 | 0.9 |
| Town's overall tax revenue | 3.6 | 1.1 |
| Quality of life in general | 3.4 | 0.9 |
| Courtesy and hospitality toward strangers | 3.3 | 0.9 |
| Attitude toward work | 3.1 | 0.6 |
| Mutual confidence among people | 3.0 | 0.6 |
| Morality | 2.9 | 0.8 |
| Politeness and good manners | 2.9 | 0.8 |
| People's honesty | 2.9 | 0.6 |
| Sexual permissiveness | 2.7 | 0.7 |
| Alcoholism | 2.6 | 0.6 |
| Drug addiction | 2.5 | 0.7 |
| Organized crime (crimes which are the products of groups or organizations) | 2.4 | 0.7 |
| Individual crimes (planned and conducted by individuals) | 2.3 | 0.7 |
| Traffic conditions | 1.6 | 0.8 |
| Grand Mean | 2.9 | |

[a] 1 = Significantly worsen
2 = Worsen somewhat
3 = Not make any difference
4 = Improve somewhat
5 = Significantly improve

When asked whether local residents would willingly take jobs in the tourism and hospitality industry, 63.1% of the respondents said they would. In addition, 75% of the respondents said that they would suggest to their friends or relatives to take jobs in the tourism industry.

To determine the respondents' level of respect towards a tourism occupation, they were asked to choose their preferred occupation, from a limited list of occupations that included one hotel occupation (hotel receptionist). The majority of the respondents chose school teacher followed by salesman, hotel receptionist, officer in the armed forces, and foreman in a factory (Table 4).

Despite the fact that the list of occupations was limited and inexhaustive, it is still possible to suggest that Central Floridians perceive the relatively low level of hotel receptionist to be in the range of medium desirability in comparison to the other four occupations.

*General Attitude Toward Tourists*  A few questions addressed the residents' perception of tourists. The majority of the respondents (about 56%) found domestic tourists to be similar to themselves (Table 5), but foreign tourists were found to be dissimilar (Table 6).

When asked about social relationships with tourists, the majority of the respondents (about 70%) said that they had contacts with tourists (Table 7). Since only about 20% of the tourists coming to Florida have friends and relatives in the region (Florida Division of Tourism 1985), it is safe to assume that for the large majority of residents the relationships that they maintain with tourists are not based on previous friendships.

*Present Attitudes Towards Tourism*  Respondents were asked to express their overall attitude towards the tourism industry in Central Florida. As indicated in Table 8, 79% favor or strongly favor tourism. Only 5% of the respondents were opposed to the industry's existence in Central Florida. In addition, 58% of the respondents said that the number of tourists visiting this area should increase, 30% said it should not change, and the rest (11.5%) said that the volume of tourists in Central Florida should decrease (Table 9).

To analyze the effect of socio-demographics on respondents' support for the tourism industry, a series of bivariate analyses was conducted. These analyses measured the association between respondents' level of support for the tourism industry and their socio-demographic characteristics.

**Table 4** Appeal of Certain Occupations

| Occupation | Percentage |
| --- | --- |
| School teacher | 31.9 |
| Salesman | 24.5 |
| Hotel receptionist | 18.1 |
| Officer in the armed forces | 14.4 |
| Foreman in a factory | 11.2 |
| Total | 100.0 |

**Table 5** Perceived Degree of Similarity Between the Tourists and Residents

| Degree of Similarity | Percentage |
|---|---|
| Very different (1) | 6.0 |
| Somewhat different (2) | 17.9 |
| In some ways different and in others similar (3) | 19.9 |
| Somewhat similar (4) | 38.8 |
| Very similar (5) | 17.4 |
| | 100.0 |

Mean 3.4
Standard Deviation 1.1

The level of support for the tourism industry was measured by an index composed of the sum of our three dependent variables: "feeling about the presence of tourists" (Table 1), "feelings about controlling the number of tourists" (Table 9), and "overall opinion about the tourism industry in Central Florida" (Table 8). The ten socio-demographic variables analyzed were sex, marital status, presence of children under 18 in the household, number of children, education, age, number of years living in the area, household income, employment in the tourism industry, and family employed in the tourism industry.

Pearson product-moment correlations between age, number of children, and years living in the area, on one hand, and the level of support for the tourism industry, on the other, resulted in low and insignificant correlations ($-.13$; $.04$; $-.13$, respectively).

One-way analyses of variance between marital status, education level, household income, and the level of support for the tourism industry found that level of support does not vary significantly among different categories of marital status, education, and income. The only difference that was found was in the respondents who had an annual household income of $40,000–$50,000. Those respondents had a higher level of support for the tourism industry than respondents in the $20,000–$30,000 category (mean = 12.8 vs. 11.3; $F = 2.6$; $p = .01$). All other income categories did not differ significantly from each other in level of support.

**Table 6** Perceived Degree of Similarity Between American and Foreign Tourists

| Degree of Similarity | Percentage |
|---|---|
| Very different (1) | 19.7 |
| Somewhat different (2) | 29.8 |
| In some ways different and in others similar (3) | 27.3 |
| Somewhat similar (4) | 17.2 |
| Very similar (5) | 6.1 |
| Total | 100.0 |

Mean 2.6
Standard Deviation 1.2

**Table 7** Social Relationships with Tourists

| Type of Relationship | Percentage |
| --- | --- |
| Have no contact with tourists (1) | 30.5 |
| Have some contact with tourists (2) | 56.7 |
| Have constant contact with tourists (3) | 12.8 |
| | 100.0 |

Mean 1.8
Standard Deviation 0.6

A series of $t$-tests on the variables of sex, presence of children under 18 in the household, employment in the tourism industry, and family employed in the tourism industry found the following results: male respondents had a higher level of support for the tourism industry than female respondents (mean = 12.1 vs. 11.4; $t = 1.96$; $p = .05$); respondents with children under 18 in the household did not differ significantly in their level of support from respondents who did not have children under 18 in the household (mean = 11.7 vs. 11.8; $t = .18$; $p = .86$); respondents who were employed in the tourism industry had a higher level of support for this industry than respondents who were not employed in this industry (mean = 13.3 vs. 11.6; $t = -4.85$; $p = .0001$); and respondents whose families were employed in the tourism industry had a higher level of support for this industry than employees whose families were not employed in this industry (mean = 12.8 vs. 11.6; $t = 2.76$; $p = .009$).

Therefore, the results here indicate that most demographic variables did not affect respondents' level of support for the tourism industry in Central Florida. The only notable exceptions were found to be sex, respondents' family employed in the tourism industry, and respondents' employment in the tourism industry. The later confirms the results reported in previous studies such as Pizam (1978) and Rothman (1978).

*Predictors of the Level of Support*   Three stepwise multiple regressions were conducted to determine what factors affect respondents' overall opinion of the tourism industry in Central Florida. The dependent variables were: "feelings about the

**Table 8** Overall Opinion of the Tourism
Industry in Central Florida

| Opinion | Percentage |
| --- | --- |
| Strongly oppose it (1) | 0.5 |
| Oppose it (2) | 5.4 |
| Neither oppose nor favor it (3) | 15.3 |
| Favor it (4) | 50.2 |
| Strongly favor it (5) | 28.6 |
| | 100.0 |

Mean 4.0
Standard Deviation 0.8

**Table 9** Opinion on the Volume of Tourists
         Visiting Central Florida

| Opinion | Percentage |
|---|---|
| Should significantly decrease (1) | 3.0 |
| Should decrease somewhat (2) | 8.5 |
| Not change (3) | 30.0 |
| Should increase somewhat (4) | 42.8 |
| Should significantly increase (5) | 15.4 |
| | 100.0 |

Mean 3.6
Standard Deviation 0.9

presence of tourists" (Table 1); "controlling the number of tourists" (Table 9); and "overall opinion about the tourism industry in Central Florida" (Table 8). The independent variables consisted of 34 variables: sixteen impact variables; ten socio-demographic variables; and eight variables describing perceptions and social relations with tourists and willingness to work in the tourism industry.

The results indicated that several independent variables significantly predicted respondents' level of support for the tourism industry in Central Florida. The amount of variance explained in each of the three regressions was in the medium range (max R square = 0.44). Since the three dependent variables were found to be correlated with each other (Table 10), a new dependent variable (index) was created by summing the three dependent variables.

Table 11 shows the results of the multiple regression with the new dependent variable. As can be seen from this table, 8 out of the 34 variables entered the equation and explained 50% of variance of the residents' attitude towards tourism. More specifically it was found that Central Floridians who support the tourism industry have the following perceptions and personal characteristics:

- Believe that their quality of life is improved by the tourism industry.
- Believe that the tourism industry is improving the image of their community.
- Do not believe that the tourism industry is having any impact on drug addiction.
- Believe that the tourism industry is improving their income and standard of living.
- Would suggest a job in the tourism industry to a friend.
- Are employed in the tourism industry themselves.
- Do not believe that tourists are different than themselves.
- Do not believe that the tourism industry is having any effect on the introduction of organized crime.

**Table 10** Correlation Matrix Between Variables Explaining Overall Opinion of Tourism in
          Central Florida

| | DV2 | DV3 | |
|---|---|---|---|
| DV1 | 0.48 | 0.62 | DV1 = Controlling n. of tourists (Table 9) |
| DV2 | — | 0.52 | DV2 = Feeling about presence of tourists (Table 1) |
| DV3 | | — | DV3 = Overall opinion of tourism industry (Table 8) |

**Table 11** Multiple Regression of Level of Support for Central Florida Tourism Industry on Specific Opinions and Personal Characteristics

| Variable | Standardized Regression Coefficient | F | Zero Order Correlation Coefficient | Cumulative R Square |
|---|---|---|---|---|
| Quality of life | .22 | 63.3[a] | .37 | .24 |
| Community image | .29 | 57.9[a] | .48 | .37 |
| Drug addiction | .14 | 45.9[a] | .35 | .41 |
| Income & Standard of living | .15 | 39.3[a] | .39 | .44 |
| Suggestion of job in the tourism industry | .12 | 33.4[a] | .33 | .46 |
| Employment in the tourism industry | .11 | 29.3[a] | .21 | .47 |
| Difference between tourists & residents | .11 | 26.2[a] | .26 | .48 |
| Organized crime | .13 | 23.8[a] | .37 | .50 |

$N = 203$
R Square $= 0.50$
[a]$p < .001$

It is interesting to note that only one out of the ten socio-demographic variables, namely "employment in the tourism industry," entered the regression equation. Other socio-demographic variables like age, marital status, number of children, sex, income, and education did not have a combined effect on the residents' attitude toward tourism.

To test for multicollinearity in some of the independent variables, a set of correlations among the sixteen impact variables was concluded. The results showed that out of a possible 120 correlations, 15 (12.5%) had a coefficient higher than .40, and 6 (5%) had a coefficient higher than .50 (the highest coefficient being .66). Despite the fact that normally this would not be considered a problem of multicollinearity in the regression, it was decided to conduct a factor analysis of these sixteen variables and then regress the factor scores and the other eighteen independent variables against the new combined dependent variable.

The method of factor analysis used squared multiple correlations as communality estimates, and Varimax rotation on the sixteen variables representing the current level of tourism impacts. The rotated solutions yielded three factors explaining 43.6% of the variation. Considering loadings over 50%, the three factors essentially reflected the following constructs: legal factors, social factors, and economic factors (Table 12).

Following this procedure, a new regression was conducted to determine which of the three factors and the other eighteen independent variables affect respondents' overall opinion of the tourism industry in Central Florida. This procedure was conducted by using the new index variable ($DV1 + DV2 + DV3$) as a dependent variable and the three factors (legal, economic, social) as replacements for the 16 impact variables used in the previous runs.

The results indicated that 6 out of the 21 variables significantly predicted

**Table 12** Factors Representing Current Level of Tourism Impacts

| Impact | Factor 1 "Legal" | Factor 2 "Social" | Factor 3 "Economic" |
|---|---|---|---|
| Morality | 0.41 | 0.22 | 0.26 |
| Income and standard of living | 0.04 | 0.07 | 0.97 |
| Employment opportunities | 0.07 | 0.15 | 0.55 |
| Traffic conditions | 0.23 | 0.17 | 0.11 |
| Individual crimes | 0.72 | 0.19 | 0.11 |
| Organized crimes | 0.81 | 0.06 | 0.09 |
| Alcoholism | 0.69 | 0.24 | 0.01 |
| Drug addiction | 0.68 | 0.22 | 0.09 |
| Politeness and good manners | 0.32 | 0.54 | 0.12 |
| Sexual permissiveness | 0.47 | 0.43 | 0.08 |
| Town's overall tax revenue | 0.24 | 0.29 | 0.30 |
| People's honesty | 0.34 | 0.44 | 0.00 |
| Attitude toward work | 0.07 | 0.62 | 0.14 |
| Courtesy and hospitality toward strangers | 0.11 | 0.67 | 0.01 |
| Mutual confidence among people | 0.15 | 0.63 | 0.17 |
| Quality of life in general | 0.23 | 0.44 | 0.28 |

respondents' level of support for the tourism industry in Central Florida (Table 13). Residents who supported the tourism industry were found to have the following perceptions and personal characteristics:

- Believe that the tourism industry was improving the image of the community.
- Would suggest a job in the tourism industry to a friend.
- Do not believe that the tourism industry was impacting negatively on legal factors.
- Believe that the tourism industry was improving the economy of the area.

**Table 13** Multiple Regression of Level of Support for Central Florida Tourism Industry on Impact Factors and Personal Characteristics

| Variable | Standardized Regression Coefficient | F | Zero Order Correlation Coefficient | Cumulative R Square |
|---|---|---|---|---|
| Community image | 0.36 | 60.3[a] | 0.48 | 0.23 |
| Suggestion of a job in the tourism industry | 0.19 | 43.8[a] | 0.33 | 0.30 |
| Legal factor | 0.24 | 38.6[a] | 0.33 | 0.36 |
| Economic factor | 0.20 | 32.7[a] | 0.30 | 0.40 |
| Employment in the tourism industry | 0.13 | 27.9[a] | 0.21 | 0.42 |
| Tourists are similar to tourism industry | 0.12 | 24.5[a] | 0.26 | 0.43 |

N = 203
R Square = 0.43
[a]$p < .001$

- Were employed in the tourism industry themselves.
- Believe that tourists are similar to local residents.

Again, as in the previous case, only one socio-demographic variable ("employment in the tourism industry") entered the equation. It is interesting to note that the difference between the two regression models was not significant. The first regression (which contained the original 16 impact variables) explained 50% of the variance, while the second model (which contained the three factor scores) explained slightly less, namely 44% of the variance. Furthermore in both cases, the same independent variables (more or less) entered the equation. Therefore, the interpretation of the two models appear to be the same.

*Discussion and Conclusions*

The results of the above study suggest that support for the tourism industry in Central Florida is strong among its residents. Furthermore, residents not only supported the current magnitude of this industry, but also favored its expansion.

Considering that the industry at present is close to eight million visitors per year, any support for further expansion must be interpreted as a complete vote of confidence in the tourism industry, and decision makers both at the public and the private sectors should execute their current expansion policies.

Residents of Central Florida looked upon domestic tourists in their town as fellow residents that were away from home. Therefore, their presence brings no objection, nor does it create any xenophobic feelings. The same, however, cannot be said for international tourists who are viewed as somewhat different than American tourists.

Despite this overall positive feeling towards tourists and the tourism industry, Central Floridians were able to point out some specific negative impacts that in their opinion the tourism industry had on their community. These impacts were perceived to be traffic conditions, individual crimes, organized crimes, drug addiction, and alcoholism. The major positive impacts were mostly economic: employment opportunities; income and standard of living; town's overall tax revenue; and quality of life.

As to the question of which were the factors that influenced residents' attitudes towards the tourism industry, this study found that residents with the highest overall level of support for Central Florida tourism tended to be people who believed that the tourism industry was improving the image and the economy of their community; believed that the tourism industry was not causing illegal activities such as drugs, crimes, and organized crime; viewed tourism jobs as relatively respectable; and were themselves employed in the tourism industry.

This study is an addition to the body of work on perceptions of local residents on the presence of tourism. Similar studies highlighted the dilemma of the cost-benefit involved by the presence of tourism. What is apparent is that tourism impacts are never universal. Rather, the intensity and direction of the impacts are a function of tourist activities, the cultural and economic distance between tourists and hosts, and the rapidity and intensity of tourism growth. Furthermore, it is obvious that residents' perception of these impacts are not necessarily objective, and is affected unequally by some factors more than others. For example, the perception that tourism induces crimes of various sorts, creates almost automatically a negative attitude toward tourism regardless of whether these crimes are the results of tourism or not.

To make the results of this and other similar studies applicable to other destinations, it is necessary to have a more exhaustive and comparative analysis of results in different situations. When the results of the other six countries participating in this project will be available (i.e., the Vienna Center project), a cross-national comparison will be conducted. If the above results are confirmed in these studies, then one has contributed some building blocks and hypotheses towards the development of a theory on the social impacts of tourism.

### References

Belisle, Francois J., and Ron R. Hoy. "The Perceived Impact of Tourism by Residents: A Case Study in Santa Maria, Columbia." *Annals of Tourism Research*, Vol. 7, no. 1 (1980), pp. 83–101.

Boissevain, J. "The Impact of Tourism on a Dependent Island: Gozo, Malta." *Annals of Tourism Research*, Vol. 6, no. 1 (1979), pp. 76–90.

Cant, G. "The Impact of Tourism on the Host Community—The Queenstown Example" in *Tourism in the South Pacific: The Contribution of Research and Development to Planning*, ed. D. G. Pearce, pp. 87–97. Christ Church, New Zealand: University of Canterbury, Department of Geography.

Florida Department of Commerce. *Florida Visitor Study 1985*. Tallahassee, Fl.: Florida Department of Commerce, 1986.

Gamper, Josef A. "Tourism in Austria: A Case Study of the Influence of Tourism on Ethnic Relations." *Annals of Tourism Research*, Vol. 8, no. 3 (1981), pp. 432–446.

Kendall, K. W., and Turgut Var. "The Perceived Impact of Tourism: The State of the Art." Occasional paper No. 6. Honolulu: The University of Hawaii School of Travel Industry Management and the Social Science Research Institute, 1984.

Liu, Juanita C., and Turgut Var. "Resident Attitudes Toward Tourism Impacts in Hawaii." *Annals of Tourism Research*, Vol. 13, no. 2 (1986), pp. 193–214.

Pearce, J. A. "Host Community Acceptance of Foreign Tourists." *Annals of Tourism Research*, Vol. 13, no. 2 (1980), pp. 224–233.

Pizam, Abraham. "Tourism Impacts: The Social Costs to the Destination Community as Perceived by Its Residents." *Journal of Travel Research*, Vol. 16, no. 4 (1978), pp. 8–12.

Rothman, Robert A. "Residents and Transients: Community Reaction to Seasonal Visitors." *Journal of Travel Research*, Vol. 16, no. 3 (1978), pp. 8–13.

Sethna, Rustum J., and Bert O. Richmond. "U.S. Virgin Islanders' Perceptions of Tourism." *Journal of Travel Research*, Vol. 17, no. 1 (1978), pp. 30–31.

Sternquist-Witter, Brenda. "Attitudes About a Resort Area: A Comparison of Tourists and Local Retailers. *Journal of Travel Research*, Vol. 24, no. 1 (1985), pp. 14–19.

Thomason, Pamela, John L. Crompton, and B. Dan Kamp. "A Study of the Attitudes of Impacted Groups Within a Host Community Toward Prolonged Stay Tourist Visitors." *Journal of Travel Research*, Vol. 17, no. 3 (1979), pp. 2–6.

### Key Concepts

appreciation of strangeness and
  novelty
beneficial social contacts

conduct of visitors
contemporary institutionalized
  tourism

contrasting cultures and cultural
  distance
democratization of travel
drifter
effects of travel experiences
environmental bubble
explorer
group travel arrangements
handicapped travelers
income and social class
individual mass tourist
isolation of the mass tourist
mass follows class
national understanding
negative social effects on host society
organized mass tourist

population changes and travel interests
reduced fare schemes
resentment toward visitors
social tourism
standardization of facilities
strangeness versus familiarity
tourism and crime
transformation of attractions
travel patterns change with age,
  family life stages
travel patterns change with age,
   family life stages
travel preferences of international
  tourists
trips as family highlights
world as a global village

## For Review and Discussion

1. As a manager of a resort hotel popular with families, what social and/or educational activities would you offer your guests?
2. You have decided to take a trip to a country whose culture is very much different from your own. Would you participate in a group tour or go alone? Why?
3. Would a child's learning experience during a trip to another part of his or her country be comparable to school learning for that period of time? In what ways might parents maximize the educational benefits of such a trip?
4. Describe how a hotel's food and beverage manager might avoid the "universal waiter uniform" image.
5. In what ways could an overpopular resort city discourage further tourism growth?
6. Discuss the effects of television news coverage of global and national events on tourism.
7. Give some examples of how tourism suppliers accommodate handicapped travelers. How important is this segment of the market?
8. As a tour wholesaler sales rep, you are about to make a call on a large auto dealership concerning the possibility of setting up a travel incentive program. What arguments would you use?
9. Is there a potential for increased social tourism in your country?
10. How might the four extremes relating to the preferences of present-day international tourists affect a resort hotel's social and recreational program? Give some specific examples.
11. How do your travel interests differ from your parents'? from your grandparents'?
12. You are president of a tourist promotion association. Which of Cohen's four tourist types would you try to attract? Why?

## Case Problems

1. Mr. Alfred K. is a widower 67 years old. He has not had an opportunity to travel much, but now as a retiree he has the time and money to take extensive trips. As a travel counselor, what kinds of travel products would you recommend?

2. Mrs. Sadie W. is president of her church missionary society. She has observed that many visitors to her fairly small city in England are interested in the local history. Her church is a magnificent cathedral, the construction of which began in the year 1083. Mrs. W. and her colleagues believe that missionary work begins at home. By what methods could her group reach and become acquainted with the cathedral visitors?

3. A U.S. group tour conductor wishes to maximize the mutual social benefits of a trip to an underdeveloped country. Describe possible kinds of social contacts that would be beneficial to the hosts and to the members of the tour group.

4. A popular beach resort hotel is located in a tropical country which, unfortunately, has a high crime rate. One section of the city nearby has some "South Seas" atmosphere gambling casinos. Many guests would like to visit them. How might the hotel's staff control this situation?

5. Ms. Nadia P. is Minister of Tourism for a small West African country. This country has become a very popular winter destination for Scandinavians. The tourists seem to be mainly interested in the beaches, which are among the finest in the world. However, it is customary for these visitors to wear very scanty clothing, especially when bathing. In fact, nude bathing is occasionally practiced.

   About 90 percent of the indigenous population of the host country are Moslems. The appearance and sometimes behavior of the visitors, especially when shopping and otherwise contacting local citizens, often seems improper to their hosts.

   Tourism is increasing each year. The economic benefits are considerable and are very much needed. However, the social problem is becoming more acute. What should Ms. P. do about this?

## Selected References

AIEST. *The Role and Impact of Mega-Events and Attractions on Regional and National Tourism Development.* St. Gallen, Switzerland: AIEST, 1987.

Bello, Daniel C., and Michael J. Etzel. "The Role of Novelty in the Pleasure Travel Experience." *Journal of Travel Research,* Vol. 24, no. 1 (Summer 1985), pp. 20–26.

Brougham, J. E., and R. W. Butler. *The Social and Cultural Impact of Tourism: A Case Study of Sleat, Isle of Skye.* Edinburgh: Scottish Tourist Board, 1977.

Buck, Roy C. "Boundary Maintenance Revisited: Tourist Experience in an Old Order Amish Community." *Rural Sociology,* Vol. 43, no. 2 (Summer 1978), pp. 221–234.

Canadian Broadcasting Corporation. *Welcome to Paradise.* Ottawa: The Corporation.

Cohen, Erik. "Rethinking the Sociology of Tourism." *Annals of Tourism Research,* Vol. 6, no. 1 (January–March 1979), pp. 18–35. Special Issue on Sociology of Tourism.

Cohen, Erik. "Traditions in Qualitative Sociology of Tourism." *Annals of Tourism Research,* Vol. 15, no. 1, 1988, pp. 29–46.

*Development of Leisure Time and the Right to Holidays.* World Tourism Organization, 1983.

Eadington, William R. *Gambling and Society.* Springfield, Ill.: Thomas, 1976.

Farrell, Bryan H. *The Social and Economic Impact of Tourism on Pacific Communities.* Santa Cruz: Center for South Pacific Studies, University of California at Santa Cruz, June 1977.

Getz, Donald, and Wendy Frisby. "Evaluating Management Effectiveness in Community-Run Festivals." *Journal of Travel Research,* Vol. 27, no. 1 (Summer 1988), pp. 22–27.

Hornback, Kenneth E. "Social Trends in Outdoor Recreation." *Proceedings of the National Outdoor Recreation Trends Symposium II,* Vol. 1 (1985), pp. 37–48. Atlanta, Georgia: National Park Service Science Publications Office.

Jafari, Jafar. "Tourism and Social Science: A Bibliography." *Annals of Tourism Research,* Vol. 6, no. 2 (April–June 1979), pp. 149–195. Special Issue on Sociology of Tourism.

deKadt, Emanuel. "Social Planning for Tourism in the Developing Countries." *Annals of Tourism Research,* Vol. 6, no. 1 (January–March 1979), pp. 36–48. Special Issue on Sociology of Tourism.

MacCannell, Dean. *The Tourist: A New Theory of the Leisure Class.* New York: Schocken Books, 1976.

O'Leary, Joseph T. "Social Trends in Outdoor Recreation." *Proceedings of the National Outdoor Recreation Trends Symposium II,* Vol. 1 (1985), pp. 24–36. Atlanta, Georgia: National Park Service Science Publication Office.

Pizam, Abraham, and Ady Milman. "The Social Impacts of Tourism." *Tourism Recreation Research,* Vol. 11, no. 2. Lucknow, India: Lucknow Publishing House 37, 1986.

Richter, Linda K. *The Politics of Tourism in Asia.* Honolulu: University of Hawaii Press, 1989.

Smith, Ralph W. "Leisure of Disabled Tourists: Barriers to Participation." *Annals of Tourism Research,* Vol. 14, no. 3 (1987), pp. 376–389.

"Social Tourism for All—The Swiss Travel Saving Fund." *Tourism Management,* Vol. 4, no. 3 (September 1983), pp. 216–219.

Turner, Louis, and John Ash. *The Golden Hordes.* London: Constable, 1975.

Van Doren, Carlton S. "Social Trends and Social Indicators: The Private Sector." *Proceedings of the National Outdoor Recreation Trends Symposium II,* Vol. 1 (1985), pp. 13–23. Atlanta, Georgia: National Park Service Science Publications Office.

Woodside, Arch G., Ellen M. Moore, Mark A. Bonn, and Donald G. Wizeman. "Segmenting the Timeshare Resort Market." *Journal of Travel Research,* Vol. 24, no. 3 (Winter 1986), pp. 6–12.

# PART THREE

# Tourism Supply, Demand, Economics, and Development

# CHAPTER 7

# Tourism Components and Supply

## LEARNING OBJECTIVES

- Know the four major supply components that any tourist area must possess.
- Become familiar with the newer forms of accommodations—condominium apartments and timesharing arrangements.
- Be able to use the mathematical formula to calculate the number of guest rooms needed for the estimated future demand.
- Develop the ability to perform a task analysis in order to match supply components with anticipated demand.
- Discover methods of adjusting supply components in accordance with fluctuating demand levels.

Considering that tourism is a composite of activities, services, and industries that deliver a travel experience, it is important to identify and categorize its supply components. The quality and quantity of these determine in considerable measure tourism's success in any area.

## COMPONENTS

Tourism supply components can be classified into four main categories:

1. *Natural resources.* This category constitutes the fundamental measure of supply —the natural resources that any area has available for the use and enjoyment of visitors. Basic elements in this category include air and climate, land forms, terrain, flora, fauna, bodies of water, beaches, natural beauty, and water supply for drinking, sanitation, and similar uses.
2. *Infrastructure.* The infrastructure consists of all underground and surface developmental construction such as water supply systems, sewage disposal systems, gas lines, electrical and communications systems, drainage systems, other constructed facilities such as highways, airports, railroads, roads, drives, parking lots, parks, night lighting, marinas and dock facilities, bus and train station facilities, resorts, hotels, motels, restaurants, shopping centers, places of entertainment, museums, stores, and similar structures.
3. *Transportation and transportation equipment.* Included are items such as ships,

airplanes, trains, buses, limousines, taxis, automobiles, cog railroads, aerial tramways, and similar passenger transportation facilities.

4. *Hospitality and cultural resources.* These are all the cultural wealth of an area that makes possible the successful hosting of tourists. Examples are the tourist business employees' welcoming spirit ("aloha" in Hawaii, for example), attitude of the residents toward visitors, courtesy, friendliness, sincere interest, willingness to serve and to get better acquainted with visitors, and other manifestations of warmth and friendliness. In addition, the cultural resources of any area are included here — fine arts, literature, history, music, dramatic art, dancing, shopping, sports, and other activities.

There is a wide range of tourist resources created by combining cultural resources. Such examples would be sports events and facilities, traditional or national festivals, games, and pageants.

## NATURAL RESOURCES

A great variety of combinations of natural resource factors can create environments attractive to tourism development. Thus, no general statements can be formulated. Probably the most noticeable are the pronounced seasonal variations of temperature zones and the changes in demand for recreational use of such areas. To even out demand, the more multiple-use possibilities, the better. For example, it is more desirable that an area be used for golf, riding, fishing, hunting, snow skiing, snowmobiling, mushroom hunting, sailing and other water sports, nature study, and artistic appreciation such as painting and photography than for hunting alone. The wider the appeal throughout the year, the greater the likelihood of success.

Another highly important consideration is that of location. As a rule, the closer an area is to its likely markets, the more desirable it is and the more likely to have a high demand. User-oriented areas (such as golf courses) should be close to their users. By contrast, an area of superb natural beauty such as a U.S. national park could be several thousand miles from major market areas and yet have very satisfactory levels of demand.

Productivity of the natural resources of the area for tourism is a function of the application of labor and management. The amounts and proportions of these inputs will determine the quality and quantity of the output. The terrain, vegetation, and beaches of the natural resource will be affected by the intensity of use. Proper planning, taking such concentrations of use under consideration, and planning accordingly for permanent aesthetic appreciation will help to maintain the quality of the natural resources for the enjoyment of present and future users.

The quality of the natural resources *must* be maintained to sustain tourism demand. Proper levels of quality must be considered when planning is undertaken, and the maintenance of quality standards after construction is undertaken is absolutely necessary for continued satisfaction of the visitor. In fact, tourism is very sensitive to the quality of recreational use of natural resources, and unless high standards are maintained, a depreciation of the demand will inevitably result. Thus, ecological and environmental considerations are vital.

Vail, Colorado, is an example of how a world-class resort can be developed using natural resources. (Photo by David Lokey, courtesy of Vail Associates)

## INFRASTRUCTURE

The ground and service installations described as infrastructure are of paramount importance to successful tourism. These installations must be adequate. For example, the diameters of the pipes in various utility systems should be ample for any future increase in use. Electrical installations, water supply systems, communications installations, waste disposal, and similar service facilities should be planned with a long-term viewpoint so that they can accommodate future expansion.

Airport runways should be built to adequate standards for use by the newest group of jets so that future costly modifications will not be necessary.

Hotel or lodging structures are among the most important parts of the infrastructure. The goal should be to produce an architectural design and quality of construction that will result in a distinctive permanent environment. A boxlike hotel typical of any modern city is not considered appropriate for a seaside resort dominated by palms and other tropical vegetation, nor is it likely to attract tourists.

A tourist is often more attracted by a facility designed in conformance with local architecture as a part of the local landscape than the modernistic hotel that might be found at home.

Attention must be given to this subject since people often travel to immerse themselves in an environment totally different from their own. Modern amenities such as air conditioning, central heating, and plumbing, however, should be used in buildings otherwise characteristic of a particular region.

Interior design should also be stimulating and attractive. Lodging structures need local decor and atmosphere as well as comfort. To minimize the expense of obsolescence, high-quality materials and furnishings and first-rate maintenance are necessary.

Infrastructure is expensive and requires considerable time to construct.

## Auto Traveler Service

In developed countries, automobile transportation is most common. As the economy of a country develops, the usual pattern is from walking, to using horses or other working animals, to bicycles, to motorcycles, and finally to small and then larger automobiles, augmented by public transport.

In the case of roads, they should be hard, all-weather surfaced, be properly graded and drained, and be built to international standards for safe use. Small, inadequate roads will only have to be torn up and replaced with better and more adequate systems.

Auxiliary services, such as gasoline stations, roadside eating facilities, motels,

A trained travel counselor provides advice to a visitor at an official travel information center. Travelers may call, free of charge, anywhere in Michigan to make reservations or obtain information. These centers are part of Michigan's integrated system of highway signing, travel information, and service for motorists. (Photo courtesy of the Michigan Department of Transportation)

roadside parks, roadside picnic facilities, rest parks that have toilet facilities, scenic turnouts, marked points of interest within easy access of the road, and auto repair and service facilities are all needed for successful auto tourism. The number and spacing of essential services depend on the nature of the area, but a spacing of about one hour's driving distance is recommended.

## Road Planning and Road Signs

In the planning of new roads, long-term consideration must be given to "tourist" or "scenic routes" that present the most impressive scenery. A good example is the scenic Mississippi River route in the United States. Such routes should have specially colored markers and be indicated on road maps as "scenic tourist routes" or some similar designation. The marking or sign program for the roads should show points of interest—including directions—and have sufficient information concerning the availability of food, lodging, and gasoline.

Some type of classification for such signs indicating the nature of the accommodations and services available is desired. One method is to provide signs with the logos of the various hotel, motel, restaurant, and gasoline service stations. This type of sign identifies for the traveler the type of facilities he or she can expect. Adequate sign facilities including the international auto-road symbols are essential as are adequate supplies of maps that translate road signs into the most needed language of visitors.

Attractive road signs giving historical information enhance the visitors' enjoyment of an area. This historical marker tells of the difficulties pioneers faced in their efforts to pass Mt. Hood. (Photo courtesy Oregon Department of Transportation)

Another aspect of signs concerns their control along the highways. It is the authors' belief that the most satisfactory way to provide information (and advertising) for the tourist and at the same time protect the beauty of the countryside is to control the placement of signs as follows:

> Within one mile (1609 meters) from the outskirts of the city or community, signs along the highways will be permitted. These signs will be located in any convenient place, with one stipulation—that signs be maintained in excellent physical condition. No obvious deterioration of the signs will be allowed, and if such deterioration takes place, the highway authorities would have the mandate to remove the sign at the expense of the owner. The countryside between cities beyond the one-mile radius of each city would have no advertising signs. Only highway marker signs to indicate road conditions, curves, warning signs, and similar highway directional information would be found in this area.

An exception to these rules might be made in the case of major intersections where highway directional signs exist and a cluster of informational signs of tourist accommodations and other tourist services could be permitted.

## Roadside Parks

Auto tourists use and enjoy roadside parks, picnic tables, rest areas, scenic turnouts, and similar roadside facilities. These facilities are sometimes abused by inconsiderate motorists who litter the area with their trash. Thus, the rule "If you can't maintain it, don't build it" is a cardinal principle of tourism development, and regular maintenance to keep the park in an orderly condition is essential. If the parks are not properly maintained, the tourist is disappointed and the investment in the park is largely wasted.

Some states provide deluxe roadside parks with a fine information building, free refreshments, tourist hosts and hostesses, and rest rooms. These parks are equipped with supplies of folders, maps, pictures, and other amenities for a refreshing informative stop.

## Gasoline Stations

Service stations should be provided in sufficient quantity to avoid delays for service. An automobile patron should not wait more than five minutes for service. Station attendants need to be schooled in courteous service and in the importance of friendliness, hospitality, and knowledge of the tourist attractions in the immediate vicinity (such as within a radius of 50 miles). They should be knowledgeable concerning accommodations, shopping, and entertainment in their community.

## Accommodations

For successful tourism, accommodations must be available in sufficient quantity to match the demand of the travelers who arrive at the destination. Accommodations should precede any other type of development; their importance cannot be overemphasized.

Hotels vary tremendously in their physical facilities, level of maintenance and cleanliness, and services provided. Unless all of these factors are at satisfactory levels, tourism cannot succeed. The hotels must provide the physical facilities, price ranges, locations, and services that meet the expectations, wants, and needs of the travelers. Should the quality of facilities and services drop, demand will fall off — a serious blow to the tourism industry in the area.

## Types of Accommodations

*Hotels*  Hotels are of several types: commercial, resort, motor, airport, and residential. In relation to tourism, residential hotels are probably not important, although there are usually some rooms available to tourists in most residential hotels. The primary type is the resort hotel situated in attractive surroundings and usually accompanied by a large mix of services, including entertainment and recreational activities for the traveler and vacationer.

The commercial hotel is usually a downtown structure located conveniently for the business traveler, convention attender, and vacationer.

The demand for accommodations varies according to the price guests are willing to pay, services required, and similar considerations. Many successful tourism areas have no multistoried, expensive, contemporary-looking hotels. For example, a bungalow-type accommodation constructed with native materials, built to modern standards of comfort and safety, and kept immaculately clean will be acceptable to a large segment of the market.

An elaborate world-class hotel, Tahara's Tahiti, is a creation of exciting design, skilled engineering, and construction in a beautiful setting. (Photo courtesy of Wimberly, Allison, Tong & Goo)

The motor hotel is of primary importance for tourists traveling by car and is of major importance in the United States, Canada, and Mexico.

Suitable accommodations should be available for all segments of the market. American companies such as Marriott, Ramada, Holiday Corporation, and Quality International now offer accommodations under different names that are aimed at specific price levels of the market. Thus they compete for various segments of the travel market. Expensive hotel accommodations may be demanded by those who "want the best" and are willing and able to pay accordingly. On the other hand, youth tourism and adults unable or unwilling to pay for top-level accommodations should have facilities available, such as hostels, pensions, and bed and breakfast. Camping or caravanning facilities are often needed. Other types of accommodations include marina hotels, airport hotels, gambling resort hotels, and rustic cabins in wilderness areas. All accommodations should be harmonious with one another.

Certain places are known as expensive destination areas, and travelers expect to find higher-quality accommodations there. Conversely, other areas are expected to be inexpensive, and the high-priced hotel would be out of place in such a locality.

*Condominium apartments*   Individual buyers of condominium units typically use the apartment for their own enjoyment, or they rent it to tourists for all or part of the year. This form of accommodation has become increasingly important and, in some resort areas, constitutes considerable competition to the resort hotels. Real estate management firms often manage such apartments or groups of "condos" within a building or complex and thus serve as agents for the owners. They rent the condos as managers of the group, charging a fee for this service to the absent owner. Such arrangements can be made through a local travel agent in the prospective traveler's home city. The agent will book the reservation through the real estate management firm.

*Timesharing*   Timesharing is a technique for the multiple ownership and/or use of resort and recreational properties. Timesharing has been applied to hotels, motels, condominiums, townhouses, single-family detached homes, campgrounds, and even boats and yachts. It involves both new construction and conversion of existing structures, along with properties devoted solely to timesharing and projects that integrate timesharing and nontimesharing properties. While most programs may be classified as either ownership or nonownership (right to use), there are wide variations in program and legal format.

The attraction of timesharing is simple: it permits purchasers to own or have occupancy rights at a resort accommodation for a period of time each year for a fraction of the purchase price of the entire unit. Timeshare owners pay for exactly what they plan on using, and when they leave they don't have to think about where they'll be vacationing next year. Another option or advantage of timesharing is the exchange program. The exchange system affords vacation flexibility by allowing owners to trade or swap their timeshares for other locations and times. Finally, a well-designed timeshare program can be a hedge against inflation in resort accommodations.

The benefits of timesharing are substantially borne out by the high degree of consumer satisfaction it has achieved. In a survey of approximately 10,000 timeshare buyers, conducted by the National Timesharing Council of the American Land Development Association, 86.3 percent of the respondents said they were "very satisfied" or "satisfied" with their purchase. About 40 percent indicated that they were interested in purchasing additional timeshares. Additional information on timesharing is available from the National Timesharing Council, 1220 L Street N.W., Suite 510, Washington, D.C. 20005.

## Hotel Management

As mentioned in the previous section, the management of a hotel should ideally be the same group that was involved in the planning and construction of the hotel. To do otherwise is unadvisable because the hotel business is not overly profitable, and any efficiency that can be built into the design or layout of the hotel as recommended by an experienced management group helps to assure a better chance of success.

For best results, the manager should be a graduate of a hotel school so there is a proper depth of understanding and appreciation of the industry as well as training for the job.

All decisions pertaining to the management of the hotel should begin with the customers and guests. What is the likely reaction to each management decision? Implementation of such a policy favors success for the hotel as the policy most likely to produce a high measure of guest satisfaction.

Success in hotel management also depends on organization and the functioning of each department. Each department head should be considered a manager of his or her own department. The goals of each should affect and support the overall goals of the hotel. The personal goals of each employee should contribute to and buttress the goals of the department. Each employee should be taught high standards of service, sanitation, and personal conduct, essential for the success of the hotel.

Thorough training sessions must be conducted for new employees, and recurring training should be provided for all employees. A wide selection of home study courses (also suitable for group use) is available, in English, from the Educational Institute, American Hotel and Motel Association, 1407 So. Harrison Road, East Lansing, Michigan 48824.

Assistance in training staff and managers can also be obtained from colleges and universities, state departments of education and public instruction, trade associations, and private management institutes or associations as well as from resources from within the organization or from larger affiliates or chain staff personnel.

*Local Charm* A principal appeal of travel is the enjoyment of people of other cultures, and guests will inevitably become acquainted with the staff of the hotel. In fact, at a resort hotel, the guest probably gets to know his or her waiter or waitress better than anyone else in the hotel or local area.

Tourists expect all hotel personnel to serve them with courtesy and efficiency. Thus, all hotel employees should be indoctrinated into the importance of this relationship and its success-building potential.

The use of local costumes, the retention of unsophisticated charm, and the practice of friendliness and cleanliness are integral to achieving good hotel management.

*Inspection*  The most common types of hotel inspection relate to water supplies, sewage and waste disposal, general cleanliness, kitchen and food storage, and safety. Such inspection can be accomplished by local-, area-, or state-level authorities. Inspections of these conditions should be made no less than annually, and semiannually would be preferred.

Inspection to prevent fires is also important. Rigid inspections of electrical systems, heating systems, ventilating systems, air-conditioning systems, fuel storage, elevators, and storage areas are all important. Cleanliness and orderliness are essential ingredients in the prevention of fires. Fire prevention systems such as automatic sprinklers or similar warning devices should be inspected, and installation of fire prevention devices should be encouraged, if not required.

*Regulations*  Regulations of hotels take many forms depending on local conditions and requirements. Regulations often relate to fairness and minimum standards of wages, hours, and ages of employees. Others relate to the licensing for selling alcoholic beverages; various tax structures for hotels; the disposal of wastes; hours of operation for public eating and drinking facilities; registration of guests; the importation of various food and drink items; equipment, unemployment, and disability insurance and other staff benefits; passport identification; zoning and building regulations; and fair employment and civil rights regulations.

Many states regulate the sale of alcoholic beverages and the licensing of serving establishments, usually via a special agency.

*Hotel Classification*  Hotels are classified using a number of different systems. Then, too, many tourist countries have no classification system whatsoever. Many in the industry prefer the five-star rating system, which grades hotels according to specific criteria (usually by the national tourist organization) from the highest (five stars) to the most modest accommodations (one star) suitable for travelers. Countries such as Spain also classify nonhotel accommodations, such as pensions. Criteria used for star ratings are public rooms, bathrooms, climatization, telephone, bar, dining rooms, and other characteristics. The inspections and classifications in Spain are conducted by the director general of Touristic Enterprise and Activities.

Other classifications are *deluxe, superior* and *good,* or *super deluxe,* and *first-class reasonable.* Still another classification is A, B, C, D, or E. A uniform worldwide classification truly indicative of the grades of hotels in any country would be a real plus to tourism. Of course, differences in general standards of development in various countries would be understood. A five-star hotel in a highly developed country would likely be more deluxe than would a five-star hotel in a less developed area.

*Promotion Through Referral and Franchise Groups*  A substantial number of U.S. hotels and motels belong to some kind of an endorsing or referral association. Examples are Best Western, American Automobile Association (AAA), or Preferred Hotels. The main purpose of group membership is to obtain substantial numbers of reservations from other properties in the group and from the association's computerized reservation system.

Accommodations firms can also hold a franchise such as Holiday Inns, Hilton Inns, or Marriott Inns. All members of the franchise encourage their guests to make free reservations at another property in the group. Franchise companies operate sales offices in major cities (called hotel rep firms) and also provide national and international reservations services. All of this effort is aimed at increasing members' annual volume of reservations.

## TRANSPORTATION AND TRANSPORTATION EQUIPMENT

All factors concerning transportation should be considered in developing tourism, beginning with taxis, limousines, and bus service from the place of lodging to the departure terminals. Such services must be adequate and economical.

### Air

As described in Chapter 3, the airline industry dominates public intercity transportation systems, capturing about 92 percent of the common carrier passenger mile market. Thus, planners looking to improve tourism must evaluate the adequacy of air transportation. Flight frequencies as well as size and type of aircraft are important. Air service from important origins for tourists is, of course, essential.

Airport facilities must be adequate. Major problems frequently encountered are the accessibility to the airport and the loading-unloading-parking space sequence. Newly built airports seem to have solved these to a considerable degree and also reduced walking distances due to design improvements. There is also frequent shuttle bus service for interline passengers.

### Motorcoach

Motorcoaches intended for tour use should have large windows, air conditioning, comfortable seats, and rest room facilities. Springs or other suspension systems in the coaches should be designed so that the joggling of passengers is kept to a minimum or eliminated. Multilingual guide service or multilingual tape recording facilities with earphones for each passenger are desirable in communities or on tours where an interpretation of the points of interest is desirable.

Personnel assigned to buses should be selected for suitable temperament, courtesy, and spirit of hospitality. For example, if a bus is staffed by a driver and an interpreter, the interpreter can assist passengers on and off the bus as well as inform them of local environment, particularly attractions of interest. Interpreters or guides should be trained and educated for this duty. Too often, the interpretation of points of interest is superficial (and inaccurate). A program of certification for guides should be conducted by a special school or provided in the curriculum of an institution of higher learning. In such a program, competent instructors should educate potential guides in the history, archeology, ethnology, culture, and economic system of the area in which the tour is being conducted. Competency in the various languages commonly encountered with tourists is also an essential qualification.

The Dallas-Fort Worth airport exemplifies good planning for traveler convenience. Note the narrow terminal buildings requiring only a short walk to taxi and parking areas. There are airport hotels, multilevel parking ramps, and elevated highways connecting each terminal complex. An automated shuttle train provides passengers with transportation to the other terminals. Land area for future expansion has been included. (Photo courtesy of American Airlines)

## Ship and Boat

Water travel is a major part of tourism and contributes considerably to the development of travel on land and by air.

Forms of water travel include cruise ship, passenger travel on freighters, ferry boats, river stern wheelers, chartered boats and yachts, houseboats, and smaller family boats and canoes.

Cruise ships and other large vessels need convenient piers and good land-air transportation connections for their passengers. Smaller boats need docks and loading-unloading ramps for easy accessibility to water. Charter boat operators must have reliable weather forecasting and ready availability of needed supplies and repair services. Where rental canoes are popular, delivery and pickup services are often necessary as are campgrounds in wilderness areas where canoeists can stay overnight. Persons owning their own boats appreciate good public access points for launching.

## Rail

Travelers worldwide often prefer rail travel, particularly because of its unparalleled safety record and the convenience and comfort of viewing the scenery from an air-conditioned car. Also the frequent schedules of trains in many countries appeal to travelers. The recent advent of high-speed trains further enhances their appeal. Some trains have stewardesses or hostesses, which travelers seem to appreciate.

Adequate taxi, limousine, or bus service from the railroad station to hotels and

Breathtaking Glacier Bay is one of the scenic attractions that draw many people to Holland America's flagship *Rotterdam* for Alaska Inside Passage cruises. (Photo courtesy of Cruise Lines International Association)

Superliner family bedrooms provide a feature not formerly available on conventional U.S. sleeping cars—bedrooms that extend the full width of the car with windows on both sides. Able to accommodate three adults and two children, the family bedrooms have one wide lower berth, one upper berth, and two children's berths. (Amtrak photo)

downtown points is essential. Such transportation service must be frequent enough to get the traveler to the destination promptly. Conversely, the traveler should be able to get to the railroad station in ample time to make connections with the train as well.

Amtrak's Superliner diners set a new standard for luxurious rail travel. Operating on long-distance routes in the West, each bilevel diner has a seating capacity of 72 persons at 18 tables. The dining area, which is divided by a maitre d's and waiters' station in the center, is located on the upper level. Food is prepared on the lower level and then transported by dumbwaiters to the dining area above. (Amtrak photo)

## Taxis

Adequate taxi and limousine services are essential in a tourist area. Ideally, taxis should have removable and washable seat covers so the car always presents a clean appearance to the passenger. Also, the taxi driver, to make the best impression, should dismount from the driver's seat and open the door for the passenger. He or she also should assist in stowing the luggage in the trunk or elsewhere in the cab and be courteous at all times.

Taxi drivers that are multilingual are highly desirable and, in fact, essential if tourism is to be an important element of the economy of the state. Training taxi drivers in foreign languages should be no more difficult than training of tourist guides or front desk clerks.

Where taxi drivers have no foreign language ability, hotels may provide written directions for the tourist to give to the driver concerning the destination and the return to the hotel at the end of the excursion.

## HOSPITALITY AND CULTURAL RESOURCES

The development of hospitality resources is perhaps the most important factor in tourism. The finest physical facilities will be worthless if the tourist feels unwelcome. For example, we suggest having a welcoming sign and a special reception area for visitors at airports and other entry points. A favorable attitude toward the visitor can be created through programs of public information and propaganda. Public relations and publicity designed to convince local citizens of the importance of tourism are helpful. Courses at tourist hospitality schools for all persons who have direct contact with visitors are useful. In these schools, store clerks, gasoline station attendants, hotel clerks, and other persons who are directly in contact with the visitor are given indoctrination on the importance of tourism to their community and are

Theme parks and amusement centers are among the most important types of tourist attractions. (Photo courtesy of Sea World)

taught the location of important points of interest. Other parts of the program include the importance of appearance and good grooming, greeting of visitors, providing information, and being helpful, gracious, friendly, and cooperative.

Cultural programs such as "Meet the Danes" (home visitation arrangements) help greatly in this respect. Adequate training of personnel by tourist hospitality businesses can also create the desired hospitable attitude.

## Activities Tourists Enjoy Most

One of the most important functions of a tourism promotion organization is to ascertain what activities visitors would enjoy. When substantial data are accumulated, the findings should be reported to those who accommodate and entertain. They are thus guided into more successful methods and programs.

The best method of obtaining this information is by interviewing both the visitors and their hosts. Questionnaires can also be placed in guests' rooms. Public contact employees can be instructed to inquire politely as to guests' interests and entertainment preferences. Careful recording and thorough analysis of these data will result in findings of real value. When those responsible for attracting and hosting visitors provide the requested entertainment activities, the community will likely be a preferred destination area. There is no better advertising than a satisfied visitor. See Chapter 11, "Travel and Tourism Research."

## Shopping

Shopping is an important tourist activity and thus an essential element in the tourism supply as it affects the success of the tourist destination area. The most important single element in shopping is the authenticity of the products offered for sale as they relate to the local area. A product that is supposedly a "native handicraft" should be that. If it is an import, the purchaser may be disappointed if he or she expected an authentic, locally made item.

Tourists who are shopping are particularly interested in handicraft items that are typical or indigenous to that particular locale or region. Of course, they are also interested in essential items such as toothpaste, but our discussion here is confined to purchases that tourists make as souvenirs or special gifts.

Tourists can be encouraged to spend more money on shopping if displays are high quality, imaginative, and attractive. Hotels are excellent places for shops, and if these shops are exquisitely furnished and stocked, the tourist is attracted to the shop and is more likely to make purchases.

*Native Marketplaces* Another shopping experience concerns the local market or so-called "native marketplace." Such areas are rich in ethnicity and have much local color. They are popular with visitors, even though the visitor may not understand the language and may have trouble making a purchase. Although many persons in native shopping places do not understand any foreign languages, the sign language of bargaining is fairly universal.

Tourism is a "people" industry, and cheerful, friendly service makes visits memorable. (Photo by Fred W. Marvel, courtesy of Oklahoma Tourism Department)

*Shops and Clerks* Shopkeepers and clerks themselves should be amiable and courteous. Furthermore, the shopkeeper should not be so anxious to close a sale that the tourist is pressured. A tourist who is courteously served in a store and who makes a good purchase will tell friends back home. Thus, future business can be developed in this way. Salespeople should also take the time to explain the value of the item and relate something of its history that would be otherwise unknown to the purchaser. Of course, this information should be accurate and truthful.

Salespersons must have sufficient language ability to conduct conversations with the visitors. The most common language is English, but a knowledge of other languages that are commonly spoken by tourists who visit a particular area is a necessary qualification of clerks who serve these visitors. Salespersons must be patient and understanding and try to help the prospective purchaser cheerfully at all times.

*Prices and Unethical Practices* One of the most important considerations in shopping is the pricing of the goods. Probably resented more than any other single factor of tourism is higher prices for tourists than for local residents. Since many shoppers compare prices from one store to another, prices should be as consistent as possible and in line with costs.

If the shopkeeper resorts to unethical methods of selling such as deception, selling imitation goods or products of inferior quality, refusing to exchange damaged goods, or short-changing or short-weighting, the seller is hurting the tourist trade and should be prosecuted by local authorities.

### Entertainment, Recreation, and Other Activities

The recreation and other activities engaged in by tourists at their destination comprise a major component of tourism. Thus, considerable thought and effort should be devoted to the type of activities that visitors are likely to enjoy.

*Entertainment*  The most satisfying entertainment for visitors is native to the area. In any country, there are expressions of the culture in the music, dance, drama, poetry, literature, motion pictures, television, ceremonies, festivals, exhibits, shows, meetings, food and beverage services, and tours (or local excursions) that portray the best the area has to offer.

Not all forms of entertainment can be successfully described or illustrated in tourist promotional literature. One of the best ways to bring these entertainment opportunities to the attention of the visitor is with a social director whose desk is in the lobby of hotels, resorts, and other forms of accommodation so that the visitor can readily find out what is going on and make arrangements to attend. In European hotels this desk is traditionally staffed by the concierge who provides an amazing amount of information concerning all types of entertainment and activities available. An appropriate substitute is a knowledgeable person at the front desk to provide information concerning recreation and entertainment.

Embarking on the sternwheeler steamboat *Natchez* provides an experience that combines water travel, history, entertainment, and dining. (Photo courtesy of Louisiana Office of Tourism)

Bulletin board displays or posters and verbal announcements of outstanding events made in the dining room or other areas where guests gather can also provide entertainment information. A local newspaper that features articles concerning everyday as well as special entertainment events and opportunities is a valuable method of distributing information. These newspapers or bulletins are presently provided in popular vacation destination areas such as Miami Beach and Honolulu, but the idea is not widespread. In metropolitan centers, a weekly magazine is normally provided to hotel guests to give current information on entertainment, recreational, and cultural opportunities in the city.

*Special Events*  Entertainment can be provided very effectively as a special promotional event to attract visitors during an off-season. One of the best examples of this is "Aloha Week," which was inaugurated in Hawaii in the early 1960s to bolster tourist traffic in the fall. This festival is enthusiastically supported by local tourism interests and is very successful in attracting tourists. Musicians, dancers, exhibits, floral displays, and special programs are assembled and give the visitor an unusual opportunity to enjoy the beauty and excitement of cultural expression that this state offers.

The musical productions at Opryland theme park feature Country Music U.S.A., tracing the history of country music. (Photo courtesy of Tennessee Tourist Development)

Rodeo events are popular tourist attractions in the American and
Canadian West. (Photo courtesy of Arizona Office of Tourism)

Expositions and festivals are very attractive to visitors and deserve adequate
promotion.

***Museums and Art Galleries***   Museums and art galleries are another major attraction
for tourists. They provide some of the highlights in many of the world's most
important tourist destinations such as New York, Washington, D.C., Chicago, Paris,
London, Madrid, Rome, Singapore, Tokyo, Buenos Aires, Mexico City, and many

Located in the San Jose Plaza, the Pablo Casals Museum is a tribute to the renowned
cellist/composer Pablo Casals, who spent the last 20 years of his life in Puerto Rico. The
museum houses his cello, manuscripts, photographs, and a library of videotapes of Casals
Festival concerts. (Photo courtesy of Puerto Rico Tourism News Bureau)

others. The quality and magnitude of these institutions are an important consideration for attracting and satisfying tourists.

*Sports*  Golf and sports such as tennis, surfing, swimming, mountain climbing,
skiing, hunting, fishing, hiking, prospecting, or any other outdoor sports activity
require properly publicized facilities and services. Guides, equipment, charter boats,
and other services needed to enjoy these sports must be readily available at fair
prices. Convenience and accessibility are key factors in this type of entertainment.

## MATCHING SUPPLY WITH DEMAND

Providing an ample tourism supply to meet anticipated demand is a challenge for the
planner.

The following formula can be used to calculate the number of hotel rooms (or
other types of lodging) required:

$$\text{Room demand per night (100\% occupancy)} = \frac{\text{no. tourists} \times \text{\% staying in hotels} \times \text{average length of stay}}{365 \times \text{average no. of persons per room}}$$

$$R = \frac{T \times P \times L}{S \times N}$$

where

$T$ = number of tourists
$P$ = percentage staying in hotels
$N$ = average number of persons per room (obtained from hoteliers); this is the total
  number of guest nights divided by the number of guests, during any period of
  time
$R$ = room demand per night, at 100 percent occupancy
$O$ = hotel occupancy used for estimating (for 70 percent occupancy); divide number
  of rooms needed at 100 percent occupancy by 70 percent
$S$ = number of days per year in business
$L$ = average length of stay

Illustrating application of the formula,

$T$ = 1,560,000 visitors
$P$ = 98%
$L$ = 9 days
$N$ = 1.69
$O$ = 70%
$S$ = 365 days per year open for business

$$R = \frac{1,560,000 \times 0.98 \times 9}{365 \times 1.69} = \frac{13,759,200}{616.85} = 22,306 \text{ (rooms needed at 100\% occupancy)}$$

$$R = \frac{22,306}{.70} \text{ (as more rooms will be needed at 70\% occupancy than at 100\%)}$$

$R$ = 31,866 rooms needed

Infrastructure factors in supply will largely be determined by the number of guest rooms as well as restaurants, stores, and similar installations. Infrastructure appropriate to the size of the development is an engineering problem and is readily ascertained as the plans are developed.

Transportation equipment is generally supplied by commercial firms as well as publicly owned or quasi-public transportation facilities and services.

Regarding hospitality resources, the recruiting and training of staff for the various elements of supply is a critical one. The traveler generally enjoys being served by unsophisticated local persons who have had proper training and possess a hospitable attitude. Such persons may be recruited through government and private employment agencies as well as through direct advertisement to the public. Newly hired employees must be indoctrinated in the importance of tourism, how it affects their own personal welfare as well as that of their community, the importance of proper service to the visitors, and how their economic welfare is closely related to their performance.

Museums, art exhibits, festivals, craft shows, and similar cultural resources are usually created by community cooperation and the willing assistance of talented people. A chamber of commerce or tourism body is the best mechanism for organizing the creation of these hospitality resources.

## Task Analysis

The procedure used in matching supply with demand is called a task analysis. Suggested steps are as follows:

1. *Identification of the present demand*
   a. By mode of transportation and by seasons of the year
   b. For various forms of tourism such as activities, attendance at attractions, and similar categories
   c. For special events such as conventions, celebrations, fairs
   d. Group and tour visitors
   e. Family and individual visitors
   f. Business visitors
2. *A quantitative and qualitative inventory of the existing supply*
3. *The adequacy of present supply with present demand*
   a. Natural resources
   b. Infrastructure
   c. Transportation and equipment
   d. Hospitality and cultural resources
4. *Examination of present markets and the socioeconomic trends*
   a. Geographic market segmentation and orientation
   b. Demographic market segmentation and orientation
      (1) Population age, sex, occupation, family life stages, income, and similar data
      (2) Leisure time and work patterns

      c. Psychographic market segmentation

        (1) Motivations, interests, hobbies, employment orientation, skills, professional interests

        (2) Propensity to travel, responsiveness to advertising

5. *Forecast of tourism demand*

    a. Computer systems simulation method

    b. Trend analysis

    c. Simple regression — linear least squares

    d. Multiple regression — linear least squares

    e. Executive judgment or Delphi method

6. *Matching supply with anticipated demand*

    a. If adequate, no further action necessary

    b. If inadequate, inauguration of planning and development procedures

To perform the task analysis, certain skills are required, with statistical research techniques employed to identify and quantify the present demand. Suggestions for doing this will be found in Chapter 8, "Measuring and Forecasting Demand."

When making a quantitative and qualitative inventory of the existing supply, the aid of specialists and experts is usually needed. For example, the adequacy of the present supply in relation to present demand requires the work of tourism specialists such as travel agents, tour company and hotel executives, tourism promotion people, ground operators (companies that provide baggage transfers, taxi services, local tours, and similar services), shopkeepers, and perhaps a sample of the tourists themselves.

Examining the present markets and the socioeconomic trends that will affect future markets requires specialized market research activities. These should include determination of market characteristics, development of market potentials, market share analysis, sales analysis, competitive destination studies, potentials of the existing and possibly new markets, short-range forecasting, and studies of travel business trends. A number of sophisticated techniques are now available. The engagement of a reputable market research firm is one way to obtain this information.

Forecasting tourism demand is a perilous business. However, a well-structured statistical analysis coupled with executive judgment is most likely the best approach to this difficult problem. See Chapter 8 for several methods for accomplishing this.

Finally, matching supply with the anticipated demand must be done by knowledgeable planners. A tourism development plan within the master plan is recommended. Supply items are essentially rigid. They are elaborate and expensive and, thus, cannot be expanded rapidly. An exception would be transportation equipment. Additional sections of planes, buses, trains, or cars could be assembled quite rapidly to meet an unusually high-demand situation.

## Peaks and Valleys

The foregoing discussion dealt with matching supply and demand in a long-run context. Another important consideration is that of fluctuations in demand in the short run (seasonality) and the resulting peaks and valleys in demand. This is a vexing problem.

The reason for this is simply that tourism is a service and services cannot be placed in inventory. If a 400-room hotel rents (sells) 350 rooms on a particular night, it cannot place the other 50 rooms in inventory, for sale the following night. Regardless of how many rooms went unoccupied in the past, a 400-room property can only rent up to 400 rooms on any given night. By way of contrast, consider the case of some tangible good, say, television sets. If some television sets are not sold in one month, the storekeeper can keep them in inventory and sell them the next month. Of course, the storage charges, interest payments, and other expenses incurred in inventorying a particular item reduces the item's economic value. But in tourism, the economic value of unsold items such as the 50 hotel rooms mentioned is exactly *zero*.

It should be clear then, that while in most cases, firms selling tangible goods can deal with demand fluctuation through the inventory process, this option is not available to firms providing travel services. In the travel industry, an effort must be made to reduce seasonal fluctuations as much as possible. Because of the high economic cost involved, no effort should be spared in attempting to limit the amount of seasonal variations in demand. Nor can the problem be dealt with by simply selecting an appropriate supply level. The following charts illustrate various supply situations associated with fluctuating demand levels.

Suppose that the demand for a particular destination exhibits the seasonal pattern depicted in Figure 7.1*a*. If no action is taken to "level off" the demand, then three possible levels of supply can be considered. In Figure 7.1*b*, the level of supply is provided so that demand in the peak season is fully satisfied. This implies that tourists coming to the destination in the peak season will be accommodated comfortably and without overcrowding. However, during the slack season, the destination will suffer from extremely low occupancy levels, with obvious implications for profitability. If, on the other hand, the supply is set at a low level (Figure 7.1*c*), the facilities during the peak season will be overcrowded enough to detract from the tourist experience. Visitor satisfaction will be at a low level, and the future of such a resort area will be doubtful. Last, if supply is set in between the level of demand during the peak and the off season (Figure 7.1*d*), the problems are somewhat mitigated. Nevertheless, low occupancy will result during low demand periods, and overcrowding will result in peak periods—neither is desirable. To maximize customer satisfaction and to utilize the facilities year around, some action must be taken. Two strategies for dealing with this situation are

1. *Multiple use.* This involves supplementing peak-season attractions of a destination with other attractions that would create demand for travel to that destination during off-season periods. In effect, the peak season for the destination is extended. Examples of such efforts abound. In Michigan, for example, the current demand for off-season travel (during the fall, winter, and spring) has been successfully increased and sustained at much higher levels than 10 years ago. While Michigan was once viewed primarily as a summer destination, the development and promotion of winter sports in resort areas, foliage tours, and superb salmon fishing in the fall and spring have created new markets for these off-season periods.

    Festivals, special celebrations, conventions, and sports activities sponsored and promoted during off-seasons are other examples of multiple use strategies.

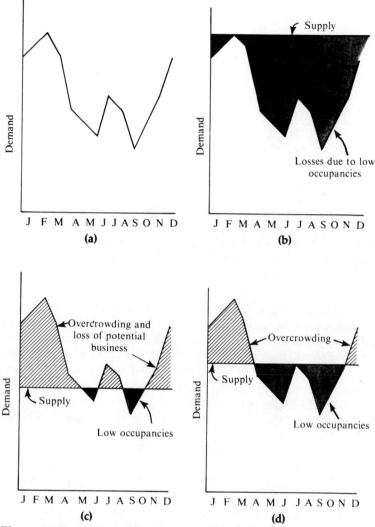

**Figure 7.1** Fluctuating Demand Levels and Supply.

2. *Price differential.* This technique, as contrasted with the multiple use strategy, creates new markets for the off-season periods by employing price differentials as a strong tool to shift demand away from the peak season in favor of the off-season. Florida and destinations in the Caribbean have used this strategy rather effectively. The prices in these destinations during the off-seasons are considerably less than during the peak seasons. In addition, the development of promotional fares by airlines and other carriers, and the expansion of the number, timing, and variety of price-discounted tours have all helped to stimulate demand in the off-season. Increased efficiency and effectiveness of promotional campaigns and better marketing also tend to offset the traditional seasonal patterns of demand.

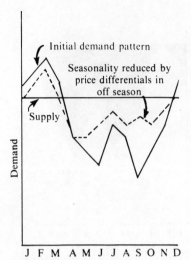

**Figure 7.2** Reducing Seasonality
Through Price Differentials.

In addition to these strategies implemented by destination areas, some trends in the employment and leisure patterns of Western societies further contribute to the leveling of demand between off and peak seasons. The staggering of holidays, the increasing popularity of three-day weekends with a holiday on Friday or Monday, the splitting of vacations between various seasons of the year all lend themselves to leveling the demand for travel. Once the demand is evened out, the destination is then able to maximize customer satisfaction during the peak season *and* during the off-season. Also, facilities are utilized at a considerably higher level than previously.

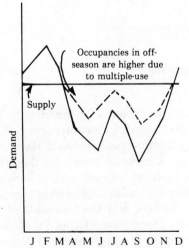

**Figure 7.3** Reducing Seasonality
Through Multiple Use.

The importance of boosting off-season demand and, therefore, utilization level is further underscored by the fact that in most tourist service businesses, fixed costs are quite high in relation to operating costs. This implies that increasing total yearly revenue, even modestly, produces proportionally larger profits. There may be some softening of demand during the peak season due to those who might switch to the off-season because of the lower prices. (See Figure 7.2.) However, this is believed to be minimal. When off-season demand is boosted by the multiple-use strategy, peak season demand is unaffected. Therefore, overall demand for the entire year will be substantially higher (See Figure 7.3).

# SUMMARY

Certain broad classifications of supply components must be provided by any area that is attractive to tourists. The components consist of natural resources, infrastructure, transportation-transport equipment, and hospitality and cultural resources. These factors may be combined in many ways to create the environment, facilities, and services that the planners hope will attract and please the customers.

Creation of supply components necessarily involves financing — a critical element.

Ideally, all of the supply components perfectly match the demand at any given time. However, this is unrealistic. Too much supply means unused facilities, which is uneconomic. Too little supply results in overcrowding with resultant depreciation of the vacation experience. A moderate supply level is recommended.

Supply can be matched with demand using a mathematical formula. When confronted with a supply problem, the proper level of supply to meet the anticipated demand can be estimated by using the formula provided in this chapter. The process is refined and completed by a six-step task analysis.

## Key Concepts

accommodations
entertainment, recreation, and other
     activities
financing
government financed components
hospitality resources
hotel management
infrastructure
matching supply with demand
multiple use
natural resources

peaks and valleys of demand
price differentials
reducing seasonality
regional planning
seasonality
shopping
task analysis
timesharing
total planning effort
transportation and transportation
     equipment

## For Review and Discussion

1. In planning supply components for a development in an entirely new area, which one of the four components should be considered first? Last? Why?

2. When a gorgeous new hotel is opened for business, are the attractive physical facilities more important than the quality and training of the staff?
3. As a resort hotel manager, do you believe there is any need to educate your guests about environmental protection? Is there a need to educate your staff?
4. In a poor, developing country, a world-class hotel uses about half of the community's water supply. This requires rationing of water by the local people, which creates resentment. Suggest a partial solution to this problem.
5. For new developments, should the access roads be supplied by a government agency, the developer, or both? If both, who should supply what?
6. What might be appropriate costumes and uniforms for waiters and waitresses in various localities?
7. A motor hotel manager states, "I can't seem to sell any souvenirs that cost over $5." How could this situation be improved?
8. The sports director of a large resort hotel has been instructed to upgrade the hotel's physical fitness program. Provide some suggestions as to how this might be done.
9. Is changing the prices of hotel rooms, meals, and entertainment the best way to mitigate fluctuating levels of demand? Are there nonprice methods? Could combinations of methods be used?

## Case Problems

1. In order to maintain and even enhance the appeal and quality of its area's natural resources, the city council has decided it needs to enact protective laws to help ensure its future tourism success. What specific laws and regulations might these be?
2. The director of the city's planning department has received an inquiry from a prominent hotel and motel systems company. This firm wants to find out if there is a need for a new concept budget motel there. How should the director proceed to ascertain this need?
3. Resort City is anxious to attract more tourists. The chamber of commerce has been successful in attracting several new tourist firms to the community. These firms plan to develop new hotels, motels, shops, and restaurants. However, an influential member of the chamber of commerce expresses the viewpoint that the community should enact some strict zoning and building code laws before these construction projects get underway. The prospective developers and many other members of the chamber disagree. What do you think should be done to resolve this situation and why?
4. A national tourism organization is seeking ways in which to improve the proficiency of accommodations management. It is exploring the possibility of installing a computer-based accommodations information system. This system provides data comparisons between similar operations considering size, location, and countrywide averages. What do you see as advantages for implementing such a system? How might the system be implemented in your country? What other management improvement incentives or programs could be provided?

## Selected References

Arbel, Avner, and Abraham Pizam. "Some Determinants of Urban Hotel Location: The Touristic Inclinations." *Journal of Travel Research,* Vol. 15, no. 3 (Winter 1977), pp. 18–22.

Clawson, Marion, and Jack L. Knetsch. *Economics of Outdoor Recreation.* Baltimore, Md.: Johns Hopkins University Press, 1966.

McCool, Stephen F. "Recreation Use Limits: Issues for the Tourism Industry." *Journal of Travel Research,* Vol. 17, no. 2 (Fall 1978), pp. 2–7.

Smith, Stephen L. "Room for Rooms: A Procedure for the Estimation of Potential Expansion of Tourist Accommodations." *Journal of Travel Research,* Vol. 15, no. 4 (Spring 1977), pp. 26–29.

Trowbridge, Keith W. *Resort Timesharing.* New York: Simon & Schuster, 1981.

Var, Turgut, R. A. D. Beck, and Patrick Loftus. "Determination of Touristic Attractiveness of the Touristic Areas in British Columbia." *Journal of Travel Research,* Vol. 15, no. 3 (Winter 1977), pp. 23–29.

Waddell, Joseph M. "Hotel Capacity: How Many Rooms to Build?" *The Cornell Hotel and Restaurant Administration Quarterly,* Vol. 18, no. 2 (August 77), pp. 35–47.

World Bank. *Tourism Supply in the Caribbean Region.* Washington, D.C.: The Bank, November 1974.

# Measuring and Forecasting Demand

## LEARNING OBJECTIVES

- Know the definition of demand and its application and importance in tourism development planning.
- Understand the factors determining the magnitude and fluctuations of demand.
- Become able to apply various methods to measure and forecast demand.

Economists define demand as a schedule of the amount of any product or service that people are willing and able to buy at each specific price in a set of possible prices during some specified period of time. Thus, there exists at any one time a definite relationship between the market price and the quantity demanded.

## WHY DEMAND IS IMPORTANT

The amount of demand for travel to a particular destination is of great concern to anyone involved in tourism. Vital demand data would include (1) how many visitors arrived, (2) by what means of transportation, (3) how long did they stay and in what type of accommodations, and (4) how much money was spent. There are various measures of demand; some are much easier to obtain and are usually of more general interest than are others. Techniques also exist for making forecasts of future demand. Such estimates are of great interest to anyone planning future tourism developments. The availability of financing will largely depend on reliable forecasts of the future gross sales or revenues from the project in order to determine if the proposal will be financially feasible.

Marketing and sales promotion programs are, of course, aimed at increasing demand. Sometimes this effort is focused on increasing demand at certain periods of the year or to a particular market. But the basic purpose is the same—to increase demand.

## DEMAND TO A DESTINATION

In somewhat more specific terms, the demand for travel to a particular destination will be a function of the propensity of the individual to travel and the reciprocal of the resistance of the link between origin and destination areas. Thus,

$$D = f(\text{propensity, resistance})$$

where $D$ is demand.

Propensity can be thought of as a person's predisposition to travel. In other words, how willing is the individual to travel, what types of travel experiences does he or she prefer, and what types of destinations are considered. A person's propensity to travel will, quite obviously, be largely determined by his or her psychographic profile and travel motivation, as discussed in previous chapters. In addition, a person's socioeconomic status will also have an important bearing on propensity. It follows that to estimate a person's propensity to travel, we must understand both psychographic and demographic variables concerning the person. Propensity is *directly* related to demand.

Resistance, on the other hand, relates to the relative attractiveness of various destinations. This factor is, in turn, a function of several other variables, such as economic distance, cultural distance, the cost of tourist services at destination, the quality of service at destination, effectiveness of advertising and promotion, and seasonality. Resistance is *inversely* related to demand.

## Economic Distance

Economic distance relates to the time and cost involved in traveling from the origin to the destination area and back. The higher the economic distance, the higher the resistance for that destination, and consequently the lower the demand. It follows, conversely, that between any origin and destination point, if the travel time or travel cost can be reduced, then demand will increase. Many excellent examples of this are available, such as the introduction of the jet plane in 1959 and the introduction of the wide-bodied jets in the late 1960s. They first cut travel time between California and Hawaii, for example, from 12 hours to 5 hours, and demand grew dramatically. A similar surge in demand was experienced with the introduction of the wide-bodied planes for transatlantic flights. The introduction of these planes cut the travel cost by almost 50 percent between the United States and most countries of the European continent.

## Cultural Distance

Cultural distance refers to the extent to which the culture of the area from which the tourist originates differs from the culture of the host region. In general, the greater the cultural distance, the greater will be the resistance. In some cases, however, the relationship might be the opposite. For example, the higher the cultural distance between particular origin and destination areas, the more an allocentric person may wish to travel to that destination, to experience this extreme difference.

## Cost of Services

The higher the cost of services at a destination, the higher the resistance to travel to that destination will be and, therefore, the lower the demand. This variable captures the familiar inverse relationship between the price of a good or service and demand for it.

### Quality of Service

Clearly, the higher the quality of service at a destination, the lower the resistance will be for travel to that destination. Although the relationship between quality of service and demand is straightforward enough, a difficulty arises in the interpretation and evaluation of "quality." Evaluation of quality is a highly personal matter, and what is quality to one tourist is not necessarily quality to another. Second, if a tourist does not have previous travel experience at a destination, can the tourist accurately judge the quality of services there? In such case, the tourist must select a destination based on what the quality of service is *perceived* to be. Often, due to misleading advertisements or inaccurate input from others, the tourist's perception of the quality of service may not be realized at the destination. Such a situation has serious implications for establishing a repeat clientele, which is an important ingredient for success in the tourist business. Consequently, a destination area must be meticulous in projecting an accurate image.

### Seasonality

The effect of seasonality on demand is quite apparent. The relative attractiveness of a given destination will depend on the time of year for which a vacation is planned. For a ski resort, for example, the demand will be at the highest level during the winter months. Resistance is at a minimum in this season.

The following illustrates the relationship between propensity, resistance, and demand, in terms of these variables as just described:

$$\text{Demand} = f(\text{propensity, resistance})$$

| *Propensity Depends on:* | *Resistance Depends on:* |
|---|---|
| Psychographics | Economic distance |
| Demographics (socioeconomic status) | Cultural distance |
| Marketing effectiveness | Cost of tourist services |
| | Quality of service |
| | Seasonality |

## MEASURING DEMAND

Demand is strongly affected and limited by the supply. If the supply aspects are not taken into consideration when using demand figures, then planners might be led into a false assumption that, in a particular area, the supply should be increased to meet the demand when, in actuality, the increased supply may be needed much more elsewhere.

There are several measures of actual demand:

1. Visitor arrivals
2. Visitor-days or -nights
3. Amounts spent

## Visitor Arrivals

Simply counting the number of people who arrive at a destination is a measure of demand, although not a particularly adequate one. However, when visitors arrive by ship or aircraft, for example, to an island, quite accurate data are obtainable. Those who are en route to someplace else should not be included in the arrival data. Visitor arrivals are the easiest type of data to obtain, especially if public transportation is the principal mode used. Regular reporting of visitor arrivals is of value in measuring broad changes in demand. Variation in the number of arrivals month by month is quite significant as it indicates the rise and fall of demand during the course of a year.

Arrival data become more of a problem if a large proportion of visitors arrive by private automobile on many major highways. In this case, a sampling method is employed, sometimes involving a tourist information center. Those stopping at the center are asked to fill out a card with data about their trip. The total number of visitors is then estimated, based on the sample obtained.

Visitors coming through seaports should be classified according to the United

Convenience creates demand. Visitors are shown bound for the slopes of Steamboat, Colorado, after deplaning from their direct flight to Yampa Valley Regional Airport. Three carriers, American Airlines, Northwest Airlines, and American West Airlines, fly nonstop to Steamboat from six different cities, helping Steamboat increase skier visits. (Photo by Larry Pierce, courtesy of Steamboat)

Nations' definition of tourists and excursionists. Excursionists remain in an area for less than 24 hours; tourists stay 24 hours or longer. Arrival statistics should not include those who illegally enter the country, air travelers who do not leave the airport transit area, or analogous cases.

## Visitor-Days or -Nights

These types of data are much more valuable to tourism planners than are the number of arrivals data. To calculate the former, the number of visitors is multiplied by their average length of stay. Public park planners and beach managers are interested in visitor-day figures. Hotel and other accommodations people want data on visitor-nights. When such data are obtained, it is not difficult to make an estimate of the likely expenditures made per visitor per day or night. But these expenditure figures are at best only estimates and need to be used carefully. Data on visitor-days and -nights are of great benefit to planners who are working on public facilities for tourists such as utility systems, parking, and recreation areas. Likewise, private developers planning new hotels or other accommodations or services want and need visitor-night information. Thus, visitor-days and/or -nights are the most practical data to obtain and are useful to tourism people.

$$D = \text{no. of visitors} \times \text{av. no. of days or nights at destination}$$

## Amounts Spent

This is the most meaningful measure of demand, if accurately determined. However, it is the *most difficult measure* to obtain. Statistics of this type tend to be hidden or partially forgotten by the visitor. Thus, they are not as accurate as desired. However, to members of legislatures and the public, total tourist expenditures are the most easily understood and the most impressive.

The most common method of estimating tourist expenditures is to multiply visitor-days or -nights by the average per day or per night expenditure. Thus,

$$D(\$) = \text{no. of visitor-days or -nights} \times \text{avg. expenditure per day/night}$$

Total expenditures in an area would be the sum of the visitor-day and visitor-night expenditures over a specified period of time.

## Measuring Tourism Expenditures Through Tax Collections

Many states have a sales and use tax on consumer items. These tax collections provide a statistical base for calculating tourist expenditures. Suppose that a state has a 4 percent use tax on hotel and motel rooms. If we know what percentage of the average tourist dollar is spent for lodging, we could make an estimate of how much is spent on lodging and total expenditures, as illustrated in the following hypothetical example:

Rooms tax collections                   = \$5 million
Rooms use tax rate                      = 4 percent
Total lodging spending                  = \$5 million ÷ 0.04 = \$125 million
Lodging expenditures                    = 25 percent of total spending
Total expenditures                      = \$125 million ÷ 0.25 = \$500 million
                                          (visitor-nights)

Estimated spending of those
   not using commercial lodging
   + visitor-day spending               = \$600 million

Total $D(\$)$ = \$500 million + \$600 million = \$1.1 billion

### Research in Measuring Demand

Considerable interest exists in improving methods of measuring current demand. Tourism is a labor-intensive service industry. As such, it is looked upon by state governments as a promising business to relieve unemployment. But one of the main problems is to determine its present financial dimensions.

Official tourism organizations are typically charged with the responsibility of undertaking research to measure economic impact and current demand. In this task they are assisted greatly by the U.S. Travel Data Center. Details on research are found in Chapter 11.

The next research task is to make an estimate of what the future demand might be, should certain steps be taken by the concerned destination area.

## PROJECTION METHODOLOGY

Several statistical methods or econometric analyses can be used to project demand. All require a degree of statistical or mathematical sophistication, familiarity with computers, and a clear understanding of the purpose (and limitations) of such projections. Listed are several such methods with brief explanations. (For more complete review, see references at the end of this chapter.)

### Trend Analysis Method

This method involves the interpretation of historical demand data. For instance, if a record of the number of tourist arrivals in an area on an annual basis is available, then demand for future years can be projected using this information.

The first step is to plot the available data on a graph — time (in years) against the tourist arrivals. Once this has been done, a linear trend can be established, which best captures the changes in demand levels in the past. Demand projections for future years can now be made by extending the trend line up to the relevant year and reading the demand estimate off the graph. Figure 8.1 illustrates this procedure. The points represent the levels of demand for the six-year period for which data are available.

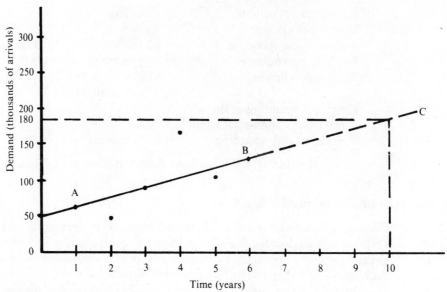

**Figure 8.1** Trend Analysis.

A linear trend in demand levels can then be determined (say, line *AB*). If a demand projection for year 10 were needed, the trend line *AB* can be extended to a point such as *C*. Finally, the projected demand level in year 10 can be determined to be approximately 180,000 arrivals as shown in Figure 8.1.

The advantage of using trend analysis is that the data needed are rather basic and easy to obtain. Only one data series is required — visitor arrivals, or some other measure of demand on a quarterly or on an annual basis for the past few years. In addition, the method is simple and does not require a great deal of mathematical sophistication. Characteristically, however, the simplicity of the model is to a large extent a trade-off for the usefulness of the results. For instance, the future demand estimates obtained in this manner should be interpreted with a great deal of caution. There are several reasons for this. First, trend analysis does not "explain" demand in any way. In other words, if demand changes from year to year, we would expect this to be due to changes in the components of demand (propensity and resistance, as discussed earlier in this chapter). Trend analysis does not acknowledge the influence that these variables have on demand levels and, therefore, cannot explain why it changed. Second, to *extrapolate* from a linear trend (extending the trend line *AB* to point *C*) is to assume that past growth trends will continue without change. Such an assumption is tentative at best. Estimates based on a constant growth rate tend to become very unrealistic in rather short periods of time, due to the nature of compounding.

## *Simple Regression — Linear Least Squares Method*

In this method, information on demand levels for past years is plotted against one important determinant of demand, say, income or prices. Then, through the application of a statistical technique called least squares regression, a straight line is used to "explain" the relationship between demand and the particular variable being considered (such as income levels of tourists). Consider, for example, the hypothetical data in Table 8.1 for demand levels for 10 years and the income levels of tourists for these same years.

By plotting the pairs of arrivals—income data on a graph—we obtain a relationship between income and travel demand, illustrated in Figure 8.2. The points represent the annual observations, and the line *AB* represents the line of "best fit." It is obtained by the least squares method.

We can now obtain demand projections from this method based on what we *expect* income levels to be in the future. Suppose we wish to estimate demand for year 15. In this year, income is projected to be $8300 per capita. As shown in the figure, the estimate of demand for this income level is 128,000.

Since income is a major determinant of demand, simple regression "explains" demand to some extent. It is superior to trend analysis for this reason. Besides, the methodology is still relatively simple and can be presented visually. Data needed for this method are relatively easy to collect, when compared to the data needs of the two following projections methods.

## *Multiple Regression — Linear Least Squares Method*

The major drawback of simple regression is that only one variable can be considered at a time. In reality, demand is affected by all the factors that influence propensity and resistance, as discussed earlier. It may not be feasible to include all these variables at one time, but it is certainly practical to isolate a few that are particularly relevant to determining demand and deal with these in one model. Multiple regression is one way to do this. It is essentially the same as simple regression, except that now more than one variable can be used to explain demand. Through a mathematical formula, a relationship is established between demand and the variables that we have chosen to consider in the model. For example, suppose that we had data on the prices of tourist services at a destination in addition to the incomes of the tourists. We

**Table 8.1** Demand and Income Data

| Year | No. Tourist Arrivals (thousands) | Per Capita Income of Tourists ($) |
|---|---|---|
| 1 | 75 | 6300 |
| 2 | 90 | 7200 |
| 3 | 100 | 7000 |
| 4 | 105 | 7400 |
| 5 | 95 | 6800 |
| 6 | 110 | 7500 |
| 7 | 105 | 7500 |
| 8 | 100 | 7200 |
| 9 | 110 | 7600 |
| 10 | 120 | 7900 |

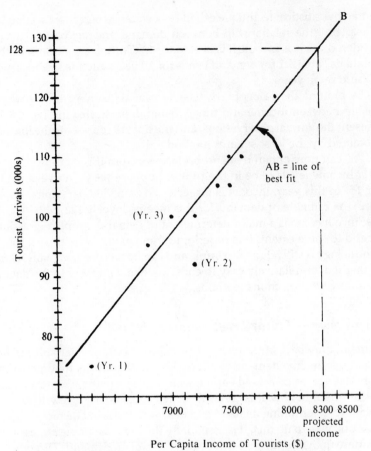

**Figure 8.2** Relationship Between Income and Travel Demand.

could then regress demand on these two variables (income and prices) and obtain a mathematical relationship between them. To estimate future demand, projected income and price levels for the relevant year can simply be substituted into the mathematical formula. The resulting estimate of demand will be more reliable than will one obtained by the simple regression method, since the former incorporates the *combined* effect of income and price on demand.

Indeed, the analysis is not restricted to these two variables alone. Conceptually, any number of variables can be used to explain and predict demand levels. But there are some practical limitations. As the number of "explanatory" variables increases, the calculations become increasingly complex. In addition, the costs involved in collecting the additional data and solving the mathematics of the technique are considerable. In some instances, the incremental reliability of the estimates may not justify these expenses, because estimates are after all estimates, and not certain to materialize—no matter how comprehensibly they may be calculated.

In addition to the expense involved, another drawback of multiple regression is that the relationships cannot be depicted graphically, as the results of the two earlier

Greatly increased demand for cruising has brought about a
remarkable expansion in the number of cruise ships and has also
spurred numerous mergers of cruise line companies. (Photo
courtesy of Cruise Lines International Association)

methods can be. The reason is, of course, that we get into multidimension planes. Up
to three dimensions can be depicted visually, but beyond that, it becomes impossible.

### Computer Systems Simulation Method

An approach to projecting demand based on a computer systems simulation method
is most promising. There are two features of primary significance in this approach.
First, the prediction of tourism demand at the destination is broken into two phases.
Phase I involves the use of *observed* participation rates *at the origin* correlated with
socioeconomic data to give estimates of future demand *at the origin.* Phase II consists
of predicting the probable future distribution of this demand *at the destinations* by
simulating the flows of visitors on the computer with the model appropriately
modified to represent future conditions. Many sophisticated approaches to demand
distribution prediction are severely handicapped because they become too complicated when the entire process is attempted in one step.

The second outstanding feature of this approach is that the computer simulation takes into consideration all the demand at all the origins simultaneously and
distributes it to the destinations. It is a *dynamic* model of a *dynamic situation.*

Let us examine the entire procedure in some detail to see how it works.

When gaming became legal in Atlantic City, New Jersey, hotels, restaurants, and other service businesses had to make demand estimates in order to plan remodeling or expansion. Many new properties were built to satisfy the increased demand. (Photo courtesy of New Jersey Division of Travel and Tourism)

*Demand at the Origin*  A sampling is done in important origin centers to ascertain how many visitors spent how many days at the destination(s). This will then give the total estimated number of visitors from that origin point.

*Model Structure*  The model consists of three basic groups of components: (1) origin countries, (2) destination countries, and (3) the transportation link in between.

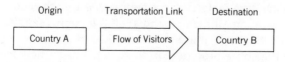

In setting up the model, the centers of population of a country can be treated as *nodes* from which the flow of visitors emanate. Similarly, the main destinations in a country can be designated as *destination nodes*. The most direct transportation routes between these *nodes* then become the "transportation links" for those particular origins' destination.

Each of the transportation links should be measured for distance and also assigned an average speed and cost where applicable.

In constructing the computer systems model, simulation equations are written based on the principle that

$$\text{Demand (for any link)} = f(P \times \text{resistance of the link})$$

where $P$ is the propensity to participate at the origin. The resistance of a link is a function of distance and cost, as previously described.

It will be readily seen that the number of calculations needed to simulate this flow during one model run on the computer can be fantastic based on the number of origins that can feed visitors to each of the various destinations through a variety of combinations of linkages. Let's look at just four countries to see the possible combinations:

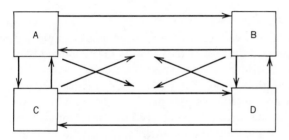

Here there is a total of 12 possible direct flow routes. This means 12 equations to be solved in the model.

*Tuning the Model*   Once the origin data are assembled and the model program written, an initial test run can be made whereby the *known demand* at the origin is "distributed" to the destinations. A subroutine in the program can compare the predicted distribution with the actual measured distribution of this demand at the destinations. The difference between the predicted value and the actual value is expressed as a percentage of error on the computer printout. A "tuning" procedure can then follow whereby certain constants in the program are adjusted until the individual and gross errors are brought within acceptable limits. In other words, the model can be tuned until it represents reality within reasonable limits.

*Predicting Future Demand*   Once the model was shown to be giving reasonably accurate distributions for the known base year, it could be used to predict probable future distributions. For example, in one simulation, the 1995 demand at the origin can be computed using the observed 1988 participation rates and applying these to the official state projections of 1995 population. There can also be an implied assumption that the *composition* of the origin populations would be basically the same in 1995 as it was in 1988 since a substantial change in the socioeconomic structure of the origin populations would probably result in a change in participation rates.

Another could be 1995 simulations of certain changes in the supply aspects of the model. The capacity of the country for tourism could be increased. An increase in capacity due to greater public and private access development could be accomplished. Information on planned improvements to the highway system or airport facilities, aircraft, and travel time from airport to city could be used as a basis for the changing of distances, speeds, and costs.

The 1995 demand distributions that resulted from these simulations could then be related numerically to the estimated 1995 supply of tourism facilities in each distribution area. The resultant values for either a projected surplus or deficit could then be computed.

The computer systems simulation method of predicting demand is emerging as a very promising technique. Its main advantages are

1. It is basically simple yet a reasonably realistic representation of the real world.
2. The future demand for all major tourism activities can be predicted by this approach.
3. The destination zones can and should be reasonably *small*.
4. The origin areas should also be *small*. However, by "small" is meant that demographic data are available for such areas. For example, a major city or a county is the standard unit for census reports in the United States.
5. Demand estimation for the base year is based on actual measurements rather than on the application of unreliable national or regional demand data.
6. The problem of how to forecast the probable distribution of predicted origin demand at the destinations has been solved by a mechanical procedure. It does not rely entirely on the individual planner's interpretations and judgments. In view of this, and since it is tuned using measured relationships, it is reasonable to believe that the technique has a fair degree of reliability.
7. Interaction between components is a basic characteristic of the approach so it is appropriately used to simulate the behavior of a complex dynamic situation involving much interaction.
8. Demand is expressed in the same units as supply, so the two can be related numerically.
9. The process is relatively fast and repeatable so a number of alternative situations or solutions can be modeled.
10. The amount of personal judgment involved in the process is identified and controlled.
11. Once the program is set up and satisfactorily tested, much of the routine application can be done by technicians following a manual, thus releasing more highly trained tourism planners for analysis of results and plan formulation.

There are obviously some problems with the technique. Specially trained personnel are required to set up the original model and data processing programs, plus a large amount of special data. These are serious problems that have to be faced by any tourism organization that might consider using the computer systems simulation method.

## Executive Judgment (Delphi) Method

Mathematical and statistical models are most useful and often produce accurate results. However, the combined experience of tourism executives is also valuable. The Delphi method, in essence, consists of a systematic survey of such experts. A series of questions is asked, and then the results, as a consensus, are reached.

Mathematical-statistical tools cannot incorporate the influences of variables not explicitly included in the model. For example, under multiple regression, income and travel prices were the only two variables used to predict demand. However, other factors such as the political situation, fuel situation, changes in taste, amounts of leisure, and the effectiveness of promotion campaigns obviously have an impact on demand levels. By the Delphi method, the combined effects of all such factors are carefully considered from the base of the executive's experience.

For estimating tourism demand, then *a combination of various mathematical-statistical methods and the Delphi method* is believed to produce the most reliable demand estimates in any given situation.

## SUMMARY

Demand, without doubt, is the fundamental measure of any area's success in attracting visitors. All planning activities are ultimately intended to increase or control demand. Marketing programs are aimed at increasing demand, sometimes at certain periods during the year, and/or to attract particularly identified market segments.

Understanding demand requires a knowledge of its definition, what comprises demand, what affects the levels of demand, and how future demand can be identified and estimated. Thus, use of demand data is essential in any tourist business situation.

Development of a destination area, whether by public authority, private developers, or both requires demand data that are as accurate as possible. Providing such data is one of the most important responsibilities of an official tourism organization. Similar data are provided by research organizations and consulting firms, usually when commissioned to make feasibility studies. Any development proposal must have ample estimates of expected demand before any financing can be committed.

Becoming familiar with methods of measuring or estimating present and future demand, as described in this chapter, should enable you to produce such data. With the current high cost of land and construction, reasonably accurate demand statistics are of paramount importance.

## Key Concepts

| | |
|---|---|
| amounts spent | demand measures |
| arrivals | economic distance |
| computer systems simulation | executive judgment (Delphi method) |
| cost of services | increasing demand |
| cultural distance | linear least squares method |
| demand forecasts (projection) | multiple regression |

projection methodology              tax collections
propensity                          trend analysis
quality of service                  visitors
resistance                          visitor-days
seasonality                         visitor-nights
simple regression


## For Review and Discussion

1. Why is demand data so important? Give examples. By whom is demand data used?
2. Explain why resistance to make a trip is inversely related to demand. Are there situations with which you are familiar?
3. Describe in detail the three factors that determine propensity. Create an example using all three of these major elements.
4. What determines the degree of resistance to travel experiences? Considering the five factors described in this chapter, give an example involving: (1) an irresistible travel offer, and (2) a seasonal travel product.
5. Using the three measures of demand presented, describe a situation in which each one of these would be the most meaningful.
6. A state tourism director wants to convince the legislature to increase the promotion budget for the next fiscal year. What measure of demand should be used? How might this data be obtained?
7. How much faith should be placed in mathematical models of demand projection? What characteristics of input data affect the degree of reliability?
8. A national lodging chain is planning expansion. What are the best methods for estimating future demand?
9. How valuable is trend analysis?
10. What is the Delphi method?


## Case Problems

1. The federal government has imposed an increase in the gasoline tax of 50¢ per gallon, effective in three months. How might a motel franchise headquarters organization estimate the effect on demand that this new tax would have for their member motels, which are located in all parts of the country? How could a restaurant chain organization operating turnpike food services make such an estimate? How could a regional airline?
2. William D. is executive vice-president of his city's chamber of commerce. John A., representing a major hotel chain, visited Mr. D. and stated that his company was contemplating construction of a 280-room deluxe motor hotel in the city. But, before doing so, the company needed travel and hotel demand estimates. How could Mr. D. proceed to supply these?

## Selected References

Calatone, Roger J., Anthony Di Benedetto, and David Bojanic. "A Comprehensive Review of the Tourism Forecasting Literature." *Journal of Travel Research,* Vol. 26, no. 2, pp. 28–39.

Clawson, Marion, and Jack L. Knetsch. *Economics of Outdoor Recreation.* Baltimore, Md.: Johns Hopkins University Press, 1966.

Committee on Assessment of Demand for Outdoor Recreation Resources. *Assessing Demand for Outdoor Recreation.* Washington, D.C.: Assembly of Behavioral and Social Sciences, National Research Council, National Academy of Sciences, The Committee, 1975.

Mak, James. "Taxing Hotel Room Rentals in the U.S." *Journal of Travel Research,* Vol. 27, no. 1 (Summer 1988), pp. 10–15.

Marzella, Dennis A., George R. Conrade, and Samuel S. Shapiro. *Characteristics of Demand for Miami Beach Hotels, Phase I—Marketing Research Report.* Miami: Florida International University, no date.

Marzella, Dennis A., Samuel S. Shapiro, and George R. Conrade. *Characteristics of Demand for Miami Beach Hotels, Phase II.* Miami: Florida International University, 1976.

Recreation Resources Center. *Upper Great Lakes Regional Recreational Planning Study.* Part 2, *Recreation, Demand Survey and Forecasts.* Madison: University of Wisconsin, The Center, 1974.

Ritchie, J. R. Brent, and Michael Sheridan. "Developing an Integrated Framework for Tourism Demand Data in Canada." *Journal of Travel Research,* Vol. 27, no. 1 (Summer 1988), pp. 3–9.

U.S. Travel Data Center. *National Travel Survey—Full-Year Report.* Washington, D.C.: USTDC. Annual.

U.S. Travel Data Center. *Travel Printout.* Washington, D.C.: USTDC. Monthly.

U.S. Travel Data Center. *1989 Outlook for Travel and Tourism.* Washington, D.C.: USTDC, 1988.

U.S. Travel Data Center. *1977 National Travel Expenditure Study.* Washington, D.C.: USTDC, 1979. Plus appendices.

Uysal, Muzaffer, and John L. Crompton. "An Overview of Approaches Used to Forecast Tourism Demand." *Journal of Travel Research,* Vol. 23, no. 4 (Spring 1985), pp. 7–15.

Waters, Somerset R. *Travel Industry World Yearbook, The Big Picture.* New York: Child and Waters. Annual.

Witt, Stephen F., and Christine A. Martin. "Econometric Models for Forecasting International Tourism Demand." *Journal of Travel Research,* Vol. 25, no. 3 (Winter 1987), pp. 23–30.

# CHAPTER 9

# The Economics of Tourism

## LEARNING OBJECTIVES

- Know the economic place and impact of tourism.
- Perceive the relationship between tourism and employment.
- Understand multipliers.
- Know about balance of payments.
- Recognize the concepts of demand and supply.
- Comprehend elasticity and inelasticity.

## OPTIMIZATION

Economics is concerned with the attainment of an optimum return from the use of scarce resources. Whether it is an individual seeking psychological benefit from travel, or a business interested in providing tourists goods and services at a profit, or a host community government viewing tourism in terms of the economic benefits resulting from tourist expenditures, the principle is the same. Economic agents seek to fulfill psychological and physical wants (which, as a rule, are limited). The problem that economics attempts to solve is how these scarce resources should be allocated in the pursuit of a variety of unfulfilled needs and wants.

### Goals

As indicated, at least three major goals can be identified in tourism:

1. Maximize the amount of psychological experience for tourists.
2. Maximize profits for firms providing goods and services to tourists.
3. Maximize the primary and secondary impacts of tourist expenditures on a community or region.

These goals are often compatible; maximizing psychological experience creates happy clientele, which causes them to return, to spend money, and to make everyone in the industry and the region satisfied. In certain situations, they can also be incompatible. A short-run profit-maximizing goal may cause the development of facilities beyond capacity of the site, thus leading to overuse and a decline in psychic enjoyment. Extreme emphasis on tourism as an element in economic development might have the same result. There can also be clashes between use of resources for tourism and for other kinds of development.

## Constraints

The second half of the optimizing situation is occupied by those factors that place obstacles in the way of goal attainment. We assume that it is desirable to have unlimited amounts of psychic enjoyment, profits, and local impacts. But that is not possible because something is always getting in the way. Tourism, being extremely broad and diverse, must deal with a large number of constraints. To make an analysis of relationships, it will be necessary to classify them.

*Demand*   Every firm providing goods and services to tourists is constrained by the demand functions of its customers. These relate quantity purchased to price, wealth, and income.

*Supply of Attractive Resources*   Possibly one of the most important constraints faced by the industry as a whole is the limited amount of resources available for tourist enjoyment. This is particularly true when geographic distribution of these sites is considered. Some areas are simply better attractions for tourists than others.

*Technical and Environmental Constraints*   These are usually related to a particular site or situation. They involve such things as the relationship between sewage effluent disposal and the environment, numbers of fish and numbers of fishermen, number of people who can walk in a given area without causing unacceptable damage, number of elephants supportable on a wildlife range, impact on lions' behavior of observing them from a car, number of campsites possible in a given area without harming the environment, and so on.

*Time Constraints*   The amount of vacation time available limits what the vacationer can do. The length of the tourist season influences profitability of tourist-oriented businesses and the impact of tourist expenditures on the local economy.

*Indivisibilities*   Many times it is necessary to deal with all of something or nothing. It is not possible to fly half an airplane, even though the seats are only half filled. It may not be profitable to build a hotel under a given size. A road has to be built all the way from one point to another.

*Legal Constraints*   There are several types of legal constraints affecting tourism. Activities of the government tourist bureau might be one. Laws concerning environmental problems could be another. Zoning and building codes may influence the construction of facilities. Laws concerning contractual relations may limit activities.

*Self-Imposed Constraints*   This type of constraint arises from a need to reconcile conflicting goals. The conflicts may arise within a firm or among firms, government agencies, and so on that are seeking to develop a particular area or concept.

*Lack of Knowledge*   Many activities are limited because little is known about particular situations. Businesspeople are used to living with a certain amount of uncertainty, but there are inevitable limits to the amount they are willing to countenance. Ignorance influences governmental operations as well.

*Limits on Supportive Resources*   There are always limits to the amount of money, managerial talent, workers, construction materials, social capital, and so on. And these, in turn, limit chances to provide psychic experiences, take advantage of profit-making opportunities, or develop local attractions.

Many times these individual constraints interact, creating compound constraints on given activities.

## Optimizing the Experience

Maximization of the tourist experience is subject to a number of constraints and is manifested in the demand function. Demand for tourist experience is peculiar in the sense that the product being purchased is not easy to identify directly and is frequently purchased sight unseen.

The tourist is particularly constrained by time and budget. To optimize the experience, it is necessary to determine the combination of destinations preferred and then the possibilities within the money and time constraints. This explains some of the popularity of package tours, where both time and cost can be known in advance. There are some exceptions. Retired persons and young people often have time but limited resources. A few people have neither constraint.

## Optimizing Returns to Businesses

Since goods and services provided to tourists are really inputs to the process of producing the experience, demand for them is derived from demand for tourism as a whole. Some goods and services are complementary, and their demand is interrelated in a positive fashion. Others are substitutes and are characterized by limited area competition.

Packaged tours have the characteristic of putting all parts and services together, so they become complementary. Competition occurs among tours. Tour operators can maximize profits by selling tours of different value and costs, in order to cater to as many people as possible along the demand curve. The number of people to be accommodated can be determined from the marginal cost of the tour and the marginal revenue to be derived from a given price level.

Goods and services sold to tourists are subject to severe peaking in demand. That is, the heaviest tourist season is usually limited. During that period, demand is intense and must be met with facilities that are excess in the off-season. This means that investment necessary to provide the excess capacity must be paid for from revenues received during the peak period. During off-peak periods, only variable cost is of interest, but, since demand is low, some capacity will not be utilized.

As owner of the facilities, firms are concerned with providing adequate long-run capacity and with choosing those investments that will give optimum returns. In the tourist industry, a number of interrelationships must be considered. Sometimes, low benefit-cost investments are made so that higher yielding investments can succeed. Consequently, it is not always true that investors choose the highest-yielding opportunities.

Generally, it is considered the long-run business of the firm to remove constraints on operations. But in tourism there are a number of constraints to expansion. These include demand for the tourist experience and environmental constraints.

## Optimizing for the Local Economy

Tourism affects a region during periods of intense investment activity and afterward when the investments are producing. The effects are dependent upon linkages among economic units.

Money spent for investment will go to construction and a few other industrial sectors. These will have links to economic units varying from households to manufacturing plants. Money spent by tourists will also be introduced through a few sectors that will also be linked to the economy.

The multiplier effects in both cases are dependent upon the strength of the linkages. The multiplier reflects the amount of new economic activity generated as basic income circulates through the economy. Some sectors have strong links to other sectors in an economy and a large multiplier effect. Others have weak links and small multipliers. It is possible to have a thriving tourist industry and abject poverty in the local populace, if there are not links. For example, linkages will be strong and the income multiplier high if the year-round resorts in a particular destination area hire all local labor; buy their flowers, fruit, and vegetables and poultry products from local farmers; hire local entertainers; and buy furnishings for guest rooms from local manufacturers. Linkages would be weak if most of these goods and services were imported from another state or country.

## Tourism Exports and Imports

The host region is defined loosely as a country, a state, or a nation, depending on the level at which the problem is being considered. For a county-level government, the income of the county is of primary interest. A state government would perceive the maximization of the combined income of the entire state to be its objective and so on.

Regardless of which definition of host region is being considered, expenditures in this area by tourists coming from another region represent *injections* into the area's economy.

West Germans traveling to the United States presumably earned their income in Germany. When spending money in the United States as tourists, they are "injecting" money into our economy that wasn't here before. As such, expenditures by foreigners in this country (for travel purposes) represent *tourism exports* for the United States. This may be somewhat confusing since we are accustomed to thinking of something leaving the country as an export. When we export computers or cars, for example, these commodities are sent out of the United States. In the example of the German tourists, the tourists are coming *into* this country. So how is it an export? There seems to be a contradiction in terminology. As the astute student would note, however, when tourists come into this country, they are purchasing travel experiences. When they leave, they take these experiences back with them. We have exported travel experiences, which are, after all, what tourism is all about.

Figure 9.1 clarifies this concept. When U.S. tourists travel to Germany and spend money there, this becomes a tourism *import* to the U.S. economy. For the Germans, their money spent in the United States is a tourism *import* for the German economy.

In tourism exports, the flows of tourists and payments are in the same direction, whereas in commodity exports, the two flows are in opposite directions. Therein lies

Tourists arriving from Japan will spend money in the United States and take travel experiences home with them. These tourists create export income. (Photo courtesy of the Boeing Company)

the confusion. However, if one were to look at the *direction of payment flow* to determine what is an export, there is no contradiction between the two cases. When payment flows into the United States, something has been exported—travel experiences, for instance, or commodities. Both payment flows are in the same direction.

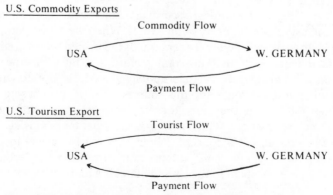

**Figure 9.1** Economic Comparison—Commodity Flows and Tourist Flows.

## Balance-of-Payments Effects

Tourism is one of the world's largest international industries. As such it has a noticeable impact on the balance of payments of many nations. We have heard much about the balance-of-payments problems of the United States, and, indeed, tourism imports do affect the balance of payments and economic conditions generally. We define tourism imports as those expenditures made by American tourists in foreign countries. An easy way to remember this is "Who got the money?" If for example, Britain received American funds, it makes no difference whether we bought some English china or an American tourist visited England.

Our balance-of-payments situation directly affects the gross national product of the United States $(Y)$. The formula is

$$Y = C + I + G + (X - M)$$

where

$$Y = \text{GNP}$$
$$C = \text{consumer expenditures}$$
$$I = \text{investments}$$
$$G = \text{government expenditures}$$
$$X = \text{exports}$$
$$M = \text{imports}$$

By looking at the formula, we can see that if imports $(M)$ exceed exports $(X)$, it will be a negative number and $Y$ will, thus, be smaller. So it is advantageous to us in our American economy to attract more visitor spending in the United States. These "tourism exports" are like credits and help our economy. It is economically better to have foreign visitors come to the United States than it is to have U.S. citizens travel abroad. However, this should be tempered with the realization that the situation is not entirely positive or negative.

Expenditures by U.S. tourists abroad make possible purchasing power in foreign countries for those countries to buy American-made products. For example, most airlines of the world use American-made equipment. Purchase of these aircraft, parts, supplies, repair services, and so forth makes an important contribution to the export trade of the United States, and thus, we cannot charge the tourist industry with all the problems of our negative balance of payments. The purpose of the foregoing discussion is simply to point out the relationships.

Tourism exports become very desirable as far as the gross national product and the prosperity of the country are concerned. Efforts on the part of the United States Travel and Tourism Administration to attract foreign visitors have a great impact on the balance-of-payments situation. Business firms, which serve the foreign visitor, provide desired services, and stimulate sales, materially help our national economy. However, during periods when the U.S. dollar is high against foreign currencies, a dampening effect occurs on our tourism exports as this situation is seen as unfavorable by prospective foreign visitors. Conversely, if the dollar is low, more foreign tourists will visit the United States. This increases our tourism exports, improves our balance of payments, and raises the gross national product. These same relationships of comparable currency values exist between any country that exports tourism and the countries of its tourists' origin.

World-famous attractions draw tourists from many countries and create a favorable balance of payments. (Photo courtesy of the Boeing Company)

## Investment Stimulation

The tourist industry has a unique structure. It is characterized by, and, in fact, is, an agglomeration of a large number of very small units, covering a variety of different service trades—the small restaurants, motels, guest houses, laundries, arts and crafts shops, and others. Thus, investment in infrastructure and sometimes expensive superstructure by the government stimulates investment in numerous smaller businesses. Because of the small size of these businesses, capital requirements are relatively low and investment generally proceeds at a rapid pace. In this respect, too, governments view tourism rather favorably. The initial investment in tourism brings forth a large investment in supporting and tertiary industries. This also includes large investments in major hotels, restaurants, shopping centers, marinas, airports, and so on.

## Tourism Increases Tax Revenue

Tourists must pay taxes like most other people. Since they come from other regions or countries, their expenditures represent an increased tax base for the host government. In addition to the usual sales tax, tourists sometimes pay taxes in less direct ways. Airport taxes, exit fees, customs duty, and charges assessed for granting visas are just a few examples of commonly used methods of taxing tourists. The wisdom of imposing such special taxes on tourists is questionable, since it merely serves to reduce demand. In some countries, for instance, the room rate at a hotel can be different for tourists (generally higher) than for residents. This is a questionable practice, for it leaves the tourist with a feeling that he has been "taken."

Apart from these special cases, the usual taxes collected from both tourists and residents increase due to tourism expenditures.

Is tourism, then, a panacea for all the economic woes of a region or country? It has been claimed that tourism increases incomes, employment, investment, tax revenues, and so forth, so it might indeed appear to be one. However, there are constraints that limit the extent to which governments can maximize the benefit from these aspects of tourism. These constraints are of two types: social and economic. The social constraints have already been discussed. The economic constraints are in the form of potential economic costs that the tourism industry may impose. These merit further scrutiny to gain a better understanding of the government's optimization problem.

## Inflationary Pressure

Tourists inject money (earned elsewhere) into the destination economy. While this increases the income of the region (as discussed earlier), it also might cause inflationary pressures. Tourists typically have a higher expenditure capability than the residents do—either because tourists have higher incomes or because they have saved for the trip and are inclined to "splurge" while on vacation. Hence, they are able to somewhat bid up the prices of such commodities as food, transportation, and arts and crafts. This causes inflationary pressures, which can be detrimental to the economic welfare of residents of the host community. This is particularly true when inflation affects the prices of essentials such as food, clothing, transportation, and housing. Land prices have been known to escalate rapidly in tourist destination areas. The prices that foreigners are willing to pay for "vacation homes" in the area can decrease the demand for "first homes" by residents.

Lundberg[1] notes that as the tourist industry developed in an area, land prices rose sharply. In a particular underdeveloped area, the amount of investment in land constituted just 1 percent of the total investment for a hotel project. By contrast, this ratio increased to 20 percent in an area where tourism was already overdeveloped. With such increases in land prices, it can be expected that local residents (with their lower incomes) are effectively "chased out" of the housing market in a tourism-developing section.

## ECONOMIC MULTIPLIERS

### Direct Effect

In addition to the direct impact of tourism expenditures on an area, there are also indirect impacts. The indirect or "multiplier" impact comes into play as visitor spending circulates and recirculates. The direct effects are the easiest to understand

[1] Donald E. Lundberg, "Caribbean Tourism," *The Cornell Hotel and Restaurant Administration Quarterly*, Vol. 14, no. 4, February 1974, pp. 30–45.

Tourism has a powerful economic impact because tourists inject money into the destination economy. New York City is the world's top tourist destination, as well as the site of the world headquarters for the United Nations Organization (building in foreground). (Photo courtesy of New York Division of Tourism)

This chartered motorcoach tour, carrying about 40 people, will generate about $3500 for the local economy. The tourists' expenditure for meals, lodging, shopping, admission fees, discretionary spending, and other expenses will ultimately become widely distributed and will be multiplied during the ensuing year. (Photo courtesy of National Tour Association)

as they result from the visitor spending money in tourist enterprises and providing a living for the owners and managers and creating jobs for employees.

## Indirect Effect

This visitor expenditure gives rise to an income that, in turn, leads to a chain of expenditure-income-expenditure and so on, until leakages bring the chain to a halt. Consequently, the impact of the initial income derived from the tourist's expenditure is usually greater than the initial income, because subsequent rounds of spending are related to it. For example, a skier purchases a lift ticket for $30. This money received by the ski area will be used to pay the wages of the lift operators. The lift operator spends the money on groceries; the grocer uses the money to pay part of his rent to the local landlady; the landlady uses it to pay for her dry cleaning; the dry cleaner spends it in a restaurant for a dinner; the restaurant owner spends it for steaks shipped in from Kansas City; and the cycle stops as the money is lost to the local economy. This last transaction is known as "leakage" from the economy.

The combination of the direct and indirect effects of an expenditure pattern determines the impact. In a typical situation, not all of the income generated in each round of expenditure is respent. Some portion tends to be saved, and some portion tends to be spent outside the local economy. The greater the proportion of income spent locally, the greater will be the multiplier.

The degree to which a local area is able to retain tourist income depends on how self-sufficient the local economy is. If the local economy is able to produce the goods and services tourists buy, the greater will be the multiplier effect. The more goods that have to be imported from outside the region, the smaller the multiplier will be.

From the discussion, it is clear that when a tourist's spending injects funds into the economy of a host area, an economic effect occurs that is a specified number of times what was originally spent. Initially this effect is thought of as an *income multiplier*, as tourist expenditures become income directly and indirectly to local people. However, there are additional economic phenomena. Increased spending necessitates more jobs, which results in an *employment multiplier*. Because money changes hands a number of times during a year, there is a *transactions multiplier*. This is of particular interest to governmental tax officials where sales taxes are imposed. As business grows in a tourist destination area, more infrastructure and superstructure are constructed. This results in a *capital multiplier*. Examples are provided here of how an *employment multiplier* and an *income multiplier* were determined.

## Employment Multiplier

This multiplier varies from region to region depending on its economic base. In a study entitled *Recreation as an Industry*, by Robert R. Nathan Associates, county employment multipliers calculated for the Appalachian region provide a good illustration of what typical multipliers are and how they work.[2]

The multipliers estimated in this study were based on county employment data.

[2] *Recreation as an Industry* (Washington, D.C.: Robert R. Nathan Associates and Resource Planning Associates, 1966), p. 57.

They represent the approximate measure of the direct and indirect employment associated with each addition of direct employment to the export sector of a county. There are 375 counties and 3 independent cities for which multipliers were estimated. The smallest multiplier was 1.13 and the highest was 2.63. Thus, the county with the smallest multiplier value would provide other employment opportunities for approximately 0.13 persons for each person directly employed in servicing export demand, and the county with the highest multiplier value would provide other employment opportunities for approximately 1.63 persons for each person directly employed in servicing export demand. In general, county employment multipliers vary directly with the population or total employment size of the counties: as county population size grows, so does the multiplier value. This relationship is as might be expected, insofar as import leakages would tend to be less where diversity of occupations is greater, and diversity is positively associated with county population or total employment.

## Income Multiplier

Jobs mean income, which stimulates the economy of the area in which the development occurs. How much stimulation depends on several factors. Using a hotel as an example, the management takes one of two actions concerning the revenue earned — it either spends the money on goods and services, or it saves part of such funds. Economists refer to such action as *MPC* (marginal propensity to consume) or *MPS* (marginal propensity to save — removing funds from the local economy). Such removal of these marginal (extra) funds can be made in two ways: (1) they can be saved and thus not loaned to another spender, or (2) they can be used to purchase imports. In either case, so doing removes the funds and thus does not stimulate the local economy.

Economic research is needed in a tourist destination area to determine what these income relationships are. If the results of such economic research were made available, many beneficial results might be possible. For example, governmental bodies might be more inclined to appropriate additional funds for tourism promotion to their areas if they knew more about the income that was generated by tourist expenditures. Also, improved and added developments of facilities to serve tourists might be more forthcoming if prospective investors could have more factual data upon which to base decisions.

To understand the multiplier, we must first make some approximation as to what portion of the tourist dollars that are received in a community are spent (consumed) and saved (leakage). To illustrate this, suppose that we had a total of $1000 of tourist spending in a community and that there was an *MPC* of 1/2. The expenditure pattern might go through seven transactions in a year. These are illustrated in Table 9.1.

The other formula for the multiplier is 1/*MPS*. This is a simpler formula, as it is the reciprocal of the marginal propensity to save. If the marginal propensity to save were 1/3, the multiplier would be 3. This is shown in Table 9.2.

Leakage, as defined, is a combination of savings and imports. If we spend the money outside of our country for imports, obviously it does not stimulate the economy locally. Also, if it is put into some form of savings that are not loaned to another

**Table 9.1** Formula for the Multiplier

$$\text{Multiplier} = \frac{1}{1 - MPC}$$

where

$M$ = marginal (extra)

$P$ = propensity (inclination)

$C$ = consume (spending) $MPC$

$S$ = savings (money out of circulation) $MPS$

Suppose $1000 of tourist expenditure and an $MPC$ of 1/2. Then,

| | |
|---|---|
| $1000.00 | |
| + | |
| 500.00 | $1/2 \times 1000$ |
| + | + |
| 250.00 | $(1/2)^2 \times 1000$ |
| + | + |
| 125.00 | $(1/2)^3 \times 1000$ |
| + | + |
| 62.50 | $(1/2)^4 \times 1000$ |
| + | + |
| 31.25 | $(1/2)^5 \times 1000$ |
| + | + |
| 15.63 | $(1/2)^6 \times 1000$ |
| + | + |
| 7.81 | $(1/2)^7 \times 1000$ |
| . . . | |

$2000.00 (approx.)

$$\text{Multiply: } \frac{1}{1 - 1/2} \times \$1000, \text{ or } 2 \times \$1000 = \$2000$$

Thus, the original $1000 of tourist expenditure becomes $2000 of income to the community.

**Table 9.2** "Leakage"

$$\text{Leakage} = \begin{cases} \text{Savings} \\ \text{Imports} \end{cases}$$

Savings = not loaned to another spender

Imports = spending on tourism needs in sources outside country (state)

$$\text{Multiplier} = \frac{1}{MPS}$$

$$MPS = 1/3$$

$$\text{Multiplier} = \frac{1}{1/3}$$

$$\text{Multiplier} = 3$$

spender within a year, it also has the same effect as imports — not stimulating the economy. Thus, to get the maximum benefits economically from tourist expenditures, we should introduce as much of the tourist funds as possible into the local economy for goods and services rather than save the proceeds or buy a large amount of imports.

Here, also, more economic research is needed. Some studies have indicated that the multiplier might be as high as 3 in some areas, but economic research in other localities indicate that it may be more typically lower than this.

### Economic Benefits Widely Distributed

Using a conceptual approach, you should realize that tourism is characterized by the existence of a large number of very small businesses that support and are ancillary to the industry. The receipts from tourism quickly filter down to an extremely broad cross section of the population, so that the entire community shares the economic benefits. Figure 9.2, based on a partial hypothetical example, illustrates how quickly tourism receipts seep through the economy and the diversity of the businesses that benefit from tourism. As the figure indicates, the tourism dollar is shared by over 45 distinguishable types of enterprises in just two rounds of spending.

### Structural Changes

In countries that primarily rely on a single industry, such as agriculture, the introduction of tourism has often led to a decrease in the agricultural base of the country. Agriculture is an extremely low-productivity industry in the developing countries. The promise of much higher wages in the tourism industry draws people away from farming. Agricultural output declines as a result, just when the demand for food is increasing due to the influx of tourists. The inflationary pressure on food prices is further aggravated and can lead to considerable social upheaval. In the mid-1970s, some Caribbean countries experienced a wave of protests and even direct attacks on tourists, as the resident population expressed its dissatisfaction over rising prices.

Another major implication of the structural change is that instead of diversifying its economic base, the country's tourism sector merely "cannibalizes" its other major economic sector. Diversity is the foundation of economic stability. When one sector (or industry) is experiencing a slump, another sector is booming, thus reducing the probability of a severe depression and, indeed, reducing its impact if a depression does occur. Thus tourism, instead of diversifying an economy, sometimes replaces agriculture as a "subsistence" sector.

### Dependence on Tourism

Permitting tourism to become the subsistence industry is not desirable for a number of reasons. First, tourism is by its very nature subject to considerable seasonality. While seasonal fluctuations in demand can sometimes be reduced, they cannot be eliminated. Thus, when tourism is the primary industry in an area, the off-season periods inevitably result in serious unemployment problems. Such areas find that

| VISITORS SPEND FOR | TRAVEL INDUSTRY SPENDS FOR | ULTIMATE BENEFICIARIES |
|---|---|---|
| | | Accountants |
| | | Advertising and Public Relations |
| | | Appliance Stores |
| Lodging | | Architects |
| | | Arts and Crafts Producers |
| | Wages and Salaries | Attorneys |
| | | Automobile Agencies |
| | Tips—Gratuities | Bakers |
| | | Banks |
| Food | | Beach Accessories |
| | Payroll Taxes | Butchers |
| | | Carpenters |
| | Commissions | Cashiers |
| | | Charities |
| | | Chemists |
| Beverages | Music & Entertainment | Clerks |
| | | Clothing Stores |
| | Administrative and General Expenses | Clubs |
| | | Confectioners |
| | | Contractors |
| | | Cooks |
| Entertainment | Legal and Professional Services | Cultural Organization |
| | | Dairies |
| | | Dentists |
| | | Department Stores |
| | Purchases of Food, Beverages, etc. | Doctors |
| | | Dry Cleaning Establishments |
| | | Electricians |
| Clothing, etc. | Purchases of Goods Sold | Engineers |
| | | Farmers |
| | | Fishermen |
| | | Freight Forwarders |
| | Purchases of Materials and Supplies | Garages and Auto Repairs |
| Gifts and Souvenirs | | Gardeners |
| | | Gift Shops |
| | Repairs and Maintenance | Government |
| | | Education |
| | | Health |
| | Advertising, Promotion and Publicity | Roads & Railroads |
| Photography | | Utilities |
| | | Development & Others |
| | | Greengrocers |
| | Utilities—Electric Gas, Water, Etc. | Grocery Stores |
| | | Financiers |
| | | Furniture Stores |
| | | Importers |
| Personal Care | Transportation | Insurance Agencies |
| Drugs and Cosmetics | | Landlords |
| | Licenses | Laundries |

**Figure 9.2** Distribution of Tourism Expenditures. *Source:* Pannell Kerr Forster and Belt Collins and Associates.

the seasonal character of tourism leaves severe economic and social effects on the host region.

Another very important reason relates to the source of demand for tourism. The demand for tourism depends largely on the income and the tastes of tourists, both of which are beyond the control of the host region. If the American economy is going through a slump, demand for travel to a foreign destination by Americans will fall off. There is precious little a destination area can do, in this case, to increase the level of demand. If the tastes of the people in the tourist-generating area change — they decide to travel to a new destination — tourism in the old area will decline, causing economic and social problems. Again, there will be little or nothing the destination can do to avoid this. In fact, as Plog[3] points out, there is reason to believe that such a decline in an area's popularity may be largely inevitable. Quite clearly, then, tourism should not be allowed to grow to an extent that the destination area becomes totally dependent on it.

In other words, total dependence on a single industrial sector is undesirable. If it cannot be avoided, then dependence on domestic agriculture is in many ways preferable to dependence on tourism. The country has presumably adapted itself economically and socially to dependence on agriculture over several centuries. The demand for agriculture output is also unlikely to suffer from a secular decline since people must eat. Also, it is the residents, not foreigners as in tourism, who directly benefit from agricultural production.

Moreover, tourism imposes certain environmental and social costs on the host region and its residents. Permitting it to develop to the extent that the host region becomes totally dependent on tourism poses this dilemma: if further development were curtailed, economic devastation would result; if tourism were permitted to continue growing, the natural and cultural resources could be depreciated due to overexploitation. Hawaii is a case in point. When demand for travel to Hawaii showed a 2.7 percent decline in February 1973, many scholars and researchers welcomed this trend, pointing to the adverse environmental and social impacts implied by continued growth of tourism. They contended that further growth of tourism, especially on Oahu, would cause havoc with the natural resource base of Hawaii and cause the Hawaiian society to be overwhelmed by the sheer number of tourists. Both these effects were considered undesirable. Jonish and Peterson,[4] on the other hand, pointed to the enormous economic burden that a reduced *rate of growth* in demand (let alone a decline) would impose on the economy of Hawaii. Clearly, Hawaii had reached this impasse because over the years tourism had replaced the sugar and pineapple industries as the civilian mainstay of Hawaii's economy. The solution may well be intractable in such cases.

## Investment Priorities

Sometimes, governments of developing countries take an overly optimistic view of tourism. They undertake aggressive investment programs to develop tourism, as-

[3] Stanley C. Plog, "Why Destination Areas Rise and Fall in Popularity," *The Cornell Hotel and Restaurant Administration Quarterly*, Vol. 14, no. 4, February 1974, pp. 55–58.
[4] James E. Jonish and Richard E. Peterson, "Impact of Tourism, Hawaii," *The Cornell Hotel and Restaurant Administration Quarterly*, Vol. 4, no. 2, August 1963, pp. 5–12.

signing it top priority in their development plans. In extreme cases, such an approach can lead to the neglect of more fundamental investment needs of the country. For example, funds can be channeled into tourism development at the cost of education, health, and other social services. The education, health, and other aspects of the social well-being of the population should be of primary concern for a developing country. Not only is undue glamorization of tourism unwise because it usurps this position, but such a strategy only speeds up the process of dependence on tourism, which, as discussed earlier, is itself undesirable. Moreover, investment in tourism at the cost of health and education programs also slows down the rate at which the local population is assimilated into the modern market economy of the country. Under certain circumstances, it may actually retard development rather than enhance it.

The conclusion is that, although tourism has tremendous potential as a tool in economic development, it is no panacea. Governments should attempt to optimize (not maximize) the benefits that tourism provides, being ever mindful of the costs that it can impose. It should be noted also that the probability and the intensity of the economic costs of tourism are greater for developing nations (or regions) than for wealthy ones. Wealthy nations, by definition, possess robust economies that can more easily absorb the costs of tourism. Typically, such economies are well diversified, and government investment programs are not so central to development efforts.

The social benefits and costs of tourism should be viewed similarly. While the host community seeks to maximize the benefits, it must weigh these against the social costs. The social costs are likewise higher in both probability and magnitude when tourism is being considered for development in an area that still possesses a traditional social structure.

## Demand for Tourism

Economically speaking, demand for tourism may be defined as the *quantity* of tourism goods and services that will be purchased at a given *price* and within a given time *period*. The concept of "quantity" is a difficult one to define in tourism. We briefly addressed this problem when the various measures of demand were discussed. Regardless of the particular definition of demand used — arrivals, visitor-days, or tourism expenditures — we can usually conclude that the higher the price of a tourist service, the lower the quantity demanded.

This relationship can be discussed by using the concept of a demand schedule. A demand schedule shows the levels of demand at various prices. Table 9.3 shows a hypothetical demand schedule for travel to a destination.

The demand pattern shown in this table can be presented in the form of a demand curve, by plotting the prices against the corresponding levels of demand. Figure 9.3 is the demand curve based on the data given. Since demand is inversely related to price, the demand curve is *always* downward sloping. A few exceptions to this will be discussed later.

The demand curve contains considerable information of use to practitioners of tourism. It indicates what the level of demand will be at a given price. It also provides information about the total revenue earned at each price. Also, we can derive

**Table 9.3** Demand Schedule

| Cost of Vacation (dollars) | Quantity Demanded (arrivals) |
|---|---|
| $ 600 | 140,000 |
| 800 | 120,000 |
| 1000 | 100,000 |
| 1200 | 80,000 |
| 1400 | 60,000 |

information about the elasticity of demand, which is an extremely important concept for tourism planners at all levels.

### Total Revenue

Total revenue is the product of price and the quantity sold at that price. It can be computed readily using the demand curve.

Suppose that the cost of a vacation (in the example) is $1100. Demand at this price can be read off immediately from the demand curve. As shown in Figure 9.3 the demand will be 90,000 arrivals. Total revenue at this price will be

$$90,000 \times \$1100 = \$99,000,000$$

On the graph, total revenue is simply the *area* beneath the demand curve, at any

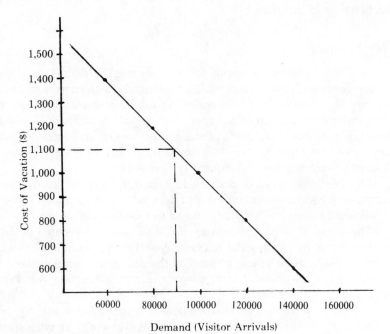

Figure 9.3 Demand Curve.

given price. In Figure 9.4, total revenue at a price of $1100 is shown by the shaded area under the demand curve.

## Quantity Demanded and Price Elasticity

For some products, even a large change in price over a certain range of the demand curve results in only a small change in quantity demanded. In this case, demand is not very responsive to price. For other products, or for the same product over a different range of prices, a relatively small change in price elicits a much larger relative change in quantity demanded. Demand can be classified as inelastic or elastic on the basis of the relative responsiveness of quantity demanded to changes in price. Specifically, price elasticity of demand may be defined as the percentage change in demand resulting from a given percentage change in price.

## Computation of Elasticity

Having presented the definition of price elasticity of demand, we may now introduce a method for computing price elasticity ($\epsilon_p$):

$$\epsilon_p = \frac{\% \text{ change in quantity demanded}}{\% \text{ change in price}}$$

$$= \frac{\Delta Q/Q}{\Delta P/P}$$

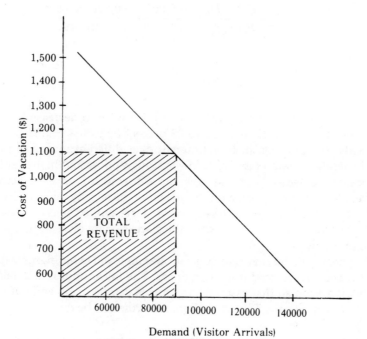

Figure 9.4 Demand and Total Revenue.

where

$$\Delta = \text{read as a "change in"}$$
$$Q = \text{quantity demanded}$$
$$P = \text{price}$$

Returning to the demand schedule in Table 9.3, we can calculate price elasticity of demand at various price levels. We can compute the elasticity of demand at a price of $800, as follows: (Examples show demand decrease and increase.)

$$\epsilon_p = \frac{Q/Q}{P/P} = \frac{(Q_1 - Q_0) \div Q_0}{(P_1 - P_0) \div P_0}$$

where the subscripts 1 and 0 refer to new and initial prices and quantities, respectively. Using this formula and applying values of demand from Table 9.3, we obtain, considering a price change to $600,

$$\epsilon_p = \frac{(140,000 - 120,000) \div 120,000}{(\$600 - \$800) \div \$800} = \frac{0.167}{-0.25}$$

(at $800)

$$= -0.668$$

This number, $-0.668$, means that if the price were to increase by 10 percent, quantity demanded would decrease by 6.68 percent ($10\% \times -0.668$).

Similarly, price elasticity can be computed at an initial price of $1400, by considering a lowering of price to $1200:

$$\epsilon_p = \frac{(Q_1 - Q_0) \div Q_0}{(P_1 - P_0) \div P_0} = \frac{(80,000 - 60,000) \div 60,000}{(\$1200 - \$1400) \div \$1400}$$

(at $1400)

$$= \frac{0.333}{-0.143} = -2.329$$

An elasticity of $-2.329$ means that if price were to decrease by 10 percent, quantity demanded would increase 23.29 percent ($-10\% \times -2.329$).

Clearly, the price elasticity is different over different ranges of the demand curve. In *absolute value*, elasticity is lower at high prices and higher at low prices. And because the demand curve always slopes downward, price elasticity is always negative. It is customary, for simplicity, to ignore the negative sign and refer to price elasticity by its absolute value. To keep the reader reminded of its negative value, we shall denote price elasticity as $|\epsilon_p|$ when the discussion involves the consideration of its absolute values.

The linear demand curve (such as the one employed in the examples) is a special case. Demand curves need not all be linear. The linear approach is taken here to simplify discussion so that essential arguments can be made without introducing unnecessary complexity. The results can, nevertheless, be directly applied to nonlinear demand curves.

As noted, price elasticity is different over different ranges of the demand. As indicated in Figure 9.5, three regions can be identified on a demand curve—the regions where elasticity $|\epsilon_p|$ is greater than 1, equal to 1, and less than 1.

We can now define elastic and inelastic demand, which we referred to earlier rather loosely, on the basis of the *absolute value* of price elasticity. Thus, if elasticity is greater than 1, demand is said to be *elastic*, whereas if elasticity is less than 1, demand is *inelastic*. At a value of 1, demand is *unitary* elastic. In terms of Figure 9.5, demand is elastic above $P$, inelastic below $P$, and unitary elastic at $P$. For a linear demand curve, unitary elasticity occurs at the midpoint of the demand curve (in relation to the horizontal axis). That is, if point $A$ is exactly midway between 0 and $B$, then price elasticity is unity at the price of $P$.

## Price Elasticity and Total Revenue

Price elasticity and total revenue are directly related. If price elasticity is larger than 1, quantity response is (by the definition of elasticity) relatively larger than the corresponding price change. Recalling that total revenue is the price multiplied by quantity demanded, it becomes clear that when demand is elastic, a decline in price will result in a higher total revenue, since the negative change in price will be "outweighed" by the relatively larger increase in quantity demanded. If price were

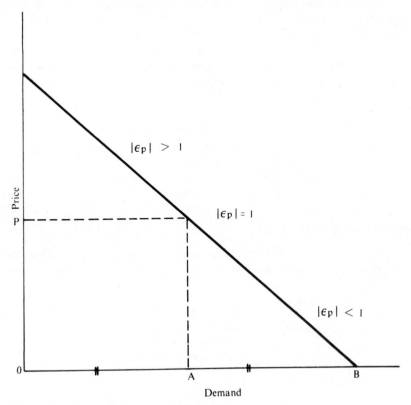

**Figure 9.5** Demand Curves and Elasticity.

to increase, total revenue would decline because the positive increase in price is outweighed by the larger relative decrease in quantity demanded.

By contrast in the range where demand is inelastic, price and total revenue change in the same direction. A decrease in price reduces total revenue, and vice versa. Finally, at unitary elasticity, a small change in price produces no change in total revenue. Table 9.4 summarizes these relationships.

The implications from this discussion are fairly obvious. First, we can talk of demand as being elastic or inelastic *only* over a particular range of prices or quantities demanded. Second, it becomes clear that raising prices may not be beneficial, such as when demand is elastic, since total revenue will fall as will the number of customers served. Similarly, if demand is inelastic, it may be wise not to lower prices. To do so would mean that lower revenues will be earned as *more* customers are served.

## Veblen Effect — Exception of Price-Quantity Relationship

Some people claim that for certain goods that have a "snob" appeal, such as Yves St. Laurent dresses or Rolls-Royce autos, price and quantity can be directly related. This is called the Veblen effect.

In the tourism industry, a very small group of people for whom neither time nor budget seems important, are commonly referred to as "jet setters." Jet setters are members of the leisure class, whose demand patterns were investigated by the economist Veblen.

Veblen claimed that whenever a high price for a good or service is perceived by buyers as enhancing the "quality" or "snob" appeal of the good, the demand for it will increase if price increases. Veblen effects may be operable at the most expensive resorts, hotels, and special attractions. Because of the high prices, the wealthy clients of these resorts are assured that they will associate only with people they consider their social equals.

When the Veblen effect is in operation, the demand curve is positively sloped. Higher prices are associated with higher level of demand. It should be noted that the Veblen effect can only apply within a *specified* range of prices. If it applied to the entire range of prices, the prices of such goods would go to infinity. Every increase in price will lead to higher levels of demand.

## Income Elasticity of Demand

As income rises, more travel is demanded at any given price. Thus the relationship between income and demand is positive. The responsiveness of demand to changes

**Table 9.4** Relationships Between Price Elasticity and Total Revenue (TR)

|  | Elastic Demand ($|\epsilon_p| > 1$) | Unitary Elasticity ($|\epsilon_p| = 1$) | Inelastic Demand ($|\epsilon_p| < 1$) |
|---|---|---|---|
| Price rises | TR falls | No change | TR rises |
| Price falls | TR rises | No change | TR falls |

in income is called income elasticity of demand. It is defined as the percentage change in quantity demanded in response to a given percentage change in income, price remaining unchanged.

The effect of a shift in income is depicted graphically in Figure 9.6. $D_1$ is demand curve for travel at an income level of $Y_0$. If income increases from $Y_0$ to $Y_1$, the

Ten miles of wide beach; pools for all ages; more than 12 miles of paved bicycle paths; a mile-long physical fitness trail; two tennis clubs with a total of 28 courts; two 18-hole golf courses; a 21-acre recreation park; villas, cottages, and homes (many of which are on the vacation rental market); shops, restaurants, and lounges; a 150-room inn; and beautiful scenery with the ocean, lagoons, the Kiawah River, sand dunes, maritime forests, wildlife, and a community designed to complement the environment: This is an example of tourism investment on Kiawah Island. (Photo courtesy of Kiawah Island Company)

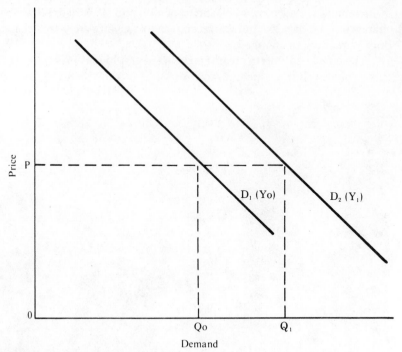

**Figure 9.6** Income Elasticity of Demand.

quantity demanded at any given price will be higher. This means that the *entire* demand curve shifts, say, to $D_2$. At a price of $P$, the quantity demanded was initially $Q_0$ (from the original demand curve $D_1$). With an increase in income to $Y_1$, demand at the same price of $P$ increases to $Q_1$ (from the new demand curve $D_2$).

The income elasticity of demand, according to the definition can be expressed as

$$\epsilon_y = \frac{\Delta Q/Q}{\Delta Y/Y} \quad \text{or} \quad \epsilon_y = \frac{(Q_1 - Q_0) \div Q_0}{(Y_1 - Y_0) \div Y_0}$$

where $Q$ is quantity demanded and $Y$ is income.

In general, income elasticity is *positive* since quantity demanded will increase (decrease) due to an increase (decrease) in income. It can range from 0 to infinity. When the income elasticity is between 0 and 1, demand is said to be income *inelastic*. An elasticity of greater than 1 implies demand is income *elastic*. Finally, demand is *unitary* elastic if elasticity is exactly equal to 1.

Inferior goods are exceptions to the positive relationship between income and quantity demanded. A family accustomed to consuming margarine (which is cheaper than butter) may purchase *less* margarine and buy butter instead when family income increases. Tourism as a whole is a normal good, although particular segments may exhibit inferior good characteristics.

Therefore, a family whose income has increased can be expected to travel more. However, the family may now choose to stay in a hotel rather than camp (or fly instead of drive). Thus, camping or driving may be considered inferior goods since an increase in income led to a decreased demand for them. At the same time, travel increased, and therefore tourism is a normal or superior good.

In general, tourism is believed to be income elastic ($\epsilon_y > 1$). It is a discretionary expenditure and thus highly sensitive to changes in income. Tourism is one of the first expenses to be curtailed when income declines and can be expected to increase by a larger proportion when income rises. However, some people believe that tourism is income inelastic ($\epsilon_y < 1$), at least in affluent countries. The contention is that people in the United States, for instance, have come to expect an annual vacation as an integral part of the family calendar. In the event that family income declined in a particular year, other things will be given up to afford vacations. It may be true that income elasticity declines as a nation becomes wealthier, but there is no evidence to support the claim that travel demand is actually income inelastic, even in the United States.

The erroneous conclusion arises because the various ways of reducing travel demand without altogether eliminating the annual vacation are not considered. For instance, instead of traveling to California, an East Coast family may instead spend less by taking its vacation in New England. In fact, most empirical estimates of income elasticity have yielded values significantly larger than 1. This means that tourism demand appears income elastic.

## COMPLEMENTS AND SUBSTITUTES

The tourism product, as mentioned earlier, has several major suppliers and activities: transportation, accommodation, shopping, and entertainment (or, synonymously, activities and attractions). Each of these four components is, in turn, comprised of several subcomponents called elements. For example, accommodations can take the form of resorts, hotels, motels, or campsites. The list of elements within a category is almost endless. The demands for the four parts and for the elements in each part are closely related, though in different ways.

Complementary goods (or services) are goods that are consumed in combination, for instance, bread and butter. If more bread is consumed (say, due to a decline in the price of bread), then the demand for butter will rise. Even if the price of butter is unchanged, more of it will be demanded, since it is consumed in conjunction with bread.

Similarly, in tourism, the supply categories are consumed in combination. A tourist on vacation requires transportation to get to a destination. Once there, the tourist needs food and lodging and will also participate in some activities related to the trip. Thus, the demands for the parts are directly related. If demand for one part increases, so will the demand for other parts.

The demands for the elements within a part are, on the other hand, inversely related to each other. A tourist can stay either at a hotel or at a motel and cannot possibly stay in both facilities simultaneously. Therefore, if due to a decrease in hotel room rates, the tourist chooses to stay in a hotel rather than a motel, what has happened? The demand for hotels increased in response to a change in hotel prices and, as a consequence, the demand for motels declined. Thus, hotels and motels are substitutes for each other.

The purpose of this discussion is to underscore the interdependence of the various parts of the tourist industry. A hotel manager, for instance, must realize that what happens in other parts of tourism is critical to the future of the hotel industry. The hotel manager should view the hotel industry not in isolation, but as an integral part of overall tourism (that is, the major parts and the elements in each of these parts). Keeping abreast of developments and trends in all segments of the industry will lead to better decision-making capability.

## SUMMARY

Domestic and international tourism are major economic strengths to many of the world's countries, states, cities, and rural areas. Thus, those who live there are affected by the economic results of tourist spending. This chapter explains why these resulting effects vary greatly and what brings about a large measure of benefits or possible detriments to a community. The main economic phenomena described are various multipliers, balance of payments, investments, tax consideration, inflationary pressure, dependence on tourism, demand considerations, price and income elasticity as related to buying travel experiences, Veblen effect, complements and substitutes in travel products, and optimization.

Many people do not understand or appreciate the economics of tourism. The following list summarizes the principal economic effects:

1. Expenditures by foreign visitors in one's country become exports (mainly of services). The economic effects are the same as those derived from exporting tangible goods. If there is a favorable exchange rate (foreign currency buying appreciably more of one's own country's currency) the country that has the devalued currency will experience a higher demand for visitor services than before devaluation.

2. If citizens of one's country spend money in foreign countries, these expenditures become imports for the tourists' originating country.

3. Sums of the values of national exports and imports are used when calculating a nation's balance of payments. A plus balance results when exports exceed imports, thus increasing a nation's gross national product (GNP).

4. Tourism developments typically require large investments of capital. Thus, local economies where the developments take place are stimulated by such investments.

5. Tourists pay various kinds of taxes directly and indirectly while visiting an area. Thus tax revenues are increased for all levels of government.

6. As tourists usually spend more per day at a destination than they do while at home, these extra expenditures may cause inflationary pressures and rising prices for consumer goods in the destination area.

7. Tourism expenditures injected into the economy produce an income multiplier for local people. This is due to the diversity of expenditures made by those receiving tourist payments. Tourist receipts are used to buy a wide variety of goods and services over a year's time. The money turnover creates additional local income.

8. The amount of income multiplication, however, will depend on how much leakage takes place. Leakages are a combination of (1) imported goods and services purchased by tourism suppliers, and (2) savings made of tourist receipts not loaned to another spender within one year of receipt. Thus, the more tourist goods that are supplied locally, the higher will be the multiplier.

9. Income multiplication caused by tourist expenditures necessitates hiring more people. Thus, they also effect an employment multiplier.

10. As increased spending produces more financial transactions, they create a transactions multiplier. These are of particular interest to governments that have a sales or value-added tax on such transactions.

11. As a tourist area grows, more capital is invested in new facilities. This results in a capital multiplier.

12. It is an unwise policy for a society to place too much dependency on tourism as a subsistence industry.

13. Although tourism often has an excellent potential in economic development, it is not a panacea for economic ills. Its economic benefits should be optimized rather than maximized.

14. We believe that tourism products are mainly price elastic, meaning that as prices rise, the quantity demanded tends to drop.

15. In general, we believe that tourism is income elastic. This means that as family income rises, or a particular market's income rises, and tourism prices do not rise proportionally, the demand for travel to that particular area will increase.

16. If a tourism commodity or service is perceived as having snob appeal, an increase in price will create an increase in demand. However, this is limited to a specific range of prices. This exception is termed the *Veblen effect.*

17. The economic contributions of tourism to a community can be measured, in part, by estimating revenues received by accommodations businesses and parks plus expenditures of day visitors.

### About the Reading

Tourism's economic contributions include employment, income, and taxes. Measuring the economic impact of these contributions is of great value. This reading looks at the economic contribution of travel to state economies and examines both the direct and multiplier effects.

## READING 9-1

### The Economic Contribution of Travel to State Economies

By James Mak
Department of Economics
University of Hawaii at Manoa

### U.S. Travel Data Center Studies

Each year, the U.S. Travel Data Center (USTDC) publishes estimates of the economic impact of U.S. resident travel on the economies of all 50 states, and Washington D.C., using its Travel Economic Impact Model (TEIM).[1] The purpose of the model is to produce individual state estimates of employment, payroll, and tax revenues generated by travel spending in the United States. The model uses estimated annual U.S. travel expenditures in the 50 states and the District of Columbia derived from national survey data on travel activity levels which are combined with the estimated average costs of each unit of travel activity to produce total dollar amounts of spending in a number of different categories of travel-related goods and services. The spending estimates include all U.S. resident travel expenditures on overnight trips, and day trips of 100 miles or more, away from the traveler's origin.

The USTDC economic impact estimates include only the *direct* effects and do not include the multiplier (i.e., trickle-down) effects of tourist spending in the individual states. Another source of underestimation is the exclusion of the economic impact of foreign visitor expenditures on state economies.

### Regional Input-Output Model: RIMS II

It is now possible to measure more completely the economic impact of travel spending on state economies by using an input-output model of each state developed recently by the U.S. Department of Commerce, Bureau of Economic Analysis (BEA).

The model, known as RIMS II (for Regional Input-Output Modeling System), adapts the national input-output table to derive input-output tables for individual states. From these state tables BEA has generated total output, employment, and earnings multipliers by industry for all 50 states and the District of Columbia, and has published them in a handbook (1986).[2] RIMS II multipliers are intended to show the *total* economic impact of initial changes in a state's economic activity. They can be used to estimate the impacts of projects and program expenditures by industry on *business output* (i.e., business gross receipts or sales), *earnings* (i.e., the sum of wages and salaries, proprietors' income, and other labor income less employer contributions to private pension and welfare funds), and *employment* (i.e., full-time equivalent jobs). Empirical tests have shown that estimates based on expensive survey-based state input-output models and RIMS II estimates are similar in magnitude.[3]

In this brief paper, we apply the RIMS II total multipliers for each state to USTDC estimated state travel expenditures for 1983 to determine the total impact of travel expenditures on gross business sales, earnings, and employment in the 50 states and the District of Columbia. We chose 1983 for two reasons. First, it is the only year for which state-by-state travel expenditure data are also available on foreign visitors.[4] Second, it is also a convenient year, because the RIMS II multipliers published in the 1986 handbook used 1983 data.[5] Had a different year been selected, it would have required a different set of multipliers for the states.

### Comparison of RIMS II and USTDC Models

The results produced here using RIMS II multipliers are not comparable to USTDC annual estimates of the economic impact of U.S. travel on state economies for a number of reasons.

The estimates here include the impact of foreign visitor spending in the individual states, but the USTDC annual estimates do not. In 1983, foreign visitors spent only $13 billion in the United States, compared with nearly $196 billion spent by U.S. travelers. Although, in the aggregate, foreign travel spending in the United

States was only 6.7 percent of U.S. resident travel spending, there were very large differences among the states, ranging from .5 percent (West Virginia) to 48.8 percent (Hawaii). Arizona, California, Florida, Hawaii, New York, and Washington, D.C., all had foreign travel expenditures that exceeded 10 percent of U.S. resident travel expenditures. Thus, the exclusion of foreign travel spending would have significantly understated the economic contribution of travel in several important states.

Further, as already noted, RIMS II estimates include the multiplier effects, but the USTDC estimates do not. RIMS II generates estimates of earnings; however, the USTDC Travel Impact Model produces estimates of payrolls. "Earnings" are a broader measure of household income than "payroll" since they include proprietors' income. RIMS II produces estimates of full-time equivalent jobs generated by travel spending, but the USTDC employment estimates count full- and part-time jobs equally. However, the latter is a more convenient measure to use to determine the *relative* importance of travel-generated employment to total employment since it is consistent with the U.S. Department of Labor data series on nonagricultural payroll employment. Finally, USTDC also estimates the impact of travel on tax revenues, but RIMS II does not. Hence, the estimates presented here using RIMS II multipliers should not be regarded as substitutes for the USTDC estimates of the economic impacts of travel on state economies, but as providing additional information that can be useful in a number of situations.

*RIMS II Estimates*

The estimates of the state-by-state contribution to total gross business receipts, earnings, and employment attributable to United States and foreign travel spending in 1983 are presented in Table 1 without detailed discussion. Overall, in 1983, U.S. and foreign visitors spent $209 billion on travel in the United States and generated $435 billion in gross business sales/receipts, nearly $145 billion in household income (or earnings), and 10.5 million full-time equivalent jobs. In computing these estimates, we applied the RIMS II total multipliers in the "transportation" sector to USTDC estimated travel expenditures on public and automobile transportation, the total multipliers in the "hotels and lodging places and amusements" sector to "lodging and entertainment and recreation" expenditures, the total multipliers in the "eating and drinking places" to "food service" expenditures, and the total multipliers in the "retail trade" sector to "general retail trade" expenditures.[6]

*Advantages of RIMS II*

The availability of RIMS II multipliers enable the individual states to determine the total economic contribution of travel expenditures to their economies without having to spend large sums of money to develop their own input-output models. However, in those states that have survey-based input-output models, it would still be desirable to compare the estimates of travel-generated economic impacts using their own models against the RIMS II estimates. There are two additional advantages in using RIMS II: (1) The multipliers are regularly updated, and (2) BEA will generate, for a modest fee, total multipliers for any region composed of one or more counties so that planners, consultants, investors, and researchers can use them to estimate the economic impacts of planned projects or expenditures in smaller areas. For more information or to order the tables, contact the Analysis Branch, Regional Economic

**Table 1** The Total Economic Contribution of Travel on State Economies: 1983

| State | Total Travel Expenditures (millions $) | Total Gross Business Sales (millions $) | Total Earnings (millions $) | Total FTE Jobs (thousands) |
|---|---|---|---|---|
| Alabama | $ 1,398.4 | $ 2,818.6 | $ 948.7 | 84.8 |
| Alaska | 834.3 | 1,435.0 | 478.0 | 20.9 |
| Arizona | 3,476.3 | 6,386.9 | 2,312.6 | 180.6 |
| Arkansas | 1,680.8 | 3,470.3 | 1,126.0 | 107.1 |
| California | 28,573.4 | 65,121.1 | 21,441.0 | 1,299.2 |
| Colorado | 4,162.8 | 8,748.2 | 2,930.6 | 220.0 |
| Connecticut | 2,207.7 | 4,193.1 | 1,613.9 | 97.0 |
| Delaware | 482.0 | 848.7 | 259.4 | 24.0 |
| Florida | 19,267.5 | 37,788.5 | 12,784.3 | 990.8 |
| Georgia | 4,903.0 | 10,414.7 | 3,483.6 | 240.5 |
| Hawaii | 3,575.1 | 6,715.4 | 2,268.1 | 157.0 |
| Idaho | 907.0 | 1,661.0 | 574.9 | 60.9 |
| Illinois | 5,921.2 | 14,029.1 | 4,772.5 | 289.4 |
| Indiana | 2,409.1 | 5,158.3 | 1,731.4 | 146.7 |
| Iowa | 1,609.2 | 3,264.3 | 1,143.1 | 105.0 |
| Kansas | 1,575.8 | 3,421.3 | 1,100.4 | 90.2 |
| Kentucky | 2,139.7 | 4,520.5 | 1,492.7 | 109.7 |
| Louisiana | 3,308.2 | 7,036.7 | 2,142.4 | 152.0 |
| Maine | 1,522.6 | 2,721.7 | 930.8 | 109.9 |
| Maryland | 3,504.5 | 7,141.6 | 2,515.7 | 179.1 |
| Massachusetts | 4,995.5 | 9,628.6 | 3,523.5 | 237.9 |
| Michigan | 5,545.4 | 10,316.3 | 3,664.2 | 277.1 |
| Minnesota | 4,584.2 | 9,796.8 | 3,294.9 | 264.5 |
| Mississippi | 1,108.5 | 2,330.2 | 776.0 | 69.2 |
| Missouri | 4,398.6 | 9,793.2 | 3,171.6 | 227.3 |
| Montana | 672.7 | 1,238.7 | 417.9 | 48.0 |
| Nebraska | 1,078.3 | 2,162.9 | 742.1 | 67.2 |
| Nevada | 6,254.3 | 10,400.5 | 3,538.2 | 230.8 |
| New Hampshire | 1,154.0 | 2,083.2 | 712.3 | 71.1 |
| New Jersey | 8,568.8 | 18,702.9 | 6,187.6 | 386.7 |
| New Mexico | 1,548.9 | 2,939.8 | 963.8 | 87.7 |
| New York | 15,166.9 | 30,938.1 | 9,730.7 | 587.1 |
| North Carolina | 4,486.0 | 9,100.9 | 3,086.1 | 274.7 |
| North Dakota | 681.5 | 1,315.8 | 452.9 | 39.1 |
| Ohio | 5,884.2 | 12,851.6 | 4,386.2 | 306.7 |
| Oklahoma | 2,606.3 | 5,532.2 | 1,744.6 | 139.6 |
| Oregon | 2,247.0 | 4,503.7 | 1,530.3 | 128.0 |
| Pennsylvania | 7,545.0 | 16,465.4 | 5,531.7 | 409.7 |
| Rhode Island | 355.7 | 633.2 | 236.1 | 19.1 |
| South Carolina | 2,644.6 | 5,148.7 | 1,739.0 | 162.6 |
| South Dakota | 477.3 | 913.3 | 320.2 | 34.9 |
| Tennessee | 2,996.1 | 6,520.5 | 2,170.6 | 171.7 |
| Texas | 14,643.5 | 33,918.8 | 10,782.6 | 731.9 |
| Utah | 1,456.2 | 2,989.5 | 990.6 | 92.0 |
| Vermont | 1,019.7 | 1,735.5 | 586.7 | 62.6 |
| Virginia | 3,731.7 | 7,621.1 | 2,555.8 | 194.9 |
| Washington | 2,908.4 | 6,226.9 | 2,087.2 | 149.2 |

**Table 1** *(Continued)*

| State | Total Travel Expenditures (millions $) | Total Gross Business Sales (millions $) | Total Earnings (millions $) | Total FTE Jobs (thousands) |
|---|---|---|---|---|
| West Virginia | 1,158.4 | 1,917.3 | 660.0 | 59.3 |
| Wisconsin | 3,640.5 | 7,553.5 | 2,516.3 | 244.3 |
| Wyoming | 625.9 | 1,051.5 | 361.0 | 36.5 |
| Dist. of Columbia | 1,351.0 | 1,706.3 | 268.6 | 16.4 |
| Total | $208,993.7 | $434,931.9 | $144,785.4 | 10,492.6 |

*Source:* U.S. Travel Data Center, *Impact of Travel on State Economies, 1983*; also U.S. Travel Data Center, *Impact of Foreign Visitors on State Economies,* 1983.
*Note:* Information is unavailable on the distribution of foreign travel spending by expenditure categories. It is assumed that foreign spending has the same distribution as U.S. travel spending.

Analysis Division, Bureau of Economic Analysis, U.S. Department of Commerce, Washington, D.C. 20230 (phone 202-523-0528 or -0594).

## Reading Endnotes

1. See for example, U.S. Travel Data Center, *Impact of Travel on State Economies 1986* (Washington D.C., 1988).
2. U.S. Department of Commerce, Bureau of Economic Analysis, *Regional Multipliers: A User Handbook for the Regional Input-Output Modeling System (RIMS II)* (Washington D.C.: U.S. Government Printing Office, May, 1986).
3. U.S. Department of Commerce, Bureau of Economic Analysis, *Regional Input-Output Modeling System (RIMS II): Estimation, Evaluation, and Application of a Disaggregated Regional Impact Model* (Washington D.C.: U.S. Government Printing Office, 1981).
4. U.S. Travel Data Center, *Impact of Foreign Visitors on State Economies, 1983* (Washington D.C., April, 1985).
5. The employment multipliers used 1983 employment-earnings ratios.
6. For illustrations on how to use the RIMS II multipliers, see Chapter IV of the handbook, pages 16 to 18. The correct procedure is to apply the RIMS II output, income, and employment multipliers to changes in "final demand" rather than to changes in tourist spending. In the handbook, changes in tourist spending and changes in final demand are assumed to be the same, except in the case of retail trade, where changes in final demand comprise of the sum of operating expenses, profits, sales taxes and excise taxes only (see page 16). The handbook uses national estimates to convert expenditures to final demand since individual estimates are unavailable. If we apply the handbook method to the two states with the largest (California) and smallest (Rhode Island) tourist retail spending, the estimates of total output, income, and employment would be as follows: California: output = $61,771.3 million, income = $20,133.2 million, employment = 1,217,147; Rhode Island: output = $590.4 million, income = $218.1 million, and employment = 17,599. For California, these estimates are 7 to 8 percent smaller than the estimates in Table 1; for Rhode Island the estimates are 5 to 7 percent smaller.

   The USTDC has suggested that RIMS II multipliers be applied not to travel expenditures but to business receipts, which are expenditures minus state and local sales and excise taxes. The difference between the two is approximately 3 percent.

## Key Concepts

| | |
|---|---|
| balance of payments | income inelasticity |
| complements-substitutes | inflationary pressure |
| demand | investment stimulation |
| demand curve | leakage |
| demand schedule | multipliers |
| economic base | optimization |
| economic impact | price elasticity |
| employment | price inelasticity |
| exports and imports | supply categories |
| gross national product | tax revenue |
| income | Veblen effect |
| income elasticity | |

## For Review and Discussion

1. What is meant by *optimization?*
2. Discuss how an airline executive might use tourism economics relating to passenger load factors, ticket prices, discounts, frequent flyer programs, joint fares, and flight frequencies.
3. Selecting one form of public transportation, enumerate the economic constraints that affect this business.
4. A full-service restaurant is considering having an elaborate buffet dinner three nights a week. What constraints are likely to bear upon this consideration?
5. Define *tourism exports and imports* in terms of national economies.
6. Explain how international tourism could assist in reducing the current sizable U.S. trade deficit. How could it increase the deficit?
7. Give several reasons that a hotel's purchasing director should be familiar with the income multiplier phenomenon.
8. Trace how tourist expenditures in a community provide financial support to the public library.
9. Enumerate various methods by which a tourist-dependent community can at least partially overcome seasonality of tourism demand.
10. What is the Veblen effect and how might it influence the development of a tourist facility?

## Case Problems

1. Mr. and Mrs. Henry B. are considering taking their first trip abroad. Deciding to buy a group tour, they find that some countries in which they are interested seem to offer a much better value than do others. Assuming that the ingredients of the tours being considered are very similar, what factors are likely to account for this price difference?
2. A tour operator is planning next year's tours to South America — a new destination for this firm. As the planning progresses, two main types of tours emerge: (1) a quite expensive tour using top quality transportation, accommodations, and local cultural exchanges and experiences, and (2) a much cheaper tour with standard types of services and accommodations.

The staff and funds of the tour company are quite limited, so only one type of tour can be offered. The company wishes to maximize profits.

Identify the essential economic and marketing considerations that must be evaluated to make the best decision.

## Selected References

Archer, Brian. "Tourism in Mauritius: An Economic Impact Study with Marketing Implications." *Tourism Management,* Vol. 6, no. 1 (March 1985), pp. 50–54.

Cicchetti, Charles J. *Forecasting Recreation in the United States.* Lexington, Mass.: Lexington Books-Heath, 1973.

Clawson, Marion, and Jack L. Knetsch. *Economics of Outdoor Recreation.* Baltimore, Md.: Johns Hopkins University Press, 1975.

Edwards, Anthony. *Choosing Holiday Destinations: The Impact of Exchange Rates and Inflation.* London: The Economist Intelligence Unit, 1987.

Fresenmaier, Daniel R., Lonnie Jones, Seoho Um, and Teofilo Ozuna, Jr. "Assessing the Economic Impact of Outdoor Recreation Travel to the Texas Gulf Coast." *Journal of Travel Research,* Vol. 28, no. 1 (Summer 1989), pp. 18–23.

Kealy, Walter G. "International Travel and Passenger Fares, 1987." *Survey of Current Business,* Vol. 68, no. 5 (May 1988), pp. 47–49. Published by the Bureau of Economic Analysis, U.S. Department of Commerce, Washington, D.C.

Kottke, Marvin. "Estimating Economic Impacts of Tourism." *Annals of Tourism Research,* Vol. 15, no. 1 (1988), pp. 122–133.

Latimer, Hugh. "Developing-Island Economies—Tourism vs. Agriculture." *Tourism Management,* Vol. 6, no. 1 (March 1985), pp. 32–42.

Liu, Juanita C. "Relative Economic Contributions of Visitor Groups in Hawaii." *Journal of Travel Research,* Vol. 25, no. 1 (Summer 1986), pp. 2–9.

Mak, James. "Taxing Hotel Room Rentals in the U.S." *Journal of Travel Research,* Vol. 27, no. 1 (Summer 1988), pp. 10–15.

Mak, James, and Edward Hishimura. "The Economics of a Hotel Room Tax." *Journal of Travel Research,* Vol. 17, no. 4 (Spring 1979), pp. 2–6.

Mescon, Timothy S., and George S. Vozikis. "The Economic Impact of Tourism at the Port of Miami." *Annals of Tourism Research,* Vol. 12, no. 4 (1985), pp. 515–528.

Milne, Simon S. "Differential Multipliers." *Annals of Tourism Research,* Vol. 14, no. 4 (1987), pp. 499–515.

O'Connor, William E. *An Introduction to Airline Economics.* New York: Praeger, 1978.

Powers, Terry A. "Economic Appraisal of International Tourism Projects." *Journal of Travel Research,* Vol. 15, no. 2 (Fall 1976), pp. 10–13.

Rose, Warren. "The Measurement and Economic Impact of Tourism on Galveston, Texas: A Case Study." *Journal of Travel Research,* Vol. 19, no. 4 (Spring 1981), pp. 3–11.

Schulmeister, Stephan. *Tourism and the Business Cycle.* Vienna: Austrian Institute for Economic Research, 1979.

Summary, Rebecca M. "Tourism's Contribution to the Economy of Kenya." *Annals of Tourism Research,* Vol. 14, no. 4 (1987), pp. 531–540.

U.S. Travel Data Center. *The 1988-89 Economic Review of Travel in America.* Washington, D.C.: USTOC, 1989.

Vickerman, R. W. *The Economics of Leisure and Recreation.* London: Macmillan, 1975.

World Tourism Organization. *Economic Review of World Tourism.* Madrid: WTO, annual.

World Tourism Organization. *Tourism Multipliers Explained.* Madrid: WTO, 1981.

Young, George. *Tourism: Blessing or Blight?* Baltimore, Md.: Penguin Books, 1973.

# Tourism Planning, Development, and Social Considerations

## LEARNING OBJECTIVES

- Discover what the goals of tourism development should be.
- Recognize that there are some serious barriers to tourism development that must be overcome if a desired growth is to occur.
- Learn the political and economic aspects of development including those related to developing countries.
- Appreciate the importance of architectural design and concern for heritage preservation, local handicrafts, and use of indigenous materials in creating tourist facilities.

## WHY TOURISM PLANNING IS NECESSARY

The decision to develop tourism or expand present tourism development in a community, a region, or a country must be studied carefully. The socioeconomic benefits from tourism are powerful. Tourism development looks attractive to both developed and underdeveloped countries with the right preconditions — some combination of natural, scenic, historical, archaeological, cultural, and climate attractions. Tourism is a growth industry, and while that growth may show some slowing in the short run, the long-run prospects are good. The expected continued growth is based on continually rising per capita incomes, lower travel costs, increased leisure time, and changes in consumers' tastes and preferences toward travel, recreation, and leisure goods and services.

Many advocates have looked at tourism as a panacea for solving an area's development problems. This view is unrealistic because benefits may be accompanied by detrimental consequences. A review of some advantages and disadvantages arising from tourism development will indicate why careful planning is necessary.

Major arguments for tourism are that it

1. Provides employment opportunities, both skilled and unskilled, because it is a labor-intensive industry
2. Generates a supply of needed foreign exchange
3. Increases incomes
4. Creates increased gross national product

5. Requires the development of an infrastructure that will also help stimulate local commerce and industry
6. Justifies environmental protection and improvement
7. Increases governmental revenues
8. Helps to diversify the economy
9. Creates a favorable worldwide image for the destination
10. Facilitates the process of modernization by education of youth and society and changing values
11. Provides tourist and recreational facilities that may be used by a local population who could not otherwise afford developing facilities
12. Gives foreigners an opportunity to be favorably impressed by little-known country or region

Some disadvantages of tourism are that it

1. Develops excess demand
2. Creates leakages so great that economic benefits do not accrue
3. Diverts funds from more promising forms of economic development
4. Creates social problems from income differences, social differences, introduction of prostitution, gambling, crime, and so on
5. Degrades the natural physical environment
6. Degrades the cultural environment
7. Poses the difficulties of seasonality
8. Increases vulnerability to economic and political changes
9. Adds to inflation of land values and the price of local goods and services

Consequently, tourism is not always a panacea. On the contrary, overdevelopment can generate soil and water pollution and even people pollution, if there are too many visitors at the same place at the same time. Consider automobile and bus traffic congestion, inadequate parking, hotels dwarfing the scale of historic districts, and the displacement of the local community serving businesses by tourist-serving firms leading to degradation of the quality of life rather than improving it.

Then, too, too many visitors can have a harmful impact on life in the host country and on the visitors themselves. A beautiful landscape can suffer through thoughtless and unwise land development and construction methods. And customers and crafts can be vulgarized by overemphasis on quantity and cheapness.

These responsibilities cannot really be blamed on tourism, but rather on over-commercialization. Tourism is one of the world's greatest and most significant social and economic forces. But government officials and business people must weigh the economic benefits against the possible future degradation of human and natural resources.

Tourism development must be guided by carefully planned policy, a policy not built on balance sheets and profit and loss statements alone, but on the ideals and principles of human welfare and happiness. Social problems cannot be solved without a strong and growing economy that tourism can help to create. Sound development policy can have the happy result of a growing tourist business *and* the preservation of the natural and cultural resources that attracted the visitors in the first place.

Viewed comprehensively, the relationship between tourism and the community, state, regions, and countries requires consideration of many difficult issues: the quality of architecture, landscape, and environmental design; environmental reclamation and amenity; natural conservation; land-use management; financial strategies for long-term economic development; employment; transportation; energy conservation; education, information and interpretation systems; and more.

These are the reasons sound tourism planning is essential. Planning can ensure that tourist development has the ability to realize the advantages of tourism and reduce the disadvantages.

## THE PLANNING PROCESS

Proper planning—of the physical, legal, promotion, finance, economic, market, management, social, and environmental aspects—will help to deliver the benefits of tourism development.

Good planning defines the desired result and works in a systematic manner to achieve success. The following steps briefly describe a logical sequence:

*Define the System*   What is the scale, size, market, character, and purpose?

*Formulate Objectives*   Without a set of objectives the development concept has no direction. The objectives must be comprehensive and specific and should include a timetable for completion.

*Data Gathering*   Fact finding, or research, provides basic data that are essential to developing the plan. Examples of data gathering are preparing a fact book, making market surveys, undertaking site and infrastructure surveys, and analyzing existing facilities and competition.

*Analysis and Interpretation*   Once collected, the many fragments of information must be interpreted so the facts gathered will have meaning. From this step results a set of conclusions and recommendations that leads to making or conceptualizing a preliminary plan.

*Preliminary Planning*   Based on the previous steps, alternatives are considered and alternative physical solutions are drawn up and tested. Frequently scale models are developed to illustrate the land-use plans; sketches are prepared to show the image the development will project; financial plans are drafted from the market information, site surveys, and the layout plan to show the investment needed in each phase of the project and the cash flow expected; and legal requirements are met.

*Approving the Plan*   The parties involved can now look at plans, drawings, scale models, estimates of costs, estimates of profits, and know what will be involved and what the chances for success or failure will be. While a great deal of money may have been spent up to this point, the sum is a relatively small amount compared to the expenditures that will be required once the plan is approved and master planning and implementation begin.

*Final Plan*   This phase typically includes a definition of land use; plans for infrastructure facilities such as roads, airports, bike paths, horse trails, pedestrian walkways, sewage, water and utilities; architectural standards; landscape plans; zoning and other land-use regulations; economic analysis, market analysis, and financial programming.

*Implementation*   Implementation carries out the plan and creates an operational tourism development. It also follows up and evaluates. Good planning provides mechanisms that give continuing feedback on the tourism project and the levels of consumer satisfaction achieved.

Good planning should eliminate problems and provide user satisfaction. The final user is the judge in determining how successful the planning process has been.

Figure 10.1 shows a model for the tourism planning and development process and illustrates the large number of variables that come into play. The advantage of utilizing such a model is that it requires the planner to view the total picture and guides the thinking process. While no model can depict all interrelated facts of a planning process or eliminate all guesswork, such a model deserves inclusion in the initial phases of planning as a tool that helps to order, coordinate, and control the process.

# GOALS OF TOURISM DEVELOPMENT

Tourism development should aim at

1. Providing a framework for raising the living standard of the people through the economic benefits of tourism
2. Developing an infrastructure and providing recreation facilities for visitors and residents alike
3. Ensuring types of development within visitor centers and resorts that are appropriate to the purposes of those areas
4. Establishing a development program consistent with the cultural, social, and economic philosophy of the government and the people of the host country or area
5. Optimizing visitor satisfaction

## Obstacles to Development of Supply

The first obstacle to overcome in turning potential supply into actual supply is the lack or inadequacy of transportation and access routes to the tourist nucleus or center.

It is, of course, not enough to get there. The tourist should also be induced to stay. To this end, another basic obstacle to the development of actual supply should be overcome—the lack or shortage of accommodation.

Tourists inevitably require a series of goods and services. Some may be found on the spot and may be economically flexible enough to adapt to the fluctuations of demand. The infrastructure capacity must meet maximum demand. Financing can be a major obstacle.

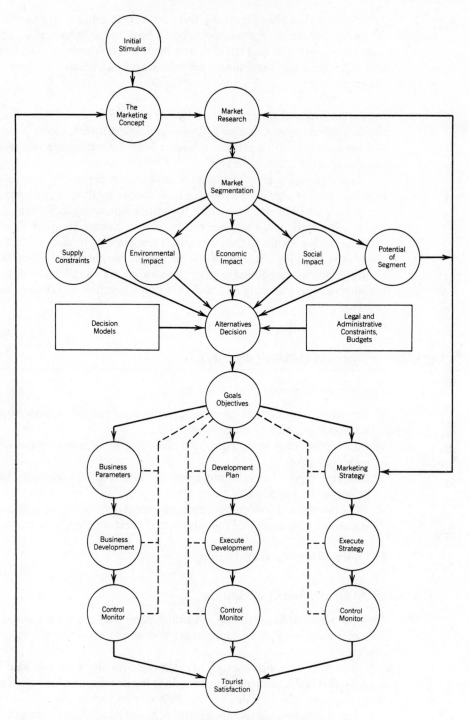

**Figure 10.1** Model for the Tourism Planning and Development Process.

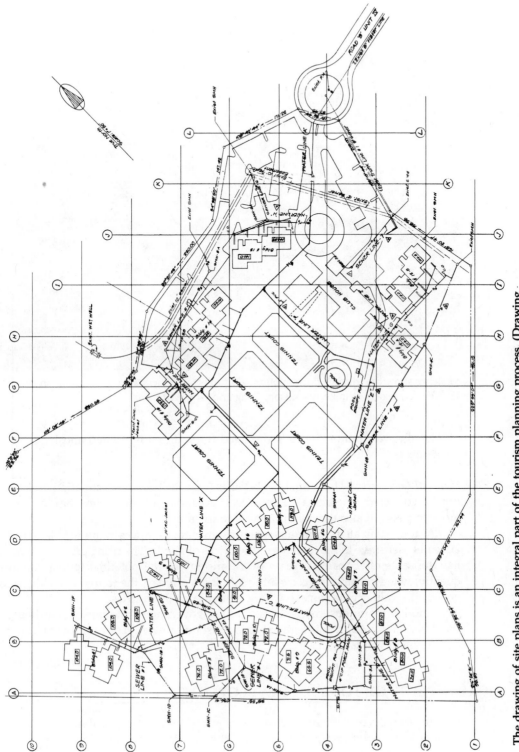

The drawing of site plans is an integral part of the tourism planning process. (Drawing courtesy of Wimberly, Allison, Tong and Goo Architects)

Sketches show the image a development will project and facilitate the planning process. (Sketch courtesy of Wimberly, Allison, Tong and Goo Architects)

Finally, we cannot overlook the need for sufficiently trained and hospitable personnel.

*Internal Obstacles*   These are the obstacles found within the destination area that can be corrected or eliminated by direct, voluntary means. They may occur in incoming as well as outgoing or internal tourism.

As tourism in all its forms absorbs consumer goods, prices in this field tend to be extremely sensitive to movements in the prices of goods. The rising price of tourism has the same effect as a decrease in the income of the potential tourist. Consequently, when considering costs and planning a holiday, the tourist will choose to go—if the value is the same—where money goes the furthest.

Another major obstacle is the attitude of government and business leaders in the destination area. If this leadership is resistant or even passive toward tourism, development will lag.

## POLITICAL ASPECTS OF TOURISM DEVELOPMENT

Like any significant element of an area's economy, there are political aspects that can and often do have major influences on the creation, operation, and survival of tourism projects. Many examples can be cited. One is the land-use regulations (zoning) for commercial or public tourism developments, which can be emotionally and politically sensitive topics. Another is the degree of involvement of governmental agencies in creating and maintaining tourism infrastructure. A third is the type and extent of publicity, advertising, and other promotional efforts.

## Land Use (Zoning)

Zoning ordinances specify the legal types of land use. But the final determination of the land use and the administration of the zoning ordinances are typically assigned to a publicly employed zoning administrator and a politically appointed or elected zoning board. Thus, the government decides on how land is to be used and rules on any request for changes in the zoning districts or rezoning to accommodate a non-conforming proposed development.

Attitudes of these public bodies toward tourism development will be influenced by the general public's perception (if any) of the desirability of a specific development. Creating a favorable public image is the responsibility of the developer and the managers of all tourism supply components. The public tourism promotion organization bears responsibility as well. If the public feels that tourism is desirable, rational zoning regulations and administration should result. Furthermore, if principles of tourism planning and development, as presented in this chapter, are faithfully implemented, the result should be well-planned projects. These will be accepted in the community as welcome sources of employment and tax revenues.

## Creation and Maintenance of Infrastructure

Any tourism development will need infrastructure. Whether this is provided by government agencies, the private developer, or both, is basically a political question. What troubles many local people is that their taxes are spent in part to provide roads, water systems, sewers, airports, marinas, parks, and other infrastructure that they perceive as benefiting mainly tourism. Is this fair or desirable from their point of view? Those having a common concern in tourism must realize that it is their responsibility to convince the public that such expenditures by government *are* desirable and *do* benefit the local economy. One way to achieve this understanding is through an intelligent lobbying effort. Another approach is to address service clubs, social organizations, and school groups. A third method shows how much money was spent by tourists or convention delegates.

Maintenance policies are also a vital factor in successful tourism development. Any element of infrastructure, once created, needs maintenance. The level of this maintenance can greatly affect successful tourism. An example is the promptness and adequacy of snow removal from public roads servicing ski resorts. Another is the quality and adequacy of public water and sewage systems. Many other examples could be given. Political influence to obtain good maintenance can be brought to bear by hotel and motel associations, chambers of commerce, convention and visitors' bureaus, and promotion groups. Such efforts can be very effective as public service agencies tend to be receptive if the demands are frequent and forceful.

Government and private industry *must* interact cooperatively if tourism development is to be successful. Political friction can develop when government officials think that private industry should do more to help itself and businesspeople believe that the government should do more to assist them. A knowledgeable outside consulting firm can study the situation and make recommendations in the best interests of both factions.

### Promotional Efforts

Publicly funded promotional programs are an essential part of the industry. However, the level or degree of participation in such publicity is largely a political process. To convince lawmakers and local political decision makers of the desirability of tourism, produce accurate data on the economic impact of tourism spending. An "investment" concept is the preferred way to view government programs. Pointing out industry diversification in the economy is another good approach. Other benefits cited could be employment, income multipliers, additional investments, preservation and enhancement of local industries, crafts, and the arts, as well as building local pride and recognition.

Lobbying efforts need to be convincing and persistent. Organizations representing tourism must have both moral and monetary support in sufficient measure to bring about successful political influence. Nothing succeeds like success. If tourism booms, the politicians can well take pride in their important contribution. We repeat—as in all other aspects of the tourist business, cooperation pays!

## DEVELOPMENT OF TOURIST POTENTIAL

### Official Tourism Body

A tourism body or organization should be created to keep abreast of socioeconomic developments in the various market countries or areas to provide a reasonably early forecast of the size, type, and structure of probable tourism demand. It would be equally useful to have a report on developments in the tourist industry of supplying centers or areas and on activities and projects undertaken to promote development.

Since tourism is such a complex phenomenon, distinct ministerial departments are responsible for finding solutions to developmental problems.

The stabilization of general and tourist prices should be a constant objective, as rising prices automatically reduce the volume of demand. Land speculation should be discouraged.

The inventory of potential national tourist resources (parks, attractions, recreational facilities, and so on) should be kept up to date and extended so that these resources may be duly incorporated into actual tourist trade in accordance with quantity and quality forecasts of demand.

Tax pressures that directly affect operating costs also influence prices. Because of the export value of tourism, a fiscal policy similar to that applied to the conventional or classical export trade should be devised.

Publicity campaigns should be organized and implemented every year according to the forecasts. These should be to-the-point, detailed, and constructive and should zero in on socioeconomic developments and activities in the market. Financing to cover this activity should be obtained from annual tourist earnings and other identifiable funds at a rate of not less than 1 percent and perhaps not more than 4 percent of total earnings.

Customs facilities should be as lenient as possible while ensuring control and maintenance of order and avoiding fraud or other crimes.

For their own benefit, host countries should make the tourists' sojourn as agreeable as possible. But proof that tourists have the financial means to cover the costs of their stay may be desired.

The seasonal nature of mass tourism causes congestion in the use of services required by tourists. Some services, such as accommodation, cannot adapt easily to seasonal fluctuation. On the other hand, some, such as transportation and communications, can adapt. Government provision of public services are important for development.

## Transportation

Because of its role in tourist development, the following measures with regard to transportation are recommended:

1. Continual, detailed study of transport used for tourism with a view toward planning necessary improvements and extensions.
2. Establishing a national or international plan of roads relevant to tourism, building new roads if necessary, improving those in a deficient state, and improving road sign systems. Such activities should be included in the general road plans with priorities according to economic necessity and the significance of road transport in tourism.
3. Improving rail transport (where needed) for travelers on lines between the boundary and the main tourist centers and regions as well as short-distance services in these regions of maximum tourist influx.
4. Improving road frontier posts, extending their capacity to ensure smoother crossings, organizing easier movement of in- and outgoing tourist flows. Crossing the frontier is always either the prologue or the epilogue to any journey between countries and is therefore important for the favorable impression the tourist will retain.
5. Providing adequate airport services and installations to meet demand. The rapid progress of technology in air transport makes reasonable forecasts possible.
6. Planning for ports and marinas equipped for tourism.
7. Extending car-hire services (with and without drivers) for tourists who arrive by air or sea.

## Accommodations

Accommodations must be properly placed in the regional plan. Hotels are permanent structures and grace the landscape for a long time. Planning considerations are vital. Figure 10.2 shows a specific site development plan.

One of the first considerations to be made by any planning body should be where hotels will be located. This can be accomplished by using zoning laws. Hotels

Harbour Town in Sea Pines Plantation on Hilton Head Island, South Carolina, is a good example of a well-planned resort development in a picturesque location. (Photo courtesy of South Carolina Department of Parks, Recreation and Tourism)

are commonly allowed in "commercial" zones. Also to be decided is the number of hotel rooms needed in relation to the anticipated demand. Then to be considered is a provision for expansion of hotels as demand increases.

One consideration in hotel planning is intelligent spacing of hotels in a given area. Hotels spaced too close together tend to have a mutual value-reducing effect. Views are cut off or inhibited, and structures are lowered in value.

Also important is the ratio of the number of persons on the beach to the number of rooms in the hotel. Research in the Department of Natural Resources of the state of Michigan indicates that the optimum capacity of an average-sized ocean or Great Lakes beach is approximately 1000 persons for each 400 lineal feet of beach. Typically, about 50 percent of those vacationers in a resort or beach area will actually be on the beach, and of this group, 25 percent will be in the water and 75 percent will be on the beach.

Another consideration is the topography. In rolling or hilly country, more accommodations can be placed close together without a feeling of interference with one another than in a flat area. Also, the type of vegetative cover affects the density of the accommodations. A heavy, thick cover tends to obscure the view, and more accommodations can be successfully placed in a limited area than if the vegetation is sparse or absent entirely.

Clusters of accommodations in reasonably close proximity, surrounded by extensive natural areas, is recognized as superior planning, as opposed to spreading out accommodations over a wide area. The beauty of the natural environment can be more fully appreciated in such an arrangement.

Before any investment in hotels and similar lodging facilities is made, the traveling and vacation habits of the prospective guests should be studied to tailor the facilities to the requirements and desires of guests. This is extremely important and

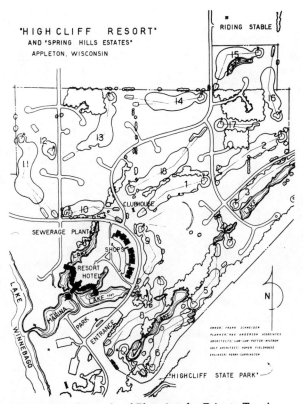

**Figure 10.2** Example of Planning for Private Tourism
Development Adjacent to a State Park. Note
integration of infrastructure and recreational facilities.
(*Source:* Recreational Land Development, Wisconsin
Department of Natural Resources, Division of
Resource Development, Bureau of Recreation)

conforms to the "market orientation" concept in which major decisions on investment begin with the desires of the potential customers.

Another factor is the harmony required between the various elements of the
travel plan, the local environment, and infrastructure.

Finally, when resort development is to be limited (and it usually is), it is best to
select the most desirable location and create a hotel of real distinction at this site.
Then, later, if proper planning and promotion have been accomplished, expansion
to other nearby sites can be achieved. Distinctive design of other hotel sites will
encourage the visitor to enjoy the variety, architectural appeals, and other satisfactions inherent in each resort hotel.

## Financing

Possible procedures for financing construction include a mortgage guarantee plan
and direct loans from a variety of sources.

Hotel accommodations should be planned to blend in with the surrounding environment to enhance the tourist experience. (Photo courtesy of Wimberly, Allison, Tong and Goo Architects)

*Mortgage Guarantee Plan*   Under this plan the government would guarantee mortgage loans up to 80 percent of the approved and appraised value of the land, building, furnishings, and equipment when the resort is completed. The approved mortgage would carry interest at prevailing mortgage rates and would require a schedule of amortization for the full retirement of the loan in not more than perhaps 30 years.

A guarantee fund would be established that at all times would be maintained at 20 percent of the total outstanding principal amount of mortgages guaranteed under this plan. The guarantee fund would be managed by trustees who would make any payments of interest and principal certified to them by the agency in charge of the mortgage loan plan. This agency would supervise the status of all approved loans and would investigate the facts and situations whenever it might become necessary to rely upon the guarantee fund to make the required interest and amortization payments. In such cases, an assignment of assets and income would be taken from the resort in default, which would have to be made up from subsequent earnings before any other use could be made of it.

Under this plan, the investor in the resort project would secure a mortgage loan from a lending institution or issue bonds or mortgage certificates to one or more sources of the borrowed capital. With the guarantee of payments of interest and principal and the existence of the guarantee fund for that purpose, mortgage loans under this plan should be attractive to lending institutions and other sources of borrowed capital.

With an approved resort development project and a guaranteed mortgage loan equivalent to 80 percent of the total financing required for land, building, furniture and equipment, 20 percent of the cost could be invested as equity risk capital. The ability to finance on this basis would provide incentive to those directly interested in the business, as well as other investors, to participate in new resort development projects.

*Financing Procedures*  A group interested in building a resort must convince the local city, regional, or national authorities that the resort should be built. The next step is to obtain a suitable site designated for construction under a previously completed tourist development plan for the area. A third-party feasibility study should be undertaken.

To indicate that this group is seriously interested in building a resort, architects, engineers, consultants, and other specialists should be contacted during the planning phase. The organization that is to *operate* the resort should be the same group that *builds* the hotel. An important planning ingredient is the recommendation of experienced resort managers concerning design and layout of the project.

The next step is to obtain construction capital either from local sources or from government or foreign sources. Also, capital must be secured for equipment, supplies, and services, including opening expenses and pre–break-even expenses. Government aid in obtaining imported supplies and equipment is often necessary. Governmental consideration should be given for reduction or elimination of taxes for an adequate length of time to help insure the financial success of the resort venture. Elimination of import duties on materials needed to build and run resorts is also desirable.

## SUMMARY

The quality of tourism planning and development will determine the ultimate success and longevity of any destination area. Thus, time, effort, and resources devoted to planning are essential investments.

Thoughtful planners have formulated the goals for tourism development, and these should be guiding principles everywhere. Obstacles must be overcome by sound planning augmented by political means, if growth is desired. This is often accomplished by the official tourism body. Tourism development should be a part of the overall regional or urban land-use development plan.

Tourism developments almost always involve both government and private developers. Each sector can best contribute certain parts of a project. Government typically provides the infrastructure, such as roads, water supply, sewers, public transportation terminals, and parks. Private developers supply superstructure, such as hotels, restaurants, recreation facilities, and shopping areas.

Government can also help considerably in making financing available. The private sector must deem an investment in a tourist facility attractive from the standpoint of financial return and risk before funds will be committed.

### About the Readings

The first brief reading provides a development example in a small city provided by the organization Partners for Livable Places.

Allison's article emphasizes the wisdom of incorporating local architectural designs, materials, decor, handicraft products, and other manifestations of local culture into tourist facilities. Doing so helps to make the developments an asset to the country instead of a detriment.

The third reading examines tourism's future in developing countries. It explores how tourism can benefit local residents as well as serve tourists.

## READING 10-1

### Development Example in a Small City

"Destination? Where? Putting Cities Without Surf, Slopes and Slot Machines on the Map," Partners for Livable Places, Washington, D.C.

Jonesborough (population 3000), Tennessee, is the oldest town in the state, a living historic community and seat of the short-lived State of Franklin that offers a rare glimpse into the past. The restoration of the town's historic district, initiated less than two decades ago, boasts the preservation of many Victorian, Neo-Classical, Federal and Greek Revival style buildings. The cornerstone of the district is the Christopher Taylor House, a log cabin that once housed President Andrew Jackson. Visitors can also view historic churches, the 1779 courthouse in which Jackson was admitted to the bar, charming houses, and can dine and shop along the town's Main Street.

A multi-purpose tourist facility was recently constructed to serve as a welcome and orientation to the preserved historic district. The center provides an introduction to Tennessee's first town through an audiovisual program and museum displaying the city's history and artifacts. As it has no hotels, Jonesborough promotes itself as a day-visitor destination.

Jonesborough's efforts to preserve an important part of American history and culture have added to tourist-related expenditures in the upper East Tennessee region. These funds amounted to $145 million in 1981, and produced $5.7 million in state tax revenues and $2 million in local tax receipts.

## READING 10-2

### Special Places in Special Places

By Gerald L. Allison, FAIA, RIBA
President, Wimberly Allison Tong and Goo Architects, Ltd.

Special places in special places—redundant? Not really. In the context of resort travel, those words are a fair description of what we all seek when we become travelers for pleasure. Certainly when we head for a resort in anticipation of cherished days of respite, we look forward to finding a special place within a special place.

Furthermore, this expectation often influences travel decisions even when the primary purpose is not an unalloyed holiday. Otherwise, why would resort hotels offer extensive convention facilities or corporate conferences be held in exotic places?

Speaking for myself — with everything else being equal — I am far more likely to accept an invitation to speak in Portugal, for example, over the same opportunity in Chicago. I have never experienced Portugal. It holds great promise of pleasure. I have been to Chicago and experienced Chicago. I stayed in a Chicago hotel. And I also stayed in a Chicago hotel in Hong Kong. And in Tokyo. And in Singapore. A couple of them in Sydney, another in Auckland, and a whole list of other places around the world. Also Athens, the wellspring of architectural history. It is truly amazing how widespread Chicago hotels are. Even in Kuala Lumpur and Bali you can wake up in the morning and say, "What a nice hotel — for Chicago."

That's what I want to talk about — how it is not necessary or even desirable to design Chicago hotels around the world. They belong in Chicago.

Please understand, this is not meant to denigrate Chicago, the city. Or special places appropriate to Chicago, where they reflect the special character of that city.

The repetition of the architecture of any particular place — over and over in other places — and mindlessly superimposed out of context — inevitably adds up to sameness and usually inappropriateness. This homogenizing sameness means, at best, overlooking the vast potential that awaits sensitive, responsible development. Sameness in hotel design has the effect of watering down the individuality of place — the very thing that should be enhanced, spotlighted. This sameness is — by inference — disrespectful of the character and culture of the host community. Further, it tends to limit rather than contribute to guest opportunities to experience the place chosen for special qualities. These clone hotels are anything but special places.

I concede they routinely offer the basics for comfortable travel — plumbing that works, hot water for bathing, safe water for drinking, and clean sheets — but not deeply rewarding travel.

And I would gladly accept a little sag in the bed in exchange for a little lift of the spirit.

Do you think this is a bit overstated? I don't think so. There are highly successful premium priced resorts in which all rooms have views and none have telephones, radios, TVs, or mini-bars. Let's consider the implications of "travel for pleasure." What does it mean? It means that for reasons of pleasure we leave one place to go to another. Why? The expectation of change, relaxation, escape, newness, excitement, enrichment, fantasy. Rejuvenating experience.

A successful resort, then, is one that satisfies these expectations. Put another way: The realization of these expectations is what sells hotel rooms and dining seats. And that's really what spells success in the hospitality industry; because if you don't fill those rooms and those seats, you are destined for failure.

So what are we talking about in terms of satisfying this wish list of expectations?

First — and I know this is repetitive, one thing we are not talking about is cookie cutter sameness, because change, not sameness, is what the pleasure traveler seeks.

Note of caution, however. Never underestimate the power of the cookie cutter. As rich as the possibilities are for individuality and appropriateness in hotel design, the cookie cutter mold is an ever-present temptation. It's always there, available, quick, cost efficient (in the short haul), ready to stamp out more and more copies of itself. It is often sneaked in under the guise of expediency, among other things. Perhaps one of the most heavily weighted reasons for reliance on cookie cutter hotels has been guest acceptance. Fortunately, this is eroding. Discrimination in matters of taste is an acquired, or developed, attribute. Jet travel, growing affluence, the opening up of heretofore undeveloped areas, renovation of the grand old hotels of Europe and America, and a rapidly expanding inventory of truly fine new hotels worldwide all contribute to the growing pool of pleasure travelers who grow more and more discriminating as they amass travel experiences. Thus, the more success the travel industry enjoys, the more dedicated to excellence it must become—to keep pace with the enlightened, discriminating traveler it is in the process of producing.

If we disdain cookie cutter hotels, we endorse hotels that are an expression of their particular environment and its people, that have a vibrant sense of place, and provide guests a rich array of optional pleasures. These hotels work, in part, because they recognize the name of the game is "pleasure" and they do afford guests the means whereby their individual expectations of pleasure can be realized. And because people are as individual in their preferences as in their personalities, the potential for creating uniquely wonderful—special—places is limitless.

While the ideal site for your special place may be in the Swiss or New Zealand Alps or mountains of Colorado, my fantasies may focus on the shores of Bora Bora or Cannes.

Australian rain forests and desert sands of the American Southwest have strong appeal.

Country lanes and, surely, city streets have allure.

Both the exoticism of Bangkok and the familiarity of American apple pie in Memphis attract, as surely as the warmth of the California or Riviera sunshine, or Scandinavia's bracing winds and weather.

History and culture buffs are drawn, as if by a magnet, to Williamsburg and New Orleans, London and Paris, Rome and Lisbon. . . .

How about castles in Spain? Or—Italy? Surely they too capture the imagination.

Fly to the Pacific for safe viewing of primeval furies of Hawaii's volcanoes; or, to the Atlantic for leisure listening to mellifluous songs and vibrant rhythms of the Caribbean.

Sip a Singapore Sling at fabled Raffles Hotel and talk about the tiger that was killed in the bar and the writers who created legends there.

Small jewel-like resorts—simple to sophisticated, informal and formal, each catering to a single facet of recreation—are cutting a nice niche in the marketplace —for example, the European and African resorts of Serena Hotels.

Leave your *istana* (ancient palaces of Malaysian sultans) inspired quarters in Trengganu to watch the ageless ritual of a giant sea turtle lumbering ashore, laying and burying her eggs and then with silent dignity returning to the deep from whence she came.

Is the picture emerging? Growing in your mind's eye?

You ask, am I talking business or am I caught up in my own dreams and imaginations?

The answer is—both!

The business of pleasure travel is the business of creativity, creating special places in special places — to translate everyone's dreams into reality. Call it the Pleasure Principle, if you like. But never lose sight of this very real fact: In this business, pleasure is paramount. Believe it — there is a correlation between the degree of success we achieve in pleasing people and the color of the bottom line.

To deviate slightly, I would like to encourage you to feel good about all this "leisure." Americans as a group are probably burdened excessively with our Puritan work ethic. Hotel management attracts many Germans, who may have originated the super disciplined approach to work. Unless, of course, it was of Chinese derivation. Whatever the roots of our dedication to work, I think we sometimes need reminding that it's OK — even desirable for good health — for humans to indulge, on a regular basis, in periods of pure pleasure. Recreation, in the sense of re-creation.

This business we're engaged in has a very valid *raison d'etre*. It is not simply a modern version of Louis XIV opulence. For all the super rich who can afford to spend their lives doing nothing but trekking from one resort to another, there are thousands of ordinary people who work diligently on a year-round basis, subjected to highly stressed lifestyles. They need and are willing to pay for the rejuvenation that comes from a complete change of pace — pleasure in a special place.

This is our major market segment, our growth potential.

What does it take, in a hotel, to richly reward our travel expectations? What is required to keep it out of the cookie cutter class and assure its role as a destination of distinction?

Keeping in mind that the primary function or service provided is pleasure — although the hotel is eminently practical — attractiveness and the ambiance of the physical structure are vital to its economic success. Every hotel needs thoughtful, imaginative design. Resort hotels, which exist solely for the pleasure of their users, demand it.

But it is not simply a matter of serving up a physically beautiful hotel. We recreational travelers seeking new experiences in exotic places are looking for far more than that. We want to observe and to experience that which makes our destinations different from the places we have left. Universally, we seek that special place in a special place. That is what drives us to other parts of our own countries and to other parts of the world. We seek other cultures, other lifestyles, and the uniqueness of the region we visit.

Toward fulfilling these goals, the hotel design can be a key element. Generally, the first unhurried introduction to a new region is the hotel in which we are to stay. It becomes our temporary home base. The place where we may eat, sleep, exercise, socialize, shop, listen to music, look at art, or simply "hang out" as the younger generation would say. It should be very much a part of our escape objective, not simply where we sleep and change clothes. It is also at our hotel that we may have the closest relationship with natives of the host locale. This offers an opportunity for good social interchange between guest and host. Both benefit. The hotel provides a captive audience eager to learn.

However . . .

Considering the salient and comprehensive role of the hotel in the guest's holiday experience, it naturally follows that hotel design should address the matter as creatively and effectively as possible.

There are other reasons for appropriate design. If the hotel design is sensitive to and appreciative of the culture and arts of the host area, this encourages and reinforces pride of heritage in the native resident and tends to make him or her more receptive to nonresidents. Sensitive, responsible design may also make significant contributions to the preservation and/or enhancement of a region's particular heritage. This works to the benefit of everyone.

From the developer's and operator's points of view, design appropriate to the region will quite likely result in cost savings as the facilities will be easier to construct and maintain. The design will often make use of readily available materials and technology appropriate to local construction techniques. Proper design may even eliminate the need for elevators, air conditioning and numerous other high maintenance building elements.

Designing with this kind of approach should lead to a degree of guest satisfaction that results in solid demand, excellent occupancy rates, enviable room charges, and long stays. It should also result in return visits and a generous number of referrals, each looking for a special place of escape.

Successfully meeting these goals is not a project confined to design of buildings. It is, rather, a highly complex matter encompassing the whole project continuum from master planning, design, approvals, and financing right through construction to maintenance, management, and even marketing, and in some cases periodic additions and renovations.

Meeting the challenge requires a lot of understanding—understanding by management of the challenges inherent in creating a design that fits the locality and cultural mores, and understanding by the design team of management's problems in providing services to guests and of maintaining the property in top condition. At times, it is difficult for clients, particularly in developing countries, to understand that locally inspired designs and native materials in new buildings can be as marketable as ancient temples.

Generally speaking, America has only recently begun to understand what Europe has long known—saving old landmarks and/or constructing new buildings near landmarks in such a manner as to respect and complement them is a responsibility. And a privilege.

There are many examples of this enlightened philosophy in Europe, where tourism plants are frequently integral parts of the regional cultural heritage. Ironically, many of the most successful projects are, by their very nature, difficult to find—which may be a good part of the reason for their success. They so blend into their immediate environment that they are hardly distinguishable as part of the tourist industry. Many, in fact, originally were not. Villas and houses, taverns and castles, have been converted to hotels, lodges, resorts. That they are, practically speaking, inseparable from the architecture and tapestry of life in their respective communities is a large part of their grace and appeal.

To summarize this relationship between special places and success in the pleasure travel arena: In the long run, the hotel providing the strongest possible sense of place will become the most desirable. The pleasure traveler seeks novel experiences, not a rerun of "Chicago." If the hotel patronized provides all the amenities required, while reinforcing the sense of being in an exotic location, the satisfaction quotient should be high—and this means the traveler will stay longer, return sooner, and pay more for the travel experience.

One price I paid as a traveler, I hadn't really bargained for; but with the added perspective of time, I can now treasure it as a priceless experience. Imagine a business conference in Japan with twelve stark naked men and one equally naked woman — the secretary — sitting chest deep in a steaming hot-spring bath discussing redesign of the world's largest enclosed communal "jungle bath." Also imagine being the only 6'2" blond-haired, blue-eyed Caucasian in the group. The meeting wears on; an hour later you are still sitting stark naked in that steaming bath trying to sketch design solutions before you and the paper wilts into oblivion. Making the challenge even more interesting — you are surrounded by bathers of both genders. They are curious, and slightly amused, about the way you look. Imagination is probably not vivid enough to match the reality that was.

Now, let's bring theory into focus by looking at specific projects, each with its own unique characteristics, challenges, and requirements. Ideally, there is no typical resort.

Much of what has been presented so far can be pulled together in a single case study of a small resort project that relies much less on fantasy for guest satisfaction, than on its integration with the culture of the beautiful east coast of West Malaysia. Exoticism, romance, seclusion, are key words to describe the resort. It is an unusual one, too, in that facilities are split in two sections five miles apart. They are the hotel and resort facilities at Tanjong Jara Beach and visitor center facilities at Rantau Abang.

Genesis of the design process was preparation of a tourism study in which Wimberly, Allison, Tong and Goo Architects participated. The study concluded that the economic success of a Malaysian visitor development program venture would depend in large on the country's ability to maintain and enhance Malaysia's distinctive character — its historic, cultural, and scenic attractions.

Five years later, the Malaysian Tourism Development Corporation engaged WAT&G to transform the development plan from a dream to reality, to create a hotel which would become the first step towards actualization of the master plan. The architects were charged with site selection as well as design and project development of what would become the first major tourist facility on West Malaysia's picturesque east coast.

One of the principal attractions of the area — giant sea turtles in their migration and egg laying rituals — presented both an opportunity and a responsibility. The architects felt visitors should be acquainted with the turtles' delicate life cycle and also the relationship that exists between Malaysia and the surrounding sea. On recommendation of the architects, the Malaysian government agreed to establish, as part of the overall project, a museum and visitor center near the middle of the hatching grounds, five miles from the hotel site. The two separate yet complementary parts of an integrated whole.

Throughout concept development and the working out of details there was strong motivation to create a project so appropriate to its total environment that it would not only look and feel right but seem an inevitable outgrowth of the whole.

Before starting with the actual hotel design, extensive research took place. This involved photographs and sketches and the study of whatever documents we could obtain that dealt with the unique cultural aspects of West Malaysia's east coast.

The design team then searched the area for craftsmen whose work could be incorporated into the construction. Trengganu is fortunate in having an abundance of talent capable of doing excellent wood carving, kite making, fine weaving, and mat making plus other crafts suitable for incorporation into design plans.

Ultimately, work of these craftsmen was well utilized and integrated into the construction and interiors of the facilities. As a side effect, this involvement provided a whole new ongoing economic outlet for their production and encouraged further development of traditional crafts.

The final step in our research was into the historic architectural styles of Trengganu. We determined that the unique and handsome, 100-year-old *istanas* (Sultan's palace) were an architectural form that could be adapted for hotel use. Their design and construction was such that natural ventilation could drastically reduce the need for energy-consuming airconditioning. Using the *istanas* as the architectural theme, we designed a resort master plan facility in the manner of a Malaysian riverside village with an existing stream as a focal point and the hotel placed on a curve of white sand beach at the foot of lush green mountains.

Architecture of the *istana*-like buildings is eminently practical in relationship to local weather conditions, makes use of materials plentiful in the area, and features traditional Malaysian art forms and craftsmanship. A salient feature of the two-story hardwood construction is that buildings are three to five feet above the ground for purposes of security, flood protection, and air circulation. Other ventilating elements are open-sided rooms, lattice soffits, steep pitched roofs with gable grilles, and locally-made bisque roof tiles left exposed "to breathe" on the inside. Buildings are constructed of native hardwood allowed to weather naturally.

Decorative motifs utilize Malaysian arts and crafts including wood carvings, woven mats, baskets, kites, shadow puppets and ceramics that are an integral part of the design and made by local artisans using traditional methods.

Rantau Abang Visitor Centre, with its sea life museum, depicts the strong traditional link between Malaysians and the sea. It serves, further, to protect the giant sea turtle during one step of its migratory life. The site is sandwiched between the coastal road and ocean with the Kabang River lying between the two.

The project consists of a complex of Malaysian-style buildings that include the museum/visitor center, a bazaar featuring Malaysian craftsmen with their wares, a Malaysian cuisine restaurant, a botanical garden featuring Malaysian plants used for food, shelter, and medicinal purposes, and a group of bungalows for overnight guests.

Structures are raised on piers above the river and sand dunes to avoid disruption of the site's natural characteristics. The height also affords a sweeping view of the turtle hatching grounds. Buildings, entirely of native hardwoods from nearby forests, are built in the centuries-old tradition of Malaysian construction by carpenters and craftsmen of the area.

Was the project well received? Very much so. It has been critically acclaimed internationally; the client is well-pleased, Rantau Abang was awarded an American Institute of Architects Excellence in Design citation, and in 1983 Tanjong Jara/Rantau Abang captured the prestigious Aga Khan Award for Architecture. The jury commended WAT&G for having "the courage to search out and successfully adapt and develop an otherwise rapidly disappearing traditional architecture and craft, to meet the demands of contemporary architecture. The consistency and seriousness with which this approach has been pursued at all levels of design and execution has generated an architecture that is in keeping with traditional values and esthetics, and of an excellence matching the best surviving traditional examples."

By the way, sometimes the process of learning foreign customs can be embarrassing — if somewhat humorous. A personal example happened while I was designing the project in Malaysia, where it is the usual Muslim custom in an Islamic country to wash your hands prior to partaking of food. At a business meeting, we were all served tea and each received an individual dish of delicacies. Folded neatly at the side of the dish was a thin, damp, chartreuse green sponge. I unfolded it and was diligently wiping my hands when I was shocked to see the Malaysian across from me eating his. A closer look at my ritual hand washing "sponge" revealed that it was, in fact, a coconut filled crepe.

Among WAT&G's work is a group of resort projects in several countries of the South Pacific. These projects have been extremely successful. Each is uniquely different from the others, and without exception — design for these hotels was derived from the culture of the particular host area.

Let's consider a few of them, briefly.

First, the Fijian Hotel, on Yanuca Island. The site plan of this hotel reflects the traditional Fijian village layout, with buildings clustered around a central court. Design and construction of the public rooms drew heavily on the indigenous architectural style of the Fijian *bure* (house), which is characterized by a high, steep roof and projecting ridge pole. Construction throughout was done by local natives using techniques familiar to them. The architectural firm sent a sculptor, Mick Brownlee, to work with natives in reestablishing the all but lost art of Fijian wood carving. As a result, newly trained artisans were employed to carve Fijian-motif artifacts to be used in the public rooms and established a shop on the site to sell their wares to the visitor.

One of WAT&G's most spectacularly romantic and equally as understated projects is the world renowned Hotel Bora Bora in French Polynesia. On a palm-studded promontory facing Bora Bora Lagoon are 65 beach and garden bungalows designed in the manner of the traditional Tahitian *fare* (house). Fifteen over-water luxury bungalows are perched at the reef's edge. Each unit has a view of the azure lagoon and reef, white sand beach, tropical flowers, and distant mountains. The open-air buildings, cooled by prevailing tradewinds, have bamboo walls with screened openings and roofs constructed of *lauhala* thatching. At Hotel Bora Bora, don't expect such intrusions as radios and televisions.

In almost every instance, native solutions to climatic problems — representing centuries of trial and error — are good responses to local conditions. We found this to be particularly true in American Samoa while working on design solutions for the Hotel Pago Pago Intercontinental. The Samoan *fale* (house) effectively solves the problems of building in a hot, humid climate. The traditional thatched roof protects from rain without impeding air movements; the open sides let prevailing winds pass through; palm-leaf "blinds" can be lowered to keep rain out. To base our design on this vernacular architecture and yet speak to modern requirements for comfort and sanitation, we devised a contemporary version of the *fale* combining its form and response to climate with modern materials to obtain a simple and economical structure adaptable to a variety of conditions. Our hotel *fales* were constructed by native workmen using traditional methods. Timbers were hand hewn by adzes, fitted together with wooden pegs and lashed with coconut fiber sennet. The project won a Hawaii Society American Institute of Architecture Design Award.

## READING 10-3

### Tourism's Future in Developing Countries

#### Economic Benefits and Costs

Successful tourism brings about numerous economic benefits, including increased employment, improved incomes, more business transactions, improved balance of payments, and larger foreign exchange earnings. In addition, tourism leads to improved infrastructure components such as roads, water systems, sewage systems, and communications, besides the hotels, motels, and shopping areas. These benefit local residents as well as serve the tourists. Natural history resources—parks and other natural areas—are frequently enlarged and enhanced to increase nature tourism.

At the same time, to serve tourists successfully, many countries have found that they must import a fairly large variety of items which are needed to accommodate travelers at international standards of comfort, sanitation, and aesthetic satisfaction. Quite commonly, various materials for hotel construction must be imported, as well as some food and beverage items and other commodities needed to serve the tourist. Other "imports" that appear on a tourism balance-of-payments account include the cost of promotion in foreign markets, leakages such as repatriation of profits by foreign investors, interest paid on borrowed foreign capital, and, possibly, imported labor of a specialized nature that is not available locally. Another somewhat negative factor, depending on the location, is the seasonal aspect of tourism, which leads to uneven levels of employment. Finally, tourist demand, as manifested in tourist expenditures, sometimes creates inflationary effects within the economy.

Because of these factors, when the possibility of increasing or improving tourist investments in a particular country is being considered, care should be exercised that the economic benefits from tourism are at least comparable to the economic costs. Calculation of the true values of capital/output ratios must take into account the total investment actually involved in tourist developments, not just the direct investment in hotels and immediately associated supply elements. Thus, investments in infrastructure, for example, which are exclusively required by new tourist developments, ought to be included in any calculation of the capital/output ratio.

The balance between negative and positive effects of international tourism varies in different countries. The effects are complex, and insufficient work has been done to try to assess the full impact on particular societies. Careful planning and regulation can mitigate the negative effects, but the responsible public authorities must take these effects into account in formulating tourist development policies and programs.

#### Maintaining Existing Levels of Tourism

While industrialized countries are concerned with expanding tourism, developing countries are challenged to maintain existing tourism levels. Growing competition among the world's tourist destinations requires these countries to offer ever-improving vacation experiences which are considered to be good values for prices paid.

One of the best opportunities to maintain demand is to increase the quality and extent of reception and guest activities. This can be accomplished by providing a more personal welcome to each arrival and offering expanded recreational, cultural, social, and instructional programs (such as sports instruction) and activities for children.

In addition, marketing programs must be planned by the most capable people available and conducted with verve and imagination. All supply components must cooperate fully, so that destination promotion is included in individual business advertising and all other promotions.

Upgrading all types of facilities and services is also an essential ingredient to assure success in retaining guests and customers. Word-of-mouth endorsements are the most credible and effective of all promotions.

### Planning Procedures

In our experience, improvement in an existing tourism plant or planning for additional facilities and services is best undertaken using the following steps in the order given.

*Review of Likely Demand*  Understanding the expected visitor is fundamental and of highest priority — likes, dislikes, interests, prices and willingness to pay, susceptibility to marketing programs, location and identification of markets, and description of target markets. Most tourism development programs that fail do so because they have not properly evaluated these factors. Thorough studies of the dimensions of the market and the qualities and preferences of the expected visitors are absolutely fundamental to success. Researching the existing and potential markets will make possible a much more intelligent approach to supplying the needs and wants of those markets. Thus, market research should be the foundation upon which tourism is intelligently built (see Chapter 11, "Travel and Tourism Research").

*Provision of Supply Components*  The supply components needed and desired by visitors — now and expected — can then be predicated upon the findings of the market research (see Chapter 7, "Tourism Components and Supply").

*Assessment of Accessibility*  Another important consideration is accessibility. Can the tourist conveniently reach the destination? How adequate are the various forms of transportation available to reach this particular area?

*Securing of Technical Know-How*  Planners, engineers, land use and resource experts, landscape architects, managers, transportation experts, economists, financiers, and others must be available. They are needed to provide the technical knowledge required for successful planning and development.

*Development of Financing Plan*  The financing plan makes or breaks the proposal, as adequate financing must be available to assure adequacy of the project. If financing is not done properly in the first place, the project is not very likely to succeed. Shortage of capital is the most frequent limiting factor in tourism development.

*Establishment of Time Schedule*  A time schedule for planning and implementation must be established. Planning without a time schedule is mainly an academic exercise. What is to be done and when it is to be done are integral parts of successful planning for tourism.

*Determination of Optimum Capacities*  An ideal capacity plan that prevents overuse, deterioration, and pollution is extremely desirable. Tourism planning must be done from a long-range viewpoint. Permanent improvements and developments should continue to be assets for at least 40 years. Future expansion should likewise be considered. There are constant improvements in technology, transportation, and marketing methods. If the development is to be expanded in the future, adequate allowances and provisions for such expansion should be considered at the outset.

An innovative method of establishing new or enlarged national parks and/or protecting other natural resources from exploitation has succeeded in some Central and South American countries. It is called "swapping debt for conservation." Through this arrangement the World Wildlife Fund, Conservation International, and other powerful international conservation organizations purchase some of the developing country's international debt, typically at substantial discounts. In exchange for the retirement of these debts, the country's central government agrees to purchase (if necessary) and manage enlargements and improvements to their national parks. Also included may be protection of game preserves, tropical forests, and other areas of natural beauty and interest to visitors and scientists. An example is an agreement between Bolivia and Conservation International. This pact provides that in return for $650,000 of Bolivia's outstanding debt purchased by Conservation International, Bolivia will provide a 3.7 million-acre expansion of the Beni Biosphere Reserve in the heart of the Amazon rain forest wilderness. Over a decade or so, the cumulative effect of this imaginative program in various countries will be to create very substantial appeals and attractions for visitors as well as for the local population. Similar programs in other underdeveloped areas of the world are very likely, as magnificent national parks and potential parks currently exist in many underdeveloped countries.

*Wildlife, Natural Areas, and Nature Tourism:*
*An Example for Development*

Widespread recognition of the world's dwindling wildlife resources has become a concern of many people and particularly of conservation organizations who wish to focus attention on this alarming situation and to do something about it. These organizations have provided expert advice and funds to countries that possess a relative abundance of wildlife and unspoiled natural areas. Many countries rich in natural history resources have continued to enlarge and enhance these areas because they have experienced an ever-increasing demand by visitors who wish to see them. Some African countries are good examples. By using expert game management techniques and sound conservation and protective measures, they have made their natural resources attractive and have created such a satisfying environment that visitors interested in enjoying such an experience come from many parts of the world. An increase in tourism benefits the host country, as this provides a means to generate foreign exchange earnings and increases employment. Organizations such as the World Wildlife Fund have made important contributions to countries striving

Establishing vast natural resource parks and game areas in Kenya has brought about substantial nature tourism. Viewing herds of elephants in their natural surroundings is a thrill for visitors to Marsabit National Game Parks, Kenya. (Photo courtesy of Kenya Tourist Office)

to enhance their wildlife, as in Kenya, Botswana, and Rwanda. These countries have outstanding national parks and game reserves. In Botswana, national parks comprise 17 percent of the entire country, sheltering an estimated 50,000 elephants as well as large numbers of other exciting animals for visitors to observe and photograph. Rwanda, a small country in southeastern central Africa, is home to mountain gorillas. In the Parc des Volcans located in the Virunga Mountains, a highly successful project has ensured the protection and actually increased the numbers of one of the world's two remaining populations of mountain gorillas.[1] A carefully controlled tourism trade based on observing the gorillas has flourished, providing economic benefits to local people. This has become a strong incentive not to convert gorilla habitats to farmland.

Many other countries in Africa and elsewhere have wildlife and protected forests as well as related natural history resources of global interest and quality.

### Sea Life Conservation and Marine Parks

In many instances, coral reefs and other attractive underwater natural resources are being destroyed by illegal fishing activities. These include using dynamite or dropping weights onto coral formations to herd fish into nets. Siltation from adjacent land erosion is also greatly destructive to reefs. In locations where tourists can visit and observe the beauty of the reef life, tourism is a desirable employment alternative, as providing tourists services is more economically rewarding than catching fish or collecting shells. Tourists enjoy underwater observations and delight in seeing and even touching harmless and attractive underwater creatures.

Keeping coral reefs and other underwater attractions in pristine condition and protecting them from siltation and other forms of destruction are basic for tourism, and creating a marine park is the best method of protection. In addition, marine parks have the advantage of being listed along with land-based parks. Such parks are unique and provide interesting subjects for publicity and good tourist advertising, especially when sites of shipwrecks are protected by placing them in marine parks; this protection creates an alluring attraction for scuba divers.

If tourism can be encouraged and accomplished, it has the double advantage of creating long-term jobs and income as well as protecting a natural resource vital to the preservation of underwater life and beauty.

## Obstacles to Development

The most common obstacle to development is a poor attitude on the part of government, industry, and business leaders, who often do not understand the implications of tourism and the benefits it can provide. Because of this lack of understanding, proper research, planning, and preparation, including the gathering of adequate data, should be undertaken to provide the information needed to eliminate this very significant obstacle.

Inadequate transportation and accessibility are other obstacles. Adequate transportation facilities must be available so that visitors can visit the area conveniently and economically. A deficient infrastructure is also a common obstacle to proper development. If an area's infrastructure and tourist facilities are not adequate, attractive, clean, and suitable for tourist use, tourism will not grow and prosper.

Another major obstacle, as previously noted, is lack of finances. It is better to have a pilot area where exemplary development can be created than to try to develop tourism widely without sufficient capital to do an outstanding job. In fact, no facilities at all are preferable to a poorly conceived, cheap, inadequate, and unattractive development.

Finally, a major obstacle to development is a lack of adequate personal and professional services. Essential elements of tourism development are hotel, restaurant, and tourism training schools, as well as schools for wildlife management personnel and game wardens. Adequate facilities and instruction must be available to prepare workers for skilled and semiskilled jobs, and these schools should possess instructional staffs of high caliber and other adequate resources. If the industry is to grow, it needs skilled persons available for employment in all tourist services, including not only hotels, restaurants, and transportation services, but also travel agencies, tour wholesaling companies, tour operators, tourist guide services, tourism marketing organizations, parks, game areas, and wildlife sanctuaries.

Professional services such as those provided by consultants and technicians in various fields are also needed by tourist enterprises. Sometimes these professional services have to be imported, but when they can be provided locally, a boost to the tourist business and the local economy will result.

## The Final Balance

The economic benefits of tourism are substantial. Developments such as charter flights, package tours, promotional and discounted fares have brought possibilities of greatly expanded tourist markets. These favorable factors can provide the basis for an advantageous diversification of national economies.

The environmental, ecological, cultural, and social impacts of tourism development, however, should be estimated and carefully considered in any plans. Also important are the ownership, capacities, and use of various kinds of land and other natural resources for tourism purposes. The tourist attractions and facilities of a particular country should be developed with due regard to the costs of infrastructure and other supply components. The development of well-planned resort areas at priority sites to serve relatively large concentrations of visitors is likely to be much more economical and desirable than scattered developments. This is true from the viewpoints of both tourists and residents of the host country.

In many areas of the world, tourism has produced great disparities between the standards of amenities provided for visitors and those for the local population. These inequalities cannot be avoided entirely, but, in the longer run, the improvement of standards for local residents should be the primary condition of successful tourism development. The upgrading of amenities provided for the local population is thus an integral part of a well-planned project. When this concept becomes the guiding principle of the development, its contribution to the welfare of local people is most likely to be maximized.

## Reading Endnote

1. Debbie Crouse, "Up Close with Gorillas, " *International Wildlife,* December, 1988, 4–11.

## Key Concepts

architectural recommendations
area tourism development plan
creating of infrastructure
economic and financial aspects
economic dependence on tourism
goals of tourism development
government tourism program
heritage preservation
land use
management of government tourism
 program

obstacles to development
official tourism body
policy formulation
political aspects
preservation and environmentalism
problems of unplanned growth
promotional efforts
role of local or state governments
total planning effort
transportation
zoning

## For Review and Discussion

1. Basically, what is the purpose of planning?
2. Discuss the importance of transportation to tourism development.
3. Discuss the most important factors that would influence the success of a newly built resort.
4. Why is tourism developmental planning so necessary?
5. What are some of the most significant relationships between a large-sized resort development and its nearby community?
6. Referring to the previous question, if the community is a rather small one, should any input be solicited from residents of the community before major remodeling or new construction is undertaken?

7. What goals should guide the land use plan of a small lakeshore village that is popular with summer visitors?
8. Provide some descriptions of the importance of infrastructure to the following: ski resort, summer campground, fishing pier, public marina, shopping center, resort apartment condominium project.
9. From planning to completed project, name the principal individuals and organizations that would be involved.
10. Do you agree with the statement that if a community's government and business leaders are resistant or passive toward tourism, development will lag?
11. Currently, heritage preservation is a popular trend. Is it a desirable one?
12. Would you encourage tourism development if your community and area were already very prosperous ones?
13. Enumerate various kinds of environmental pollution that unwise developments can create.
14. How could greater emphasis be placed on the importance of a development process in which meticulous attention is given to the environment to create a harmonious combination of natural assets and human-made facilities?
15. Architect Gerald Allison states that he would "gladly accept a little sag in the bed for a little lift in the spirit." What does he mean by this? Do you agree? Explain.
16. Explain nature tourism and enumerate its advantages for a developing country.

## Case Problems

1. A real estate developer, aware of a growing demand for a lakeshore resort condominium, planned for 126 apartments plus a 56-slip marina. Upon submission of his plan, the township planning board informed him that only one apartment and one boat slip would be allowed for each 100 feet of lakeshore. As he did not own that much lakeshore, plans were redrawn to construct the planned development back from the lakeshore. Access to the lake would be provided via a canal, using one of the lakeshore lots — a "keyhole" plan. This proposal was also rejected. The developer then sued the township board to force approval. What should the court or judge decide?
2. You have accepted a United Nations Development Program assignment in tourism to a small Central American country. Your first task is to make financial calculations concerning the economic feasibility for such development. What factors do you consider when beginning this process? Assuming your findings result in a favorable conclusion, what would your next step be?
3. Hotels built in a box-like manner are cheaper to construct and maintain than those with more elaborate designs. Hotel companies normally aim to maximize profits. Thus, should all hotels be built in that manner?

## Selected References

Baud-Bovy, Manuel, and Fred Lawson. *Tourism and Recreation Development.* London: Architectural Press; Boston: CBI, 1977.
Bell, Charles Anderson. "Crosscultural Construction: Designing Hotels Overseas." *The Cornell Hotel and Restaurant Administration Quarterly*, Vol. 27, no. 2 (August 1986), pp. 25–28.

Bosselman, Fred P. *In the Wake of the Tourist.* Washington, D.C.: The Conservation Foundation, 1978.

Cater, Erlet A. "Tourism in the Least Developed Countries." *Annals of Tourism Research,* Vol. 14, no. 2 (1987), pp. 202–226.

Culpan, Refik. "International Tourism Model for Developing Economies." *Annals of Tourism Research,* Vol. 13, no. 4 (1986), pp. 541–552.

Davern, Jeanne M. *Places for People: Hotels, Motels, Restaurants, Bars, Clubs, Community Recreation Facilities, Camps, Parks, Plazas, and Playgrounds.* New York: McGraw-Hill, 1976.

Gearing, Charles E., William W. Swart, and Turgut Var. *Planning for Tourism Development.* New York: Praeger, 1976.

Gee, Chuck Y. *Resort Development and Management.* East Lansing, Mich.: Educational Institute of the American Hotel and Motel Association, 1988.

Getz, Donald. "Models in Tourism Planning." *Tourism Management,* Vol. 7, no. 1 (March 1986), pp. 21–32.

Gunn, Clare A. *Tourism Planning.* New York: Taylor & Francis, 1988.

Gunn, Clare A. *Vacationscape Designing Tourist Regions.* New York: Van Nostrand Reinhold, 1988.

Hawkins, Donald, Elwood Shafer, and James Rovelstad. *Tourism Planning and Development Issues.* Washington, D.C.: George Washington University, 1980.

deKadt, Emanuel. *Tourism: Passport to Development?* Washington, D.C.: Oxford University Press for UNESCO and the International Bank for Reconstruction and Development/ The World Bank, 1979.

Kaiser, Charles, Jr., and Larry E. Helber. *Tourism Planning and Development.* Boston: CBI, 1978.

Kariel, Herbert. "Tourism and Development: Perplexity or Panacea?" *Journal of Travel Research,* Vol. 28, no. 1 (Summer 1989), pp. 2–6.

O'Reilly, A. M. "Tourism Carrying Capacity: Concept and Issues." *Tourism Management,* Vol. 7, no. 4 (December 1986), pp. 254–258.

Pearce, Douglas. *Tourist Development.* Essex, U.K.: Longman House, 1981.

Portman, John, and Jonathan Barnett. *The Architect as Developer.* New York: McGraw-Hill, 1976.

Richter, Linda K. *Land Reform and Tourism Development.* Cambridge, Mass.: Schenkman, 1982.

"Selecting and Planning for Tourists — The Case of Cyprus." *Tourism Management,* Vol. 4, no. 3 (September 1983), pp. 209–211.

Smith, Stephen L. J. "Regional Analysis of Tourism Resources." *Annals of Tourism Research,* Vol. 14, no. 2 (1987), pp. 254–273.

*Tourism USA: Guidelines for Tourism Development.* Columbia, Mo.: Department of Recreation and Park Administration, University Extension, University of Missouri.

Turgut, Var, Juanita C. Liu, Pauline Sheldon, and Kevin Boberg. "Tourism and Computers: Quo Vadis?" *Annals of Tourism Research,* Vol. 13, no. 1 (1986), pp. 109–117.

Warner, Raynor M., Sibyl M. Groff, and Ranne P. Warner. *Business and Preservation.* New York: Inform, 1978.

Williams, Alan M., and Gareth Shaw. *Tourism and Economic Development, Western European Experiences.* London: Belhaven Press, 1988.

Woodside, Arch G., and Jeffrey A. Carr. "Consumer Decision Making and Competitive Marketing Strategies: Applications for Tourism Planning." *Journal of Travel Research,* Vol. 26, no. 3 (Winter 1988), pp. 2–7.

World Tourism Organization. *Presentation and Financing of Tourist Development Projects.* Madrid: WTO.

Yesawich, Peter C. "Planning: The Second Step in Market Development." *The Cornell Hotel and Restaurant Administration Quarterly,* Vol. 28, no. 4 (February 1988), pp. 71–81.

# PART FOUR

# Essentials of Tourism Marketing and Research

# CHAPTER 11

# Travel and Tourism Research

## LEARNING OBJECTIVES

- Know the role and scope of travel research.
- Know the travel research process.
- Know about secondary data.
- Know the methods of collecting primary data.
- Know who does travel research.

Information is the basis for decision making, and it is the task of travel research to gather and analyze data to help travel managers make decisions. Travel research is the systematic, impartial designing and conducting of investigations to solve travel problems. Examples of travel research are

1. Delta Airlines investigating consumer attitudes and behaviors to enable the airline to serve the flying public
2. Marriott Hotels and Resorts studying the leisure travel market
3. The City of Denver conducting a feasibility study to determine whether the city should build a large new airport
4. The Aspen Skiing Company conducting a market profile study to understand its customers
5. The U.S. Travel Data Center measuring the economic impact of travel in the United States

Although travel research does not *make* decisions, it does help travel decision makers operate more effectively. Managers can plan, operate, and control more efficiently when they have the facts. Thus, research, which reduces the risk in decision making, can have a great impact upon the success or failure of a tourism enterprise.

## ILLUSTRATIVE USES OF TRAVEL RESEARCH

Some of the uses or functions of travel research are

1. *To delineate significant problems.* The constant pressure of day-to-day business operations leaves the travel executive with little time to focus on problem areas

that handicap operations. The isolation of causes and problems that are creating inefficiency is often one of the most important single contributions that travel research makes to management.

2. *To keep an organization or a business in touch with its markets.* Travel research identifies trends, interprets markets, and tracks changes in markets so that policies can be developed that are aimed in the right direction and are based on facts rather than on hunches or opinions. Research reduces the risk of unanticipated changes in markets. In a way, research is insurance against these changes to make sure that a business does not stick with a product until it becomes obsolete.

3. *To reduce waste.* Research has always been effective in measuring methods of operation to eliminate those methods that are inefficient and to concentrate on those that are the most effective. Automation of travel makes this use even more important. The energy crisis led to research that has produced dramatic savings in aircraft fuel requirements.

4. *To develop new sources of profit.* Research can lead to the discovery of new markets, new products, and new uses for established products. Research can show the lodging industry the types of rooms and the type of lodging facilities that should be offered to meet customers' needs.

5. *To aid in sales promotion.* Many times the results of research are interesting not only to the firm but also to the public and can be used in advertising and promotion. This is particularly true of consumer attitude research and research where consumers are asked to rank products and services.

6. *To create goodwill.* Consumers react favorably to travel research; they feel that the company that is involved in research really cares about them and is trying to create a product or service that will meet their needs.

## THE STATE OF THE ART

Travel research today runs from the primitive to the sophisticated—from simple fact gathering to complex, mathematical models. For those who really wish to dig into the subject, there are several references worth noting. The most important is *Travel, Tourism and Hospitality Research: A Handbook for Managers and Researchers,* published by John Wiley and Sons in 1987; a second is "Analysis, Methods, and Techniques for Recreation, Research and Leisure Studies," published by the Ontario Research Council on Leisure; a third is an article that appeared in the *Journal of Travel Research* entitled "Some Critical Aspects of Measurement Theory and Practice in Travel Research"; a fourth and one of the most useful documents is "Identifying Traveler Markets, Research Methodologies," published by the U.S. Travel Service in September 1978; and a fifth is a six-part series on marketing research by Robert C. Lewis, University of Massachusetts, which appeared in *The Cornell Hotel and Restaurant Administration Quarterly* in 1984 and 1985.

Measurement is a critical element in research activity, and the lack of standard or precise definitions has hampered the development of travel research. Without definitions, measurement cannot be taken and data cannot be generated and compared from study to study. Economic projections or analytical findings made by sophisticated models or pure intuition must be based on some kind of data. Without a quantitative record of past experiences, only individual, isolated studies making a limited contribution to the state of the art are possible. That is basically where we stand in the area of travel research at the present time. Giant strides are being made, improving travel research by adopting techniques developed by other disciplines and utilizing new and more sophisticated techniques; however, the existing body of literature largely consists of individual isolated studies utilizing different definitions that were set up only to solve the immediate problem at hand.

## THE TRAVEL RESEARCH PROCESS

The key to good travel research is to define the problem and work through it in a systematic procedural manner to a final solution. The purpose of this section is to describe briefly the basic procedures that will produce a good research result.

1. *Identify the problem.* First, the problem must be defined or identified. Then you are in a position to proceed in a systematic manner.
2. *Conduct a situation analysis.* In this step you gather and digest all the information available and pertinent to the problem. The purpose is to become familiar with all the available information to make sure that you are not repeating someone else's work or that you have not overlooked information that will provide a ready solution to the problem. The situation analysis is an exhaustive search of all the data pertinent to the company, the product, the industry, the market, the competition, advertising, customers, suppliers, technology, the economy, the political climate, and similar matters. Knowledge of this background information will help you to sort out the likely causes of the problem and will lead to more efficient productive research. The organization will get the most from the research result when you understand the organization's internal environment and its goals, strategies, desires, resources, and constraints.
3. *Conduct an informal investigation.* After having gotten background information from available sources, you will talk informally with consumers, distributors, and key people in the industry to get an even better feel for the problem. During both the situation analysis and informal investigation, you should be developing hypotheses that can be tested. The establishment of hypotheses is one of the foundations of conducting research and is a valuable step in the problem-solving process. An hypothesis is a supposition, a tentative proposal, a possible solution to a problem. In some ways it could be likened to a diagnosis. If your automobile quit running on the interstate, you might hypothesize that (1) you were out of gas or (2) the fuel pump had failed or (3) you had filter problems. An investigation would enable you to accept or reject these hypotheses.
4. *Develop a formal research design.* Once adequate background information has been developed and the problem has been defined against this background, it is time to develop the specific procedure or design for carrying out the total investigation or research project. This step is the heart of the research process. Here you have to develop the hypotheses that will be tested and determine the types and sources of data that are to be obtained. Are secondary sources available, or will it be necessary to conduct primary research? If primary research has to be con-

ducted, then it is necessary to develop the sample, the questionnaires, or other data collection forms and any instruction sheets and coding methods and tabulation forms. Finally, it is necessary to conduct a pilot study to test all of the foregoing elements. The results are then written up in a detailed plan that serves as a guide that any knowledgeable researcher should be able to follow and conduct the research satisfactorily.

5. *Collect the data.* If the data are available from secondary sources, then collecting the data becomes primarily desk research. However, if primary data are collected, this step involves actual fieldwork in conducting survey research, observational research, or experimental research. The success of data gathering depends on the quality of field supervision, the caliber of the interviewers or field investigators, and the training of investigators.

6. *Tabulate and analyze.* Once the data have been collected, they must be coded, tabulated, and analyzed. Both this step and the previous one must be done with great care; it is possible for a multitude of errors to creep into the research process if collection, tabulation, and analysis are not done properly. For example, if one is going to use the survey method, then interviewers must be properly selected, trained, and supervised. Obviously, if instead of following the carefully laid out sample the interviewers simply fill out questionnaires themselves, the data will not be useful.

   In today's environment, it is likely that tabulation will take place on the computer. A number of excellent packages are available for this purpose. One of the most used is SPSS, the Statistical Package for the Social Sciences.

7. *Interpret.* Tabulation results in stacks of computer printout, with a series of statistical conclusions. These data must now be interpreted in terms of the best action or policy for the firm or organization to follow — a series of specific recommendations of action. This reduction of the interpretation to recommendations is one of the most difficult tasks in the research process.

Research involves a complete understanding of the client's needs, planning a research design, analyzing data, and presenting results. (Photo courtesy of Davidson-Peterson Associates, Inc.)

8. *Write the report.* Presentation of the results of the research is extremely important. Unless the data are written up in a manner that will encourage management to read them and act upon them, all of the labor in the research process is lost. Consequently, emphasis should be put on this step in the research process to produce a report that will be clearly understood with recommendations that will be accepted.

9. *Follow up.* Follow up means precisely that. A study sitting on the shelf gathering dust accomplishes nothing. While many people will consider the researcher's task to be done once the final report or presentation has been made, the work is *not* completed until the results of the survey are put into action. Research is an investment, and an ultimate test of the value of any research is the extent to which its recommendations are actually implemented and results achieved. It is the task of the researcher to follow up to make the previous investment of time and money worthwhile.

## SOURCES OF INFORMATION

Primary data, secondary data, or both may be used in a research investigation. Primary data are original data gathered for the specific purpose of solving the travel research problem that confronts you. In contrast, secondary data have already been collected for some other purpose and are available for use by simply visiting the library or other such repositories of secondary data. When researchers conduct a survey of cruise passengers to determine their attitudes and opinions, they are collecting primary data. When they get information from the Bureau of Census on travel agents, they are using a secondary source.

The situation analysis step of the travel research process is emphasized as it focuses on the use of secondary sources; however, their use is not confined to this step. One of the biggest mistakes in travel research is to rush out and collect primary data without exhausting secondary source information. Only later do you discover you have duplicated previous research when existing sources could have provided information to solve your problem for a fraction of the cost. Only after exhausting secondary sources and finding you still lack sufficient data to solve your problem should you turn to primary sources.

### Secondary Data

In the last 10 years there has been a virtual explosion of information related to tourism, travel, recreation, and leisure. A competent researcher must be well acquainted with these sources and how to find them. Appendix B contains a concise list of major secondary sources of travel information.

If you are fortunate enough to find secondary sources of information, you can save yourself a great deal of time and money. Low cost is clearly the greatest advantage of secondary data. When secondary data sources are available, it is not necessary to construct and print questionnaires, hire interviewers, pay transportation costs, pay coders, pay keypunchers, and pay programmers; it is easy to see the cost advantage of utilizing secondary data. Secondary data can also be collected

A library is a good source of secondary data for a situation analysis. Gin Hayden, Project Director, Travel Reference Center, University of Colorado, is in charge of maintaining the largest collection of travel research studies in North America. She can conduct literature searches of the collection by 973 descriptions. (Photo courtesy of Business Research Division, University of Colorado)

much more quickly than can primary data. With an original research project, it typically takes a minimum of 60 to 90 days or more to collect data; secondary data could be collected in a library within a few days.

Secondary data are not without disadvantages; for example, many times information does not fit the problem for which you need information. Another problem is timeliness — many secondary sources become outdated. For example, the Census of Population and Housing is conducted every 10 years; as we get to the end of that time period, the data are not very useful. The last Census Bureau *National Travel Survey* was conducted in 1977; in the rapidly changing travel world, it now serves as a historical document.

## Evaluating Secondary Data

While it is not expected that everyone will be a research expert, everyone should be able to evaluate or appraise secondary data. Any study, no matter how interesting, must be subjected to evaluation: "Is it a valid study? Can I use the results to make decisions?" On such occasions the researcher must evaluate the secondary data and determine whether they are usable.

The following criteria may be used to appraise the value of information obtained from secondary sources:

1. *The organizations supplying the data.* What amount of time went into the study? Who conducted the study? What experience did the personnel have? What was the financial capacity of the company? What was the cost of the study? An experienced research firm will put the proper time and effort into a study to yield results whereas a novice or inexperienced organization may not.

2. *The authority under which the data are gathered.* For example, data collected by the IRS are likely to be much better than data collected by a business firm. Data that are required by law, such as census data, are much more dependable than is information from other sources.

3. *Freedom from bias.* One should always look at the nature of the organization furnishing the data. Would you expect a study sponsored by airlines to praise the bus industry for providing the lowest-cost transportation on a per mile basis in the United States?

4. *The extent to which the rules of sampling have been rigidly upheld.* What is the adequacy of the sample? Adequacy is frequently difficult to evaluate because deficiencies in the sampling process can be hidden. One indication of adequacy is the sponsor's willingness to talk about the sample. Will the sponsor release sampling details? Are the procedures well-known, acceptable methods?

5. *The nature of the unit in which the data are expressed.* Here even simple concepts are difficult to define. In defining the term "house," how do you handle such things as duplexes, triplexes, mobile homes, and apartment houses? Make sure that good operational definitions have been used throughout the research so there will be no problems in understanding it. Research results that are full of terms such as "occasionally" and "frequently" are not likely to be useful; these terms have different meanings to different people.

6. *The accuracy of the data.* The need here is to examine the data carefully for any inconsistencies and inquire into the way in which the data were acquired, edited, and tabulated. If at all possible, check the data against known data from other sources that are accurate. For example, check the demographics in a study against known census data.

7. *Pertinency to the problem.* You must be concerned with fit. You may have a very good study, but if it does not pertain to the problem at hand, it is not worth anything to you. The relevancy of secondary data pertaining to the problem must stand up; otherwise, the study cannot be used.

8. *Careful work.* Throughout your evaluation always look for evidence of careful work. Are tables constructed properly? Do all totals add up to the right figures or 100 percent? Are conclusions supported by the data? Is there any evidence of conflicting data? Is the information presented in a well-organized, systematic manner?

## Primary Data

When it is not possible to get the information you need from secondary sources, it is necessary to turn to primary sources — original, firsthand sources of information. If you need information on travelers' attitudes, you would then go to that population and sample it. As stated earlier, you should turn to collecting primary data only after exhausting all reasonable secondary sources of information.

Once you have determined that you are going to collect primary data, then you must choose what method of gathering primary data you are going to use. The most widely used means of collecting primary information is the survey method. Other methods are the observational method and the experimental method. It is not uncommon to find one or more of these methods used in gathering data. These basic methods are discussed in the next section.

## BASIC RESEARCH METHODS

### The Survey Method

If we look at the methods of collecting travel research data, we will find that the survey method is the most frequently used. The survey method, also frequently referred to as the questionnaire technique, gathers information by asking questions. The survey method includes factual surveys, opinion surveys, or interpretive surveys, all of which can be conducted by personal interviews, mail, or telephone techniques.

*Factual Surveys* A quick look at the types of surveys will reveal that factual surveys are by far the most beneficial. "In what recreational activities did you participate last week?" is a question for which the respondent should be able to give accurate information. While excellent results are usually achieved with factual surveys, all findings are still subject to certain errors, such as errors of memory and ability to generalize or the desire to make a good impression. Nonetheless, factual surveys tend to produce excellent results.

*Opinion Surveys* In these surveys, the respondent is asked to express an opinion or make an evaluation or appraisal. For example, a respondent could be asked whether tour package A or B was the most attractive or which travel ad is the best. This kind of opinion information can be invaluable. In studies of a ski resort conducted by the University of Colorado, vacationer respondents were asked to rate the resort's employees' performance as excellent, good, average, or needs improvement. The ratings allowed resort management to take action where necessary. Opinion surveys tend to produce excellent results if they are properly constructed.

*Interpretive Surveys* On interpretive studies the respondent acts as an interpreter as well as a reporter. Subjects are asked why they chose a certain course of action — why they participated in a particular recreation activity the previous week (as well as what activity), why they flew on a particular airline, why they chose a particular vacation destination, why they chose a particular lodging establishment.

While respondents can reply accurately to "what" questions, they often have difficulty replying to "why" questions. Therefore, while interpretive research may give you a feel for consumer behavior, the results tend to be limited. It is much better to utilize motivational and psychological research techniques, which are better suited for obtaining this information.

In summary, try to get factual or opinion data via the survey method and utilize in-depth interviewing or psychological research techniques to get "reason why" data.

It was mentioned earlier that surveys can be conducted by personal interviews, telephone, or mail. The purpose of a survey is to gather data by interviewing a limited number of people (sample) that represents a larger group. Reviewing the basic survey methods, one finds the following advantages and disadvantages.

*Personal Interviews* These are much more flexible than either mail or telephone surveys because the interviewer can adapt to the situation and the respondent. The interviewer can alter questions to make sure that the respondent understands them or probe if the respondent does not respond with a satisfactory answer. Typically one can obtain much more information by personal interview than by telephone or mail surveys, which by necessity must be relatively short. Personal interviewers can observe the situation as well as ask questions. For example, an interviewer in a home can record data on the person's socioeconomic status, which would not be possible without this observation. The personal interview method permits the best sample control of all the survey techniques.

A major limitation of the personal interview method is its relatively high cost. It tends to be the most expensive of the three survey methods. It also takes a considerable amount of time to conduct, and there is always the possibility of personal interviewer bias.

*Telephone Surveys* Respondents are interviewed over the telephone with this approach. Telephone surveys are usually conducted much more rapidly and at less

Survey Sampling, Inc., is one of the many firms that utilize the survey technique to conduct travel research. (Photo courtesy of the Travel and Tourism Research Association)

**CAREY AMERICAN LIMOUSINE** Colorado Springs Shuttle Service

Please take a moment to respond to the following questions. This information will be used to evaluate areas of service to afford you quality service for your next trip. Thank you.

1. Was the vehicle on time? Yes _____ No _____ (Delay time: _____ Reason given                                    )
2. What was the condition of the equipment? Clean _____ Average _____ Unkempt _____
3. Was your driver courteous? Yes _____ No _____
4. How was your service: Excellent _____ Fair _____ Poor _____ (Why?                                    )
5. Was it easy to make your reservation? Yes _____ No _____ (Why:                                    )
6. Where did you find out about our company? Travel agent _____ Advertisement _____ Referred by:
7. Was the scheduled time convenient for you? Very _____ Acceptable _____ Inconvenient
8. Were you traveling on Business _____ Pleasure _____
9. Will you recommend our service to others? Yes _____ (Name & Address                         ) No _____
Comments:


Name:                                                              If you represent a company or travel agency, please include that
Address:                                                          information:
City: _____ State: _____ Zip: _____
**COLORADO TRANSPORTATION GROUP**                 Telephone (      )

Self-administered questionnaires are an excellent way to receive feedback from customers. This short questionnaire is illustrative of how Carey American Limousine evaluates its service.

cost than are personal interviews. The shortcomings of telephone surveys are that they are less flexible than personal interviews, and of necessity they are brief. While a further limitation of phone surveys is that not everyone has a telephone, those with telephones tend to have the market potential to travel or buy tourism products. Consequently, this limitation is not very serious for travel research. Speed and low cost tend to be the primary advantages of telephone interviews.

*Mail Surveys*  Mail surveys have the potential of being the lowest-cost method of research. As would be expected, mail surveys involve mailing the questionnaire to carefully selected sample respondents and requesting them to return the completed questionnaires. This survey approach has a great advantage when large geographical areas must be covered and when it would be difficult to reach respondents. Other advantages of this approach are that personal interview bias is absent and the respondent can fill out the questionnaire at his or her convenience.

The greatest problem in conducting a mail survey is having a good list and getting an adequate response. If a large percentage of the target population fails to respond, you will have to question whether those who did not respond are different from those who have replied and whether this introduces bias. Length is another consideration in mail questionnaires. While they can be longer than telephone surveys, they still must be reasonably short. Another limitation of mail surveys is that questions must be worded carefully and simply so that respondents will not be confused. While questions may be very clear to the person who wrote them, they can be very unclear to the respondent.

*Electronic Devices*  A relatively new way of conducting survey research is the use of computer-type electronic devices to ask the consumer questions and immediately record and tabulate the results. This equipment can be placed in a hotel lobby, mall, or other high-traffic location and attract consumers to record responses to questions. Use of these machines is a low-cost method of getting consumer information because the questions are self-administered, saving the cost of interviewers, and the results are tabulated automatically. A disadvantage is that children, who like to play with such machines, may distort the results. However, it is predicted that such devices will become increasingly popular in the future.

## Observational Method

The observational method relies upon the direct observation of physical phenomena in the gathering of data. Observing some action of the respondent is obviously much more objective and accurate than is utilizing the survey method. Under the observational method, information can be gathered by either personal or mechanical observation. Mechanical recorders on highways count the number of cars that pass and the time that they pass. Automatic counters at attractions observe and count the number of visitors.

Advantages of the observational method are that it tends to be accurate and it can record consumer behavior. It also reduces interviewer bias. Disadvantages are that it is much more costly than the survey method and it is not possible to employ in many cases. Finally, the observational method shows what people are doing but does not tell you why they are doing it. It cannot delve into motives, attitudes, or opinions. If the "why" is important, this would not be a good method to use.

## Experimental Method

This method of gathering primary data involves setting up a test, a model, or an experiment to simulate the real world. The essentials of the experimental method are the measurement of variations within one or more activities while all other conditions and variables are being controlled. The experimental method is very hard to use in tourism research because of the difficulty of holding variables constant. There is no physical laboratory in which tourism researchers can work. However, it is possible for resort areas to run advertising experiments or pricing experiments or to develop simulation models to aid in decision making. Such test marketing is being conducted successfully, and as time passes, we will see the experimental method being used more and more.

## WHO DOES TRAVEL RESEARCH?

Many organizations are involved in the use and conduct of travel research. The types of firms and organizations that engage in travel research include government, educational institutions, consultants, trade associations, advertising agencies, media, hotels and motels, airlines and other carriers, attractions, and food service organizations.

## Government

The federal government has been a major producer of travel research over the years. Appendix B indicates the role of the government in travel research, citing work by the Bureau of the Census, the Department of Transportation, the Bureau of Economic Analysis, the Department of State, and the Senate. The U.S. Travel and Tourism Administration conducts studies on international visitors, focusing on both marketing information and economic impact. State and local governments also employ travel research to assist in making marketing and public policy decisions. Examples are studies of highway users, the value of fishing and hunting, the economic impact of tourism on various geographic areas, inventories of tourism facilities and services, tourism planning procedures, and visitor characteristics studies. In other countries, research inaugurated by the official tourism organization of a state or country often has very significant ramifications for tourism development and promotion. Research done in Mexico, England, Spain, France, and some of the Balkan countries, particularly Yugoslavia, Bulgaria, and Rumania, has been outstanding.

## Educational Institutions

Universities conduct many travel research studies. The chief advantage is that the studies are usually conducted without bias by trained professionals. Many of the studies have contributed greatly to the improvement of travel research methods. Institutions of higher learning, particularly universities with departments of hotel and restaurant management, hospitality management, and tourism, have a vital need for such information. Such educational organizations are concerned with the teaching of tourism or related subjects and need the most current available research findings to do an effective teaching job. Research is also needed by such academic departments as geography, fisheries and wildlife, resource development, park and recreation resources, and forestry. All these departments have an interest in the effect on the environment because of the use of the natural landscape for recreation and tourism.

Many departments of universities are qualified to accomplish pure research or applied research in tourism. Bureaus of business and economic research are often active in this field. An example is the research accomplished by the Business Research Division of the University of Colorado at Boulder. This organization has published many tourism research findings, including a bibliography of tourism and travel research studies, reports, and articles. Departments of universities that can be helpful include psychology, sociology, economics, engineering, landscape architecture and urban planning, management, hotel and restaurant administration, theater, home economics, human ecology, forestry, botany, zoology, history, geography, and anthropology.

## Consultants

Numerous organizations specialize in conducting travel research on a fee basis for airlines, hotels, restaurants, ski areas, travel agents, resorts, and others. Consultants offer the service of giving advice in the planning, design, interpretation, and application of travel research. They will also provide the service of conducting all or a part of a field investigation for their clients.

The primary advantage of consultants or consulting firms is that they are well trained, experienced specialists who have gained their experience by making studies for many different clients. They also provide an objective outsider's point of view, and they have adequate facilities to undertake almost any job. The disadvantage of consultants is that of any outsider—the lack of intimate knowledge of the internal problems of the client's business; however, management can provide this ingredient. Many travel firms with their own research departments find it advantageous to use consultants or a combination of their own internal staff and consultants.

There are many well-known firms specializing in travel research. A few of these are Laventhol and Horwath and Pannell Kerr Forster (CPA firms that have specialized in the lodging and hospitality fields for years), Opinion Research Corporation, Davidson-Peterson Associates, Economic Research Associates, the Gallup organization, International Research Associates Ltd., Arthur D. Little, Midwest Research Institute, Nettleton Travel Research Center, Plog Research, Robinson's, SRI International, Starch INRA Hooper, Travel and Tourism Consultants International, Somerset R. Waters, and Simmons Market Research Bureau.

Davidson-Peterson Associates, Inc., is illustrative of the many firms available to conduct travel and tourism research studies. (Photo courtesy of Davidson-Peterson Associates, Inc.)

### Trade Associations

Extensive travel research is conducted by trade associations. Appendix B also indicates the role of trade associations as a source of travel information. The trade association often provides facilities for carrying on a continuous research service for its members, particularly in the area of industry statistics.

### Advertising Agencies

Today advertising agencies typically maintain extensive research departments for both their own and their clients' needs. The agency must have basic facts if it is to develop an effective advertising campaign for its travel client in today's rapidly changing world. Advertising agencies that have been leaders in travel research are Ogilvy and Mather; J. Walter Thompson; BBDO Worldwide; Foote, Cone and Belding; Leo Burnett; and DOB Needham Worldwide.

### Media

Trade journals often conduct outstanding tourism research. Experts in various disciplines are brought together in symposia to discover relationships and applications of their disciplines to problems and opportunities in tourism. Travel Weekly's comprehensive study of the travel agency market is a classic example of good media research. The 1988 edition represents the publication's ninth in-depth probe of the travel agency industry. Consumer magazines have also been active producers of travel research. *Time, U.S. News and World Report, Newsweek, Better Homes and Gardens, National Geographic, New Yorker, Sunset, Southern Living, Sports Illustrated,* and *Travel/Holiday* are all known for their travel research.

### Hotels and Motels

Hotels and motels constantly use current research findings concerning their markets, trends in transportation, new construction materials, management methods, use of electronic data processing, human relations techniques, employee management, advertising, food and beverage supplies and services, and myriad other related information.

### Airlines and Other Carriers

This group offers services designed for the business and vacation traveler. Because of their needs and the importance of research to their operations, airlines and other carriers will usually have their own market research departments to conduct ongoing studies of their customers and the market. They are also frequent employers of outside consultants.

### Attractions

The most ambitious private attractions in the country are the major theme parks, and research has played a major role in the success of these enterprises. That research has run the gamut from feasibility studies to management research. Walt Disney's thinking still dominates the industry. The Disney formula of immaculate grounds, clean and attractive personnel, high-quality shops, tidy rest rooms, and clean restaurants are the consumers' preferences today. Research shows that if attractions are not clean, they are not likely to be successful.

## Food Service

Much of the pioneering work in the use of research by restaurants has been done by franchises and chains because what will work in one location will typically work in others, resulting in a large payoff from funds invested in research. All travel firms, whether they are restaurants, airlines, hotels, or other hospitality enterprises, need to be in touch with their markets and find new and better ways of marketing to sell seats, increase load factors, and achieve favorable occupancy ratios.

## THE U.S. TRAVEL DATA CENTER AND THE
## TRAVEL AND TOURISM RESEARCH ASSOCIATION

Two unique organizations serve the travel research area: the U.S. Travel Data Center (USTDC) and the Travel and Tourism Research Association (TTRA). Following is a brief description of the operations of these organizations.

The U.S. Travel Data Center is a nonprofit, privately supported agency that devotes its resources to measuring the economic impact of travel and monitoring changes in travel markets. The Data Center has become a recognized source for current data used by business and government to develop tourism policies and marketing strategy. Market and economic research provided by the Data Center is utilized by all major sectors of the travel industry. Its members represent lodging; food service; transportation; entertainment; attractions; federal, state, county, and city promotion agencies; travel-related media; marketing organizations; universities; and tourism associations.

The objectives of the Data Center are to (1) develop and encourage standard, sound travel research terminology and techniques; (2) develop and encourage consistent estimates of travel activity over time and geographic areas; (3) monitor trends in travel activity and the travel industry over time; (4) measure the economic impact of travel over time and on geographic areas; (5) evaluate the impact of major government programs affecting travel and the travel industry; (6) monitor, evaluate, and help develop techniques to forecast travel supply and demand; and (7) develop techniques to measure the cost and the benefits of travel in the United States.

The Data Center holds an annual outlook for travel and tourism each fall and carries on an active research and publications program. The majority of its publications are available for purchase by writing its office. The Data Center also conducts a *National Travel Survey* on a monthly basis, performs custom research, has developed the Travel Economic Impact Model, and maintains the U.S. Travel Data Bank. The U.S. Travel Data Center is located at 1133 21st Street N.W., Washington, D.C. 20036.

The Travel and Tourism Research Association is an international organization of travel research and marketing professionals devoted to improving the quality, value, scope, and acceptability of travel research and marketing information. The association is the world's largest travel research organization, and its members represent all aspects of the travel industry, including airlines, hotels, attractions, transportation companies, media, advertising agencies, government, travel agencies, consulting firms, universities, students, and so on.

TTRA's mission is to increase the quality, value, effectiveness and use of research in travel marketing, planning, and development with the following specific objectives:

- To serve as a forum for the exchange of ideas and information among travel researchers, marketers, planners, and development people.
- To encourage the professional growth of travel researchers, marketers, planners, and development people.
- To encourage cooperation between producers and users of travel research.
- To collect and disseminate research of interest to the travel and tourism industry.
- To support the continuation and improvement of timely and relevant government research of interest to the travel and tourism industry.
- To encourage travel and tourism research in college and university programs.
- To improve the effectiveness of the management process in the travel and tourism industry.

TTRA has chapters: in Canada, CenStates, Florida, New School Student Chapter, New York, Mountain States, San Francisco, Southeast, Southern California, Northern California, Hawaii, South Central States, and Washington, D.C. TTRA publishes the *Journal of Travel Research,* the TTRA newsletter, annual conference proceedings, and other special publications. The organization helped establish the Travel Reference Center located at the Business Research Division, University of Colorado, Boulder, Colorado 80309. This service was established to assist the travel industry in finding information sources and solving business problems. Those wishing further information on TTRA should write to Mari Lou Wood, TTRA Executive Secretary, Bureau of Economic and Business Research, University of Utah, P.O. Box 58066, Foothill Station, Salt Lake City, Utah 84158.

## SUMMARY

Travel research provides the information base for effective decision making by tourism managers. Availability of adequate facts allows managers to plan, operate, and control more efficiently and decreases risk in the decision-making process.

Useful travel research depends on precise identification of the problem; a thorough situation analysis supplemented by an informal investigation of the problem, careful research design; and meticulous collection, tabulation, and analysis of the data. The researcher must also present a readable written report with appropriate recommendations for action and then follow up to ensure that the recommendations are actually implemented so that results can be achieved.

The research itself may use secondary (preexisting) data or require collection of primary data (original research). Primary data may be gathered by survey—personal interview, mail, or telephone surveys—or by the observational and experimental methods. Numerous organizations and agencies use and conduct travel research. Two professional organizations serve the field: the U.S. Travel Data Center and the Travel and Tourism Research Association.

### About the Readings

Knowing how travel research is accomplished and actually doing it are very different. The first reading provides an example of how a major lodging firm used consumer-product oriented research to determine what travelers wanted in accommodations. The research findings then became the basis for continuing changes and improvements in the lodging facilities. This firm's growth and success (world's largest) are testimonials to the value of research.

The second reading summarizes the findings of a study of the American pleasure travel market. The study is the most comprehensive examination of the perceptions and preferences of U.S. travelers ever undertaken.

## READING 11-1

### Researching Travel the Procter and Gamble Way

By Russell A. Bell,
Past President, Travel and Tourism Research Association

Reprinted from *Innovation and Creativity in Travel Research and Marketing, 12th Annual Conference Proceedings,* Travel and Tourism Research Association, 1981.

Unquestionably, research has grown in importance across America over the last decade, proving very emphatically that the businesses that prosper are those that utilize research to chart the course of action.

At Holiday Inns we have expanded our horizons considerably over the past several years, primarily because of research. When we began our hotel chain in 1952, the major criterion for highly satisfactory accommodations was a clean, comfortable room. Then, as lifestyles improved appreciably over the years, expectations of the hotel guest skyrocketed. The increasingly sophisticated traveler demanded accommodations equal to or even better than what he left at home.

Consequently, the old philosophy of merely providing a serviceable room suddenly became obsolete. We were faced with the necessity for drastic improvements of our entire operation if we were to successfully compete in the market place. So, we began to develop an overall strategy that would position us much more aggressively in the hotel market. Intense consumer-products research proved to be the catalyst that was needed to accomplish this.

I will tell you about the methodology and findings of two of our research projects a little later on which will illustrate this new strategy, but first I would like to give you an overview of our Research Department and the businesses that we support. We have a staff of 21 people who handle the research function, a function that costs close to $2 million a year to operate. That figure gives you an idea of the importance which management places on our area. We are organized into four research groups—two for lodging, one for gaming and one for restaurants.

The lodging groups are responsible for all research that involves the more than

1,700 Holiday Inn hotels in 59 countries. One lodging group tracks the chain's performance in the marketplace, including traveler mix, size of market share and product quality. The other lodging group handles the advertising, promotional, and room development activities.

The restaurant group handles research for our hotel restaurants as well as the entire Perkins Cake & Steak chain, acquired by Holiday Inns in 1979, today the fourth largest full-service family restaurant in the U.S.

And finally, our gaming group is devoted to research for Harrah's Casino which Holiday Inns acquired a year and a half ago, and which along with our interest in a Las Vegas casino now comprises the largest gaming operation in the country, in terms of square footage.

So you can see that we have wide areas of interest and responsibilities. Our research staff represents a good cross-section of the country and most have advanced degrees in marketing, marketing research or related fields. A number of our people have had previous research experience within the consumer products industry.

Here's how our staff usually functions: First, we define the basic problem and then design a research project to match the criteria that have been set down. Next, we contract with a research supplier who handles the interviewing and computer processing necessary for the project. Our department then does the analysis and writes reports.

Now, let me talk in more detail about the research strategy I mentioned earlier. When we decided it was imperative to market more aggressively, we directed our attention specifically to large-scale consumer products market analysis. Obviously, we had to modify our methods to the specific needs of the lodging industry, but, overall, we believe we have achieved the type of research knowledge about our customer that exists throughout the consumer products industry. And we have learned to utilize this information to build effective and aggressive promotions. For example, just as Procter & Gamble markets soap with coupons, we have turned to promotions such as the $5 guest check certificate, good for $5 off the price of the next Holiday Inn room. This was a promotion we had on the shelf, waiting for a lull in business, and which we were able to implement quickly when last summer's slump in travel occurred.

To me, one of the most unusual facets of our Holiday Inn research department is its total integration into the management decision process. This is one of the major reasons why we operate as a completely self-funded department. This fact gives us substantial leeway in deciding what projects we wish to work on and the priorities involved since we are not working from someone else's budget. And, at the same time, we are challenged by management to justify each project and the methods which we employ.

Also, because of the way management perceives the research function, we actively participate in the effective utilization of research information. For example, the research function is organized into the Product Management division and we are jointly charged with the implementation of research findings. As a result, research has become an integral part of the planning, development and execution stages of systemwide operations.

This attitude gives us a refreshing break from the all too frequent "thanks for the report, good job" comments we sometimes receive in the research industry while at the same time, never hearing another word about the report which we have labored on so painstakingly. In contrast, Holiday Inn officials often ask for advice about implementation of a new product, a new promotion, or advertising theme, based on what we have learned through extensive research.

A study on various room configurations illustrates what I mean about effective research follow through. We wanted to develop a room concept which in general was conceived as a "home away from home." We started with secondary research on various items in the home that had the most dramatic appeal, such as bedding quality, mattress size, or the type of showerheads that were most popular.

Then we created room prototypes. We took photographs of these prototypes and asked people what they found most appealing about the various room components. Shopping malls and hotel lobby intercepts among travelers were utilized to obtain this information. From there, we installed rooms in hotels specifically for research purposes. We recruited guests in the hotels and walked them through the rooms. We showed them the new rooms along with the traditional double/double configurations. We asked them what they liked or did not like about the rooms.

From that, we developed two room concepts . . . King Leisure, which includes a king-size bed and enlarged work/leisure area with a table and two upholstered chairs; and King Sofa, which includes all the amenities of King Leisure with the addition of a sofa bed, so four people can be accommodated.

The final stage involved the installation of enough rooms in geographically dispersed hotels in order to obtain live-in research information. Then we called guests after they had spent at least one night in the new rooms, and from these findings, developed standards for the rooms. These rooms are now well into the process of installation in our hotels and are guided by the guest mix at each property.

Our research shows that King Leisure rooms enjoy a high guest preference over the conventional double/double room and that guests are more willing to pay a few dollars more for these improved accommodations. As a result of the popularity of King Leisure amenities, we have introduced several systemwide standards such as thicker towels, glass tumblers rather than plastic, larger bars of soap and massaging showerheads.

Another study which we call the Anatomy of the Lodging Experience is a good example of consumer products-oriented research approach. The purpose of this study was to find out in great detail how guests used the hotel facilities . . . where they put their suitcase, what electrical outlets they used, and so on.

The study was made during two different seasons, summer and winter. We intercepted people in the lobbies after check-in and conducted short interviews, concentrating on details such as method of travel, size of party, purpose of the trip and length of stay.

We gave the guests questionnaires, along with complimentary gifts, and asked them to fill out the questionnaires after checkout and then mail them to us. Forty-five percent responded which provided us with an excellent base. The surveys worked well, I believe, because we carefully explained to guests that we wanted to improve the quality of their lodging experience, and then we gave them a gift in advance to make them feel a little guilty if they didn't return the questionnaires.

I would like to point out that we took a very broad sample from a number of

Holiday Inns and then did a complete folio audit on everyone who stayed at the hotels involved. This gave us necessary in-depth information that helped us adjust our research findings accordingly. For instance, we found that we had greatly under-represented the single night lodgers in our sample and used that information to weight the results.

You might be interested in some of the things we learned about how people use our hotels, so let me mention some of the findings. First, the people — they came to our properties mostly by car; 58 percent in their own, 23 percent in a rental car, and 17 percent arrived by plane.

Most are men, but a growing percentage of our guests are women — some 24 percent. The vast majority, 81 percent — have reservations. Seventy-three percent of our guests are traveling alone or with their spouses which makes you wonder why the hotel industry usually puts two double beds in the room.

Sixty-seven percent have only one or two pieces of luggage aside from their briefcase and 80 percent don't want the bellhop to give them help. Thirty-six percent put their luggage on top of the dresser; 23 percent on the bed (the one they have no other use for) and 8 percent put it somewhere else. Ninety-four percent hang something in the closet.

Once they get their luggage all settled:

46 percent use a vending machine
30 percent use the pool area
50 percent make a local phone call
61 percent make a long distance phone call
and 67 percent use our ice machines and ice buckets.

You might be interested to know that use of the ice buckets is highest among people traveling with children — 74 percent — which is clear statistical evidence that kids really can drive you to drink!

The average guest spends two hours in the room when he or she is not asleep. Ninety-two percent of all travelers watch TV an average of one hour each night. Business travelers work in their rooms about 50 minutes each night. You'd think some hotel company would give them a comfortable place to work, wouldn't you?

Twenty percent of our guests take baths — mostly in the evening. You may find it interesting that only 5 percent of salesmen take baths. After a good night's sleep, 40 percent of our guests are greeted by a wake-up call. But it is worth noting that another 37 percent of our guests bring their own alarm clock.

Once out of bed, 95 percent take a shower, in case you ever wondered at 7:15 what happened to the hot water.

I could go on and on with these tidbits. To what point have I told you this? Specifically, I want to illustrate how Holiday Inns has set about achieving product supremacy in its segment with this well-researched lodging knowledge. We are now designing, constructing, and furnishing our properties in accordance with the way people use them today, and that is, in many ways, vastly different from the way they used them just ten years ago.

This is a very significant difference. It was, in retrospect, product superiority that spurred Holiday Inn growth during the decade of the 60s. And it is, we believe, the re-establishment of this superiority which will spur very impressive growth in the new decade we have entered. Undoubtedly, research will continue to play a very important role in making this happen.

## READING 11-2

### A Look At the American Traveler: The U.S. Pleasure Travel Market Study

By Jerry M. Dybka
Tourism Canada

Reprinted from *Journal of Travel Research,* Vol. 15, no. 3, Winter 1987.

In 1985, following a decade of at first declining and then stagnant levels of American visitation to Canada, the federal government commissioned a major study of the United States pleasure travel market. Conducted by Longwoods Research Group, the study became the most comprehensive examination of the perceptions and preferences of U.S. travelers ever undertaken by a Canadian source.

Since 87% of overnight person-trips to Canada are taken by Americans, the health of the Canadian tourism industry obviously depends on attracting visitors from south of the border. In 1984, 11.3 million overnight travelers came from the U.S. to Canada and spent more than $3 billion.

While such figures are impressive, Canada's market share of U.S. travelers has not kept pace with the rapidly escalating numbers of Americans who are traveling. A number of factors, such as increased leisure time and higher incomes, mean that Americans are taking millions of additional pleasure trips every year.

To draw its share of these pleasure trips, Canada must ensure that it is competitive in the international marketplace. Remaining competitive is imperative to Canada's economic well being, since each percentage point increase in long-term visitors to Canada means $30 million added to the economy, 800 person-years of employment, $17 million in direct income for Canadians and $11 million in federal, provincial and municipal government revenues.

### The Raison d'Etre

With this economic imperative at play, Canada had to discover how to garner the economic spin-offs that accrue from more tourists coming to the country. This meant an improved marketing campaign which, in turn, hinged on thorough research of the target audience.

Also in 1985, the federal government was involved in a national consultative process on the tourism sector. Coast-to-coast public meetings, a national conference, specialized seminars and meetings of officials from all orders of government were conducted. The objective was to devise a tourism strategy for Canada based on cooperation and coordination among all partners in the sector.

A study of the U.S. pleasure travel market fit nicely into the process because its findings would be available to all the partners. Accessible to everyone and relevant at both the "macro" (government) and "micro" (individual operators) levels, the study would provide a framework of information for common planning and action.

*Methodology*

The study findings are based on 9,000 personal, in-home 50-minute interviews. Field work was conducted in the fall of 1985 with 1,000 interviews in each of the nine census divisions in the U.S.

A sequential probability plan, by quota, sampled area segments, housing units and eligible consumers within households. Three levels of urbanization were represented: central cities, suburban, and non-metropolitan. The criteria for participating in the study were that respondents must be at least 16 years of age, have taken one pleasure trip in the past 36 months requiring travel more than 100 miles one way, have spent at least one night away from home, and used commercial accommodation or transportation. Americans meeting these criteria represent 75% of the U.S. public 16 years of age or older.

The large sample size was necessary because a number of publics, both government and private-sector, would be using the data base and they requested that it be sufficiently representative to allow for statistically reliable segmentation by geographical regions.

On the basis of quantitative research, the study design divided the U.S. pleasure travel market into eight vacation-type segments: a visit to friends or relatives; a close-to-home leisure trip; a touring trip; a city trip; an outdoors trip; a resort trip; a cruise; and a trip to a theme park, exhibition or special event. Each of these trip types was examined in terms of: the size of the market (both in the past year and travelers' intentions for the next two years); Canada's market share; the consumers' wants, needs and activities; and image strengths and weaknesses of Canadian destinations.

The study dealt with pleasure travel generically as well as by each of the eight identified trip types, and the results include conclusions and implications as well as "hot buttons" that must be pushed if Canada is to increase its share of the U.S. pleasure travel market.

*Findings*

What insights does this in-depth examination offer to the Canadian tourism sector?

First, the study makes clear that Canada could be doing much better in attracting American pleasure travelers. While the U.S. pleasure travel market is enormous (annually, over 130 million Americans take 468 million personal pleasure trips averaging four days in length), Canada's market share is small. In the 12 months preceding the interviews, from the fall of 1984 to the fall of 1985, 4.3% or some 5.6 million American pleasure travelers visited Canada, staying for a total of 49.6 million trip-nights. This accounts for only 2.6% of all trip-nights of pleasure travel taken by Americans.

According to the study, Canada's poor showing is largely attributable to a lack of awareness by Americans. Fewer than one in five U.S. travelers even thinks of Canada as a place to consider for a vacation. In other words, for about 85% of Americans, Canada is not even on the list.

On the other hand, the study found a strong link does exist between thinking about a Canadian destination and intending to go there. The problem appears to be one of "out of sight, out of mind." Given the positive link between awareness and choice of Canada as a destination, real opportunity exists to increase Canada's share of the U.S. market through intensive advertising.

*The Importance of the Touring Trip*   As stated above, Americans spend only 2.6% of their total trip-nights of pleasure travel in Canada. Examined on the basis of trip type, Canada's share of American travel is as follows:

| | |
|---|---|
| touring trip | 6.8% |
| outdoors trip | 5.4% |
| city trip | 2.8% |
| trip to theme park, exhibition, special event | 2.1% |
| cruise | 1.5% |
| visit to friends or relatives | 1.4% |
| close-to-home leisure trip | 1.2% |
| resort trip | 0.8% |

The most surprising finding to emerge from the research is that the touring trip, and not the outdoors trip, is Canada's greatest asset in the pleasure travel market. Over the past years, a major assumption has been that the great outdoors, Canada's natural beauty, scenery and wilderness, was our key selling point. The study dispels this prevailing belief.

A touring trip is defined as one by bus, car, or train through areas of scenic beauty or of cultural or general interest. In regional terms, the most preferred area for touring is the Pacific coast (38%), followed by Quebec (21%), Ontario (20%), the Rockies (15%), and the Maritimes (9%). However, the study also revealed that Canada's individual products, including our outdoors, cities and resorts, are not perceived by Americans as being superior to those found in their own country.

On the positive side, Canada's primary strength in terms of image is that Americans see Canada as a foreign destination, close and familiar yet somehow different. "The essential difference is the people of Canada—their British and French heritage, their ethnic diversity and their regional and local traditions," the study posits, adding "Canada's strength as a pleasure travel destination does not lie in its emulation of American destinations, but rather in its points of difference." The Canadian cultural mosaic has appeal to our southern neighbors.

*The Implications*   What implications do these findings have on Canada's marketing approach in the U.S.? If Canada is to launch a "concerted and intrusive advertising campaign," as the study recommends, what factors must be taken into account? The following observations focus on the newly discovered strength of the touring market and on an enhanced role for culture as a tourist attraction.

- There is an immediate opportunity to market Canada actively as a destination for a touring trip.
- Since touring involves sampling a potpourri of our products, the focus must be regional, encompassing a number of individual products that may not be sufficient travel generators on their own, but which, when packaged together, make Canadian touring destinations attractive prospects.
- Much remains to be done at the regional level to identify the most promising regional touring "products." In addition, the private sector can play a significant role in putting together touring packages tailored to the very specific needs of particular lifestyle segments.

- Our major cities can gain from being positioned not just as destinations on their own, but also as gateways to an enjoyable touring trip, one that can include our countryside, towns and villages, resorts, cruises, theme parks and special events, as well as the great outdoors.
- Emphasis on Canada's foreign mystique in national advertising and communications is important, and should include the exciting things offered in the way of hotels, food, landmarks and things to do and see. While Canada's great outdoors translates into Canada's second largest market, the evidence is that our real opportunity lies in portraying Canada as an exciting foreign place. Our image of vast open spaces is already well established. We now need to begin the job of filling in those open spaces.
- Awareness of Canada can be increased through advertising designed specifically to enhance Canada's visibility in the eyes of U.S. travelers. To meet this objective, regional and national campaigns must be coordinated as much as possible and a central theme must be developed for use in all U.S.-directed advertising.

*"Barriers" and "Hot Buttons"*   The study also identifies what are labeled as "barriers" and "hot buttons" — an overview of Canada's strengths and weaknesses vis-a-vis the U.S. pleasure travel market. Like the preceding observations, these insights are aimed at facilitating the design and implementation of marketing strategies by both the public and the private sector.

For example, in general Americans have a positive image of Canada, but (and this is a key point) they tend to view their own country in the same positive light. In other words, although they consider Canada beautiful, scenic, natural, clean, etc., they hold the U.S. in the same high regard. Thus, marketers must not only search for areas in which Canada is doing well; they must also find areas in which we can demonstrate a clear edge and advantage over the U.S. One such area is a touring trip which highlights our "foreignness," our different cultures and different ways of living as compared to the U.S.

In regard to the marketing of cities, the study notes that Canada's image of vast open spaces has worked against it in the city trip market. Canadian cities are perceived as clean, safe and walkable, but Americans do not consider them sophisticated in terms of shopping, entertainment, restaurants, and cultural events. The gap between how our cities are perceived and what they do in fact offer can be narrowed through effective communications programs.

The matter of prices also drew attention and the research found that Canada's price image is on the whole more favorable than that of the U.S. Canadian prices for touring or outdoor trips are deemed to be similar to those in the U.S. while Canadian cities and resort areas are perceived as less expensive than American cities and resorts. The study found no evidence that American pleasure travelers are dismissing Canada as a destination because of prices.

Of course, the above material is merely a synopsis of the study's key findings and recommendations. With a sample size of 9,000 and a national scope, the study contains a wealth of information that can be examined from a number of perspectives, including product-by-product analysis of market size and share; demographics; product strengths and weaknesses; image strengths and weaknesses; market identification; trip activities; and trip planning.

*The Impact of the Study*

Although the study findings were only released in February of 1986, they have already had a significant impact on the number of tourism initiatives. Indeed, the insights provided by the study had an immediate impact on the federal government and its 1986 U.S. marketing campaign. With an up-to-date, comprehensive profile of the American pleasure traveler in its hands, the federal government went to work re-designing its marketing campaign in the U.S. to reflect the findings of the study.

By early March, television and magazine advertisements were launched in the U.S., promoting Canada as a tourist destination. Aimed at enhancing Canada's image, the ads focus on the country's "old world" (our cultural and historic destinations), "wild world" (our scenic outdoors and wilderness areas) and "new world" (our exciting and sophisticated urban centers). Viewed together, the three themes portray Canada as a land of variety, a multi-faceted destination, an ideal locale for a touring trip. With a heavy penetration in the U.S., the marketing campaign also serves to overcome the "lack of awareness" problems mentioned previously. By the time the campaign ends in the early summer, by which time most decisions concerning vacation plans will have been made, millions and millions of Americans will have been exposed to Canada and its travel potential.

The significance of culture as a tourist attraction also led to the signing of an agreement between Canada's Ministers of Tourism, Communications and Multiculturalism. Over $1 million will be committed to a series of pilot projects which will evaluate the tourism impact of select Canadian cultural and multicultural destinations promoted in the U.S. market in 1986 and 1987. As well, a national conference on Tourism and Culture will be held this fall.

These are just a few of the immediate impacts that have resulted from the study findings. As the data base is examined in greater detail by more government and industry representatives at all levels, its relevance and utility as a marketing instrument will become more clearly evident. At this early date, of course, the economic return from the better designed marketing campaigns is not clear. The total impact of the campaigns may not be fully known for a few years when the statistics on American visitation to Canada for 1986 and onwards become available.

*Conclusion*

In releasing the findings, Canada's Minister of State for Tourism, the Honorable Jack B. Murta, stressed that the study was conducted for the benefit of all participants in the Canadian tourism sector and that the wealth of information it contains should be used by them to attract more American visitors to Canada. According to the Minister, the $1.2 million cost of the study will be repaid through the revenues generated from increased levels of visitation, triggered by marketing initiatives by governments and businesses alike.

The Government of Canada is providing a "Highlights Report" of the U.S. pleasure travel market study free of charge to interested parties. For those individuals who may require more detailed information, the report in its entirety, complete data tables and/or the data tape will be available for a fee. Inquiries about data availability should be directed to the Manager, Research and Analysis, Tourism Canada, 235 Queen Street, 4th Floor East, Ottawa, Ontario Canada K1A0H6 or phone (613) 993-4328.

## Key Concepts

advertising agencies
airlines and other carriers
analytical findings
attractions
basic research methods
collection and analysis of data
consultants
consumer attitude studies
consumer-products research
data
decision making
definitions
economic impact study
economic projections
educational institutions
experimental method
facts
feasibility studies
follow-up
food service firms
government
hotel and motel firms
identification of the problem
impartial

information
intuition
investigations
measurement
media
methodology
observational method
primary data
recommendations for action
report
research design
risk
secondary data
situation analysis
sophisticated models
sources of information
surveys
systematic
trade associations
travel research process
Travel and Tourism Research Association
uses of travel research
U.S. Travel Data Center

## For Review and Discussion

1. What does a situation analysis cover?
2. What problems can travel research solve?
3. When should you use primary data? Secondary data?
4. What are the basic research methods?
5. Why are research findings so important to intelligent decision making?
6. If you were director of a major city's convention and visitors bureau, how would you use travel research?
7. As a consultant, you are researching the feasibility of a new resort hotel project. What procedures would you use, step by step?
8. How would a resort developer use a consultant's report when the report is completed? Once the resort is built, does the manager need further research?
9. What methods could be used by a state tourist office to survey out-of-state visitors?
10. Should a state tourist office conduct its own research or hire an outside supplier? Why?
11. Why would your office consider being a supporter of the U.S. Travel Data Center?
12. Would you join TTRA? Explain your answer.

## Selected References

Barnett, Lynn A. *Research About Leisure: Past, Present, and Future.* Champaign, Ill.: Sagamore Publishing, 1988.

Baron, Raymond. *Travel and Tourism Data.* London: Euromonitor, 1989.

Bureau of the Census. *National Travel Survey: Travel During 1977.* Washington, D.C.: U.S. Department of Commerce, 1979.

Butler, Richard W., and Geoffrey Wall. "Themes in Research on the Evolution of Tourism." *Annals of Tourism Research,* Vol. 12, no. 3 (1985), pp. 287–296.

Camacho, Frank E., and D. Matthew Knain. "Listening to Customers: The Market Research Function at Marriott Corporation." *Market Research: A Magazine of Management and Applications,* Vol. 1, no. 1 (March 1989), pp. 5–14.

Dann, Graham, Dennison Nash, and Philip Pearce. "Methodology in Tourism Research." *Annals of Tourism Research,* Vol. 15, no. 1 (1988), pp. 1–28.

Geller, Neal. "How to Improve Your Information System." *The Cornell Hotel and Restaurant Administration Quarterly,* Vol. 26, no. 2 (August 1985), pp. 19–27.

Gitelson, Richard, and Deborah Kerstetter. "The Focus Group Interview: An Untapped Resource." *Visions in Leisure and Business,* Vol. 6, no. 3 (1987), pp. 60–67.

Goodrich, Jonathan N. "Respondents' and Nonrespondents' Views on Stimulating Response to Mail Surveys in Travel Research." *Journal of Travel Research,* Vol. 17, no. 3 (Winter 1979), pp. 7–11.

Hartmann, Rudi. "Combining Field Methods in Tourism Research." *Annals of Tourism Research,* Vol. 15, no. 1 (1988), pp. 88–105.

Lewis, Robert C. "The Basis of Hotel Selection." *The Cornell Hotel and Restaurant Administration Quarterly,* Vol. 25, no. 1 (May 1984), pp. 54–69 (Part 3 of a six-part series).

Lewis, Robert C. "Getting the Most from Marketing Research." *Cornell Hotel and Restaurant Administration Quarterly,* Vol. 24, no. 3 (November 1983), pp. 81–85 (Part 1 of a six-part series).

Lewis, Robert C. "The Market Position: Mapping Guests' Perceptions of Hotel Operations." *The Cornell Hotel and Restaurant Administration Quarterly,* Vol. 26, no. 2 (August 1985), pp. 86–99.

Lewis, Robert C. "Theoretical and Practical Considerations in Research Design." *The Cornell Hotel and Restaurant Administration Quarterly,* Vol. 24, no. 4 (February 1984), pp. 25–35 (Part 2 of a six-part series).

Perdue, Richard R., and Martin R. Botkin. "Visitor Survey Versus Conversion Study." *Annals of Tourism Research,* Vol. 15, no. 1 (1988), pp. 76–87.

Platek, R., F. K. Pierre-Pierre, and P. Stevens. *Development and Design of Survey Questionnaires.* Ottawa: Statistics Canada, 1985.

Potter, Dale R., et al. *Questionnaires for Research: An Annotated Bibliography on Design, Construction and Use.* Portland, Oreg.: Pacific Northwest Forest and Range Experiment Station, Forest Service, U.S. Department of Agriculture, 1972.

Potter, Robert B., and John Coshall. "Sociopsychological Methods for Tourism Research." *Annals of Tourism Research,* Vol. 15, no. 1 (1988), pp. 63–75.

Reuland, Ruud, Janet Choudry, and Ans Fagel. "Research in the Field of Hospitality." *International Journal of Hospitality Management,* Vol. 4, no. 4 (1985), pp. 141–146.

Ritchie, J. R. Brent, and Charles R. Goeldner, eds. *Travel, Tourism and Hospitality Research: A Handbook for Managers and Researchers.* New York: John Wiley & Sons, 1987.

Sheldon, Pauline J., Juanita C. Liu, and Chuck Y. Gee. "The Status of Research in the Lodging Industry." *International Journal of Hospitality Management,* Vol. 6, no. 1 (1987), pp. 89–96.

Smith, Stephen L. J. *Tourism Analysis.* Harlow, England: Longman, 1989.

The Tourism Research Planning Committee. *Standard Definitions and Classifications for Travel Surveys.* Ottawa: Federal-Provincial Conference on Tourism, The Committee, February 1975.

U.S. Travel and Tourism Administration. *Identifying Traveler Markets: Research Methodologies.* Washington, D.C.: U.S. Department of Commerce, The Administration, 1979.

Van Raaij, W. Fred. "Consumer Research on Tourism: Mental and Behavioral Constructs." *Annals of Tourism Research,* Vol. 13, no. 1 (1986), pp. 1–10.

Welch, Joe L. "Focus Groups for Restaurant Research." *The Cornell Hotel and Restaurant Administration Quarterly,* Vol. 26, no. 2 (August 1985), pp. 78–85.

World Tourism Organization. *Guidelines for the Collection and Presentation of Internal Travel Statistics.* Madrid: WTO

World Tourism Organization. *Guideline on Methodology for the Preparation, Application and Control of the Results of Market Research.* Madrid: WTO

World Tourism Organization. *Handbook of Market Research Methods.* Madrid: WTO

# C H A P T E R   1 2

# The Consumer Market

## L E A R N I N G   O B J E C T I V E S

- Determine how population trends impact travel and tourism.
- Understand the major social forces that determine the magnitude of the travel market.
- Examine current life-styles and the inclusion of travel experiences.
- Evaluate statistical data in any market area to ascertain the likely dimensions of the demand for travel.

Certain basic factors affect the market for travel. To be marketed successfully, tourism, like any other product, requires qualified buyers — people with income and a willingness to spend. Major factors that affect the market for travel include population trends; income; race; gender; education; occupation; time; attitudes; fashion; custom, habit, and tradition; energy; and life-styles. This list does not represent all the factors affecting tourism, but it illustrates major factors a tourism manager or planner must be concerned with to make forecasts and develop marketing plans.

## POPULATION TRENDS

Let's examine briefly some of the changes in population occurring in the United States that are important to tourism.

### Population

It takes people to create a tourism market. The population of the United States has been increasing rapidly. In 1950 it was 151 million; in 1960 the total was 179 million; in 1970 the population totaled 203 million; and the 1980 Census counted some 226.5 million.[1] In 1987 the population count was estimated to be 243.8 million. Future population counts are expected to be 249.3 million in 1990, and 267.5 million in 2000.[2]

Today's population trends determine tomorrow's tourism. If the U.S. birth rate

---

[1] U.S. Bureau of Census, *Statistical Abstract of the United States, 1989* (Washington, D.C.: Government Printing Office, 1989), p. 7, and U.S. Bureau of the Census, *Current Population Reports,* Series P-25, No. 922 (Washington, D.C.: Government Printing Office, n.d.).

[2] Ibid.

remains below the expected replacement level of 1.9 children per woman of child-bearing age, the total U.S. population will increase an average of less than 1 percent per year. Declining birth rates do not necessarily mean less travel; they can favorably alter population composition. As the average age increases, a greater portion of the population will be in its productive years, and the net economic effect will be an increase in discretionary income. Industries that are sensitive to changes in discretionary income, such as tourism, recreation, and leisure, should benefit. So, at the present time, population trends appear to be favorable for tourism and recreation.

## Age

The population's changing age profile affects virtually every business in one way or another. Age is of greater interest to tourism managers than is the actual population count. Because children and institutionalized elders are not travel consumers, it is worthwhile to look at what is happening to the age segments of our population and identify their impact on tourism demand.

Table 12.1 presents data from the U.S. Travel Data Center's *National Travel Survey* and illustrates the importance of the various age groups in travel. In this survey, more than half (63 percent) of the travelers were between the ages 25 and 54. The inclination to travel seems to be a characteristic of the three 10-year subclassifications within this age group, all three groups accounting for more travelers than their population numbers. Table 12.2 shows the 35–44 age group as particularly significant, accounting for 13.7 percent of the population and 19.0 percent of trips. Travelers under 25 made up 38 percent of the population but represented only 27 percent of the trips. At the other end of the age spectrum, those 65 and over made up 12.0 percent of the population but took 8 percent of the trips. Figure 12.1 shows the age distribution of three segments of the U.S. resident population and indicates the trend toward an older population.

**Table 12.1** Travelers by Age Groups

| Category | U.S. Adult Population | Total Travelers |
|---|---|---|
| 18–24 years | 15% | 15% |
| 25–34 years | 24 | 27 |
| 35–44 years | 19 | 21 |
| 45–54 years | 13 | 15 |
| 55–64 years | 12 | 12 |
| 65–74 years | 10 | 8 |
| 75 and over | 7 | 3 |
| Average Age | 45% | 41% |

*Source:* U.S. Travel Data Center, *1987 Travel Executive Briefing, A National Travel Survey Summary* (Washington, D.C.: The Center, 1988).

Will tomorrow's customers be different from today's? (Photo courtesy of United Airlines)

*Babies*  A mini baby boom took place in the 1980s and will continue into the early 1990s as the post-World War II baby boomers are having their own children. Even though these people are delaying marriage until they are older and having fewer children, this mini-boom results from the sheer number of women in the child-bearing years. Approximately 3.7 million babies a year are being born, and this rate is expected to continue through the early 1990s. After the early 1990s, it is predicted,

**Table 12.2** Person-Trips by Age Groups

| Category | Millions | Population | Person-Trips 1987 | 1986 |
|---|---|---|---|---|
| Less than 18 | 63.3 | 26.3% | 15% | 13% |
| 18–24 | 27.7 | 11.5 | 12 | 13 |
| 25–34 | 42.8 | 17.8 | 22 | 21 |
| 35–44 | 33.1 | 13.7 | 19 | 18 |
| 45–54 | 22.8 | 9.5 | 14 | 12 |
| 55–64 | 22.2 | 9.2 | 10 | 12 |
| 65 years & over | 29.1 | 12.0 | 8 | 10 |
|  | 241.0 | 100.0% | 100 | 100 |

**Millions of Persons**

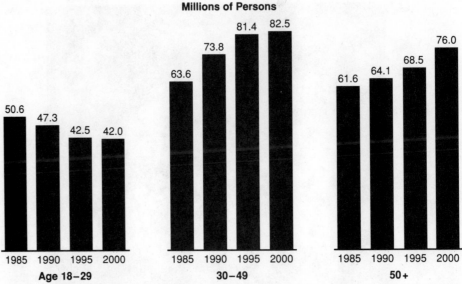

**Figure 12.1** Population Growth by Age Segments. *Source:* U.S. Census Current Population Reports Series p. 25, #952.

there will never again be more than 3.7 million births a year, because of a decline in the female population of child-bearing age. Instead, the number of births are expected to fluctuate between 3.4 and 3.7 million a year. At the moment this is not a particularly desirable circumstance for tourism managers, because families with babies and young children tend to have to stay home and take care of them. In addition, young children create a drain on income which might otherwise be used for travel. However, these babies are potential customers for the future, and in the long run this is a healthy sign.

*Teenage Market*   The teenage population is now declining after record growth in the 1960s and early 1970s. Although the total population of the United States is projected to grow about 10 percent during the next 10 years, there will be a decrease in the number of teenagers ages 14 to 17; in 1990 there will be 12.9 million versus 16.1 million in 1980. In 1995 the number of teenagers ages 14 to 17 will total 14.0 million; in 2000 they will total 15.4 million, an increase over 1990, but still substantially below the 1980 total.[3]

Nevertheless, teenagers comprise an important market because they have a great deal of individual spending power and a great deal of influence on family spending patterns, especially when it comes to deciding where the family will vacation. In families with teenage children, the head of the household is usually at the peak of his or her earning power, and the largest number of women who work outside the home comes from these families. Families with teenagers also tend to spend the largest percentage of their incomes and save the least.

[3] Ibid., and U.S. Bureau of Census, *Projections of the Population of the United States, By Age, Sex, and Race: 1983 to 2080* (Washington, D.C.: Government Printing Office, 1984), pp. 7–8.

Teenagers also tend to travel on their own. Many American teenagers own their own cars, a phenomenon that greatly increases their opportunity to travel. Additionally, teenagers generally have much more positive feelings about flying than do their parents; 84 percent of teenagers state positive feelings about flying versus 55 percent of adults. More teenagers indicate that they plan to fly in the future than do their parents—about 90 percent versus 76 percent.[4]

*Young Adult Market*   The young adult market is made up of two age segments, 18–24 and 25–34 years. Because of its numerical strength, this group's buying power and influence cannot be denied. In 1980, there were more than 30 million young adults aged 18 to 24 and more than 37.5 million aged 25 to 34, making a total of over 67.8 million. In 1990 the 18–24 age group will decline, numbering 25.8 million, while the 25–34 age group will increase, reaching 43.5 million (its peak) giving a total of 69.3. In the year 2000 the numbers in both age segments will decline, numbering 24.6 million (18–24) and 36.4 million (25–34), for a total of 61.0 million.[5] These declines will take place because of the aging of the last of the baby boom generation, putting them out of these age categories. Although this group is at its peak now, it cannot be overlooked in the future. Even with a decline, 61.0 million in the year 2000 will be a potent market for travel.

Because this is such a large group, its composition needs to be examined to reflect trends toward later marriages, delays in having a first child, fewer children

White water rafting is a vacation travel experience that has strong appeal to the young adult market segment. (Photo by Ron Snow, courtesy of West Virginia Department of Commerce)

---

[4] Behavior Science Corporation, *New Markets for Air Travel*, BSC, Panorama City, California, n.d.), p. 12.
[5] U.S. Bureau of the Census, *Statistical Abstract of the United States, 1988*, p. 17, and U.S. Bureau of the Census, *Projections of the Population of the United States, By Age, Sex, and Race: 1983 to 2080* (Washington, D.C.: Government Printing Office, 1984), pp. 7–8.

per family, small households, and an emphasis on careers for both family members. Two subgroups—young singles and young childless couples—have both expanded notably.

*The 35–44 Market (Baby Boomers)*   Consider the fact the years 1954 to 1964 are the only years in which the United States recorded 4 million or more births per year and this over 40 million wave carries forward and determines the future.

As baby boomers born in the 1950s enter middle age in the next decade, the number of households headed by 35- to 45-year-olds will be the fastest-growing segment until the year 2000, when their numbers will peak. Because the baby boom generation is much larger than the generations that surround it, its influence is enormous. Its life-styles become America's life-styles, whether traveling, eating out, or joining exercise clubs. This group is also inclined to travel. As indicated earlier, the 35–44 age group currently makes up 13.7 percent of the population and accounts for 19.0 percent of person-trips. Those in this group are about 40 percent more likely to travel than is the average person.

People in the 35–44 age group tend to travel by air and to populate destination resorts. They tend to spend the most on travel and lodging. In 1990 the 35–44 age group numbers 37.8 million, and by 2000 will grow by 5.9 million, a 16 percent increase over 1990, swelling its numbers to 43.7 million people, which will be its peak size.[6]

Baby boomers tend to be better educated and more widely traveled than their parents. Consequently, they are more comfortable traveling than previous generations have been. They also place a high priority on personal growth and experiences and have been known to consider travel as a necessity, not a luxury. Meeting the needs of this group is essential to the future success of the travel business.

*The 45–54 Market*   The 45- to 54-year-old segment is becoming another rapidly growing group as our population ages and baby boomers move into it. The 45 to 54 segment numbered a modest 22.8 million in 1980, grew to 25.4 million in 1990, will reach 31.4 million in 1995 and 37.1 million in 2000.[7] This is also a very important segment. Like those in the 35–44 age group, members of this group tend to populate destination resorts, travel by air, and spend a great deal on travel and lodging. At the present time they account for about 9.5 percent of the population and 14 percent of person-trips.

The population increases projected for this age group and the 35–44 age segment bodes well for the future of travel during the decade of the 1990s. These two age groups currently account for 23.2 percent of the population and 33 percent of person-trips. The rapid growth of these key age segments will more than offset the decline in the 25–34 age segment.

*Senior Citizen Market*   Another major trend to be watched is the growth of the over-65 senior citizen market and semi-senior citizen market, the over-55-year-olds. Many have dubbed this the mature market, senior market, retirement market, or

[6]Ibid.
[7]Ibid., pp. 53 and 63.

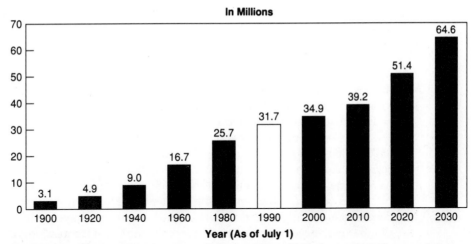

**In Millions**

**Figure 12.2** Number of Persons 65 and Over, 1900 to 2030. *Source:* U.S. Bureau of the Census and AARP.

elderly market. Others look at it as the 50-plus market because 50 is the age for American Association of Retired Persons (AARP) membership.

Whatever it is called, it is an important and growing market. The over-65 group totaled 25.7 million in 1980 and 31.7 million in 1990. This segment is expected to grow to 33.9 million in 1995; then, because of the small birth cohorts of the Depression, the group will grow more slowly to 36.2 million in 2005. After that it is expected to grow rapidly to 64.6 million in 2030 as the members of the baby boom reach this age.[8] See Figure 12.2.

Older population segments are like other segments in that they are not homogeneous. From the travel point of view, there are three important divisions, 55 to 64, 65 to 74, and 75 and older.

The 55–64 age group has substantial amounts of discretionary income, the head of household at peak earning power, smaller households, and, typically, freedom from mortgage payments, education expenses, and durable goods costs. Its population totaled 21.1 million in 1990 and is expected to grow to 23.8 million in 2000. This age group dominates the luxury travel market. Members of this group typically work full time and have the highest per capita income; however, since 1970 men 55 to 64 have been dropping out of the labor force in record numbers, so that in 1990 one-third were retired.

Only a decade ago almost all the statistics showing population by age stopped at 65-and-over. Today we have statistics showing even 100-and-over. The over-65 population can really be divided into three different groups or markets. The young old, aged 65 to 74, are considered active retirees. They comprise an important market for travel, accounting for 10 percent of the population and 8 percent of travelers, as shown in Table 12.1. In 1990 there were 18.0 million people aged 65 to 74, and in 2000 there will be 17.6 million (Figure 12.3).

The old elderly are defined as aged 75 to 84. Compared with the first group,

[8] Ibid.

they are not as active, are often widowed, and are less likely to travel, but still represent 3 percent of travelers 18 and over.

The 85-and-over are defined as the very old, and represent the fastest-growing group of elderly. In 1990 they numbered 3.3 million, and in 2000 they are expected to number 4.9 million. As people grow older they tend to become less active, and there is a tendency to write them off as not having market potential. Marketers need to ask these questions: What is the potential of the 85-and-over market? How can it be fully developed and penetrated?

If the senior market is defined as 55 or older, its members currently account for $575 billion in personal household income, or nearly one-third of the U.S. total.[9] It currently controls 28 percent of all U.S. discretionary income. People in this category have money and they spend it. Those 65 and over who fall in the high-income categories make up a high-spending segment, looking for luxury goods, cruises, and deluxe foreign and domestic travel. A large segment of travelers in the over-65 age group experienced the economic hardship of the Great Depression, which has given them a value orientation not typical of people born in the post-World War II years. Because of this value orientation, many older travelers cannot justify the cost of luxury accommodations even if they can afford them. Consequently, this age group favors midprice or budget properties where they can justify extended vacations because of lower rates.

Although both past and present trends show that pleasure travel declines with age, particularly after age 65, there are now offsetting factors. An increasing portion of the total market is retiring at a relatively early age, leaving additional time for travel. Even though the over-65 segment of the population is the least mobile, many of these people have the time, money, and interest to travel if appropriate facilities are available and promoted properly. Travel by people 65 and over is strong and does not appear to decline until after age 75. Growth in travel by this group continues, and its potential for the future cannot be overlooked.

Because of its growing importance, research has been conducted on the senior market by the U.S. Travel Data Center and AARP. Some of the characteristics of over-65 travelers are that they are very similar to the rest of the traveling public when considering the purposes of travel; outdoor recreation is not a high priority; older travelers travel just about when everyone else does, but they spend almost twice as long away from home and twice as many nights in hotels and motels; they have an increased tendency for lodging with friends and relatives; and their journeys are triple the distance of those of the rest of the market. In regard to transportation, the 65-plus fly more frequently than the overall population. They also are more likely to use package tours, consult travel agents, have dual residences, and take cruises.

Communication with this significant older market is important. Older travelers do not want to be reminded of their age; consequently communication with this segment of the market is difficult. Yet their needs and desires are specific to their age group. Typically, they seek travel experiences that do not require a great deal of physical exertion. On the other hand, their life-style does not confine them to a

[9] The Conference Board, *A Marketer's Guide to Discretionary Income* (New York: The Board, 1983), p. 23.

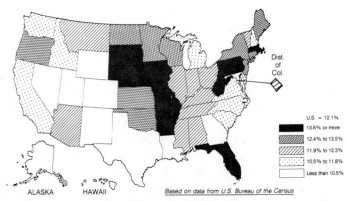

U.S. = 12.1%

■ 13.6% or more

▨ 12.4% to 13.5%

▧ 11.9% to 12.3%

⬚ 10.5% to 11.8%

□ Less than 10.5%

*Based on data from U.S. Bureau of the Census*

**Figure 12.3** Percentage of Population 65 and Over, by State, 1986.

specific season or length of time, as is the case for the younger groups, and they are often more affluent than younger travelers.

Many firms have designed programs aimed at senior citizens. Examples are TWA's VSP Senior Pass, which gave people aged 65 and over a full year of travel on TWA for one low fare. United Airlines Silver Wings Club has discounts and special deals for members. Northwest Airlines has a program, World Horizons, that offers senior citizens discounted fares. It has had an innovative promotion by which it gave senior citizens fare cuts equal to their ages; thus discounts ranged from 65 percent to 100 percent, depending on the customer's age. Days Inns of America has the September Day's Club for people 55 years old and over. It requires a one-time annual membership fee, and members are entitled to receive discounts on lodging, air fares (Delta is the official airline), insurance, car rentals, gifts, food, and pharmaceuticals. The Tennessee Office of Tourism has sponsored an imaginative vacation promotion entitled "The Senior Class" in conjunction with Greyhound Bus Lines. This program, in which food and lodging establishments and attractions offer special discounts to seniors, has been extremely successful in stimulating group travel. The American Association of Retired Persons also has a long history of serving this market segment and is active in the travel area. Individuals over 50 are eligible for membership.

In recognizing new trends and the huge potential of senior citizens, not only do older households have more to spend, but they also have fewer needs. Typically the children are grown, educated, and gone, making a smaller household; the mortgage on the home was purchased decades earlier so payments are modest or the home is paid for, and the appliances and furniture are paid for. The mature household measured by ability to spend is an attractive market for luxuries, food, second homes, and domestic and foreign travel.

*Singles* There are more single people in America than ever before, a development that has brought about substantial change in our society. In 1980, 54.9 million people aged 18 or over were single, widowed, or divorced, an increase of 17.4 million over 1970. In 1986 the total was 64.5 million. Such increases have never been approached before. The number of persons living alone rose from one in every six households in 1965 to nearly one in four in 1980. Most of these are young adults, not burdened by the costs of raising children, who devote expenditures to recreation, travel, restaurant meals, and the "good life." Young singles travel more than the average adult does and more than others their age who are married. They are also more likely to travel by air and to travel outside the continental United States.

Singles data are divided into three categories: never married, widowed, and divorced. The 1986 population figures were 37.6 million, 13.4 million, and 13.5 million, respectively. The never married account for the majority (58 percent), while the widowed account for 21 percent, and the divorced account for 21 percent. The divorced population increased by 3.6 million between 1980 and 1986. The widowed segment was relatively stable, growing by 700,000 from 1980 to 1986.[10]

The singles population will probably not continue to grow; the percentage of young people in the teenage and young adult years is shrinking, the widowed group is relatively stable, and the size of the divorced segment depends on the rate of remarriage, which is high. The singles market segment thus appears to have reached its peak.

*Population Shifts*  The nation's population growth during the 1980s was concentrated in the South and West. Figure 12.4 shows how this population growth is expected to continue from 1990 to 2000. The states of California, Alaska, Nevada, Arizona, New Mexico, Georgia, Florida, and New Hampshire are expected to have the largest percentages of population increase. Although the South and West dominate in population growth, the Northeast and Midwest continue to grow slowly, even with 15 of their combined 21 states experiencing net outmigration. Most states have shared in the national growth of population under 5 years of age, and all states have shared in the increase of elderly population. The nation's metropolitan areas are the home of 77.6 percent of its population and have grown at a faster rate than nonmetropolitan areas. In metropolitan areas, the proportion of people living in the suburbs continues to increase.

# INCOME

Buying power is another factor for the tourism manager to consider. People must have buying power to create a market. There is no question that a large and increasing percentage of the population today has sufficient discretionary income to finance business and pleasure travel, although some families may be limited to inexpensive trips. The frequency of travel and the magnitude of travel expenditures increase rapidly as income increases. All travel surveys, whether conducted by the Census Bureau, U.S. Travel Data Center, market research firms, or the media, show a direct relationship between family income and the incidence of travel. The greater the income, the more likely a household will travel. The affluent spend more on just

[10] U.S. Bureau of the Census, *Statistical Abstract of the United States, 1988* (Washington, D.C.: Government Printing Office, 1988), p. 39.

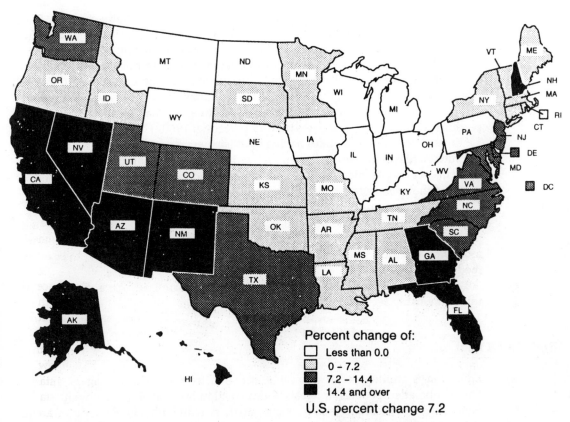

**Figure 12.4** Projected change in state populations: 1990 to 2000. *Source:* Bureau of Census, *Projections of the Population of States, by Age, Sex, and Race: 1988 to 2010.*

about everything, but spending on travel is particularly strong. The value placed on time increases with household income, which is one of the reasons air travel attracts the higher-income consumer.

How the travel dollar is spent obviously depends on income. When the income of the population is divided into fifths, less than 33 percent of the lowest fifth report an expenditure for travel, whereas 85 percent of those in the top fifth report a travel expenditure. Almost half of all consumer spending for vacation and pleasure trips comes from households in the top fifth of the income scale. The affluent spend more on lodging, all-expense-paid tours, food, and shopping, but transportation expenditures are a smaller share of their total travel outlays than with those at the bottom of the income scale — 32 percent versus 43 percent. This results from the fact that it is more difficult to economize on transportation than on food, lodging, and miscellaneous expenses.[11]

[11] Fabian Linden, "The Business of Vacation Traveling," *Across the Board*, Vol. 27, no. 4 (April 1980), pp. 72–75.

If current trends continue, the U.S. population will be wealthier by the year 2000. The Bureau of the Census reports that median family income rose to $30,850 in 1987. Since 1982, real median family income (after adjusting for inflation) increased by 11.8 percent. In addition to a rise in real wage rates, an exceedingly important factor was the growth in dual wage earners. The increase in the number of women who work outside the home has been dramatic and has boosted household income. Both husband and wife are employed in about half of all marriages (51 percent), an increase over the less than 29 percent in 1960. This trend is expected to continue, 57 percent of families having both partners working by the year 2000. As incomes increase, it bodes well for travel, but with husbands and wives both working, it may be more difficult to find time for travel and vacation. It is believed that this is one of the reasons for the trend toward shorter and more frequent vacations.

Travel expenditures historically have had an income elasticity exceeding unity; as per capita real incomes continue to rise, consumers should spend an increasing proportion of their incomes on travel. Besides making more trips in the future, increasing numbers of consumers can be expected to choose air travel over other modes of travel.

Income, education, and occupation are closely correlated. For a discussion of this relationship see the Occupation section.

## EDUCATION

Education is another factor deserving attention from tourism managers, since it tends to broaden peoples' interests and thus stimulate travel. People with college educations take more pleasure trips than do those with high school educations, and those with high school educations take more trips than do those with grade school educations. Educators are forecasting continued increases in the average educational level, which would result in a continued positive impact on pleasure travel.

Studies uniformly show that the well educated account for the most travel and the most dollars spent for vacation and pleasure trips. Only about 50 percent of the homes where the household head did not earn a high school diploma report an expenditure for vacation trips. Where the head holds a high school diploma, about 65 percent report vacation expenditures; where the head has some college, 75 percent spend on vacations; and where the head has a degree, 85 percent report vacation expenditures. Income accompanies education as an important factor. In the approximately 35 percent of the homes where the head of the household has had some college, approximately 55 percent of the expenditures for vacation travel are made. Where the head has more than four years of college, vacation expenditures run two to three times the U.S. average.

There appears to be no question that increased education levels heighten the propensity to travel, and with expanding higher education levels within the population, air travel should also expand.

The nation's educational level continues to rise. Fifty years ago, a high school diploma was nearly as rare a credential as a four-year college degree is today. As of 1986, 75 percent of all adults 25 years of age and older had completed four years of high school. The proportion of the population completing college has also increased considerably. In 1950 only 7.3 percent of men and 5.2 percent of women had completed college. In 1985 the proportion of persons 25 and over completing four years of college or more grew, so that 23 percent of men and 16 percent of women were college graduates. If we look at just the 25- to 29-year-old age group for both sexes, we see that about 21 percent of women and 23 percent of men had completed four years of college. Today, the majority of college students (53 percent) are women.[12]

Education is closely correlated with income and occupation, so the rising level of education should help to increase the demand for travel.

# OCCUPATION

All the factors that determine tourism are interrelated. For example, occupation is closely related to both income and education, and certain life-styles are associated with certain occupations; all this has an impact on travel. Discretionary income is a key requirement for travel. Examining the relationship of income, education, and occupation, one finds that the discretionary dollar is a well-educated dollar. While less than 35 percent of the nation's household heads have had at least some exposure to college, they account for 60 percent of total discretionary spending power. Of all homes where the head earned a college degree, substantially over half are in the discretionary income class. While less than 19 percent of all households are headed by persons with that amount of schooling, they wield over 43 percent of total discretionary buying power. Homes of high school graduates account for 35 percent of the population but for only 28 percent of aggregate discretionary money.[13]

As the educational figures suggest, those engaged in professional and managerial occupations account for a disproportionately large segment of the discretionary income class. Households headed by persons in those occupations account for less than a quarter of the population, but for half of total spendable discretionary resources.

Blue-collar workers, who also represent about a quarter of the population, have only 18 percent of all discretionary income. Homes headed by sales and clerical workers account for slightly over 12 percent of the population and for only a slightly higher proportion of the discretionary income population.[14]

As has been the case throughout the post-World War II period, the labor force participation rates for men and women in the 1980s moved in opposite directions. The long-term decline in labor force participation for men, reflecting in part a move toward earlier retirement, continued as their rate dropped from 77.4 in 1980 to 76.3 in 1985. Conversely, the rate for women continued to climb, from 51.5 in 1980 to a record 54.5 in 1985.

[12] U.S. Bureau of the Census, *Statistical Abstract of the United States, 1988,* p. 149, and U.S. Bureau of the Census, *Population Profile of the United States 1984/85,* 1987.
[13] The Conference Board, *A Marketer's Guide to Discretionary Income,* p. 11.
[14] Ibid., p. 11.

Since white-collar workers take many more trips than do blue-collar workers, and managers and administrators take the greatest number of trips each year, occupation trends are currently favorable to travel. Figure 12.5 presents the percentage distribution of employed men and women by occupations and shows the heavy distribution of executive, professional, and technical occupations which favor travel. Employment growth has been greatest for office workers, especially in executive, administrative, and managerial positions (a 6-percent increase).

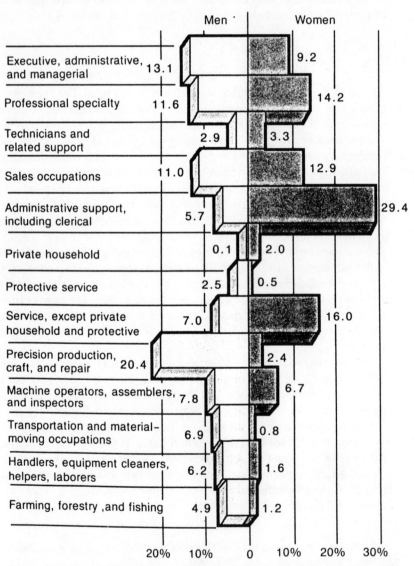

**Figure 12.5** Percent Distribution of Employed Men and Women by Occupation: 1985. *Source:* U.S. Bureau of the Census, *Population Profile of the United States 1984/85* (Washington, D.C.: Government Printing Office, 1987).

The fluctuations in the economy are reflected in most of the blue-collar occupations. Blue-collar workers are the hardest hit occupational group when the economy falls into a recession because so many are employed in manufacturing industries and are the first to be laid off when demand falls. While the tourism marketing manager should focus on the most productive target markets — managers, administrators, professionals — he or she should not overlook the blue-collar segment. The income level of this market is anything but low. Consumers no longer fit neatly into categories of income, age, gender, and occupation. Some blue-collar workers now have the income of university professors, but their spending habits are quite different; they tend to spend less on travel and take a smaller number of air trips than the national average. The potential is there, but this market segment has not fully emerged as active travelers. It deserves more attention from the tourism manager.

# RACE

Hispanic, black, and other minority populations will continue to increase during the next century. In 1985, persons of Spanish origin or descent in the United States numbered about 17 million, or 7 percent of the population. The Hispanic population is expected to increase to 25.2 million by the year 2000, 46 percent over their 1985 population, or 9.4 percent of the total population in 2000. Their numbers will grow to 60 million by the year 2080, when the Hispanic population will represent 19 percent of the nation's total.

The black population, numbering 29 million, represented 12 percent of the U.S. total in 1985, and is expected to increase to 36 million (13.3 percent of the total population) in the year 2000. The numbers of blacks is expected to reach 56 million in 2080, representing 18 percent of the population.

The populations of other races in the United States (American Indians, Alaskan Natives, Asians, and Pacific Islanders) is projected to grow from 6.4 million to 9.5 million in 2000, and reach 23.4 million in 2080, using the U.S. Census Bureau's middle series projections. Their proportion of the population will increase from 2.7 percent in 1985 to 3.6 percent in 2000.

The white non-Hispanic population is not expected to grow proportionately as fast as other groups. In 1985, white non-Hispanics numbered 187 million, 78 percent of the total U.S. population. Their numbers are likely to peak at approximately 205 million in about 2020, then decline to 176 million by 2080, when they will represent 57 percent of the U.S. total population.

Because of their large numbers, the black and Hispanic populations will continue their gains for an equal share in American society. Owing to antidiscrimination legislation and fair hiring practices, nonwhites are making income gains. College enrollment of black Americans today is about triple the 1960 enrollment; however, there is concern about a current decline.

When the tourism managers digest these trends, they recognize that the black travel market is growing rapidly, representing a market segment larger than the population of Canada. The second largest minority group, Hispanics, is also growing rapidly, and by the year 2000 will be the size of Canada's population.

# GENDER

The question of how a family decides whether to buy, where to buy, and which brand to buy has fascinated and puzzled marketers of a variety of products and services for many years. Marketers wonder who is the prime mover — the husband or the wife — or does each play an equal part? If one is the decision maker, what are the influence and role of the other? There is no question that women play a very important role in determining travel decisions. According to the U.S. Travel Data Center, women make up 49 percent of travelers; therefore, they make important travel decisions of their own and influence family travel decisions.

It is obvious that women are becoming much more important in the travel picture. More than 51 percent of the adult population are women, and their relative longevity continues to increase. These factors, plus their growing social, political, and economic independence, must necessarily increase women's share of the travel market. Women currently hold about 48 percent of the nation's driver's licenses (up from 43.2 percent in 1970). Women today are more likely to be employed, live alone, have a college education, and own a home than just a decade ago. Travel marketers are just beginning to recognize the potential of women as customers for travel.

In 1970 there were more housewives than women employed outside the home. In 1973 it was startling news that there were as many women in the work force as there were staying home and keeping house. Now women working outside the home far outnumber housewives. In 1980, 52 percent of all women aged 16 and over were employed outside the home, and this figure rose to 55.8 percent in 1987. This rate is expected to rise to 61.5 percent by the year 2000. The current participation rate for men is 76.6 percent.

According to the Bureau of Labor Statistics, there were 52.4 million women in the labor force in 1986, and projections show 66 million in the labor force in 2000. With this growth, women would make up 47 percent of the labor force in 2000.

Working women have increased family income, thereby providing more discretionary income necessary for pleasure travel. They are clearly better customers for pleasure travel than are women who do not work outside the home. The presence of young children is a strong deterrent to travel; therefore, single working women with no children or working wives with no children or with grown children are better customers than are working men with family responsibilities. Among working women, the most valuable prospects for travel are career-oriented women. In 1973, one in four business travelers was likely to be a woman; today, one in three business travelers is a woman.[15]

Smaller families, smaller and better equipped homes, and demand for brain power instead of physical power have all altered women's traditional role. For many women, maintaining the home has ceased to be a full-time occupation, and women have earned increasing responsibilities in the traditional work of men, leading to new levels of female education and greater degrees of economic and social independence. As a result, women represent a large new travel market quite different from

---

[15] U.S. Travel Data Center, *1987 Travel Executive Briefing: A National Travel Survey Summary* (Washington, D.C.: USTDC), p. 27.

that of previous generations. Thus gender roles are undergoing dramatic change in the United States and are causing changes in consumer behavior. Changes in this area deserve increasing attention of the tourism manager.

## ATTITUDES

Attitudes toward leisure have changed over the centuries. From the beginning of the sixteenth century until only recently, the Protestant ethic was a dominating philosophical force in our culture. Today its tenets of piety, hard work, and thrift as a means of achieving individual salvation are fading, as are the beliefs that self-discipline and unflagging labor are necessary to attain eminence in the community, material wealth, and spiritual reward.

The American workweek has grown considerably shorter over the past 125 years. In 1850 the average workweek spanned 70 hours; it was even longer for agricultural workers. Forty years later the average week had shrunk to 53 hours and by 1920 to 50 hours. This trend can partially be explained by the reduced number of people employed in agriculture, an occupation that traditionally has had long hours.

The length of the average workday in the United States has been compressed from about 12 hours to 8, and the number of days worked per week has declined from 7 to 5 or even fewer. The strength of the unions, new attitudes, and the paid vacation have eroded the historical American emphasis on work and a reluctance to spend time and money on leisure activities. It now seems clear that future generations will view leisure quite differently from those of the past. They will view it as a birthright, as one of the most meaningful aspects of their lives.

## TIME

Another factor affecting tourism is free time. Not only does travel require income, it takes time. All the income in the world will not help if an individual does not have the time to travel. In today's society the lack of time is a major travel constraint. Time also affects the mode of transportation chosen, the places visited, and the activities engaged in.

During the past century, leisure time has increased spectacularly. Reductions in the average workweek, flex-time, longer vacations, more holidays, greater opportunities for part-time work, the exodus from farming, changes in education, and wider retirement opportunity have all played a role.

The amount of free time or leisure time available to the average person in the United States has increased for many years, but it is now shrinking. The practice of granting paid vacations and holidays, however, will continue to grow. The greatest impact on travel happens when employees are given blocks of free time, which may extend anywhere from three days to six weeks. The Uniform Monday Holidays Act added four three-day weekends to the year. The Martin Luther King holiday added another. Thus, people now have more time to take tours or vacation trips and frequently take more than one vacation each year. As the three-day weekend becomes more and more popular, the convenience of air travel becomes more attractive; people can get to destinations in a very short time for mini-vacations.

The blocks of time achieved through longer vacations, more holidays, and shorter workweeks have had a great impact on travel, and it appears that these will continue. However, recent studies contradict the predictions of social scientists that increased leisure time and shorter workweeks will be the wave of the future. Harris surveys indicate that the trend is now toward more work and less play, largely because women joining the work force are juggling jobs plus work at home, thus having less leisure time, and both men and women, in increasing numbers, are finding professional, technical, and managerial jobs that require more than a 40-hour week. See Figure 12.6. Data in this area will have to be monitored carefully to see if new trends are developing, as there are conflicting reports. For example, John P. Robinson in the July 1989 issue of *American Demographics* states: "Despite the belief that Americans are facing a time famine, we have more free time today than we did 20 years ago."

## FASHION, CUSTOM, HABIT, AND TRADITION

Fashion is universal in U.S. marketing today. It applies to all products, be it clothing, transportation, homes, beverages, or recreation. The tourism industry is fortunate because travel experiences are now more important than material possessions. However, certain kinds of experiences are more fashionable than others. In the transportation area, it is not fashionable today to go by bus (although if current trends persist, this may change); cruises and air travel are fashionable items. Back in the 1920s, hot springs resorts were fashionable; today, they are very low on the consumers' priority lists. Taking their place as fashionable items are tennis and ski resorts.

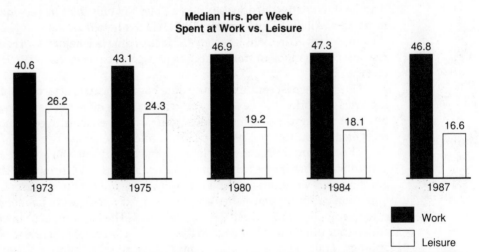

Figure 12.6 America's Shrinking Leisure Time. *Source:* Louis Harris and Associates, 1988.

Other factors to be reckoned with in the market for tourism and recreation are custom, habit, and tradition. Profiles of tourists indicate that about 40 percent of all travel is for the purpose of visiting with friends and relatives. This has been confirmed by the Census Bureau's *National Travel Survey* and the U.S. Travel Data Center's *National Travel Survey.*

By far the most frequently used mode of travel is the automobile, and most auto travelers stay with friends and relatives. This is even more likely for lower-income families. Upper-income families take more business trips, stay much more frequently in commercial lodging, and use air travel more often. The wealthier families also take more trips for entertainment and sightseeing.

Attitude surveys have shown that an important factor in American travel is the feeling of obligation or the desire to visit friends or relatives. Beyond this, a vacation destination is often chosen based on custom or habit. Vacationers are likely to return to places they have been before.

Nostalgia is a major market segment for tourism. Increasing technology and the faster pace of modern life make people interested in recapturing the past. History is a powerful tourist attraction. The pulling power of the Smithsonian, the Holy Land, the King Tut exhibit, Athens, Rome, Colonial Williamsburg—the list is endless—

The Delta Queen Steamboat Co. provides a historical travel experience in modern comfort. (Courtesy of the Delta Queen Steamboat Co.)

amply demonstrates this. Preservation today is taking the form of exhibits as working objects; thus it is possible for tourists to visit railroad museums where old steam locomotives work, antique car museums where early auto models operate, and living history farms where farm work is done with actual equipment from past years.

A prime example of nostalgia is the San Francisco cable car. This obsolete transportation system with questionable safety and comfort is a strong tourism force. The system was shut down for a lengthy period for a major overhaul in the early 1980s amid protests from tourists, conventioneers, and the general public that they could not use their beloved system. The major work was completed in the summer of 1984 and the cable cars are again a permanent feature of the San Francisco tourism experience.

The *Delta Queen,* the old Mississippi River paddle steamer, and the Durango-Silverton narrow-gauge railroad are other good examples of how nostalgia has been developed into successful tourism enterprises.

## CHANGING LIFE-STYLES

In the past, society cast people in rigid roles — man, the breadwinner; woman, the housewife. On weekends they trimmed the yard or painted the bedroom; in August they spent his two-week vacation together. Travel was viewed as a luxury.

Today, pleasure has become an integral part of the American life-style. Two-thirds of Americans have taken a pleasure trip the past year, during which they spent at least one night away from home.

The San Francisco cable car is a symbol of the city, and no visit is complete without a ride on this unique form of transportation. (Photo by Tom Vano, courtesy of San Francisco Convention and Visitors Bureau)

The *Marriott Report on Leisure Travel* published in 1987 shows that the traditional two-week American vacation is no longer the norm for American leisure travel. Most Americans prefer taking several weekend pleasure trips rather than one longer trip. While many Americans continue to take long vacation trips, the majority (72 percent) take short trips of three days or less, and most of these short trips are over weekends.

This is one of the most significant trends taking place now. People are taking shorter trips and more frequent trips. Pleasure travelers now take an average of about 4.7 trips a year. This preference for short weekend trips reflects the modern American life-style. It has evolved for a variety of reasons. Americans are attracted to a quick vacation fix that does not disrupt the routine of home and job; the aging baby boomers and two-career households have more disposable income but less time to spend in one large block; with today's time and work pressures people are looking for a break from their everyday routines; and, finally, the lodging industry has made a major effort to attract the "getaway" market and serve the weekend pleasure traveler.

In addition to weekend getaways, other "hot" items that appeal to today's

Changing life-styles call for more adventure travel and participation activities. Rock climbing for beginners and professionals is one of many summer activities to choose from at Winter Park, Colorado. (Photo by Grafton Smith, courtesy of Winter Park)

life-styles are adventure travel, experience travel, "healthy" travel, trips for women and mature travelers, and Canada, Mexico, and Caribbean destinations.

Today people are concerned with self-fulfillment and self-gratification, trying out new life-styles and searching out new pleasures. They are more committed to self-knowledge and introspection, and society has strongly supported this individualism and quest for self-expression and self-realization.

Experiments with life-style, the sexual revolution, weekend vacations, and the women's movement have given the travel industry new groups of travelers to accommodate. Working couples eat out more and travel more; childless couples have greater discretionary income and travel more than do couples with children; unmarried couples travel together; single women and older women travel alone or together for business and pleasure.

New concepts of the family often make contradictory demands on the travel industry. Some people reject the idea of doing everything together; husbands and wives may vacation separately. Other couples go together, yet demand separate activities for their children. Some demand resorts that offer facilities for everything, yet they actually use very few of them. Whatever the choice, there is more and more involvement by women in the purchasing decision.

Today, as millions of people become more financially and physically mobile, there is a great merging of tourism and recreation life-styles with less distinction between the social classes. An analysis of demographics is no longer a sure guide to patterns of travel; it must be supplemented by life-style analysis and psychographics.

Once a tourism manager gets a handle on life-style patterns, it is likely they will change. While the 1960s brought profound change and created new market segments, the process did not stop. Today we see the aging of the U.S. population, the renewal of traditional values and patriotism, and a new intensity of young people in pursuing their vocational goals. Managing change requires a continuing dedication to knowing your customers better through market research, constant customer feedback and attention to the ever-changing needs of key markets through an alert, aggressive marketing organization. We must not simply respond to change; we must manage it. The years ahead promise to be challenging and exciting and full of additional change. To survive in the marketplace, it will be necessary to deliver value. People will be more particular, they will be more selective, and they will look for consistency and quality.

## SUMMARY

Because there would be no tourism industry if there were no consumers willing to spend their income on travel rather than on other products and services, it is important to analyze factors that determine the market for travel and tourism.

The first of these factors is the population and population trends; the utility of using these data has been shown. Population data are readily available in almost all libraries. One can examine a market segment such as 18-year-olds and know that that segment will move through the age cycle; this enables one to project the future.

Other key demographic variables such as income, education, occupation, race, and gender also affect tourism. Such forces as women entering the labor force, dual-income consumer units, income erosion by inflation, early retirement, childless families, and more divorces make demographic forecasting difficult.

Factors such as time play a role and can be a major barrier to travel. New values and attitudes toward marriage, leisure, work, self-actualization, and self-improvement create changing markets. Energy constraints alter traditional tourism patterns. New life-styles are emerging and must be studied.

These factors point out that in the tourism, recreation, and leisure marketplace, it is necessary to recognize that people and market conditions will change in the coming decades. If the tourism planner is to forecast trends with a profitable foresight, he must be a student of the factors affecting the tourism scene. Tourism businesses will have to examine their markets more carefully than ever to serve them well and profitably. Market information is essential to identify market segments and to develop marketing strategy and plans. These are discussed in Chapter 13.

## Key Concepts

| | |
|---|---|
| attitudes about leisure and travel | leisure ethic |
| buying power | nostalgia |
| changing life-styles | occupation |
| custom, habit, tradition | population trends |
| dual-income households | race |
| educational levels | senior citizens market |
| fashion | singles |
| free time | teenage group |
| gender of travel buyer | women and travel |
| | young adult market |

## For Review and Discussion

1. Using demographic and income factors, describe the segment that would be the best market for a ski vacation.
2. What changes in consumer demand are likely to result from the fact that the over-65 age segment of our population is growing rapidly?
3. Is the number of people in an area an accurate index of its importance as a market?
4. How does the time factor affect consumer travel patterns? Airline operations? The lodging industry?
5. Give several examples of tourism products or services whose market demand would be affected by (a) age, (b) marital status, and (c) gender.
6. Do you feel that discretionary income is the most important factor affecting travel markets? Why or why not?
7. What marketing opportunities do minorities present?
8. Who are the airlines' best customers?

9. What impact does education have on travel?
10. You have just opened a luxury destination resort. What occupation groups will you try to attract to your resort?
11. Today, leisure, recreation, and travel are considered a right, not a privilege or luxury. Discuss.
12. The automobile is the traditional mode of travel for a family vacation. How could this habit or custom of behavior be changed?
13. Discuss the impact of the values of your generation on travel versus those of your parents.
14. How will the baby boomers segment affect the market for travel in 2000? In 2010?

## Selected References

Allan, Carole B. "Measuring Mature Markets." *American Demographics*, March 1981, pp. 13–17.

Anderson, Beverlee B., and Lynn Langmeyer. "The Under-50 and Over-50 Travelers: A Profile of Similarities and Differences." *Journal of Travel Research*, Vol. 20, no. 4 (Spring 1982), pp. 20–24.

Bartos, Rena. *The Moving Target, What Every Marketer Should Know About Women.* New York: The Free Press, 1982.

Blazey, Michael A. "The Differences Between Participants and Non-participants in a Senior Travel Program." *Journal of Travel Research*, Vol. 26, no. 1 (Summer 1987), pp. 7–12.

Brown, Barbara I. "How the Baby Boom Lives." *American Demographics*, May 1984, pp. 35–37.

Butz, William P., et al. *Demographic Challenges in America's Future.* Santa Monica, Calif.: The Rand Corporation, 1982.

The Conference Board. *A Marketer's Guide to Discretionary Income.* New York: The Board, 1983.

Goodrich, Jonathan N. "Black American Tourists: Some Research Findings." *Journal of Travel Research*, Vol. 24, no. 2 (Fall 1985), pp. 27–28.

Hawes, Douglass K. "Travel-Related Lifestyle Profiles of Older Women." *Journal of Travel Research*, Vol. 27, no. 2 (Fall 1988), pp. 22–32.

Lazer, William, and Eric H. Shaw. "How Older Americans Spend Their Money." *American Demographics*, Vol. 9, no. 9 (September 1987), pp. 36–41.

Longino, Charles F., Jr. "The Comfortably Retired and the Pension Elite." *American Demographics*, Vol. 10, no. 6 (June 1988), pp. 22–25.

Riche, Martha F. "The Postmarital Society." *American Demographics*, Vol. 10, no. 11, pp. 22–26, 60.

Robinson, John P. "Time's Up." *American Demographics*, Vol. 11, no. 7 (July 1989), pp. 32–35.

Shipp, Stephanie. "How Singles Spend." *American Demographics*, Vol. 10, no. 4 (April 1988), pp. 22–27.

Shoemaker, Stowe. "Segmentation of the Senior Pleasure Travel Market." *Journal of Travel Research*, Vol. 27, no. 3 (Winter 1989), pp. 14–21.

Stipp, Horst H. "What Is a Working Woman?" *American Demographics*, Vol. 10, No. 7 (July 1988), pp. 24–27, 59.

Tongren, Hale H. "Travel Plans of the Over-65 Market Pre- and Postretirement." *Journal of Travel Research*, Vol. 19, no. 2 (Fall 1980), pp. 7–11.

Travel Industry Association of America. *Emerging Travel Markets: The Woman Traveler.* Washington, D.C.: TIAA, 1978.

*Travel Weekly. The Mature Traveler.* New York: Murdoch, 1988.

Waldrop, Judith. "The Fashionable Family." *American Demographics,* Vol. 10, no. 3 (March 1988), pp. 22–26.

World Tourism Organization. *Summary of Developments in the Fields of World Economy, Demography and Energy: Prospects for Tourism.* Madrid: WTO, 1983.

# CHAPTER 13

# Tourism Marketing

## LEARNING OBJECTIVES

- Recognize the extreme importance of a well-planned, vigorous marketing program to the success of any tourist business and how this must be based on research.
- Become familiar with the marketing mix and be able to formulate the best mix for a particular travel product.
- Appreciate the importance of the relationship between the marketing concept and product planning and development.
- Understand the vital relationship between pricing and marketing.
- Know about distribution systems and how this marketing principle can best be applied to a variety of travel products.
- Be able to do market segmentation to plan a marketing program for the business you are the most interested in.

## NATURE AND SCOPE

Tourism marketing is

- The State of New York creating a tourism promotion fund, developing a marketing plan, and creating an advertising campaign around the theme "I Love New York."
- Quality International segmenting its lodging product into four separate chains: Sleep Inns, their new no-frills concept; Comfort Inns for the value-conscious guest—the price-sensitive traveler who wants a good bed, limited services and facilities, a good night's sleep, and a low price; Quality Inns aimed at the largest travel segment—the midprice traveler who seeks clean, comfortable, well-appointed rooms at a moderate price; and Clarion, appealing to the luxury traveler who wants nothing but the best and is willing to pay the price.
- United Airlines offering different classes of service, supersaver fares, Mileage Plus, advertising the "friendly skies," developing a logo, adding new routes and schedules, using their own reservation system and travel agents, and working with tour groups.

Marketing includes all of the above and much more. Marketing has been defined in a variety of ways. The American Marketing Association defines marketing as "the performance of business activities that direct the flow of goods and services from the producer to the consumer or user." Others have stated that marketing is the delivery of the standard of living to society. You are no doubt acquainted with the old adage, "nothing happens until somebody sells something."

Most people have little idea what marketing is all about and would probably say that it has something to do with selling or advertising. However, marketing is a very broad concept, of which advertising and selling are only two facets. Marketing is goal-oriented, strategic, and directed. It both precedes and follows selling and advertising activities. Marketing is the total picture in getting goods and services from the producer to the user.

Unfortunately, "marketing" often conjures up unfavorable images of used car salespeople, TV furniture advertisers, high-pressure selling, and gimmicks, leading to the perception of marketing in terms of stereotypes. In fact, marketing plays a critical role in all organizations whether they are nonprofit educational institutions, tourist resorts, or manufacturers. The role of marketing is to match the right product or service with the right market or audience.

Marketing is an inevitable aspect of tourism management. Marketing can be done effectively and well, with sophistication, or it can be done poorly in a loud, crass, intrusive manner. It is the goal of this chapter to discuss the basic elements of marketing so that it can be done effectively, with style, and with a favorable economic impact.

## MARKETING CONCEPT

The heart of good marketing management today is the marketing concept, or a consumer orientation. Tourism organizations which practice the marketing concept find out what the consumer wants and then produce a product that will satisfy those wants at a profit. The marketing concept requires that management thinking be directed toward profits rather than sales volume.

Assume that you are going to develop a new major resort area. This is a difficult exercise in planning that requires that the designs that are developed be based on how consumers view the product. One of the first steps is to employ the marketing concept and do research to understand the consumer's (the market's) needs, desires, and wants. Designers of products and consumers of products often perceive them differently. Architects, for example, may see a hotel in terms of such things as space utilization, engineering problems, and design lines or as a monument; consumers may see the hotel as a bundle of benefits — as being attractive, as offering full service and outstanding food, as having recreational facilities, and so on. Once consumer views are determined, the task is to formulate strategic marketing plans that match the resort and its market. In today's competitive environment where consumers have choices, firms need to employ the marketing concept.

## THE MARKETING MIX

The marketing program combines a number of elements into a workable whole — a viable, strategic plan. The tourism marketing manager must constantly search for the right marketing mix — the right combination of elements that will produce a profit. The marketing mix is composed of every factor that influences the marketing effort:

1. *Timing.* Holidays, high season, low season, upward trend in the business cycle, and so on must all be considered.

Good marketing requires expert handling of guests from the
beginning to the end of their experience. Cypress Gardens has
gracious Southern belles who greet visitors and welcome them to
the Central Florida theme park. (Photo by David Woods, courtesy
of Cypress Gardens)

2. *Brands*. The consumer needs help in remembering your product. Names,
   trademarks, labels, logos, and other identification marks all assist the consumer
   in identifying and recalling information about your product.
3. *Packaging*. Although tourism services do not require a physical package,
   packaging is still an important factor. For example, transportation, lodging,
   amenities, and recreation activities can be packaged and sold together or separately. Family plans or single plans are other forms of packaging.
4. *Pricing*.  Pricing affects not only sales volume but also the image of the product.
   A multitude of pricing options exist, ranging from discount prices to premium
   prices.
5. *Channels of distribution*. The product must be accessible to the consumer. Direct selling, retail travel agents, wholesale tour operators, or a combination of
   these methods all comprise distribution channels that must be developed.
6. *Product*. The physical attributes of the product help to determine its position against the competition and provide guidelines on how to best compete.
7. *Image*. The consumer's perception of the product depends to a great extent
   on the important factors of reputation and quality.
8. *Advertising*. Paid promotion is critical, and the questions of when, where,
   and how to promote must be carefully considered.
9. *Selling*. Internal and external selling are essential components for success,
   and various sales techniques must be incorporated in the marketing plan.

A good marketing plan attracts visitors, filling hotels, restaurants, and other enterprises with tourists. (Photo by Fred W. Marvel, courtesy of Oklahoma Tourism Department)

10. *Public relations.* Even the most carefully drawn marketing plan will fail without good relations with the visitors, the community, suppliers, and employees.

The preceding list makes it obvious that the marketing manager's job is a complex one. Using knowledge of the consumer market and the competition, the marketing manager must come up with the proper marketing mix for the resort, attraction, or other organization. The marketing manager's job begins with planning to allow direction and control of the foregoing factors.

The many elements in the marketing mix have been defined most frequently as "the four Ps," a term popularized by E. Jerome McCarthy, author of *Basic Marketing* and *Essentials of Marketing.*[1] While the four Ps are an oversimplification, they do provide a neat, simple framework in which to look at marketing and put together a marketing program. The four Ps are product, place, promotion, and price.

[1] E. Jerome McCarthy, *Essentials of Marketing* (Homewood, Ill.: Richard D. Irwin, 1979), p. 32.

The product includes not only actual physical attributes of the product but also product planning, product development, breadth of the line, branding, and packaging. Planning the product should consider all these aspects in order to come up with the "right" product.

Place is really concerned with distribution. What agencies, channels, and institutions can be linked together most effectively to give the consumer easy access to the purchase of your product? Where is the "right" place to market your product?

Promotion communicates the benefits of the product to the potential customers and includes not only advertising but sales promotion, public relations, and personal selling. The "right" promotional mix will use each of these promotional techniques as needed for effective communication.

Price is a critical variable in the marketing mix. The "right" price must both satisfy customers and meet your profit objectives.

## Product Planning and Development

The objective of most firms is to develop a profitable and continuing business. To achieve this objective, companies must provide products and services that satisfy consumer needs, thereby assuring themselves of repeat business. Product planning is an essential component in developing a profitable, continuing business and has frequently been referred to as the "five rights" — planning to have the right product, at the right place, at the right time, at the right price, in the right quantities.

A product is much more than a combination of raw materials. It is actually a bundle of satisfactions and benefits for the consumer. Product planning must there-

Logos identify products and companies, assisting the consumer in identifying and purchasing products and services.

High quality and good service are important elements of the product mix. (Photo courtesy of Cunard Lines)

fore be approached from the consumer's point of view. Creating the right service or product is not easy; consumer needs, wants, and desires are constantly changing, and competitive forces typically carry products through a life cycle, so that a product that is successful at one point declines and "dies" at a later time.

Figure 13.1 shows the phases that a new product goes through from inception to decline, namely, (1) introduction, (2) growth, (3) maturity, (4) saturation, and (5) decline. Because of the rapidly changing consumer life-styles and technological changes, the life cycle for products and services has become shorter, but the product life cycle remains a useful concept for strategic planning. Each stage of the product life cycle has certain marketing requirements.

*Introduction*   The introductory phase of the product's life cycle requires high promotional expenditures and visibility. (The most productive time to advertise a product or service is when it is new.) Operations in this period are characterized by high cost, relatively low sales volume, and an advertising program aimed at stimulating primary demand; in this stage of the life cycle, there will be a high percentage of failures.

*Growth*   In the growth period, the product or service is being accepted by consumers. Market acceptance means that both sales and profits rise at a rapid rate, frequently making the market attractive to competitors. Promotional expenditures remain high, but the promotional emphasis is on selective buying motives by trade name rather than on primary motives to try the product. During the growth stage, the number of outlets handling the product or service usually increases. More com-

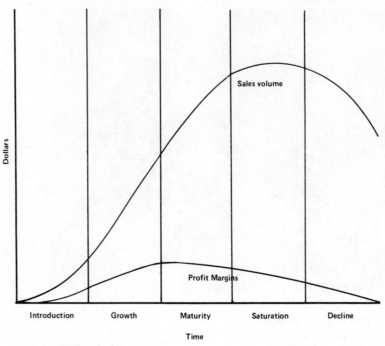

**Figure 13.1** Product Life Cycle.

petitors enter the marketplace, but economies of scale are realized and prices may decline some.

*Maturity* The mature product is well established in the marketplace. Sales may still be increasing but at a much slower rate; they are leveling off. At this stage of the product's life cycle, many outlets are selling the product or service, and they are very competitive, especially with respect to price, and firms are trying to determine ways to hold on to their share of the market. The ski resort is an excellent example of a mature product. After years of spectacular growth, sales are now leveling off, and the resorts are looking for ways to hold market share and diversify.

*Saturation* In the saturation stage, sales volume reaches its peak; the product or service has penetrated the marketplace to the greatest degree possible. Mass production and new technology have lowered the price to make it available to almost everyone.

*Decline* Many products stay at the saturation stage for years. However, for most products, obsolescence sets in, and new products are introduced to replace old ones. In the decline stage, demand obviously drops, advertising expenditures are lower, and there is usually a smaller number of competitors. While it is possible for a product to do very well in this stage of the product life cycle, there is not a great deal of comfort in getting a larger share of a declining market. Hot springs resorts are a good example of a tourist product in the decline stage. These facilities, at their peak in the 1920s, are no longer the consumer's idea of an "in" place to go.

*Pricing* One of the most important marketing decisions is the pricing decision. Price determines how consumers perceive the product and strongly affects other elements of the marketing mix.

Firms have a choice of three strategies in pricing their products. First, they may decide to sell their product at the market price, which is the same price that everyone else charges. They then compete on nonprice terms. Selling at a price equal to competitors' tends to prevent price cutting and protect margins, and customers are not driven away by price. However, because there is no price individuality, there can be no price demand stimulation.

Second, firms may decide to price below the current market price. Firms that adopt such a discount policy are trying to create the reputation of having the lowest prices and underselling all competitors. To be successful, such firms must make sure that demand is elastic; otherwise, they will gain only at the expense of their competitors and start a price war. This pricing strategy is more successful when it is based on the elimination of services. Motel 6, Inc., for example, took its name from its original $6-a-night charge and built its network on a no-frills philosophy. Today it is one of the top budget chains in the United States, owning 452 properties and 51,572 rooms and ranking thirteenth among the 100 largest world hotel chains.

The third approach is to charge above-market prices. Premium pricing strategy must be coupled with the best service in the industry and other features and amenities to make this higher price attractive. Such an approach emphasizes quality, which many consumers think is a function of price; provides higher margins; generates more revenue for promotion; and makes better service possible. However, premium pricing reduces volume, raises overhead costs, and encourages substitution. Nevertheless, numerous tourism firms successfully use this approach, including the Fairmont, Hyatt, and Westin hotels.

Some firms choose to employ two or three pricing strategies and develop a product to appeal to consumers in each market segment. The lodging industry has moved to employing this strategy in the last decade. Ramada, Quality, Marriott, Holiday Corporation, and others have developed products to appeal to a broad range of market segments.

The tourism marketing manager must consider the following factors that influence price policies:

1. *Product quality.* The quality of the product really determines the price-value relationship. It is common sense that a product that offers greater utility and fills more consumer needs than a competitive product can command a higher price.
2. *Product distinctiveness.* A staple or standard product with no distinctive features offers little or no opportunity for price control. However, a novel and different product may be able to command higher prices. The Hyatt Corporation, for example, features lobby atriums; this attractive novelty combined with excellent service and facilities makes it possible for the Hyatt Hotels to command higher prices.
3. *Extent of the competition.* A product that is comparable to competitors' products must be priced with the competitors' prices in mind. The product's price to some extent determines its position in the market.
4. *Method of distribution.* The price of the product must include adequate margins for tour operators, travel agents, or the company's own sales force.

5. *Character of the market.* It is necessary to consider the type and number of possible consumers. If there is a small number of consumers, then the price must be high enough to compensate for a limited market. However, one must also consider the ability of consumers to buy and their buying habits.
6. *Cost of the product and service.* It should be obvious that price must exceed cost over the long run or else the business will not survive. Both cost and market conditions should serve as guides to pricing.
7. *Cost of distribution.* Distribution costs must also be included in the pricing equation. Unfortunately, in many cases they are much more difficult to estimate than other costs.
8. *Margin of profit desired.* The profit margin built into the price of the product must be more than returns realized on more conventional investments in order to compensate for the risk involved in the enterprise.
9. *Seasonality.* Most tourism products are affected by seasonality because of school year patterns and vacation habits; consequently, the seasonal aspects must be considered in developing prices.
10. *Special promotional prices.* Many times it is good strategy to offer introductory prices and special one-time price offers to acquaint consumers with your product. However, these must be carefully planned so that they fill the proper intent and do not become a regular discount price.
11. *Psychological considerations.* Throughout our economy we see psychological pricing employed, usually using prices that are set in odd amounts such as 19¢, 99¢, $19.95, or $29.99. Consumers respond well to odd pricing, and there seems to be something particularly magical about prices that end in nine.

*Price Skimming*    In the pricing of a new product or service, the two pricing philosophies that prevail are called price skimming and penetration pricing. A price-skimming strategy sets the price as high as possible. No attempt is made to appeal to the entire market, but only to the top of the market; consequently, this approach is frequently called skimming the cream. The strategy is to sell the product to as many consumers as possible at this price level; then, as either buyer resistance or direct competition develops, the seller will lower prices step by step. This approach typically results in higher profits and more rapid repayment of development and promotion costs. It also tends to invite competition. Skimming is appropriate when the product or service has the following characteristics: (1) price inelasticity, (2) no close substitutes, (3) high promotion elasticity, and (4) distinct market segments based on price.

*Penetration Pricing*    The opposite approach to price skimming is market penetration, in which the seller attempts to establish the price of the product as low as possible to penetrate the market as completely as possible. A low price makes the product available to as many income levels as possible, and the sellers are likely to establish a large market share quickly. When penetration pricing is used, this introductory price tends to become the permanent price of the product. It results in a slower recovery of fixed costs and requires a greater volume to break even. The factors that would recommend a penetration pricing approach would be (1) high price elasticity, (2) large savings from high-volume production (economies of scale), and (3) an easy fit of the product into consumer purchasing patterns.

## Place (Distribution)

Another difficult decision for the marketing manager concerns what distribution channel or channels will be used. The distribution decisions affect the other elements of the marketing mix, and in the best marketing mix all aspects will be compatible with each other. Figure 13.2 provides a simple illustration of the travel distribution system.

Channels of distribution are selected by (1) analyzing the product, (2) determining the nature and extent of the market, (3) analyzing the channels by sales, costs, and profits, (4) determining the cooperation you can expect from the channel, (5) determining the assistance you will have to give to the channel, and (6) determining the number of outlets to be used. For example, if you want intensive distribution, exposing your product to maximum sale, you will use many travel agents. In contrast, with an exclusive distribution policy, you would sell your product through one or a few agents, who would have the sole right to sell your product or service in a given area.

More research needs to be conducted on the travel distribution system and its operation, though some study has been undertaken. One of the better studies is by Mary J. Bitner and Bernard H. Booms, whose article, "Trends in Travel and Tourism Marketing: The Changing Structure of Distribution Channels," appeared in the Spring 1982 issue of the *Journal of Travel Research*. Their study focused on the intermediaries who link travelers with the suppliers of travel services (airlines, hotels, car rental firms, and others). Bitner and Booms define three main categories of travel intermediaries: tour packagers, retail travel agents, and specialty channelers. The specialty channeler category includes incentive travel firms, meeting and convention planners, hotel representatives, association executives, corporate travel offices, and others as shown in Figure 13.2.

Each intermediary has the power to influence when, where, and how people travel. In other words, they control to some degree how much business an individual airline, hotel, or cruise line or car rental firm gets. Even among the three main

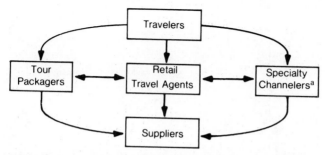

[a]Incentive Travel Firms, Business Meeting and Convention Planners, Corporate Travel Offices, Association Executives, Hotel Representatives, and Supplier Sales Offices.

**Figure 13.2** Travel Distribution System. *Source:* M. J. Bitner and B. H. Booms, "Trends in Travel and Tourism Marketing: The Changing Structure of Distribution Channels," *Journal of Travel Research*, Vol. 20, no. 4 (Spring 1982), p. 40.

intermediary categories, different combinations and interactions occur, resulting in a wide range of channel configurations (Figure 13.3). Each vertical bar represents a possible channel linking travelers with travel suppliers. The uninterrupted bar on the far left represents the channel whereby travelers book their own transportation, reserve accommodations, and make other travel arrangements directly with suppliers. Each of the other bars represents a form of indirect channel involving one or more travel intermediaries. These are the channel choices that the tourism marketing manager must study to select the best channel or combination of channels to market his firm's service. The manager must also be aware of changes in the distribution system, especially under deregulation. With new competitors entering the system more competition and additional distribution methods can be expected.

## Promotion

The aim of promotion activities is to create demand for a product or service. Promotion is a broad term that includes advertising, personal selling, public relations, publicity, and sales promotion activities such as give-aways, trade shows, point of purchase, and store displays.

To sell the product it is necessary to (1) attract attention, (2) create interest, (3) create a desire, and (4) get action. Either personal selling or advertising can carry out all of these steps in the selling process; however, the two used together tend to be much more powerful. Advertising is ideally suited to attract attention and create interest in the products and services. Personal selling is best suited to creating desire and conviction on the part of the customer and to closing the sale. Advertising and personal selling are even more effective when supplemented by publicity and sales promotion activities.

*Advertising*   Advertising has been defined as any nonpersonal presentation of goods, ideas, or services by an identified sponsor. In travel marketing, these paid public messages are designed to describe or present a destination area in such a way

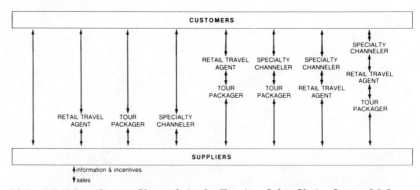

**Figure 13.3**  Distribution Channels in the Tourism Sales Chain. *Source:* M. J. Bitner and B. H. Booms, "Trends in Travel and Tourism Marketing: The Changing Structure of Distribution Channels," *Journal of Travel Research*, Vol. 20, no. 4 (Spring 1982), p. 40.

as to attract consumers. This can be done through the use of the major advertising media such as newspapers, magazines, direct mail, television, outdoor, or radio. Effective advertising gains the attention of the prospective visitor, holds the attention so the message can be communicated, and makes a lasting positive impression on the prospect's mind.

Each advertising medium has advantages and disadvantages. A key decision in developing promotional strategy is to select the right medium to maximize advertising expenditure. To assist in media selection, turn to Standard Rate and Data Service, 5201 Old Orchard Road, Skokie, Ill. 60077. SRDS publications contain advertising rates and other media information required to make intelligent decisions. The advantages and disadvantages of the major media are as follows.

**Newspapers** Newspapers give comprehensive coverage of a local market area, are lower in cost than other media, are published frequently, are flexible (short lead time) and timely, have a wide audience, and get a quick response. Most newspapers have travel sections. The major disadvantages are low printing quality and short life.

**Direct Mail** Although mail costs have increased rapidly, direct mail is one of the most important advertising methods for tourism enterprises. It is the most personal and selective of all the media; consequently, it is the most effective medium in minimizing waste circulation. Direct mail gets the message directly to the consumers one wishes to contact. Direct mail advertising is self-testing when it asks for a response. The critical problem with direct mail is obtaining and maintaining the right mailing lists. Many types of lists are commercially available through firms specializing in this activity. (One source of such information is Standard Rate and Data Service.)

For the tourism industry, previous visitors comprise the most important mailing list sources. However, names and addresses must be correct, and the lists must be kept in ready-to-use form, such as address plates or on a computer. Other good sources of prospects are the inquiry lists.

**Television** Television presents both an audio and visual message and comes as close to approximating personal selling as a mass medium can. Television requires minimal exertion on the part of listeners and is very versatile. However, television is not a flexible medium, commercials have a short life, and advertising on television is expensive relative to the costs of using other media. Nevertheless, despite television's expense, many destinations are using television and finding it is very cost effective.

**Magazines** The major advantage of magazines is their print and graphic quality. Other advantages are secondary readership, long life, prestige, and favorable cost per 1000 circulation. Many special interest magazines reach specialized market segments effectively, making it possible to target markets. Regional editions allow further selectivity, with a minimum of waste circulation. Some of the unfavorable characteristics of magazines are that they require long lead times and that changes cannot be made readily. Magazines also reach the market less frequently than do newspapers, radio, and television.

## Where is it written that paradise has to be tropical?

Swaying palms may be just fine for some people. But if you've ever strapped on a pair of skis, this is pure paradise.

Mountain peaks glistening against an endless blue sky. Snow that's sparkling light perfection. And more trails than you could hope to ski in one lifetime. If that's more your idea of a day in the

sun, send for your free Colorado Vacation Kit. Or call toll-free and ask for ext. 101.

You'll get everything you need to see paradise in a whole new light.

## COLORADO

1 - 8 0 0 - 4 3 3 - 2 6 5 6

Colorado Tourism Board, Box 38700 Dept. BXCFOP, Denver CO 80238

Have you ever skied Colorado?

Yes ☐                                  No ☐

Name _____

Address _____

City _____

State _____ Zip _____

BXCFOP

In 46 states, advertising is directed toward stimulating inquiries. This Colorado Tourism Board advertisement is an example. Travel offices reported a total of 12 million general and advertising-generated inquiries received during 1987, or approximately 267,000 inquiries per state, according to the U.S. Travel Data Center. (Ad courtesy of the Colorado Tourism Board by Karsh and Hagan, Denver, Colorado)

**Radio**   Radio has the advantage of outstanding flexibility and relatively low cost. While the warmth of the human voice adds a personal touch to the selling message, radio has the disadvantage that it presents only an audio message. Tourists driving in their automobiles are typically radio listeners, and many attractions find radio an excellent medium.

**Outdoor Advertising**   Outdoor advertising has been used with great success by many tourism organizations. It is a flexible, low-cost medium that reaches virtually the whole population. It has made the Wall Drugstore in Wall, South Dakota, world famous. Outdoor advertising has the disadvantage that the message must be short; however, it does reach travelers. An additional problem is highway signing laws, which are making it more difficult to advertise tourism attractions.

## Your request for a return to childhood has been approved.

There's something about the snow here. Something about this light, fluffy, powdery stuff that does more than just make for the finest skiing in the world.

It seems to wash away the years. And take you back to the kind of fun you used to have before you started to care much about what other people thought.

So if acting all grown up has become a

full time job, send for a free Colorado Vacation Kit. Or call and ask for ext. 103. You'll get all you need to plan your trip. Even a coupon for up to $50 off the airfare from Continental, the Official Airline of Colorado.

**COLORADO**

1 - 8 0 0 - 4 3 3 - 2 6 5 6

Colorado Tourism Board, Box 38700, Dept. RWCFOD, Denver CO 80238

Have you ever skied Colorado?

Yes ☐                            No ☐

Name _____

Address _____

City _____

State _____ Zip _____

RWCFOD

Travel offices reported 1988–89 advertising budgets totaling $122,435,863. States spend these advertising dollars to attract summer, winter, and other target market visitors. This ad is another in a series published by the Colorado Tourism Board in their campaign to attract winter visitors. (Ad courtesy of the Colorado Tourism Board by Karsh and Hagan, Denver, Colorado)

**Using an Advertising Agency**  While promotion managers must know the fundamentals of marketing, advertising, personal selling, and public relations, the specialized skill and experience of an advertising agency can greatly increase business—and can do it profitably. An advertising agency will

1. Work with ideas in copy and layout. "Copy" is the term used to describe written messages; "layout" refers to the arrangement of copy, art, and pictures.
2. Advise on the choice of media to convey advertising messages, devising an organized and carefully worked-out plan using newspapers, magazines, radio, TV, guide books, posters, direct mail, postcards, folders, or other advertising media.
3. Conduct market analysis and research so that advertising efforts can be directed to the best prospects.
4. Assist in planning and carrying out a public relations program.

The advertising program must be planned objectively by setting forth specific, achievable goals. The advertising agency can help to establish such goals. When seeking the services of an advertising agency, look at the agency's experience in promoting tourism, and check the agency's past advertising campaigns and clients to determine the campaigns' effectiveness.

**The Advertising Budget**   No magic formula exists for setting the advertising budget. How much to spend is always a perplexing question. Commonly used methods include a percentage of last year's sales, a percentage of potential sales, or the industry percentage. These methods are all flawed because advertising should create sales and cause things to happen, not react to what has happened in the past or in other companies. Consequently, the best method of setting advertising budgets is to determine the objectives to be performed and allocate the proper amount to reach these objectives.

Promoting a new tourist destination area will require more money than will promoting one with an established clientele. The specific amount to budget for advertising and sales promotion will depend on each situation. However, as a rule of thumb most resorts spend about 3 percent of sales on media advertising and about 3 percent on other sales promotion activities.

No matter what expenditures are, efforts should be made to coordinate the promotion program so it is consistent with the product offered and consumer expectations will be met. Word of mouth is the least expensive, most convincing form of personal advertising. A friendly and capable host encourages this type of communication. Visitors who are treated as very important persons will not only come back, they will recommend the area to their friends. All facilities, services, hospitality, and pricing policies must be directed to this one goal—a satisfied, happy visitor.

*Research*   Successful tourism marketing depends in large part on research. Tourism promotion efforts undirected by research are largely wasted effort. Unless the following characteristics are known, advertising expenditures cannot be productive:

1.  Who are the present visitors and where do they live?
2.  What do you know about their likes and dislikes?
3.  Who are your potential customers and where do they live?
4.  What are their travel and vacation preferences and interests?
5.  What are your visitors' travel destination preferences?
6.  What are your visitors' preferences for shopping and entertainment?
7.  What is your competitive situation?
8.  What are the trends in competition?
9.  What are the likely future trends in your share of the market?
10. What are the prospects for increasing demand for your area?
11. What kind(s) of marketing program(s) appears to be needed?
12. How will these programs be implemented?

Carefully review questions of this kind; adequate answers to them are obtained only through research.

Market research can be classified into three main categories: geographic market orientation (where present and potential visitors reside), demographic market orientation (age, sex, levels of education, income, population distribution, family status, and similar data), and psychographic market orientation (motivations, interest, hobbies, responsiveness to advertising, and propensity to travel). Guidance of the subsequent marketing program will rest largely on the results of such research and the success of the marketing upon the adequacy of the research. See Chapter 11 for methods of conducting tourism research.

*Personal Selling* Personal selling is the most used and oldest method of creating demand. Because it is adaptable to the prospect, it is the most compelling and effective type of selling. In contrast to advertising, which is the impersonal component in the promotional mix, personal selling consists of individual, personal communication. The U.S. economy depends on salespeople; there are over 10 million compared to about 400,000 working in advertising. In many companies, personal selling is the largest operating expense item, ranging from about 8 to 15 percent of sales. Expenditures for salespersons' compensation, expenses, training, and supervision and the cost of operating sales offices make management of the sales force an important task.

Personal selling is so widely used because it offers maximum flexibility. Sales representatives tailor their presentation to each individual customer. They can tell which approaches are working and which are not and adjust accordingly. Prospects can be identified so target market customers are approached and efforts are not wasted.

Counterbalancing these advantages is the fact that personal selling is the most expensive means of making contact with prospects, and productivity gains are unlikely. Another limitation is that it is not always possible to hire the caliber of person needed for the sales job.

Because of the importance of personal selling, all staff should be sales-minded.

Cheerful, friendly employees are an important part of the selling process. (Photo courtesy of Delta Airlines)

All salespeople must be trained to offer sales suggestions to prospects when opportunities present themselves. This includes expert selling on the telephone as well as the telephone receptionist, who can create a favorable image for a resort. Inquiries can often be the opening for a polite and skillful sales effort. Obviously, an unfriendly manner can discourage customers and sales.

*Public Relations*  Public relations may be defined as an attitude—a "social conscience" that places first priority on the public interest when making any decisions. Public relations permeates an entire organization, covering relations with many publics: visitors, the community, employees, and suppliers.

Acceptance of any tourist destination by the public is of utmost importance. No business is more concerned with human relations than is tourism, and all public interests must be served. Serving one group at the expense of another is not sound public relations. Furthermore, each individual business manager and the group he or she represents must be respected and have the confidence of the community. There is no difference between a personal reputation and a business reputation.

Favorable public relations within the firm emphasize respect for people. Employees must have reasonable security in their jobs and be treated with consideration. Externally, tourism employees have a powerful influence on the public as they represent the owners in the public's eye. Employees should be trained to be courteous, respectful, and helpful to guests. Little things make a big difference, and the attitude of employees can make or break a public relations effort.

Considerations for the public relations effort include being aware of public

Pictures and press releases are an integral part of public relations. This photo distributed by the South Dakota Department of Tourism features Mount Rushmore, site of the world's most famous mountain carving.

The handicapped comprise a market segment that has special
needs and numbers 37 million. A number of travel agencies have
identified this segment as a target market they wish to serve and
specialize in meeting its needs. (Photo by Fred Marvel, courtesy of
Oklahoma Tourism Department)

attitudes toward present policies — ask some of the visitors for feedback. Communication is the lifeblood of good relations. In publicizing the firm, first do good things
and then tell the public about them. Above all, give the public factual information
about your area. False information is detrimental; you must describe conditions as
they exist.

## MARKET SEGMENTATION

The strategy of market segmentation recognizes that few vacation destination areas
are universally acceptable and desired. Therefore, rather than dissipate promotion
resources by trying to please all travelers, you should aim the promotional efforts
specifically to the wants and needs of likely prospects. One of the early steps in
marketing tourism, then, is to divide the present and potential market on the basis of
meaningful characteristics and concentrate promotion, product, and pricing efforts
on serving the most prominent portions of the market — the target markets.

An effective market strategy will determine exactly what the target markets will
be and attempt to reach only those markets. The target market is that segment of a
total potential market to which the tourism attraction would be most salable. Target
markets are defined geographically, demographically (age, income, education, race,
nationality, family size, family life cycle, gender, religion, occupation), or psycho-
graphically (values, motivations, interests, attitudes, desires). See Figure 13.4.

Once target markets have been determined, appropriate media are chosen to
reach these markets. For example, if tennis players are a target market, advertising in
tennis magazines would give comprehensive coverage of this market. This would be

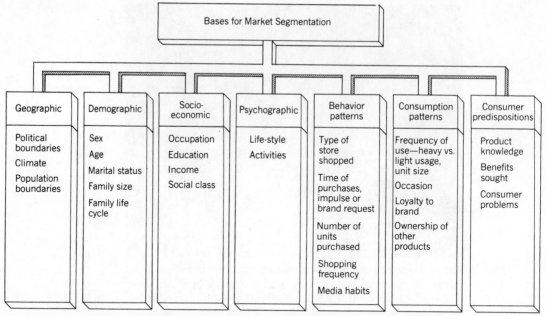

**Figure 13.4** Typical Bases for Market Segmentation. *Source:* Zikmund and D'Amico, *Marketing,* copyright © 1984, John Wiley & Sons, Inc., New York; adapted by permission of Prentice-Hall, Inc., Englewood Cliffs, N.J., from Philip Kotler, *Principles of Marketing,* copyright © 1980, p. 297.

using a "rifle approach" to zero in exactly on the market in which you are interested. In contrast, a "shotgun approach" would be to advertise in *Time* magazine, which would reach only a small number of your target market and result in large waste circulation.

Market segmentation must be employed in the marketing programs if a shotgun approach is to be avoided. Every tourism attraction can appeal to a multitude of market segments, and market segments can overlap a great deal. The marketing manager must look at market segments and determine which ones offer the most promising potential for his or her services. An excellent example of target marketing to a particular segment is provided by the LaQuinta Motor Inns, headquartered in San Antonio and now the world's twenty-fourth largest hotel chain and still expanding. The product was designed to appeal to the business traveler with a moderate price and an attractive room. LaQuinta has been very successful in attracting this market segment.

Tourist resorts typically segment in a variety of ways. One of the most common is geographic. Here the segments tend to be destination visitors (those visitors traveling long distances to vacation at the resort), regional visitors (those who live within the region of the resort and can arrive within four hours' driving time), and local residents.

Proximity of the destination area to the market is an important factor. Generally, the nearer the tourist destination is to its major market, the more likely it is to attract large numbers of visitors. For example, Boblo Island is just a few miles from Detroit and may be reached by excursion boat. As might be expected, this vacation destination receives many times the number of visitors from the greater Detroit area than does Bermuda or the Bahamas.

It follows then that the prime target area for promotion of any given tourist destination area will be that area of greatest population density nearest the vacation area. In the United States, the best concentration of markets for tourism promotion are the metropolitan statistical areas (MSAs), formerly called standard metropolitan statistical areas (SMSAs). These are defined by the U.S. Bureau of Census as a county or group of contiguous counties containing at least one city of 50,000 inhabitants or more. An authoritative source of market data concerning these areas is found in *Survey of Buying Power* published by Sales and Marketing Management, 633 Third Avenue, New York, N.Y. 10017.

Demographics also provide good segmentation variables. Age groups are an excellent example. Many demographic characteristics were presented in Chapter 12 on Consumer Markets and can form the basis for determining profitable market segments.

### Psychographic Market Segmentation

As marketing becomes more competitive, many marketing managers wish to go beyond geographic and demographic variables as a way of describing consumers. They will use motivation research, psychographics, or life-style analysis. William D. Wells, in his paper "Life Styles in Selecting Media for Travel Advertising,"[2] presented at the third annual conference of the Travel and Tourism Research Association, offered the following interesting concepts:

Using computerized cluster analysis, marketers produce life-style segments that take into consideration simultaneously all of the answers to questions about respondents' activities, interests, beliefs, perceptions, values, and needs. One of the earliest attempts at cluster analysis of life-style data produced consumer groups with names like the Self-indulgent Pleasure Seeker, the Active Achiever, the Business Executive, the Blue-Collar Worker, and the Traditional Homebody.

**The Self-Indulgent Pleasure Seeker's** responses to the life-style questions show that he is a young man with a routine, uninteresting job. His chief satisfactions come from real and imagined action and adventure out of doors. He likes hunting, fishing, baseball, and expensive, powerful cars. He has a good income, but he is an impulse buyer and a heavy user of credit, so he is always short of cash. He does not make long-range plans. He is not very interested in any of the print media, but he is a heavy viewer of sports and of action and adventure programs on TV.

**The Active Achiever** combines ability and energy in pursuit of upward mobility. He is interested in his job, liberal and contemporary in his opinions on many subjects, sure of his skills, and sure of himself. He seeks new experiences of many kinds, including sailing, skiing, and foreign travel. He reads magazines that keep him abreast of current events and the latest trends in popular culture. He watches sports programs, talk shows, and news analysis on TV.

[2] The Travel Research Association, *The Values of Travel Research: Planning, Techniques, Applications* (Salt Lake City: TTRA, 1972), pp. 63–74.

**The Business Executive** is, in a sense, the Active Achiever who has "arrived." Considerably more affluent than the Active Achiever, he has the discretionary funds to allow him to purchase club memberships, expensive vacations, second homes. He is also less geographically mobile than the Active Achiever, having now settled down more or less permanently with a completed family. He is a reader of business magazines and news magazines, and a viewer of news and news analysis, travel specials, and nature specials on TV.

**The Blue-Collar Worker** is to be found in small towns and in the industrial suburbs of big cities. He has very strong beliefs in conventional values, including the primacy of patriotism, morality, and hard work. His idea of a fine vacation is to take the family camping. He likes to hunt and fish. On television, he would rather watch bowling or pro football than tennis or golf.

**The Traditional Homebody's** main problem is maintaining his equilibrium in the face of a rapidly changing world. He admits he is old-fashioned, and he wishes everyone else would be that way too. He tries hard to wring the greatest value from every dollar he spends. He avoids anything that is fancy, frivolous, risky, or extravagant, and he is dead set against going into debt. With his wife, he is the backbone of the TV situation comedy audience. His major source of information about national and world events is the TV early evening news.

Again, it is possible only to skim the surface of what such data have to offer, but it should be obvious, from even these thumbnail sketches, that life-style segments revealed by cluster analysis have dramatically different sets of needs and values. Each segment represents a prime market for a special travel package. Demographic data specify each segment's physical and financial capacities and limitations. Life-style data show what each segment wants and needs. Data on media habits show how each segment can best be reached.

While this analysis has obviously been conducted on males, the concept is equally applicable to females.

In an effort to improve the economic impact of tourism, the Michigan Travel Bureau performed a market segmentation study on the state's tourism industry. A consumer survey conducted in Michigan, five adjacent states, and Ontario, Canada, produced new attitudinal and behavioral data. From this data six vacation activities preference types were developed on the basis of factor analysis.

These were noninclusive groups; that is, an individual could belong to more than one of the types. For communication purposes, they were given names descriptive of the kinds of activities they liked to do on vacation. The types are illustrated in Figure 13.5 with the activities which ranked highest on the factors that described them: young sports, outdoorsman/hunter, winter/water, resort, sightseer, and nightlife activities.

The market segmentation study pointed out the segments not being reached and demonstrated where advertising should be increased or introduced. Strategies were developed and implemented, resulting in a 12 percent growth in the state's tourist industry.

A popular segmentation system used today is VALS, which stands for Values, Attitudes, and Life-styles and was developed by SRI International. Its use as a tool

**YOUNG SPORTS TYPE**

Bicycling
Canoeing
Camping
Hiking
Horseback Riding
Swimming
Tennis

**OUTDOORSMAN HUNTER**

Power boating
Fishing
Hunting
Ice fishing
Snowmobiling

**WINTER/WATER TYPE**

Sailing
Canoeing
Snow skiing
Snowmobiling
Tennis
Water skiing

**RESORT TYPE**

Golf
Tennis
Casino gambling

**SIGHTSEER TYPE**

Seeing natural resources
Seeing historical sites
Culture-concerts/plays
    art shows
Man-made attractions
Museums
Special festivals

**NIGHTLIFE ACTIVITIES**

Professional sports
Major amusement parks
Man-made attractions
Nightclubs & restaurants
Casino gambling

**Figure 13.5** Vacation Activity Preference Types.

for tourism market research in Pennsylvania has been reported by David Shih.[3] Mr. Shih, of the Pennsylvania Department of Commerce, reports:

The basis of the Value and Life-style Program is the VALS typology. It divides Americans into nine life-styles or types, which are grouped in four categories based on their self-images, their aspirations, their values and beliefs, and the products they use. The four categories and nine life-styles are the following:

[3] David Shih, "VALS as a Tool of Tourism Market Research: The Pennsylvania Experience," *Journal of Travel Research*, Vol. 24, no. 4 (Spring 1986), pp. 2–11.

- Need-driven groups
  Survivor life-style
  Sustainer life-style
- Outer-directed groups
  Belongers life-style
  Emulator life-style
  Achiever life-style
- Inner-directed groups
  I-am-me life-style
  Experiential life-style
  Societally conscious life-style
- Combined outer- and inner-directed group
  Integrated life-style

The VALS program can be a useful tool for tourism marketing. Life-style variables reveal something beyond demographics and are real, meaningful, and relevant. The key VALS segments — belongers, achievers, and the societally conscious — provide valuable information about market segmentation, advertising copy appeals, and media selection.

VALS research conducted in Pennsylvania substantiates the "friendly people" theme as an effective message for the state. Overall, no radical change is indicated in the Pennsylvania tourism campaign's creative approach. However, an objective should be to strengthen the "belonger" base traveling to Pennsylvania, while at the same time to attract more achievers and societally conscious persons. Also, in-state TV advertising should be continued, and additional print advertising in appropriate publications is warranted to attract the achievers and the societally conscious.

One thing that can be counted on in marketing is change; consequently, Standard Research International has come up with a new VALS 2, see Figure 13.6. The nine original VALS psychographic segments have been replaced by eight new psychographic groups. The eight VALS 2 groups and some of their characteristics are

- *Actualizers*  Have highest incomes, high self-esteem, abundant resources. Consumer choices are directed toward "the finer things in life."
- *Fulfilleds*  Mature, responsible, well-educated professionals, open to new ideas. High-income, practical, value-oriented consumers.
- *Achievers*  Successful, work-oriented, receive satisfaction from jobs and family. Favor established products.
- *Experiencers*  Youngest of segments, median age of 25. Seek variety and excitement. Avid consumers spending on clothing, fast food, music, and other youthful favorites.
- *Believers*  Lives centered on family, church, community, and nation. Conservative and predictable consumers who favor American products and established brands.
- *Strivers*  Have values of achievers but few resources. Style is important as they strive to emulate the people they wish they were.
- *Makers*  Practical people who value self-sufficiency. They focus on the familiar.
- *Strugglers*  Have lowest incomes. Lives are constricted. Within means tend to be brand-loyal consumers.

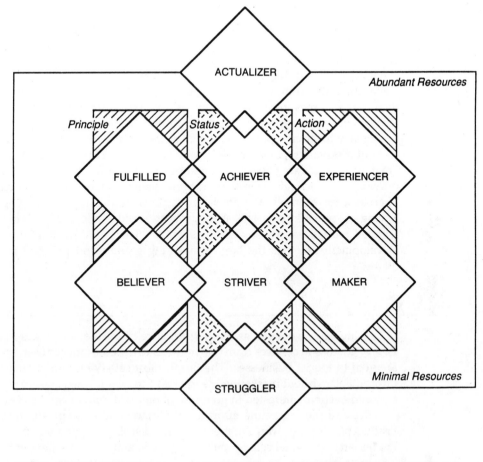

**Figure 13.6** The VALS™ 2 Segmentation System, developed by the Values and Lifestyles Program at SRI International, is a new psychographic system for segmenting American consumers and predicting consumer behavior. *Source:* SRI International.

## JOINT MARKETING EFFORTS

In the majority of cases, a tourism organization will want to market its product and services individually; however, in other cases, joint cooperative efforts will be the most profitable. Typically these efforts are launched through associations or government agencies. Colorado Ski Country, USA, and the Utah Ski Association are groups that jointly promote the services of their members, many of whom are in competition with each other. Publishing posters and directories, answering inquiries, and providing snow reports promote the industry in the most cost-effective way. In addition to these joint marketing efforts, the areas have their own individual marketing programs. They may also work with other private firms such as airlines, rental car companies, and credit card firms to stretch their marketing dollars.

Experience to date has shown that tourism promotion on a country or state basis is best accomplished by a cooperative effort of private industry and government. Joint promotion by private interests and official government tourist organizations is an effective and efficient procedure. One of the best examples of the pooling of private and government funds is the Hawaii Visitors Bureau, an independent non-profit organization that conducts tourism promotion under contract with the State Department of Planning and Economic Development. Approximately one-third of the funding comes from private sources and two-thirds from state sources.

In some states, specific "matching funds" are provided by a government tourism agency for tourist promotion, such as the provision of a portion of advertising costs of a private regional tourist promotion association. Various combinations of "matched" funds are possible, depending on the amount of funds available and the provisions of the legislation that authorizes such expenditures of public funds. In Michigan, for example, the official government tourism promotion agency is the Michigan Travel Bureau. This agency is authorized to allocate funds to each of four regional tourist associations within the state. The Pennsylvania Bureau of Travel Development operates the largest matching grants fund program in the United States.

## SUMMARY

Marketing can be defined as the performance of business activities that direct the flow of goods and services from the producer to the consumer or user. Such activities are vital to tourist businesses. The finest, most satisfying tourist facility would be unprofitable without marketing. People have to be informed about a travel destination and become interested in going there before a market can be created.

Basic to the marketing effort are the marketing concept, the marketing mix, product planning and development, pricing, distribution channels, promotion, market research, personal selling, public relations, and market segmentation.

Joint marketing efforts among official tourism organizations, public carriers, and providers of accommodations or even with nearby competing destination areas are strategically sound and typically successful.

### About the Readings

The first reading presents a short case example of the use of tourist promotion by a small city. Traverse City, Michigan, has grown to national prominence through good tourism planning and successful promotion. This reading covers the highlights of that effort.

The second reading deals with promotion and describes how to develop a promotional plan to achieve a marketing objective.

## READING 13-1

### *Successful Tourism Promotion — The Case of Traverse City, Michigan*

In 1984 Traverse City was designated as an "All-America City" by the National Municipal League — one of only nine so honored in the United States. Also, with its population of 15,516, it was the smallest city so honored. The five-county area surrounding the city has a population of about 58,000.

What is the allure of this area? What marketing methods are used to attract an average of about 100,000 visitors each day during the summer season and a substantial number during other seasons of the year?

First the community of Traverse City appeals to its residents. One resident stated, "Traverse City has a spiritual pull of some kind. Its beauty entrances you and makes you want to stay. To me, it's a fantastic town. It's a real 'can do' place. There's a positive attitude, the quality of life is great, and the people are tremendous. The physical beauty can't be beat. Everything looks good and crisp and clean. It's a great place to live."

Second, several miles of the main highway skirt both Grand Traverse Bays (of Lake Michigan), so that passing motorists can't help but see and admire the community's natural setting. Finally, Traverse City is a center for medical and hospital services, oil production, food processing (mainly cherry and bakery products), boating, golf, cultural events, and winter sports. There are numerous government offices, and retirees often choose the community as a place to live.

*Tourism Promotion Problems Identified—Partially Solved*

The evolution of good tourism promotion since the 1950s has brought about a solution to a major problem—myopia in individual business promotion. Now, businesses do not promote just their own interests; they also consistently advertise their geographical area as an attractive destination. This philosophy is thus a broad-based one, reflecting conviction that the destination *must* be marketed along with the individual business. An example of this is the cooperative marketing program of the five-area ski resorts. Although they are competitors under different ownership, their sales reps attend travel shows as a group. Each resort is individually promoted, of course, but skiing in the entire area is also publicized. The resorts also market a "ski free" midweek program for children during the holidays and a gold and silver ski pass honored at any of the resorts. The passes are marketed through the Chamber of Commerce and receipts are kept by the chamber to be used for ski promotion.

A problem that so far has been only partially solved is that of local people who are overly optimistic about the community's tourism success. Many feel that visitors will come regardless of the amount of effort expended to attract them, and such a philosophy is hard to change. This philosophy, when coupled with a fairly wide-spread feeling that their area should be kept secret and the sense of protectiveness that prevails, makes all-out tourism promotion difficult. A major strategy to overcome this resistance to promotion has been the creation of the Traverse City Area Convention and Visitors Bureau, which markets the area to any type of visitor, including families, groups, conventions, or tours. The bureau is financed by a small levy on local commercial lodging receipts.

*Development of Supply Components*

The most urgent continuing problem is to increase publicly owned recreational land. Most desirable is that of beaches along the two bays. Removing unsuitable structures from the waterfront areas and creating elongated parks have been major accomplishments in the past decade, and today miles of beautiful parkways attract motorists who stop to enjoy the views and are often inclined to return for a vacation.

A new boardwalk along the downtown riverside is a recent example of improving the infrastructure; this feature is enjoyed by locals as well as visitors. New resorts of the "world class" have also been built near the city. Such developments include convention facilities and adjacent condominium construction as well as golf courses and sports resources.

Increasing demand for transportation has brought about more adequate air travel services with one major airline and two regionals providing about 18 flights per day. For motorists, only two-lane highways service the area. This situation is viewed as a major limiting factor for increasing tourism.

### How Target Markets Are Decided Upon

*Geographic Considerations*   The East North Central states comprise the primary market, with emphasis on Michigan, Illinois, and Indiana.

*Psychographic Considerations*   Focus is on outdoor sports, cultural activities, and agriculture. Special promotion is devoted to the National Cherry Festival, one of the 10 top festivals in the nation. Other promotion features cherry blossoms in the spring, fishing and boating, golf, tennis, racquetball, canoeing, public beaches, rainy day activities, colored-leaf tours in fall, and winter sports. Cultural assets include an opera house, Interlochen Center for the Arts, antique shops, and indigenous arts and crafts.

*Demographic Considerations*   Efforts are made to attract all age categories and a wide range of income groups. Public parks with campgrounds as well as deluxe accommodations are featured.

The mode of transportation to be used by those who respond to marketing efforts is consistently included in advertisements. For example, air travel is emphasized in convention promotion, motorcoach in promoting group tours, and the auto for family vacations.

### A Goal-Setting Process

Two major objectives have been stated as slogans: "fill every guest room every night" and "make ski resorts year-round vacation places." To accomplish these goals, all-season community promotion is undertaken. At ski resorts, all-year operation is made possible by providing golf courses, indoor-outdoor swimming pools, and other athletic facilities; expanding numbers of guest rooms; adding more restaurants; and developing real estate such as condominiums and sale of building sites.

Along with these goals, however, is the less exciting but meaningful objective of maintaining and improving the livability of the area. The promotion people sincerely believe that this is indeed accomplished by effective tourism marketing and by increasing the amount and quality of the infrastructure and superstructure. These activities benefit not only the community's visitors, but the local inhabitants as well. Increased employment and raised standards of living are brought about by visitor spending. An added benefit is the economic impact of the construction and maintenance of these facilities, which results in increased direct or indirect incomes for all of the area's residents.

*How the Promotion Program Is Organized*

Staff members of the Traverse City Area Convention and Visitors Bureau prepare an annual marketing plan. This includes a situational analysis, goals, target markets, potential markets, programs to reach these markets, budgets, and a system of evaluation of results.

This plan is reviewed by the marketing committee with final reconsideration and approval by the board of directors.

There are three main thrusts:

1. Creating a vigorous demand for holding meetings, seminars, and conventions in their area
2. Marketing the area as a destination or stopover for motor coach tours
3. Expanding the visitor industry of family vacations, sports, festivals, cultural events, and similar activities

These programs are under the direction of two account executives who specialize in (1) group marketing and (2) vacation travel promotion.

Elements of the various programs include media selection, publicity materials, a meetings planner booklet, newspaper supplements, editorial solicitation, coordination of promotions with the Michigan Travel Bureau (official), distribution of promotional literature, and direct personal sales, including those at travel and sports shows.

Something unique is their community volunteer program in which qualified volunteers help at convention registration desks and also serve as guides for local tours.

A guiding philosophy of the bureau is that, for the most part, the Chamber of Commerce helps to create and enhance the tourism product and the bureau sells the product in the area's travel markets. The bureau is thus a strictly promotional-sales-marketing organization for tourism.

*Measuring Marketing Effectiveness*

Immediately after Labor Day, the Chamber of Commerce, in cooperation with the bureau, surveys 200 area firms to ascertain what percentage change in business was experienced in the past season compared with the previous year. These surveys have been conducted each year since 1979. The same firms are surveyed each year, which assures good continuity and comparability. Lodging places (in representative groupings) are asked to compare occupancy percentages; all other businesses compare dollar volume. Businesses are selected by category: lodging, restaurants, wholesale beverage distributors, major department stores, other retailers, campgrounds, attractions, farm markets, travel agencies, gift shops, wineries, tourist inquiries received by the chamber, and even visits to the emergency rooms of area hospitals! Results of the survey are reported to all members in the October issue of the chamber's business publication.

*Future Challenges*

A primary effort must be made to better identify potential markets. When pinpointed, how are these markets to be reached? What amounts of supply components will be needed to successfully accommodate these? Should these primary efforts be successful, how will the necessary investments in infrastructure and superstructure be attracted to the area?

The feasibility of such investments rests upon the effectiveness of tourism promotion. Thus, intelligent development and productive marketing are inseparably interchanged. They must be if satisfactory contributions to the area's economy and ways of life are to be achieved.

## READING 13-2

### *Developing the Promotional Plan*

Reprinted from *Tourism U.S.A.*, Volume III, *Marketing Tourism,* U.S. Department of Commerce.

. . . The basic procedure in the development of a promotional plan is summarized below:

- Forecast expected revenues considering the planned budget expenditures for the forecasted period.
- Clearly define the specific market target(s) to be cultivated.
- Determine the motivational factors possessed by the target market(s) which will attract them to the tourism site.
- Develop specific promotional goals.
- Develop the overall campaign theme, the "big idea" or creative strategy which will allow an integration of all the foregoing points in its implementation.
- Develop a media strategy.
- Compose and create the specific advertisements in the campaign.
- Test the effectiveness of the individual ads and the campaign itself.

The paragraphs which follow will provide a brief discussion and application of the planning procedure shown above.

#### Forecast Expected Revenues

In the absence of the sophisticated forecasting methods, even a crude estimate of the expected tourism demand will be useful. In most instances the starting point will be the history of demand for previous years. The average growth rate then can be projected into the next year.

It must be remembered, however, that the projection into the future assumes a continuation of past marketing effectiveness. By the same token any improvement in effectiveness will raise the original forecasted estimate. Most importantly, the promotional budget for the upcoming period may cause the estimate to be changed significantly. If, for example, last year's 10% increase in budget provided a 20% increase in revenues, we might assume a doubling of last year's 10% budget increase to 20% this year, might cause revenues to go up by 40% if your effectiveness remains the same. A reverse condition could also be true, however, if the budget is contracted. The important point to remember is that a simple mathematical projection of an estimate must be modified to consider the new investment you are willing to commit to a marketing or promotional plan for the forthcoming period. The modified forecast in effect, then, becomes the tourist site's overall goal.

*Specify Market Targets*

One certain way to fail is to try to please everyone. Everyone is not an equally avid tourist and therefore, everyone is not equally important as a potential tourism visitor. Markets can be defined in a number of ways. *Geographic segmentation,* for example, might allow the tourism promoter to focus on a particular city or group of cities or, perhaps, only on locations within a specified distance of the site. Similarly, the *age of tourists,* or, perhaps, the *stage in family life cycle* may provide a very good basis for market segmentation. By examining past research you might find, for example, a heavy incidence of travelers at a particular site are families with children in the 6- to 15-year-old category. Similarly, you may find that few young unmarrieds or visitors under age 25 visit that particular site.

Other segmenting bases are available which may be even superior. The major precaution must be the necessity of locating good market descriptors so that a few specific markets can be actively cultivated while others may be entirely passed over. Seldom are budgetary resources so abundant that promotion can use a shotgun approach to market development. Moreover, it is virtually impossible to write advertising copy which will motivate everyone. It is much more effective to study intensively your major market segments or a specific potential target which has a good probability of being developed.

*Determine Tourist Motivations*

Once the target market(s) has been defined, the segment(s) must be studied to discover why they travel and why they would choose to travel to your specific site. Again, it is best not to use a shotgun approach with too many appeals directed at a specific targeted segment. People who choose to visit historical attractions or communities of restored older buildings are not motivated in the same way as those who travel to man-made attractions which offer athletic activities, gambling casinos or musical shows.

The objective is to sell, for example, the mystique which is created by a site's historical importance, or the mystique of witnessing a past era. The main reason people travel is to experience a new or different environment. Modern hotel facilities may be appreciated and even play a vital part in any tourism site; however, it is not the magnet which attracts the visitor. The impetus for travel must remain focused on the benefits offered by the core attractions which provide the new or different experiences which will be enjoyed by the traveler.

*Develop Specific Promotional Goals*

Goals play an important part in developing promotional strategies. A well thought out goal should, if possible, be expressed quantitatively and should be measurable. Goals should also be expressed in terms of a given time period during which the goal should be accomplished. Goals should be written and be as specific as possible. Finally, it is generally agreed that promotional goals which are stated in terms of their communicative purposes are more realistic than expressing them in more general terms, such as expected sales or revenues.

The following, to illustrate, could be developed as communications goals:

- To create and measure the *awareness* of a particular tourism attraction in a specific market.
- To communicate a specific tourism appeal in your promotion to a specific market and then determine how many people can recall it.
- To communicate a basic campaign theme to a specific market and then determine how many people can restate the premise without aided recall.
- To communicate a particular image or try to create a particular attitude about a tourism site and then determine if the message registered in the potential prospect's mind creates the correct image.
- To promote and measure the usage of a coupon in the advertisement as a means for locating interested prospects and mailing out information.

The above are only illustrative and should be stated quantitatively and more fully. To be of value there should be a "before" and "after" measurement to determine the effectiveness of the promotion, a measurement of how effectively it produced.

### Develop the Campaign Theme

One of your promotional goals could be to increase awareness of the tourism site to targeted residents in a neighboring state which research data shows produces many travelers for you. An overall theme may be developed which will encompass this stated goal. The campaign theme is primarily an exercise in creativity and often performed by specialists at an advertising agency. To illustrate, Illinois Tourism is currently using a theme aimed at tourists in Missouri. Expressed in a musical jingle is a theme which states, "Right at your own back door is a state called Illinois." This theme in all advertisements provide a thread of continuity to the individual ads and pulls them together in a series. Using this theme the Illinois Department of Tourism points out a number of special tourism attractions in Illinois which can be reached conveniently by Missouri travelers. Each advertisement, moreover, is well planned to convey the special mystique of the individual site. It is clearly evident to most observers of these ads that each is part of an overall theme relating to Illinois tourism.

### Develop a Media Strategy

Because the market has been carefully segmented, it becomes much easier to locate effective media to channel the message. Radio stations and magazines, for example, are highly selective means of reaching specific market segments. Geographic segmentation can often be accomplished through newspapers and regional editions of magazines. Mailing lists are highly specialized in reaching particular tourist groups such as campers, historical societies, educators, and the like.

Cost efficiency will play a large part in the particular vehicle which is finally chosen. It is best expressed in terms which measure cost per target market reached.

Timing is also an important element of media strategy. Generally it is difficult to interest people in traveling when they are not inclined to do so. While the tourism season might be extended somewhat by advertising earlier in the season and/or later in the season, it would be difficult to encourage tourism in the off-season. The largest part of the budget should be placed to anticipate by a few weeks the best tourism periods.

As a concluding comment, it is recognized that certain media may be more effective than others in their special ways of presenting ads. No doubt television, because of its ability to visualize and demonstrate, is very effective in a communicative sense. On the other hand, the cost is very often prohibitive. Radio, however, cannot show a beautiful scene even though the driver and family may be traveling or vacationing at the very time a radio commercial is heard. Newspapers may offer the inducement of a travel section which helps to segment the tourism market for the newspaper and newspaper-reading tourist. On the other hand outdoor advertising, while it is not especially effective in transmitting information or major benefits, may attract attention very well and direct a traveler in the immediate area to your particular tourism site.

*Composition of Specific Advertising Copy*

Following the procedure shown above, the task of good and effective copy writing should be much easier. It is easier to write copy when you know to whom (market target) you are writing, what motivates the target market, the goals which are intended to be accomplished, the basic theme which is to be used, and the advantages and disadvantages of using specific mediums to convey the copy writer's message. All of the above influences should clearly direct the copy writer into producing more effective messages. At the copy writing stage it is again the creativity of the individual writer which dominates. The foregoing procedure will allow the copy writer to channel his/her energy and talents into producing more relevant and effective commercials.

*Test Advertising Effectiveness*

It should be obvious that if a goal-oriented approach to promotion is to be used, there must be some way to measure the degree to which those goals have been accomplished. How are you to judge your effectiveness if there are no "before" and "after" benchmarks to evaluate performance?

Promotional research is necessary in four basic areas:

- It is necessary to use research to determine the motivations, attitudes, and opinions of your potential customers.
- Once advertising copy is created it should be tested *before* it is placed in the media to determine whether there is reason to believe you have empathized with the target market, whether he understands your message as intended, and whether he draws conclusions from it which allow your goals to be accomplished.
- In most instances, it is worthwhile to investigate the demographic characteristics of the promotional vehicle being considered. It is also often worthwhile to judge the effectiveness of competing media available to you through their ability to produce inquiries, coupons for tourism brochures, and the like. The coupons or "departments written to" can be coded to help judge the effectiveness of the vehicle and the advertisement itself.
- The overall effectiveness of the campaign should be researched in order to determine the degree of accomplishment you have attained in reaching the specific communication goals spelled out early in the planning procedure.

## Key Concepts

| | |
|---|---|
| advertising | marketing mix |
| advertising agency | packaging |
| channels of distribution | place |
| consumer orientation | pricing |
| definition of marketing | product |
| demographics | product life cycle |
| four Ps | product planning and development |
| image | promotion |
| individual business-destination marketing | psychographics |
| | public relations |
| joint marketing efforts | selling |
| market research | *Survey of Buying Power* |
| market segmentation | target market |
| marketing concept | timing |

## For Review and Discussion

1. What is the marketing concept?
2. Do you regard the concept of consumer-oriented marketing as a step forward? Why or why not?
3. What are the stages in the product life cycle? What are the marketing implications of each stage?
4. What are the key factors a tourism marketing manager must consider in setting price?
5. Discuss the conditions when penetration pricing should be used. Price skimming?
6. Discuss how a tourism firm's pricing strategy may influence the promotional program.
7. How are channels of distribution selected? Using an example, explain.
8. As the manager of a tourism enterprise, what can you do when customers complain that the price of your product is too high?
9. What are the advantages and disadvantages of the various advertising media?
10. What can an advertising agency do?
11. What is the objective of advertising?
12. The cost of running an ad on the back cover of *Time* magazine is more expensive than is hiring a salesperson for a year. As the marketing manager for a leading hotel chain, you have just been told by the president of the company to eliminate ads and hire more salespersons. You feel that this would be a serious mistake. What would you do to change the president's mind?
13. What are some examples of realistic objectives of a tourism marketing program? Use a resort hotel, a motorcoach, and a tour company.
14. Explain the statement "tourism promotion efforts undirected by research are largely a waste of effort." Do you agree?
15. What are the advantages of marketing vacation packages?

16. Give an example of a vacation package that might be marketed in your area. How would you market it? To whom?
17. What value do you see in market segmentation? Give an example.
18. If you were a hotel manager in a resort community, how would you use the marketing concept? Give details.
19. You are the assistant vice-president for marketing of a regional airline. Your current target market is youth. Give the marketing mix you would propose to your boss.
20. As the planner of a new wing on your resort hotel, how does product planning and development in a marketing context apply?
21. You are a restaurant manager in a popular year-round resort area. How do you decide on the price levels of your meals?
22. As a tour operator you are trying to improve the distribution system for marketing your tours. How might this be done?
23. What kind of advertising program is best for a cruise company?
24. As president of your local convention and visitors bureau, propose a joint marketing scheme that would have surefire results.
25. As a resort hotel manager, would you *always* advertise your destination area along with your individual resort property? Explain why or why not.

## Case Problem

A Midwest lakeshore community is economically depressed. By 1989 industrial employment had fallen to 50 percent of its 1970 level. Tourism seems to be a logical industry to expand. The county has 25 miles of beautiful Lake Michigan sandy beaches and is adjacent to a 1.5 million-acre national forest. The forest has many fine rivers and inland lakes, offering bountiful year-round recreation. This area is only about a five hours' drive from Chicago or Detroit and has thrice-daily air service from Chicago.

The chamber of commerce has virtually no budget for tourist promotion. State law authorizes an added 2 percent local tourism promotion tax to the 4 percent state rooms tax. However, enacting the added tax must be approved by local lodging establishments. Vote is apportioned by number of rooms owned. Managers of the two larger motels are in favor of the tax, but they suspect that the smaller motel owners will not collect all or part of the tax, lowering their room rates proportionally and creating a price advantage over the honest larger motels. Added tourism is greatly needed to stimulate the local economy. How can this impasse be resolved?

## Selected References

Abbey, James R. *Hospitality Sales and Advertising.* East Lansing, Mich.: The Educational Institute of the American Hotel and Motel Association, 1989.

Burke, James F. "Computerized Management of Tourism Marketing Information." *Tourism Management,* Vol. 7, no. 4 (December 1986), pp. 279–289.

Crompton, John L., and Charles W. Lamb, Jr. *Marketing Government and Social Services.* New York: Wiley, 1986.

Davidoff, Philip G., and Doris S. Davidoff. *Sales and Marketing for Travel and Tourism.* Rapid City, S.D.: National Publishers, 1983.

Etzel, Michael J., and Russell G. Wahlers. "The Use of Requested Promotional Material by Pleasure Travelers." *Journal of Travel Research,* Vol. 23, no. 4 (Spring 1985), pp. 2–6.

Fisk, Raymond P., and Patriya S. Tansuhaj. *Services Marketing.* Chicago: American Marketing Association, 1985.

Gartner, William, and John D. Hunt. "A Method to Collect Detailed Tourist Flow Information." *Annals of Tourism Research,* Vol. 15, no. 1 (1988), pp. 159–165.

Gartrell, Richard B. *Destination Marketing for Convention and Visitor Bureaus.* Dubuque, Iowa: Kendall/Hunt, 1988.

Greene, Melvyn. *Marketing Hotels into the 90s.* London: Heinemann, 1982.

Hawkins, Donald E., Elwood L. Shafer, and James M. Rovelstad. *Tourism Marketing and Management Issues.* Washington, D.C.: George Washington University, 1980.

Harris, Godfrey, and Kenneth M. Katz. *Promoting International Tourism.* Los Angeles: The Americas Group, 1986.

Holloway, J. C., and R. V. Plant. *Marketing for Tourism.* London: Pitman, 1988.

*Journal of Travel Research,* Special Marketing Issue, Vol. 20, no. 4 (Spring 1982), 9 articles. Business Research Division, University of Colorado, Boulder, Colorado.

Lefever, Michael M., and Alistair M. Morrison. "Couponing for Profit." *The Cornell Hotel and Restaurant Administration Quarterly,* Vol. 28, no. 4 (February 1988), pp. 57–64.

Lewis, Robert C. "The Incentive Travel Market: How to Reap Your Share." *The Cornell Hotel and Restaurant Administration Quarterly,* Vol. 24, no. 1 (May 1983), pp. 19–27.

Lewis, Robert C., and Richard E. Chambers. *Marketing Leadership in Hospitality: Foundations and Practices.* New York: Von Nostrand Reinhold, 1989.

Lickorish, Leonard, and Alan Jefferson. *Marketing Tourism: A Practical Guide.* Harlow, U.K.: Longman, 1989.

Lovelock, Christopher H. *Services Marketing.* Englewood Cliffs, N.J.: Prentice-Hall, 1984.

Maas, Jane. *Better Brochures, Catalogs and Mailing Pieces.* New York: St. Martin's Press, 1981.

Mazanec, Josef A. "Allocating an Advertising Budget to International Travel Markets." *Annals of Tourism Research,* Vol. 13, no. 4 (1986), pp. 609–634.

McCarthy, E. Jerome. *Essentials of Marketing.* Homewood, Ill.: Richard D. Irwin, 1982.

McCleary, Ken W. "A Framework for National Tourism Marketing." *International Journal of Hospitality Management,* Vol. 6, no. 3, pp. 169–175.

Metelka, Charles J. "Tourism Advertising: A Window to the World, a Reflection of Ourselves?" *Hospitality Education and Research Journal,* Vol. 11, no. 3 (1987), pp. 77–81.

Meyer, Robert A. "Understanding Telemarketing for Hotels." *The Cornell Hotel and Restaurant Administration Quarterly,* Vol. 28, no. 2 (August 1987), pp. 22–26.

Middleton, Victor T. C. *Marketing in Travel and Tourism.* Oxford, England: Heinemann, 1988.

Morrison, Alastair M. *Hospitality and Travel Marketing.* Albany, N.Y.: Delmar, 1989.

Moutinho, Luiz. "Role of Budgeting in Planning, Implementing, and Monitoring Hotel Management Strategies." *International Journal of Hospitality,* Vol. 6, no. 1 (1987), pp. 15–22.

National Technical Information Service. *Psychographic Marketing.* Springfield, Va.: NTIS, 1989.

Nykiel, Ronald A. *Marketing in the Hospitality Industry.* Boston: CBI, 1983.

Peters, Clarence H. "Pre-Opening Marketing Analysis for Hotels." *The Cornell Hotel and Restaurant Administration Quarterly,* Vol. 19, no. 2 (May 1978), pp. 15–22.

Reilly, Robert T. *Travel and Tourism Marketing Techniques.* Albany, N.Y.: Delmar Publishers, 1988.

Smith, Valene L., Arlene Hetherington, and Martha D. Brumbaugh. "California's Highway 89: A Regional Tourism Model." *Annals of Tourism Research,* Vol. 13, no. 3 (1986), pp. 415–433.

Stanton, William J., and Charles Futrell. *Fundamentals of Marketing.* New York: McGraw-Hill, 1987.

Starr, Nona S. *Marketing for the Travel Industry.* Wellesley, Mass.: Institute of Certified Travel Agents, 1984.

Stevens, Peter J., and Ken W. McCleary, eds. *The Marketing of Hospitality Services.* Okemos, Mich.: Hospitality Publications, Inc., 1986.

Vladimir, Andrew. *The Complete Travel Marketing Handbook.* Lincolnwood, Ill.: NTC Business Books, 1989.

Witt, Stephen F., and Luiz Moutinho. *Tourism Marketing and Management Handbook.* London: Prentice-Hall, 1989.

Wood, Malcolm. *Tourism Marketing for the Small Business.* London: English Tourist Board, 1980.

Woodside, Arch G., and Laurence W. Jacobs. "Step Two in Benefit Segmentation: Learning the Benefits Realized by Major Travel Markets." *Journal of Travel Research,* Vol. 24, no. 1 (Summer 1985), pp. 7–13.

# PART FIVE

# Tourism Practices and Prospects

# Consumerism in the Travel Industry[1]

## LEARNING OBJECTIVES

- Recognize that travel products, like manufactured goods, are subject to consumer protection laws.
- Realize that the public's interest in consumerism has fluctuated over many years but is currently at a high level.
- Know that several different types of federal and state agencies now regulate various components of tourism.
- Understand the need, benefits, and limitations of regulations for the tour business.

## HISTORICAL DEVELOPMENT

Each year, several hundred thousand Americans have a disappointing experience because travel producers and marketers did not deliver the promised services. Unlike physical products that are offered with warranties, guarantees, service contracts, and the right to return the merchandise in the event of poor performance, the travel product, as a service, is produced and consumed at the same time. Any fault, mistake, or below-par performance is irreversible and irreparable. A person who has allocated the time and money for a trip, once departed, usually must continue, whatever the circumstances. Imagine a honeymoon couple who have reserved a suite at a secluded luxury hotel at the seaside to enjoy a carefully planned and rather expensive two weeks. Upon arrival they discover that the hotel has overbooked. Their honeymoon suite becomes a double room, close to the elevator and overlooking the backyard of the hotel. How can tourists be protected from such obviously unacceptable service performance, and how can their rights be preserved?

Today, the American consumer rightfully feels entitled to protection. Over the past two decades the demand for protection has become a comprehensive movement—consumerism—to protect the consumer from unsafe or defectively manufactured products or services or from misleading labeling, packaging, or promotion practices and to protect the environment from undue harm.

Generally, consumer dissatisfaction with products and services rises during periods of economic recession, when incomes decline and prices rise. Consumerism is least noticeable during periods of economic well-being and expansion.

[1] This chapter was prepared with the assistance of Carl Walther, California State University, Sacramento.

The history of consumerism in the United States can be divided into three distinct periods: the early 1900s, the mid-1930s, and the current period, which started in the early 1960s. This third period has been the strongest of all three, a fact well reflected in the consumer protective legislation passed since 1962. The Consumer's Bill of Rights stated four basic rights for the consumers: the right for safety, the right to be informed, the right to choose, and the right to be heard. From 1966 to 1975, extensive legislation and activity demonstrated the extent of the third movement:

- Ralph Nader published two popular books—*Designed for Death* and *Unsafe at Any Speed.*
- Nine consumer protection acts were passed:
    The Fair Packaging and Labeling Act
    The Cigarette Labeling Act
    The Child Protection Act
    The Truth in Lending Act
    The Child Protection and Toy Safety Act
    The Public Health and Smoking Act
    The Fair Credit Reporting Act
    The Consumer Goods Pricing Act
    The Magnusson-Moss Warranty Act
- The Action for Children's Television was organized.
- The Office of Consumer Affairs was established.
- The Consumer Product Safety Commission was established.
- The FTC Verification of Claims Ruling was established.

In 1969 Senator Warren Magnusson (D., Wash.) was quoted as saying that deceptive selling is the nation's most serious form of theft. Every year unscrupulous operators net more money from consumers than the combined damage from robbery, larceny, auto theft, embezzlement, and forgery. The bulk of complaints against business can be placed into four basic categories: deceptive promotion, hidden charges, poor service, and unsafe and impure products.

Although no specific act to protect travelers in general exists, the categories of complaints illustrate the potential for claims in the travel and tourism industry. A series of fires and structural failures has forced the hotel industry to deal specifically with these problems. Complaints about deceptive promotions, hidden charges, and poor service are occasionally made against the lodging, restaurant, and tour industries. But how in particular is the traveler protected against inappropriate business practices?

## Travel Industry Regulations

Some legislation does exist governing the practices of various industries that make up the tourist industry. Air travel is controlled by both the Department of Transportation and the Federal Aviation Administration. Ship travel is regulated by the Federal Maritime Commission. Bus and rail travel are governed by the Interstate Commerce Commission. The lodging and restaurant industries are regulated by federal, state, and local law. Various industry organizations such as the U.S. Tour

Operators Association, American Society of Travel Agents, the National Tour Association, and the American Hotel and Motel Association encourage and require high standards of operation. In very general terms, the Federal Trade Commission regulates unfair trade practices in the travel and tourist industry.

Although a fair amount of regulation of the various components of the tourism industry protects the tourist, much of the regulatory protection is very broad and imprecise. Even worse, the existing protective regulation does not provide for easy or inexpensive legal procedures to enforce the tourist's rights. Also the existing regulation ceases when travel is across state or national borders or when the tour ingredients, such as lodging and transportation, are assembled in a package and offered as a new product entity (for example, a fully inclusive, packaged vacation tour).

The package tour business in the United States has grown in a period of less than 30 years into a sizable industry. In 1983, 200 million people participated in tours and spent over $10 billion. If the development and success of the European tour industry is any indication of the future growth potential of this industry in the United States (and there is reason to believe it is), the outlook for the package tour industry is bright.

At the same time the consumer movement has not bypassed the travel industry. In a typical year, about 5 percent of the tourists have problems and file complaints regarding inadequate services provided. The number of dissatisfied travelers is probably significantly larger. Because no specific protective legislation exists, there have been suggestions for the need of such regulation. The comptroller general in his report to the U.S. Congress in 1979 clearly expressed this need and made recommendations for future regulation of the tour industry. An analysis of the proposed regulation follows.

## ANALYSIS OF CONSUMER COMPLAINTS

According to the study done by the comptroller general,[2] complaints in the tour industry fall into four broad categories.

### Failure to Provide Advertised Items

The bulk of all complaints, 36 percent, fall into this category. The difference between what is promised and what is delivered may range from partially to wholly unacceptable. Minor unacceptable experiences would include not receiving daily breakfast or promised flowers. Totally unacceptable would be transportation to the wrong destination. Envision the buyer of a packaged tour to the Super Bowl who fails to receive his admission tickets to the game. Refunding money or other attempts to remedy such a situation are ineffective; the travel product is perishable instantaneously.

[2] *Report to the Congress of the United States, Protecting Consumer Rights in the Tour Industry: Who Is Responsible?* The U.S. General Accounting Office, Distribution Section, Room 1518, 441 G Street N.W., Washington, D.C. 20548 (1979).

When travel expectations are met, happy, satisfied consumers result. (Photo courtesy of Royal Cruise Line)

## Lack of Notification of Change

This is the second most frequent complaint category. Unnotified changes range from minor to major changes. Typical unnotified minor changes are changing departure or arrival points, or days or time, or changes in the class or location of the hotel at the destination. A change of major significance might be eliminating Turkey from a Greece/Turkey program and substituting Israel for it. In all complaints, notification was given too late—at boarding of the airplane or not at all.

## Omission of Significant Information

The consumer decision as to which travel service to purchase is very complicated; unlike shelf products, the object of purchase cannot be visually and physically inspected. The consumer tries to make an intelligent choice from several packages of similar nature and must decide between a tour package and the option of traveling independently and buying all ingredients separately. The prospective traveler therefore must have appropriate information to make the best choice. A typical complaint is that the inquirer did not receive the appropriate information and did not know that a less appealing, off-beach hotel would be substituted for the beach hotel pictured. Often the consumer is not informed that the destination and departure city are uncertain and subject to change or that the price of the tour package is subject to change. Often no instructions are provided as to how information is to be received regarding trip changes.

Clearly, if changes occur after the consumer has made a decision, these changes may very well make the decision appear inferior to other original options. Further, if no information is received about the changes, then the gap between the expected and the realized service level increases, leaving a dissatisfied traveler with an unsatisfactory travel experience.

### Limitations of Liability for Changes

Travel brochures in most cases are the only form of printed information about the tour package, its features, and its conditions. Brochures should contain a clear statement about the limitations of liability of the tour company. After all, the tour consists of the services of many suppliers, many of whom are in different states or countries. Travel depends on the weather, political and economic circumstances, and human behavior, each of which may greatly affect the success of a planned trip. In many instances, the tour company is not directly at fault if changes from the original schedule occur. Travelers' complaints with respect to liability clauses were that they were phrased too broadly, were unreadable (in fine print), and were so narrow that tour operators excluded themselves from almost any liability.

Consumers are irritated by unreasonably narrow limitations of liability and are often discouraged from actively ascertaining their rights. A printed disclaimer can be very powerful and persuasive, thus contributing to the failure to report a claim.

## THE CHARACTERISTICS OF THE TOUR INDUSTRY

Many of the present complaints may be justified and are either directly or indirectly caused by inappropriate business practices. A tour wholesaler (for the present discussion no distinction is made between a tour wholesaler and tour operator) is by definition a business entity engaged in the planning, preparation, marketing, making of reservations, and operation of a vacation tour. Such tours consist of some form of transportation, with other individual ground services included. There is a date or series of dates for departure to a specific destination at predetermined prices. The tour wholesaler assembles the components but typically does not produce any of the service ingredients except sometimes the tour escort. The four categories of complaints discussed earlier can be attributed either directly to the faulty planning and organization of the tour or indirectly to the delivery of unsatisfactory service provided by third parties, called suppliers. In the long run, however, the tour wholesalers can control the quality of these services by choosing reputable suppliers.

The increasing number of complaints in the tour industry seems to be caused by two factors. First, within the context of the current wave of consumerism, the American traveler is becoming more price and value conscious. Today's budget-constrained travelers are more inclined to insist on their rights, thus increasing the number of complaints.

Second, reputable and well-established firms are more likely to offer satisfactory products to their customers than are poorly managed firms. Over the last decade the package tour industry has been growing significantly, and the expansion of demand for tours has led new, inexperienced firms to enter the tour industry. The

Good employee performance keeps complaints at a minimum.
(Photo courtesy of National Car Rental)

tour industry appears very attractive to newcomers; the initial capital requirements
are low, and the return on equity is high compared with that in other industries.
Thus, the rising number of complaints may partly be attributable to increased participation of tour companies that are less experienced and resourceful. Although reputable and well-established tour companies have grown with the rising demand for
package tours, the market share of newer companies has increased proportionately
to the total supply and probably contributed to the increase in the number of

Quality food, outstanding service, and good entertainment keep
consumers smiling rather than complaining. (Photo courtesy of
Florida Division of Tourism)

dissatisfied customers. If satisfaction cannot be delivered by the tour industry, it is likely that consumers will demand some kind of protection.

## TOUR INDUSTRY REGULATION

Regulation of the tour industry is intended to help assure that the marketing and sale of tours or particular components of a tour meet or exceed widely accepted industry standards and practices. The consequences of a failure to do so would be twofold. First, an increasing number of complaints would damage the reputation of the tour industry—both well-established and reputable tour companies as well as less acceptable ones. Thus, the demand for tours overall would suffer. Second, at a certain point, drastic regulation would be enacted that would stifle the development of a creative, innovative, and healthy industry.

### Forms of Regulation

Regulation in the industry can be directed toward two purposes—prevention and correction. Regulation to help assure that the business practices of tour companies are of high standard and that the travel product offered is of high quality may be called preventive regulation. Regulation providing a mechanism to assure that the rights of the tourist are preserved and that the tourist receives adequate compensation in the case of error or mistreatment may be called corrective or remedy regulation. See Figure 14.1. Both types could be accomplished by legislation or self-regulation.

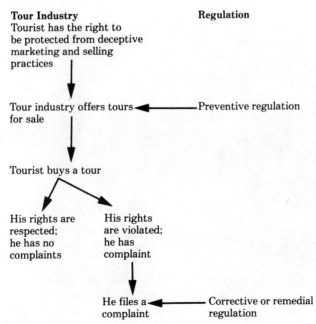

**Figure 14.1** Tour Company Regulation Procedures.

As pointed out earlier, current regulation is either very broad or exists only for transportation companies and other individual suppliers. Unclear responsibilities and no specific regulations for tour companies represent a regulatory gap. The key question is: Would the consumer be better off with or without regulation? Various regulatory alternatives have been proposed, including extension of agency controls (DOT, ICC, etc.) to cover the tour industry. Another suggestion has been to have each state develop its own regulations of the tour industry.

For example, California passed a "travel promoters" law which took effect January 1, 1989. Under the law, a travel promoter is defined as anyone who "sells, provides, furnishes, contracts for, arranges or advertises" air or sea transportation without airline or cruise line appointments. Travel promoters are required to register, pay a $50 annual fee, maintain a trust account, and submit discount certificates to the attorney general for review.

A third alternative is that the tour industry regulate itself, establishing a consumer protection trust fund to provide arbitration of consumer claims against tour operators and necessary compensation payments to consumers. A final proposal might be to pass legislation giving the Federal Trade Commission the primary responsibility to set standards and enforce fair trade practices in the tour industry.

The proposed tour industry self-regulation and establishment of a consumer protection trust fund would fall into the category of corrective or remedial regulation. Extended responsibility for the FTC to enforce standards and fair trade practices would represent preventive regulation (refer to Figure 14.1). Perhaps an ideal solution would be a combination of both proposals. In fact, in 1979 the comptroller general recommended in his report to the Congress a combination of industry self-regulation and FTC responsibility to set standards and enforce trade practices. Decisions have yet to be made and implemented.

Productive and efficient employees who deliver accurate travel documents prevent complaints. (Photo courtesy of Delta Airlines)

The strongest voice for self-regulation is that of the United States Tour Operators Association. In the foreword to a recent publication, *Ethics in U.S. Tour Operations, Standards for Integrity,* this organization contends that "substantial need does not exist for any such regulation" and suggested instead that both the government and the industry should encourage adherence to an industry-developed program of performance standards for operators and other suppliers. In 1978 the USTOA appointed a special ad hoc committee to produce a definitive industry-developed, realistically practicable compendium of *The Ethics in U.S. Tour Operations/Standards for Integrity.* All of the data produced by the committee were given to Jack Yohe, former consumer advocate of the CAB, to harmonize the contents for final production. Active members of the USTOA have now pledged to adhere to these ethics and standards; adherence has been made a requirement of continuous membership in the organization.

Mr. Yohe, in commenting on this achievement, stated, "The USTOA members have gone and continue to go a long way in presenting a face of responsibility to the consumer public. Not only do they work constantly at maintaining and honoring their own ethical standards and knowledge of their industry, but also they go beyond the limits of their own responsibility; they spell out for the consumer his or her duties and responsibilities. And that makes for informed consumers."[3]

The tour operator's code follows:

## Principles of Professional Conduct and Ethics

1. It is the responsibility of Active and Affiliated Active Tour Operator Members of the United States Tour Operators Association (USTOA) to conduct their business affairs forthrightly, with professional competence and factual accuracy.
2. Representations to the public and retailers shall be truthful, explicit, and intelligible and avoid deception and concealment or obscuring of material facts, conditions, or requirements.
3. In advertising and quoting of prices for tours, the total deliverable price, including service charges and special charges, shall be stated or clearly and readily determinable, and the pendency of any known condition or contingency, such as fares subject to Conference and/or Government approval, shall be openly and noticeably disclosed.
4. Advertising and explanation of tour features shall clearly state and identify the facilities, accommodations, and services included; any substitutions of features or deviation from the advertised tour shall be communicated expeditiously and the cause thereof be explained to agents and/or clients involved.
5. Each Active and Affiliated Active Tour Operator Member of USTOA shall so arrange and conduct its business as to instill retailer, consumer, and public confidence in such Member's financial stability, reliability, and integrity and shall avoid any conduct or action conducive to discrediting membership in USTOA as signifying allegiance to professional and financial "Integrity in Tourism."

[3] *Ethics in U.S. Tour Operations, Standards for Integrity* is published by the U.S. Tour Operators Association (1982). It spells out in detail what the tour industry feels are the responsibilities and ethics of the tour operator, tour components, retail travel agents, and the consumer. This organization is located at 211 East 51st Street (Suite 4b), New York, N.Y. 10022.

The National Tour Association (NTA) is equally concerned with the operating practices and ethics of its members. The members of NTA have adopted the following ethical standards and guidelines for conduct to promote and maintain high standards of public service so that the public can have confidence in the integrity of NTA, and its members, and that the motorcoach industry will serve the public interest.

**Ethical Standard No. 1:**  Each member should obey all laws and regulations and should avoid any conduct or activity that would cause unjust harm to others.

A. In the conduct of business activities, no member should engage in any act or omission of a dishonest, deceitful, or fraudulent nature.
B. No member should allow the pursuit of financial gain or other personal benefit to interfere with the exercise of sound professional judgment and skills.

**Ethical Standard No. 2:**  Each member should seek continually to maintain and improve professional knowledge, skills, and competence.

A. Each member should keep informed on those financial and operational matters that are essential to the maintenance of the member's professional competence in assembling or furnishing the components of a tour program and providing reliable and efficient service to the tour patron.
B. Each member should endeavor to participate in educational seminars and programs that are designed to improve the level of professional competence among members.
C. Each member should assist in maintaining and raising professional standards in the motorcoach tour industry and support the development, improvement, and enforcement of such regulations and codes as will foster competence and ethical conduct on the part of all members and benefit the public.

**Ethical Standard No. 3:**  Each member should endeavor to ensure the development and marketing of sound group tour offerings.

A. Each member should develop and complete tour planning on the basis of good and reliable information and exercise selectivity in arrangements with suppliers of the components of a tour.
B. Each member should conduct business on the basis of firm and clear contracts and provide reasonable assistance for consumer satisfaction in the event of deficient performance.

**Ethical Standard No. 4:**  Each member should provide accurate and informative solicitation material.

Each member should develop solicitation material that contains sufficient information to enable the purchaser to make an informed purchasing decision.

**Ethical Standard No. 5:**  Each member should endeavor to promote public confidence in NTA's code of Ethics and respect for the integrity and reputation of those doing business in the group tour industry.

A. Each member should use the NTA logo as an emblem of the highest standards of professional conduct.

B. No member should commercially disparage the business activities of any other member of the Association.

C. Each member should assist in maintaining the integrity of the NTA Code of Ethics, should report promptly to the Association any information concerning a violation of the Code, or the Ethical Standards and Guidelines for Conduct, and, upon request, should disclose any unprivileged information concerning any alleged violation to the Association to facilitate an investigation of any such alleged violation.

NTA's Code of Ethics is shown in Figure 14.2.

## The Limits of Regulation

The advantages of consumerism and resulting legislation, and of regulation in general and in the tour industry in particular, are that the consumer enjoys more protection. Regulation leads to the elimination of undesirable marketing practices and provides for the preservation of consumers' rights. However, consumerism and the associated regulation, particularly if carried too far, can also limit choice of products, innovation, and competition, and it can create a cumbersome bureaucratic structure. The result of all this may be increased costs of doing business, increased prices to the consumers, and a more limited variety of tours from which to choose in the future.

## CONSUMER ASSISTANCE

Self-regulation is one of the most effective ways of improving industry-client relations and serving the public. The American Hotel and Motel Association operates a complaint referral service to help consumers handle problems. The American Soci-

---

**NTA CODE OF ETHICS**

**Preamble**

These established principles of professional conduct of the National Tour Association are to guide the members in their relationship to one another and the membership in its combined quality services to the traveling public.

**As a member:**

I will be guided in all activities by truth, accuracy, fairness and integrity.

I pledge loyalty to the association and agree to pursue and support its objectives.

I pledge to keep informed on the latest techniques, developments and knowledge pertinent to my professional improvement.

I will help my fellow members reach personal, corporate and professional fulfillment.

I will utilize every opportunity to enhance the public image of the group tour industry.

---

**Figure 14.2** NTA Code of Ethics.

ety of Travel Agents (ASTA) maintains a consumer affairs department that handles disputes brought to its attention by both consumers and travel agencies. They try to mediate disputes and will handle almost any kind of consumer complaint. The ASTA consumer affairs department functions much like the Better Business Bureau. The most common complaint received by the consumer affairs department is that "expectations of the tour are not met." In addition to having an active consumer affairs department, ASTA has also been a leader in developing ethical conduct. Its brochure, "Principles of Professional Conduct and Ethics," is reproduced as Reading 14-1. Finally ASTA provides items such as their "Packing Tips" brochure as a public service to consumers.

Tourism firms frequently offer consumer information aids. For example, lodging organizations publish directories and small booklets which contain advice on packing, late flights, bumping, damaged and lost baggage, renting a car, tipping, and medical care. American Express publishes information that discusses how travelers can protect themselves against credit and charge card fraud.

Many times state tourism offices, local visitor bureaus, resort associations, and chambers of commerce operate a complaint service and handle inquiries and problems of travelers.

Government agencies at all levels periodically distribute consumer education literature. The U.S. government publishes the *Consumers' Resource Handbook*, which lists agencies the consumer can seek help from.

## CONSUMER RIGHTS

Consumers of travel products and services have the same rights and protections as consumers of other products sold in the business area. While most legislation and regulation was created for other industries and is quite broad, it has some applicability to the travel industry. This is particularly true in the advertising area.

In air transportation a number of consumer rights have been established covering baggage, denied boarding, smoking, charter flights, access by the handicapped, and unfair and deceptive advertising. These are administered by the Department of Transportation. The DOT also requires the provision of detailed information to consumers about on-time performance. Congress has been debating a massive airline consumer protection bill that covers everything from baggage to bankruptcy. Although it is intended to improve service for air travelers, it is so complicated that it could actually harm consumers in a number of areas.

In regard to complaints on airline service, which can be made to the DOT, the carriers closed out 1988 with vastly improved numbers. The DOT reported its consumer complaint volume dropped 47 percent in 1988 compared with 1987, a decline from 44,857 to 23,844. In December 1988 the carriers generated only 724 gripes, the lowest monthly total in four years.

## COMPLAINING

The government has provided commonsense advice on how to resolve legitimate complaints. While it is directed at air travelers, much of the advice is applicable to other travel situations. We present this information here from the DOT to indicate the options that consumers have in resolving complaints.

When passengers comment on airline service, most airlines do listen. They analyze and keep track of the complaints and compliments they receive and use the information to determine what the public wants and to identify problem areas that need special attention. They also try to resolve individual complaints.

Like other businesses, airlines have a lot of discretion in how they respond to problems. While you do have some rights as a passenger, your demands for monetary compensation will probably be subject to negotiation, and the kind of action you get depends in large part on the way you go about complaining.

## Start with the Airline

Before you write to the DOT or some other agency for help with an air travel problem, give the airline a chance to resolve it.

As a rule, airlines have troubleshooters at the airports (they're usually called customer service representatives) who can take care of most problems on the spot. They can arrange meals and hotel rooms for stranded passengers, write checks for denied boarding compensation, arrange luggage repairs, and settle other routine claims or complaints that involve relatively small amounts of money.

If you can't resolve the problem at the airport and want to file a complaint, it's best

Surveys indicate that cruise passengers have the highest satisfaction level of vacation travelers. Delivering promised benefits and ensuring that guests have a good time are essential to producing satisfied guests and eliminating complaints. (Photo courtesy of Cruise Lines International Association)

to send a letter to the airline's consumer office. Take notes at the time the incident occurs, and jot down the names of the carrier employees with whom you dealt. Keep all of your travel documents (ticket receipts, baggage check stubs, boarding passes, etc.) as well as receipts for any out-of-pocket expenses that were incurred as a result of the mishandling. Here are some tips to help you write your letter.

- Type the letter and, if possible, limit it to one page in length.
- No matter how angry you might be, keep your letter businesslike in tone and don't exaggerate what happened. If the complaint sounds very vehement or sarcastic, you might wait a day and then consider rewriting it.
- Start by saying what reservations you held, what happened, and at which ticket office, airport, or flight the incident occurred.
- Send copies, *never* the originals, of tickets and receipts or other documents that can back up your claims.
- Include the names of any employees who were rude or made things worse, as well as anyone who might have been especially helpful.
- Don't clutter up your complaint with petty gripes that can obscure what you're really angry about.
- Let the airline know if you've suffered any special inconvenience or monetary losses.
- Say just what you expect the carrier to do to make amends. An airline may offer to settle your claim with a check or some other kind of compensation, possibly free transportation. You might want a written apology from a rude employee or reimbursement for some loss you incurred—but the airline needs to know what *you* want before it can decide what action to take.
- Be reasonable. If your demands are way out of line, your letter might earn you a polite apology and a place in the airline's crank file.

If you follow these guidelines, the airline will probably treat your complaint seriously. Your letter will help them to determine what caused your problem, as well as to suggest actions the company can take to keep the same thing from happening to other people.

## Writing to the DOT

If you want to put your complaint about an airline on record, you should write to the Consumer Affairs Division, Room 10405, Office of Community and Consumer Affairs, Department of Transportation, 400 Seventh Street S.W., Washington, D.C. 20590.

That agency will make sure your letter reaches someone at the airline who will review the way your complaint was handled and get back to you. They will also provide information about what rights you may or may not have under federal laws. If your complaint still does not produce the desired results, and if you want to pursue it, they will try to refer you to an office in your community that can help you.

If your complaint is about something you feel is a safety hazard, write to the Federal Aviation Administration:

Community and Consumer Liaison Division
APA-400
Federal Aviation Administration
800 Independence Avenue S.W.
Washington, D.C. 20591

### Local Consumer Help Programs

In most communities, there are consumer help groups that try to mediate complaints about businesses, including airlines and travel agencies.

Most state governments have a special office that investigates consumer problems and complaints. Sometimes it is a separate division in the governor's or state attorney general's office. Check your telephone book under the state government's listing.

Many cities and counties have consumer affairs departments that handle complaints. Often you can register your complaint and get information over the phone or in person.

A number of newspapers and radio or TV stations operate "Hot Lines" or "Action Lines" where individual consumers can get help. Consumer reporters, with the help of volunteers, try to mediate complaints and may report the results as a news item. The possible publicity encourages companies to take fast action on consumer problems when they are referred by the media. Some Action Lines, however, may not be able to handle every complaint they receive. They often select the most severe problems or those that are more representative of the kinds of complaints they receive.

Local consumer help offices can sometimes be helpful even when they can't persuade a company to meet your demands. This is because they are usually up to date on local small claims courts. They can tell you how to file a complaint and what documents you will need to back up your claim—and they may even provide important moral support to make you feel less nervous about taking legal action.

### Your Last Resort

If nothing else works, small claims court might be the best way for you to help yourself. Many cities have these courts to settle disputes involving relatively small amounts of money and to reduce the red tape and expense that people generally fear when they sue someone.

You can usually get the details of how to use the court in your community by contacting your city's office of consumer affairs or the clerk of court. As a rule, court costs are low, you don't need a lawyer, and the procedures are much less formal and intimidating than they are in most other types of courts.

Finally, the court can order the airline to pay you if you are able to convince the judge or arbitrator that you are entitled to compensation.

## SUMMARY

Consumerism has been a force in the United States since the early 1900s. Its force rises and falls with economic fluctuations; currently, it is at a high level. Numerous federal laws have been enacted since 1966 to protect consumers from deceptive promotion, hidden charges, poor service, and unsafe and impure products.

The tourism manager of the future will confront a growing and continuing surge of consumerism. Consumers are expecting and demanding greater value from the marketplace. As consumers continue to become more affluent, better educated, and more aware, tourism firms must improve their performance to meet consumer expectations.

Consumerism is caused by discontent; consequently, if firms are socially responsible and deliver the products and services promised, there is no need for consumers to bring pressure on government to correct business conduct thought to be unethical. If value is not received and consumers organize, legislation frequently results. Regulation has its limits, and in many cases the consumer is better off without government regulation. Self-regulation has proven to be popular with both industry and consumers.

But no amount of regulation can guarantee a happy vacation trip. Too much regulation can offset preservation of consumers' rights with higher prices, more limited choices, and less innovation and competition in the industry.

### About the Reading

ASTA is one of the world's largest travel organizations. In an attempt to bring professionalism and consumer protection to the travel industry they require their members to adhere to a code of professional conduct and ethics. This code is reproduced in its entirety in this reading.

## READING 14-1

### The ASTA Code

#### Preamble

We live in a world in which travel has become increasingly important and intricate. The travel industry is now highly specialized and travelers, faced with a myriad of alternatives as to transportation, accommodations and other travel services, must depend upon accredited travel agencies to guide them competently and honestly in the choices they must make. Similarly, carriers, hotels and other suppliers which appoint travel agencies to represent them depend upon the travel agency to follow the best traditions of salesmanship and ethical conduct. In recognizing the vital role of travel agencies, all ASTA members voluntarily pledge themselves to observe this spirit in all their activities and to conduct their business in accordance with the following Principles of Professional Conduct and Ethics.

#### Part I: Travel Agency Relations With Consumers

1. ASTA members should attempt to ascertain and inform their customers of all pertinent facts concerning tours, transportation, accommodations or other travel services offered to consumers.
2. ASTA members should be factual and accurate when called upon to give an opinion of a service provider.
3. ASTA members should endeavor to keep their employees informed in an accurate and timely manner on domestic and international travel in order to give consumers competent travel advice and to secure for them travel services and accommodations suitable to their needs and desires.
4. ASTA members should try to protect consumers against any fraud, misrepresentation or deceptive practices in the travel industry. Members should endeavor to eliminate any practices which could be damaging to consumers or to the dignity and integrity of the travel agency business.

5. ASTA members should consider every transaction with a customer to be confidential unless the person authorizes disclosure or such disclosure is required by law.

6. ASTA members should advise their customers in writing about cancellation policies and any service charges prior to the time initial payment is made for any booking.

7. ASTA members should avoid false and misleading statements and doubtful superlatives in their advertising. Phrases such as "our services are free" or "it costs no more," or words of similar import should not be used unless such statements are true.

8. ASTA members should clearly disclose to their customers their agency-principal relationship with service providers prior to the time initial payment is made. In the event of a failure by a service provider to provide a service booked through an ASTA member, the member should assist its customers in trying to reach a satisfactory settlement of the matter with the service provider.

## Part II: Travel Agency Relations With Service Providers (Carriers, Hotels, and Other Industry Members)

9. ASTA members should follow the best traditions of salesmanship and fair dealing by according fair, objective and impartial representation to all service providers which they represent.

10. ASTA members should attempt to make themselves conversant with all applicable rules and regulations of service providers. They should take appropriate steps so that their employees and representatives know of these rules.

11. ASTA members should not attempt in any illegal manner or through actions or means that violate the policies of a service provider to influence the employees of service providers for the purpose of securing preferential consideration in the assignment of space or for any other purpose.

12. ASTA members should release reserved, but unsold, space and return cancelled accommodations. Members should refrain from suggesting or making duplicate bookings or reservations.

13. ASTA members who undertake to recruit sales representatives or to franchise new locations should avoid misrepresentations and unrealistic promises in statements relating to such activities.

14. In the event of a complaint or grievance by a customer against a service provider, ASTA members should, as a first step, notify the service provider involved so that it may have an opportunity to resolve the matter.

## Part III: Travel Agency Relations With ASTA Members

15. ASTA members should share with members the lessons of their experience and study which will improve the professionalism, competence and services of all travel agencies.

16. ASTA members should so conduct their business as to try to avoid controversies with fellow members. In the event of a controversy between ASTA members, such controversy should be referred to ASTA for mediation or arbitration, where appropriate.

17. If an opinion is sought about a competitor, ASTA members should render it with professional integrity and courtesy.
18. ASTA members should not deliberately interfere with or induce the cancellation of a definite sale made by another member or otherwise cause a customer to break a contractual obligation.
19. ASTA members should not take advantage of the former affiliation of a new employee by use of unauthorized lists or records which may accompany the employee.
20. When a written complaint is lodged against an ASTA member, the member should, upon notification of the complaint, cooperate with any inquiry initiated by ASTA.
21. ASTA members should encourage and promote membership in the Society so that the entire travel industry and the public may benefit from the training, experience and high standards of ASTA members.

### Part IV: Allied Member Relations With Active Members

22. Allied members should strive to do their best to provide travel services that satisfy the needs and expectations of the public.
23. Allied members should provide travel agencies and consumers with complete and accurate information about their services, schedules and other relevant information, and give priority to informing travel agencies of any changes.
24. Allied members should inform travel agencies about their policies concerning business relationships with travel agencies and should abide by those announced policies until they have informed travel agencies of any changes.
25. Allied members should cooperate with travel agencies and ASTA in attempting to resolve consumer complaints and inquiries about services.
26. Allied members should assist travel agencies in marketing and promoting their services to the public. This marketing and promotion should be accurate in its descriptions and should avoid any misleading or false statements or pictures.
27. Allied members should stand behind any program in which their name or logo is used, with their permission, in advertising and/or promotional material.

### Conclusion

Adherence to these Principles of Professional Conduct and Ethics signifies competence, fair dealing and high integrity. Failure to adhere to these Principles may subject a member to disciplinary action, as set forth in ASTA's Bylaws.

## Key Concepts

| | |
|---|---|
| code of ethics | Department of Transportation |
| consumer dissatisfaction | evolution of consumerism |
| consumerism | Federal Aviation Administration |
| consumers' complaints | federal legislation |
| consumer movement | Federal Maritime Commission |
| corrective legislation | Federal Trade Commission |
| deceptive promotion | forms of regulation |

| | |
|---|---|
| industry organizations | self-regulation |
| Interstate Commerce Commission | service contracts |
| limitations of liability | tour operators |
| poor service | tour wholesalers |
| preventative regulation | trade associations |
| regulation limitations | travel industry regulation |
| reputable tour firms | travel products |

## For Review and Discussion

1. Senator Brown states, "Our state should license all travel agencies and tour operators!" Do you agree or disagree? Explain.
2. Discuss: When the government insures competition, it adequately protects the interests of consumers.
3. Explain why the consumer movement gained strength in the 1960s.
4. What would you recommend as the most effective way to convey information to travel consumers?
5. Which is preferable: industry self-regulation or government regulation?
6. There is an identity of interest between travel suppliers and consumers. Do you agree with this statement?
7. Discuss what consumerism means to you.
8. Are consumer protection laws really necessary?
9. What and whom is the government trying to protect when it legislates?
10. What are the social responsibilities of tourism managers?
11. What are business ethics? What do they have to do with social responsibility?
12. Consumerism, social responsibility, and government regulation all affect travel. Discuss the impact of each.
13. The president of a travel agency has just had his best clients, Jack and Joan Smith, return from Beautiful Islands and complain that their vacation was terrible. The plane was six hours late, original hotel reservations were not honored, the substitute facility had poor housekeeping, a broken TV, and excessive noise. How do you handle this situation?
14. You have just received your credit card bill for your vacation trip and discover unwarranted charges. What should you do?

## Selected References

Freed, David H. "Why Can't Customers Complain Better?" *International Journal of Hospitality Management*, Vol. 7, no. 2 (1988) pp. 95–98.

Gay, Jeanne, ed. *Travel and Tourism Law Bibliography*. Quarterly. San Francisco: International Forum of Travel and Tourism Advocates.

Gieseking, Hal. *Consumer Handbook for Travelers*. Washington, D.C.: High Street Press, 1977.

Hannigan, John A. "Reservations Cancelled: Consumer Complaints in the Tourist Industry." *Annals of Tourism Research*, Vol. 7, no. 3 (1980), pp. 366–384.

Lewis, Robert C. "When Guests Complain." *The Cornell Hotel and Restaurant Administration Quarterly*, Vol. 24, no. 2 (August 1982), pp. 23–32.

Moser, Martin R. "Answering the Customer's Complaint: A Case Study." *The Cornell Quarterly*, Vol. 28, no. 1 (May 1987), pp. 10–15.

U.S. Department of Transportation. *DOT Guide to CAB Sunset*. Washington, D.C.: DOT, 1985.

# CHAPTER 15

# Tourism's Future

## LEARNING OBJECTIVES

- Appreciate the giant strides that have occurred in technology related to tourism.
- Recognize the powerful and positive impact that the environmental movement has made on tourism development.
- Understand the social and economic forces in industrialized civilizations that have brought about greater education and purchasing power—essential factors in creating demand for tourism.
- Imagine the tourism implications inherent in a gradual growth of these forces during America's third century.
- Evaluate the contributions that international tourism can make toward world peace.

## FUTURE PROSPECTS

As vast numbers of people become increasingly aware that they are citizens of the world as well as of their own country, the market for trips will expand, and travel experiences, especially purposeful ones, will have an even greater effect on individuals, families, and societies than in the past several decades. Greatly enhanced access to information and promotional messages will increase the worldwide demand for all forms of travel, and awareness of other places and cultures will be instilled in people's minds far more than ever before. Generally higher levels of education and vastly expanded instruction in foreign languages will aid in this heightened awareness.

As cultural distances shrink, individual international travelers will find managing their trip resources of money and time much easier than did their parents. Visitors will be much more interested in life-seeing tourism because deeper immersion into local ways of life will be more meaningful. Acquired foreign language skills and increased awareness of a host country's culture will prepare travelers to absorb and appreciate the new environment, so that their travel will provide a higher level of personal enrichment as well as greater appreciation and understanding of other lands and peoples.

It is likely that in the future the trend will continue for marriages to take place a bit later in life, divorce rates will be lower, and travel will be seen as an important way to further strengthen family life. Because they are better prepared for travel,

**448**

families will more easily maximize a trip's benefits. The children (families will average only two children) will have had a better education in geography, history, foreign languages, and cultures, and typically parents will want to make a family trip an enjoyable adventure as well as an educational experience. Easily available audio-visual destination descriptions will facilitate planning and increase the family's excitement and anticipation of the trip.

The effects of visitors on host societies will be also much improved, especially when tourists from industrialized countries visit underdeveloped areas. Greater awareness of other cultures and sincere interest in knowing about the host country will produce a more positive overall influence and lead to both social and economic benefits for both groups. For example, mingling socially with locals will become customary and universal, because hotels and local tourism organizations will routinely arrange such social occasions as part of the area's life-seeing and hosting programs. Hotels, especially resort hotels, will feature local art and handicraft items in their furnishings and shops, and social directors will encourage hotel guests to participate in activities sponsored by local groups for social, cultural, and recreational purposes.

All of these trends, then, will be positive. Trip planners and travel suppliers will, of course, continue to emphasize the pleasures and recreational opportunities provided by vacation travel. But they will also be keenly aware of their clients' heightened interest in the cultures of other societies and will plan trips to provide genuine opportunities for social contact with their indigenous hosts. Such occasions will help greatly to fulfill desires for better understanding and appreciation by both guests and hosts.

## DEMOGRAPHIC CHANGES

While increased cultural awareness will be one factor that affects the travel industry, there will be several demographic changes that comprise other factors. The world's industrialized societies will continue to grow in population at a moderate rate, thus increasing the total travel market. The U.S. population, for example, is expected to rise from 241.6 million in 1986 to 268.3 million in 2000, a 0.8 percent annual increase.[1] As this growth occurs, occupational shifts from manufacturing to distribution and services will continue, and arts and crafts will increase as a proportion of total production. In addition, early retirement and long-term leisure opportunities will expand, so that travel and tourism become a much more important part of life patterns than at present. Because of higher levels of education and greater interest in other cultures, the number of people who travel for pleasure will increase significantly, and shortened travel time and lower costs will allow them to travel farther. Foreign travel in particular will have great appeal.

The result of these changes will be increased travel product values in relation to incomes, leading to greater demand for all forms of pleasure travel. As the industry expands, there will also be an increase in demand for travel supplier staff and for all

[1] U.S. Department of Labor, *Projections 2000*, Bulletin 2302, March 1988, p. 19.

types of equipment and supplies needed by the transportation and accommodations industry (see Figure 1.2, p. 16).

Because of the prevalence of interest in travel, larger employers will provide travel kiosks in employees' rest and recreation rooms. These kiosks will present descriptions of many travel destinations and cruise ships, as well as complete tour offerings. Travel offices within factories and businesses will be common, and vacation periods will be more frequent and longer. Sabbatical leaves for study and travel customarily will be available after a required period of employment.

Although population will grow moderately, the labor force will be aging; the median age of employees will rise from the present 35 years to 45 years by the year 2050. This significant change will create a demand for travel products designed for a more mature market — products that offer the comfort and conveniences demanded by a more mature, sophisticated traveler.

In the United States, the composition of the labor force will also change significantly between now and the year 2000. Blacks, Hispanics, Asians, and other non-white minority groups are projected to account for 57 percent of labor force growth. If non-Hispanic white women are included, the combined share of future growth reaches more than 90 percent.[2] This forecast implies a much enlarged market for travel by groups which previously did not participate fully in the travel industry marketplace.

Children in school will have a much better education overall, especially in studies of various world cultures. Foreign languages will generally be required, beginning when the students are about 10 years old or even younger. Virtually all schools will offer summer study programs for the purpose of increasing knowledge of the students' own state or country, other countries, and differing ways of life among the world's people. Student travel opportunities will be abundant and costs will be low, so that almost every child can have at least one opportunity for travel to another state or country. Student exchange programs are forecast to be greatly expanded as educators recognize the value of experiences in the country where the student's foreign language is used.

With the possibility of world peace becoming a permanent reality, the world's advanced industrial societies may be eager to help raise the standards of living in less developed countries. Technical assistance teams in myriads of specializations will be available. Any country will be able to request assistance through the revitalized United Nations Development Program, and considerable funding previously spent on armaments may be available for agricultural and other economic development projects, including tourism.

## LEISURE AND DISCRETIONARY INCOME

Future populations in all of the world's industrialized countries will be characterized as having an enhanced "quality of life." Recreation, travel, hobbies, and the arts will flourish. Working hours, although not expected to decrease much, will be more

---

[2] Ibid., p. 2.

flexible, and workers who wish to take extended leaves of absence for study or travel will be encouraged to do so. Two people might perform the work and responsibilities of one full-time position. A compressed workweek will be common in many industries; a 36-hour workweek comprised of four 9-hour days would free up a full three-day weekend for travel, cultural, and recreational pursuits.

Long-term leisure will also be a major social force in the future. With a much larger middle-aged and older population, the numbers of those in retirement status will be greatly expanded. Furthermore, early retirement options for workers will become common — a retirement age of 60 is expected to be popular for a substantial portion of the work force. Also adding length to the leisure years is increased longevity; life expectancies for women might be 80 years or longer, and those for men 77 years plus.

Prosperity will spread worldwide. With world production of food at abundant levels in virtually all countries, cost-of-living to income ratios will be moderate. For example, revolutionary technologies in manufactured housing have made possible comfortable housing at reasonable costs.

Real disposable income (actual gains over inflated costs of living) in the United States is projected to grow 1.6 percent per year to year 2000, to $13,421 per capita from $10,780 in 1986. This growth rate reflects primarily the projected faster rate of productivity growth.[3] Travel outlays will be an important use of these available funds. Spending on hobbies, home entertainment, sports activities, and other recreational and cultural pursuits will also rise substantially. Employment in amusement and recreation services is estimated to grow by 2.3 percent per year to year 2000, a substantial increase.[4]

## *Market Growth Potential*

Because of an expected rise in standards of living worldwide and increased discretionary incomes, travel markets will expand both in the principal tourism-generating countries and in lesser developed countries. Efforts by the United Nations to expand education to all people in the world, including those in the poorest of countries, will greatly heighten the interest of people everywhere in their fellow world citizens, and as a result most of the world's population will have an increasing desire to travel away from their home environments, for even short trips if they cannot afford longer ones.

In the developed industrialized countries, rising education levels, standards of living, and discretionary incomes will power a much expanded demand for travel. Excellent values for all types of trips will make travel highly attractive to large segments of the population.

International travel markets will continue to grow worldwide as telecommunications and information-processing technologies continue to evolve and increase in efficiency, speed, and services performed. Complete arrangements will be made with one telephone call, for either an individual traveler or a group, regardless of the

[3] Ibid., pp. 2, 14.
[4] Ibid., p. 41.

distance of the destination. The ease with which these arrangements can be made will add to the travel market's growth.

## EVOLVING MARKETING TECHNOLOGY

Advances in technology will also aid in the marketing of travel services. Consider the following highly realistic scenario: A prospective traveler obtains travel information simply by dialing a special number on a device that is part of a home television set. A selected travel agent responds by displaying on the client's screen a series of full-color pictures or a descriptive audiovisual program of a desired travel destination, tour, or cruise ship. If the client is prepared to decide on the spot, all arrangements are completed, and the client's checking account or credit card number is debited by the travel agency for the deposit or for the cost of the entire trip. The complete travel arrangements may include numerous attached services, such as care for a pet while the owner is gone, having the driveway plowed of snow, mowing the lawn, stopping the newspaper, notifying the post office to suspend mail delivery, or other similar domestic arrangements for a person who is away from home. Once the trip is under way, it proceeds smoothly, as every detail has been arranged in advance through instantaneous communication. As much as possible, problems have been anticipated and alternatives established to ensure an enjoyable, rewarding trip.

This scenario can be augmented with further details. For example, every home television receiver will have several channels devoted to travel programs. Published weekly schedules will list domestic and foreign travel destinations, various kinds of tours, cruises, and automobile trips. For each travel program presented, simple instructions will be provided as to how to book or arrange any of the trips shown, typically with the local travel agency that sponsors the program.

More important, however, marketing will be influenced greatly by the increased motivation of travelers to learn more about other peoples and their ways of life. Opportunities to do this will be included in most promotional programs. Travel suppliers will have videocassettes describing destinations, tours, and equipment, including cruise ships, for use in the marketing distribution system. Marketers in this system can then provide adequate information and pictures of the destination area and its population—not only descriptions of accommodations, local tours, and transportation but also cultural and entertainment programs available, shopping opportunities, and recreation suggestions.

Video marketing technology is easily expanded to video sales machines in banks, savings and loan offices, hotel lobbies, larger stores of various kinds, shopping centers, and office buildings. An interested person can then select a destination, tour, or cruise ship by pressing the appropriate keys and obtain a brief video screen color presentation. If the viewer decides to purchase this travel product, then he or she can press the appropriate keys to make a reservation and obtain tickets and passes for the entire trip, all debited to the would-be traveler's credit card account or checking account. A viewer who has a question or wants counseling is able to use a telephone connected directly to the travel agency owning the video sales machine. A prospective traveler who visits the travel agency, public carrier, or cruise sales office would use a similar system of video presentation and automated reservation and ticketing immediately available there.

# ENVIRONMENTAL AND
# LAND-USE PLANNING CONSIDERATIONS

The anticipated increase in demand for travel is already affecting forward-looking communities in industrialized countries, which are recognizing the need for land-use planning to create environmentally sound tourist accommodations, parks, or other tourist attractions and facilities. In the past, recreational areas usually got the leftovers. Land unacceptable for local housing, commercial, or manufacturing uses was dedicated to recreational uses regardless of its suitability. However, strategic recreation and tourism planning will allow recreational facilities and open space to serve a variety of interests that might otherwise be incompatible.

An excellent example of such forward thinking is the downtown Detroit Linked Riverfront Parks Plan. The Detroit plan began by listing *peoples' activities* rather than by describing facilities. That is, the planners started with a focus on meeting peoples' needs through a changed riverfront. Then, two regional riverfront attractions about two and a half miles apart — Belle Isle, a 1000-acre park in the Detroit River, and the Hart Plaza, a 20-acre, two-level urban festival plaza — were designed to serve as "anchors" for the project (see Figure 15.1). Hart Plaza, a public park, is the site for the enormously popular Detroit Ethnic Festivals which attract about 600,000 people during each summer season; Belle Isle is a traditional public park.

Within the project, each major recreational land use is coordinated by planners as a juxtaposition of business, industry, housing, and recreation. The Stroh River Place development is an example of private development cooperating with the overall plan. This 31-acre property, formerly owned by the Parke-Davis pharmaceutical company, is being redeveloped into a new office and commercial center, and has become the largest mixed-use historic renovation project in the United States.

Regardless of the proposed land use, planning bodies at all levels — village, city, township, county, regional, and state — are now taking a watchful and guarded look at any proposed development projects. The economic and environmental impacts that a project might produce are carefully studied and evaluated, and often public hearings are held to provide additional considerations. For each project there must

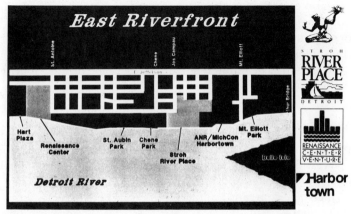

**Figure 15.1** Downtown Detroit Linked Riverfront Parks Plan.
*Source: Michigan Planner,* Fall, 1987.

also be provision for the sanitary disposal of all kinds of waste products. Because of this posture, any developmental project intended to serve vacationers or tourists is now very likely to be scrutinized closely before planning and zoning bodies decide the project's fate.

Any proposed growth in a supply component that disregards possible adverse effects on the environment is likely to be disallowed by local governmental planning and administrative land-use control groups. Citizens of industrialized societies leave little doubt about how they feel with respect to their natural environment and its preservation. Outdoor air, ground and surface waters, beaches, and forests must remain in wholesome condition, unpolluted and protected. The same principle is applied to wildlife and marine life. Thus, proposed developments must be planned so that the environment is safeguarded, and possibly even enhanced, by the project under consideration.

## TOURISM SUPPLIERS AND ACTIVITIES

### Natural and Cultural Resources

Maintaining and enhancing natural and cultural resources is fundamental to successful tourism growth. As previously noted, the environmental factors in tourism development have become major considerations in any type of project. Planning and zoning commissions at all levels of government will play critical roles. The majority of local people now feel that developments intended for visitor use must be harmonious with other land uses in the community.

In the future, plans for recreational and tourist facilities will become part of overall master plans for any particular area. The environmental and economic impacts must be investigated thoroughly and determined completely before construction begins, so that natural and cultural resources that have or will have attraction for visitors can be maintained and enhanced as part of public policy.

Intelligent, carefully considered landscape and architectural designs will be mandatory. A balanced approach to all of the supply and anticipated demand estimates is also essential for ultimate aesthetic and economic fulfillment.

Another major concern will be to avoid inappropriately designed and poorly located or constructed buildings and other facilities. Incorporating an area's cultural heritage into architectural design will be strongly favored, and indigenous designs in all improvements will be strongly advocated because of their tourist appeal and benefit to the community itself.

### Shopping

Shops in resort hotels and shopping areas visited by tourists will continue to be popular places. Because of their heightened interest in international affairs and knowledge of other states and foreign countries, shoppers will want to purchase authentic, high quality art and handicraft works. Where feasible, shops will strive to incorporate actual working places for artists so that shoppers can observe the creative process. This effort to offer high quality local or regional souvenirs will not only be welcomed by visitors but will provide expanded sales outlets for an area's crafts-people and artists.

In addition, sales staffs will be educated in the creative processes so they can fully explain the methods, background, or history of the work and can describe how the items are actually created and how they should be properly used or displayed. Clerks will also be educated in the languages most frequently used by their visitors. They will be knowledgeable about packing and shipping methods best suited to the individual shopper's needs, so that shipping to any place in the world will be facilitated.

## Recreation

The worldwide trend toward more healthful living is expected to heighten, and most accommodations will offer recreational equipment and facilities for exercising and various sports. Because of the prevalence of three-day weekends and longer vacation times, maintaining an exercise program during a vacation will be a priority. Resort hotels will provide instructional programs led by pros. Package vacations will commonly include a course of instruction in some recreational pursuit, and recreational use will boom in national parks, national and state forests, wildlife and nature sanctuaries, ski resorts and other types of outdoor recreational areas. Those states and countries that have anticipated this growth, provided funds to acquire more public recreational lands, and made improvements in them are now reaping the rewards. An ever-growing demand for these outdoor recreational resources has resulted in economic growth as well. Tourism developed from such recreational assets has likely repaid development costs.

## Attraction Visits

Although natural, scenic, historical, cultural, and entertainment attractions are expected to grow modestly in number, worldwide the total attendance is expected to increase substantially. Attractions of all kinds will be more accessible because of improved roads and airports. Facilities are expected to be upgraded and enlarged. Attractions that feature historical and international themes especially will prosper, because of the increased interest in world cultures, and parks that feature samples of the cultures of other countries will have a powerful lure. The quality of these attractions will increase and be maintained as the traveling public becomes more sophisticated, having visited much of their own country as well as, usually, several others.

## Business, Trade, and Conventions

The proliferation of new technology in electronic and satellite audiovisual transmission may result in a decline in the travel market in this category. Meetings can be held without those interested being present in a given place. Instruction to each participant will be provided in advance, and those in charge and the speakers will be present in a telecasting studio to conduct the meeting. Participants will be able simply to tune in their TV sets to a prearranged channel to listen and observe the entire proceedings. Voting or individual participation can be transmitted by telephone and summarized by computer, and the results or summary then transmitted by telecast to participants in their homes or places of employment.

This technology also holds the potential for a great expansion in meeting travel, as a major meeting at one location with key speakers and a live audience can be transmitted easily to other hotel sites across the country, thus creating additional attendance travel.

Stores and factories will order materials, supplies, and equipment by radiotelephone or television. New lines of merchandise will be displayed via television, and orders will be transmitted by videophone.

Attendance at business and trade meetings which include a pre- and postconvention tour will be increasingly popular. Meetings planners will offer complete packages, including all elements of the meeting or convention as well as before-and-after activities as an option. The majority of all large meetings and conventions will be planned by professional meetings planners. Most associations and corporations will have such planners as regular staff members, as meetings and conventions that are planned by such specialists are far more worthwhile, effective, and enjoyable than those planned without such expertise. Meetings planners consistently improve their abilities by participating in meetings planners' professional organizations.

## Studies

A great increase is expected in study tours, international student exchanges, study of foreign languages, adult education programs, and "elderhostel" studies for senior citizens, and international education centers will flourish in larger colleges and universities in all parts of the world. University campuses, which are already important tourist attractions for sports, cultural events, entertainment, conferences, and short courses, will be even more attractive to visitors as societies become more highly educated the world over. Typically, enlightened citizens will consider education to be a life-long process and will use every opportunity to participate in seminars, conferences, or courses that contribute to their understandings and appreciations. In the future, these offerings that relate to other places and other cultures will be especially sought after.

## Sports

Both the winter and summer Olympic Games have powered a rising world interest in international sports events, and sports competitions of virtually all kinds will increase in popularity. Regional competitions will expand not only in number but also in the breadth of sports that are included. Furthermore, as world peace makes steady gains, countries will consider their outstanding athletes and sports teams to be evidence of their prowess and achievement.

## Accommodations

Perhaps furthest in the future are hotels in space orbiting around the earth, on the moon's surface, and on Mars. These are, of course, the most incredible developments foreseen in lodging. However, earthbound accommodations already have changed in that they provide much wider ranges of comforts and services than have been offered in the past, and these improvements make staying in them most satisfying and memorable experiences. Not far away are business services such as videophones in each guest room and special communication rooms for sending or receiving any kind of written or audio message. Letters will be typed automatically and in perfect form simply by a person's talking into a dictating machine and then, if needed, transmitted by satellite to the desired receiving unit located anywhere in the world.

Guest room selection in the future will be determined by many more criteria than those used today. These will include all the special features desired by the guest, plus the selection of room decor most complementary to the guest's complexion and hair color. Bathrooms will be equipped with whirlpool baths and special massaging machines designed to stimulate circulation and relax tired muscles, and for entertainment each guest will be able to select from thousands of video titles to receive any type of instructional program, entertainment, or informational topic of interest. The videos will be delivered automatically to the guest room and operated on playback equipment using the guest room television set.

Growing in popularity will be "boutique" hotels — older, often small properties that have been well maintained and beautified within to become charming, comfortable accommodations. Outstanding food service is a part of such hotels. Even today bed-and-breakfast places are growing in popularity because of their homey atmosphere, owners' hospitality, and reasonable prices. Accommodations directories will list these types along with modestly priced and luxury properties.

The old. Pictured above is the first Holiday Inn hotel in Memphis, circa 1952. Compare this with Holiday Inn's growth around the world since that time and the firm's entry into airport hotels and downtown highrises. (Photo courtesy of Holiday Inns)

The new. The Holiday Inn Crowne Plaza at the San Francisco
International Airport represents a new top-of-the-line Holiday
Inns hotel brand, targeted primarily toward the frequent business
traveler. (Photo courtesy of Holiday Inns)

### Food Service

Food and beverage places will offer an even wider range of choices than in past
decades. As the public becomes more world-minded, ethnic restaurants with beverage services will proliferate, and restaurants and bars with exotic themes will be
particularly favored. Authentic music and entertainment, including strolling musicians, will become more common in areas where they have not previously been
featured.

### Transportation

Future trips by air will occur at amazingly increased speeds. Long trips, such as from
New York to Sydney, Australia, (10,000 miles) will take only three hours; New York
to London will take two hours, and New York to Moscow, two and a half hours.
In-flight movies will include easily understood diagrams and pictures explaining
how the plane functions and how the pilot navigates to the destination, and optional
programs available on individual TV screens at each seat will provide pictures and
descriptions of the trip's destination in sufficient detail to inform passengers adequately. There will be suggestions for places to see and things to do upon arrival.
Addresses and phone numbers of sources of additional information, such as tourism

Newest versions of the B-737 and B-747 aircraft are forerunners of planes designed for vastly increased speed. (Photo courtesy of the Boeing Company)

At 46,052 gross registered tons, Carnival Cruise Lines' new SuperLiner *Holiday* is the largest ship ever built exclusively for cruising. The $170 million vessel features nearly two acres of Burmese teak decks, a revolutionary double-width promenade, and main showroom extending two full decks. State-of-the-art technology includes satellite navigation and an on-board desalinization plant capable of producing 560 tons of potable water daily. (Photo courtesy of Carnival Cruise Lines)

offices, will also be included in the program. Passengers traveling by motorcoach on trips of more than 150 miles will also enjoy similar TV screens at each seat, with destination descriptions available at an extra charge.

Cruise ships will offer short educational courses on myriads of subjects by videotape and other specialized equipment, with live instructors supplementing the video instruction in particular fields. There will be greater emphasis on having ship personnel help passengers to learn more about ports of call prior to arrival. Shore excursions will be planned carefully to maximize awareness and appreciation of people living in the countries being visited.

All public carriers and tour operators will promote people-to-people programs heavily because of their popularity. Because global thinking and awareness by most people are now a reality, purposeful trips will be the most popular. Those who travel want to know more about the culture of the places they visit and demand that trips provide high quality learning and observational opportunities.

## SPACE TRAVEL

In the not-too-distant future, space travel (about 100 to 200 miles above the earth) to distant cities will be commonplace. People willing to pay the price will travel by space shuttle from New York to Tokyo, for example, on a trip that will take only 45 minutes.[5] Connections to other distant major cities of the world via space shuttle will likewise be available.

Of trips to places off the earth's surface, a journey to the moon will be the most popular vacation tour; a space station located between Earth and the moon will be used for a stopover. NASA will operate the tours, since private airlines cannot afford the cost, and NASA will build a beautifully appointed hotel on the moon, sited at the base of a spectacular lunar mountain range. Moon visitors will have an opportunity to view space manufacturing of many products made advantageously in zero gravity and will learn about scientific experiments taking place on the moon. During their visit to the moon, tourists will be provided space suits for walks on the surface, so that everyone can enjoy the exhilaration of low-gravity moon walking as well as the spectacular vistas of moon mountains and craters and the eerie view of the earth in the sky.

By operating these exotic and very expensive tours, NASA can recoup some of the money spent on developing the space program. A tremendous demand for lunar tours has developed; although the tours would be high priced, the prestige of being able to tell friends about a walk on the moon will be well worth the cost to the adventurous affluent.

Trips to other planets will be the ultimate in travel—the epitome of one's lifetime of travel experiences. Mars will be the most popular destination. As on trips to the moon, passengers will wear ordinary street clothes and will be accommodated in a passenger module seating 40 to 50 people. The space vehicle's first stop will be at a luxury space hotel orbiting the earth about 100 miles up. Here the passengers are refreshed and rested for a few days while receiving instructions and preparing for their 280-day flight to Mars. Passengers will be divided into two groups. Those of

[5] I. Kaufmann III, "Tourism in the Twenty-first Century," *Science Digest*, April 1983, pp. 52–55.

Tours to the moon will begin in a passenger version of the space
shuttle. (Photo courtesy of Florida Division of Tourism)

normal range of weight to height remain alert during the entire trip, and they are
required to participate in rigorous physical exercise each day to keep up their physical well-being. Those who are quite overweight will spend most of the trip in a
comatose state, reached by being wrapped in a refrigerated blanket. This device
slowly lowers body temperature to 78 degrees Fahrenheit, inducing hibernation (it is
believed that being in this condition is perfectly safe) until they almost reach the Red
Planet.

At an appropriate time prior to arrival, the refrigeration blankets are removed
by the flight crew. Each passenger gradually warms up to normal body temperature.
A series of exceptionally nourishing meals is served prior to arrival to renew body
strength and vigor.

Upon arrival, passengers are transferred to a beautiful NASA hotel where
complete recovery from the long trip is accomplished under the guidance of experienced space physicians.

462 Tourism Practices and Prospects

Donning streamlined space suites, the Mars visitors can explore the most interesting features of the Red Planet by battery-operated automobile and, if they desire, ski cross-country on the north polar ice cap.

After a two-week visit, it is time to prepare for the long homeward trip. Again, hearty meals are served in the hotel to help to rebuild those needing fat reserves. When this has been accomplished, passengers embark for the trip back to the space-orbiting hotel and thence to the starting point. Upon return to Earth, they are awestruck by the lush greenery and beautiful blue waters of their earthly home, and they are amazed by the changes that have taken place since their departure into space.

## TOURISM AND PEACE

The future of tourism is heavily dependent on peace, as tourism can prosper only in a peaceful environment. As pointed out in Chapter 4, fear (concern for safety) is a powerful deterrent to travel. To ensure the continued growth of the industry, travelers need to be confident that they can move about in safety. This section explores some contributions tourism can make to peace and the vital relationship between peace and tourism.

### *Tourism — A Vital Force for Peace*

In October 1988, the first global conference on the theme "Tourism — A Vital Force for Peace" was held in Vancouver, B.C., Canada. Some 500 delegates from 65 countries attended. The purpose of the conference was to explore ways in which the world's hundreds of millions of international travelers could, by increasing interests, improving attitudes, and engaging in various social and other activities, contribute to better mutual understanding and appreciation — an important contribution toward world peace.

The conference provided a forum to examine tourism and its many dimensions as a force for peace. It brought recognition that tourism has the potential to be the largest peace-time movement in the history of humankind because tourism involves people, their culture, their economy, their traditions, their heritage, and their religion. Tourism provides the contacts that make understanding other peoples and cultures possible. The conference clearly demonstrated that tourism has the potential to make the world a better place in which to live.

One of the outcomes of the conference was the distribution of the following:

#### Credo of the Peaceful Traveler

Grateful for the opportunity to travel and to experience the world, and because peace begins with the individual, I affirm my personal responsibility and commitment to

- Journey with an open mind and gentle heart
- Accept with grace and gratitude the diversity I encounter
- Revere and protect the natural environment which sustains all life

The International Peace Garden spans the border along the longest unfortified boundary in the world. It is a symbol of peace between Canada and the United States. (Photo courtesy of North Dakota Tourism Promotion)

- Appreciate all cultures I discover
- Respect and thank my hosts for their welcome
- Offer my hand in friendship to everyone I meet
- Support travel services that share these views and act upon them and, by my spirit, words and actions,
- Encourage others to travel the world in peace.

## A PHILOSOPHY OF TOURISM AND PEACE

Great leaders in many fields have extolled the social benefits to humanity that result from travel. Travel is one of man's noblest occupations. The famous Greek statesman, Solon, in 550 B.C. recommended that we travel "in order to see." To see is to increase understanding and appreciation of other peoples, other cultures, and other lands. Jason, leader of the Argonauts — those incessant sailors in Greek mythology who were searching for the Golden Fleece — said, "The essential thing is not to live, the essential thing is to navigate."

Marco Polo became a prince of merchants, papal envoy, governor of a Chinese city, favorite of Kublai Khan, master of exotic languages, war correspondent, and the first travel writer. His book, written in 1296 A.D. describing his adventures, established the first bond between East and West. Polo was wonderstruck at splendors that he saw and of which he heard. During the Renaissance, his book was the chief and almost the sole Western source of information on the East.

This brief dip into history and mythology has but one purpose—to emphasize that travel—and often written accounts of it in later years have done more to create bonds and mutual understanding between various peoples of the world than any other single force throughout civilization's long existence.

There's no better way in which to gain a panoramic view of civilization than making a trip around the world. Being a guest for dinner is probably the best way to sense the unity that exists among peoples throughout the world. Here, people joined by blood or friendly spirit gather to break bread under the same roof. A few examples might include a dinner with a Japanese family, marveling at the swift movement of chopsticks gracefully picking rice from small snow-white porcelain bowls. Or a meal with Thais in the floating markets of Bangkok where sampans loaded with pyramids of tropical fruits, vegetables, and fish ply the klongs in search of buyers. With Arabs in Tunisia, it may be having a delicious lunch in the shade of a tent out on the Sahara desert—in a landscape of stark, wild beauty, enriched by the lively warm hospitality of these friendly people.

Whatever happens in any home—be it

- a modest wooden house furnished with straw mats and rice paper windows in Kyoto
- a solemn British mansion on Victoria Hill
- a mud hut on the banks of the Nile
- a Cape Cod bungalow
- a Rio de Janiero apartment

being born, living, eating, drinking, resting, and dying are the same the world over.

World travel is broadening and leads to an appreciation of other cultures. (Photo courtesy of the Boeing Company)

Meeting people from other parts of the world can be one of the
most rewarding aspects of travel. (Photo courtesy of the Boeing
Company)

These similarities reflect the basic unity of people. This unity is really well understood by people but, alas, too often forgotten by nations and their rulers and leaders.

There are many ways in which a traveling family can meet and become acquainted with families in other lands. One of the best known of these plans is the
"people-to-people" program. Arrangements can be made by a travel agent through
a local contractor, say, in Copenhagen, to provide a program of social contacts and
other activities to enrich the visitor's acquaintanceship and understanding of the
Danish people. Arrangements can be made to stay in a private home or to attend a
seminar or similar program. Such opportunities can be and are operating in
hundreds of places, in many parts of the world. A greater awareness of such possibilities and more widespread use of this type of program would increase understanding, friendship, and appreciation of other people.

A tourist standing on the balcony of a $100-per-day hotel room looking at the passersby below obtains little real knowledge of the people in the country being visited. However, if opportunities are readily available for social contacts with locals of that country, increased understanding and appreciation for the people of that area will take place.

Can tourism contribute to peace? If understanding and increased appreciation for other people's way of life, mores, culture, and language make us more a part of a world community, then the answer must be "yes." This is especially so if at least casual acquaintance can be made with residents of the host country. Tourism provides a vehicle whereby people from one area become acquainted with people of another. Efforts to build that acquaintance will contribute to understanding. And understanding is at least the first step in creating and maintaining friendly national relationships.

Countries whose leaders understand and encourage tourism (at least in-tourism) are making an effort to improve the personal relationship between their citizens and those of other countries. Although economic considerations may be uppermost, the importance of social contacts is also recognized.

Tourism flourishes in a climate of peace and prosperity. Political unrest, wars, depressions, recessions, and civil strife discourage tourism.

Tourism, if properly planned, organized, and managed can bring understanding, appreciation, prosperity, and a better life to all who are involved. Let it grow and

One of the best ways to meet people in other lands is to sign up for a "people-to-people" program. (Photo courtesy of the Boeing Company)

its positive effects increase. Tourism, if not a passport to peace, is at least a worthy effort toward building peace. Wherever and whenever visitor and host meet and greet each other with mutual appreciation, respect, and friendship, a movement toward peace has been made.

The Holiday Inn *Passport,* which lists and describes worldwide properties associated with this company, contains this statement:

> In today's shrinking world, neighbors are across the ocean, down the continent, and in every corner of the world. Time is different. So is dress, language, even food. But for all to live as neighbors, mankind must understand each other.
>
> Understanding is impossible without communication. That which is unknown often seems forbidding, even wrong. People must learn other ways of life besides their own.
>
> Only travel and communication closes this gap of knowledge. By world tourism it is possible to discover distant neighbors, how they live and think as human beings.
>
> World tourism and understanding go hand in hand. For travel is the way to knowledge. So let everyone do his part, traveling about the earth, keeping his mind and heart open. And the world will become a better place for all.

## FINAL THOUGHTS

> The world is a great book, of which they who never stir from home read only a page.
>
> St. Augustine of Hippo (354–430 A.D.)
> Christian theologian and philosopher

> Of journeying the benefits are many: the freshness it brings to the heart, the seeing and hearing of marvelous things, the delight of beholding new cities, the meeting of unknown friends, the learning of high manners.
>
> Saadi (1184–1291 A.D.)
> Persian poet

> Voyage, travel, and change of place impart new vigor to the mind.
>
> Lucius Annaeus Seneca (4 B.C.–65 A.D.)
> Roman statesman and philosopher

## SUMMARY

Social and economic trends in developed countries seem to favor a long-term growth in both domestic and international travel demand. More long-term leisure, increased disposable income, higher levels of education, and more awareness of other countries and peoples are significant factors influencing a growing market for travel.

Technological trends are also favorable. Transportation equipment is now more efficient and more comfortable; hotel and motel accommodations have become more complete, attractive, convenient, and comfortable; and new developments have given much more attention to environmental considerations.

Tourism is believed to have a positive effect on world peace. As people travel from place to place with a sincere desire to learn more about their global neighbors, knowledge and understanding grow. Then at least a start has been made in improving world communication that seems so important in building bridges of mutual appreciation, respect, and friendship.

We trust that you are now ready to contribute your part toward making this world a bit more prosperous and peaceful through tourism.

### About the Readings

The first reading considers how science and technology can dramatically affect demand and supply patterns within the tourism phenomena. Science and technology are the wild cards in the tourism strategic planning game, appearing unexpectedly, creating entirely new markets, or causing further segmentation of current ones. Coping with the uncertainty of science and technology is an essential aspect of tourism planning.

Tourism, along with its obvious international economic pact, transcends governmental boundaries by bringing peoples of the world closer together through the understanding of different cultures, environments, and heritage. It is potentially one of the most important vehicles for promoting understanding, trust, and goodwill among peoples of the world. The second reading explores these opportunities to achieve peace through tourism.

The third reading describes a space age suite that is available today.

## READING 15-1

### Future Encounters with Science and Technology

By Elwood L. Shafer
Department of Recreation and Parks
Pennsylvania State University

Reprinted from the *Journal of Travel Research*, Vol. 27, No. 4, Spring 1989.

### Introduction

The one thing public and private tourism managers have to prepare for in the future is — the future. No matter what the future may bring, examining current and potential break-throughs in science and technology (S & T) can help tourism to be prepared. Exploring S & T allows the tourism industry to anticipate the future needs and use patterns of tourists, so that the solutions provided today may work tomorrow. Solutions that last will help sustain a positive customer perception of public and private tourism programs. Further, lasting solutions embody professional commitment to connect science and technology developed in the past with that which will exist years from now.

Modern managers and strategic planners have emphasized that every public or private organization or industry that wants to prosper must invoke the "law of the situation." That is, the organization or industry must ask itself what business it is *really* in (Iacocca, 1984; Naisbitt, 1982; Naisbitt and Aburdene, 1985). The classic definition of tourism's business is attracting visitors and catering to their needs and expectations (McIntosh and Goeldner, 1984). However, as the demand for tourism has increased, consumer behavior has not necessarily conformed to classic economic and marketing theory—because of rapid and sometimes unexpected advances in S & T (Massey, 1979; Naisbitt, 1987).

The conventional ways of looking at consumer behavior—especially in tourism—are becoming outdated very quickly. For example, no longer can the purchasing habits of consumers of a product or service be predicted simply by labeling a group as a new segment of the market. A world of paradoxes in tourism and leisure behavior is emerging, where existing opposites operate simultaneously (Naisbitt and Aburdene, 1985) and greater sameness and greater diversity, as well as greater security seeking and greater risk taking, occur side by side. For example, some accountants skydive, and some campers drive air-conditioned vans to their site for "roughing it" in the woods. Other people drive air-conditioned cars to air-conditioned gyms, where they work out hard to sweat as much as they can. An individual may shop at both K mart and Neiman-Marcus, own a sizeable investment portfolio but trade it with a discount broker, fill a BMW with inexpensive self-serve gas, or go to McDonalds for lunch and a four-star restaurant for dinner. Leisure life-style mosaics are often elusive, inconsistent, and contradictory (Massey, 1979; Perry, 1987; Plawin and Blum, 1987; Smith, 1985; Fensom, 1984).

A high degree of market segmentation is occurring throughout the leisure and tourism industry, and leading forecasters emphasize that the multiple-profile consumer is here to stay (McIntosh and Goeldner, 1984; Naisbitt, 1982). If any service industry provides anything without acknowledging that consumer tastes, preferences, and perceptions are changing rapidly because of new S & T, that industry is in for an expensive shock (Iacocca, 1984). As a result, (1) the conventional way of looking at tourism behavior is not only outdated but dangerous, and (2) new approaches for analyzing the market must consider the effects of oncoming S & T on future demand and supply (Naisbitt, 1987; Miller, 1986; Sivy, 1985; Kaufmann, 1983). Furthermore, in the tourism strategic planning game, many times it is the S & T *outside* the normal sphere of tourism research that can affect tourism demand and supply patterns most dramatically. Breakthroughs in these areas of S & T are the wild cards in the planning process. They often seem to appear on the scene unexpectedly, creating entirely new markets or significantly segmenting current ones.

This article describes some of the oncoming S & T that may profoundly influence tourism planning and development in the coming decades. More than 100 popular and scientific articles were explored to provide visions of how S & T will create new challenges and solutions in future tourism programming and planning. Areas of S & T examined include video, transportation, medicine, recreation equipment, the natural sciences, the built environment, and the contributions of computers, robotics, and space exploration.

*Video Breakthroughs*

Just as the invention of movable type in the 1400s made mass literacy possible and changed Western society from an oral to a written culture, so the video S & T of the twentieth and twenty-first centuries will revolutionize traditional patterns of supply and demand for tourism.

Breakthroughs in video S & T over the next 10 to 20 years will have countervailing effects on tourism demand and the need to supply natural environments for tourism activities. The following expected scientific advances, which will allow individuals to enjoy various attributes of natural environments in their own homes, may also generate a stronger desire to visit the actual environments. However, the direction of change in demand for natural environments is not clear at this time.

• Videocycles—a combination of a stationary exercise bike and a TV/VCR—will be used extensively by cyclists at home to "tour" scenic routes in forested and urban environments, complete with exciting background music (*Country Technology* 1987–88).
• Image libraries available for home viewing will contain all the world's best art. Inexpensive flat panel-display devices will be available throughout the house, with such high resolution that viewing a projection will be like looking at the original oil painting (Long, 1987; Booth, 1986).
• People will be able to create their own images and scenes on their TV screens; the viewer will be able to simulate just about anything. For example, someone who wanted to enjoy a raft trip down the Grand Canyon of the Colorado River could call up the image on a wall-sized TV and experience the sensation of the trip (Hartley, 1987; Rochester, 1986).
• TV images will rival 35mm film quality and emanate from wall-projection units. Digital TV will allow the viewer to become a participant in the actual production. For example, a person who put a wager on the wrong football team will be able to take a picture of the quarterback, superimpose him scoring the winning play, and at least get the thrill of having the play turn out satisfactorily (Long, 1987).
• Sensavision TV will allow the viewer to feel temperature and humidity as well as to smell and walk around in the scene, because the whole room will be part of the TV set. With sensavision, viewers will be able to feel the thrill of victory or the agony of defeat in whatever activity they care to be in (Long 1987).
• As simulators become more realistic, people will be able to enjoy the breath-taking thrills of high-risk recreational experiences such as skydiving, mountain climbing, or underwater explorations with scuba gear without leaving home (*Newsweek,* 1987).

Video S & T at tourism locations will help to increase demand and create a greater need to supply on-site facilities. Some examples include the following:

• Videotapes will be used on location in specific recreational environments to train tourists to become more skilled at whatever they are doing—skiing, scuba diving, or sailing, for example—so participants can apply almost instantly what they have seen on videotape to their activity (Sybervision, 1987).
• In-room checkout to menu-driven displays on guest-room televisions will be commonplace in resorts and hotels (McCoy, 1987; Cetron and Rocha, 1987).
• Rather than read about a tourist destination in a travel guide, the average consumer will view travel videotapes of several possible destinations prior to making a decision about which trip to take (Kennedy, 1987; International Video Network, n.d.).
• Existing flight simulators generally place a person behind the controls of comparatively tame private planes. In the future, computer programs will not only teach

basic flying skills, but also provide instructions on advanced maneuvers and stunts. The characteristics of many different kinds of planes will be simulated — from World War I classics to rocket planes and experimental aircraft. Viewers will be able to put them all through their paces in the privacy of their own homes (Electronic Arts, 1987).

### Transportation

The overall effect of advances in S & T in transportation will be a greater increase in demand and supply for tourism activities. Future transportation will be faster, easier, and more comfortable.

- Cars will contain many of the sights, sounds, and comforts of home, such as video map displays of the car's position, car phones, facsimile machines, lap-top computers that can send and receive data, answering machines, and sound systems for high-tech compact disc players (Cook, 1987; Wiener, 1987).
- Magnetic trains — trains that fly between cities on cushions of electromagnetism — will be making short trips (for example, Los Angeles to Las Vegas) faster and more comfortably than airlines can manage today (Black, 1984; Lemonick, 1987).
- A new X-ray scanner will be used in airports to detect plastic weapons used by terrorists (Tracy, 1986).
- A new car in the year 2020 will have an average price of $70,000 and get 100 miles per gallon (Naisbitt, 1986).
- An aerospace plane, about the size of a Boeing 727 and able to take off and land at regular airports, will fly coast-to-coast in about 12 minutes (Kristof, 1987; Siwolop, 1985).
- Scheduled commercial flights from New York to Tokyo will take about two hours (Yeager, 1986).
- A 25-passenger tilt-rotor aircraft will be used to provide short trips between major cities in Europe that are 600 miles or less apart. It will take off from downtown heliports and when aloft change to a conventional cruise flight; it will cost half as much to operate but fly twice as fast as most helicopters (Siwolop, 1987).
- Future commercial airplanes will be safer, cheaper to operate, more flexible in seating, and more comfortable than those of today (Schefter, 1987).
- Multiple-transportation cars that convert to airplanes will be fuel efficient and economically accessible to the tourist (Kocivar, 1987; Hoyt, 1986).
- Vertical take-off and landing vehicles that cruise 225 mph above daily traffic will be used for everyday personal and commercial use (Moshier Technologies, 1987).

### Medicine

Major medical advances will enable people to live longer, healthier lives as science discovers new treatments for major disorders and pushes back the frontiers of aging. Consequently, the tourist population probably will be comprised of a greater proportion of more mature, physically active, healthier individuals who will seek a greater level of adventure and physical challenge than ever before. Some of those medical advances include the following:

- Many of the diseases that plague humans today — cancer, arteriosclerosis, arthritis, diabetes, and many infectious diseases — will fade from the scene in the next

20 years, because effective ways to prevent or treat them will be found (Kluger, 1987; Bezold, 1985; Carey, 1985; Garr, 1987).

- Genetic manipulation will help to eliminate congenital defects that have plagued society for so long (Cetron and O'Toole, 1982).
- Research in combating AIDS will allow science to deal more effectively with problems of the immune system, and out of this will come, among other things, a dramatic increase in the success and number of transplant operations (Kluger, 1987; Carey, 1986).
- In the next 20 years, transplants of all kinds will become possible: heart, lung, and brain-cell among them (Long, 1987). Artificial organs will also be developed: liver, spleen, and pancreas (Cetron and O'Toole, 1982).
- The discovery of a mechanism for regenerating nerve tissue will be a great advance leading to the rehabilitation of paraplegics and quadriplegics (Long, 1987).
- A portable, all-purpose defense against bites from snakes, scorpions, fire ants, bees, and wasps will be developed, a sort of stun gun that short-circuits the consequences of the bite (Franklin and Davis, 1987).
- Nonaddictive painkillers more powerful than morphine will be commonplace (Pelt, 1982).
- Medicines will be developed to improve and restore memory, stave off senility, cure Parkinson's and Alzheimer's diseases, and heal spinal cords (Kluger, 1987; Bezold, 1985; Cusumano, 1985). Other medicines will cure addictions to drugs and alcohol (Bloom, 1985).
- Pills will be available to counteract fear of flying and fear of heights (Cetron and O'Toole, 1982).
- Synthetic hormones will be developed for controlling weight, memory, and growth (Cetron and O'Toole, 1982).
- Artificial hands, arms, and limbs will be available (Walker, 1985; Kashi, 1987), and artificial blood will be developed which is compatible with any blood type and which carries none of the risks that human blood can (Pelt, 1982).

*Recreation Equipment*

Like developments in the field of video, S & T advances in recreation equipment will cause both increases and decreases in tourism demand and supply; however, the overall effect probably will be that more people spend more time, day and night, in natural environments year-round.

- Outdoor recreation clothing, although extremely lightweight and breathable, will resist cold, rain, heat, and tearing, allowing the user to wear just one outfit for all climates and conditions (Scherer, 1987; Beercheck, 1986, Doran, 1986).
- Night-vision glasses will allow individuals to participate in outdoor recreation activities in the dark; off-road vehicles will be driven at night without headlights, and electronic and other devices will be available to outdoor enthusiasts to improve hearing, touch, sense of smell, strength, and coordination (Shaker and Finkelstein, 1987).
- Skycycles—one-person light aircraft with wingspans of a DC-9 jet—will be used to travel 25 miles or more at 15 mph via pedal power (Ashley, 1987), and ultralight two-person aircraft will be popular for touring and soaring in the 1990s (Campbell, 1986).
- Inflatable boats that can be stored in a closet, carried to the water in the smallest

car, and used in places that are not accessible by conventional boats will be used extensively in the future (Bignami, 1987).

- Lazer tag, complete with space-suit uniforms and starelyte guns that fire harmless beams of invisible infrared light at opponents day or night, will increase in home and outdoor recreation environments (The Sharper Image, 1986).
- Because more people can be expected to participate in tourism and outdoor recreation activities if they can quickly learn and enjoy the skills required, sports equipment manufacturers will invent new equipment that enhances participant success (Wendland, 1986).
- Pocket-sized audio communication transceivers will be used by vacationers to report emergencies, communicate with their workplace or home, remotely turn on and off home appliances, and participate in certain types of work (Lundberg, 1985).
- Technology for extracting oxygen from seawater will be used to fuel underwater recreational vehicles for exploring shipwrecks and underwater environments (Hoban, 1987).
- Solar-powered bubbles (sunpods) will permit bathers to relax outdoors at home for an all-over tan even in below-freezing temperatures (Brody, 1984).
- Innovations in equipment will allow off-road vehicles to be converted for wheelchair riders (Nachtivey, 1986).
- A supersub will be developed as a kind of undersea tour bus with oversized windows and passenger-plane interior (Sitwell and Sedgwick, 1984).

*The Natural Sciences*

The overall impact of new S & T in the natural sciences will be to increase both demand and supply for tourism. Emerging technology will immensely improve the quality of natural environments, probably more in the next several decades than in previous centuries. The resultant increase in environmental quality will likely stimulate demand and supply for leisure activities in natural environments.

- A chemical process will exist to embalm plants and young trees so they permanently retain their life-like appearance in home environments (Bronson, 1987).
- Rainbow trout weighing as much as 100 pounds and maturing five times faster than normal will be developed through genetics research. Similar developments will occur for salmon, tuna, and other commercial fish (*The Futurist*, 1985).
- Techniques will be devised to communicate with one or more animal species, which could eventually lead to the development of a universal translator device (Nobbe, 1987b).
- Science will develop a grass that is self-weeding, can be grown in almost any climate or soil, needs no watering or fertilizer, and needs to be mowed only two or three times a year (*Newsweek*, 1987; Rayl, 1987).
- Biotechnology will develop waste-eating bacteria to reduce or eliminate water pollution and toxic waste (Wallace, 1987).
- Hunters in the United States will be able to hunt exotic wildlife from other parts of the world within a few hours' drive of their residence (Hass, 1983).
- Marine biology research will provide a means to understand, predict, and perhaps even control the behavior of more useful or commercially valuable species, not just for human use but also for the species' own good (Nobbe, 1987a).

- Extended weather forecasts of two or more weeks will be possible (Kiester, 1986, Heckman, 1987).
- Science will develop a practical way to make drinking water from the ocean (Bowker, 1987; Glenn and O'Leary, 1985).

*The Built Environment*

S & T in the built environment will cause both increases and decreases in tourism demand-supply phenomena. Some of the developments that may create increases include the following:

- Massive multistoried floating hotels moored off-shore will contain restaurants, shopping arcades, gymnasiums, and glass-enclosed elevators that carry tourists directly to the sea floor (Lawren, 1985).
- Underwater hotels will attract the more adventurous leisure travelers who can peer at the undersea life through their bedroom windows (Barol and Belleville, 1987).
- Glass, one molecule thick, that bends like plastic wrap and molds into many shapes will be used in creating tourism structures that blend esthetically with natural environments to provide interiors with summer temperatures throughout the year (Stewart, 1986).
- Geotextiles, filaments produced from a variety of sources to form a nonbiodegradable fabric, will be used to stabilize erosion of scenic forest roads and trails (Schmidt, 1985).
- Energy-efficient earth shelters that use soil and sod for insulation will be used in outdoor recreation facilities in hostile climates (Maranto, 1987).
- Geothermal generators that use different water temperatures found layered through the ocean's depths will power underwater villages (Lawren, 1987).
- Electrolytic accretion — a process that uses matter dissolved in seawater — will be used to build artificial reefs and grow startling reeflike submarine cities (Lawren, 1985; Phoebe, 1984).
- Restaurants will use spatial image projections in which holograms in the shapes of mystical figures will appear magically beside customers' tables to take their orders (Simmons, 1987).

On the other hand, certain other kinds of S & T related to the built environment may cause tourism demand to decrease:

- Many homes of the future will become self-contained islands in terms of leisure life-style and entertainment potential. Developers will build homes that cater to the individual recreational appetites of the buyer (Sternlieb and Hughes, 1985; Lurz, 1985; Smay, 1985).
- The theme parks of the future will be individual-experience centers where people can engage in role play in almost any situation. For example, a Victorian-style high-tech house is presently being constructed to transport visitors back into a romantic version of the previous century. The house includes a three-dimensional film theater with vibrating chairs to simulate motion, a scent-projection device that is coordinated with images on the screen, and a state-of-the-art sound system (Simmons, 1987).

*Computers, Robotics, and Space*

The coming revolution in computers, robotics, and space will cause major changes in demand-supply conditions of tourism that stretch imagination to the limit.

- Fifty years from now, more of the world's surface may be used for farms, parkland, and wilderness because considerable quantities of industry will be moved into space (Asimov, 1983).
- Robots in the form of buildings will provide most of the services of modern hotels and be run by an administrative computer (Barrett, 1985), and robots will eventually play a large part in planning many tourism-related facilities and services such as restaurants, landscaping, park design, and entertainment (Barrett, 1985; Reeve, 1987).
- Robots will be used to perform hazardous tasks, such as rescue operations in remote environments (Kashi, 1987; *Newsweek*, 1987).
- Artificial intelligence in human form will be used in educational courses designed to enhance human negotiation, management, and leadership skills. These machines will instruct, counsel, and evaluate the student's participation (Knasel, 1986; Frand, 1987; Rogers, 1987).
- Natural language software will be popular for mainframe and personal computers because of the higher proportion of novice users (Knasel, 1986).
- Computer programs that can draw conclusions will be used by tourism managers to help formulate the best program mix for clientele and to manage vast natural resources for a multiplicity of uses (Chait, 1985; Kelly, 1985).
- Computers will make it possible to display and read almost any journal or magazine of particular interest to an individual — a mass medium tailored to the individual (Dolnick, 1987).
- A pocket-sized, voice-activated computer will be available to translate English into two or three languages (Stone, 1986).
- Resource managers will use conflict-negotiation computer games to define and choose alternative courses of action regarding tourism development versus non-development in wildland areas (Zweig, 1986).
- Vandal-proofed computers at hiking trailheads and along the trails will explain the value of the environment and interpret what is being observed (McCann, 1984).
- Computers eventually will possess artificial intelligence and mimic human senses and attitudes (Rogers, 1987; Waterbury, 1987; Hoban, 1987).
- A passenger module developed for the space shuttle will carry passengers to an orbiting space hotel or act as a hotel module itself (Alcestis, 1983; Eskow, 1986; Davies, 1985; Wolkomir, 1986).
- Today's commercial airliner will be modified to become a space transport to deliver payloads to a low orbit for only 10 percent of the cost of a NASA shuttle flight (Lawren, 1986).
- Eventually, robotic immortality will be possible. In such a "deathless" universe, computer copies of our minds could be transferred (or downloaded) into robotic bodies. Once one copy of a brain's contents has been made, it would be possible to make multiple backup copies, so that anyone could embark on any sort of adventure without having to worry about aging or death. As decades pass into centuries, one could travel the globe and then the solar system and beyond (Fjermedal, 1986; Maranto, 1987; Dewitt, 1987).

*Summary*

To adapt to tomorrow's fast-unfolding world of tourism, professionals at all levels must come to grips with a series of paradoxes created by science and technology that may set some conventional management wisdom on its ear. Management principles of long standing are being relentlessly attacked and are succumbing because of events in S & T that were unimagined even a decade ago. Today's successful tourism professionals will be those who are most flexible in adapting to new S & T. A continuing ability to embrace new planning and management ideas, routinely challenge old ones, and live with paradox will be an essential trait.

Basically, the tourism industry must plan on uncertainty — the gap between what is known and what needs to be known to make correct decisions. Dealing sensibly with uncertainty is central to responsible tourism decisions and demands that tourism professionals be Renaissance women and men, able to imagine, perceive, and gauge the future. The tourism of tomorrow will be managed by those who look now to the future and shape it into a strategic vision.

*References*

Alcestis, O. "NASA's Space Hotel." *Science Digest* (April 1983), p. 58.

Ashley, S. "88-Pound Pedal Plane." *Popular Science* pp. 70–73, 118–120.

Asimov, I. "The 21st Century: Squinting into the Crystal Ball." *U.S. News and World Report* (May 9, 1983), p. A41.

Barol, B., and B. Belleville. "Sleep Tight, Underwater." *Newsweek* (April 1987), p. 56.

Barrett, F. "The Robot Revolution." *Futurist* (October 1985), pp. 37–40.

Beercheck, R. "Engineering: The Winning Edge." *Machine Design* (June 1986), pp. 26–32.

Bezold, C. "Drugs and Health in the Year 2000." *The Futurist* (June 1985), pp. 36–40.

Bignami, L. "Blow-Up Boating." *Boat Pennsylvania* (Summer 1987), pp. 4–7.

Black, R. "Magnetic Trains Take Off." *Science Digest* (August 1984), p. 26.

Bloom, F. "Brain Drugs." *Science* (November 1985), p. 58.

Booth, S. "Future Vision." *Popular Mechanics* (July 1986), pp. 67–69.

Bowker, M. "Fresh Water from the Ocean." *Popular Science* (April 1987), pp. 57–58.

Brody, R. "Sun Bubble." *Omni* (June 1984), p. 52.

Bronson, G. "Vegetable Taxidermy." *Forbes* (May 1987), p. 145.

Campbell, J. "Flying Wing Built for Two." *Popular Mechanics* (October 1986), p. 60.

Carey, J. "The Brain Yields Its Secrets to Research." *U.S. News and World Report* (June 3, 1985), pp. 64–65.

Carey, J. "Genetics and Heart Disease." *U.S. News and World Report* (July 28, 1986), p. 58.

Cetron, M., and T. O'Toole. *Encounters with the Future: A Forecast of Life into the 21st Century.* New York: McGraw-Hill, 1982.

Cetron, M. J., and W. Rocha. "Travel Tomorrow." *The Futurist* (July–August 1987), pp. 29–34.

Chait, L. *Direct Marketing.* New York: Hoke Communication, Inc., 1985.

Cook, W. "Cars of the 90's." *U.S. News and World Report* (August 1987), pp. 38–44.

*Country Technology.* "Vital Signs." (Gay Mills, Wis., 1987–88).

Cusumano, J. "Designer Catalysts." *Science* (November 1985), p. 12.

Davies, O. "Space Tourists." *Omni* (November 1985), pp. 30–32.

Dewitt, P. "Dreaming the Impossible at MIT." *Time* (August 31, 1987), pp. 52–53.

Dolnick, E. "Inventing the Future." *The New York Times Magazine* (August 23, 1987), pp. 30–33, 41, 59.

Doran, P. "Winter World—Getting Technical." *Runner's World.* (1986), pp. 21, 43–48.

Electronic Arts *Chuck Yeager's Advanced Flight Simulator* (video) San Mateo, Calif., 1987.

Eskow, D. "Space City." *Popular Mechanics* (June 1986), pp. 27–30.

Fensom, R. "Self Enrichment Travel." *USA Today* (September 1984), pp. 40–42.

Fjermedal, G. "Surrogate Brains." *Omni* (October 1986), p. 38.

Frand, E. "Some Terrific New Product Ideas." *Research and Development* (July 1987), p. 19.

Franklin, D., and L. Davis "Shocking Snakebites." *Hippocrates* (May/June 1987), pp. 8–9.

*Futurist, The.* "Superfish: Genetics Seeks 100-Pound Trout." (February 1985), p. 3.

Garr, D. "Conic Painkiller." *Omni* (May 1987), p. 128.

Glenn, E., and J. O'Leary "Productivity and Irrigation Requirements of Halophytes Grown with Seawater in the Sonoran Desert." *Journal of Arid Environments* (July 1985), pp. 1–11.

Hartley, C. "Video Dreamland." *Audio-Visual Communications* (June 1987), p. 41.

Hass, R. "Global Reforestation." *Resources for the Future* (Washington, D.C., 1983), p. 21.

Heckman, J. "Tomorrow's Weather." *The Futurist* (March/April 1987), pp. 27–29.

Hoban, P. "Artificial Intelligence." *Omni* (February 1987), pp. 24, 111.

Hoyt, W. "Driving the Future." *Popular Mechanics* (October 1986), pp. 77–79, 115.

Iacocca, L. *Iacocca: An Autobiography,* New York: Bantam Books, 1984.

International Video Network (n.d.), *Video Travel Library,* San Ramon, Calif.

Kashi, E. "Part of Life." *Hippocrates* (May/June 1987), pp. 46–53.

Kaufmann, W. "Tourism in the Twenty-first Century." *Science Digest* (April 1983), pp. 53–60.

Kelly, K. *Computer in Landscape Architecture.* Landscape Architecture Technical Information Series 8 (Washington, D.C.: American Society of Landscape Architects), 1985.

Kennedy, H. "Travel Videos." *U.S. News and World Report* (August 3, 1987), p. 65.

Kiester, E. "Rain or Shine." *Science Digest.* (1986), pp. 94, 48–53, 83.

Kluger, J. "Body Doubles." *Omni* (August 1987), pp. 48–49, 106.

Knasel, T. *Artificial Intelligence in Manufacturing: Forecasts for the Use of Artificial Intelligence in the USA, Robotics.* New York: Elsevier Science Publishers, B.V., 1986, pp. 357–362.

Kocivar, B. "Flying Porsche." *Popular Science* (May 1987), p. 39.

Kristof, N. "12-Minute Trip to Coast Is Plane's Goal." *The New York Times* (December 2, 1987), *Business Day,* D-1.

Lawren, B. "Floating Hotel." *Omni* (February 1985), pp. 27–28.

Lawren, B. "Private Affordable Space Planes." *Omni* (December 1986), p. 157.

Lawren, B. "The Cities of Neptune." *Omni* (July 1987), pp. 37–40, 88.

Lemonick, M. "Superconductors!" *Time* (May 1987), pp. 62–72.

Long, M. "The 1987 Seer's Catalog." *Omni* (January 1987), pp. 37–40, 94–100.

Lundberg, O. "Proposed Mobile-Satellite Systems Will Offer Users a Wide Range of Services." *Communications News* (June 1985), p. 51.

Lurz, W. "Introducing N.E.S.T. '85—An Exciting Housing Concept." *Professional Builder* (February 1985), pp. 1–10.

Maranto, G. "Earth's First Visitors to Mars." *Discover* (May 1987), pp. 28–43.

Massey, M. *The People Puzzle: Understanding Yourself and Others,* Reston, Va.: Reston Publishing Co, 1979.

McCann, R. "Communications Is the Goal in the Computer World." *Parks and Recreation* (November 1984), pp. 33–35.

McCoy, M. "Technology Update." *Lodging Hospitality* (May 1987), pp. 72–73.

McIntosh, R. W., and C. R. Goeldner. *Tourism: Principles, Practices, Philosophies,* 5th ed. New York: John Wiley & Sons, Inc., 1984.

Miller, W. F. "Emerging Technologies and Their Implications for America." *USA Today* (November, 1986), pp. 60–64.

Moshier Technologies. "The Dawn of a New Era in Transportation May Be Closer Than You Think." *Discover* (May 1987), p. 15.

Nachtivey, R. "In High Gear." *Sports and Spokes* (January/February 1986), p. 17.

Naisbitt, J. (1982), *Megatrends,* New York: Warner Books, Inc.

Naisbitt, J. "A Nation on Wheels." *Popular Mechanics* (July 1986), pp. 173–190.

Naisbitt, J. *John Naisbitt's Trend Letter,* Washington, D.C., 1987.

Naisbitt, J., and P. Aburdene. *Re-inventing the Corporation.* New York: Warner Books, 1985.

*Newsweek.* "Now, Artificial Reality" (February 9, 1987), p. 56.

Nobbe, G. "Fish Talk." *Omni* (March 1987a), p. 28.

Nobbe, G. "Flippernauts." *Omni* (May 1987b), p. 37.

Pelt, D. "Next Best Thing to Whole Blood?" *Insight* (October 12, 1982), p. 51.

Perry, N. "The Economy of the 1990's — What the Sober Spenders Will Buy." *Fortune* (February 2, 1987), pp. 35–38.

Phoebe, H. "Sponge Power." *Omni* (September 1984), p. 2.

Plawin, P., and A. Blum. "Great Family Vacations." *Changing Times* (July 1987), p. 35–39.

Rayl, A. "Dreamgrass." *Omni* (May 1987), p. 36.

Reeve, R. "Where Are the Robots?" *Chemtech* (February 1987), pp. 72–75.

Rochester, P. "The Unreal Thing." *Omni* (December 1986), p. 3.

Rogers, M. "The Next Computers." *Newsweek* (April 1987), pp. 60–62.

Schefter, J. "Engineering Tomorrow's Airlines." *Popular Science* (April 1987), pp. 49–52, 98.

Scherer, M. "New Wrinkles in Old Clothing." *Sierra* (January/February 1987), pp. 121–124.

Schmidt, D. "Building Better Blacktops." *American City and Country Administration, Engineering and Operations.* Communication Channels, Inc. (June 1985), pp. 1–3.

Shaker, S., and R. Finkelstein. "The Bionic Soldier." *National Defense* (April 1987), pp. 3–7.

Simmons, J. C. "Christopher and Goddard: Variations on a Theme." *American Way* (July 15, 1987), pp. 21–25.

Sitwell, N., and J. Sedgwick. "Super Sub of the Future." *The Futurist* (June 1984), pp. 60–65.

Sivy, M. "What We Don't Know." *Money* (November 1985), pp. 209–212.

Siwolop, S. "Unsteady as She Flows." *Discover* 6 (1985), pp. 67–69.

Siwolop, S. "It's a Chopper — It's a Plane — It's Europe's New Air Shuttle." *Business Week* (January 19, 1987), p. 75.

Smay, V. "Bolt and Glue Arched Panels Cut Costs." *Popular Science* (August 1985), p. 13.

Smith, J. O. "Mysterious Weekends." *County* (January 1985), pp. 28–29.

Sternlieb, G., and J. Hughes. "The Good News About Housing." Dow Jones and Co. (August 1985), pp. 1–5.

Stewart, D. "Fiber Fabric Structures." *Science Digest* (March 1986), pp. 58–62.

Stone, C. "Computer Translator." *Omni* (December 1986), p. 157.

Sybervision. *Sybervision* (video). Newark, Calif., 1987.

The Sharper Image (October 1986), pp. 1–2.

Tracy, E. "A New X-ray Scanner to Hinder Hijackers." *Fortune* 28 (April 1986), p. 12.

Walker, P. "Joints to Spare." *Science* (November 1985), p. 57.

Wallace, J. "Pollution Solutions." *USAIR* (January 1987), pp. 58–62.

Waterbury, R. "Computer/Human Interface 2000." *Assembly Engineering* (June 1987), pp. 70–73.

Wendland, M. "New Wave Gear." *American Health* (July/August 1986), pp. 50–53.

Wiener, L. "All the Sights, Sounds and Comforts of Home." *U.S. News and World Report* (August 1987), p. 45.

Wolkomir, R. "Beyond the Challenger Era." *Omni* (February 1986), pp. 27–30.

Yeager, C. "America's Orient Express." *Popular Mechanics* (August 1986), pp. 73–75.

Zweig, C. "Mayan Vacation." *Omni* (December 1986), p. 157.

# READING 15-2

## *Tourism — The World's Peace Industry*

By Louis D'Amore
L. J. D'Amore and Associates

Reprinted from the *Journal of Travel Research*, Vol. 27, No. 1, Summer 1988.

### The Economic Significance of Tourism

Tourism has been one of the world's most consistent growth industries of the past 30 years. Prospects for the continued growth of world tourism appear to be most promising. Societal trends are favorable to the continued growth of demand and low-cost air travel is becoming increasingly available. As well, the governments of many nations are playing a stronger role in encouraging the growth of both domestic and international tourism as a means of job creation, economic diversification, and source of foreign exchange.

Current forecasts suggest that international travel will double by the year 2000 and will account for fully 10% of international trade.

Beyond its economic significance, there is a growing realization of the role of international travel in promoting understanding and trust among people of different cultures. This is not only a precondition for additional trade in goods and services, particularly with newly emerging trading partners, but also a foundation on which to build improved relationships towards the goal of world peace and prosperity.

### What Is Peace?

Peace is commonly viewed as "the absence of war." Negatively defined as such, our efforts as a society are on national defense through the building of armaments and armies, and the formation of military coalitions with other nations who have common interests.

For nearly half a century now, there has been a military confrontation among the world's major powers. From this perspective, most of the world has been at peace (negatively defined as above). Yet, in 1986, the United Nations "Year of Peace," some 3–5 million people died in 36 wars and armed conflicts around the world. Beyond the 41 nations directly engaged, other countries are involved in providing weapons and support — particularly the United States and Soviet Union who support opposing factions in virtually every conflict. In the continuing Persian Gulf War between Iran and Iraq, some 53 countries have sold arms to one side or the other since the war started in 1980.[1]

Beyond these situations of actual armed conflict, the threat of nuclear war and the havoc it would bring us profoundly affected the people of the world, particularly the young. (Recent developments toward the reduction of nuclear weapons in the arsenals of the United States and Soviet Union, as this is being written, offer some hope for optimism in this area.)

More recently, peace researchers have suggested that the opposite of peace is not war, but violence. At some point during the summer of 1987, world population reached 5 billion people. Nearly one third of its population is living in absolute poverty (a number equal to the total world population at the start of the century);

nearly one half does not have access to basic health services; more than half a billion are seriously undernourished.

In just the last three years, the drought-triggered crisis in Africa resulted in the death of about a million persons and put 35 million at risk; an estimated 60 million people (mostly children) died of diseases related to unsafe drinking water and malnutrition; and the world witnessed the technological tragedies of Bhopal and Chernobyl.

It is difficult to conclude that we are living in a peaceful world, given this second definition of peace as "the absence of violence."

There have been successes nonetheless, and the signs of hope are many. Infant mortality is falling; human life expectancy is increasing; the literacy rate is climbing; the proportion of children starting school is rising; and global food production has increased more rapidly than population. But clearly, we have a large agenda to complete before we can claim that world peace is a reality for most of the world's population, if our criterion for peace is "the absence of violence."

Beyond violence to humanity, we have experienced an escalating rate of violence to our environment, which in turn is threatening the survival of a wide range of species and the lives of humans as well. More than 11 million hectares of forests are destroyed yearly. Over three decades this would equal an area approximately the size of India. The world's deserts are expanding at a rate of 6 million hectares a year.

In developed countries, acid precipitation is killing forests and lakes and is damaging the artistic and architectural heritage of nations. Toxic wastes and chemicals are penetrating our water systems and the food chain.

Environmental threats might indeed be the most serious threats to global security in the 21st century. A United Nations study group recently concluded that, "there can no longer be the slightest doubt that resource scarcities and ecological stresses constitute real and imminent threats to the future well-being of all peoples and nations." [2]

Within this global context, more than $1 trillion U.S. was spent on weapons and warfare in 1987. To this amount we are now adding billions more in the "war on terrorism" and for "security" against terrorists. This is more than $200 for every man, woman and child in the world — the per capita income of most nations. It is the aggregate GNP of some 130 nations.

One-tenth that amount could feed all the people of the world. Another one-tenth could educate all school aged children. One-tenth could provide new towns and communities with housing for the displaced persons of the world. Less than one-tenth would provide clean water, sanitation and basic health services to the one-third of the world's population who lack these services.

The philosophy and ethic of "industrial man" originating with Descartes, Bacon and other philosopher/scientists who ushered in the industrial era, was one of domination and control over nature. The environmental "alerts" of the late 1960s and current issues including acid rain and toxic waste, have caused a re-evaluation of our relationship with nature. We are now recognizing that sustainable development requires a custodial relationship with our environment and living in harmony with nature.

Similarly, international terrorism. Third World debt and nuclear arms proliferation are the "alert signals" of the 1980s which call for a re-conceptualization of man's relationship to man in the global village of an information age.

Long term global security in relationships with our neighbors in the global village will not come from a growing proliferation of weapons, wars, and swift retaliatory strikes to acts of terrorism. Former Canadian Prime Minister Lester B. Pearson warned us a quarter century ago that "no planet can survive half slave, half free; half engulfed in misery, half careening along toward the joys of an almost unlimited consumption . . . neither ecology nor our morality could survive such contrasts."

### Toward a Positive Definition of Peace

Perhaps the most powerful and symbolic photographs ever taken were the photographs of planet earth as the first U.S. astronauts began their probe into space. Edgar Mitchell described what he saw from space as "a beautiful, harmonious, peaceful looking planet, blue with white clouds, and one that gave you a deep sense . . . of home, of being, of identity."

The photographs brought back from space generate similar reactions of awe, connectedness, and mutual dependency among people on earth, a heightened awareness of the relationship between humanity and the planet, and the need to live in harmony with one another and our environment.

Historians may well conclude that this vision of planet earth will have a greater impact on the future direction of human thinking than the Copernican Revolution of the 16th century which revealed that the earth was not the center of the universe. From space, we view the world as one living organism where the health of the total organism is necessary for the health of each component part, and the health of each component part, in turn, contributes to the health of the total organism.

Once we accept the perspective of an organic and interconnected world as described above, we can begin to think in terms of a *positive* definition of peace. In this context the Russian word for peace and its various meanings are illuminating. The word is "mir" which means:

   the universe
   planet earth
   the human race
   peace and tranquility
   concord in relations between people and states
   freedom from war

The Russian definition of peace is both multidimensional and positive. It implies peace and tranquility within ourselves; peace with our fellow humans and between nations; peace with nature and our spaceship earth; peace within the universe (and perhaps we can add—with our God).

To achieve such a positive concept of peace, we must first have a vision of what peace in positive terms can be. The vision of a world at peace so defined. Once we have created that vision, we have already set the forces in motion to bring about the actualization of that vision. We must be armed with new insights rather than new weapons. Insights which harness the resources of nature and the intelligence of humans for the common good of all. New visions will be required from fields other than politics—from fields such as anthropology, psychology, sociology, and geography; from the scientific community with visions for the constructive use of science and technology; from the environmental and ecological sciences with visions of ecological harmony; from the cultural community and the full range of creative art forms for a spirit of celebration in cultural diversity; and from the business community for a vision of the benefits from international trade and the free flow of goods, people, and ideas.

Most importantly, we must as individuals and ordinary people work towards and contribute to a positive vision of our common destiny, new visions of how to relate and ways of relating. President Dwight D. Eisenhower said in 1959, "I like to believe that people in the long run are going to do more to promote peace than are governments. Indeed, I think that people want peace so much that one of these days, governments had better get out of their way and let them have it."

*Images of the "Enemy"—The "Other"*

Throughout human history, our "mental map" of the rest of the world and the people of that world, has been constructed from behind borders—behind city walls; political borders; or the mental borders of political ideology and ethnocultural differences.

World history provides many examples of how closed societies are prone to suspicion, hostility, and armed conflict. It is the separateness from other nations and cultures that creates the psychological distance and mind-set conducive to nurturing fears and suspicions and contributes subsequently to the potential for destructive conflict. "The unleashed powers of the atom has changed everything, save our modes of thinking," wrote Albert Einstein in 1946, "and thus we drift toward unparalleled disaster."

Some forty years after this warning, scientists and scholars from the Soviet Union and the United States came together to explore a new "mode of thinking" appropriate to an interdependent world with jet planes, computer technology, global communications, and a proliferation of nuclear weapons.

The focus of two of the scientists, Dr. Jerome Frank, Professor of Psychiatry at Johns Hopkins University and Dr. Andrei Melville, of the Moscow Institute on U.S.A. and Canadian Studies, was on "perception of the enemy." They concluded that "the mutual image of the enemy is always similar, no matter who the enemies are, and they mirror each other. That is, each side attributes the same virtues to itself and the same vices to the enemy. 'We' are trustworthy, peace loving, honorable and humanitarian; 'They' are treacherous, warlike and cruel . . . because of the belief that what is bad for the enemy is good for us, any efforts toward peace are seen as weak or naive on 'Our' part, and cunning and treacherous on 'Theirs'."

Images of the enemy are sustained by a disposition to accept as truth only those facts or assertions that meet our preconceived beliefs. Thus we tend to believe only the worst of our enemies and the best of ourselves.

Survey research tends to support these conclusions. A 1983 Gallup Poll found that only 9% of the U.S. public had favorable views toward the Soviet Union. In a separate poll taken by Daniel Yankelovich, most Americans expressed their belief that the Soviet Union would attack the U.S. or its allies if the U.S. were weak (65%); that the Soviets saw U.S. friendly gestures as weaknesses (73%); that force was the only language understood by the Soviets (62%); and that the U.S. should weaken the Soviets at every opportunity "because anything that weakens our enemies makes us more secure." [3]

The survey also found however, that these sentiments were mainly directed at the leaders of the Soviet Government. Nearly 90% of the American public agreed that "the Russian people are not nearly as hostile to the U.S. as their leaders are and, in fact the Russians could be our friends if their leaders have a different attitude." This is confirmed by the many travelers to the Soviet Union who are impressed by the high regard most Soviets have for the American people.

*Track Two Diplomacy*

In a seminal article on citizen diplomacy, written in the Winter 1981–82 issue of *Foreign Policy*, William D. Davidson and Joseph V. Montville defined the official channel of governmental relations as "track one diplomacy" and the unofficial channel of people-to-people relations as "track two diplomacy." Their article suggests that the two tracks run parallel. Track two diplomacy is "supplement to the understandable shortcomings of official relations." To defend their nation's interests, track one diplomats must make worst case assumptions about an adversary's intentions, but these very assumptions can set in motion a chain reaction of mutual distrust, threats, and hostilities that can culminate in war. Track two diplomats, they argued, create an alternative set of relationships that can prevent such a chain reaction.

"Track two diplomacy is unofficial, non-structured interaction. It is always open-minded, often altruistic, and . . . strategically optimistic, based on the best case analysis. Its underlying assumption is that the actual or potential conflict can be resolved or eased by appealing to common human capabilities of reason and goodwill." They concluded that "both tracks are necessary for psychological reasons and both need one another."

Tourism operates at the most basic level of "track two" diplomacy by spreading information about the personalities, beliefs, aspirations, perspectives, culture and politics of the citizens of one country to the citizens of another.

*The Role of Tourism in Building Bridges of Reality and Understanding*

To develop a world view that is realistic — that conforms to the reality of the world and our role in it — we must constantly revise and extend our understanding to include new knowledge of the larger world. Louis Brandeis, one of America's great jurists and thinkers, once said that there could be no true community "save that built upon the personal acquaintance of each with each."

Travel and tourism provide such an opportunity; the opportunity for individuals to gain first-hand knowledge of the larger world.

Some thirty years ago, the European Economic Community was established with the objective of reconciling the enemies of two world wars. The EEC was based on the premise that if the peoples of these countries got to know each other better, there would be less likelihood of war. One of the main cornerstones of EEC policy is freedom to travel and minimizing frontier controls.

The People's Republic of China, a nuclear-armed country widely regarded as a "yellow menace" in the 1960s, has in the past fifteen years become a friend. The key to a changed political relationship between the United States and the People's Republic of China has been an opening to travel and the web of relationships that have developed through cultural exchanges, conferences, sports, twinning of cities, trade, and a growing set of common interests.

The People's Republic of China opened its doors to the outside world in 1978 following visits from Canadian Prime Minister Pierre Trudeau and U.S. President Richard Nixon. Visitor arrivals have grown annually by 20–30% since 1978. More than 2.0 million foreign visitors will travel to China in 1988. By the year 2000, foreign visitors are expected to number 7–8 million.

It is interesting to note that over the past two years, the People's Republic of China has been reducing the size of its army by a million soldiers.

### U.S.-Soviet Relations

In the Soviet Union, the leadership of Mikhail Gorbachev, with his policies of "glasnost," "perestroika," and "demokratizatsiya," is signalling a new era in relationships with Western nations. The new generation of Soviet leadership is recognizing that it cannot continue to expend 13% of its GNP on the military establishment and at the same time meet the requirements of its domestic economy. The annual demand for consumer goods exceeds supply by more than $30 billion. The task of acquiring needed supplies for a family of four alone requires some 20 hours a week of effort.

Gorbachev's policy of "perestroika," or economic restructuring, calls for a doubling in economic output by the year 2000. To achieve this goal, requires a relaxation of international tensions and the focus of energy and resources on domestic reform. It will also require constructive economic relations with the West to which the Soviets already are turning to learn about motivation and modern principles of management. The U.S.S.R. will also have a need for the technological tools of Western nations. Therefore the potential exists for the Soviet Union to become a major trading partner with the West and eventually to become integrated with the world economy.

It is becoming increasingly clear that the United States as well, is losing its economic capacity to sustain a large military establishment and ever-growing expenditures for a sophisticated nuclear arsenal. Paul Kennedy, in a recent article "The (Relative) Decline of America," points out that in 1945, the U.S. commanded a 40% share of the world economy. Today that share is 20%. Yet military commitments have grown dramatically.[4] Along with a diminished share in the world's economy has come a weakening of the U.S. financial position in terms of staggering deficits in international trade and the Federal budget. The U.S. Federal debt by the end of 1988 will be approximately $2.5 trillion or almost three times greater than the $0.9 trillion debt at the start of the decade in 1980. The trade deficit persists in a range of $140–150 billion a year.

These deficits are supported by importing ever larger amounts of capital. In the space of a few short years, the U.S. international position has shifted from being the world's leading creditor nation, to the position of being the world's leading debtor nation. At the end of 1987, U.S. liabilities were approximately $400 billion. (Brazil, the Third World's largest debtor nation, has a debt of $104 billion.)

The net foreign assets of Japan, on the other hand, have soared and approached some $300 billion by the end of 1987.

Kennedy states that, "while the U.S. devotes 7% of its GNP to the Defense budget and the military establishment utilizes the majority of the country's ablest scientists and engineers, Japanese and West Germans concentrate their financial and human resources on the design of commercial products." He goes on to suggest that a heavy investment in armaments "while bringing greater security in the short term, may so erode the commercial competitiveness of the American economy that the nation will be less secure in the long term."

Clearly, the easing of tensions between the U.S. and the Soviet Union would also help to restore balance between U.S. military commitments and the economic capacity to sustain those commitments.

The Geneva Summit, in November 1986, sent forward a clear signal to the world that the relaxation of tensions was possible, and had begun. Recognizing the benefits of travel in achieving better relationships among the two countries, Secretary Gorbachev and President Reagan declared in their joint statement following the Summit: "There should be greater understanding among our peoples and to this end we will encourage greater travel."

A few days before President Reagan met with Secretary Gorbachev, he gave what has since been called his "People to People" speech:

"Imagine how much good we could accomplish, how the cause of peace would be served, if more individuals and families from our respective countries could come to know each other in a personal way. . . .

"I feel the time is ripe for us to take bold new steps to open the way for our peoples to participate in an unprecedented way in the building of peace . . .

"Such exchanges can build in our societies thousands of coalitions for cooperation and peace. Governments can only do so much; once they get the ball rolling, they should step out of the way and let people get together to share, enjoy, help, listen, and learn from each other. . . .

"It is not an impossible dream that our children and grandchildren can someday travel freely back and forth between America and the Soviet Union; visit each other's homes; work and study together; enjoy and discuss plays, music, and television; and root for teams when they compete."

Some 120,000 Americans will visit the Soviet Union in 1988, making approximately 1 million visitors overall. What is also significant is the types of visitors traveling to the Soviet Union. They include environmentalists, developers, economists, movie producers, political leaders, professors and others who are meeting with their professional counterparts in the exchange of ideas and exploration of joint projects.

Various conferences have included an International Peace Forum in February 1987, and the Seventh Annual Convention of Physicians for the Prevention of Nuclear War. Other events have included a Walk for Peace, a Moscow Marathon for Peace, a Bering Strait Swim For Peace, a Conference of High School Students for Peace, and an Ice Cream Exchange for Peace.

### Tourism — The World's Peace Industry

As we travel and communicate in ever-increasing numbers, we are discovering that most people, regardless of their political or religious orientation, race, or socioeconomic status, want a peaceful world in which all are fed, sheltered, productive, and fulfilled.

The story is told about a Senator approaching Abraham Lincoln amidst the passions of the Civil War and saying, "Mr. President, I believe that enemies should be destroyed." Lincoln replied, "I agree with you sir, and the best way to destroy an enemy is to make him a friend."

Through travel, people are finding friends in every corner of the earth: finding common bonds with the rest of humanity and spreading messages of hope for a peaceful world.

Tourism properly designed and developed, has the potential to help bridge the psychological and cultural distances that separate people of diverse races, colors, religions and stages of social and economic development. Through tourism we can come rather to an appreciation of the rich human, cultural, and ecological diversity that our world mosaic offers; to evolve a mutual trust and respect for one another and the dignity of all life on earth.

The tourism industry, combined with our world parks systems, can make a contribution to living in harmony with our environment as well. The tourism industry makes possible the setting aside and preservation of vast tracts of land as national parks and wilderness areas. More than 3,000 protected areas in 120 countries and covering more the 4 million square miles are now preserved in their natural state. Visitors to these areas experience the beauty and majesty of the world's finest natural features and come away with a heightened appreciation of environmental values. In national parks townsites such as Banff and Jasper, we have the opportunity for "Man" to be co-creators with nature, bringing the best of human design in juxtaposition with the best of nature.

Transfrontier parks, or border parks, provide a special category of national parks. These are protected areas located along the boundaries of countries and are increasingly recognized as "Peace Parks." Border parks, on each side of a frontier, offer the benefits of larger, contiguous protected areas, increased cooperation between nations, and improved international understanding.

Tourism contributes to both preservation and development of the world's cultural heritage. It provides governments with the rationale for the preservation of historical sites and monuments and the motivation for indigenous groups to preserve unique dimensions of heritage in the form of dance, music, and artifacts. Tourism also provides both the audience and the economic engine for museums, the performing and visual arts, and the restoration of historical areas.

Severe poverty, stemming from under-development, is not only an active cause of conflict, but is inherently a form of violence. Pope Paul VI once said that "development is the new name for peace." The tourism industry is a human resource-intensive industry. It has the capacity to generate foreign exchange and a high ratio of government revenues as a proportion of total expenditures. As well, it has a capacity for both forward and backward linkages with other sectors of the economy. Properly designed, it can contribute to social and cultural enrichment as well as economic development. For these reasons, it is increasingly attractive as an industry among developing nations.

The 5,000 international conferences held each year increasingly draw on people of all nations to share their concerns; propose solutions to problems; exchange ideas; and create "opportunity networks." The growth in student exchanges, cultural exchanges, twinning of cities, and international sporting events not only give us an appreciation of our differences, but also show us the commonality of our goals and aspirations as a human family. The collective outcomes of these travel and tourism experiences help all humankind to appreciate the full meaning of the "Global Village" and the bonds that people everywhere have with one another.

Approximately 400 million persons will travel to another country in 1988. This number is growing by 5–7% each year. Millions more will act as "hosts" to these travelers as part of their daily job and/or as interested residents of the host country.

These millions of daily person-to-person encounters are potentially a powerful force for improved relations among the people and nations of the world; relations which emphasize a sharing and appreciation of cultures rather than the lack of trust bred by isolation.

### Conclusion

The countdown to the 21st century has begun. Less than 15 years remain before the dawning of a new millenium, a period in which the late Buckminster Fuller believed humankind would be taking its "final exam."

Humankind will pass its "final exam" when we recognize the need to live in harmony with our fellow human beings, as well as with nature — when we recognize that we are our brother's keeper. We will have passed our "final exam" when the one-half of the world's scientists who are currently conducting research into weaponry and destruction have shifted their focus to human and social development and a sustainable environment. We will have passed our "final exam" when the U.S. and the Soviet Union join together, with other nations, in a program of de-militarization and the re-allocation of vital resources to achieve sustained global development for the benefit of all humankind.

For the first time in human history, all the problems which the world faces are man-made problems. And so too, humankind has the capacity to solve them. Ninety per cent of the scientists who ever lived are alive today, and our scientific knowledge base continues to expand exponentially.

The key to solving global issues is the human, institutional, corporate, and political will to do so.

In the 1960s, President John F. Kennedy had a vision of putting a man on the moon within that decade. The articulation of this vision brought about the marshalling of human, scientific, and fiscal resources to make that vision a reality.

So too, the year 2000 offers an occasion for visionary thinking. There are roughly 40–50 million persons engaged in the tourism industry around the world. The value of the global tourism plant is in the trillions of dollars.

Just as John Kennedy's vision put a man on the moon within a decade, the vision of tourism leaders around the world can marshall immense human and physical resources to help achieve global peace in this century.

The tourism industry has achieved its goal of becoming the world's largest industry. It now has the promise of becoming the world's first "Peace Industry;" an industry which recognizes, promotes and supports the belief that every traveler is potentially an "Ambassador for Peace," an industry which will be a model for other industries to follow.

*Reading Endnotes*

1. Findings of the Stockholm International Peace Research Institute as reported in the *Montreal Gazette,* June 18, 1987.
2. World Commission on Environment and Development (1987), *Our Common Future,* U.S.A.: Oxford University Press. p. 300.
3. Don Carlson and Craig Comstock (ed.) (1986), *Citizen Summitry — Keeping The Peace When It Matters Too Much To Be Left To Politicians,* U.S.A.: Jeremy P. Tarcher, Inc., p. 11.
4. *The Atlantic Monthly,* August 1987.

## READING 15-3

### Space Age Suite Provides Unique Stay

Reprinted from *Travel Trade,* July 24, 1989.

The crew of the Starship Enterprise and the adventurous Star Wars gang landed in some unusual places, but would feel right at home in Carnival's Crystal Palace Resort & Casino during a stay in its extravagant Galactica suite.

This one-of-a-kind suite provides guests with a look into the twenty-first century through the eyes of designer Diane Sepler. It promises to be an exciting — and at $25,000 a night, an expensive — era.

Guests of the Galactica suite are whisked by limousine from the airport, and upon arrival at Carnival's Crystal Palace Resort & Casino are escorted to a guest lounge in the hotel's Casino Tower, where they are given a silver "prox" card. The concierge activates the suite's electronic "set" mode at the touch of a button, and as the guests walk the corridor toward Galactica, futuristic music welcomes them. An etched-glass panel with fiberoptic stars and planets announces the guests' arrival at the "Galactic Fantasy".

The suite's stainless-steel doors slide open a la the Starship Enterprise, providing the guests' first glimpse of the Spielbergian experience to come.

#### White and Silver Decor

The entire suite is white and silver, with the exception of the blue neon glow emanating from bent-steel ceiling soffits.

The guests' entrance past heat-sensitive columns summons the suite's permanent occupant, Ursula. The sophisticated, friendly robot greets guests by name and advises them of all the electronic systems available at the touch of a button, from the $40,000 audio-visual system to the $98,000 lighting extravaganza.

A circular sofa in the center of the living area faces a two-story, 8-foot-square screen which displays an ever-changing art abstraction. The screen also acts as the suite's television and movie display. Guests can experience their favorite movies, which are pre-stocked in the VHS movie library, in Sensurround.

#### Central Control Panel

The "brains" of the suite reside in a panel in the sofa's armrest, where guests can control the art screen, stereo, television, movies, compact disc and cassette players, the suite's lighting and the return of Ursula. The sofa rotates so that all areas of the room can be seen, including the lucite piano and a space-age reef aquarium, which produces "bubble shows" around the tank's primary occupant: an undulating sting-ray.

"Galactica is designed to make the guests feel transported into the next century," says designer Diane Sepler. "We've used exclusively white, silver, and lucite throughout the suite, combined with the state-of-the-art in electronics, lighting, and robotics to create a futuristic environment that is both exciting and inviting."

Incorporated into the utopian setting is the floor-to-ceiling view of the Bahamian beach and ocean through the two-story glass walls of the multi-faceted living area.

The ceiling perpetuates the "view" of sky as it is painted in subtle shades of a night sky through which fiberoptic stars and planets shine brightly.

*Spiral Staircase*

The second-floor bedroom is reached via illuminated spiral lucite staircase, and contains its own bar, art light sculpture, and large bathroom with glowing light strips accenting the floor.

The suite's master bedroom, located on the main floor, contains a circular bed on raised platform surrounded by windows. A mirrored ceiling soffit also illuminates and highlights the bed, while the room's lighting and window fashions are controlled from a panel located in the bed. The bathroom's jacuzzi allows guests to bet on the roll of holographic tumbling dice while soaking. When summoned, Ursula appears bearing fresh towels.

Included with the suite are a butler, masseur or masseuse, all meals at Carnival's Crystal Palace Resort & Casino, and a limousine on call 24 hours a day.

After an evening in one of Carnival's Crystal Palace Resort's exotic gourmet restaurants, taking in the Palace Theater's show JUBILATION!, and playing the odds in the 30,000-square-foot casino, a night in the Galactica suite provides still more excitement.

In the master bedroom, even the atmosphere is at your command. With the touch of a button, the lights dim and a screen slides silently into place. Far away, wind blows softly, and clouds begin to gather on the screen. As the wind picks up, the clouds become heavier, darker, and finally angry. The wind sounds brisk now, pushed along by the distant thunder. You are surrounded by the storm, and it finally breaks around you — thunder crashing, lightning sizzling around the room, and the sound of a driving rain.

Guests to the Galactica suite at Carnival's Crystal Palace Resort & Casino have the opportunity to experience the twenty-first century beginning this fall on The Bahamian Riviera.

## *Key Concepts*

| | |
|---|---|
| aircraft | demographic changes |
| built environment | discretionary income |
| challenge of leisure | environmental trends |
| changing attitudes toward leisure | land use |
| computers | leisure trends |
| cultural understanding | medical advances |

recreation equipment
robotics
science and technology
space travel
study tours
technological trends

telephone-computer tourist information
transportation
tourism and peace
universality of humankind
video marketing technology

## For Review and Discussion

1. As a travel counselor, what questions might you ask of a prospective tourist to determine his or her interest in a life-seeing or local hosting program?
2. What might be an obstacle to the optimistic projections of increased international tourism forecast in this chapter?
3. Intelligent, creative, sensitive tourism developments can actually improve the environment and heighten the appeal of an area. Give examples of how this might happen.
4. Can tourism enhance and improve a destination area's cultural and hospitality resources? Provide actual or hypothetical examples.
5. What is the expected trend in health-oriented accommodations and programs? Food services?
6. Evaluate your campus as a center for an elderhostel, international education, conferences, study tours, and short courses.
7. What are the realistic prospects for a four-day workweek?
8. Does early retirement appeal to most workers?
9. How can tourism interests obtain a growing share of leisure market expenditures?
10. Specifically, in what ways can world peace be enhanced by tourism?

## Selected References

Bureau of Labor Statistics. *Projections 2000.* Washington, D.C.: U.S. Department of Labor, 1988.

Cutter, Blayne. "Anything for a Thrill." *American Demographics,* Vol. 10, no. 8 (August 1988), pp. 38–41.

D'Amore, L. J., and Jafar Jafari. *Tourism—A Vital Force for Peace.* Montreal: First Global Conference, 1988.

Goodrich, Jonathan N. "Touristic Travel to Outer Space: Profile and Barriers to Entry." *Journal of Travel Research,* Vol. 26, no. 2 (Fall 1987), pp. 40–43.

Hodgson, Adele. *The Travel and Tourism Industry Strategies for the Future.* Oxford: Pergamon Press, 1987.

Hyatt. *Hyatt Travel Futures Project: Report on Business Travelers.* Chicago: Hyatt Corporation, 1988.

Kelly, John R. *Recreation Trends Toward the Year 2000.* Champaign, Ill.: Sagamore Publishing, 1987.

Papson, S. "Tourism—World's Biggest Industry in Twenty-first Century?" *Futurist* (August 1979), pp. 249–257.

*Proceedings 1980 National Outdoor Recreation Trends Symposium,* 3 vols. Broomall, Pa.: North-eastern Forest Experiment Station, 1980.

U.S. Travel Data Center. *Highlights of Discover America 2000.* Washington, D.C.: Travel Industry Association of America, 1988.

Van Doren, Carlton S. "Outdoor Recreation Trends in the 1980s: Implications for Society." *Journal of Travel Research,* Vol. 19, no. 3 (Winter 1981), pp. 3–10.

# A P P E N D I X  A

# Key Travel Industry Contacts

## ASSOCIATIONS AND ORGANIZATIONS

Air Transport Association of America
1709 New York Avenue N.W.
Washington, D.C. 20006

Airport Operators Council International
1220 19th Street N.W.
Suite 800
Washington, D.C. 20036

American Association of Retired Persons
1909 K Street N.W.
Washington, D.C. 20049

American Automobile Association
8111 Gatehouse Road
Falls Church, Virginia 22047

American Bus Association
1025 Connecticut Avenue N.W.
Washington, D.C. 20036

American Car Rental Association
2011 Eye Street N.W.
5th Floor
Washington, D.C. 20006

American Hotel and Motel Association
1201 New York Avenue N.W.
Washington, D.C. 20005

American Resort and Residential Devel-
    opment Association
1220 L Street N.W.
Suite 510
Washington, D.C. 20005

American Recreation Coalition
1331 Pennsylvania Avenue N.W.
Suite 726
Washington, D.C. 20004

American Sightseeing International
309 Fifth Avenue
New York, New York 10016

American Society of Travel Agents
1101 King Street
Alexandria, Virginia 22314

American Youth Hostels
P.O. Box 37613
Washington, D.C. 20013

Association of Retail Travel Agents
25 South Riverside
Croton-on-Hudson, New York 10520

Association of Travel Marketing Executives
P.O. Box 43563
Washington, D.C. 20010

Bureau of Economic Analysis
U.S. Department of Commerce
1401 K Street N.W.
Washington, D.C. 20230

Bureau of the Census
Demographic Surveys Division
U.S. Department of Commerce
Washington, D.C. 20233

Caribbean Tourism Association
20 East 46th Street
New York, New York 10017

Caribbean Tourism Research and Devel-
    opment Centre
Mer Vue, Marine Gardens
Hastings, Christ Church
Barbados, West Indies

Conference of National Park Conces-
    sioners
P.O. Box 29041
Phoenix, Arizona 85038

Cruise Lines International Association
500 Fifth Avenue
Suite 1407
New York, New York 10110

European Travel Commission
630 Fifth Avenue
New York, New York 10111

Federal Aviation Administration
800 Independence Avenue S.W.
Washington, D.C. 20591

Federation of International Youth Travel
    Organizations (FIYTO)
Islands Brygge 81, DK-2300
Copenhagen S, Denmark

Gray Line Sight-Seeing Association
350 Fifth Avenue
Suite 1409
New York, New York 10118

Highway Users Federation
1776 Massachusetts Avenue N.W.
Washington, D.C. 20036

Hotel Sales and Marketing Association
    International
1300 L Street N.W.
Suite 800
Washington, D.C. 20005

Institute of Certified Travel Agents
148 Linden Street
Wellesley, Massachusetts 02181

International Academy of Tourism
4 rue des Iris
Monte Carlo, Monaco

International Academy for the Study of
    Tourism
WTO Building
Capitan Haya, 42
28020 Madrid, Spain

International Air Transport Association
    (IATA)
IATA Building
2000 Peel Street
Montreal, Quebec
Canada H3A 2R4

International Airline Passengers Associa-
    tion
4301 Westside Drive
Dallas, Texas 75209

International Association of Amusement
    Parks and Attractions
4230 King Street
Alexandria, Virginia 22302

International Association of Convention
    and Visitors Bureaus
P.O. Box 758
Champaign, Illinois 61820

International Association of Scientific Ex-
    perts in Tourism (AIEST)
Varnbuelstrasse 19
CH-9000 St. Gallen
Switzerland

International Bureau of Social Tourism
    (BITS)
7 bd de l'Imperatrice
B-1000 Brussels, Belgium

International Civil Aviation Organization
    (ICAO)
International Aviation Square
1000 Sherbrooke Street West
Montreal, Quebec
Canada H3A 2R2

International Touring Alliance (AIT)
2 quai Gustave-Ador
CH-1207, Geneva, Switzerland

National Air Carrier Association
1730 M Street N.W.
Suite 710
Washington, D.C. 20036

National Campground Owners Association
11706 Bowman Green
Reston, Virginia 22090

National Caves Association
Route 9, P.O. Box 106
McMinnville, Tennessee 37110

National Park Service
Statistical Office
P.O. Box 25287
Denver, Colorado 80225

National Recreation and Park Association
3101 Park Center Drive
Alexandria, Virginia 22302

National Restaurant Association
1200 Seventeenth Street N.W.
Washington, D.C. 20036

National Ski Areas Association
20 Maple Street
Springfield, Massachusetts 01101

National Tour Association
546 East Main Street
P.O. Box 3071
Lexington, Kentucky 40596

National Trust for Historic Preservation
1785 Massachusetts Avenue N.W.
Washington, D.C. 20036

Pacific Asia Travel Association (PATA)
One Montgomery Street
West Tower, No. 1750
San Francisco, California 94104

Recreation Vehicle Industry Association
P.O. Box 2999
1896 Preston White Drive
Reston, Virginia 22090

Society of American Travel Writers
1120 Connecticut Avenue N.W.
Suite 940
Washington, D.C. 20036

Society of Incentive Travel Executives, Inc.
271 Madison Avenue
Suite 904
New York, New York 10016

Tourism Canada
235 Queen Street
Ottawa, Ontario
Canada K1A 0H6

Tourism Industry Association of Canada
130 Albert Street
Ottawa, Ontario
Canada K1P 5G4

Travel and Tourism Government Affairs
  Council
Two Lafayette Center
1133 21st Street N.W.
Washington, D.C. 20036

Travel and Tourism Research Association
P.O. Box 58066, Foothill Station
Salt Lake City, Utah 84158

Travel Industry Association of America
Two Lafayette Center
1133 21st Street N.W.
Washington, D.C. 20036

United Bus Owners of America
1300 L Street N.W.
Suite 1050
Washington, D.C. 20005

United States Tour Operators Association
211 East 51st Street
New York, New York 10022

U.S. Travel and Tourism Administration
U.S. Department of Commerce
Washington, D.C. 20230

United States Travel Data Center
Two Lafayette Center
1133 21st Street N.W.
Washington, D.C. 20036

Universal Federation of Travel Agents' Associations (UFTAA)
1, rue Defacqz, boite 1
B-1050 Brussels, Belgium

World Tourism Organization
Calle Capitan Haya 42
E-28020, Madrid, Spain

# STATE CONTACTS

Alabama
Alabama Bureau of Tourism and Travel
532 South Perry Street
Montgomery, Alabama 36104-4614

Alaska
Alaska State Division of Tourism
P.O. Box E
Juneau, Alaska 99811

Arizona
Arizona Office of Tourism
1100 West Washington Street
Phoenix, Arizona 85007

Arkansas
Arkansas Department of Parks and
  Tourism
1 Capitol Mall
Little Rock, Arkansas 72201

California
California Office of Tourism
1121 L Street, Suite 103
Sacramento, California 95814

Colorado
Colorado Tourism Board
1625 Broadway, Suite 1700
Denver, Colorado 80202

Connecticut
Connecticut Department of Economic
   Development
210 Washington Street
Hartford, Connecticut 06106

Delaware
Delaware Tourism Office
99 Kings Highway
P.O. Box 1401
Dover, Delaware 19903

District of Columbia
Washington Convention and Visitors
   Association
1212 New York Avenue N.W.
Suite 600
Washington, D.C. 20005

Florida
Florida Division of Tourism
Department of Commerce
107 West Gaines Street
Collins Building, Room 505
Tallahassee, Florida 32301

Georgia
Georgia Tourist Division
Department of Industry & Trade
P.O. Box 1776
Atlanta, Georgia 30301

Hawaii
Hawaii Visitors Bureau
2270 Kalakaua Avenue
Suite 801
Honolulu, Hawaii 96815

Idaho
Division of Travel Promotion
Department of Commerce
State Capitol Building
Boise, Idaho 83720

Illinois
Illinois Office of Tourism
State of Illinois Center
100 W. Randolf, Suite 3-400
Chicago, Illinois 60601

Indiana
Indiana Tourism Development Division
Department of Commerce
One North Capitol, No. 700
Indianapolis, Indiana 46204

Iowa
Bureau of Tourism and Visitors
Department of Economic Development
200 East Grand Avenue
Des Moines, Iowa 50309

Kansas
Kansas Travel and Tourism Division
400 West 8th Street
5th Floor
Topeka, Kansas 66603-3957

Kentucky
Kentucky Department of Travel Develop-
   ment
Capital Plaza Tower, 22nd Floor
Frankfort, Kentucky 40601

Louisiana
Louisiana Office of Tourism
P.O. Box 94291
Capitol Station
Baton Rouge, Louisiana 70804-9291

Maine
Office of Tourism
Department of Economic and Community
   Development
189 State Street
Augusta, Maine 04333

Maryland
Maryland Office of Tourist Development
45 Calvert Street
Annapolis, Maryland 21401

Massachusetts
Massachusetts Office of Travel and
   Tourism
100 Cambridge Street
Boston, Massachusetts 02202

Michigan
Travel Bureau
Michigan Department of Commerce
P.O. Box 30226
Lansing, Michigan 48909

Minnesota
Minnesota Office of Tourism
375 Jackson Walkway
250 Skyway Level
St. Paul, Minnesota 55101

Mississippi
Division of Tourism
Mississippi Department of Economic
  Development
1301 Walter Sillers Building
Jackson, Mississippi 39205

Missouri
Missouri Division of Tourism
308 East High Street
P.O. Box 1055
Jefferson City, Missouri 65102

Montana
Montana Promotion Division
Department of Commerce
1424 Ninth Avenue
Helena, Montana 59620-0411

Nebraska
Nebraska Travel and Tourism Division
Department of Economic Development
P.O. Box 94666
Lincoln, Nebraska 68509

Nevada
Nevada Commission on Tourism
600 East Williams
State Capitol Complex
Carson City, Nevada 89701

New Hampshire
New Hampshire Office of Vacation Travel
105 Loudon Road
P.O. Box 856
Concord, New Hampshire 03301

New Jersey
New Jersey Division of Travel and Tourism
Department of Commerce and Economic
  Development
CN 826
Trenton, New Jersey 08625-0826

New Mexico
New Mexico Tourism and Travel Division
Economic Development and Tourism
  Department
1100 St. Francis Street
Santa Fe, New Mexico 87503

New York
New York Division of Tourism
State Department of Economic Develop-
  ment
One Commerce Plaza
Albany, New York 12245

North Carolina
Division of Travel and Tourism
North Carolina Department of Commerce
430 North Salisbury Street
Raleigh, North Carolina 27611

North Dakota
North Dakota Tourism Promotion
Liberty Memorial Building
State Capitol Grounds
Bismarck, North Dakota 58505

Ohio
Ohio Division of Travel and Tourism
Department of Development
P.O. Box 1001
Columbus, Ohio 43266-0101

Oklahoma
Oklahoma Tourism and Recreation
  Department
500 Will Rogers Building
Oklahoma City, Oklahoma 73105

Oregon
Oregon Economic Development Depart-
  ment
Tourism Division
595 Cottage Street, N.E.
Salem, Oregon 97310

Pennsylvania
Pennsylvania Bureau of Travel Develop-
  ment
Department of Commerce
Room 453 Forum Building
Harrisburg, Pennsylvania 17120

Rhode Island
Tourist Promotion Division
Rhode Island Department of Economic
    Development
7 Jackson Walkway
Providence, Rhode Island 02903

South Carolina
South Carolina Department of Parks,
    Recreation and Tourism
Edgar A. Brown Building, Suite 106
1205 Pendleton Street
Columbia, South Carolina 29201

South Dakota
South Dakota Department of Tourism
P.O. Box 6000
Pierre, South Dakota 57501

Tennessee
Tennessee Department of Tourist
    Development
320 Sixth Avenue, North
Nashville, Tennessee 37219

Texas
Texas Tourism Division
Department of Commerce
P.O. Box 12008, Capitol Station
Austin, Texas 78711-2008

Utah
Utah Travel Council
Capitol Hill
300 North State
Salt Lake City, Utah 84114

Vermont
Vermont Travel Division
Agency of Development and Community
    Affairs
134 State Street
Montpelier, Vermont 05602

Virginia
Virginia Division of Tourism
202 North 9th Street, No. 500
Richmond, Virginia 23219

Washington
Tourism Development Division
Department of Trade and Economic
    Development
101 General Administration Building
Building AX-13
Olympia, Washington 98504-0613

West Virginia
West Virginia Department of Commerce
Tourism Division
2101 Washington Street, East
Charleston, West Virginia 25305

Wisconsin
Wisconsin Division of Tourism
123 West Washington Avenue
P.O. Box 7970
Madison, Wisconsin 53707

Wyoming
Wyoming Travel Commission
Frank Norris Junior Travel Center
I-25 and College Drive
Cheyenne, Wyoming 82002-0660

## PROVINCE CONTACTS

Alberta
Alberta Department of Tourism
18th Floor, Imperial Oil Building
10025 Jasper Avenue
Edmonton, Alberta
Canada T5J 3Z3

British Columbia
Tourism British Columbia
Ministry of Tourism
1117 Wharf Street
Victoria, British Columbia
Canada V8W 2Z2

Manitoba
Manitoba Department of Industry, Trade
    and Tourism
155 Carlton Street, 7th Floor
Winnipeg, Manitoba
Canada R3C 3H8

New Brunswick
Department of Tourism, Recreation and
    Heritage
Marysville Place
P.O. Box 12345
Fredericton, New Brunswick
Canada E3B 5C3

Quebec
Ministere du Tourisme
710 Place d'Youville
3e etage
Quebec, Quebec
Canada G1R 4Y4

Newfoundland
Newfoundland Department of Development and Tourism
4th Floor, Confederation Building Complex
P.O. Box 4750
St. John's, Newfoundland
Canada A1C 5T7

Northwest Territories
Division of Tourism and Parks
Northwest Territories Department of Economic Development and Tourism
Northern United Place, Box 1320
Yellowknife, Northwest Territories
Canada X1A 2L9

Nova Scotia
Nova Scotia Department of Tourism and Culture
P.O. Box 456
5151 Terminal Road
Halifax, Nova Scotia
Canada B3J 2R5

Ontario
Ontario Ministry of Tourism and Recreation
77 Bloor Street West
Toronto, Ontario
Canada M7A 2R9

Prince Edward Island
Prince Edward Island Department of Tourism and Parks
Shaw Building, 3rd Floor
105 Rochford Street
P.O. Box 2000
Charlottetown, Prince Edward Island
Canada C1A 7N8

Saskatchewan
Saskatchewan Department of Economic Development and Tourism
7th Floor, 1919 Saskatchewan Drive
Regina, Saskatchewan
Canada S4P 3V7

Yukon
Tourism Planning and Development Branch
Heritage and Cultural Resources
Government of Yukon
P.O. Box 2703
Whitehorse, Yukon
Canada Y1A 2C6

# APPENDIX B

# Data Sources for Travel and Tourism Research

The sources of secondary information available on tourism, travel, and recreation continue to grow. In the rapidly expanding, dynamic world of tourism, practitioners must know what is available and where to find it. Information gathering requires a great deal of tourism executives' time; yet little exists to guide them to the best sources of data for their particular concerns. Thus, this appendix provides a comprehensive list of numerous sources along with a summary of the type of information available in each.

This appendix is organized into eight main categories: (1) Indexing Services, (2) Bibliographies and Finding Guides, (3) Periodicals, (4) Trade and Professional Associations, (5) Government, (6) Yearbooks, Annuals, Handbooks, Etc., (7) Databases, and (8) Some Final Suggestions. The sources are arranged alphabetically within each heading.

There has been considerable effort to make the list up-to-date and give enough information to enable users who cannot find the information in their own libraries or the public library to send requests to the sources indicated. Readers should be aware that names, addresses, and prices change frequently.

One of the biggest mistakes in travel and tourism research is to rush out and collect primary data without exhausting secondary source information. Only later do researchers discover they have duplicated previous research. Existing sources can often provide information to solve the problem for a fraction of the cost. Therefore, users should exhaust secondary sources before turning to primary research for additional data.

In selecting sources of information, efforts have been made to (1) emphasize prime data, (2) list sources that can be used to locate more detailed data, and (3) keep the list brief enough to be actually read and used rather than just filed. Effective utilization can save money, hours of time, and provide useful information that might otherwise be missed.

## 1. INDEXING SERVICES

Unfortunately, there is no one convenient heading under which you can look and automatically find travel research information listed. Travel research studies may be found under many headings. The most important subject heading in the indexes is Tourist Trade. Examples of other headings that contain useful information are Travel, Travel Agents, Vacations, Transportation, Tourist Camps, Motels, Hotels, Recreation, and National Parks.

*Business Periodicals Index* (New York: H. W. Wilson, monthly, except August). A cumulative subject index covering periodicals in the fields of accounting, marketing, finance, advertising, banking, and so on.

*Predicasts F & S Europe* (Cleveland, Ohio: Predicasts, Inc., monthly). Devoted exclusively to Europe. Covers the European community, Scandinavia, other West European countries, the Soviet Union, and other East European countries.

*Predicasts F & S International* (Cleveland, Ohio: Predicasts, Inc., monthly). Indexes articles from foreign publications. Information arranged by (1) industry and product, (2) country, and (3) company. Covers Canada, Latin America, Africa, Middle East, Oceania, and other Asian countries.

*Predicasts F & S Index United States* (Cleveland, Ohio: Predicasts, Inc., weekly). Indexes articles from the United States and from foreign sources that may affect U.S. business.

*PAIS Bulletin (Public Affairs Information Service)* (New York: Public Affairs Information Service, monthly). A selective list of the latest books, pamphlets, government publications, reports of public and private agencies, and periodicals relating to economic and social conditions, public administration, and international relations.

*PAIS International* (New York: Public Affairs Information Service). A computerized index of information contained in the *PAIS Bulletin*, with the addition of some foreign language material. Fee based.

*Reader's Guide to Periodical Literature* (New York: H. W. Wilson, semimonthly). An index of the contents of the nation's general magazines.

## 2. BIBLIOGRAPHIES AND FINDING GUIDES

Baretje, R. *Touristic Analysis Review* (Aix-en-Provence, France: Centre des Hautes Etudes Touristiques, Fondation Vasarely 1, Avenue Marcel Pagnol 13090). Published every three months, this review printed on 40 heavy-duty pages gives complete references of studies and a short synopsis of their contents. Each issue analyzes 160 books or articles dealing with tourism.

Goeldner, C. R., and Karen Dicke *Bibliography of Tourism and Travel Research Studies, Reports and Articles* (Boulder: Business Research Division, College of Business, University of Colorado, 1980), 9 vols., 762 pp., complete set $60. This nine-volume bibliography is a research resource on travel, recreation, and tourism. Volume I, *Information Sources*, covers bibliographies, classics, books, directories, proceedings, list of travel and tourism trade and professional publications, list of U.S. travel and tourism associations, list of universities involved in travel and tourism research, list of U.S. travel contacts, selected list of Canadian travel contacts, and list of world travel contacts. Volume II, *Economics*, covers general, analysis, balance of payments, development, employment, expenditures, feasibility studies, impact, indicators and barometers, international, and multipliers. Volume III, *International Tourism*, covers general; Africa; Asia and the Pacific; Canada; Central, Latin, and South America; Europe (excluding the United Kingdom); Middle East; and the United Kingdom. Volume IV, *Lodging*, covers general, financial aspects, innovations, management, marketing and market research, statistics, and second home development. Volume V, *Recreation*, covers general, boating, camping, carrying capacity, demand, economics, forecasts, forests, hiking, hunting and fishing, land development, management, parks, planning, public input, research and research methodology, rural, skiing, snowmobiling, sports, statistics, urban, user studies, and water.

Volume VI, *Transportation,* includes transportation—general and forecasts; air—general, costs, commuters, deregulation, economics, fares, forecasts, international, passengers, planning, and statistics; highways and roads—bus, auto, and recreational vehicles; rail; water; and other. Volume VII, *Advertising-Planning,* covers advertising and promotion, attitudes, business travel, clubs, conferences and conventions, education, energy, environmental impact, food service, forecasts, gambling, handicapped traveler, hospitality, leisure, management, and planning. Volume VIII, *Statistics-Visitors,* includes statistics, tourism research, travel agents, travel research methodology, vacations, and visitors. Volume IX, *Index,* includes several indices to the material in Volumes I–VIII.

*The Hospitality Index: An Index for the Hotel, Food Service and Travel Industries* (Washington D.C.: American Hotel and Motel Association, quarterly and annual), $99.00. This comprehensive database comprising citations of articles, reports, and research from more than 40 different hospitality journals and periodicals has been published by the Consortium of Hospitality Research Information Services (CHRIS), a joint effort of Cornell University's School of Hotel Administration, the University of Wisconsin-Stout, and the Information Center of the American Hotel and Motel Association. Information contained in the published index is organized under more than 1500 subject headings.

Jafari, Jafar. "Tourism and the Social Sciences: A Bibliography." *Annals of Tourism Research.* (Elmsford, N.Y.: Pergamon Press) Vol. 6, No. 2 (April–June 1979), pp. 149–194. $4.00. The purpose of this bibliography is to bring together a selection of publications dealing with the study of tourism. This list of bibliographies is from 1970–1978.

Jafari, Jafar, and Dean Aaser. "Tourism as the Subject of Doctoral Dissertations." *Annals of Tourism Research* (Elmsford, N.Y.: Pergamon Press), Vol. 15, No. 3 (1988), pp. 407–429. This article discusses tourism as a field of study and presents the results of a computer search of doctoral dissertations on tourism. The search resulted in 157 titles with a touristic focus written between 1951 and 1987. Titles, authors, and schools are given.

Jafari, Jafar, Philip Sawin, Christopher Gustafson, and Joseph Harrington. *Bibliographies on Tourism and Related Subjects* (Boulder: Business Research Division, College of Business, University of Colorado, 1988), 81 pp., $25.00. A bibliography of bibliographies dealing with tourism and associated fields. There are 271 annotated entries, and information is arranged in three ways: (1) alphabetical listing, (2) author index, and (3) subject index. Also included is a listing of the tourism bibliographies available from the Centre des Hautes Etudes Touristiques in Aix-en-Provence, France.

*Leisure, Recreation and Tourism Abstracts* (formerly *Rural Recreation and Tourism Abstracts*). (Oxford: Commonwealth Agricultural Bureaux, quarterly). Annual subscription rate is $128.00. The abstracts, arranged by subject, provide short informative summaries of publications with full bibliographical details and often a symbol for locating the original documents.

Pisarski, Alan. *An Inventory of Federal Travel and Tourism Related Information Sources* (Boulder: Business Research Division, University of Colorado, 1985), 107 pp., $25.00. This inventory of existing federal data programs relevant to travel and tourism provides a comprehensive listing and description of pertinent government sources.

Pizam, A., and Z. Gu. *Journal of Travel Research Index and Abstracts, Volumes 6–24* (Boulder: Business Research Division, College of Business, University of Colorado, 1988), 182 pp., $48.00. Comprehensive index and abstracts of the articles that have been published in the *Journal of Travel Research* and its predecessor, the *Travel Research Bulletin.* Covers articles through volume 24. Articles indexed by author, title, subject, and destination outside the United States.

*Recent Acquisitions*   (Ottawa, Ontario: Tourism Research and Data Centre, Tourism Canada, 235 Queen Street, K1A 0H6, monthly). This is a listing of publications received by the Tourism Reference and Documentation Centre of Tourism Canada.

*Tourism: A Guide to Sources of Information*   (Edinburgh: Capital Planning Information Ltd., Castle Street, Edinburgh EH2 3AT, Scotland, 1981), 73 pp. This publication gives a selected and evaluative listing of tourism literature primarily about the United Kingdom; however, it also includes some international sources.

*Tourism and Vacation Travel: State and Local Government Planning*   (Springfield, Va.: National Technical Information Service, U.S. Department of Commerce, May 1988), 50 pp., $40.00. Economic and socioeconomic aspects of vacation travel and tourism in various localities of the United States are documented. Most of these studies deal with the use of tourism for the economic development of local communities. Special attention is given to wilderness, coastal zone, lake, waterway, and Indian reservation areas. This updated bibliography covers the period 1970 to May 1988 and provides 175 citations.

*The Travel and Tourism Index*   (Laie, Hawaii: Brigham Young University Hawaii Campus, quarterly). This quarterly index covers 47 travel and tourism publications.

"The Travel Research Bookshelf,"   *Journal of Travel Research* (Boulder: Business Research Division, College of Business, University of Colorado). A regular feature of the quarterly *Journal of Travel Research.* "The Travel Research Bookshelf" is an annotated bibliography of current travel research materials. Sources and availability of materials are shown for each entry.

*University Research in Business and Economics*   (Morgantown, W.V.: Bureau of Business Research, College of Business and Economics, West Virginia University, for the Association for University Business and Economic Research (AUBER), annual), $25.00. This bibliography covers the publications of members of AUBER and member schools of the American Assembly of Collegiate Schools of Business for the calendar year. Subject classifications 531, 615, 635, 721, and 941 cover travel and tourism subject matter.

## 3. PERIODICALS

The following are periodicals that contain travel research information.

*Annals of Tourism Research*   (Elmsford, N.Y.: Pergamon Press, quarterly), DM260.00.

*ASTA Agency Management Magazine*   (New York: ASTA Agency Management, monthly), United States and Canada, $10.00 a year; $12.00 elsewhere.

*The Cornell Hotel and Restaurant Administration Quarterly*   (Ithaca, N.Y.: School of Hotel Administration, Cornell University, quarterly), $30.00 a year in the United States, $40.00 elsewhere.

*Courier*   (Lexington, Ky.: National Tour Association, monthly), $24.00 a year.

*Hospitality and Tourism Educator*   (Washington, D.C.: Council on Hotel, Restaurant and Institutional Education, three times a year), $35.00 a year in the United States, $45.00 international.

*Hospitality Education and Research Journal*   (Washington, D.C.: Council on Hotel, Restaurant, and Institutional Education, three times a year), $50.00 a year in the United States.

*Hotel and Motel Management*  (Duluth, Minn.: Edgell Communications, 18 times per year), $25.00 a year in the United States, $50.00 in Canada, $100.00 elsewhere; single copies $2.50 in the United States, $5.00 in Canada, $10.00 elsewhere.

*Hotels: The International Magazine of the Hotel and Restaurant Industry*  (Des Plaines, Ill.: Cahners, 12 times a year), $50.00 per year in the United States, $65.00 in Canada and Mexico, elsewhere $85.00 (add $50.00 if air mail is desired); single copy $10.00.

*International Journal of Hospitality Management*  (Elmsford, N.Y.: Pergamon Press, quarterly), DM250.00 a year.

*International Tourism Reports*  (London: The Economist Publications, Ltd., quarterly), $316.00 a year.

*Journal of Leisure Research*  (Alexandria, Va.: National Recreation and Park Association, quarterly), United States, $20.00 a year; foreign, $33.00; $30.00 nonmember.

*Journal of Travel Research*  (Boulder: Business Research Division, College of Business, University of Colorado, quarterly), free to members of the Travel and Tourism Research Association; nonmembers $70.00 a year in the United States, $75.00 Canada and Mexico, $85.00 elsewhere.

*Leisure Sciences*  (New York: Taylor & Francis, quarterly), $75.00 a year, institutions; $42.00, personal; single copies $21.00.

*Lodging*  (New York: American Hotel Association Directory Corporation, monthly except August), $35.00 a year.

*Meetings and Conventions*  (Secaucus, N.J.: Reed Travel Group, monthly), $45.00 a year in the United States, $65.00 elsewhere; single copies $5.00 in the United States, $12.00 elsewhere.

*Revue de Tourisme—The Tourist Review—Zeitschrift fur Fremdenverkehr*  (St. Gallen, Switzerland: AIEST, Varnbuelstrasse 19, CH-9000 St. Gallen, quarterly), 50 Sfr.

*Tour and Travel News*  (Manhasset, N.Y.: CMP Publications Inc., weekly), $40.00 a year in the United States.

*Tourism Management*  (Guildford, U.K.: Butterworth, quarterly), $193.83 a year in the United States, single copies $58.90.

*Tourism Recreation Research*  (Indira Nagar, Lucknow, India: Centre for Tourism Research, semiannually), $35.00 a year.

*The Travel Agent*  (New York: American Traveler Division, Capital Cities ABC, Inc., weekly), $79.00 a year in the United States.

*Travel & Tourism Analyst*  (London: The Economist Publications, Ltd., 6 times a year), $795.00 a year in North America.

*Travel-log*  (Ottawa: Statistics Canada, quarterly), $40.00 a year in Canada, $44.00 in other countries.

*Travel Printout*  (Washington, D.C.: U.S. Travel Data Center, monthly), $70.00 a year in the United States, Canada, and Mexico; $80.00 elsewhere.

*Travel Trade*  (New York: Travel Trade Publications, weekly), $10.00 a year in the United States, $13.00 in Canada, $25.00 elsewhere.

*Travel Weekly*  (Secaucus, N.J.: Reed Travel Group, twice weekly), $26.00 a year in the United States, Canada, and Mexico, $44.00 elsewhere; single copies $1.00.

There are also many other periodicals and journals dealing with the travel field. The sources for locating these are

*Business Publications Rates and Data*   (Skokie, Ill.: Standard Rate and Data Service, monthly). A listing of more than 3800 U.S. and about 200 international business, trade, and technical publications.

*TIA International Travel News Directory*   (Washington, D.C.: Travel Industry Association of America, annual). A listing of some 1400 key editorial and advertising contacts at travel trade and consumer publications in more than 40 countries.

*Ulrich's International Periodicals Directory*   (New York: R. R. Bowker, annual). Includes entries for more than 65,000 in-print periodicals published throughout the world.

## 4. TRADE AND PROFESSIONAL ASSOCIATIONS

Many trade and professional associations publish valuable data on the travel industry. Examples are

Association Internationale d'Experts Scientifiques du Tourisme (AIEST), Varnbuelstrasse 19, CH-9000, St. Gallen, Switzerland. AIEST is composed primarily of academicians interested in tourism research and teaching. It publishes the *Tourist Review* and annual proceedings of its meetings.

Pacific Asia Travel Association (PATA), One Montgomery Street, West Tower, No. 1750, San Francisco, California 94104, publishes the *PATA Annual Statistical Report* and other publications and holds research seminars.

Travel and Tourism Research Association (TTRA), P.O. Box 8066, Foothill Station, Salt Lake City, Utah 84108, helps sponsor the *Journal of Travel Research* and publishes proceedings.

Travel Industry Association of America, Two Lafayette Center, 1133 21st Street N.W., Washington, D.C. 20036, has a publication program that includes special reports and newsletters.

The World Tourism Organization (WTO), Calle Capitan Haya, 42, E-28020 Madrid, Spain. One of the main tasks of the WTO is to give members continuing information on tourism and its influence on the social, economic, and cultural life of nations. It offers a number of publications and educational programs. A publications list can be received by writing the organization.

Some other associations are the Tourism Industry Association of Canada, 130 Albert Street, Ottawa, Ontario, Canada K1P 5G4; Air Transport Association of America, 1709 New York Avenue N.W., Washington, D.C. 20006; International Air Transport Association, IATA Building, 2000 Peel Street, Montreal, Quebec, Canada H3A 2R4; American Hotel and Motel Association, 1201 New York Avenue N.W., Washington, D.C. 20005; International Association of Amusement Parks and Attractions, 4230 King Street, Alexandria, Virginia 22302; International Association of Convention and Visitors Bureaus, P.O. Box 758, Champaign, Illinois 61820; Association of Travel Marketing Executives, P.O. Box 43563, Washington, D.C. 20010; American Society of Travel Agents, 1101 King Street, Alexandria, Virginia 22314; National Tour Association, 546 East Main Street, P.O. Box 3071, Lexington, Kentucky 40596; Institute of Certified Travel Agents, 148 Linden Street, Wellesley, Massachusetts 02181; National Recreation and Park Association, 3101 Park Center Drive, Alexandria, Virginia 22302.

If you are in doubt about trade associations in the field, you can check

*Encyclopedia of Associations:* 1990, 24th ed. (Detroit: Gale Research, 1989), Volume I, *National Organizations of the United States,* 3194 pp.; Volume 2, *Geographic and Executive Indexes,* 859 pp.; Volume 3, *New Associations and Projects,* Volume 4, *International Organizations.*

## 5. GOVERNMENT

Probably no group collects more information on the tourism industry than government agencies. The government agencies vary according to the objectives of the particular country and, in most cases, to the degree of importance of the tourism sector. Generally, the following public agencies are involved in tourism and travel research activities: (1) ministries of tourism; (2) undersecretarial or underministiral tourism organizations; (3) specific governmental organizations for tourism and travel; (4) statistical agencies for collection, analysis, and publication of data related to tourism and travel, such as Statistics Canada and the U.S. Census Bureau; and (5) state or provincial tourism organizations.

Most government travel organizations are members of the World Tourism Organization (WTO), Calle Capitan Haya, 42, E-28020 Madrid, Spain. Researchers can write for a list of members and associate members.

The major U.S. government tourism development organization is the U.S. Travel and Tourism Administration, Department of Commerce, Washington, D.C. 20230. An inventory of federal agencies involved in tourism by Pisarski is listed in Section 2, "Bibliographies and Finding Guides."

Selected examples of useful government publications in the travel field include

*Canadian Travel Survey: 1988* (Ottawa: Statistics Canada, Travel, Tourism and Recreation Section, quarterly). This report provides statistics on travel by Canadians on trips of 80 kilometers or more with destinations in Canada. Information is provided on who the travelers are, why they traveled, when they traveled, how they traveled, where they stayed, how much they spent, and what they did. A general summary of the travel situation in Canada is given and the importance of domestic travel is demonstrated.

*A Conceptual Basis for the National Tourism Policy Study* (Washington, D.C.: Committee on Commerce and National Tourism Policy Study, U.S. Senate, October 1976), 70 pp., 85¢. This report identifies the federal programs and policies that significantly impact tourism research, planning, development, and promotion. It also contains an overview of legislation that directly and indirectly affects one or another aspect of tourism, a discussion of the national interests in tourism and other interacting interests, a discussion of the definitional problem with tourism and how the term is defined for purposes of the report, and a review of federal tourism and tourism-related legislation. Order from the Superintendent of Documents, U.S. Government Printing Office, Washington, D.C. 20402.

"International Travel and Passenger Fares, 1987," *Survey of Current Business* (Washington, D.C.: Bureau of Economic Analysis, U.S. Department of Commerce, May 1988), $18.00 (second-class mail) or $43.00 (first-class mail) a year in the United States, $22.50 elsewhere; single copy $6.50 in the United States, $8.13 elsewhere. This article reviews development affecting the travel accounts that appear in the U.S. balance of international payments. Total spending by U.S. residents traveling abroad, spending by foreign visitors to the United States, and data on passenger fares for transoceanic transportation are covered.

The United States Travel and Tourism Administration's *In-flight Survey of International Air Travelers* (Washington, D.C.: U.S. Department of Commerce, United States Travel and Tourism Administration, quarterly), $100.00 per quarter, $400.00 per year. The in-flight survey provides a comprehensive consumer marketing database on international travel to and from the United States. Some 25,000 foreign visitors and 35,000 U.S. residents traveling abroad respond to the survey annually. One series analyzes inbound travel to the United States, and another focuses on travel from the United States. Tables profile international travelers by residency, trip characteristics, and regional destinations.

*National Tourism Policy Study—Final Report* (Washington, D.C.: Committee on Commerce, Science and Transportation, U.S. Senate, 1979), 361 pp. This report by Arthur D. Little, Inc. presents the findings of the final phase of the *National Tourism Policy Study*. It was designed to develop a proposed national tourism policy for the United States; to define appropriate roles for the federal government, the states, cities, private industry, and consumers in carrying out, supporting, and contributing to the national tourism policy; and to recommend organizational, programmatic, and legislative strategies for implementing the proposed national tourism policy.

*Touriscope: International Travel 1987* (Ottawa: Statistics Canada, 1988). The report presents significant trends on travelers to Canada and the Canadians traveling abroad.

*Tourism in Canada, A Statistical Digest, 1988* (Ottawa: Statistics Canada, 1988). The report is full of current facts and figures on the demand and supply sides of tourism. Issues that are vital to the tourism industry are presented by experts.

*U.S. International Air Travel Statistics* (Cambridge, Massachusetts: Transportation Systems Center, U.S. Department of Transportation, monthly). The report is compiled using data collected by the U.S. Immigration and Naturalization Service. It contains world area travel statistical data and is available as a subscription service to anyone who wishes to acquire the information.

## 6. YEARBOOKS, ANNUALS, HANDBOOKS, AND OTHER SOURCES

*Air Transport 1989* (Washington, D.C.: Air Transport Association of America, annual), 16 pp., free. The official annual report to the U.S. scheduled airline industry containing historical and current statistical data on the industry.

*Economic Analysis of North American Ski Areas, 1987–88* (Boulder: Business Research Division, University of Colorado, annual), 144 pp., $55.00. The major objective of this survey of ski operations for the 1987–88 operating season was to provide ski area characteristics and financial figures in understandable tabulations so ski area operators and others could assess the characteristics and the economic health of the ski industry.

*The 1988–89 Economic Review of Travel in America* (Washington, D.C.: U.S. Travel Data Center, annual), $60.00. This annual report on the role of travel and tourism in the American economy reviews the economic contributions of travel away from home, developments in the travel industry, and the effects of economic changes on travel and tourism.

*National Travel Survey* (Washington, D.C.: U.S. Travel Data Center, quarterly and annual). In March 1979, the U.S. Travel Data Center began conducting a monthly *National Travel Survey*. Since that time, quarterly and annual summaries of the results have been published to provide researchers with timely, consistent, and relevant data on major trends in U.S. travel activity.

*PATA Annual Statistical Report, 1987* (San Francisco: Pacific Asia Travel Association, 1988), 109 pp.; $70.00 to members, $100.00 to nonmembers. This report presents the visitor arrival statistics and other relevant data reported by PATA member governments. The report gives visitor arrival data for the individual countries by nationality of residence and mode of travel. Selected market sources of visitors to the Pacific area are given, along with data on accommodations, length of stay, visitor expenditures, and national tourist organization budgets.

*Compendium of Tourism Statistics* (Madrid: World Tourism Organization), approximately 200 pp., $15.00. This book provides quantitative and qualitative data covering many aspects of domestic and international tourism. It contains major statistical series relating to levels and trends in tourist movements by countries, by regions, and worldwide, and assessments of tourism's economic effect on both generating and receiving countries.

*Tourism Policy and International Tourism in OECD Member Countries* (Paris: The Organisation for Economic Co-operation and Development, annual). This is an annual report on tourism statistics in Australia, Austria, Belgium, Canada, Denmark, Finland, France, Federal Republic of Germany, Greece, Iceland, Ireland, Italy, Japan, Luxembourg, the Netherlands, New Zealand, Norway, Portugal, Spain, Sweden, Switzerland, Turkey, the United Kingdom, and the United States.

*Travel Industry World Yearbook: The Big Picture-1989* (New York: Child and Waters, annual), 152 pp., $78.00 in the United States, $84.00 foreign airmail. This annual issue presents a compact up-to-date review of the latest happenings in the world of tourism.

*Travel Trends in the United States and Canada* (Boulder: Business Research Division, University of Colorado, 1984), 262 pp., $45.00. This document provides statistics on visits to recreation areas, number of tourists, tourist expenditures, length of stay and size of party, economic impact of tourism, tourism-related employment, mode of transportation used, tourism advertising, passport statistics, international travel, foreign visitor arrivals, travel costs, and highlights from national travel surveys. Data have been compiled from 260 sources.

*Trends in the Hotel Industry, International Edition* (Houston: Pannell Kerr Forster, annual), $50.00. A statistical review incorporating operational and financial data on hotels. Data included represent voluntary contributions by 1600 establishments located outside the United States.

*Trends in the Hotel Industry, USA Edition* (Houston: Pannell Kerr Forster, annual), $50.00. Statistical highlights are analyzed, and data are provided on operating results as measuring guides for hotel and motel operators. The data included represent voluntary contributions by 1000 establishments. Current trends are compared with previous years, and graphs and charts illuminate the statistics.

*U.S. Lodging Industry* (Philadelphia: Laventhol and Horwath, annual), $50.00. This annual report on the lodging industry covers comments from around the country, market data, the trends of business, percentages of occupancy, hotel earnings, payrolls, taxes, restaurant operations, credit and collection data, balance sheet statistics, and statements of income.

*World Air Transport Statistics* (Geneva: International Air Transport Association, annual). This is an annual compilation of facts and figures illustrated with numerous graphs and charts, representing the most up-to-date and complete source of data on the air transport industry.

*World Travel Overview 1988/1989* (New York: American Express Publishing Corporation, annual), $95.00. This annual review of worldwide travel covers global markets, the U.S. market, and travel trends.

*World Wide Lodging Industry* (New York: Horwath and Horwath International, annual),

$50.00. This annual edition provides information on market data, performance measures, sales, occupancy, length of stay, payroll, income, operating expenses, and restaurant operations.

*Yearbook of Tourism Statistics* (Madrid: World Tourism Organization, annual). Published in two volumes, this work gives detailed breakdowns of international tourist arrivals and nights by country of residence and nationality, and of average foreign tourist expenditures.

# 7. DATABASES

In this era of the computer we would be remiss if we did not mention databases. Several databases containing travel and tourism information are available now. One of the quickest ways of finding information is to conduct a computer search of these databases. Some databases available are

CENTRE DES HAUTES ETUDES TOURISTIQUES, Fondation Vasarely 1, Avenue Marcel Pagnol, 13090, Aix-en-Provence, France. This center maintains a comprehensive collection of the world literature on tourism which has now been computerized. The Centre publishes *Touristic Analysis Review* every quarter. Rene Baretje heads the center and requests all researchers to send him complimentary copies of their tourism studies.

DIALOG, Information Services, Inc., 3460 Hillview Avenue, Palo Alto, California 94304; (800) 334-2564. Included in Dialog are the CAB Abstracts, a comprehensive file of the 26 journals published by Commonwealth Agricultural Bureaux in England. CAB Abstracts include a subfile entitled "Leisure, Recreation and Tourism Abstracts." Subject areas covered in LRTA are leisure, recreation, and tourism; natural resources; tourism; recreation activities and facilities; culture and entertainment; and home and neighborhood activities.

IATA Statistical Information System (ISIS), I. P. Sharp Associates Ltd., Suite 1900, Exchange Tower, 2 First Canadian Place, Toronto, Ontario, Canada M5X 1E3; (416) 364-5361. IATA's computerized information service on airline traffic, capacity, revenue, and costs is now available to member airlines and affiliated interests. It provides timely, easily accessible statistics on commercial air transport. ISIS consists of a centralized database and a number of easy-to-use programs enabling retrieval, processing, analysis, and display of information compiled by IATA.

INFORMATION CENTER, American Hotel and Motel Association, 888 Seventh Avenue, New York, New York 10106; (212) 265-4506. Contains information on more than 1300 subjects related to hotel/motel operation. Divided into two divisions, the five-year files (information printed in the last five years) and "historical" files, information is provided on 30 major subject categories.

INS-U.S. INTERNATIONAL AIR TRAVEL STATISTICS, Center for Transportation Information, Transportation Systems Center, Kendall Square, Cambridge, Massachusetts 02142; (617) 494-2450. Maintains monthly time series showing the number of passengers flying between the United States and other ports. Data are broken down according to passenger citizenship, flight type, and the nationality of the carrier.

SIRLS, Faculty of Human Kinetics and Leisure Studies, University of Waterloo, Waterloo, Ontario, Canada N2L 3G1; (519) 885-1211, ext. 2560. A computerized, bibliographical database and documentation center in the areas of leisure, sport, recreation, play, games, and dance. More than 12,000 citations are listed at the present time and the system is accessible from external institutions.

TOURISM RESEARCH AND DOCUMENTATION CENTRE (TRDC), 3rd Floor West, 235 Queen Street, Ottawa, Ontario K1A 0H6, Canada; (613) 954-3943. The center maintains the most comprehensive computerized collection of tourism-related information in Canada. The holdings of more than 5000 books and documents include research papers, statistics, surveys, analyses, journals, conference proceedings, speeches, proposals, feasibility studies, legislation, guidebooks, bibliographies, and more. Information on this material is held in a data bank that can be accessed by TRDC staff or by the users of remote terminals in other parts of the country.

The computer system at TRDC is a bilingual bibliographic information storage and retrieval system that allows users to search the holdings using 1500 key words or "descriptors." Information is classified into eight major sectors: transportation, accommodation, conventions, hospitality services, events and attractions, recreational activities and facilities, education, and tourist-related enterprises. The descriptors can be used singly or in combination to produce the information required. Searches can be undertaken, for instance, by subject, author, sponsor, date, document type, geography, or various combinations of these. The information has been compiled to assist the industry and officers of Tourism Canada; however, it is also available to the general public.

TRAVEL REFERENCE CENTER, Business Research Division, Campus Box 420, University of Colorado, Boulder, Colorado 80309; (303) 492-5056. The reference center was established in 1969 to assist the travel industry in finding information sources and provide a facility to house a comprehensive collection of travel studies. The center now comprises the largest collection of travel, tourism, and recreation research studies available at any one place in the United States. The present collection numbers over 10,000 documents and is growing daily. The collection was computerized in 1985, and the center can do literature searches using more than 900 descriptors. The cost for a literature search is $50.00.

## 8. SOME FINAL SUGGESTIONS

This section provides information on the U.S. Travel Data Center and identifies some well-known books and reports on travel research.

U.S. Travel Data Center, Two Lafayette Center, 1133 21st Street N.W., Washington, D.C. 20036, was organized early in 1973 as a nonprofit corporation dedicated to serving the travel research needs of the industry and nation. Today, the Data Center is the focal point of a multitude of efforts to measure and understand the travel activities of Americans and of foreign visitors to this country. In some instances, the Data Center gathers, analyzes, and disseminates statistical data published by other recognized research organizations. In other cases, the Data Center collects original data for analysis and publication. Selected programs of the Data Center are (1) National Travel Survey, (2) Impact of Travel on State Economies, (3) Survey of State Travel Offices, (4) Travel Price Index, and (5) annual travel outlook forum. A catalog of its publications is available and can be obtained by writing to the center.

*American Outdoors: The Legacy, The Challenge.* (Washington, D.C.: Island Press, 1987), 426 pp. This volume is the final report of the President's Commission on Americans Outdoors. The report makes an important contribution to our understanding of the nation's outdoor recreation needs and resources.

*The Character and Volume of the U.S. Travel Agency Market, 1988* (New York: Travel Weekly, 1988), 142 pp. This 1988 Louis Harris Survey presents the findings of the ninth comprehensive study of the travel agency business. It updates information obtained in previous studies on the dimensions and scope of the travel agency market and on the sources and components of agency business. Like the 1976, 1978, 1981, 1983, 1985, and 1987 studies, this study also describes the importance of various criteria influencing travel agents' choices of air carriers, hotels, cruise ships, car rental agencies, and package tours for their clients. The June 29, 1988, issue of *Travel Weekly* (Vol. 47, No. 57) is the Louis Harris study issue.

Gee, Chuck Y., Dexter J. L. Choy, and James C. Makens. *The Travel Industry* (New York: Van Nostrand Reinhold, 1989), 352 pp., $34.95. The emphasis in this text is on introducing concepts about travel as an industry. It provides a basic understanding of travel and tourism and provides insights into the development and operations of the various components of the travel industry.

Gunn, Clare A. *Tourism Planning* (New York: Taylor & Francis, 1988), 356 pp. This text takes a human ecology approach and describes opportunities, on the state and regional scale, for greater expansion of tourism without damage to our delicate natural resources. The book provides a unique framework for understanding and regrouping the complicated elements that make up tourism. By relating planning to tourism, constructive guides for the future are offered.

Gunn, Clare A. *Vacationscope: Designing Tourist Regions* (New York: Van Nostrand Reinhold Company, 1988), 208 pp. This volume is a sourcebook of theory, new ideas, and real-world examples for designers, tourism developers, promoters, and students.

Howell, David W. *Passport: An Introduction to the Travel and Tourism Industry* (Cincinnati: South-Western Publishing Co., 1989), 422 pp. The book is designed to help readers understand the roles played by various components of the travel and tourism industry and to help them decide which of the many different careers would best suit them.

Krippendorf, Jost. *The Holiday Makers* (London: William Heinemann, Ltd., 1987), 160 pp. This book analyzes the different forms of tourism, examines the effects on various countries and their people, and outlines positive steps to reconcile people's holiday requirements with the world's economic and social structures.

Lundberg, Donald. *International Travel and Tourism* (New York: Wiley, 1985), 254 pp., $23.95. The perspective of this book is American — why Americans go abroad, where they go, how they get there, and how they get around once they have arrived. Only the highlights of international travel are included. The amount of information presented about particular destinations varies according to their popularity for American travelers. It was written as a textbook on international travel.

Mill, Robert C., and Alastair M. Morrison. *The Tourism System* (Englewood Cliffs, N.J.: Prentice-Hall, 1985), 457 pp. A book presenting a comprehensive systems view of tourism, stressing the interrelationships and interdependencies of its various elements. The authors cover all aspects from a marketing point of view and describe how tourism works.

Powers, Thomas F. *Introduction to Management in the Hospitality Industry* (New York: Wiley, 1988), 591 pp. This book covers the hospitality industry. It discusses the management problems of institutions that offer shelter or food or both to people away from their homes.

Ritchie, J. R. Brent, and Charles R. Goeldner. *Travel, Tourism and Hospitality Research: A Handbook for Managers and Researchers* (New York: John Wiley & Sons, 1986), 512 pp. This reference handbook provides guidance for travel industry professionals and researchers. Noted scholars and experts in travel, tourism, and hospitality management contributed the book's 43 chapters.

*Tourism's Top Twenty* (Boulder: Business Research Division, University of Colorado, 1987),

118 pp., $48.00. This book, compiled in cooperation with the U.S. Travel Data Center, Washington, D.C., provides facts and figures on travel, tourism recreation, and leisure. Information is presented primarily for the United States; however, there is some coverage of world tourism. It provides fast facts on a wide array of tourism-related subjects, including advertising, airlines, attractions, expenditures, hotels and resorts, recreation, world travel, and travel statistics. Sources are given for each table, and complete addresses for the sources are provided in an appendix. An index by table number is also included for ease in locating information.

# Glossary

**Affinity group**  A group bound together by a common interest or affinity. Where charters are concerned, this common bond makes them eligible for charter flights. Persons must have been members of the group for six months or longer. Where a group configuration on a flight is concerned, the minimum number of persons to which the term would apply may be any number determined by a carrier rule-making body. They must travel together, on the departure and return flight, but they can travel independently where ground arrangements are concerned.

**Airline Reporting Corporation (ARC)**  A corporation set up by the domestic airlines that is concerned with travel agent appointments and operations.

**Air Transport Association of America (ATA or ATAA)**  The authoritative trade association maintained by domestic airlines.

**American plan**  A room rate that includes breakfast, lunch, and dinner.

**Balance of payments or trade**  Practical definition of an economic concept. Each nation is assumed to be one tremendous business doing business with other big businesses. When a business (country) sells (exports) more than it buys (imports), there is a positive balance of payments. When a country buys (imports) more than it sells (exports), there is a negative balance of trade. Tourism is a part of balance of trade classified under Services.

**Carrier**  A public transportation company such as air or steamship line, railroad, truck, bus, monorail, and so forth.

**Carrier-participating**  Means a carrier over whose routes one or more sections of carriage under the Air Waybill or Ticket is undertaken or performed.

**Charter**  The bulk purchase of any carrier's equipment (or part thereof) for passengers or freight. Legally, charter transportation is arranged for time, voyage, or mileage.

**Charter flight**  A flight booked exclusively for the use of a specific group of people who generally belong to the same organization or who are being "treated" to the flight by a single host. Charter flights are generally much cheaper than regularly scheduled line services. They may be carried out by scheduled or supplemental carriers.

**Clients**  Those persons who patronize travel agencies.

**Concierge**  This is a wonderful European invention. Depending on the hotel, the concierge is a superintendent of service, source of information, and link between the guest and city or area.

**Consolidator**  A travel firm that makes available airplane tickets, cruise tickets, and sometimes other travel products at discount prices. These are usually sold to retail travel agencies but are also sometimes sold directly to the public.

**Consortium**  A privately owned firm (not owned by its members as is a cooperative) that maintains a list of preferred suppliers. This list is made available to members, resulting in superior commissions earned.

**Continental breakfast**  A beverage, roll, and jam. Sometimes a fruit juice is added. In Spain, Holland and Norway, sometimes cheese, meat, or fish is included.

**Continental plan**  A hotel rate that includes continental breakfast.

**Cooperative**  A membership group of retail travel agencies that offers advantages to each agency member, such as lower prices on wholesale tour offerings, educational opportunities, problem solving, and other aids.

**Coupon flight**  The portion of the passenger ticket and baggage check or excess baggage ticket that indicates particular places between which the coupon is good for carriage.

**Destination**  The ultimate stopping place according to the contract of carriage. Can also be defined as a place offering at least 1500 rooms to tourists.

**Domestic independent travel (DIT)**  A tour constructed to meet the specific desire of a client within a single country.

**Eurailpass**  A special pass sold overseas for unlimited first-class rail travel in 15 European countries. Youth and children's passes are also available. They are sold for varying numbers of days.

**European plan**  A hotel rate that includes only lodging, no food.

**Excursionist**  A traveler who spends less than 24 hours at a destination.

**Familiarization tour**  A free or reduced rate arrangement for travel agents or public carrier employees that is intended to stimulate them to sell travel or tours as experienced on the "fam" tour.

**Federal Aviation Administration (US)**  A governmental regulatory agency concerned with airport operation, air safety, licensing of flight personnel, and other aviation matters.

**Foreign independent travel (FIT)**  An international prepaid tour for an individual or family planned for them by a travel agent or tour operator. It is individually designed.

**Ground arrangements**  All those services provided by a tour operator after reaching the first destination. Also referred to as land arrangements.

**Group inclusive tour (GIT)**  A tour that includes group air and ground arrangements for a minimum of 15 persons. They may or may not stay together as a group for both the land and air portions of the trip.

**Incentive tour**  A tour arranged especially for employees or agents of a company as a reward for achievement, usually sales. Spouses are typically included on the trip.

**Inclusive tour**  A travel plan for which prearranged transportation, wholly by air or partly by air and partly by surface, together with ground facilities (such as meals, hotels, etc.) are sold for a total price.

**International Air Transport Association (IATA)**  The authoritative trade association maintained by international and overseas airlines.

**Modified American plan**  A room rate that includes a full American breakfast and lunch or dinner, usually dinner.

**Package**  A prepaid tour that includes transportation, lodging, and other ingredients, usually meals, transfers, sightseeing, or car rentals. May be varied, but typically includes at least three ingredients sold at a fixed price.

**Passport** Issued by national governments to their own citizens as verification of their citizenship. It is also a permit to leave one's own country and return.

**Pension** A French word widely used throughout Europe meaning guest house or boarding house.

**Reception agency** A tour operator or travel agency specializing in foreign visitors. American Adventure Tours is such a company.

**Retail travel agency** Mostly in America. Travel agents sell carriers' tickets and wholesalers' or operators' tours. In perspective, retail agents are commissioned or subagents. Usually, all or most of the gross revenue is from commissions.

**Revalidation** The authorized stamping or writing on the passenger ticket showing it has been officially altered by the carrier.

**Run-of-the-house** A hotel term to guarantee a firm price that applies to any room in the house. Often a hotel will provide a superior room, if available, in an effort to please the guest and the tour operator.

**Spa** A hotel or resort providing hot springs or baths and other health-enhancing facilities and services.

**Supplier** An industry term meaning any form of transportation, accommodations, and other travel services used by a travel agency or tour operator to fulfill the needs of travelers.

**Tariffs** The published fares, rates, charges, and/or related conditions of carriage of a carrier.

**Tour operator** A company that specializes in the planning and operation of prepaid, preplanned vacations and makes these available to the public, usually through travel agents.

**Tour organizer** An individual, usually not professionally connected with the travel industry, who organizes tours for special groups of people, such as teachers, church leaders, farmers, and the like.

**Tour package** A travel plan that includes several elements of a vacation, such as transportation, accommodations, and sightseeing.

**Tour wholesaler** A company that plans, markets, and (usually) operates tours. Marketing is always through intermediaries such as retail travel agents, an association, club, or tour organizer—never directly to the public as is sometimes done by tour operators. The wholesaler would not operate the tour if, for example, it was functioning as a wholesaler in the United States for tours operated by a foreign firm. In industry jargon tour operator and tour wholesaler are synonymous.

**Tour-basing fare** A reduced, round-trip fare available on specified dates, and between specified times, only to passengers who purchase preplanned, prepaid tour arrangements prior to their departure to specified areas.

**Tourism** (1) The entire world industry of travel, hotels, transportation, and all other components, including promotion, that serves the needs and wants of travelers. Tourism today has been given new meaning and is primarily a term of economics referring to an industry. (2) Within a nation (political subdivision or transportation-centered economic area of contiguous nations), the sum total of tourist expenditures within their borders is referred to as the nation's tourism or tourist industry and is thus ranked with other national industries. More important than just the total monetary product value of tourism is its role in the balance of trade. Here tourism earning from foreigners truly represents an export industry. Tourism is an "invisible" export.

**Tourist**  A person who travels from place to place for nonwork reasons. By U.N. definition, a tourist is someone who stays for more than one night and less than a year. Business and convention travel is included. This thinking is dominated by balance-of-trade concepts. Military personnel, diplomats, immigrants, and resident students are not tourists.

**Travel (see Tourism)**  Often interchangeable with tourism. Actually, this term should represent all direct elements of travel. Included in the term travel are transportation, vacations, resorts, and any other direct passenger elements, including but not limited to national parks, attractions and auto use for any of the above purposes. To make a journey from one place to another.

**Visa**  Document issued by a foreign government permitting nationals of another country to visit or travel. The visa is usually stamped on pages provided in one's passport, but may also be a document fastened to the passport.

## SELECTED TOURISM ABBREVIATIONS

| | |
|---|---|
| **AAA** | American Automobile Association |
| **AAR** | Association of American Railroads |
| **ABA** | American Bus Association |
| **ABC** | Advance Booking Charter |
| **ACTO** | Association of Caribbean Tour Operators |
| **AHMA** | American Hotel and Motel Association |
| **AIT** | Academie Internationale du Tourisme |
| **AIEST** | International Association of Scientific Experts in Tourism |
| **Amtrak** | National Railroad Passenger Corporation |
| **ANTA** | Australian National Travel Association |
| **AP** | American Plan |
| **ARC** | Airlines Reporting Corporation |
| **ARTA** | Association of Retail Travel Agents |
| **ASTA** | American Society of Travel Agents |
| **ATA** | Air Transport Association of America |
| **ATC** | Air Transport Committee (Canada) |
| **ATME** | Association of Travel Marketing Executives |
| **BIT** | Bulk Inclusive Tour |
| **BTA** | British Tourist Authority |
| **CEDOK** | Czechoslovakia Travel Bureau |
| **CHRIE** | Council on Hotel, Restaurant and Institutional Education |
| **CITC** | Canadian Institute of Travel Counselors |
| **CLIA** | Cruise Lines International Association |
| **CNTA** | China National Tourism Administration |
| **CRS** | Computerized Reservations System |
| **COTAL** | Conference of Tourist Organizations of Latin America |
| **CTA** | Caribbean Travel Association |
| **CTC** | Certified Travel Counselor |
| **CTO** | Caribbean Tourism Organization |
| **DC** | Diner's Club |
| **DIT** | Domestic Independent Tours |
| **DOT** | U.S. Government Department of Transportation |
| **ECOSOC** | Economic and Social Council of the United Nations |
| **EP** | European Plan |

| | |
|---|---|
| **ETC** | European Travel Commission |
| **FAA** | Federal Aviation Administration (U.S.) |
| **FIT** | Foreign Independent Tour |
| **GIT** | Group Inclusive Tour |
| **HSMAI** | Hotel Sales Management Association International |
| **IAAPA** | International Association of Amusement Parks and Attractions |
| **IAF** | International Automobile Federation |
| **IACVB** | International Association of Convention and Visitors Bureaus |
| **IATA** | International Air Transport Association |
| **IATAN** | International Airlines Travel Agent Network |
| **ICAO** | International Civil Aviation Organization |
| **ICC** | Interstate Commerce Commission |
| **ICTA** | Institute of Certified Travel Agents |
| **IFWTO** | International Federation of Women's Travel Organizations |
| **IHA** | International Hotel Association |
| **IIT** | Inclusive Independent Tour |
| **ILO** | International Labor Organization |
| **IT** | Inclusive Tour |
| **ITC** | Inclusive Tour Charter |
| **IYHF** | International Youth Hostel Federation |
| **MAP** | Modified American Plan |
| **MCO** | Miscellaneous Charges Order |
| **NACOA** | National Association of Cruise Only Agents |
| **NRA** | National Restaurant Association |
| **NRPA** | National Recreation Parks Association |
| **NTA** | National Tour Association |
| **OAG** | Official Airline Guide |
| **OAS** | Organization of American States |
| **OECD** | Organization for Economic Cooperation and Development |
| **PATA** | Pacific Asia Travel Association |
| **RPM** | Revenue Passenger Miles |
| **SATW** | Society of American Travel Writers |
| **S & R** | Sell and Report |
| **SST** | Supersonic Transport |
| **STTE** | Society of Travel and Tourism Educators |
| **TC** | Tourism Canada |
| **TIA** | Travel Industry Association of America |
| **TIAC** | Tourism Industry Association of Canada |
| **TTRA** | Travel and Tourism Research Association |
| **UFTAA** | Universal Federation of Travel Agents Associations |
| **UNESCO** | United Nations Educational, Scientific and Cultural Organization |
| **USTDC** | United States Travel Data Center |
| **USTOA** | United States Tour Operators Association |
| **USTTA** | United States Travel & Tourism Administration |
| **WATA** | World Association of Travel Agents |
| **WEXITA** | Women Executives in Tourism Administration |
| **WHO** | World Health Organization |
| **WTAO** | World Touring and Automobile Organization |
| **WTO** | World Tourism Organization |
| **XO** | Exchange Order |

# Index